LA FRANCE

LE ROYAUME-UNI

LA MER DU NORD

LES PAYS-BAS

L'ALLEMAGNE

LA BELGIQUE

la Wallonie

LE LUXEMBOURG

LA MANCHE

Dunkerque
Calais
Boulogne
Lille
NORD-PAS-DE-CALAIS

Dieppe
Amiens
PICARDIE
Charleville-Mézières

Cherbourg
Le Havre
HAUTE-NORMANDIE
Rouen
la Seine

Caen
BASSE-NORMANDIE

ÎLE-DE-FRANCE
Versailles Paris

Reims
Verdun
Metz
LORRAINE
Nancy
Strasbourg
ALSACE

CHAMPAGNE-ARDENNE
la Seine
Troyes

Colmar
LES VOSGES

Brest
Saint-Malo
le Mont-Saint-Michel

Chartres
Fontainebleau

BRETAGNE
Rennes
Le Mans
Orléans
la Loire

Blois
CENTRE-VAL DE LOIRE

la Loire
Angers Tours

BOURGOGNE
Dijon

FRANCHE-COMTÉ
Besançon

LA SUISSE

Nantes
PAYS DE LA LOIRE

Bourges

la Saône

LE JURA

Poitiers

L'OCÉAN ATLANTIQUE

POITOU-CHARENTES

La Rochelle

Limoges
LIMOUSIN

AUVERGNE
Clermont-Ferrand

RHÔNE-ALPES
Lyon
le Rhône

le Val d'Aoste

L'ITALIE

Grenoble

Bordeaux
AQUITAINE

Rocamadour

LE MASSIF CENTRAL

LES ALPES

le Rhône

Moissac
Albi
MIDI-PYRÉNÉES

Avignon
Nîmes
Montpellier Arles

PROVENCE-ALPES-CÔTE D'AZUR

Nice
Cannes

MONACO

Biarritz
Toulouse
Carcassonne
LANGUEDOC-ROUSSILLON

Aix-en-Provence
Marseille

L'ESPAGNE

Lourdes
LES PYRÉNÉES

Perpignan

la CORSE

L'ANDORRE

LA MER MÉDITERRANÉE

Élévation en mètres
2000+
500–2000
200–500
0–200
Niveau de la mer

0 25 50 75 100 MILLES
0 50 100 150 KILOMÈTRES

la SARDAIGNE

50°
46°
44°
4°
0°
4°
8°

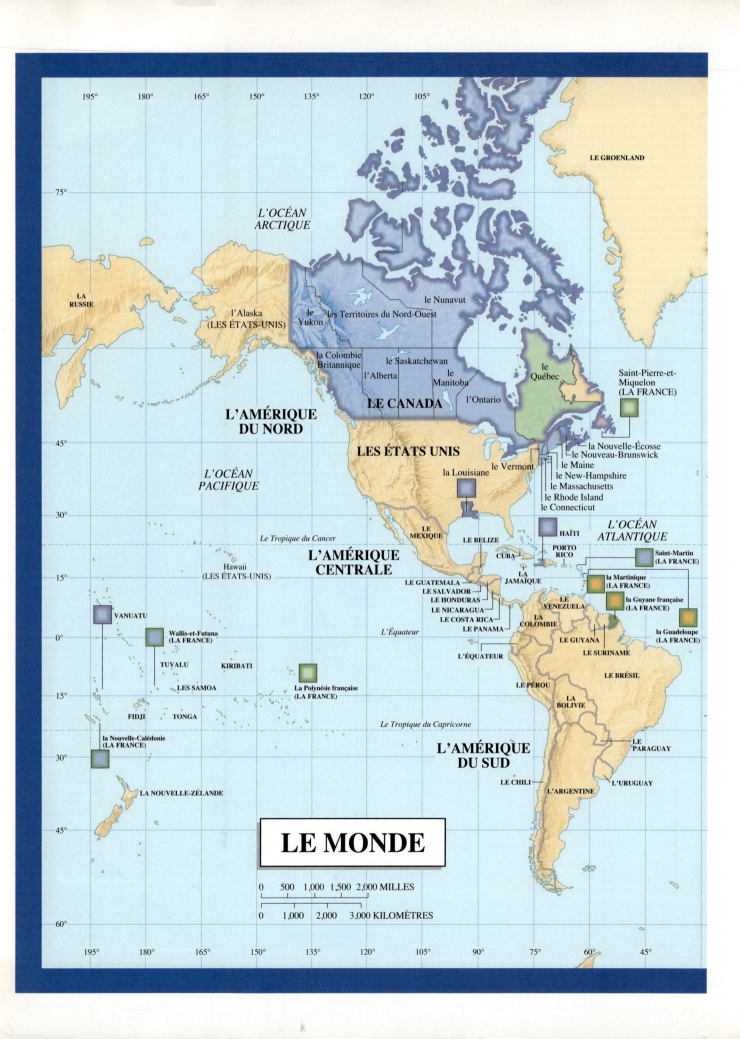

LE MONDE

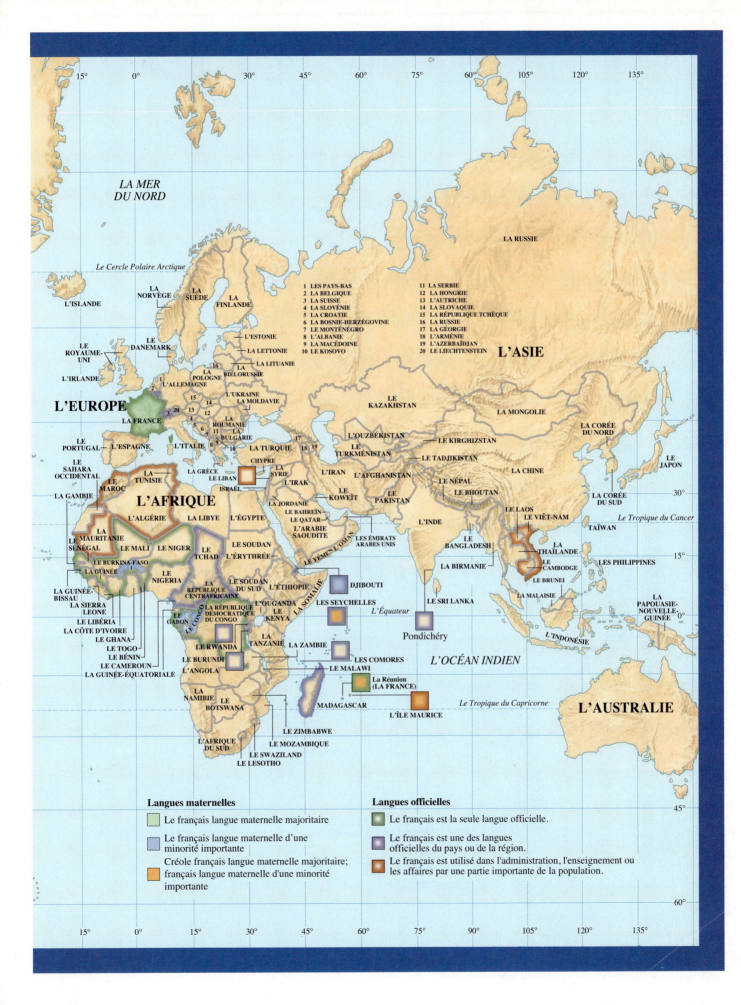

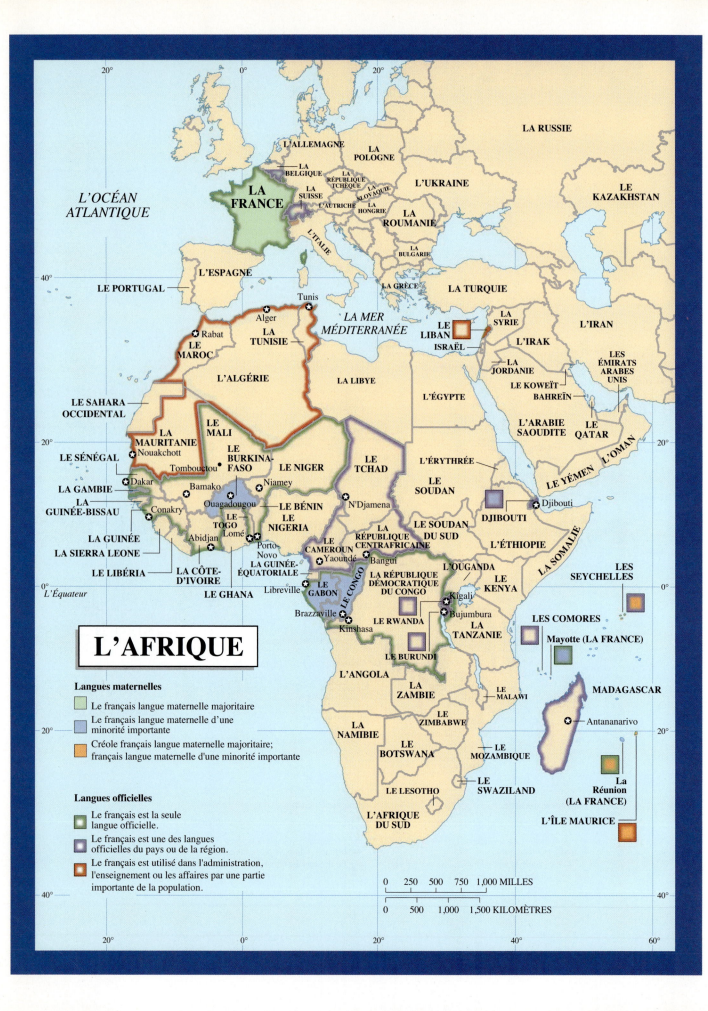

L'AFRIQUE

L'OCÉAN ATLANTIQUE

LA RUSSIE

L'ALLEMAGNE
LA POLOGNE
LA BELGIQUE
LA RÉPUBLIQUE TCHÈQUE
LA SUISSE
LA SLOVAQUIE
L'AUTRICHE
LA HONGRIE
LA ROUMANIE
LA BULGARIE
L'UKRAINE
LE KAZAKHSTAN

LA FRANCE
L'ITALIE

LE PORTUGAL
L'ESPAGNE
LA GRÈCE
LA TURQUIE
L'IRAN

Tunis
Alger
LA TUNISIE
Rabat
LE MAROC
L'ALGÉRIE
LA LIBYE
L'ÉGYPTE

LA MER MÉDITERRANÉE

LE LIBAN
LA SYRIE
ISRAËL
L'IRAK
LA JORDANIE
LE KOWEÏT
BAHREÏN
LES ÉMIRATS ARABES UNIS

LE SAHARA OCCIDENTAL
LA MAURITANIE
Nouakchott
LE MALI
LE SÉNÉGAL
Dakar
Tombouctou
LE BURKINA-FASO
LE NIGER
LE TCHAD
N'Djamena
L'ÉRYTHRÉE
LE SOUDAN
LA GAMBIE
Bamako
Niamey
LA GUINÉE-BISSAU
Conakry
Ouagadougou
LE BÉNIN
LE TOGO
LE NIGERIA
L'ARABIE SAOUDITE
LE QATAR
L'OMAN
LE YÉMEN

LA GUINÉE
LA SIERRA LEONE
Abidjan
Lomé
LE LIBÉRIA
LA CÔTE-D'IVOIRE
Porto-Novo
LA GUINÉE-ÉQUATORIALE
LE GHANA
LE CAMEROUN
Yaoundé
Bangui
LA RÉPUBLIQUE CENTRAFRICAINE
LE SOUDAN DU SUD
DJIBOUTI
Djibouti
L'ÉTHIOPIE
LA SOMALIE

Libreville
LE GABON
LE CONGO
LA RÉPUBLIQUE DÉMOCRATIQUE DU CONGO
L'OUGANDA
Kigali
LE KENYA
LES SEYCHELLES

Brazzaville
Kinshasa
LE RWANDA
Bujumbura
LA TANZANIE
LES COMORES
Mayotte (LA FRANCE)

LE BURUNDI

L'ANGOLA
LA ZAMBIE
LE MALAWI
MADAGASCAR

LA NAMIBIE
LE ZIMBABWE
Antananarivo

LE BOTSWANA
LE MOZAMBIQUE
La Réunion (LA FRANCE)

LE LESOTHO
LE SWAZILAND
L'ÎLE MAURICE

L'AFRIQUE DU SUD

0° L'Équateur

Langues maternelles

- Le français langue maternelle majoritaire
- Le français langue maternelle d'une minorité importante
- Créole français langue maternelle majoritaire; français langue maternelle d'une minorité importante

Langues officielles

- Le français est la seule langue officielle.
- Le français est une des langues officielles du pays ou de la région.
- Le français est utilisé dans l'administration, l'enseignement ou les affaires par une partie importante de la population.

0   250   500   750   1,000 MILLES

0   500   1,000   1,500 KILOMÈTRES

SECOND EDITION

LIAISONS

An Introduction To French

WYNNE WONG
THE OHIO STATE UNIVERSITY

STACEY WEBER-FÈVE
IOWA STATE UNIVERSITY

BILL VANPATTEN
MICHIGAN STATE UNIVERSITY

Australia • Brazil • Mexico • Singapore • United Kingdom • United States

Liaisons: An introduction to French, Second Edition
Wynne Wong, Stacey Weber-Fève, and Bill VanPatten

Product Director: Beth Kramer

Senior Product Manager: Lara Semones Ramsey

Product Development Manager: Katie Wade

Senior Content Developer: Isabelle Alouane

Associate Content Developer: Gregory Madan

Product Assistant: Zenya Molnar

Media Producer: Elyssa Healy

Marketing Manager: Sean Ketchem

Senior Content Project Manager: Esther Marshall

Art Director: Brenda Carmichael

Manufacturing Planner: Betsy Donaghey

IP Analyst: Jessica Elias

IP Project Manager: Farah Fard

Production Service: Lumina Datamatics, Inc.

Compositor: Lumina Datamatics, Inc.

Cover and Text Designer: Brenda Carmichael

Cover Image: Christian Heeb/Aurora Photos

© 2017, 2013 Cengage Learning

ALL RIGHTS RESERVED. No part of this work covered by the copyright herein may be reproduced, transmitted, stored, or used in any form or by any means graphic, electronic, or mechanical, including but not limited to photocopying, recording, scanning, digitizing, taping, web distribution, information networks, or information storage and retrieval systems, except as permitted under Section 107 or 108 of the 1976 United States Copyright Act, without the prior written permission of the publisher.

For product information and technology assistance, contact us at
Cengage Learning Customer & Sales Support, 1-800-354-9706
For permission to use material from this text or product,
submit all requests online at **www.cengage.com/permissions.**
Further permissions questions can be emailed to
permissionrequest@cengage.com.

Library of Congress Control Number: 2015940828

Student Edition:

ISBN: 978-1-305-26275-1

Cengage Learning
20 Channel Center Street
BOSTON, MA 02210
USA

Cengage Learning is a leading provider of customized learning solutions with office locations around the globe, including Singapore, the United Kingdom, Australia, Mexico, Brazil and Japan. Locate your local office at **www.cengage.com/global.**

Cengage Learning products are represented in Canada by Nelson Education, Ltd.

To learn more about Cengage Learning Solutions, visit **www.cengage.com.**

Purchase any of our products at your local college store or at our preferred online store **www.cengagebrain.com**

Printed in the United States of America
Print Number: 01   Print Year: 2015

SCOPE and SEQUENCE

SCOPE and SEQUENCE

SCOPE and SEQUENCE

Bienvenue! Welcome to the second edition of *Liaisons*! You are joining a community of thousands of students and instructors who, in the first edition, have found that *Liaisons* is a great introductory text for taking those first steps toward communicating in French and also for learning about the fascinating cultures of France and the Francophone world. What has proven *Liaisons* so successful among students? First, and foremost, *Liaisons* is an intriguing plot-driven movie. Filmed on location in Quebec and France, this film is a first-rate production with a stellar cast of famous actors such as Mylène Savoie (also known for her role as director of the films *Exode* and *Tar and Tea*), Guillaume Dolmans (known for his role in *Marie Curie, une femme sur le front; Road to Roland-Garros;* as well as Heineken commercials), and Johanne-Marie Tremblay (from the Oscar-winning film *Les invasions barbares*). Students who have seen this film call *Liaisons* a mystery-suspense thriller that leaves you hungry for more. We know you will enjoy watching this film as much as students before you have!

The *Liaisons* program will help you acquire a solid foundation of the vocabulary and grammar that beginning-level students need in order to express themselves well at this level. The activities have been carefully designed so that you first develop confidence with the new vocabulary and grammar before being required to produce it; that is to say write or speak it. Besides learning about the French language and France and other French-speaking cultures, you will also have the opportunity to get to know your classmates and your instructors better as well as learn interesting information from them as you engage in the language practice activities in your book.

As suggested by the title of this book and film, this program contains many **liaisons,** or *connections* and *links*. Great care has been taken to ensure that the film and the different features of the book are linked together. As you learn French with the *Liaisons* program, you will also become aware of how language and culture are intricately linked together as well as see the connections that can be made between different cultures (including your own) and the French-speaking world and with people in your class, your community, and the global world at large. So, once again welcome and enjoy your journey in learning French!

Wynne Wong
Stacey Weber-Fève
Bill VanPatten

TO THE STUDENT

 Liaisons: **The Film**

Claire Gagner, a graduate student in psychology at McGill University in Montreal, has spent most of her adult life on her own ever since her mother committed herself to a psychiatric hospital. Working as a receptionist at *l'Hôtel Delta* to put herself through school, Claire's life has been defined by work, her studies, and visits with her mother at the hospital. One day Claire receives an envelope with an anonymous prepaid trip to Quebec City. As she embarks on this journey, she encounters mysterious characters and eventually travels to France where the past and the present blend in some startling revelations.

Cast of Characters

CLAIRE
A graduate student in psychology at McGill University and hotel receptionist at *l'Hôtel Delta*

ABIA
Claire's best friend and co-worker at *l'Hôtel Delta*

SIMONE
Claire's mother and psychiatric patient at the *Clinique psychiatrique Laurier*

ALEXIS
A Parisian who is in Canada to deal with family business

ROBERT
Hotel manager of *l'Hôtel Delta* and Claire and Abia's supervisor

MADAME PAPILLON
Friend and neighbor of Claire's uncle in Paris

RÉMY
A mysterious man with an interest in Claire

Student Textbook

The Student Textbook contains the information and activities that you need for in-class use and self-study. The textbook is divided into 12 core chapters, a preliminary chapter, and a final chapter. Each core chapter contains three parts (**parties**), and each part contains a vocabulary and grammar section with presentations, explanations, activities for listening, speaking, and writing practice and cultural information. In each chapter, one page is always dedicated to French pronunciation and two pages help you understand and work with the film *Liaisons*. **Oui, je peux!** boxes at the end of each grammar section allow you to assess your ability to put new language learned to expressive use. Special end-of-chapter sections give you the opportunity to develop your reading and writing skills in French and your cultural knowledge of the French-speaking world. In odd-numbered chapters, brief cultural videos expand on the cultural theme and topics discussed in the book. In every chapter **Share It!** activities prompt you to go online to the textbook's **iLrn** component to share your reactions to what you have read with your classmates. Each chapter ends with a French-English vocabulary list of all of the chapter's active vocabulary to help you study for quizzes and exams. An additional study tool is provided for you at the end of the textbook. The tear-out cards contain the **Oui, je peux!** statements along with key vocabulary, grammar, and activities to help you execute them. Also at the end of the textbook, you will find a comprehensive reference section including verb charts, and a French-English glossary—the English-French glossary will be online.

Student Activities Manual

The purpose of the Student Activities Manual (SAM) is to give you extra practice of what you learned in your book outside of class. They represent both the workbook (comprehension and written practice of the vocabulary and grammar presented in class) and the lab manual (listening and pronunciation practice). In odd-numbered chapters, you will continue to develop your writing skills in French through a blog-style writing activity in which you react to the film *Liaisons*. Even-numbered chapters contain an e-mail-style writing activity related to the chapter's theme. You may find these activities in your Assignment Calendar or in the Activities tab in **iLrn**.

iLrn

iLrn gives you access to your textbook and all its supplements, including the Student Activities Manual, online in an interactive format. The many functions you can take advantage of also include clicking on words to hear how they are pronounced and accessing self-tests, additional activities for practice and exploration, and a media library that includes the film *Liaisons*. A calendar allows you to quickly view assignments and due dates. **iLrn** also lets you highlight, as well as take and organize notes, in your e-book. The **Share It!** feature allows you to post discussions and share activities and projects such as video projects with other students so you can form a virtual sharing community with your classmates.

Acknowledgments

We are very happy to bring this second edition of *Liaisons* to both students and instructors! As authors, we get great joy not only out of working with each other but also by connecting with the community of people who are excited about

learning and teaching French language and the French-speaking world. In our travels to visit those of you who have worked with the first edition of *Liaisons* and in our interactions with those of you who offered reviews of the first edition, we are indebted to you for your loyalty, your input (no pun intended!), and your voices. Because of you, the tremendously positive reception of *Liaisons* exceeded what we had expected—and also because of you, we launch this new edition. Combined with the captivating movie that accompanies the text, *Liaisons,* Second Edition, is something we are eager to put in your hands once again. To be sure, we pondered, talked, wrote, and rewrote, and sometimes rewrote again. This is what authors do, but we had a greater motivation this second time than the first. We knew we had something good, something special, and we wanted to make it even better. And we only knew this because of you. So, first, and foremost, we would like to thank all of our *Liaisons* students and instructors. You said *Oui!* to us and so now we say, *Voilà! La deuxième fois pour vous!* And if you are using *Liaisons* for the first time, we say welcome to the growing national team that is making *liaisons* everywhere across the country!

To be sure, we have a good number of people to thank for putting this second edition into your hands. It is thanks to the many long hours and endless efforts of editors and their dedicated team behind the scenes that authors' ideas become magically transformed into the beautifully polished product that makes its way to your desks. First, a big thank you to Product Director Beth Kramer for believing in this project from the very beginning and for her continued insightful wisdom during the development of this second edition. We are also greatly indebted to Product Manager Lara Semones and to developmental editor Denise St. Jean for working with us on a day-to-day basis. Thank you both for skillfully guiding us through the many different phases of writing this second edition that we have come to be so proud of. We also owe a debt of gratitude to Esther Marshall for her meticulous work editing texts in the second edition and for all her efforts during the production process. Esther, we are so grateful to you for making our job as authors easier! We would also like to recognize all the people on Esther's team for their invaluable work and assistance during the production process. These people include in particular Sev Champeny, copyeditor and proofreader, and Katy Gabel, Lumina Datamatics Project Manager. For those in sales and marketing, we want to say a special thank you for the important role you play for making our program a success. Your hard work does not go unnoticed. Thank you all for your dedication to our projects!

We would also like to recognize all those who generously allowed us to use their work in *Liaisons.* A special thank you to artists M.A.J. Fortier, Denis Nolet, Patrick Rodrigue, and Neal Turner for allowing us to use their paintings; and to Charles Larroque, Julie M. Nagaro, Gaëtan Paquet, and Larry Wong for their images.

Once again, we would like to thank all the people who had a hand in making the movie *Liaisons* the first-rate production that it is. Its success has exceeded our expectations! We knew we had a great story, but you all made it come to life in the magical way that it did. It's thanks to all of you that we have this incredible film that is now inspiring students all over the country to continue studying French, and that has made many of them love the French language as much as we do. A very special thank you to our director Andrei Campeanu for the ingenious vision he had for our film. Andrei, students are asking about the sequel and we can't wait to see what you have in store for *Encore.* Mylène (Savoie), Guillaume (Dolmans), Jasmine (Bouchardy Johnson), and Johanne-Marie (Tremblay), thank you for not just playing your roles so beautifully, but also for the important role you continue to play in inspiring our students to learn French. We could not have asked for a better cast. You have many fans in the U.S. following your careers on social media and they can't wait to see you in the sequel *Encore!*

Lest we be remiss, we need to step back and acknowledge the terrific people who shepherded the first edition through that led to what you have before you now. We were indebted to them then and we do not forget the faith they had in us as well as their tremendous efforts when we started some seven years ago. Without them, we would not have the *Liaisons* that we have today. Those people include Nick Agnew, P.J. Boardman, and Nicole Morinon.

Finally, we would like to thank our colleagues across the country whose valuable input and feedback led to this improved second edition.

Reviewers for the Second Edition

Antoinette Alitto	*Harrisburg Area Community College*	Vicki Leigh Earnest	*Calhoun College*
Elizabeth Allen	*Washington University in St. Louis*	Vicki Earnest	*Calhoun Community College*
Katie Angus	*University of Southern Mississippi*	Mary Ellen Eckhert	*East LA College*
Mariana Bahtchevanova	*Arizona State University*	Betty Rose Facer	*Old Dominion University*
Shelton Bellew	*Brenau University*	Timothy Farley	*Truman State University*
Carolyn Bilby	*Bellevue College*	John Fields	*Florida State College at Jacksonville*
Tom Blair	*City College of San Francisco*	Jonathan Fulk	*University of Minnesota, Twin Cities*
Anne-Sophie Blank	*University of Missouri, Saint Louis*	Janette Funaro	*Johnson County Community College*
Geraldine Blattner	*Florida Atlantic University*	Stephanie Gaillard	*Louisiana State University*
Margaret Capara	*Saint Joseph's University*	David Graham	*Clinton Community College*
Rosalie Cheatham	*University of Arkansas, Little Rock*	Jennifer Hall	*University of Mount Union*
Isabelle Corneaux	*George Fox University*	Beatrice Hallier	*University of San Francisco*
Nathalie Cornelius	*Bloomsburg University*	Cheryl M. Hansen	*Weber State University*
Mohamed Daassa	*University of Michigan*	Patricia Harrigan	*Community College of Baltimore County*
Aurélie Dargent	*University of San Francisco*		
Kelly Davidson Devall	*Valdosta State University*	Erika Hess	*Northern Arizona University*
Patrick Day	*University of Wisconsin, Eau Claire*	Mary Jane Highfield	*St. John's University*
Chris De Ville	*Pitt Community College*	Marie-Laure Hinton	*Long Beach City College*
Nicole Denner	*Stetson University*	Bette Hirsch	*Cabrillo College*
Jean-Luc Desalvo	*San Jose State University*	Martine Howard	*Camden County College*
Emilie Destruel Johnson	*University of Iowa*	Stephanie Howe	*University of Georgia*
Georges Detiveaux	*Lone Star College, CyFair*	Anna Hudson	*Dickinson College*
Nadia Duchelle	*George Mason University*	Charlotte Jackson	*Long Beach City College*

(Continued)

Reviewers for the Second Edition *(Continued)*

Judith Jeon-Chapman	*Worcester State University*
Lilia Jmiai	*Ohio State University, Lima*
Matthew Kanefsky	*Michigan State University*
Mary Helen Kashuba	*Chestnut Hill College*
Kelly Kidder	*Lipscomb University*
Ella Kirk	*Hiram College*
Elizabeth Lang	*American University*
Rebecca Leal	*Elmhurst College*
Mikle Dave Ledgerwood	*Samford University*
Marie Level	*Baylor University*
Enrique Linan	*University of Georgia*
Lara Lomicka	*University of South Carolina*
Heather McCoy	*Pennsylvania State University*
Dorothee Mertz-Weigel	*Armstrong State University*
Christiane Metral	*Smith College*
Jessica Miller	*University of Wisconsin, Eau Claire*
Nicole Mills	*Harvard University*
Aileen Mootoo	*Southeastern Louisiana University*
Martine Motard-Noar	*McDaniel College*
Linda Nodjimbadem	*University of Texas at El Paso*
Kory Olson	*Stockton University*
Marina Peters-Newell	*University of New Mexico*
Patricia Pierce	*Baylor University*
Christine Probes	*University of South Florida*
Nicole Rudolph	*Adelphi University*
Anna Sandstrom	*University of New Hampshire*
Louis Silvers	*Monroe Community College*
Maria Snyder	*Central College*
Mariagrazia Spina	*University of Central Florida*
Francoise Sullivan	*Tulsa Community College*
Valerie Thiers-Thiam	*City University of New York / CUNY- Borough of Manhattan Community College*
Ellen Thorington	*Ball State University*
Sandra Trapani	*University of Missouri, Saint Louis*
Eric Turcat	*Oklahoma State University*
Sandra Valnes Quammen	*Duke University*
Catherine Webster	*University of Central Oklahoma*
Violaine White	*University of Missouri, Saint Louis*
William L. White	*SUNY, Buffalo State*
Joseph Wieczorek	*Notre Dame of Maryland University/ Community College of Baltimore County*
Carol Wilson	*Grand Valley State University*
Valerie Wust	*North Carolina State University*
Bonnie Youngs	*Carnegie Mellon University*

Contributors to the Second Edition

Jeffrey Allen	*North Carolina State University*
Heidi Brown	*Loyola University Maryland*
Jean-Luc Desalvo	*San Jose State University*
Lara Finklea	
Charlotte Jackson	*Long Beach City College*
Jessica Miller	*University of Wisconsin-Eau Claire*
Kimberly Meurillon	
Aaron Prevots	*Southwestern University (TX)*
Catherine Webster	*University of Central Oklahoma*
Valerie Wust	*North Carolina State University*

Reviewers for the First Edition

Ellen Abrams	*Northern Essex Community College*
Antoinette Alitto-Heigl	*Harrisburg Area Community College*
Heather Willis Allen	*University of Wisconsin – Madison*
Debra Anderson	*East Carolina University*
Eileen Angelini	*Canisius College*
Renée Arnold	*Kapiolani Community College*
Genette Ashby-Beach	*Georgia Perimeter College*
Mariana Bahtchevanova	*Arizona State University*
Julie Baker	*University of Richmond*
Jody Ballah	*University of Cincinnati – Raymond Walters College*
Elizabeth Barrow	*Kent State University – Tuscarawas*
Barbara Bateman	*Georgia Perimeter College*
Dikka Berven	*Oakland University*
Carolyn Bilby	*Bellevue College*
Thomas Blair	*City College of San Francisco*
Lisa Blair	*Shaw University*
Geraldine Blattner	*Florida Atlantic University*
Sylvie Blum-Reid	*University of Florida*
John Boitano	*Chapman University*
Tammie Bolling	*Tennessee Technology Center – Jacksboro*
Amelia Bowen	*Old Dominion University*
Marie Lorraine Bruno	*Immaculata University*
Elizabeth Bull	*Northern Virginia Community College*
Thomas Buresi	*Southern Polytech State University*
Joanne Burnett	*University of Southern Mississippi*
Ruth Caldwell	*Luther College*
Anne Carlson	*Southern Illinois University – Carbondale*
Culley Carson-Grefe	*Austin Peay State University*
Krista Chambless	*University of Alabama – Birmingham*
Matthieu Chan Tsin	*Coastal Carolina University*
Rosalie Cheatham	*University of Arkansas*
Rebecca Chism	*Kent State University*
Stephanie Coker	*University of Kentucky*
Hervé Corbé	*Youngstown State University*
Nathalie Cornelius	*Bloomsburg University*
Donna Coulet du Gard	*University of Delaware*
Tamara Cox	*Gardner – Webb University*
Eddy Cuisinier	*Western Kentucky University*
Laurel Cummins	*Bronx Community College – City University of New York*
Margaret Dempster	*Northwestern University*
Nicole Denner	*Stetson University*
Jean-Luc Desalvo	*San Jose State University*
Georges Detiveaux	*Lone Star College – Cyfair*
Constance Dickey	*Syracuse University*
Sébastien Dubreil	*University of Texas – Knoxville*
John Duffy, Jr.	*University of South Carolina*
Stephanie Duisberg	*Pima Community College – NorthWest*
Catherine Dunand	*Northeastern University*
Lucile Duperron	*Dickinson College*
Brenda Dyer	*Drexel University*
Vicki Earnest	*Calhoun College*
Mary Ellen Eckhert	*East Los Angeles College*
Wade Edwards	*Longwood University*
Shirin Edwin	*Sam Houston State University*
Claudia Esposito	*University of Massachusetts – Boston*
Betty Rose Facer	*Old Dominion University*

(Continued)

Reviewers for the First Edition (Continued)

Timothy Farley	*Truman State University*
Jennifer Forrest	*Texas State University – San Marcos*
Claude Fouillade	*New Mexico State University*
Laura Franklin	*Northern Virginia Community College*
Jonathan Fulk	*University of Minnesota*
Jeanette Funaro	*Johnson County Community College*
Claire Gallou	*Phillips Academy*
Katherine Gantz	*St. Mary's College of Maryland*
Carolyn Gascoigne	*University of Nebraska – Omaha*
Christine Gaudry-Hudson	*Millersville University*
Abdou Gaye	*Ulster County Community College*
Anne George	*Whatcom Community College*
Claudine Giacchetti	*University of Houston*
Sage Goellner	*University of Wisconsin – Madison*
Katie Golsan	*University of the Pacific*
Christelle Gonthier	*Duke University*
Eve Goodhue	*Simpson College*
Marvin Gordon	*University of Illinois – Chicago*
David Graham	*Clinton Community College*
Frederique Grim	*Colorado State University*
Luc Guglielmi	*Kennesaw State University*
Sharon Hahnlen	*Liberty University*
Mark Hall	*Ithaca College*
Lana Hamon	*Trinity School*
Brigitte Hamon-Porter	*Hope College*
Cheryl Hansen	*Weber State University*
Patricia Harrigan	*Community College of Baltimore County – Essex*
Elaine Harris	*Northeastern Illinois University*
Steve Haslam	*Westminster College*
Alexander Hertich	*Bradley University*
Mary Jane Highfield	*St. John's University*
Jean-Louis Hippolyte	*Rutgers University – Camden*
Dominique Hitchcock	*Riverside Community College*
Lethuy Hoang	*Springfield College*
Martine Howard	*Camden County College*
Amy Hubbell	*Kansas State University*
Anna Hudson	*Dickinson College*
Andrew Irving	*University of Wisconsin – Madison*
Charlotte Jackson	*Long Beach City College*
Andrea Javel	*Boston College*
Judith Jeon-Chapman	*Worcester State College*
Warren Johnson	*Arkansas State University*
Caroline Jumel	*Oakland University*
Mary Helen Kashuba	*Chestnut Hill College*
Stacey Katz Bourns	*Harvard University*
Matt Kemp	*Kent State University*
Kelly Kidder	*Lipscomb University*
Angèle Kingué	*Bucknell University*
Elizabeth Knutson	*United States Naval Academy*
Nedialka Koleva	*Mesa Community College*
Christine Lac	*Carleton College*
Elizabeth Lang	*American University*
Bérénice Le Marchand	*San Francisco State University*
Mikle Ledgerwood	*Samford University*
Kathy Leis	*College of DuPage*
Jacek Lerych	*Grays Harbor College*
Marie Level	*Baylor University*
Tamara Lindner	*University of Louisiana – Lafayette*
Jane Lippmann	*University of Texas – Austin*
Gary Ljungquist	*Salem College*
Jean-Francois Llorens	*High Point University*
Lara Lomicka	*University of South Carolina*
Joanne Lonay	*Seattle Central Community College*
José Lopez-Marron	*Bronx Community College – City University of New York*
Kathryn Lorenz	*University of Cincinnati*
Amy Lorenz	*Loras College*
Jin Lu	*Purdue University – Calumet*
Paula Luteran	*Hutchinson Community College*
Mary Katherine Luton	*Charleston Southern University*
Elizabeth Martin	*California State University – San Bernardino*
Sharla Martin	*University of Texas – Arlington*
Alix Mazuet	*University of Central Oklahoma*
Stuart McClintock	*Midwestern State University*
Heather McCoy	*Pennsylvania State University*
Anne McGovern	*Mary Baldwin College*
Betty McLane-Iles	*Truman State University*
Catherine Mennear	*Wake Technical Community College*
Christiane Métral	*Smith College*
Jessica Miller	*University of Wisconsin – Eau Claire*
Isabelle Miller	*Everett Community College*
Anne-Hélène Miller	*East Carolina University*
Nicole Mills	*Harvard University*
Blandine Mitaut	*Shippensburg University*
Julie Molnar	*Columbus State Community College*
Aileen Mootoo	*Southeastern Louisiana University*
John Moran	*New York University*
Brigitte Moretti-Coski	*Ohio University*
Christine Moritz	*University of Northern Colorado*
Kristina Mormino	*Georgia Gwinnett College*
Shawn Morrison	*College of Charleston*
Martine Motard-Noar	*McDaniel College*
Markus Muller	*California State University – Long Beach*
Kathryn Murphy-Judy	*Virginia Commonwealth University*
Stéphane Natan	*Rider University*
Patricia Newman	*Trident Technical College*
Karen Nichols	*Xavier University of Louisiana*
Barbara Nissman-Cohen	*Lebanon Valley College*
Eva Norling	*Bellevue College*
Sylvette Norré	*George Fox University*
Frances Novack	*Ursinus College*
Philip Ojo	*Agnes Scott University*
Marie-Noelle Olivier	*University of Nevada – Las Vegas*
Kory Olson	*Richard Stockton College*
Geraldine O'Neill	*Pace University*
Jennifer Orlikoff	*West Virginia University*
Brahim Oulbeid	*Westfield State University*
Kate Paesani	*Wayne State University*
Keith Palka	*Central Michigan University*
Juliette Parnell-Smith	*University of Nebraska – Omaha*
Gloria Pastorino	*Fairleigh Dickinson University*
Kelly Peebles	*Clemson University*
Marina Peters-Newell	*University of New Mexico*
Janel Pettes-Guikema	*Grand Valley State University*
Brigitte Philippe	*University of South Florida*
Lewis Porter	*Walsh University*
Joseph Price	*Texas Tech University*
Bonnie Pytlinski	*St. Leo University*
Alain Ranwez	*Metropolitan State College of Denver*
Esther Ratner	*Brandeis University*
Deb Reisinger	*Duke University*
Gail Riley	*American University*

(Continued)

Reviewers for the First Edition *(Continued)*

Daniel Rivas	*Irvine Valley College*
Radonna Roark	*Oklahoma Baptist University*
Molly Robinson Kelly	*Lewis & Clark College*
Peggy Rocha	*San Joaquin Delta College*
Susan Rosenstreich	*Dowling College*
Nicole Rudolph	*Adelphi University*
Love Sanchez-Suarez	*York Technical College*
Anna Sandstrom	*University of New Hampshire*
Prosper Sanou	*State University of New York – Stony Brook*
Rosemarie Sarkis	*Riverside Community College*
Bonnie Sarnoff	*Limestone College*
Alan Savage	*Wheaton College*
Kelly Sax	*Indiana University – Bloomington*
Patricia Scarampi	*Lake Forest College*
Cheryl Schaile	*Texas A&M University*
Timothy Scheie	*University of Rochester – Eastman School of Music*
Leslie Sconduto	*Bradley University*
Sandhya Shanker	*Michigan State University*
Thomas Shealy	*Winthrop University*
Jennifer Shotwell	*Randolph – Macon College*
Patricia Siegel	*State University of New York – The College at Brockport*
Gregg Siewert	*Truman State University*
Louis Silvers	*Monroe Community College*
Lee Slater	*Old Dominion University*
Elizabeth Smith	*Southwest Virginia Community College*
Janet Solberg	*Kalamazoo College*
Emese Soos	*Tufts University*
Karen Sorenson	*Austin Peay State University*
Janet Starmer	*Guilford College*
Victoria Steinberg	*University of Tennessee – Chattanooga*
Edith Stetser	*Arcadia University*
Kathryn Stewart-Hoffmann	*Oakland Community College*
Jessica Sturm	*Purdue University*
Amye Sukapdjo	*Gainesville State College*
Kimberly Swanson	*University of Kansas*
Bernadette Takano	*University of Oklahoma*
Kendall Tarte	*Wake Forest University*
Valerie Thiers-Thiam	*Borough of Manhattan Community College – City University of New York*
Ellen Thorington	*Ball State University*
James Tomek	*Delta State University*
Fred Toner	*Ohio University*
Rick Treece	*University of Minnesota*
Madeline Turan	*Stony Brook University*
Sandra Valnes Quammen	*Duke University*
Carmen Vergès	*Virginia Highlands Community College*
Nancy Virtue	*Indiana University – Purdue University Fort Wayne*
Irene Wallaert	*Indiana University of Pennsylvania*
Andrew Wallis	*Whittier College*
Sadik Wardeh	*Valencia Community College*
Anna Weaver	*Mercer University*
Catherine Webster	*University of Central Oklahoma*
Arlene White	*Salisbury University*
William White	*Buffalo State College*
Georgeanna Wielkoszewski	*Chandler Gilbert Community College*
Leanne Wierenga	*Wittenberg University*
Donna Wilkerson-Barker	*State University of New York – The College at Brockport*
Sharon Wilkinson	*Simpson College*
Larry Wineland	*Messiah College*
Dierdre Wolownick	*American River College*
Valerie Wust	*North Carolina State University*
Bonnie Youngs	*Carnegie Mellon University*

Student Reviewers

Erin Adams	*Southern Illinois University – Carbondale*
Tim Anderson	*Old Dominion University*
David Brennan	*University of Nebraska – Omaha*
Esther Chen	*New York University*
Charles DeVita	*Virginia Commonwealth University*
Holly Doe	*Southern Illinois University – Carbondale*
Jennifer Haggard	*Camden County College*
Valerie Lamour	*New York University*
Kate Lewanowicz	*Virginia Commonwealth University*
Nicole Mattia	*Virginia Commonwealth University*
Ryan McDonnell	*University of Nebraska – Omaha*
Morgen Powell	*Virginia Commonwealth University*
Jessie Price	*Camden County College*
Lauren Shapiro	*New York University*
John Shick	*Old Dominion University*
Sarah Stevenson	*Southern Illinois University – Carbondale*
Carter Tuttle	*Virginia Commonwealth University*
Eliza Warwick	*New York University*

Advisory Board Members

Heather Willis Allen	*University of Wisconsin – Madison*
Martine Howard	*Camden County College*
Stacey Katz Bourns	*Harvard University*
Angèle Kingué	*Bucknell University*
Kathryn Lorenz	*University of Cincinnati*
Heather McCoy	*Pennsylvania State University*
John Moran	*New York University*
Kelly Sax	*Indiana University – Bloomington*

Focus Group Participants

Michele Cao Danh	*Northeastern University*
Eddy Cuisinier	*Western Kentucky University*
Cheryl Hansen	*Weber State University*
Martine Howard	*Camden County College*
Christine Lac	*Carleton College*
Kathryn Lorenz	*University of Cincinnati*
John Moran	*New York University*
José Ortiz-Batista	*County College of Morris*
Marina Peters-Newell	*University of New Mexico*
Deb Reisinger	*Duke University*
Susan Skoglund	*Kirkwood Community College*

TO THE STUDENT

Wynne's acknowledgments

As a second language acquisition researcher and a fervent admirer of the French language and Francophone culture, *Liaisons* represents a long time dream come true! Besides building a bridge between theory and practice, *Liaisons* is the manifestation of my love for Quebec and for the language that makes this culture so beautiful and distinct. A big *merci* to Cengage and to the best co-authors in the world, Stacey and Bill, for helping me make this dream a reality, and to all the students and instructors out there for making this second edition possible. I would also like to extend a special thank you to actress Johanne-Marie Tremblay for playing the role of Simone Gagner. Johanne-Marie has been one of my favorite actresses ever since I first saw her in Deny Arcand's *Jésus de Montréal* when I was a French student. I could have never imagined back then that one day she would be in *my* film! Finally, to my family, friends, colleagues, and students, I thank you for sharing this exciting journey with me. Without a doubt, *Liaisons* has led me to some of the most amazing and magical experiences of my life. I am overwhelmed by your support, and I look forward to more opportunities to connect with all of you through this second edition. *Ça me fait chaud au cœur!*

Stacey's acknowledgments

What an exciting and challenging adventure developing these two editions of *Liaisons* has been! I would especially like to thank our faithful and enthusiastic adopters, in particular Aaron Prevots and Hélène Sicard-Cowan for your correspondences and dedication to *Liaisons*. Once again, I thank my colleague and dear friend, Wynne Wong, for inviting me to join her on this adventure. I've appreciated every minute of this experience and am so pleased to have grown so much as a writer and teacher working alongside you! To Bill VanPatten, ditto.

Thank you for your expertise and unique creativity that you bring to this project and for inspiring such creativity in Wynne and me! I'd also like to thank my students and immediate colleagues at Iowa State University who've been using *Liaisons* alongside me and shared valuable feedback: Linda Quinn Allen, Jean-Pierre Taoutel, and Neysa Goodman. I also extend a very big thanks to all those at Cengage Learning for their tireless efforts in developing and promoting *Liaisons*. And finally, I wish to thank my family in the U.S. and France for their constant love and support, especially my husband Sébastien for his enduring patience, complete understanding, and infallible faith in my abilities.

Bill's acknowledgements

I would like to add here a special thank you to Wynne Wong and Stacey Weber-Fève. These are two of the best co-authors a person could have and I can't say enough good things about them. From the first edition to this second edition, they have worked tirelessly to make *Liaisons* the great textbook that it is. I admire and respect them both. I would also like to thank Adam Gammons, Erica Piper, and Matt Kanefsky who were instrumental in the development of extra on-line materials. I am very fortunate to know them and be able to work with them at Michigan State University. Although we've already thanked the folks at Cengage for all their behind-the-scenes work, I feel the need to add a special thank you here to all the sales people and regional representatives who venture out to campuses and put this book and movie in the hands of French instructors. You have a tough job and it does not go unnoticed. And I would be remiss if I didn't thank my dog Murphy, who as of the writing of this set of acknowledgements turns 11 years old. He's the best undemanding and patient company I could have. When I think about it all, life is pretty good.

Bienvenue

En bref In this preliminary chapter, you will:

- learn greetings and introductions
- learn subject pronouns
- learn the verb **être** and some of its basic uses
- learn how to form yes/no questions
- learn vocabulary for common objects in the classroom
- learn the numbers 0–60
- talk about courses and majors

- learn about articles and the gender and number of nouns
- learn some adjectives and learn about their formation, agreement, and position
- learn about the French alphabet and accent marks
- read about French as a world language and read about some famous French speakers

 You will also watch the **PROLOGUE** of the film *Liaisons*.

Ressources

 audio   video   Share It!   iLrn™   http://www.cengagebrain.com

© Zac Macaulay/Glow Images

un **1**

🔊 Comment **ça va**?

How is it going?

- The most common way to greet people in French is to say **bonjour** *(hello)*. However, in informal situations between friends and people who know each other well, **salut** *(hi)* and the **tu** form of verbs are often used.

LYDIE	**Salut, Annie! Comment vas-tu?**	*Hi, Annie. How are you?*
ANNIE	**Salut, Lydie! Je vais très bien. Et toi?**	*Hi, Lydie. I'm fine. And you?*
LYDIE	**Très bien, merci!**	*Very well, thanks!*

ALEX	**Salut, Marc! Quoi de neuf?**	*Hi, Marc. What's new?*
MARC	**Pas grand-chose. Et toi?**	*Not much. And you?*
ALEX	**Rien de nouveau. Au revoir.**	*Nothing new. Bye.*
MARC	**À bientôt, Alex.**	*See you soon, Alex.*
ALEX	**À plus!**	*See ya!*

- When greeting people in formal situations and in situations where you need to show respect to someone, **bonjour** and the **vous** form of verbs must be used.

PROFESSEUR	**Bonjour, Marie. Comment allez-vous?**	*Hello, Marie. How are you?*
MARIE	**Très bien, merci. Et vous, monsieur?**	*Very well, thank you. And you, sir?*
PROFESSEUR	**Très bien aussi. Merci.**	*Very well also. Thank you.*

MADAME GILLES	**Bonjour, Jean. Comment vas-tu?**	*Hello, Jean. How are you?*
JEAN	**Très bien, madame. Et vous?**	*Very well, Ma'am. And you?*
MADAME GILLES	**Très bien aussi. Merci.**	*Very well, too. Thank you.*
JEAN	**Au revoir, madame.**	*Goodbye, madame.*
MADAME GILLES	**Au revoir, Jean.**	*Goodbye, Jean.*

- French speakers usually shake hands when introduced to each other. Note that **enchanté** is used when the speaker is male and **enchantée** when the speaker is female.

PIERRE	**Salut, Paul. Salut, Alex. Je vous présente mon amie Marie.**	*Hi, Paul. Hi, Alex. I introduce to you my friend Marie.*
PAUL	**Bonjour, Marie. Enchanté.**	*Hello, Marie. Pleased to meet you.*
ALEX	**Enchanté, Marie.**	*Pleased to meet you, Marie.*
MARIE	**Enchantée.**	*Pleased to meet you.*

Vocabulaire complémentaire

un (meilleur) ami *(m.)* / **une (meilleure) amie** *(f.)* a best friend
un(e) colocataire a roommate
un copain *(m.)* / **une copine** *(f.)* a friend
un garçon / **une fille** a boy / a girl
un homme / **une femme** a man / a woman
un petit ami / **une petite amie** a boyfriend / a girlfriend

---

Comment t'appelles-tu? *What's your name?*
Je m'appelle Victor. *My name is Victor.*
Mon prénom est Annick. *My first name is Annick.*
Quel est ton nom (de famille)? *What is your (last) name?*
Mon nom (de famille) est Dubois. *My (last) name is Dubois.*

Comment s'appelle-t-il? *What is his name?*
Il s'appelle Henri. *His name is Henry.*
Comment s'appelle-t-elle? *What is her name?*
Elle s'appelle Isabelle. *Her name is Isabelle.*
Son nom (de famille) est... *His/Her last name is ...*

Son prénom est... *His/Her first name is ...*
Ravi(e) de faire ta *(informal)* **connaissance.** *Pleased to meet you.*
Ravi(e) de faire votre *(formal)* **connaissance.** *Pleased to meet you.*

Comment ça va? / Ça va (bien)? *How are you?*
Ça va (bien). Et toi? *Fine. And you?*
Moi aussi. *Me too.*
Pas mal. *Not bad.*

Bonsoir. *Good evening.*
Bonne nuit. *Good night.*
Bonne journée. *(Have a) Good day.*

Au revoir. *Goodbye.*
À demain. *See you tomorrow.*
À bientôt. *See you soon.*
À plus (tard). *See you (later).*

Il n'y a pas de quoi. / De rien. *You're welcome.*
Voici... *Here is ... / Here are ...*
Voilà... *There is ... / There are ...*

Note de **vocabulaire**

Copain / Copine may be used in more informal situations. Depending on context, it may mean boyfriend or girlfriend.

Liaisons musicales

© Ghnassia Anthony/SIPA/Newscom

Born in Corsica in 1984, the French singer Alizée was discovered after winning a talent show in France called *Graines de star* in 1999. One of her hits is *Mademoiselle Juliette,* a song inspired by Juliet Capulet from *Roméo & Juliette*. Find and listen to a performance of *Mademoiselle Juliette* on the Internet. How would you characterize its musical style?

Un mot sur la culture

Monsieur, madame et mademoiselle

Monsieur *(Mister)* is used to refer to adult males. It can also mean *sir* when used alone, not followed by someone's last name. The final **r** in **monsieur** is never pronounced.

Madame *(Mrs.)* is typically used for married women while **mademoiselle** *(Miss* or *Ms.)* is reserved for girls or unmarried women. In Quebec, however, all adult women are usually called **madame** regardless of marital status. In France, it is common to use **madame** for women who are over 30, regardless of marital status.

In writing, when used before a family name, **Monsieur**, **Madame**, and **Mademoiselle** are capitalized and often abbreviated as: **M. (M. Durand)**, **Mme (Mme Martin)**, and **Mlle (Mlle Leroux)**. There is no period after the feminine forms.

- Would you use **madame** or **mademoiselle** for the following people?
  1. a professor   2. your five-year-old niece   3. your boss

ACTIVITÉ A Mettez-les dans l'ordre! Put these phrases in the order in which the speakers would most likely say them.

A. _____ Très bien aussi. Merci.

_____ Ça va très bien.

_____ Salut, François! Comment ça va?

_____ Et toi, Manuel?

C. _____ À plus tard.

_____ Bonjour, Paul. Enchanté.

_____ Bonjour, Marc. Je vous présente Paul.

_____ Enchanté, Marc.

B. _____ Au revoir, madame.

_____ Bonjour, madame.

_____ Comment allez-vous?

_____ Pas mal. Merci.

D. _____ Rien de nouveau. À demain.

_____ Pas grand-chose. Et toi?

_____ Bonsoir, David. Quoi de neuf?

_____ Au revoir.

🔊 P-1 **ACTIVITÉ B Questions** You will hear some questions. Select the answer to each one.

1. a. Ça va bien.   b. Je m'appelle Carla.   c. Salut!

2. a. Ça va très bien, merci.   b. Mon nom est Auger.   c. Bonsoir.

3. a. Au revoir.   b. Moi aussi. Merci.   c. Je m'appelle Thomas.

4. a. À demain.   b. De rien.   c. Rien de nouveau.

🔊 P-2 **ACTIVITÉ C Les personnes célèbres**

Étape 1. You will hear introductions to some famous people. Select the correct first or last name to complete each introduction.

1. a. Catherine   b. Deneuve   **4.** a. Gérard   b. Depardieu

2. a. Zinédine   b. Zidane   **5.** a. Harry   b. Potter

3. a. Sasha   b. Obama   **6.** a. Marion   b. Cotillard

Étape 2. Indicate if each person is **un garçon, une fille, un homme,** or **une femme.**

Modèle: Catherine Deneuve est une femme.

ACTIVITÉ D Meilleur(e)s ami(e)s et petit(e)s ami(e)s Complete each sentence with the appropriate name.

1. Mon/Ma *(My)* meilleur(e) ami(e) s'appelle _____.

2. Mon/Ma colocataire s'appelle _____.

3. La petite amie de *(of)* Mickey Mouse s'appelle _____.

4. Le petit ami de Daisy Duck s'appelle _____.

5. Le copain de Charlie Brown s'appelle _____.

ACTIVITÉ **E** **Répondez** You will hear a series of questions and statements. What would you say in response?

P-3

1.   2.   3.   4.   5.   6.   7.   8.   9.   10.

ACTIVITÉ **F** **À vous: Faisons connaissance!**

Étape 1. Move around the room, greeting and introducing yourself to at least four people. Write down their first and last names.

Étape 2. Be prepared to introduce at least two of the people you just met.

Modèle: **Je vous présente Carrie Smith et Tom Baker.**

ACTIVITÉ **G** **Petits sketchs** Prepare a small skit with your classmates. Write out the dialogue and be prepared to act it out. Choose one or two of the following situations.

1. Good friends run into each other on campus on the way to class.
2. A student/Students run(s) into a professor on campus.
3. Your roommate introduces a friend to you at a party.
4. You run into your professor and introduce your friend to the professor.

✈ · · · · ·
Si vous y allez

Fondation Alliance française

The mission of the **Alliance française** is to promote the appreciation of French and Francophone cultures among French, Francophone, and American people through various educational and cultural activities. Most major cities have an **Alliance française**. To meet other francophiles, go to the website of your local **Alliance française** to see what activities are offered in your city.

© Stockbyte/Getty Images

Un mot sur la culture

Les salutations (Greetings)

In the French-speaking world, when people first meet each other, it is customary for them to shake hands regardless of their age or gender. When friends or family greet each other, men generally shake hands with each other while women kiss each other on the cheek. Men will kiss female family members and female friends on the cheek. The number of kisses (**les bises**) varies depending on the region and other factors and is difficult to anticipate. Two kisses, one on each cheek, is the most common combination throughout most of France. Three kisses are often exchanged in Paris and Provence or between close friends. Four kisses are reportedly exchanged in Nantes or as a sign of affection between the closest of friends or family members. However, no matter how many the number of kisses exchanged, the French always start with the right cheek.

• Do you think it is customary for the following cultures to greet with a kiss or kisses?

	Oui	Non			Oui	Non
1. les Américains	☐	☐		**3.** les Japonais	☐	☐
2. les Mexicains	☐	☐		**4.** les Africains	☐	☐

🔊 **Liaisons avec les mots et les sons**

P-4

L'alphabet et les accents

The letters in the French alphabet look the same as those in the English alphabet, but they do not sound the same.

a (a)	**h** (ache)	**o** (o)	**v** (vé)
b (bé)	**i** (i)	**p** (pé)	**w** (double vé)
c (cé)	**j** (ji)	**q** (ku)	**x** (iks)
d (dé)	**k** (ka)	**r** (erre)	**y** (i grec)
e (eu)	**l** (elle)	**s** (esse)	**z** (zède)
f (effe)	**m** (emme)	**t** (té)	
g (gé)	**n** (enne)	**u** (u)	

Some French words have written accents. These are part of their spelling and cannot be omitted. In later lessons, you will learn how these accents may change the way a word is pronounced. For now, you need to recognize these accent marks and, when you spell a word aloud, include the name of the accent after the letter.

Accent	Name	Example	Spelling
´	accent aigu	prénom	P-R-E-**accent aigu**-N-O-M
`	accent grave	très bien	T-R-E-**accent grave**-S B-I-E-N
^	accent circonflexe	hôpital	H-O-**accent circonflexe**-P-I-T-A-L
¨	tréma	Raphaël	R-A-P-H-A-E-**tréma**-L
¸	cédille	Ça va	C-**cédille**-A V-A

Pratique A. Listen to and practice spelling these French names. Don't forget the accents.

1. Noël   3. Stéphane   5. Benoît   7. Eugène

2. Anaïs   4. Béatrice   6. François   8. Zoé

Pratique B. The **h** in French is usually silent and treated as a vowel as in these names. Listen to, repeat, and practice spelling these names. Notice the silent **h** as you say the names.

Hélène   Héloïse   Henri   Hermès   Honoré   Hugh

Pratique C. Listen to and practice spelling the names of these characters from the film *Liaisons*.

Claire Gagner

Abia Ndono

Alexis Prévost

ACTIVITÉ **H** **Enchanté(e)** Greet and introduce yourself to four people in your class to find out their names and the city (**ville**) they are from. You may have to spell your name or the city. Be prepared to present your findings to the rest of the class.

Nom	Ville
1. _____	_____
2. _____	_____
3. _____	_____
4. _____	_____

ACTIVITÉ **I** **Francophone ou francophile?** Indicate where the following people are from and whether each person is **francophone** or **francophile**.

Modèle: Catherine Deneuve / Paris
Catherine Deneuve est de Paris. Elle est francophone.

1. Julia Child / Pasadena
2. Céline Dion / Charlemagne (Québec)
3. Zinédine Zidane / Marseille
4. Jodie Foster / Los Angeles
5. Gérard Depardieu / Châteauroux (France)
6. Marion Cotillard / Paris
7. Bradley Cooper / Philadelphie
8. Le professeur de français / [ville]

Un mot sur la langue

Francophones et francophiles

The term **francophone** is typically used as an adjective meaning *French-speaking* (as a primary language) and may be used to refer to individuals, groups of people, or places.

Montréal est une ville **francophone**.
Amadou est **francophone**.

The term **francophone** may also be used as a noun to refer to a native speaker of French, regardless of ethnicity or geographical location. When used in English, the "F" is capitalized.

Il y a des **francophones** à mon université.   *There are **Francophones** at my university.*

The word **francophiles** refers to people who identify themselves with speakers of French and admire the French language and its cultures. The opposite of **francophile** is **francophobe**.

• Est-ce que vous êtes francophone, francophile ou francophobe?

© Monkey Business Images/Shutterstock.com

Pour parler de nos origines

Le verbe **être** / Les pronoms sujets / Les questions

DU FILM *LIAISONS*

Un coup d'œil sur la grammaire

In the **Prologue** of the film *Liaisons*, a woman is reading a document that she has written.

Je **suis** Madeleine Prévost de Paris…
Now answer these questions about the woman's message.

1. What part of speech is the word **suis**?
   a. noun   b. verb   c. adverb

2. What do you think **je suis** means?
   a. *I am*   b. *I have*   c. *very well*

Le verbe **être**

> **Note de grammaire**
> **Être** is the infinitive form of the verb. The infinitive is the basic form of the verb that you will find in a dictionary.

•••❖ In French, the verb **être** means *to be*. One very common use of **être** is to express one's place of origin. In this case, it is used with the preposition **de** + a city, which means *from* in this particular expression.

Céline Dion **est de** Charlemagne, au Québec.

Catherine Deneuve **est de** Paris, en France.

*Céline Dion **is from** Charlemagne, Quebec.*

*Catherine Deneuve **is from** Paris, France.*

•••❖ Another common use of **être** is to express one's occupation.

Voici Monsieur Leroux. Il **est professeur.**   *Here is Mr. Leroux. He **is a professor.***

Nathan **est étudiant.**   *Nathan **is a student.***

Catherine **est étudiante.**   *Catherine **is a student.***

Les pronoms sujets

•••❖ The following are the present tense forms of the verb **être** and the subject pronouns *(I, you, he, she, it, we,* and *they)*.

> **Note de prononciation**
> The **s** of **nous, vous, ils,** and **elles** is not pronounced. However, if the word that follows these pronouns begins with a vowel, the **s** is pronounced as **z** in **vous êtes.**

être *(to be)*	
je suis *I am*	**nous sommes** *we are*
tu es *you are*	**vous êtes** *you are*
il est *he/it* (m.) *is*	**ils sont** *they* (m. pl.) *are*
elle est *she/it* (f.) *is*	**elles sont** *they* (f. pl.) *are*
on est *one is*	

There are formal and informal ways to address people in French. When talking to someone whom you do not know well, who is older, or who is in a position of respect, use **vous** *(formal)*. When talking to a friend, family member, or a child, use **tu** *(informal)*. When talking to more than one person, use **vous** *(plural, formal, and informal)*.

When talking about several persons or a group of people, use **elles** if everyone is female. Use **ils** if at least one person is male.

Carole et Sarah, **elles** sont de Paris.	*Carole and Sarah, **they** are from Paris.*
Ahmed et Nourdine, **ils** sont de Nice.	*Ahmed and Nourdine, **they** are from Nice.*
Antoine et Marie, **ils** sont de Montréal.	*Antoine and Marie, **they** are from Montreal.*

Les questions oui/non

To ask a yes/no question in French, you can make a statement and raise the pitch of your voice at the end. This is called rising intonation. Such questions are considered informal.

—**Pauline est étudiante?**	*—Is Pauline a student?*
—**Oui, elle est étudiante.**	*—Yes, she's a student.*

You can also place **est-ce que** (**est-ce qu'** before a vowel sound) in front of a statement. Your voice also rises at the end of these questions.

—**Est-ce qu'elle est de Chicago?**	*—Is she from Chicago?*
—**Non, elle est de Cleveland.**	*—No, she is from Cleveland.*

ACTIVITÉ J Quelle ville?

Étape 1. Complete each sentence with the correct information about yourself. Then share your information with the class. How many of your classmates are from the same city (**ville**) as you? How many of you are from the same city as your parents? If you have children and/or a spouse, are they from the same city as you are?

1. Je suis de *(city)*…
2. Mes *(My)* parents sont de…
3. Mes enfants *(children)* sont de…
4. Mon mari *(husband)* / Ma *(My)* femme *(wife)* est de…
5. Mes grands-parents sont de…
6. Mon/Ma colocataire est de…

 Étape 2. Now ask two people next to you where they are from. Are they from the same city as you? To ask someone which city he/she is from, you can say **Tu es de quelle ville?** To ask about a classmate's parents, grandparents, or children, say **Tes parents / Tes grands-parents / Tes enfants, ils sont de quelle ville?** To ask about a spouse or roommate, say **Ton mari / Ta femme / Ton (Ta) colocataire est de quelle ville?**

En classe

In class

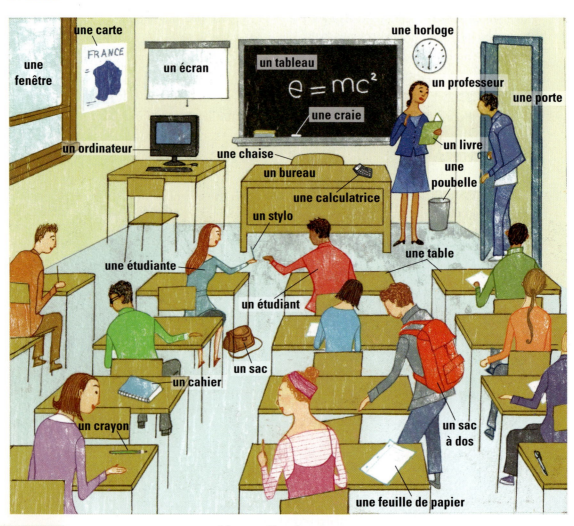

une carte

une horloge

une fenêtre

un écran

un tableau

$e = mc^2$

une craie

un professeur

une porte

un ordinateur

une chaise

un bureau

un livre

une poubelle

une calculatrice

un stylo

une table

une étudiante

un étudiant

un sac

un cahier

un crayon

un sac à dos

une feuille de papier

Une salle de classe

Note de vocabulaire

The **h** in **horloge** and in **huit** is not pronounced because the **h** in French is usually silent.

Vocabulaire complémentaire

Les nombres de 0 à 20

0 **zéro**

1 **un**	6 **six**	11 **onze**	16 **seize**
2 **deux**	7 **sept**	12 **douze**	17 **dix-sept**
3 **trois**	8 **huit**	13 **treize**	18 **dix-huit**
4 **quatre**	9 **neuf**	14 **quatorze**	19 **dix-neuf**
5 **cinq**	10 **dix**	15 **quinze**	20 **vingt**

En classe

Dans la classe, il y a... *In the classroom, there is . . . , there are . . .*
une affiche *a poster*
une agrafeuse *a stapler*
un examen *an exam*
un iPod® *an iPod®*
un ordinateur (portable) *a (laptop) computer*
un (téléphone) portable *a cell phone*

un(e) camarade de classe *a classmate*
une classe *a class*

ACTIVITÉ A **Dans notre *(In our)* salle de classe** Read these sentences and indicate whether the objects are in your classroom.

	Oui	Non
1. Il y a une porte.	☐	☐
2. Il y a une fenêtre.	☐	☐
3. Il y a une calculatrice.	☐	☐
4. Il y a un écran.	☐	☐
5. Il y a un ordinateur.	☐	☐
6. Il y a des livres.	☐	☐
7. Il y a des cahiers.	☐	☐
8. Il y a une poubelle.	☐	☐
9. Il y a une horloge.	☐	☐
10. Il y a un tableau.	☐	☐

Conclusion Notre salle de classe est bien équipée *(well equipped)*. Oui / Non

© Ferenc Szelepcsenyi/Shutterstock.com

Si vous y allez

© Ludovic/REA/Redux

If you go to France, visit the store Fnac, one of the largest retail chains specializing in cultural and electronic products such as books, DVDs, CDs, and computers. If you can't make it to France, check out their website at: www.fnac.com

ACTIVITÉ B Dans mon *(In my)* sac (à dos)

Étape 1. Indicate if these objects are in your bag.

Dans mon sac (à dos)…

	Oui	Non		Oui	Non
1. il y a une calculatrice.	☐	☐	**7.** il y a un (téléphone) portable.	☐	☐
2. il y a une affiche.	☐	☐	**8.** il y a des livres.	☐	☐
3. il y a un examen.	☐	☐	**9.** il y a une agrafeuse.	☐	☐
4. il y a un crayon.	☐	☐	**10.** il y a une feuille de papier.	☐	☐
5. il y a un iPod®.	☐	☐			
6. il y a un stylo.	☐	☐			

Étape 2. Ask a classmate if the items in **Étape 1** are in his/her bag.

Modèle: Étudiant(e) 1: **Est-ce qu'il y a une calculatrice dans ton** *(in your)* **sac (à dos)?**
Étudiant(e) 2: **Oui. / Non.**

Étape 3. Based on your findings, which statement best describes your classmate? Might he/she be a good person to borrow something from?

a. Mon/Ma *(My)* camarade de classe est bien équipé(e).

b. Ma/Mon camarade de classe n'est pas bien équipé(e) *(is not well equipped)*.

ACTIVITÉ C Les salles de classe en 1970 et aujourd'hui

Étape 1. How have classrooms changed since 1970? Make a list of typical things one would find in a classroom in the 1970s and another list of things that one would find in a typical classroom today.

1970	Aujourd'hui *(Today)*
un tableau _____	_____
_____	_____
_____	_____
_____	_____

Étape 2. Now look at your classroom and review your two lists. How would you describe your French classroom?

a. Ma *(My)* salle de classe est comme *(like)* une salle de classe de 1970.

b. Ma salle de classe est une salle de classe moderne.

ACTIVITÉ D Quel numéro le suit? *(Which number follows it?)*

P-5 You will hear a number. Select the number that follows it.

1. a. 6	b. 8	c. 10	**4.** a. 4	b. 11	c. 3
2. a. 12	b. 15	c. 18	**5.** a. 6	b. 13	c. 18
3. a. 20	b. 17	c. 9	**6.** a. 19	b. 17	c. 18

E **Combien?** *(How many?)* How many of these people or things are in your classroom?

Dans la salle de classe, il y a…

1. _____ chaise(s).
2. _____ sac(s) à dos.
3. _____ iPod(s)®.
4. _____ affiche(s).
5. _____ professeur(s).
6. _____ ordinateur(s).
7. _____ étudiant(e)(s).
8. _____ camarade(s) de classe.
9. _____ horloge(s).
10. _____ poubelle(s).

ACTIVITÉ **F** **Les courriels** *(E-mails)*

Étape 1. Write down your instructor's e-mail address. Here is some useful vocabulary to help you.

> *at* or @ = **arobase** *dash* = **tiret** *dot* = **point** *underscore* = **tiret bas**

• Le courriel de mon professeur: _____

Étape 2. Ask three students in your class to spell aloud their e-mail addresses. Write what you hear.

Modèle: Étudiant(e) 1: **Quelle est ton adresse électronique?**
Étudiant(e) 2: **Mon adresse électronique est s-m-i-t-h arobase a-b-c point e-d-u.**
Étudiant(e) 1 *writes:* **smith@abc.edu**

Un mot sur la culture

La francophonie

The term **francophonie** was created in 1880 by the French geographer Onésime Reclus (1837–1916) to refer to a community of people and countries whose culture, regardless of ethnicity and geographical location, is primarily associated with the French language. The concept of **francophonie** was popularized by Léopold Sédar Senghor in the 1960s, and gradually became institutionalized, leading to the first **Sommet de la Francophonie** in Paris in 1986. Today, **la francophonie** with a small "**f**" refers to a community of people who use French as a language of communication and in their daily life; **la Francophonie** with a capital "**F**" refers to a group of governments or countries which forms the **Organisation Internationale de la Francophonie** (OIF).

• What countries make up the **Organisation Internationale de la Francophonie**?

© tony4urban/Shutterstock.com

Pour être précis(e)

Les articles indéfinis / Le genre et le nombre

DU FILM *LIAISONS*

Un coup d'œil sur la grammaire

Here is a description of an image you will see when you watch the **Prologue** of the film *Liaisons* later in this chapter.

Il y a **une** femme avec **un** stylo qui écrit sur *(on)* **une** feuille de papier dans *(in)* **une** chambre *(room)* à Paris.

The words **une** and **un** both mean *a* or *an* in English. Why is **une** used with **femme** and **feuille de papier,** but **un** with **stylo**?

1. The article **une** is used with nouns that have _____ grammatical gender.

    a. masculine   b. feminine

2. The article **un** is used with nouns that have _____ grammatical gender.

  a. masculine   b. feminine

As in English, French nouns have number (**le nombre**): singular or plural. Unlike English, French nouns also have grammatical gender (**le genre**). Every noun (a person, an animal, a place, a thing, or an idea) is classified as being either masculine or feminine. Sometimes nouns that refer to females are feminine (**une femme** *a woman,* **une fille** *a girl*) and nouns that refer to males are masculine (**un homme** *a man,* **un garçon** *a boy*). However, in most cases, especially with inanimate nouns, gender is unpredictable. Therefore, you must learn the gender along with the noun. Gender is often expressed not only in the noun, but also in the article that introduces it.

Indefinite articles: gender and number				
	singular		**plural**	
masculine	**un** livre	*a book*	**des** livres	*(some) books*
	un ordinateur	*a computer*	**des** ordinateurs	*(some) computers*
feminine	**une** table	*a table*	**des** tables	*(some) tables*
	une horloge	*a clock*	**des** horloges	*(some) clocks*

- The indefinite articles (**les articles indéfinis**) mean *a, an,* or *some.* **Un** is used before masculine singular nouns; **une** is used before feminine singular nouns; and **des** is used before plural nouns. While *some* is often omitted in English, **des** cannot be omitted in French.

- In most cases, an **s,** which is not pronounced, is added to a singular noun to make it plural. Nouns that end in **-eau** like **un tableau** and **un bureau** add an **x: des tableaux, des bureaux.**

- Nouns that have been borrowed from the English language are usually masculine: **un CD, un iPod®, un DVD.**

- Some nouns that refer to people can be changed from masculine to feminine by adding an **e.**

un étudiant *(m.)*	*a student*	une étudiant**e** *(f.)*	*a student*
un ami *(m.)*	*a friend*	une ami**e** *(f.)*	*a friend*
un Français	*a French man*	une Français**e**	*a French woman*

Pour aller plus loin
C'est vs. *Ce sont*

To identify objects or people, use **c'est** *(this is)* followed by a singular article and noun and **ce sont** *(these are)* followed by a plural article and noun.

Qu'est-ce que c'est?	*What is this?*
C'est un stylo Montblanc.	*This is a Montblanc pen.*
Ce sont des calculatrices.	*These are calculators.*

ACTIVITÉ G **La garderie** Select the item that goes with each article. Then indicate if that item is typically found in the playroom of **une garderie** *(a daycare center).*

						Oui	Non
1.	une...	a. table	b. écran	c. stylos		☐	☐
2.	des...	a. calculatrice	b. chaises	c. livre		☐	☐
3.	un...	a. porte	b. examen	c. crayons		☐	☐
4.	une...	a. affiche	b. livres	c. tableau		☐	☐
5.	des...	a. crayon	b. livres	c. porte		☐	☐
6.	une...	a. horloge	b. écrans	c. ordinateur		☐	☐
7.	des...	a. crayons	b. tableau	c. cahier		☐	☐
8.	un...	a. feuille de papier	b. calculatrice	c. crayon		☐	☐
9.	une…	a. poubelle	b. étudiants	c. professeur		☐	☐
10.	des…	a. agrafeuse	b. amis	c. craie		☐	☐

🔊 **ACTIVITÉ** Ⓗ **Je vais acheter...** You will hear parts of statements about what
P-6 someone needs to buy for school. Pay attention to the article to determine what that
object is.

Modèle: *You hear:* Je vais acheter *(I am going to buy)* une...
You see: a. agrafeuse b. livre c. stylos
You select: **a**

1. a. calculatrice   b. cahier   c. écrans
2. a. affiche   b. chaise   c. stylos
3. a. ordinateur   b. calculatrice   c. tables
4. a. craie   b. affiches   c. crayon
5. a. iPod®   b. cahiers   c. chaise
6. a. cahiers   b. tableau   c. ordinateur
7. a. horloge   b. téléphone portable   c. agrafeuses
8. a. agrafeuse   b. sac   c. cahier

ACTIVITÉ Ⓘ **Qu'est-ce que c'est?** Listen and watch as your instructor
points to various objects in the room. Answer his/her questions with **C'est...** or
Ce sont...

Modèle: Professeur: **C'est un tableau ou une table?** *(points to blackboard)*
Étudiant(e)s: **C'est un tableau.**

👤👤👤 **ACTIVITÉ** Ⓙ **Fais-moi un dessin!** *(Draw me a picture!)*

The class will be divided into two teams to play a picture-drawing game. One person
from each team will take turns drawing. The drawers (**dessinateurs / dessinatrices**)
for each team will go to the instructor who will show them a card with a word on
it. Each drawer must then go back to his/her team and draw the picture on the card
while the rest of the team tries to guess what the object is. The first person from a
team that says the correct object and article (for example, **C'est un crayon!**) gets
a point!

ACTIVITÉ Ⓚ **Trois objets**

Étape 1. If you could only take three objects with you to class everyday, what
would they be? Complete this sentence with three objects from **Vocabulaire 2.**

• Mes trois objets sont:

_____

_____

_____.

Étape 2. Compare what you wrote with a classmate. How would you describe your partner based on his/her response? Complete the following sentence with your partner's name and select the appropriate adjective.

Conclusion _____ est pratique / original(e) / extravagant(e) parce que *(because)* ses trois objets sont _____, _____ et _____.

ACTIVITÉ **L** **Une salle de classe idéale**

Étape 1. Make a list of what should be in an ideal classroom, using vocabulary you know. Include the ideal quantity of each object. Write out the numbers in French.

• Dans une salle de classe idéale, il y a…

Étape 2. Share what you wrote with a classmate. Did you write similar things? Decide with your classmate whether the following statement is true or false for your classroom.

Conclusion Notre *(Our)* salle de classe est une salle de classe idéale. V / F

ACTIVITÉ **M** **À acheter**

Étape 1. According to the National Retail Federation, the average college student in the U.S. spends approximately $956.93 on back-to-school items every year. What do you still need to buy this semester / term for **la rentrée?** Make a list in French of what you are going to buy at the bookstore.

> **À acheter…** *(To buy …)*
>
> un stylo _____
> _____
> _____
> _____
> _____
> _____
> _____
> _____
> _____

Étape 2. Based on your list, how much do you think you will need to spend? Check the best answer.

Lexique	
< : **moins de** *(less than)*	> : **plus de** *(more than)*

☐ < $5,00   ☐ >$5,00   ☐ > $10,00
☐ > $15,00   ☐ >$20,00

Liaisons musicales

© Didier Messens/ Redferns/Getty Images

Patrick Bruel (1959–) is a French singer born in Algeria. One of his popular songs, *La place des grands hommes,* is a song about school friends wondering what their lives will be like if they meet again in 10 years. Look for the music video of this song on the Internet. Did you and your friends ever wonder about the same thing in high school?

Les études

Studies

le commerce
(international)

l'art (m.)

l'astronomie (f.)

la biologie

le journalisme

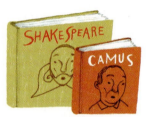

la littérature

les mathématiques
(f. pl.)

la musique

la psychologie

Les cours à l'université

Vocabulaire complémentaire

Quelle est ta spécialisation? *What's your major?*

Qu'est-ce que tu étudies? *(sing.) What are you studying?*

Qu'est-ce que vous étudiez? *(pl.) What are you studying?*

J'étudie... *I am studying . . .*

Je ne sais pas encore. *I don't know yet.*

Combien de cours *(m.)* **as-tu ce semestre?** *How many courses / classes do you have this term?*

les devoirs *(m. pl.) homework*

l'école *(f.) school*

les études *(f.) studies*

l'université *(f.) university*

Les lettres (f.), les langues (f.) et les arts (m.)

les langues
l'allemand (m.) *German*
l'anglais (m.)
le chinois *Chinese*
l'espagnol (m.)
le français
le russe *Russian*
la philosophie

Les sciences (f.) humaines / sociales

l'anthropologie (f.)
l'histoire (f.)
la psychologie
la sociologie

Les sciences naturelles

la chimie *chemistry*
la physique *physics*

L'administration (f.), l'économie

la comptabilité *accounting*
le droit *law*
l'économie (f.) *economics*
la gestion *business administration*

D'autres cours / spécialisations

le génie (civil, mécanique, électrique) *engineering*
l'informatique (f.) *computer science*
les sciences politiques (f. pl.)

Les nombres de 20 à 60

20 **vingt**	25 **vingt-cinq**	30 **trente**
21 **vingt et un**	26 **vingt-six**	31 **trente et un**
22 **vingt-deux**	27 **vingt-sept**	40 **quarante**
23 **vingt-trois**	28 **vingt-huit**	50 **cinquante**
24 **vingt-quatre**	29 **vingt-neuf**	60 **soixante**

Pour aller plus loin
Les articles définis

In French, definite articles (**les articles définis**) are used with majors and courses because one function of definite articles is to designate nouns that are used in a general sense. In this case in English, no article is used. The French definite articles are **le** (m., sing.), **la** (f., sing.), **l'** (sing. before a vowel sound), and **les** (m. pl. and f. pl.).

Tran étudie **la** psychologie.	*Tran studies psychology.*
Le français est intéressant.	*French is interesting.*

ACTIVITÉ A **Associations**

P-7

Étape 1. Indicate the item you associate with the subject matter you hear.

1. a. un microscope   b. les guerres mondiales (*world wars*)
2. a. Picasso   b. B. F. Skinner
3. a. Beethoven   b. *Les Misérables*
4. a. la Bourse (*stock market*)   b. le musée (*museum*)
5. a. la géométrie   b. les ordinateurs
6. a. Friedrich Nietzsche   b. une calculatrice

Étape 2. Go back to the items you didn't choose. Can you give a subject matter association from **Vocabulaire 3** for each one?

ACTIVITÉ B **On étudie…**

> **Note de grammaire**
> In French, **de** (*of*) is used in front of words that begin with consonants and **d'** is used in front of words that begin with a vowel or silent *h*: **un cours de chimie, un cours d'astronomie, un cours d'histoire.**

Using the following columns, make logical sentences.

Modèle: Dans un cours **d'économie,** on étudie (*one studies*) la Bourse.

Dans un cours…

1. _____ d'histoire
2. _____ d'astronomie
3. _____ d'économie
4. _____ de physique
5. _____ de journalisme
6. _____ de chimie

… on étudie

a. la gestion
b. l'actualité (*current events*)
c. les éléments chimiques
d. la rotation des planètes
e. les événements historiques
f. les réactions nucléaires

Liaisons musicales

© François Guillot/AFP/Getty Images/Newscom

French composer Bruno Coulais (1954–) composed the music for *Les Choristes,* a film about how a music teacher changed the lives of his students at a boys' boarding school in France. This soundtrack was nominated for an Oscar in 2005 in the Best Achievement in Music Written for Motion Pictures. Listen to excerpts of the soundtrack on the Internet.

ACTIVITÉ C **Quelle est sa spécialisation?**

Read these statements by several people. Can you guess what each person's major is?

1. Je m'appelle Sophie. Mes cours ce semestre sont la géométrie, le calcul et l'algèbre. Ma spécialisation est…

2. Je m'appelle Mustapha. Mes cours ce semestre sont la comptabilité, l'économie et la gestion des affaires. Ma spécialisation est…

3. Je m'appelle Anouk. Mes cours ce semestre sont la littérature française du Moyen Âge (*Middle Ages*), la grammaire avancée et le cinéma français. Ma spécialisation est…

4. Je m'appelle Jean-Marc. Mes cours ce semestre sont Freud et la psychanalyse, l'interprétation des rêves (*dreams*) et les théories de Jean Piaget. Ma spécialisation est…

ACTIVITÉ D **Et vous? Quelle est votre spécialisation?**

Ask three people what their classes are and then try to guess their major. If someone has not yet chosen his/her major, he/she can say **Je ne sais pas encore.**

Modèle: Étudiant(e) 1: **Ce semestre quels sont tes (*your*) cours?**
Étudiant(e) 2: **Ce semestre, mes cours sont le français, la comptabilité et l'économie.**
Étudiant(e) 1: **Est-ce que ta spécialisation est le commerce international?**
Étudiant(e) 2: **Oui.**

ACTIVITÉ **E** **Les nombres (Numbers)** You will hear a number. What is the most logical thing it could be referring to?

P-8

1. a. le prix *(price)* d'un livre b. le prix d'un iPod®
2. a. le prix d'un crayon b. le prix d'une calculatrice
3. a. le prix d'une agrafeuse b. le prix d'un téléphone portable
4. a. le prix d'un ordinateur b. le prix d'une chaise
5. a. le prix d'un crayon b. le prix d'une horloge
6. a. le nombre d'états *(states)* aux États-Unis b. le nombre de crédits du cours de français

ACTIVITÉ **F** **Combien?**

Étape 1. Answer these questions with the number that answers each question correctly for you. If you do not know, you can say **Je ne sais pas.**

1. Combien de cours as-tu *(do you have)* ce semestre?
2. Combien de crédits as-tu ce semestre?
3. Combien de crédits de français sont nécessaires pour *(for)* le diplôme de français?
4. Combien de devoirs as-tu ce soir?

Étape 2. Who in the class has the greatest number of credit hours this semester?

Conclusion _____ a le plus grand nombre de crédits ce semestre.

© Olga Besnard/Shutterstock.com

Un mot sur la culture

La dictée

The French **dictée** *(dictation)* is more than a spelling exercise; it is a cultural phenomenon. The French are so attached to this practice that it has been made into a popular TV show, *Les dictées de Bernard Pivot.* Host Bernard Pivot reads texts with tricky grammar and complex spelling (French does not always sound like the way it is written) to challenge participants and viewers. Besides the game show, this passion has sparked the establishment of **dictée** competitions all over the world, including the U.S., and the creation of two best-selling **dictée** books by Pivot.

- Do you think a dictation game could be popular in the U.S.?
- Would you like to participate in a **dictée** competition?

Pour décrire

Les articles définis / Les adjectifs qualificatifs

DU FILM *LIAISONS*

Un coup d'œil sur la grammaire

The film ***Liaisons*** that you will be watching in this course has a scene that takes place at McGill University. Here is what a student has to say about his courses there.

J'ai deux cours ce semestre: la sociologie et l'anglais. Pour moi, la sociologie est **fascinante**. Mon cours d'anglais est **intéressant** et il est **important** parce qu'il y a beaucoup d'anglophones à McGill.

1. The words **fascinante, intéressant,** and **important** are adjectives. Why is there an **e** at the end of **fascinante,** but not at the end of **intéressant** and **important**?

2. What two definite articles do you recognize in the student's statements?

© Arpad Benedek/iStockphoto.com

Si vous y allez

If you go to Paris, check out **la Sorbonne.** Founded by Robert de Sorbon in 1253, **la Sorbonne** is one of France's oldest universities. You can take a virtual tour at www.sorbonne.fr

Les articles définis

✦ As you saw in **Vocabulaire 3,** French has four definite articles: **le** *(m., sing.),* **la** *(f., sing.),* **l'** *(sing.* before a vowel sound), and **les** *(m. pl.* and *f. pl.).* They are often used to refer to nouns that were previously mentioned or to talk about specific nouns. In this usage, the definite article is equivalent to *the* in English.

—C'est qui?	—*Who is that?*
—C'est **le** professeur.	—*That's the professor.*
Voici **l'**agrafeuse.	*Here's the stapler.*
J'aime **le** stylo rouge.	*I like the red pen (as opposed to the blue pen).*

✦ Another use of definite articles is to designate nouns in a general sense. In this case, no article is used in English.

J'étudie **les** langues.	*I study languages.*
Ma spécialisation est **le** chinois.	*My major is Chinese.*

✦ Definite articles are also used to indicate possession with the preposition **de** and the name of a person. When the person's name begins with a vowel sound, **de** becomes **d'.**

C'est **le** professeur **de** Paul.	*This is Paul's professor.*
Ce sont **les** stylos **de** Paul et **de** Guy.	*These are Paul and Guy's pens.*
Voici **la** table **d'**Anne.	*Here is Anne's table.*

Les adjectifs qualificatifs

Adjectives are words used to describe people, places, things, and ideas: *serious student, intelligent young woman.* In French, adjectives must agree with the noun or pronoun they modify. This means that they must agree in gender and number, just as articles (**le, la, les, un, une, des**) do. Descriptive adjectives (**les adjectifs qualificatifs**) normally follow the nouns they modify.

For most adjectives, an **e** is added to the masculine form to create the feminine form. Add an **s** to the masculine and feminine forms to make them plural.

amusant(e) *funny*	**embêtant(e)** *annoying*	**intelligent(e)**
brillant(e)	**fascinant(e)**	**intéressant(e)**
charmant(e)	**impatient(e)**	**méchant(e)** *mean*
content(e)	**important(e)**	**patient(e)**
doué(e) *gifted*	**indépendant(e)**	**récent(e)**

Tom est intelligent. Sylvie est intelligent**e**.

Ils sont charmant**s**. Elles sont charmant**es**.

- When an adjective of this type describes a group of males and females or objects that are both masculine and feminine in grammatical gender, use the masculine plural form.

  Tom et Sylvie sont intelligent**s**. L'art *(m.)* et la musique sont important**s**.

- In the masculine singular form of adjectives of this type, the final consonant is silent. In the feminine singular form, the final consonant is pronounced. The final **s** of the plural forms is silent.

  Pierre est intelligen**t**. Claire est intelligent**e**.

  Ils sont intelligent**s**. Elles sont intelligent**es**.

Some adjectives have the same feminine and masculine forms. Most adjectives of this type end in **e**.

célèbre *famous*	**moderne**	**pratique**
dynamique	**modeste**	**sociable**
énergique	**nécessaire**	**timide**
facile *easy*	**optimiste**	**utile** *useful*
inutile *not useful*	**pessimiste**	

Le journalisme est **utile**. La biologie est **difficile**.
Mon professeur est **dynamique**.
Norah Jones est **célèbre**.

Note de grammaire
Adjectives like these that end in **e** and have the same masculine and feminine forms are often cognates, meaning they have the same or similar spellings and meanings in French and English. An exception is **chic**, which does not end in **e**: Il/Elle est **chic**. Ils/Elles sont **chics**.

Note de grammaire
Some adjectives are irregular and have different masculine and feminine forms. You will learn these adjectives in **Chapitre 2**.

ACTIVITÉ G Les possessions Your instructor will point to different objects that belong to you or your classmates. Indicate who that object belongs to.

Modèle: Professeur: **C'est le livre de qui?**

Étudiants: **C'est le livre de Mark.**

ACTIVITÉ H Les cours You will hear adjectives that describe various courses. Select the course you feel fits the adjective used. You may select more than one course.

P-9

1. a. le chinois	b. le français	c. le journalisme
2. a. la biologie	b. la chimie	c. la littérature
3. a. l'astronomie	b. l'astrologie	c. la danse folklorique
4. a. la comptabilité	b. la musique	c. la sociologie
5. a. l'allemand	b. l'anglais	c. le français
6. a. la comptabilité	b. l'économie	c. l'histoire

ACTIVITÉ I Quel cours? (Which class?) A French exchange student is describing courses she is taking. Listen carefully to the form of the adjectives in order to determine to which class she is referring.

P-10

1. a. la biologie	b. le français
2. a. le chinois	b. la littérature
3. a. l'art *(m.)*	b. la musique
4. a. le génie	b. la chimie
5. a. l'anglais *(m.)*	b. l'informatique *(f.)*
6. a. le journalisme	b. la gestion des affaires

ACTIVITÉ J Les Clinton

World leaders, past or present, always make the news. A journalist in Senegal recently wrote an article on the Clintons. Pay attention to the form of the adjectives to determine if they refer to Bill or to Hillary. Write either Bill or Hillary in each blank. Then, indicate whether you agree or disagree with what the journalist wrote.

DANIEL BARRY/epa/Corbis Wire/Corbis

	Je suis d'accord.	**Je ne suis pas d'accord.**
1. _____ est douée.	☐	☐
2. _____ est passionnante.	☐	☐
3. _____ est intelligent.	☐	☐
4. _____ est patient.	☐	☐
5. _____ est amusante.	☐	☐
6. _____ est content.	☐	☐

© Shaun Jeffers/Shutterstock.com

ACTIVITÉ Ⓚ **Le prince William et Catherine, la duchesse de Cambridge**

Étape 1. Does Prince William have a lot in common with his wife Kate? Decide which traits you think each one has. Select both names if you think they both have that trait. You may also decide some traits do not apply to either one.

	William	Kate
1. dynamique	☐	☐
2. timide	☐	☐
3. pratique	☐	☐
4. moderne	☐	☐
5. sociable	☐	☐
6. pessimiste	☐	☐
7. modeste	☐	☐
8. chic	☐	☐

Étape 2. Write sentences to describe Prince William and his wife Kate based on how you responded in **Étape 1.** Share your sentences with a classmate. Were your sentences similar or different?

ACTIVITÉ Ⓛ **Les cours et les professions** What course or courses do you think are **nécessaires** and **utiles** to prepare for these professions? Is there a course that is **inutile**? Share responses with a partner to see if you have similar views.

Modèle: un comptable *(accountant)*
La comptabilité est nécessaire. Les mathématiques sont utiles.
La chimie est inutile.

1. un professeur de littérature

2. un journaliste

3. un économiste *(economist)*

4. un artiste

ACTIVITÉ Ⓜ **Je suis comme…** *(I am like . . .)*

Étape 1. From the adjectives you've learned so far, select three that you think describe you well. Write three sentences.

Modèle: **Je suis très dynamique. Je suis intelligent(e). Je suis sociable.**

Étape 2. Get together with a classmate and read him/her your sentences. Based on your description of yourself, your classmate will decide which famous person you are most like. Tell your classmate whether you agree or not.

Modèle: Étudiant(e) 1: **Tu es comme** *(like)* **Jennifer Lopez.**
Étudiant(e) 2: **Oui, je suis d'accord. / Non, je ne suis pas d'accord.**

PROJECTION

**LIAISONS
PROLOGUE**

Avant de visionner

You are about to watch the **Prologue** of the film *Liaisons.* Don't worry if you do not understand all of the language you hear. As a beginning student of French, you aren't expected to! However, you should be able to grasp the central ideas of each film segment you watch. The activities in this book are designed to help you understand as much as possible.

As you may know, cinematographic elements of a film such as sound and camera techniques play a role in helping you understand what is going on in any given scene. These cinematographic elements are part of what the French call **la mise en scène** which includes: **le décor, les costumes et les objets; les couleurs; l'éclairage** *(lighting);* **le son** *(sound);* and **les mouvements de la caméra.** You may rely on context and elements of **la mise en scène** to help you understand. As your proficiency in French increases, so will your comprehension of the language.

ACTIVITÉ A Un coup d'œil sur une scène

Here is a scene from the **Prologue** of *Liaisons.*

CLAIRE Bonjour, Maman.

MME GAGNER C'est toi, Claire? Ce n'est pas une de mes hallucinations...?

CLAIRE Non, Maman. C'est moi.

With a classmate, try to answer the following questions based on the scene. You will check your answers later when you watch the **Prologue.**

1. What is the relationship between these two characters?
2. What does Madame Gagner ask Claire?
3. Where do you think this scene takes place?

▶ Regarder le Prologue

You will now watch the **Prologue** of the film *Liaisons.* Use the context and **la mise en scène** to help you understand. Also, verify your answers to **Activité A.**

Après le visionnage

ACTIVITÉ B **Le contexte** One skill you will want to develop as you study French is to guess the meaning of language from context. Here are lines between the man and the woman from the opening **Prologue.**

HOMME Maman, maman, ça va?

FEMME Oui, oui, mon fils. Ça va.

ALEXIS Tiens.

FEMME Attends! *(coughs)* Je suis Madeleine Prévost de Paris, *(coughs)* née Tremblay, femme de Henri Prévost et mère de... *(coughs)*

1. In the first line, the woman identifies herself as she dictates to the man what to write down. What is her name? Where is she from?
2. The woman also says she is **femme d'Henri Prévost.** What do you think **femme** means in this context: *wife* or *woman*?
3. The woman also says **née Tremblay.** What does this indicate?
4. Is the woman reading a will, a confession, or something else? What are your clues?
5. The man calls the woman **maman.** Can you deduce what the word **fils** means?

ACTIVITÉ C **Vérifiez votre compréhension** Answer each question based on what you remember from watching the second part of the **Prologue** in which you meet Claire Gagner.

1. C'est _____.   a. le passé   b. le temps présent
2. Claire Gagner est étudiante à _____.   a. Montréal   b. Paris
3. Claire étudie _____.   a. l'anglais   b. la psychologie

ACTIVITÉ D **Premières impressions: Claire Gagner**

Étape 1. What are your first impressions of the main character Claire Gagner? Use the verb **être** and three adjectives to describe her.

 Étape 2. Now share your impressions with a classmate. Do you have similar or different impressions of Claire?

Dans les coulisses

Some believe that the opening shots and prologue of a film sometimes contain all the information needed to understand it. What are your initial impressions of the film after viewing the prologue? What kind of film do you think it is? Can you guess what some of its themes might be?

LIAISONS
CULTURELLES

Le monde parle français... et maintenant vous aussi!

LE FRANÇAIS: LANGUE DU MONDE

By choosing to study French, you will not only learn how the French language works, you will be exposed to cultures and information that will enrich your understanding and appreciation of different perspectives of the world and its peoples.

What do you already know about French in the world? Take this quiz to find out.

1. French is spoken on how many continents in the world?
   a. two   b. three
   c. four   d. five

2. French is an official language in how many countries in the world?
   a. 6   b. 17
   c. 29   d. 38

3. French is a language of diplomacy in the world (and one of the official languages of the United Nations).
   a. True   b. False

4. French is considered a critical language by the CIA.
   a. True   b. False

5. Approximately how many people in the world speak French as a first language?
   a. 50 million   b. 100 million   c. 150 million   d. more than 200 million

6. French is an official language in the United States.
   a. True   b. False

7. Approximately how many people in the United States speak French?
   a. less than 1 million   b. more than 1 million   c. more than 2 million

8. One of the most translated books in the world is a French book. What is this book's title?
   a. *Candide*   b. *Les Trois Mousquetaires*   c. *Le Petit Prince*

Parlez-vous the language of 200 million people?

Learning French opens the doors to dozens of countries and cultures and millions of French-speakers. Across the globe there are 55 French-speaking countries, each offering a unique travel, study abroad or pen pal experience. On the Internet French is the third most common language, providing a wealth of information, networking and learning opportunities. Visit TheWorldSpeaksFrench.org to learn more about the benefits of French language education.

TheWorldSpeaksFrench.org   The French Language Initiative

The French Language Initiative is a partnership between the Embassy of France in the U.S. and the American Association of Teachers of French. © 2007 French Language Initiative. All rights reserved.

What is your current knowledge of French in the world?
15–18 points: **Bravo!** Your knowledge is quite impressive!
10–14 points: **Très bien.** You know quite a bit.
6–8 points: **Pas mal.** Not too bad. You probably learned some new facts today.
5 or less: **Courage.** You will have many more opportunities to learn.

Answers to the quiz:
1. d (3 points); 2. c (3 points); 3. a (1 point); 4. a (1 point); 5. b (3 points);
6. a, official in Louisiana along with English since 1968 (1 point) 7. b (3 points);
8. c, written by Antoine de Saint-Exupéry (3 points)

OUTILS DE LECTURE

A picture is worth a thousand words

Visuals and pictures help you interpret the message of written texts. You are going to read about some prominent personalities and a company in the Francophone world. Use the visuals to help you match the following French words to their English equivalents.

1. chanteur   a. business, company

2. entreprise   b. player

3. joueuse   c. film director

4. réalisateur   d. singer

Luc Besson: réalisateur français

Né° à Paris, le réalisateur Luc Besson (1959–) est célèbre en France et aux États-Unis pour° ses films *Le Grand Bleu* (1988), *Nikita* (1990), *The Fifth Element* (1998) et *The Messenger* (1999). Besson a aussi écrit° le scénario pour *Taken* (2008), un film mettant en vedette° Liam Neeson et Maggie Grace.

Né *Born* **pour** *for* **a écrit** *wrote* **mettant en vedette** *starring*

ITAR-TASS/Central Partnership/Landov

Paul Vreeker/United Photos/Reuters/Landov

Justine Henin: joueuse de tennis belge

Originaire de Liège (Belgique), Justine Henin (1982–) est l'une des joueuses de tennis les plus importantes des années 2003 à 2008 avec un palmarès° de 43 titres. Elle a remporté° la médaille d'or° aux jeux Olympiques en 2004.

avec un palmarès *with a list of titles* **a remporté** *won* **médaille d'or** *gold medal*

LIAISONS
CULTURELLES

© Abdelhak Senna/AFP/Getty Images

Faudel: chanteur français d'origine algérienne

Né dans une banlieue° de Paris, Faudel Belloua
(1978–), «le petit prince» du raï, rend hommage°
à ses deux cultures: la culture française et la culture
algérienne. Sa musique est caractérisée par les
rythmes orientaux et africains, le reggae et le rock.

banlieue *suburb* **rend hommage** *pays tribute*

Le Cirque du Soleil: entreprise québécoise

Entreprise québécoise de divertissement° artistique,
la compagnie a été fondée en 1984 par deux
artistes de rue°, Guy Laliberté et Daniel Gauthier.
Le Cirque du Soleil est un cirque contemporain
avec des acrobates, des costumes et de la musique
spectaculaires.

divertissement *entertainment* **rue** *street*

J L CEREIJIDO/Corbis Wire/epa/Corbis

Compréhension

1. Qui est chanteur?
2. Qui est joueuse de tennis?
3. Qui est réalisateur?
4. Quelle entreprise est connue pour le cirque
   contemporain?

PARTIE 1 P–11

LES SALUTATIONS

À bientôt.	*See you soon.*
À demain.	*See you tomorrow.*
À plus (tard).	*See you (later).*
Au revoir.	*Goodbye.*
Bonjour.	*Hello.*
Bonne journée.	*Good day.*
Bonne nuit.	*Good night.*
Bonsoir.	*Good evening.*
Comment allez-vous?	*How are you?*
(pl./sing., formal)	
Comment vas-tu?	*How are you?*
(sing., informal)	
Comment ça va?	*How is it going?*
(sing., informal)	
Ça va bien.	*Fine.*
Ça va très bien. Et toi?	*Very well. And you?*
Ça va mal. / Ça ne va pas	*Not well.*
très bien.	
Je vais très bien.	*I'm doing very well.*
Très bien aussi.	*Very well, too (also).*
Comment s'appelle-t-il?	*What is his name?*
Il s'appelle Henri.	*His name is Henry.*
Comment s'appelle-t-elle?	*What is her name?*
Elle s'appelle Isabelle.	*Her name is Isabelle.*
Son nom (de famille)	*His/Her last name is . . .*
est…	
Son prénom est…	*His/Her first name is . . .*
Comment t'appelles-tu?	*What's your name?*
Je m'appelle…	*My name is . . .*
Mon prénom est…	*My first name is . . .*
Quel est ton nom	*What is your (last) name?*
(de famille)?	
Mon nom (de famille)	*My (last) name is . . .*
est…	
De rien. / Il n'y a pas de quoi.	*You're welcome.*
Et toi? (sing., informal)	*And you?*
Et vous? (pl./sing., formal)	*And you?*
Je vous présente…	*I introduce to you . . .*
Enchanté(e).	*Pleased to meet you.*
Ravi(e) de faire ta	*Pleased to meet you.*
connaissance.	
(sing., informal)	
Ravi(e) de faire votre	*Pleased to meet you.*
connaissance.	
(pl./sing., formal)	
Merci.	*Thank you.*
Moi aussi.	*Me, too.*
Madame (Mme)	*Ma'am, Mrs.*
Mademoiselle (Mlle)	*Miss*
Monsieur (M.)	*Sir, Mr.*

Quoi de neuf?	*What's new?*
Pas grand-chose.	*Not much.*
Rien de nouveau.	*Nothing new.*
Salut.	*Hello, hi.*
Voici…	*Here is . . .*
Voilà…	*There is . . .*
un(e) meilleur(e) ami(e)	*a best friend*
un(e) colocataire	*a roommate*
un copain (m.) / une	*a friend*
copine (f.)	
une fille	*a girl*
un garçon	*a boy*
une femme	*a woman*
un homme	*a man*
un(e) petit(e) ami(e)	*a boyfriend / girlfriend*

VERBE

être	*to be*

DIVERS

de	*from*

PARTIE 2 P–12

UNE SALLE DE CLASSE

un(e) camarade de classe	*a classmate*
une classe	*a class (of students)*
un(e) étudiant(e)	*a student*
un professeur	*a professor, a teacher*
une affiche	*a poster*
une agrafeuse	*a stapler*
un bureau	*a desk*
un cahier	*a notebook*
une calculatrice	*a calculator*
une chaise	*a chair*
une classe	*a class room*
une craie	*(a piece of) chalk*
un crayon	*a pencil*
un écran	*a screen*
une fenêtre	*a window*
une feuille de papier	*a sheet of paper*
une horloge	*a clock*
un iPod®	*an iPod®*
un livre	*a book*
un ordinateur (portable)	*a (laptop) computer*
une porte	*a door*
une poubelle	*a waste basket*
un sac	*a bag, a purse*
un sac à dos	*a backpack*
un stylo	*a pen*
une table	*a table*
un tableau	*a chalkboard*
un (téléphone) portable	*a cell phone*

LES NOMBRES DE 0 À 20

0 zéro	7 sept	14 quatorze
1 un	8 huit	15 quinze
2 deux	9 neuf	16 seize
3 trois	10 dix	17 dix-sept
4 quatre	11 onze	18 dix-huit
5 cinq	12 douze	19 dix-neuf
6 six	13 treize	20 vingt

DIVERS

Dans la classe, il y a...	*In the classroom, there is . . . , there are . . .*
Qu'est-ce que c'est?	*What's that?*
C'est...	*This is . . .*
Ce sont...	*These are . . .*

PARTIE 3   P–13

LES LETTRES, LES LANGUES ET LES ARTS

l'art *(m.)*	*art*
les langues *(f. pl.)*	*languages*
l'allemand *(m.)*	*German*
l'anglais *(m.)*	*English*
le chinois	*Chinese*
l'espagnol *(m.)*	*Spanish*
le français	*French*
le russe	*Russian*
la littérature	*literature*
la musique	*music*
la philosophie	*philosophy*

LES SCIENCES HUMAINES / SOCIALES

l'anthropologie *(f.)*	*anthropology*
l'histoire *(f.)*	*history*
la psychologie	*psychology*
la sociologie	*sociology*

LES SCIENCES NATURELLES

l'astronomie *(f.)*	*astronomy*
la biologie	*biology*
la chimie	*chemistry*
la physique	*physics*

LE DROIT, L'ADMINISTRATION ET L'ÉCONOMIE

le commerce (international)	*business*
le droit	*law*
la comptabilité	*accounting*
l'économie *(f.)*	*economy*
la gestion	*business administration*

D'AUTRES COURS / SPÉCIALISATIONS

le génie (civil, mécanique, électrique)	*engineering (civil, mechanical, electrical)*
l'informatique *(f.)*	*computer science*
le journalisme	*journalism*
les mathématiques *(f. pl.)*	*mathematics*
les sciences politiques *(f. pl.)*	*political science*

DIVERS

Quelle est ta spécialisation?	*What's your major?*
Qu'est-ce que tu étudies? *(sing.)*	*What are you studying?*
Qu'est-ce que vous étudiez? *(pl.)*	*What are you studying?*
J'étudie...	*I am studying . . .*
Je ne sais pas encore.	*I don't know yet.*
Combien de cours as-tu ce semestre?	*How many courses / classes do you have this term?*
le cours	*course*
les devoirs *(m. pl.)*	*homework*
l'école *(f.)*	*school*
les études *(f. pl.)*	*studies*
l'université *(f.)*	*university*

LES NOMBRES DE 20 À 60

20 vingt	28 vingt-huit
21 vingt et un	29 vingt-neuf
22 vingt-deux	30 trente
23 vingt-trois	31 trente et un
24 vingt-quatre	40 quarante
25 vingt-cinq	50 cinquante
26 vingt-six	60 soixante
27 vingt-sept	

ADJECTIFS

amusant(e)	*funny*
brillant(e)	*brilliant*
célèbre	*famous*
charmant(e)	*charming*
content(e)	*happy, content*
difficile	*difficult*
doué(e)	*gifted*
dynamique	*dynamic*
embêtant(e)	*annoying*
énergique	*energetic*
facile	*easy*
fascinant(e)	*fascinating*
impatient(e)	*impatient*
important(e)	*important*
indépendant(e)	*independent*
intelligent(e)	*intelligent*
intéressant(e)	*interesting*
inutile	*not useful, useless*
méchant(e)	*mean*
moderne	*modern*
modeste	*modest*
nécessaire	*necessary*
optimiste	*optimistic*
patient(e)	*patient*
pessimiste	*pessimistic*
pratique	*practical*
récent(e)	*recent*
sociable	*sociable*
timide	*shy*
utile	*useful*

Une **vie** équilibrée

En bref In this chapter, you will:

- learn numbers 60–100
- learn some regular -**er** verbs
- learn the pronoun **on**
- learn how to make statements negative
- learn about stressed pronouns
- learn the days of the week

- learn adverbs of intensity and frequency
- learn some irregular adjectives
- learn how to express time
- learn the verb **avoir** and some expressions with **avoir**
- read about how people spend time in some French-speaking countries

 You will also watch SÉQUENCE **1:** **L'étranger** of the movie *Liaisons*.

Ressources

 audio ▶ video ▦ Share It! iLrn™ 🌐 http://www.cengagebrain.com

© eddie linssen / Alamy

VOCABULAIRE 1

🔊 Nos **activités**

Our activities

cuisiner et manger

déjeuner au café

dîner au restaurant

travailler au bureau

étudier à la bibliothèque

jouer *(to play)*

marcher au parc

pratiquer un sport

inviter des amis/amies

écouter de la musique

regarder la télé

voyager / aimer

Les activités de Kim-Lee pendant la semaine

Les nombres de 60 à 100

60 soixante	74 soixante-quatorze	88 quatre-vingt-huit
61 soixante et un	75 soixante-quinze	89 quatre-vingt-neuf
62 soixante-deux	76 soixante-seize	**90 quatre-vingt-dix**
63 soixante-trois	77 soixante-dix-sept	91 quatre-vingt-onze
64 soixante-quatre	78 soixante-dix-huit	92 quatre-vingt-douze
65 soixante-cinq	79 soixante-dix-neuf	93 quatre-vingt-treize
66 soixante-six	**80 quatre-vingts**	94 quatre-vingt-quatorze
67 soixante-sept	81 quatre-vingt-un	95 quatre-vingt-quinze
68 soixante-huit	82 quatre-vingt-deux	96 quatre-vingt-seize
69 soixante-neuf	83 quatre-vingt-trois	97 quatre-vingt-dix-sept
70 soixante-dix	84 quatre-vingt-quatre	98 quatre-vingt-dix-huit
71 soixante et onze	85 quatre-vingt-cinq	99 quatre-vingt-dix-neuf
72 soixante-douze	86 quatre-vingt-six	**100 cent**
73 soixante-treize	87 quatre-vingt-sept	**100% cent pour cent**

Vocabulaire complémentaire

pendant *during*
la semaine *the week*
le week-end *the weekend*

Note de vocabulaire

The number 80, **quatre-vingts**, = 4 × 20. When **quatre-vingts** is followed by another number, there is no **s** after **vingt**: **quatre-vingt-deux**.

◄)) 1-1 ACTIVITÉ A Est-ce que c'est essentiel? You will hear a series of activities. Indicate whether or not you feel they are essential for a balanced life.

1. oui / non	**5.** oui / non	**8.** oui / non
2. oui / non	**6.** oui / non	**9.** oui / non
3. oui / non	**7.** oui / non	**10.** oui / non
4. oui / non		

◄)) 1-2 ACTIVITÉ B Une vie équilibrée?

Étape 1. Listen and follow along as you hear statements about students' daily activities at Claire Gagner's university, McGill University. Select the number that you hear.

1. _____ des étudiants déjeunent tous les jours.
  a. 61%   b. 75%   c. 87%   d. 95%

2. _____ des étudiants étudient pendant le week-end.
  a. 54%   b. 68%   c. 84%   d. 96%

3. _____ des étudiants travaillent pendant le week-end.
  a. 24%   b. 68%   c. 79%   d. 88%

4. _____ des étudiants dînent avant *(before)* 8h le soir.
  a. 41%   b. 63%   c. 76%   d. 80%

5. _____ des étudiants pratiquent un sport.
  a. 69%   b. 77%   c. 83%   d. 91%

6. _____ des étudiants regardent la télévision pendant le week-end.
  a. 32%   b. 52%   c. 64%   d. 73%

Étape 2. Based on the answers to **Étape 1,** would you say that students at McGill University have **une vie équilibrée?**   oui / non

ACTIVITÉ C Quel âge? *(What age?)*

1-3

✎ **Étape 1.** You will hear how old each of these people were when they died. Write the number you hear. You do not need to spell it out.

1.

Jacques Brel

_____

5.

Léopold Sédar Senghor

_____

2.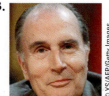

Édith Piaf

_____

6.

Mahatma Gandhi

_____

3.

François Mitterrand

_____

7.

Mère Teresa

_____

4.

Félix Leclerc

_____

8.

Martin Luther King

_____

Étape 2. These people all had special talents when it came to relating to the public. Brel, Piaf, and Leclerc were singers. Mitterrand, Senghor, and Gandhi were politicians. Mère Teresa and M.L. King were humanitarians and civil rights activists. Match these people with their special talents.

1. Brel, Piaf, Leclerc
2. Mitterrand, Senghor, Gandhi
3. Mère Teresa et M.L. King

a. travailler pour *(for)* le public
b. chanter *(sing)* pour le public
c. parler *(speak)* au public

ACTIVITÉ D Les activités

Étape 1. Indicate what percentage of time on average each week day you do the following activities. Provide the word for each number.

Pendant une journée de la semaine *(a week day):*

1. _____ %: étudier le français
2. _____ %: être à l'université
3. _____ %: travailler
4. _____ %: cuisiner
5. _____ %: pratiquer un sport
6. _____ %: regarder la télé
7. _____ %: marcher au parc
8. _____ %: manger

Étape 2. Do **Étape 1** again, but this time, for a day on the weekend. Do any of your answers change? Now select the statement that best describes you.

a. Ma vie pendant la semaine est plus *(more)* équilibrée.

b. Ma vie pendant le week-end est plus équilibrée.

ACTIVITÉ E Notre classe

Étape 1. Poll your classmates to see if they like to do the following activities. If they answer **oui,** put their names next to that item. If they answer **non,** move on and ask other classmates.

Modèle: Est-ce que tu aimes cuisiner?

_____ cuisiner	_____ dîner dans un restaurant élégant
_____ déjeuner à l'université	_____ pratiquer un sport
_____ étudier pendant le week-end	_____ jouer aux jeux vidéo
_____ regarder des émissions de télé-réalité *(reality shows)*	_____ voyager
_____ inviter des amis	_____ écouter de la musique

Étape 2. Your instructor will now poll the entire class to see how many people like these activities.

Si vous y allez

© Olivier Rieu

If you go to Paris, visit the restaurant **Des Gars dans la Cuisine** for a bite to eat. This off-beat, contemporary restaurant was started by two friends, Gil and Jean-Jacques, also known as **les gars** *(the guys).* Find the restaurant's website to take a virtual tour and read reviews.

Note de vocabulaire
The French word **gars** comes from **garçon** which means *boy.* **Gars** is a colloquial expression for *guy.*

© Jack Sullivan / Alamy

Un mot sur la culture

Téléphoner en France

French phone numbers appear in pairs and are said in pairs. For example, the phone number 06 14 36 76 89 is said like this: **zéro six, quatorze, trente-six, soixante-seize, quatre-vingt-neuf.**

- Practice saying these phone numbers for restaurants in France.

  1. Restaurant Le Marrakech: 04 93 85 81 55
  2. Des Gars dans la Cuisine: 01 42 74 88 26
  3. Couleur Café: 03 80 70 10 47
  4. Restaurant Chez Mireille: 04 93 85 27 23

Pour parler de nos activités

Les verbes du premier groupe en **-er** / Le pronom sujet **on** / La négation / Les pronoms disjoints

DU FILM *LIAISONS*

Un coup d'œil sur la grammaire

In **Séquence 1** of the film *Liaisons,* Claire makes these statements about her mother to her friend.

Elle **mange,** elle **joue** aux cartes, elle lit et elle dort. Elle **mange,** elle **joue** aux cartes, elle lit et elle dort. Elle **existe,** c'est tout. C'est trop triste...

1. You have already encountered the verb forms **mange** and **joue** in **Vocabulaire 1.** Do you remember what they mean?

2. The infinitive forms of the verbs **mange** and **joue** are **manger** and **jouer.** These verbs end in **-er.** The verb **existe** follows the same pattern. What is the infinitive form of the verb **existe?**

Les verbes du premier groupe en *-er*

Verbs in French are grouped according to the ending of their infinitive. In **Vocabulaire 1** of this chapter, you learned the meaning of several -er verbs. Now you will learn the different forms of the verbs in this group.

To form the present tense of -er verbs, you drop the -**er** from the infinitive form and add these endings: -**e, -es, -e, -ons, -ez, -ent.**

travailler *(to work)*			
je	travaill**e**	nous	travaill**ons**
tu	travaill**es**	vous	travaill**ez**
il/elle/on	travaill**e**	ils/elles	travaill**ent**

While -**er** verbs have five different written forms (the forms for **je** and **il/elle/on** are identical), there are only three distinguishable spoken forms: 1) **travaille / travailles / travaillent** (same pronunciation), 2) **travaillons,** and 3) **travaillez.**

In English, the present tense can be expressed in three ways. In French, these meanings are expressed with a single verb.

Je travaille.
{
I work.
I am working.
I do work.

Ils jouent.
{
They play.
They are playing.
They do play.

Note de **grammaire**
On can mean *one, they, you* or *people* in general. In conversation, **on** is often used instead of **nous.** There is a liaison after **on** when the next word begins with a vowel sound. **On** always takes the same verb form as **il** and **elle: On** arrive bientôt. *We are arriving soon.*

Here are some regular **-er** verbs in addition to the ones you learned in **Vocabulaire 1.** They are conjugated the same way as **travailler.**

adorer	*to adore*	**danser (avec)**	*to dance (with)*	**passer un examen**	*to take an exam*
aimer bien	*to like*	**détester**	*to hate*	**penser**	*to think*
aimer mieux	*to prefer*	**habiter**	*to live (in a place), to reside*	**rater un examen**	*to fail an exam*
				téléphoner	*to telephone*
chanter	*to sing*	**naviguer sur Internet**	*to surf the Internet*	**trouver**	*to find*
chercher	*to look for*	**parler**	*to speak, to talk*		

Verbs that end in **-ger** like **manger** and **voyager** that you learned in **Vocabulaire 1** have a spelling change in the **nous** form. They are conjugated as **nous mangeons** and **nous voyageons** (**-eons** instead of the normal **-ons** ending).

Note de **vocabulaire**
Note that **passer un examen** means *to take an exam* and not *to pass an exam.* In French, *to pass an exam* is **réussir à un examen.** You will learn this verb in **Chapitre 4.**

The following questions are useful when asking about activities.

—**Qu'est-ce que tu fais?**	—*What are you doing?*
—**Je travaille.**	—*I'm working.*
—**Qu'est-ce qu'il/elle fait?**	—*What is he/she doing?*
—**Il/Elle déjeune.**	—*He/She is having lunch.*

Sometimes two verbs can be used together to express an idea. In these cases, the first verb is conjugated and the second verb is in the infinitive form. Some common verbs that can be followed by an infinitive are **adorer, aimer, aimer mieux,** and **détester.**

J'**aime étudier** le français.	*I like to study French.*
Nous **détestons danser.**	*We hate to dance.*

Note de **prononciation**
For verbs that begin with a vowel sound, **je** becomes **j': J'aime le français!**

La négation

To make a sentence negative, place **ne** (**n'** before a vowel sound) before the conjugated verb and **pas** after it.

Je **ne** regarde **pas** la télé.	*I don't watch television.*
Vous **n'**étudiez **pas** le week-end?	*You don't study on weekends?*

In the case of two verbs used together, **ne** (**n'**)**… pas** goes around the first conjugated verb.

Je **n'**aime **pas** danser.	*I don't like to dance.*

Les pronoms disjoints

You have already learned subject pronouns in French (**je, tu, il, nous,** etc). Another category of pronouns is called **les pronoms disjoints** (*stressed pronouns*).

je → **moi**	il → **lui**	nous → **nous**	ils → **eux**
tu → **toi**	elle → **elle**	vous → **vous**	elles → **elles**

* **Les pronoms disjoints** are used after prepositions and conjunctions such as **et, mais** *(but)*, **à** or **de.**

> Alex et **toi,** vous étudiez ce soir? — *Alex and **you**, you're studying tonight?*
> Coralie est française mais pas **moi.** — *Coralie is French but not **me.***
> **Moi,** je suis américaine. — ***Me,** I'm American.*
> Je pense beaucoup à **elles.** — *I think about **them** (fem. pl.) a lot.*

* Stressed pronouns are also used after **c'est** and **ce sont.**

> —C'est Marc? — —Ce sont M. et Mme Tremblay?
> —Oui, c'est **lui.** — —Oui, ce sont **eux.**

ACTIVITÉ F Les amis Select the correct **pronom disjoint.**

1. C'est Richard? Oui, c'est _____.   a. lui   b. elle

2. Ce sont Marc et Alain? Oui, ce sont _____.   a. vous   b. eux

3. C'est Fatima? Oui, c'est _____.   a. elle   b. nous

4. C'est toi, Dien? Oui, c'est _____.   a. moi   b. vous

5. Tu penses beaucoup à moi? Oui, je pense beaucoup à _____.   a. lui   b. toi

6. Tu penses souvent à Nicole et à Anne? Oui, je pense souvent à _____.   a. eux   b. elles

ACTIVITÉ G C'est qui? Because there are only three discernible verb forms in spoken French, context is very important in determining who the speaker may be referring to. Another hint is the /z/ sound of the plural form. With verbs that begin with a vowel sound, the **s** of the plural form of **ils** or **elles** is pronounced like the sound /z/. The presence of the /z/ sound tells you that the subject is plural (**ils écoutent**) while the absence of the /z/ sound tells you the subject is singular (**il écoute**). This /z/ sound is also known as a **liaison** sound which you will learn about on p. 59 of this chapter. A reporter is interviewing a French family about their activities. Listen and determine who the reporter is referring to.

1. a. Grégoire   b. Grégoire et Pierre   6. a. Marie   b. Marie et sa maman
2. a. Marie   b. Marie et sa maman   7. a. Marie   b. Marie et sa maman
3. a. Pierre   b. Pierre et Grégoire   8. a. Grégoire   b. Grégoire et Pierre
4. a. Grégoire   b. Grégoire et Pierre   9. a. Grégoire   b. Grégoire et Pierre
5. a. Marie   b. Marie et Pierre   10. a. Marie   b. Marie et sa maman

ACTIVITÉ **H** *FLASH* **sur les actrices du film** *Liaisons*

Étape 1. Pierre Brassard, host of the talk show *FLASH* in Quebec, is interviewing the actresses of the film *Liaisons*, Mylène Savoie (Claire Gagner) and Johanne Marie Tremblay (Simone Gagner). Pay attention to the verbs to determine whom he is referring to.

1. _____ voyag**ent** toujours *(always)* pour le travail.
a. Mylène   b. Mylène et Johanne

2. _____ travaill**ent** 65 heures par semaine.
a. Mylène   b. Mylène et Johanne

3. _____ ne déjeun**ent** pas.
a. Mylène   b. Mylène et Johanne

4. _____ détest**e** le sport.
a. Mylène   b. Mylène et Johanne

5. _____ ne mang**ent** pas bien.
a. Mylène   b. Mylène et Johanne

6. _____ regard**e** des films d'horreur.
a. Mylène   b. Mylène et Johanne

Conclusion   Which sentence do you think better describes the actresses of the film *Liaisons*?

a. Leur *(Their)* vie est équilibrée.   **b.** Leur vie **n'est** **pas** équilibrée.

Étape 2. Brassard interviews actress Michèle Labonté (Mme LeGrand) who travels with her dog Demoiselle. Michèle is describing some of her activities. Do the activities refer to Michèle or to Michèle and Demoiselle?

1. _____ chant**e** souvent devant *(in front of)* le miroir.   a. Je   b. Nous

2. _____ déjeun**ons** à 11h30.   a. Je   b. Nous

3. _____ cherch**ons** des papillons *(butterflies)* au parc.   a. Je   b. Nous

4. _____ jou**e** au Frisbee®.   a. Je   b. Nous

5. _____ mang**eons** une glace *(ice cream cone)* le soir.   a. Je   b. Nous

Étape 3. *FLASH* interviews skaters Isabelle Brasseur and Lloyd Eisler. Determine if the questions are only for Isabelle or for both Isabelle and Lloyd.

1. _____ aim**ez** les émissions *(programs)* culturelles?   a. Tu   b. Vous

2. _____ aim**es** le rap?   a. Tu   b. Vous

3. _____ habit**ez** dans un grand appartement?   a. Tu   b. Vous

4. _____ pens**ez** que le français est une langue importante?   a. Tu   b. Vous

5. _____ ador**es** danser?   a. Tu   b. Vous

Et vous? How would you answer these questions if Pierre Brassard interviewed you?

ACTIVITÉ **I** Un jour avec Kelly et Michael

Étape 1. A viewer gets to spend a day with the show hosts of *Live with Kelly and Michael.* Using the following cues, create sentences to describe how she spends this day with them.

> **Activités possibles**
>
> | | | |
> |---|---|---|
> | chanter dans le studio | écouter des chansons d'Elvis | regarder le tournage de *Live with Kelly and Michael* |
> | cuisiner un repas *(meal)* français | jouer au Frisbee® | trouver une boîte de nuit *(night club)* |
> | danser le tango | naviguer sur Internet pour trouver des potins *(gossip)* | |
> | dîner dans un restaurant marocain | | |

1. Je/J' _____
2. Kelly et moi _____
3. Michael _____
4. Kelly _____
5. Kelly et Michael _____
6. Michael, Kelly et moi _____

Étape 2. Which of the activities do you adore doing, like doing, prefer doing, and hate doing?

1. J'adore...   2. J'aime bien...   3. J'aime mieux...   4. Je déteste...

ACTIVITÉ **J** Les activités

Étape 1. Create sentences indicating whether you do or do not do the following activities.

1. regarder la télé-réalité
2. parler deux langues ou plus *(or more)*
3. passer des examens pendant le week-end
4. manger trois repas par jour
5. écouter la musique de Céline Dion
6. habiter à la résidence universitaire
7. rater des examens
8. inviter des amis

 **Étape 2.** Now ask a classmate if he/she does these activities. Jot down your partner's answers so you are prepared to share information with the rest of the class.

Modèle: É1: **Est-ce que tu regardes la télé-réalité?**
É2: **Oui, je regarde la télé-réalité. / Non, je ne regarde pas la télé-réalité.**

Étape 3. What are some things that you and your partner have in common? Refer to your notes from **Étape 2** and prepare a few sentences summarizing how you and your partner are the same or different.

Modèle: **Jack et moi, nous étudions pendant le week-end.**

Liaisons musicales

© Patrick Hertzog/AFP/ Getty Images

Dur dur d'être bébé (It's Tough to be a Baby), was recorded by the French singer Jordy Lemoine in 1992 at the age of 4. The worldwide success of this dance single earned Jordy a listing in the *Guinness Book of World Records* as the youngest singer to have a #1 hit song on the singles charts. Search the Internet to find the lyrics of this song. If you had to write a song called *Dur dur d'être étudiant,* what would you say?

ACTIVITÉ **K** **Le détecteur de mensonges**

Do you know the show *Lie Detector*? The contestants give three statements about themselves. Two statements are true and one is a lie. Opponents try to guess which statement is a lie. If the opponents correctly guess which statement is false, they win! If the opponents guess wrong, the contestant wins!

Étape 1. Create four statements about yourself. At least one statement must be a negative statement, and one must be a lie.

1. _____

2. _____

3. _____

4. _____

Étape 2. In groups of 3 or 4 take turns being the contestant. The contestants read their sentences. Their opponents try to guess and say which statement is the lie. For example: **Numéro 1 est faux.** Opponents may ask the contestants questions about the statements if they wish to help them guess. Switch roles.

OUI, JE PEUX!   Here are two "can do statements" for you to check your progress so far. Look at each statement and rate yourself on how well you think you can perform the task. Then verify your ability with a partner. How did you do?

1. **"I can say three things that I typically do and three things that I typically don't do during the school week."**

   I can perform this function
   ☐ with ease
   ☐ with some difficulty
   ☐ not at all

2. **"I can ask someone else if that person does particular activities or not to see if our activities are similar."**

   I can perform this function
   ☐ with ease
   ☐ with some difficulty
   ☐ not at all

iLrn™

Are you looking for more practice? You can find it in **iLrn**.

VOCABULAIRE 2

Les **jours** de la **semaine**

Days of the week

Mon agenda

Une semaine typique pour Claire Gagner

Vocabulaire complémentaire

après *after*	**la nuit** *night*
aujourd'hui *today*	**la semaine** *week*
avant *before*	**tous les jours** *everyday*
demain *tomorrow*	**tous les soirs** *every evening*
hier *yesterday*	**Quel jour sommes-nous?** *What day is it?*
	Nous sommes mardi. *It's Tuesday.*
l'emploi du temps *(m.) schedule*	**Qu'est-ce que tu fais?** *What are you doing?, What do you do?*
	Qu'est-ce que vous faites? *What are you doing?, What do you do?*

- In French, days of the week are masculine and are not capitalized. To say that something occurs during a particular part of the day or regularly on a particular day, use the definite article **le** + the day of the week or part of the day.

  Je regarde un film **le vendredi.**   **Le soir,** j'étudie.
  *I watch a movie **every Friday (on Fridays).***   **In the evening,** *I study.*

- When an event occurs once or on a specific day, do not use **le.**

  Vendredi, je cherche un appartement.   Nous sommes **mercredi.**
  *I am looking for an apartment **on Friday.***   *It's **Wednesday.***

ACTIVITÉ A À la Clinique Laurier Listen to the passage about Nurse Nicole's activities at the **Clinique Laurier** (where Claire's mother is a patient) and determine if she does each activity weekly or just once this week.

1-5

1. a. chaque *(each)* mercredi   b. ce *(this)* mercredi
2. a. chaque jeudi   b. ce jeudi
3. a. chaque samedi   b. ce samedi
4. a. chaque mardi   b. ce mardi
5. a. chaque dimanche   b. ce dimanche

ACTIVITÉ B Quel jour sommes-nous? You will hear days of the week. Select the day that comes *after* the day you hear (**demain** *tomorrow*).

1-6

1. a. lundi	b. dimanche	c. jeudi
2. a. mardi	b. samedi	c. mercredi
3. a. jeudi	b. mardi	c. samedi
4. a. lundi	b. mercredi	c. dimanche
5. a. dimanche	b. samedi	c. vendredi
6. a. vendredi	b. lundi	c. mercredi

ACTIVITÉ C Avant et après Complete these sentences with the day *before* or *after* the day that is mentioned.

1. Le jour avant dimanche, c'est…
2. Le jour après mardi, c'est…
3. Le jour avant samedi, c'est…
4. Le jour avant mercredi, c'est…
5. Le jour après jeudi, c'est…
6. Le jour avant lundi, c'est…
7. Le jour après mercredi, c'est…
8. Le jour après dimanche, c'est…

© Brocreative/Shutterstock.com

ACTIVITÉ D Les activités de Claire Gagner You will hear a series of questions about Claire's activities. Look at her **agenda** on page 44 and answer the questions.

1-7

Modèle: *You hear:* Qu'est-ce que Claire fait samedi après-midi?
You say: **Elle travaille à l'hôtel.**

Conclusion Quelles activités est-ce que Claire fait *(does)* souvent?

ACTIVITÉ E Quel(s) jour(s) de la semaine? Quel(s) jour(s) de la semaine est…

1. Pâques *(Easter)*?
2. Thanksgiving (ou l'Action de Grâce)?
3. la fête du Travail?
4. le cours de français?
5. le week-end?
6. ton jour préféré *(your favorite day)*?

ACTIVITÉ F Le meilleur soir What day of the week is the best evening to do these activities?

Modèle: le meilleur *(best)* soir pour jouer au bingo
C'est mercredi soir!

1. le meilleur soir pour regarder un film au cinéma
2. le meilleur soir pour manger au restaurant
3. le meilleur soir pour regarder la télévision
4. le meilleur soir pour passer un examen
5. le meilleur soir pour jouer au football américain
6. le meilleur soir pour inviter des amis
7. le meilleur soir pour téléphoner aux parents
8. le meilleur soir pour étudier

ACTIVITÉ G L'emploi du temps

Étape 1. Using the table as a guide, interview a classmate to find out what days of the week he/she has classes and what those classes are. Indicate whether the classes occur **le matin, l'après-midi,** or **le soir.**

Modèle: É1: **Quels cours est-ce que tu as** *(have)* **le lundi matin?**
  É2: **français et sociologie**

	lundi	mardi	mercredi	jeudi	vendredi
le matin					
l'après-midi					
le soir					

Liaisons musicales

Andia/Alamy

Inspired by the music and texts of Bob Dylan, French singer-songwriter-guitarist, Francis Cabrel (1953–) released his first album in 1977 and remains a much appreciated and favorite artist of the Francophone world. Visit his official website and search the Internet to find videos of some of his songs.

Étape 2. Share your classmate's responses with the rest of the class.

Modèle: **Le lundi matin, Paul a** *(has)* **français et sociologie. Le mardi après-midi, il a philosophie et biologie.**

Conclusion Who has a busier schedule this quarter/semester? You or your partner?

lundi	mardi	mercredi	jeudi	vendredi	samedi	dimanche
		1	2	3	4	5
6	7	8	9	10	11	12
13	14	15	16	17	18	19
20	21	22	23	24	25	26
27	28	29	30	31		

Un mot sur la culture

Le calendrier français

In the U.S. and in English-speaking Canada, calendars list Sunday as the first day of the week. Because the Bible makes the Sabbath (Saturday) the last day of the week, it is common in Jewish and Christian practice to designate Sunday as the first day of the week. However, if you look at a French calendar, you will see that Monday is the first day of the week and not Sunday. Since, in Catholic tradition, the day of the Lord (**le jour du Seigneur**) is Sunday, the first day of the week is Monday. Another reason for this could be that modern culture views Monday as the beginning of the work week and the school week.

• Which day of the week is the first day for you?

Pour donner des descriptions

Les adverbes / Les adjectifs irréguliers

DU FILM *LIAISONS*

Un coup d'œil sur la grammaire

Elle mange, elle joue aux cartes, elle lit et elle dort. Elle existe, c'est tout. C'est **trop triste**...

In **Séquence 1** of the film *Liaisons,* Claire says this statement about her mother to her friend. You saw this statement in **Grammaire 1.** Do you remember what it means?

What do you think **trop triste** means?

a. a little sad   b. too sad

Les adverbes

✣ You have already encountered some adverbs in **Chapitre préliminaire.** You will see them again in this chapter plus additional adverbs that will help you be more precise when giving descriptions and talking about activities.

Adverbs of intensity		
trop	Je mange **trop.**	*I eat too much.*
beaucoup	Il mange **beaucoup.**	*He eats a lot.*
assez	Nous mangeons **assez.**	*We eat enough.*
un peu	Elle mange **un peu.**	*She eats a little.*

> **Note** de **grammaire**
> **Ne… jamais** functions like **ne… pas.** The **ne** goes before the conjugated verb and **jamais** goes after it. You will learn more about this and other negative expressions in subsequent lessons.

Adverbs of frequency		
toujours	Anne travaille **toujours.**	*Anne always works.*
souvent	Marc travaille **souvent** le lundi.	*Marc often works on Mondays.*
parfois, quelquefois	Je travaille **parfois** le week-end.	*I sometimes work on weekends.*
rarement	Il travaille **rarement.**	*He rarely works.*
ne… jamais	Elle **ne** travaille **jamais.**	*She never works.*

Les adjectifs irréguliers

Descriptive adjectives (**les adjectifs qualificatifs**) allow you to be more precise when talking about activities and giving descriptions. You already encountered several descriptive adjectives in **Chapitre préliminaire** and know that they must agree with the noun or pronoun they modify by adding an **e** (when they modify feminine nouns), an **s** (when they modify plural nouns) or **es** (when they modify plural feminine nouns). In French, adjectives normally follow the nouns they modify. Adjectives can also modify the subject of a sentence when they follow the verb **être**.

Je préfère **les gens** *(m. pl.)* **intéressants**.	*I prefer interesting people.*
Nadine est **une personne intelligente**.	*Nadine is an intelligent person.*
Les femmes indépendantes travaillent beaucoup.	*Independent women work a lot.*

Some Irregular Adjectives				
masculine singular	**feminine singular**	**masculine plural**	**feminine plural**	
fier	fière	fiers	fières	*proud*
naïf	naïve	naïfs	naïves	*naive*
sportif	sportive	sportifs	sportives	*athletic*
gentil	gentille	gentils	gentilles	*nice*
intellectuel	intellectuelle	intellectuels	intellectuelles	*intellectual*
travailleur	travailleuse	travailleurs	travailleuses	*hardworking*
ambitieux	ambitieuse	ambitieux	ambitieuses	*ambitious*
courageux	courageuse	courageux	courageuses	*courageous*
ennuyeux	ennuyeuse	ennuyeux	ennuyeuses	*boring*
heureux	heureuse	heureux	heureuses	*happy*
malheureux	malheureuse	malheureux	malheureuses	*unhappy*
paresseux	paresseuse	paresseux	paresseuses	*lazy*
sérieux	sérieuse	sérieux	sérieuses	*serious*
talentueux	talentueuse	talentueux	talentueuses	*talented*

Pour aller plus loin
N'est-ce pas?

In French, **n'est-ce pas** can be added to yes/no questions when one expects an affirmative answer as an expression of affirmation.

Tu aimes la philosophie, **n'est-ce pas**?	*You like philosophy, don't you?*
Le livre est intéressant, **n'est-ce pas**?	*The book is interesting, isn't it?*

ACTIVITÉ H Un bon étudiant Do these statements describe a good student? Answer **oui** or **non.** Then, select the statements that are true for you.

Un bon étudiant…

1. … rate **rarement** les examens.
   oui / non

2. … **n'écoute jamais** le professeur.
   oui / non

3. … étudie **beaucoup** le soir.
   oui / non

4. … parle **souvent** avec le professeur.
   oui / non

5. … mange **parfois** en cours.
   oui / non

6. … étudie **assez** le week-end.
   oui / non

7. … **ne** regarde **jamais** la télé.
   oui / non

8. … navigue **souvent** sur Internet en classe.   oui / non

ACTIVITÉ I Quand est-ce que vous… ? Which days of the week do you study or do other activities a lot or less frequently? Pay attention to the adverb and indicate which days of the week you do these activities with the level of frequency indicated.

Modèle: J'étudie souvent **le lundi et le jeudi soir.**

1. J'étudie **beaucoup** _____.

2. J'étudie **un peu** _____.

3. J'étudie **rarement** _____.

4. Je mange **parfois** avec des amis _____.

5. Je regarde **souvent** la télévision _____.

6. Je **ne** cuisine **jamais** _____.

©arek_malang/Shutterstock.com

ACTIVITÉ J Une vie équilibrée?

Étape 1. Indicate how often you actually do the following activities.

	rarement	parfois	souvent	toujours
1. Je pratique un sport…				
2. Je regarde la télé…				
3. J'étudie…				
4. Je voyage…				
5. Je passe des examens…				
6. Je mange…				

 Étape 2. Exchange responses with a classmate. Look at how your classmate responded and decide if he/she has a balanced life.

Conclusion Est-ce que votre camarade de classe a *(have)* une vie équilibrée?

Étape 3. Provide a complete sentence to explain why you think your classmate has a balanced life or why his/her life is not balanced.

Modèles: **Ma camarade de classe a** *(has)* **une vie équilibrée parce qu'elle étudie souvent et elle voyage parfois. / Mon camarade n'a pas** *(does not have)* **une vie équilibrée parce qu'il étudie toujours et il mange rarement.**

ACTIVITÉ **K** **Les différents types de personnes** Different types of people perform activities with different degrees of frequency or intensity. Complete each sentence with a logical adverb to describe these people's activities.

1. Les hommes sportifs pratiquent _____ un sport.
2. Les femmes ambitieuses travaillent _____.
3. Les enfants *(children)* naïfs écoutent _____ leurs parents.
4. Les étudiants paresseux étudient _____ le week-end.
5. Les parents fiers parlent _____ de leurs enfants.
6. Les gens *(people)* malheureux voyagent _____.

Note de **grammaire**
You will learn more about the position of adverbs in **Chapitre 2.**

ACTIVITÉ **L** **Barack ou Michelle Obama?** A talk show host in France recently made some comments about Barack and Michelle Obama. Pay attention to the forms of the adjectives in order to determine if the comment refers to **Monsieur Obama** or **Madame Obama**. Complete each statement with **Monsieur (M.)** or **Madame (Mme)** based on the form of the adjectives. Then indicate if you agree or disagree with the statements.

	Je suis d'accord.	Je ne suis pas d'accord.
1. _____ est gentille.	☐	☐
2. _____ est courageuse.	☐	☐
3. _____ est intellectuel.	☐	☐
4. _____ est talentueux.	☐	☐
5. _____ est travailleur.	☐	☐
6. _____ est fière.	☐	☐
7. _____ est ambitieuse.	☐	☐
8. _____ est sérieux.	☐	☐

ACTIVITÉ **M** **Les frères ou les sœurs?** A reporter is talking about Mary-Kate and Ashley Olsen and Luke and Owen Wilson. Pay attention to the forms of the adjectives in order to determine if the comment refers to **les frères Wilson** ou **les sœurs Olsen**. Complete each statement with **les frères Wilson (a)** or **les sœurs Olsen (b)** based on the forms of these adjectives. Then indicate if you feel each statement is negative or positive.

	commentaire positif	commentaire négatif
1. _____ sont heureux.	☐	☐
2. _____ sont souvent naïves.	☐	☐
3. _____ sont courageuses.	☐	☐
4. _____ sont un peu paresseux.	☐	☐
5. _____ sont toujours fiers.	☐	☐
6. _____ sont rarement talentueuses.	☐	☐
7. _____ sont ennuyeux.	☐	☐

ACTIVITÉ N Les célébrités

Étape 1. Decide whether each adjective describes the celebrities indicated. Use the negative form if you do not think the adjective describes the people. Use the appropriate form of the adjective.

Modèle: (sérieux) Jeb et George W. Bush **sont sérieux.**
Margaret Cho et Ellen DeGeneres **ne sont pas sérieuses.**

1. (ambitieux)

    Will Smith et Jada Pinkett Smith _____.

    Jessica et Ashlee Simpson _____.

2. (courageux)

    Paris Hilton et Britney Spears _____.

    Les soldats *(soldiers)* américains _____.

3. (naïf)

    Tom Brady et Gisele Bündchen _____.

    Hillary et Chelsea Clinton _____.

4. (travailleur)

    Emilio Estevez et Charlie Sheen _____.

    LaToya et Janet Jackson _____.

5. (sportif)

    Le prince William et le prince Harry _____.

    Serena et Venus Williams _____.

6. (fier)

    Bill et Melinda Gates _____.

    Elle et Dakota Fanning _____.

Étape 2. Share your answers with a classmate. Did you come up with similar statements?

✈ ..... Si vous y allez

If you go to Montreal and want to people watch, stop in the **Café Cherrier** for a drink or a bite to eat. Located on **rue St. Denis** just north of the Latin Quarter, this European style bistro is a popular gathering for intellectuals, artists, and TV personalities in Montreal.

© Megapress / Alamy

ACTIVITÉ O Nous sommes observateurs?

Étape 1. How well do your classmates know you? Let's see how observant **(observateurs/observatrices)** they've been. From the adjectives you've learned so far, select six that you think describe you or don't describe you and prepare six sentences.

Modèle: Je suis ambitieux. Je suis un peu sociable. Je ne suis pas optimiste…

Étape 2. Share your six adjectives—not your sentences—with a classmate. Your classmate will guess what sentences you wrote with those adjectives. Was your classmate able to guess correctly? Rate how observant your classmate is with the following scale.

• Mon/Ma camarade de classe est _____ observateur/observatrice.

    a. très   b. assez   c. un peu

ACTIVITÉ **P** **Les dessins animés** Prepare sentences about these cartoon characters using the verb **être** and the cues provided. You may use the adverbs more than once but each adjective can only be used once. Can you guess which cartoons **(dessins animés)** are of French or Francophone origin?

Adjectifs possibles

ambitieux	gentil	naïf
amusant	heureux	paresseux
courageux	intellectuel	sérieux
ennuyeux	malheureux	sportif
fier	méchant	talentueux

Adverbes possibles

parfois	rarement	toujours
quelquefois	souvent	trop

Modèle: Bart Simpson **est souvent paresseux.**

1. Lisa Simpson _____
2. Blanche Neige *(Snow White)* _____
3. Batgirl et Wonderwoman _____
4. Tintin et Milou _____
5. Astérix et Obélix _____
6. Anna (de *Frozen* de Disney) _____
7. Rémy (de *Ratatouille* de Disney) _____
8. Shrek et la princesse Fiona _____

OUI, JE PEUX! Here are two "can do statements" for you to check your progress so far. Look at each statement and rate yourself on how well you think you can perform the task. Then verify your ability with a partner. How did you do?

1. **"I can say two things that I do often, two things I sometimes do, and two things I rarely or never do."**

   I can perform this function
   ☐ with ease
   ☐ with some difficulty
   ☐ not at all

2. **"I can ask someone else about activities that person performs frequently, sometimes, or rarely/never."**

   I can perform this function
   ☐ with ease
   ☐ with some difficulty
   ☐ not at all

iLrn™

Are you looking for more practice? You can find it in **iLrn**.

🔊 Quelle **heure** est-il?

What time is it?

Il est une heure.

Il est deux heures.

Il est trois heures douze.

Il est quatre heures et quart.

Il est cinq heures et demie.

Il est sept heures moins vingt.

Il est neuf heures moins le quart.

Il est onze heures moins cinq.

Il est midi *(noon)*.
Il est minuit *(midnight)*.

Vocabulaire complémentaire

être en avance *to be early*
être à l'heure *to be on time*
être en retard *to be late*

À quelle heure est-ce qu'on mange? *(At) What time are we eating?*
Vers 8h30. *Around 8:30.*
Entre 10h et 11h. *Between 10:00 and 11:00.*
De 10h à 11h. *From 10:00 until 11:00.*

J'ai un cours de français à 9h. *I have a French class at 9:00.*

- To add minutes to the hour, add them after **heure(s)**.

    Il est quatre heures **seize**.　　　　　*It's 4:16.*

- Note that special words are used to mean quarter of the hour or half-hour.

    Il est trois heures **et quart**.　　　　*It's 3:15.*
    Il est onze heures **et demie**.　　　　*It's 11:30.*
    Il est midi **et demi**.　　　　　　　*It's 12:30.*

- To express a time that is approaching an hour, use the expression **moins** *(less)*.

    Il est neuf heures **moins le quart**.　*It's 8:45. (It's a quarter to nine.)*
    Il est dix heures **moins vingt**.　　　*It's 9:40. (It's twenty to ten.)*

- To distinguish between A.M. and P.M., add **du matin, de l'après-midi**, or **du soir**.

    Il est dix heures **du matin**.　　　　　*It's 10 o'clock in the morning.*
    Il est trois heures **de l'après-midi**.　*It's 3 o'clock in the afternoon.*
    Il est huit heures et demie **du soir**.　*It's 8:30 in the evening.*

Note de vocabulaire
Note that you use **moins** *le* quart but *et* quart: Il est deux heures **et quart**. Il est cinq heures **moins le quart**.

 ACTIVITÉ A **Quelle heure est-il?** Write the times you hear. Be sure to

1-8　specify A.M. or P.M.

Modèle: *You hear:* Il est une heure de l'après-midi.
　　　　You write: **1:00 P.M.**

1. _____　　　5. _____

2. _____　　　6. _____

3. _____　　　7. _____

4. _____　　　8. _____

Un mot sur la langue

Heure ou heures?

Use **heure** (singular) for one o'clock and **heures** (plural) for hours after one o'clock. Add an **e** to **demi** if it follows **heure(s)** because **heure** is feminine (**Il est cinq heures et demie**). Do not add an **e** to **demi** if it follows **midi** or **minuit** because they are masculine: **Il est midi et demi**.

- Write out these times in French.

    1. 1:30 P.M. _____
    2. 4:30 P.M. _____
    3. 12:30 A.M. _____
    4. 8:30 A.M. _____
    5. 12:30 P.M. _____
    6. 9:30 P.M. _____

ACTIVITÉ B **L'emploi du temps de Simon** You will hear statements

1-9 about Simon's (a classmate of Claire's) activities for Friday. Look at his schedule to determine if the statements are true (**vrai**) or false (**faux**).

vendredi	
7h30	cours d'anglais
9h00	cours de chimie
11h00	cours d'informatique
12h30	déjeuner
2h30	étudier à la bibliothèque *(library)*
4h15	jouer au football
6h45	dîner avec Claire

1. vrai / faux   **3.** vrai / faux   **5.** vrai / faux

2. vrai / faux   **4.** vrai / faux   **6.** vrai / faux

Liaisons musicales

© Serge Thomann/Wire Image/Getty Images

The youngest of fourteen children, Céline Dion (1968–) first started singing in shopping malls in her hometown in Charlemagne, Quebec. Today she is an international mega pop star singing in both French and English. One of her earlier songs, *Trois heures vingt* is a love song from her 1984 album *Mélanie*. Find a video clip of this song on the Internet, and visit the singer's official website.

ACTIVITÉ C **Il est l'heure** Look at each clock and say what time it is.

1. 8:00   **3.** 9:45   **5.** 5:15

2. 10:25   **4.** 3:30   **6.** 2:50

ACTIVITÉ D **Une vie saine** *(healthy)* **et équilibrée**

Étape 1. Indicate at what time one should do the following activities in order to live a healthy, balanced life. Write out the time in French.

Modèles: On prend le petit déjeuner *(have breakfast)* **à huit heures du matin.**
On va au *(goes to)* gymnase **entre neuf heures et dix heures.**

1. On déjeune _____.

2. On joue au basket-ball _____.

3. On travaille _____.

4. On dîne _____.

5. On prend un goûter *(snack)* _____.

6. On dort *(sleep)* _____.

Étape 2. Now revisit **Étape 1** and provide the time you usually do these activities.

Conclusion Est-ce que vous avez *(have)* une vie saine et équilibrée?

Étape 3. Tell a classmate at what time you do these activities. Your classmate will share his/her responses with you. Based on the responses, decide if your classmate is living a healthy, balanced life.

Conclusion Mon/Ma camarade a *(has)* une vie saine et équilibrée.   oui / non

ACTIVITÉ E À l'heure, en avance ou en retard? Indicate whether you are on time, early, or late in these situations.

Modèle: Le cours de musique est à midi. Tu arrives à midi et quart.
Donc *(So / In that case),* **je suis en retard.**

1. Le cours de biologie est à 11h. Tu arrives à 10h40.
2. Le cours de chimie est à 8h30. Tu arrives à 8h30.
3. Le cours de gestion est à 9h15. Tu arrives à 9h30.
4. Le cours de comptabilité est à 10h. Tu arrives à 9h45.
5. Le cours de génie mécanique est à midi. Tu arrives à 12h30.
6. Le cours de psychologie est à 2h. Tu arrives à 2h.
7. Le cours de journalisme est à 3h. Tu arrives à 2h30.
8. Le cours de musique est à 4h. Tu arrives à 4h20.

• En général, est-ce que tu es à l'heure, en avance ou en retard pour les cours?

ACTIVITÉ F À quelle heure? Ask a classmate at what time he/she usually does these activities.

Modèle: É1: **À quelle heure est-ce que tu écoutes la radio?**
É2: **J'écoute la radio vers 9h du matin. / J'écoute la radio de 8h à 9h du matin. / J'écoute la radio entre 8h et 9h du matin.**

1. déjeuner pendant la semaine
2. étudier le soir
3. aimer mieux pratiquer un sport
4. cuisiner pendant la semaine
5. arriver à l'université
6. regarder la télévision
7. travailler le week-end
8. aimer mieux dîner le week-end

ACTIVITÉ G Nos emplois du temps

Étape 1. Provide 1–2 things you do in the morning, in the afternoon, and in the evening for each day of the work week. Include the time when you do these activities.

	lundi	mardi	mercredi	jeudi	vendredi
le matin	10h cours de français	11h cours de musique	10h cours de français	11h cours de musique	10h cours de français
l'après-midi					travailler de 4h à 6h
le soir					

Étape 2. Ask a classmate what he/she does during the times and days that you have activities on your schedule.

Modèle: É1: **Qu'est-ce que tu fais le lundi à 10h du matin?**
É2: **J'ai un cours à 10h.**
É1: **Qu'est-ce que tu fais le vendredi à 7h du soir?**
É2: **Je travaille.**

Étape 3. Using the information you obtained in **Étape 2,** complete this statement with the appropriate adjective. Try to give two pieces of information to support your choice.

Conclusion Nos (*Our*) emplois du temps sont similaires / différents.

ACTIVITÉ H Expressions utiles Which of these expressions would you use to respond to these questions?

Expressions		
Bien sûr! (*Of course!*)	**Pas du tout!** (*Not at all!*)	**Peut-être.** (*Perhaps.*)

1. Aimez-vous passer un examen à 7h du matin?
2. Aimez-vous dîner après 9h du soir?
3. Aimez-vous dormir jusqu'à midi?
4. Aimez-vous étudier le dimanche?
5. Aimez-vous regarder les films français?
6. Aimez-vous parler français?

Un mot sur la culture

Le système des 24 heures

In most French-speaking countries, the 24-hour clock is used in formal conversations, in the news, and in publications like course schedules, train and plane schedules, movie times, and TV programs. With the 24-hour clock, you use 13 to 24 to express the hours of 1:00 P.M. through midnight. For example, 3:00 P.M. is **15h00 (quinze heures)** and 5:45 P.M. is **17h45 (dix-sept heures quarante-cinq).** The expressions **et demi(e), et quart, moins le quart, midi,** and **minuit** are not used. Thus, if your favorite TV show is on at 8:30 P.M., you will see it listed as **20h30** in the TV guide.

© Khafizov Ivan Harisovich/Shutterstock.com

● Can you convert the following times to the 24-hour clock?

1. 11:45 P.M.   2. 10:05 A.M.   3. 4:30 P.M.   4. 8:20 P.M.

Liaisons avec les mots et les sons

1-10

La liaison et l'enchaînement

Note de prononciation
In a liaison, **s** and **x** are pronounced **z**, and in an **enchaînement**, **f** is pronounced **v**.

Liaison and **enchaînement** refer to the linking of the final consonant sound of one word with the vowel sound of the following word. A **liaison** occurs when a word that normally ends in a silent consonant (**s, t, x** or **n**) is followed by a word that begins with a vowel sound. When **liaison** and **enchaînement** occur, the first word needs to modify or qualify the second word in some way as in the following examples.

Subject pronouns

Il est professeur.   Elle est professeur.   On aime le français.

Nous adorons la chimie.   Vous étudiez beaucoup.   Elles habitent à Paris.

Articles

un écran   une étudiante   les affaires   les heures

Adverbs or adjectives

C'est ambitieux.   C'est important.   C'est très intéressant.   C'est assez sérieux.

Numbers

Il est cinq heures.   Il est six heures.   Il est huit heures.

Il est neuf heures.   Il y a deux hommes.   Il y a trois étudiants.

Pratique A. Listen carefully and mark with (‿) the two letters that have a **liaison**.

1. Les étudiants mangent à neuf heures.
2. C'est une femme très intelligente.
3. Elle est très ambitieuse.
4. On est des étudiants travailleurs.
5. Il a cinq affiches dans son sac.
6. Il y a deux horloges dans la salle de classe.

Pratique B. Listen to these lines from the film *Liaisons* and indicate with (‿) where the **liaisons** should be.

CLAIRE Elle existe, c'est tout.

ABIA Et les hallucinations?

CLAIRE Elle a des moments de lucidité…

ABIA Il est presque quinze heures. Il faut travailler.

 À vos stylos! **C'est l'heure de la dictée!**

1-11 You will hear three sentences. Listen closely to them. You will then hear the sentences a second time. Write the three sentences you hear.

 Sujet Claire et Abia

Pour parler de nos possessions

Le verbe **avoir**

DU FILM *LIAISONS*

Un coup d'œil sur la grammaire

In **Séquence 1** of the film *Liaisons,* Claire makes the following statement to a friend after she returns from visiting her mother.

Elle **a** des moments de lucidité mais...

The word **a** comes from the verb **avoir.** What does this verb mean?

a. to be   b. to do   c. to have

❖ **Avoir** is an irregular verb that is used to express possession. Here are all the forms of the present tense of **avoir.**

avoir *(to have)*	
j'**ai**	nous **avons**
tu **as**	vous **avez**
il/elle/on **a**	ils/elles **ont**

Note de prononciation
Note that **as** and **a** have the same pronunciation. Make sure you pronounce the **liaison** /z/ for all the plural forms (**nous avons, vous avez, ils ont, elles ont**) and the **liaison** /n/ for **on a.**

Nous **avons** un cours de français à 10 heures.

We have a French class at 10 o'clock.

Est-ce que tu **as** un stylo?

Do you have a pen?

J'**ai** un cours le mardi et le jeudi.

I have a class Tuesdays and Thursdays.

❖ The indefinite articles **un, une,** and **des** becomes **de** (**d'** before a vowel sound) in negative sentences with **avoir** as well as with many other verbs.

Tu as **une** calculatrice?

Do you have a calculator?

Je n'ai pas **de** calculatrice.

I don't have a calculator.

Anne a **un** ordinateur.

Anne has a computer.

Marc n'a pas **d'**ordinateur.

Marc does not have a computer.

Rachid cherche **des** stylos.

Rachid is looking for some pens.

Il ne cherche pas **de** crayons.

He is not looking for pencils.

❖ The definite article (**le, la, l', les**) does not change in negative sentences.

—Vous avez **le** livre de biologie?

Do you have the biology book?

—Non, je n'ai pas **le** livre.

Non, I don't have the book.

❖ **Avoir** is also used to express age.

J'**ai** 18 ans.   *I am 18 years old.*   Ils **ont** 21 ans.   *They are 21 years old.*

Many common expressions in French also use the verb **avoir**.

avoir besoin de	*to need*	**avoir peur de**	*to be afraid of*
avoir de la chance	*to be lucky*	**avoir raison**	*to be right*
avoir envie de	*to feel like doing or having something*	**avoir sommeil**	*to be sleepy*
		avoir tort	*to be wrong*

J'**ai besoin d**'une agrafeuse.	*I need a stapler.*
Nous **avons besoin d**'étudier.	*We need to study.*
Tu **as de la chance**!	*You are lucky!*
Il n'**a** pas **envie de** travailler.	*He does not feel like working.*
Elle **a peur de** dépenser de l'argent.	*She is afraid to spend money.*
Ils **ont** très **sommeil.**	*They are very sleepy.*
Tu **as raison** mais moi, j'**ai tort.**	*You are right, but, me, I'm wrong.*
Elle **a peur de** parler français.	*She is afraid to speak French.*

The expression **avoir peur de** may be followed by a noun. Note that **de** must combine with definite articles (**le, la, l', les**) in the following ways.

de + le = du	J'**ai peur du** professeur.	*I am afraid of the professor.*
de + la = de la	Elles **ont peur de la** fille méchante.	*They are afraid of the mean girl.*
de + l' = de l'	Luc **a peur de l'**étudiant italien.	*Luc is afraid of the Italian student.*
de + les = des	Il **a peur des** cours difficiles.	*He is afraid of (the) difficult classes.*

Note de grammaire

The expression **il y a** *(there is / there are)* that you learned in **Chapitre préliminaire** also uses the verb **avoir.**

© Richard Cummins / SuperStock

Si vous y allez

Do you like haunted houses? Located in Sainte-Claire in the province of Quebec, **Québec Halloween** is a haunted house that promises to scare! Attractions include haunted mazes and ghosts and goblins of all kinds. You can even have your photo taken with your favorite horror character. **Est-ce que vous avez peur?!** Look for the website by doing a search with the words **Québec, maison hantée,** and **Sainte-Claire.**

ACTIVITÉ ⓘ Qui est-ce? / C'est qui? *(Who is it?)* You will hear statements about classes Marc and Arthur have. Listen to the verb to determine if Marc has the course or if both Marc and Arthur have the course.

1-12

1. a. Marc	b. Marc et Arthur	**4.** a. Marc	b. Marc et Arthur
2. a. Marc	b. Marc et Arthur	**5.** a. Marc	b. Marc et Arthur
3. a. Marc	b. Marc et Arthur	**6.** a. Marc	b. Marc et Arthur

ACTIVITÉ Ⓙ Les colocataires

Étape 1. Two sets of roommates are talking about their courses and things they need. Pay attention to the verbs to determine the subject of the sentence.

1. _____ **avons** un cours de musique à 8h30.	a. Nous	b. Vous
2. _____ **avez** un cours de psychologie à midi.	a. Nous	b. Vous
3. _____ **avez** un cours d'anglais à 11h00.	a. Nous	b. Vous
4. _____ **ai** besoin d'un sac à dos.	a. J'	b. Tu
5. _____ **as** besoin d'un cahier.	a. J'	b. Tu
6. _____ **ai** besoin d'une calculatrice.	a. J'	b. Tu

ACTIVITÉ K **Avoir raison ou avoir tort?** React to the following statements made by a sixth-grader with **(a) Oui, tu as raison** or **(b) Non, tu as tort.**

1. Deux plus deux font douze.
2. Onze plus cinq font seize.
3. La capitale de la France est Québec.
4. La capitale du Canada est Ottawa.
5. Les devoirs sont importants.

6. Les examens sont embêtants.
7. Je n'ai pas besoin d'étudier.
8. J'ai besoin de manger des légumes (*vegetables*).

ACTIVITÉ L **Qu'est-ce que nous avons?** *(What do we have?)*

Étape 1. Florian and Hisham will be housemates. They are making a list of things they have and don't have. Pay attention to the articles to determine whether they have or do not have the things mentioned. Remember that when **avoir** is used in the negative, the indefinite articles **un, une**, and **des** becomes **de** (**d'** before a vowel sound). Complete each sentence with **(a) Nous avons** or **(b) Nous n'avons pas.**

1. _____ **de** chaises (*f.*).
2. _____ **une** télévision.
3. _____ **des** lampes (*f.*).
4. _____ **de** table (*f.*).
5. _____ **un** réfrigérateur.

6. _____ **d'**affiches (*f.*).
7. _____ **un** ordinateur.
8. _____ **d'**horloge (*f.*).
9. _____ **des** bureaux (*m.*).
10. _____ **une** poubelle.

Étape 2. Look at the items that Florian and Hisham do not have. Write complete sentences indicating what they need. Hint: They need four items from the list. Use the expression **avoir besoin de.**

Modèle: Ils n'ont pas d'horloge.
    Ils ont besoin d'une horloge.

1. _____
2. _____

3. _____
4. _____

ACTIVITÉ M **Quel âge est-ce qu'ils ont?** *(How old are they?)* At what age are people more likely to do the following activities? Provide complete sentences using the verb **avoir** to express the persons' ages.

Modèle: Elle vote.   11 ans / 21 ans   **Elle a 21 ans.**

1. Elle cuisine un hamburger.
   5 ans / 15 ans
2. Il a une carte de crédit.
   10 ans / 30 ans
3. Elle joue à la marelle (*hopscotch*).
   8 ans / 96 ans
4. Elles adorent *Sesame Street*.
   6 ans / 56 ans

5. Ils jouent au hockey.
   22 ans / 98 ans
6. Ils dansent la polka.
   18 ans / 67 ans
7. Elles naviguent sur Internet.
   21 ans / 95 ans
8. Ils cherchent un emploi (*job*).
   34 ans / 81 ans

Étape 1. Do you know how old these famous people are? Look at the year they were born and say how old they are.

1. 1943

2. 1975

3. 1976

4. 1972

5. 1982

6. 1948

7. 1990

8. 1985

Étape 2. Answer these questions.

1. Quel âge avez-vous?

2. Quel âge a votre camarade de classe?

3. Quel âge a votre meilleur(e) (best) ami(e)?

4. Quel âge a le président de votre université?

5. Quel âge a le président des États-Unis?

6. Quel âge a le vice-président des États-Unis?

7. Quel âge a le maire (mayor) de votre ville?

8. Quel âge a votre colocataire?

Étape 3. Answer these questions.

1. Qui est le/la plus jeune (youngest) dans l'Étape 2?

2. Qui est le/la plus âgé(e) (oldest) dans l'Étape 2?

ACTIVITÉ O **Les étudiants typiques de mon université** What are typical students at your college or university like? Read the statements and determine whether the statements are true or false.

Les étudiants typiques de mon université…	Vrai	Faux
1. **ont envie de** passer des examens.	☐	☐
2. **ont envie de** parler avec leurs parents.	☐	☐
3. **ont souvent sommeil** en cours.	☐	☐
4. **ont de la chance** d'avoir de bons professeurs.	☐	☐
5. **ont de la chance** d'avoir une bonne bibliothèque.	☐	☐
6. **n'ont pas envie d**e manger au restaurant universitaire.	☐	☐
7. **n'ont pas envie d'**étudier.	☐	☐
8. **n'ont pas sommeil** le matin.	☐	☐

Et vous? Est-ce que vous êtes un(e) étudiant(e) typique de votre université? Pourquoi ou pourquoi pas?

ACTIVITÉ P **Nos envies et nos besoins**

Étape 1. Make a list of at least three activities that you feel like doing this weekend. Make another list of things that you need to do this weekend.

Modèle: **J'ai envie de regarder un film avec mes amis.**
J'ai besoin de travailler à la bibliothèque.

Étape 2. Share what you wrote with a classmate. Look at what you both want to do and what you both need to do and decide who is more likely to have a good weekend.

Conclusion Qui va passer *(Who is going to spend)* un bon week-end?

ACTIVITÉ Q **Les préférences** Poll your classmates to see if they have the following favorite things. If you find someone who does, jot down his/her name and his/her favorite thing.

Modèle: É1: **Est-ce que tu as un professeur préféré?**
É2: **Oui, j'ai un professeur préféré: le professeur de français.**

1. un cours préféré
2. un film préféré
3. un album préféré
4. un sport préféré
5. un livre préféré
6. un magasin *(store)* préféré
7. un auteur *(author)* préféré
8. un jour de semaine préféré

© Monkey Business Images/Shutterstock.com

ACTIVITÉ R **Est-ce que vous avez peur?**

Étape 1. Indicate if you are afraid of these things.

	Oui	Non
1. des professeurs	☐	☐
2. des monstres	☐	☐
3. des clowns	☐	☐
4. de voyager à l'étranger *(abroad)*	☐	☐
5. de marcher seul(e) *(alone)* sur le campus le soir	☐	☐
6. de cuisiner	☐	☐
7. de chanter	☐	☐
8. de danser	☐	☐
9. de manger des insectes	☐	☐
10. de regarder des films d'horreur	☐	☐

© 377719031?/Shutterstock.com

Étape 2. Ask a classmate whether he/she is afraid of these things.

Modèle: É1: **Est-ce que tu as peur des professeurs?**
É2: **Non, je n'ai pas peur des professeurs.**

Étape 3. Based on the information from **Étape 1** and **Étape 2,** what things are both you and your classmate afraid of?

Modèle: **Nous avons peur des clowns et de cuisiner.**

OUI, JE PEUX!

Here are two "can do statements" for you to check your progress so far. Look at each statement and rate yourself on how well you think you can perform the task. Then verify your ability with a partner. How did you do?

1. **"I can describe my weekly schedule including when I have class, when I study, and so on, and indicate on which days I do what activities."**

   I can perform this function
   ☐ with ease
   ☐ with some difficulty
   ☐ not at all

2. **"I can ask someone else about his/her weekly schedule (classes, studying, other activities) and also find out on what days that person does what activities."**

   I can perform this function
   ☐ with ease
   ☐ with some difficulty
   ☐ not at all

iLrn™

Are you looking for more practice? You can find it in **iLrn**.

PREMIÈRE PROJECTION

Avant de visionner

ACTIVITÉ A Vous rappelez-vous? *(Do you remember?)* Indicate if each sentence is **vrai** or **faux** based on what you remember from the **Prologue** of *Liaisons*.

	Vrai	Faux
1. Claire étudie à l'Université McGill.	☐	☐
2. Claire est étudiante en littérature française.	☐	☐
3. Claire va à l'hôpital après son cours.	☐	☐
4. Mme Gagner souffre de psychose.	☐	☐

ACTIVITÉ B Un coup d'œil sur une scène In this scene from **Séquence 1**, Claire talks with her co-worker Abia after visiting her mother. With a classmate, try to figure out which words—those in option a or in option b—go in the blanks. You will check your answers later when you watch this scene.

ABIA Ah, Claire. (1) _____ es déjà arrivée.

CLAIRE Oui. Quelle (2) _____ est-il?

ABIA 14h45 à peu près.

CLAIRE (3) _____?

ABIA Oui. Très (4) _____.
[noticing her expression]. Qu'est-ce (5) _____?

CLAIRE Ma mère.

1. a. Je   b. Tu
2. a. heure   b. semaine
3. a. Pas mal   b. Ça va, toi
4. a. bien   b. mal
5. a. que tu cherches   b. qu'il y a

• What do you think the questions **Qu'est-ce que tu cherches?** and **Qu'est-ce qu'il y a?** mean?

▶ Regarder la séquence

You will now watch **Séquence 1** of the film *Liaisons*. Don't worry if there are words or expressions you do not understand. Use the context and images to help you understand what you hear.

Après le visionnage

ACTIVITÉ C **Vérifiez votre compréhension!**

1. Claire travaille dans un hôpital.   V / F
2. Claire et Abia sont collègues et amies.   V / F
3. Mme Gagner mange, lit *(reads)*, joue aux cartes et dort *(sleeps)* toute la journée.   V / F
4. Un homme donne *(gives)* une enveloppe à Claire.   V / F
5. Claire rencontre Alexis Prévost qui a besoin d'une brosse à dents *(toothbrush)*.   V / F
6. Claire trouve le nom de M. Prévost dans le registre de l'hôtel *(hotel registry)*.   V / F

ACTIVITÉ D **Avez-vous compris?** Review your answers to **Activité B** of **Avant de visionner.** How did you do?

ACTIVITÉ E **Premières impressions: Abia**

Étape 1. What are your first impressions of Abia? Write 1–2 sentences to describe her, using adjectives you have learned so far.

Étape 2. Compare what you wrote with a classmate. Do you have similar impressions?

Liaisons avec la culture

Montréal—Ville internationale et cosmopolite

Montreal is the second largest city in Canada next to Toronto and the second largest French-speaking city in the world next to Paris. The official language in Montreal is French but, if you take a stroll in downtown Montreal, you are likely to hear English and many other languages because Montreal is home to many different ethnic communities including **le quartier chinois** and **le quartier italien.** Montreal is also a center for film and television production, as well as the home of many internationally-known festivals like **le festival Juste pour rire** *(Just for Laughs Festival)* and **le Festival international de jazz de Montréal.**

© Sebastian Rich/Corbis News/Corbis

LIAISONS CULTURELLES

Les études, le travail et les vacances

OUTILS DE LECTURE
Using cognates

Cognates are words that are similar in spelling and meaning in French and in English. While you may not know every word in a French text, your ability to recognize cognates will help you understand most of the meaning in a text.

1. Look at this sentence from the text **Étudier en France et au Sénégal: En général, les étudiants universitaires obtiennent une licence, qui est comparable au B.A. américain, en trois ans.** What are the cognates in this sentence?

2. Using the cognates and any other words in the sentence that you already know, what do you think this sentence means?

Étudier en France et au Sénégal

Le système universitaire du Sénégal est semblable° au système français. Pour être admis à s'inscrire° à l'université, il faut réussir° au baccalauréat, une série d'examens qu'on passe à la fin de la dernière année du lycée°. En général, les étudiants universitaires obtiennent une licence°, qui est comparable au B.A. américain, en trois ans. Il y a des différences avec° le système universitaire américain. En France et au Sénégal, les études universitaires sont presque gratuites°. Le sport est moins important qu'aux États-Unis: il n'y a pas de grandes équipes° universitaires.

© Olivier Asselin / Alamy

semblable *similar* **s'inscrire** *register* **réussir** *pass* **lycée** *high school* **obtiennent une licence** *earn a degree* **avec** *with* **gratuites** *free of charge* **équipes** *teams*

Vrai ou faux?

1. Aux États-Unis, les études universitaires sont gratuites.   V / F

2. En France et au Sénégal, le baccalauréat est très important.   V / F

3. On obtient une licence en 3 ans.   V / F

4. Il y a beaucoup d'équipes de sport universitaires en France et au Sénégal.   V / F

© Jeremy Maude/Glow Images

Au travail en France et en Suisse

La France et la Suisse sont des pays voisins°, mais leurs attitudes envers° le travail sont très différentes. En général, les Suisses travaillent entre 40 et 45 heures par semaine avec quatre semaines de vacances par an. En France, par contre°, les Français travaillent 35 heures par semaine et ils ont cinq semaines de vacances par an. Pour les Français, les vacances sont très importantes pour avoir une vie équilibrée. En effet°, pour certains Français, les vacances sont plus° importantes que l'argent°. Selon CBS news, l'argent n'est pas la priorité la plus importante parce que la France a un excellent système de soins médicaux et d'éducation qui est presque° gratuit°.

pays voisins *neighboring countries* **envers** *toward* **par contre** *on the other hand* **En effet** *In fact* **plus** *more* **l'argent** *money* **presque** *almost* **gratuit** *free*

Vrai ou faux?

1. Les Suisses ne travaillent pas beaucoup. V / F

2. Les vacances sont très importantes pour les Français. V / F

3. Les Suisses travaillent moins que *(less than)* les Français. V / F

4. La France a un excellent système de soins médicaux. V / F

En vacances au Québec

Les longs hivers sont une partie intégrante de la vie au Québec et, par conséquent, il y a beaucoup d'activités pour passer le temps durant cette saison. Le Carnaval de Québec, qui a lieu au mois de février, est un festival pour fêter° l'hiver. Pendant le carnaval, on peut pratiquer de nombreuses activités sportives et artistiques: des courses de traîneaux à chiens°, un concours° international de sculptures de glace°, la tire sur neige°, le bain de neige°, la danse folklorique, la visite du château de glace, etc. La mascotte du carnaval est le Bonhomme Carnaval. Tous les ans, les Québécois attendent° avec impatience l'arrivée de celui-ci lors du grand défilé° du bonhomme. Que la fête commence!°

© Agence Quebec Presse/Newscom

fêter *celebrate* **des courses de traîneaux à chiens** *dogsled races* **un concours** *contest* **sculptures de glace** *ice sculpture* **la tire sur neige** *taffy making on snow* **le bain de neige** *snow bath* **attendent** *wait* **défilé** *parade* **Que la fête commence!** *Let the partying begin!*

Vrai ou faux?

1. L'hiver est court *(short)* au Québec. V / F

2. Il y a des activités sportives et artistiques au carnaval. V / F

3. Le Carnaval de Québec est au mois de juin. V / F

4. La mascotte du Carnaval de Québec est le Bonhomme Carnaval. V / F

© Axiom / Glasshouse / Aurora

Le festival de théâtre d'Avignon

Le festival d'Avignon existe depuis° 1947. C'est un grand événement artistique et touristique. Ce festival de théâtre dure° de trois à quatre semaines chaque été°. La ville est remplie° d'artistes et de spectateurs. On peut voir° des pièces de théâtre classique ou expérimental. Avignon, une ville du sud de la France, a une histoire unique. Au quatorzième siècle°, les papes° de l'Église catholique vivaient° à Avignon. La ville a été contrôlée par l'Église jusqu'à° la Révolution française (1789). Aujourd'hui°, le palais des Papes d'Avignon est utilisé comme décor de théâtre pendant le festival.

depuis *since* **dure** *lasts* **chaque été** *each summer* **remplie** *filled* **peut voir** *can see* **Au quatorzième siècle** *In the fourteenth century* **les papes** *popes* **vivaient** *lived* **jusqu'à** *until* **Aujourd'hui** *Currently, Today*

Vrai ou faux?

1. Le festival d'Avignon est un festival de théâtre.   V / F

2. Le festival est en octobre.   V / F

3. Avignon est dans le nord de la France.   V / F

4. Les papes de l'Église catholique vivaient au palais à Avignon avant la Révolution française.   V / F

▶ LIAISONS CULTURELLES

Use iLrn™ to access the video **Les vacances** to learn more about where the French like to go on vacation and what they like to do. Be prepared to answer the question **Et vous? Qu'est-ce que vous aimez et n'aimez pas faire en vacances?** Share your responses with your classmates in **Share It!**

PARTIE 1   1–13

VERBES

adorer	to adore
aimer bien	to like
aimer mieux	to prefer
chanter	to sing
chercher	to look for
cuisiner	to cook
danser	to dance
déjeuner (au café)	to have lunch (at a café)
détester	to hate
dîner (au restaurant)	to have dinner (at a restaurant)
écouter (écouter de la musique)	to listen to (music)
étudier (à la bibliothèque)	to study (at the library)
habiter	to live (in a place), to reside
inviter (des amis)	to invite (friends)
jouer	to play
manger	to eat
marcher (au parc)	to walk (in the park)
naviguer sur Internet	to surf the Internet
parler	to speak, to talk
passer un examen	to take an exam
penser	to think
pratiquer un sport	to play a sport
rater un examen	to fail an exam
regarder (la télé)	to watch (television)
téléphoner	to telephone
travailler (au bureau)	to work (at the office)
trouver	to find
voyager	to travel

LES NOMBRES DE 60 À 100

60 soixante
61 soixante et un
62 soixante-deux
63 soixante-trois
64 soixante-quatre
65 soixante-cinq
66 soixante-six
67 soixante-sept
68 soixante-huit
69 soixante-neuf
70 soixante-dix
71 soixante et onze
72 soixante-douze
73 soixante-treize
74 soixante-quatorze
75 soixante-quinze
76 soixante-seize
77 soixante-dix-sept
78 soixante-dix-huit
79 soixante-dix-neuf
80 quatre-vingts
81 quatre-vingt-un
82 quatre-vingt-deux
83 quatre-vingt-trois
84 quatre-vingt-quatre
85 quatre-vingt-cinq
86 quatre-vingt-six
87 quatre-vingt-sept
88 quatre-vingt-huit
89 quatre-vingt-neuf
90 quatre-vingt-dix
91 quatre-vingt-onze
92 quatre-vingt-douze
93 quatre-vingt-treize
94 quatre-vingt-quatorze
95 quatre-vingt-quinze
96 quatre-vingt-seize
97 quatre-vingt-dix-sept
98 quatre-vingt-dix-huit
99 quatre-vingt-dix-neuf
100 cent
100% cent pour cent

DIVERS

avec	with
mais	but
pendant	during, throughout
la semaine	the week
le week-end	the weekend
Qu'est-ce que tu fais?	What are you doing?
Qu'est-ce qu'il/elle fait?	What is he/she doing?

PARTIE 2   1–14

LES JOURS ET L'EMPLOI DU TEMPS

lundi	Monday
mardi	Tuesday
mercredi	Wednesday
jeudi	Thursday
vendredi	Friday
samedi	Saturday
dimanche	Sunday
après	after
aujourd'hui	today
avant	before
demain	tomorrow
hier	yesterday
l'emploi du temps (m.)	schedule
la nuit	night
tous les jours	everyday
tous les soirs	every evening
Quel jour sommes-nous?	What day is it?
Nous sommes mardi.	It's Tuesday.

| Qu'est-ce que tu fais / vous faites? | What are you doing?, What do you do? |

ADVERBES

assez	enough
beaucoup	a lot
ne… jamais	never
un peu	a little
parfois	sometimes
quelquefois	sometimes
rarement	rarely
souvent	often
toujours	always
trop	too, too much

LES ADJECTIFS IRRÉGULIERS

fier / fière	proud
naïf / naïve	naive
sportif / sportive	athletic
gentil / gentille	nice
intellectuel / intellectuelle	intellectual
travailleur / travailleuse	hard-working
ambitieux / ambitieuse	ambitious
courageux / courageuse	courageous
ennuyeux / ennuyeuse	boring
heureux / heureuse	happy
malheureux / malheureuse	unhappy
paresseux / paresseuse	lazy
sérieux / sérieuse	serious
talentueux / talentueuse	talented

DIVERS

les gens (m. pl.)	people
l'hôtel (m.)	hotel
une personne	person

PARTIE 3   1–15

QUELLE HEURE EST-IL?

Quelle heure est-il?	What time is it?
Il est une heure. / Il est deux heures.	It's one o'clock. / It's two o'clock.
Il est midi / minuit.	It's noon / midnight.
et quart	a quarter past
et demi(e)	half past
moins le quart	a quarter to
du matin	in the morning
de l'après-midi	in the afternoon
du soir	in the evening
À quelle heure... ?	At what time . . . ?
vers 8h30	around 8:30
entre 10h et 11h	between 10:00 and 11:00
de 10h à 11h	from 10:00 until 11:00
J'ai un cours de français à 9h.	I have a French class at 9:00.
être en avance	to be early
être à l'heure	to be on time
être en retard	to be late

VERBES

avoir	to have
avoir... ans	to be . . . years old
avoir besoin de	to need
avoir de la chance	to be lucky
avoir envie de	to feel like
avoir peur de	to be afraid of
avoir raison	to be right
avoir sommeil	to be sleepy
avoir tort	to be wrong

DIVERS

donc	so, therefore
bien sûr	of course
pas du tout	not at all
peut-être	perhaps

Les **plaisirs** de la **vie**

En bref   In this chapter, you will:

- talk about the months, seasons, and weather

- learn the verb **aller** and the preposition **à**

- talk about sports and leisure-time activities

- learn the verbs **faire**, **lire**, **écrire**, and **dire**

- learn about contractions with the preposition **de**

- learn more about adverbs

- learn about silent consonants

- read about rugby in Toulouse, France

- write a brief portrait

 You will also re-watch **SÉQUENCE 1:** **L'étranger** of the film *Liaisons*.

Ressources

 audio   video   Share It!   iLrn™   http://www.cengagebrain.com

Le climat

Climate

Il fait gris.

Il pleut.

le printemps (mars, avril, mai)

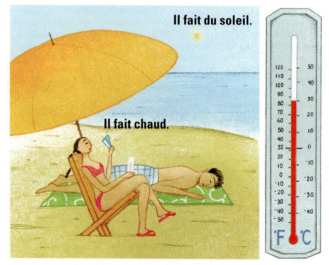

Il fait du soleil.

Il fait chaud.

l'été (juin, juillet, août)

Il fait du vent.

Il fait frais.

l'automne (septembre, octobre, novembre)

Il neige.

Il fait froid.

l'hiver (décembre, janvier, février)

Les saisons, les mois de l'année et le temps

Vocabulaire complémentaire

un an / une année *year*
un mois *month*
une saison *season*

le ciel *sky*
l'étoile (f.) *star*
la lune *moon*
la météo *weather forecast*
la neige *snow*
des nuages (m.) *(some) clouds*

la pluie *rain*
la tornade *tornado*

annoncer *to forecast*

Quel temps fait-il? *What's the weather like?*
Le ciel est couvert. *It's cloudy / overcast.*
Il fait beau. *The weather is nice.*
Il fait lourd. *It's humid / muggy.*
Il fait mauvais. *The weather is bad.*

- In most of the French-speaking world, temperature is given in Celsius, not Fahrenheit. The conversion formulas are F = (C × 1.8) + 32 and C = (F − 32) × 0.56.

  —**Quelle température fait-il?**   —*What's the temperature?*
  —**Il fait 14 degrés.**   —*It's 14 degrees Celsius. / It's 57° Fahrenheit.*

- In French, dates are expressed with **le** + the numbers 2–31 + the month. To say it's the first of the month, use **le premier**. In writing, dates are abbreviated by placing the day before the month, for example, **5/10 = le 5 octobre**.

  —**Quelle est la date aujourd'hui?**   —*What is today's date?*
  —**On est le 23 novembre.**   —*It's November 23.*
  —**Nous sommes le 23 novembre.**   —*It's November 23.*

  —**C'est quand ton / votre anniversaire?**   —*When is your birthday?*
  —**C'est le 10 janvier.**   —*It's the 10th of January.*

  —**C'est quand l'anniversaire de Samir?**   —*When is Samir's birthday?*
  —**C'est le premier mai.**   —*It's the first of May.*

- **Le temps** means both *weather* and *time* in French.

  Le temps est agréable aujourd'hui.   *The weather is nice today.*
  Olivier regarde la télé quand il a le temps.   *Olivier watches TV when he has time.*

🔊 **ACTIVITÉ A Quel mois?** Montreal, where Claire from the film *Liaisons* lives, has a four-season climate. You will hear weather expressions for Montreal. In which month of the year are these weather conditions likely to occur?

2-1

1. a. en décembre   b. en avril   c. en juillet
2. a. en avril   b. en août   c. en janvier
3. a. en octobre   b. en juin   c. en février
4. a. en septembre   b. en janvier   c. en mai
5. a. en juillet   b. en mars   c. en décembre
6. a. en février   b. en novembre   c. en septembre

🔊 **ACTIVITÉ B Quelle saison?** Listen to these weather conditions and decide if they are **vrai** or **faux.**

2-2

1. V / F   5. V / F
2. V / F   6. V / F
3. V / F   7. V / F
4. V / F   8. V / F

ACTIVITÉ C Quelle ville? With which cities or states do you associate these weather conditions?

1. les tornades   4. la pluie
2. les nuages   5. le soleil
3. la neige   6. le vent

ACTIVITÉ D Étoiles, lune ou soleil? Complete each sentence with **les étoiles, la lune,** or **(le) soleil.**

1. On voit *(sees)* _____ le matin.
2. On voit _____ le soir.
3. Les vampires aiment _____.
4. Louis XIV est le roi *(king)* _____.
5. Les astronomes étudient _____.
6. Les loups-garous *(werewolves)* aiment _____.

ACTIVITÉ **E** **Quelle saison et quel temps?** Complete these sentences with the appropriate seasons or weather conditions.

Modèle: À New York, il pleut souvent _____.
À New York, il pleut souvent **au printemps et en été.**

1. À Chicago, il fait du vent _____.

2. À Paris, il neige _____.

3. À Miami, il fait lourd _____.

4. À Los Angeles, _____ en hiver.

5. À Montréal, _____ en automne.

6. À Boston, _____ en été.

Note de vocabulaire

En is used with the months of the year (**en janvier, en décembre**) and with **automne, été,** and **hiver,** but **au** is used with **printemps.**

ACTIVITÉ **F** **La météo** Prepare sentences predicting the weather forecast for your area for the entire week starting with **lundi.**

Modèle: **Lundi, il fait beau. Mardi, il pleut.**

ACTIVITÉ **G** **Quelle est la date?** Provide the dates for these events or holidays.

Modèle: la rentrée scolaire   **C'est le 6 septembre.**

1. Halloween

2. la fête nationale américaine

3. Noël

4. la Saint-Patrick

5. la fête nationale en France

6. la Saint-Valentin

ACTIVITÉ **H** **C'est quand votre anniversaire?** Ask at least five classmates when their birthday is. Jot down the names of your classmates and their birthdays. Try to find out who has a birthday coming up. Circle the birthday that is coming up soon.

Liaisons musicales

Franck Seguin/Corbis Entertainment/Corbis

Quebecois singer Robert Charlebois (1944–) is often known as the Elvis of the French-speaking world. His songs deal with different realities of Quebec, sometimes political and often humorous, such as *Demain l'hiver* which starts with **Demain l'hiver / je m'en fous** *(I don't care)* / **je m'en vais** *(I'm going away)* **dans le sud** *(south)* **au soleil**… Look for this song as well as more information on Charlebois on his official website.

Ron Erwin/All Canada Photos/Getty Images

Un mot sur la culture

L'hiver au Québec

Winter is such a significant part of Quebec's reality that poet Gilles Vigneault wrote in a much cherished song: *Mon pays ce n'est pas un pays, c'est l'hiver!* In fact, the Quebecois have even created winter-related terms that are unique in the French language.

• Can you guess the meaning of these expressions?

1. banc de neige

2. Il fait frette.

3. la poudrerie

a. *blowing fine powdery snow*

b. *snow drift*

c. *It's very (dang) cold.*

Pour parler des destinations

Le verbe **aller** / La préposition **à**

DU FILM *LIAISONS*

Un coup d'œil sur la grammaire

Look at these photos from the film *Liaisons* and their captions, paying special attention to the verbs and prepositions used.

Claire **va au** cours de psychologie à l'Université McGill.

Claire **va à la** chambre de Madame Gagner.

1. What do you think the verb **va** means?
2. Both **à** and **au** mean *to*. Why is **au** used with **cours** and **à la** used with **chambre**?

•••‣ The verb **aller** *(to go)* is an irregular verb.

The present tense of **aller** *(to go)*	
je **vais**	nous **allons**
tu **vas**	vous **allez**
il/elle/on **va**	ils/elles **vont**

•••‣ **Aller** is often used with prepositions to indicate locations or destinations, especially the preposition **à** *(to, at)*. This preposition may appear by itself or it may contract with the definite article, depending on the gender and number of the object it is modifying.

à + le	**au** (masculine, singular)
à + les	**aux** (plural, masculine or feminine)
à + la	**à la** (feminine, singular)
à + l'	**à l'** (singular, before a vowel sound)

Les étudiants **vont** tous les jours à l'école.

*Students **go to** school everyday.*

Le professeur ne **va** pas **au** bureau.

*The professor **is not going to** the office.*

Mon professeur **va à** Paris en été.

*My professor **goes to** Paris in the summer.*

The verb **aller** may also be used to express events that will happen in the near future. Called **le futur proche** *(the near future)*, this construction consists of a form of the present tense of **aller** followed by an infinitive.

Je **vais aller** à Paris cet été.	*I **am going to go** to Paris this summer.*
Nous **allons aller** à l'université demain.	*We **are going to go** to the university tomorrow.*
Abia **ne va pas aller** au café ce soir.	*Abia **is not going to go** to the café tonight.*

ACTIVITÉ I Les activités

Étape 1. Indicate whether these activities refer to **le professeur** or **les étudiants**.

1. _____ **vont** au cours de français tous les jours. a. Le professeur b. Les étudiants

2. _____ **va** travailler à la bibliothèque. a. Le professeur b. Les étudiants

3. _____ **va** à Paris cet été. a. Le professeur b. Les étudiants

Étape 2. Select the subjects of these sentences.

4. _____ **vais** au cours de sciences politiques à 8h. a. Je b. Tu

5. _____ **vas** au cours de mathématiques à 10h30. a. Je b. Tu

6. _____ **vais** au cours de philosophie à 11h. a. Je b. Tu

Étape 3. Select the subjects of these sentences.

7. _____ **allez** au campus le lundi, le mercredi et le vendredi. a. Nous b. Vous

8. _____ **allons** au restaurant le vendredi soir. a. Nous b. Vous

9. _____ **allez** au cinéma le samedi après-midi. a. Nous b. Vous

Et vous? Est-ce que vous allez faire *(do)* ces activités aujourd'hui? Lesquelles *(Which ones)*?

ACTIVITÉ J Où je vais? Pay close attention to the prepositions in order to figure out where this person is going. Once finished, reread the sentences and decide which sentences are true for you.

1. Le lundi, je vais **à l'…**
   a. hôtel.   b. cours de français.

2. Le samedi, je vais **au…**
   a. campus.   b. université.

3. Le week-end prochain, je vais **à l'…**
   a. café.   b. université.

4. Le mercredi, je vais **aux…**
   a. cours du soir.   b. école.

5. Mardi prochain, je vais **à l'…**
   a. cours de biologie.
   b. appartement de mon ami(e).

6. Après le cours aujourd'hui, je vais **à la…**
   a. salle de gymnastique.
   b. café.

7. Le jeudi, je vais **au…**
   a. cours de musique.
   b. université.

8. Cet après-midi, je vais **à la…**
   a. école.
   b. bibliothèque.

Si vous y allez

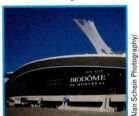

Alan Schein Photography/Documentary Value/Corbis

Si vous allez à Montréal, allez au Biodôme. It allows visitors to experience replicas of five ecosystems in the Americas: 1) Tropical Rainforest, 2) the Laurentian Wilderness, 3) St. Lawrence Marine, 4) the Arctic, and 5) Antarctic. Search for **biodôme Montréal** on the Internet and take a virtual tour.

ACTIVITÉ **K** **Qu'est-ce qu'on va faire** *(to do)*? Finish the sentences with an activity that you think the people are going to do today.

Modèle: Aujourd'hui, mon professeur **va travailler au bureau.**

1. Aujourd'hui, mes amis…
2. Aujourd'hui, mon voisin/ma voisine *(my neighbor)*…
3. Aujourd'hui, les étudiants du cours de français et moi…
4. Aujourd'hui, ma/mon colocataire…
5. Aujourd'hui, je…
6. Aujourd'hui, mon professeur…

ACTIVITÉ **L** **Quel jour de la semaine?** What day of the week do you think you will do these activities?

Modèle: danser   **Je vais danser samedi soir.**

1. cuisiner
2. dîner dans un bon restaurant
3. étudier
4. regarder la télévision
5. déjeuner à l'université
6. travailler
7. aller au cours de français
8. parler avec la famille

ACTIVITÉ **M** **Boule de cristal** *(Crystal ball)* With a partner, make real or imaginary predictions for these people. Think about what they're going to be like, what they're going to need or desire, and what they're going to do in the future. Use your knowledge of popular culture and your creativity!

Modèle: Bradley Cooper

Il va rester sexy. Il va jouer dans un autre film *Hangover*. Et il va aussi jouer dans un film français parce qu'il parle très bien français. Il ne va pas chanter dans ses films.

1. Bill Gates
2. Brad Pitt et Angelina Jolie
3. Oprah Winfrey
4. Rachael Ray et Martha Stewart
5. Prince William et Prince Harry
6. Jennifer Lawrence
7. Moi, je…
8. Claire du film *Liaisons*

Pour aller plus loin
Si

In French, **si** means *if*. **Si** becomes **s'** in front of **il** or **ils**.

Si Tom aime le sushi, on va manger au restaurant japonais.	*If Tom likes sushi, we are going to eat at the Japanese restaurant.*
S'il neige, je ne vais pas aller à l'école.	*If it snows, I am not going to go to school.*

Si, not **oui**, is also used to say *yes* in response to a negative question.

—Ils ne parlent pas français?	*— They don't speak French?*
—**Si**, ils parlent français.	*— Yes, they speak French.*
—Tu ne vas pas étudier ce soir?	*— You are not going to study tonight?*
—**Si**, je vais étudier.	*— Yes, I am going to study.*

Essayez! Answer these questions affirmatively.

1. Tu ne vas pas manger?
2. Tu n'as pas de devoirs aujourd'hui?
3. Tu n'aimes pas le français?

OUI, JE PEUX!

Here are two "can do statements" for you to check your progress so far. Look at each statement and rate yourself on how well you think you can perform the task. Then verify your ability with a partner. How did you do?

1. **"I can say one place where I am or am not going today and ask someone else if he/she is going there, too."**

   I can perform this function
   ☐ with ease
   ☐ with some difficulty
   ☐ not at all

2. **"I can say two things that I am going to do tomorrow if the weather is nice, sunny, rainy, and so on and ask someone else if he/she is going to do the same or different things."**

   I can perform this function
   ☐ with ease
   ☐ with some difficulty
   ☐ not at all

iLrn™

Are you looking for more practice? You can find it in **iLrn**.

VOCABULAIRE 2

Les sports

Sports

le baseball

le basket-ball / le basket

le football / le foot

le football américain

le golf

le hockey

le rugby

le tennis

le tennis de table

le volley-ball

Les activités sportives

Vocabulaire complémentaire

faire de l'aérobic *to do aerobics*

faire du bowling *to go bowling*

faire du cheval *to go horseback riding*

faire de la gym / du sport *to work out, to exercise*

faire du patinage *to iceskate, to go iceskating*

faire de la planche à voile *to go wind-surfing*

faire du ski (alpin) *to go (downhill) skiing*

faire du ski de fond *to go cross-country skiing*

faire du surf *to surf*

faire du yoga *to do yoga*

pratiquer *to play, to do a sport*

---

une équipe *a team*

un joueur / une joueuse *a player*

un match (de + sport) *a match, a game (of + sport)*

faire du jogging

faire de la marche

faire de la natation

faire du vélo

faire du ski nautique

Les expressions avec *faire*

- To talk about the sports you play, use an expression with the verb **faire** *(to do, to make)* or use the verb **jouer à** *(to play)* plus the name of the sport.

  J'aime faire du jogging tous les jours.   *I like to go jogging everyday.*
  Mes amis jouent souvent au foot.   *My friends play soccer often.*

Un mot sur la langue

Expressions intéressantes

Games and sports are important activities and conversation topics to many cultures. France is no exception. There are many everyday expressions in French that use games and sports-related vocabulary to express different ideas.

- Can you guess the meaning of these expressions?

  1. C'est un jeu *(game)* d'enfant *(child)*.
  2. marquer un point
  3. À vous de jouer!

  a. *It's your turn/move (now).*
  b. *It's very easy.*
  c. *to get one up, to have an advantage*

ACTIVITÉ A Quel sport? Select the famous athlete that plays the sport
mentioned in each sentence you hear.

2-3

1. a. Bob Harper	b. Andy Roddick	c. LeBron James
2. a. Hope Solo	b. Serena Williams	c. Danica Patrick
3. a. David Beckham	b. Tony Parker	c. Sidney Crosby
4. a. Roger Federer	b. Phil Mickelson	c. Martin Brodeur
5. a. Michael Jordan	b. Michael Phelps	c. Apolo Anton Ohno
6. a. Kobe Bryant	b. Payton Manning	c. Chris Froome
7. a. Jillian Michaels	b. Justine Henin	c. Venus Williams
8. a. Shawn Johnson	b. Laila Ali	c. Adelina Sotnikova

ACTIVITÉ B Les championnats Which one of the championships
corresponds to the sport you hear?

2-4

1. a. le Super Bowl   b. le Stanley Cup   c. la Coupe du Monde *(World Cup)*

2. a. la Coupe du Monde   b. le Super Bowl   c. le Gran Premio Santander d'Italia

3. a. le Stanley Cup   b. le Super Bowl   c. le tournoi de Roland-Garros

4. a. le Presidents Cup   b. le Tour de France   c. le Grand Prix de Monaco

5. a. le World Series   b. la Coupe du Monde   c. l'U.S. Open

6. a. l'Open d'Australie   b. l'Indianapolis 500   c. le Larry O'Brien Championship

ACTIVITÉ C Des athlètes ou des téléspectateurs? Is your class a group
of athletes, TV sports watchers, a mix of both, or none of the above? Select your
personal sports-related habit (a, b, c, or d) for these sports.

a. Je pratique ce *(this)* sport.   **c.** Je pratique ce sport et je regarde ce sport à la télé.
b. Je regarde ce sport à la télé.   **d.** Aucune de ces réponses. *(None of these answers.)*

1. le ski alpin	**3.** le golf	**5.** le bowling	**7.** le patinage
2. la natation	**4.** le volley-ball	**6.** le tennis de table	**8.** le football américain

ACTIVITÉ D *Faire* ou *jouer*?

Étape 1. Complete these sentences with either **jouer** or **faire.**

Les étudiants aiment _____

1. de la natation.	**3.** du cheval.	**5.** au football.	**7.** de la marche.
2. au tennis.	**4.** du jogging.	**6.** du yoga.	**8.** du vélo.

Étape 2. Finish each sentence with sports or physical activities that you like to do
or play.

1. J'aime **faire** _____ .   **2.** J'aime **jouer** _____ .

Étape 3. Which activity do you think Claire from the film *Liaisons* enjoys?

Claire Gagner aime _____ .

ACTIVITÉ **E** **Vos préférences** Pay attention to the articles to determine which sport is being referred to. Then, indicate whether each statement is **vrai** or **faux** for you.

1. J'aime faire du	a. ski nautique	b. planche à voile	V/F
2. J'aime faire de la	a. jogging	b. marche	V/F
3. J'aime faire de l'	a. aérobic	b. gym	V/F
4. J'aime faire de la	a. natation	b. yoga	V/F
5. J'aime faire du	a. planche à voile	b. surf	V/F
6. J'aime faire du	a. bowling	b. natation	V/F

Et vous? Complete the sentences with activities from this lesson.

1. Mes amis et moi, nous aimons faire _____.
2. Mon/Ma colocataire aime faire _____.

ACTIVITÉ **F** **Quel match en quelle saison?** Which professional sport games do people typically go see in each season of the year?

Modèle: en automne   **On regarde un match de football américain en automne.**

1. en automne   2. en hiver   3. au printemps   4. en été

ACTIVITÉ **G** **Les joueurs (joueuses) et les équipes** Which sports are associated with these players or teams?

Modèles: Joakim Noah   **Joakim Noah est un joueur de basket-ball.**
Les Chicago White Sox **Les Chicago White Sox sont une équipe de baseball.**

1. Serena Williams   3. Rafael Nadal   5. Les Black Hawks
2. Les Dallas Cowboys   4. Zinédine Zidane   6. Les Los Angeles Lakers

ACTIVITÉ **H** **Qu'est-ce que vos amis aiment faire?**

Étape 1. What kinds of sports do your friends like to play or what kinds of physical activities do they like to do in these weather conditions? You can also answer with what they do *not* like to do.

Modèle: **Quand il fait beau, mes amis aiment faire du jogging.**
          Quand il fait froid, mes amis n'aiment pas jouer au golf.

1. quand il fait frais   4. quand il neige
2. quand il fait beau   5. quand il pleut
3. quand il fait du vent   6. quand il fait chaud

 Étape 2. Share your answers from **Étape 1** with two or three other classmates. Do you think any of your friends would get along with your classmates' friends?

Si vous y allez

Si vous allez à Toulouse, allez au Stade Toulousain. Founded in 1907, the **Stade Toulousain** is one of the finest rugby clubs in Europe. They won the Heineken Cup in 1996, 2003, and 2005. Take a virtual tour at the **stade**'s official website.

© Alexandre Gelebart/REA/ Redux

ACTIVITÉ I Préférences

Étape 1. Do you and your classmates like or dislike the same sports or physical activities? Prepare three questions to ask your classmates based on your likes and dislikes.

Modèles: Est-ce que tu aimes faire du yoga? / Est-ce que tu joues au golf?

Étape 2. Now ask your three questions to three different students. Fill in the grid with the appropriate information. Which likes and dislikes do you have in common? Be ready to share your information in French with your instructor and classmates.

	Prénom	Réponse 1	Réponse 2	Réponse 3
É1				
É2				
É3				

ACTIVITÉ J Est-ce que vous êtes sportif/sportive?

Étape 1. Interview a classmate to find out if he/she is athletic or not. Note his/her answers. If your partner answers **non** to a question, go on to the next one. If your partner answers **oui,** indicate the frequency with which he/she does this activity: **tous les jours, régulièrement, de temps en temps** *(occasionally).*

Modèle: É1: Est-ce que tu aimes faire du jogging?
        É2: Oui.
        É1: Tous les jours? Régulièrement? De temps en temps?
        É2: Régulièrement.

		Oui	Non
1. Est-ce que tu aimes faire du jogging?		☐	☐
☐ Tous les jours ☐ Régulièrement ☐ De temps en temps			
2. Est-ce que tu aimes faire de l'aérobic?		☐	☐
☐ Tous les jours ☐ Régulièrement ☐ De temps en temps			
3. Est-ce que tu aimes faire de la marche?		☐	☐
☐ Tous les jours ☐ Régulièrement ☐ De temps en temps			
4. Est-ce que tu aimes faire de la gym?		☐	☐
☐ Tous les jours ☐ Régulièrement ☐ De temps en temps			
5. Est-ce que tu aimes faire du vélo?		☐	☐
☐ Tous les jours ☐ Régulièrement ☐ De temps en temps			
6. Est-ce que tu aimes faire de la natation?		☐	☐
☐ Tous les jours ☐ Régulièrement ☐ De temps en temps			

Étape 2. Now look back at your partner's answers to **Étape 1** and count them up. Write your partner's score and share it with him/her.

Non = 0 points	**Régulièrement = 2 points**
De temps en temps = 1 point	**Tous les jours = 3 points**

Étape 3. Write down your personal score and see what conclusion your score earns. If you finish early, share your results with another classmate or another pair of classmates.

0–3 = Pas du tout sportif/sportive. Attention! Un peu de sport est important pour une vie équilibrée.
4–8 = Pas très sportif/sportive. Vous n'êtes pas très sportif/sportive mais vous aimez faire des efforts quand même *(nevertheless)*. Essayez de faire un peu plus *(more)* d'efforts!
9–14 = Bravo! Vous êtes sportif/sportive. C'est très bien et très important pour la prévention des problèmes de santé et pour rester en forme *(stay in shape)*. Continuez.
15–18 = Très sportif/sportive. Vous êtes très sportif/sportive. En général, c'est bien d'être sportif. Mais attention! Vous risquez de vous blesser *(hurt yourself)*.

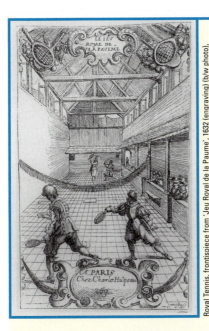

Royal Tennis, frontispiece from 'Jeu Royal de la Paume', 1632 (engraving) (b/w photo), French School, (17th century)/Bibliotheque des Arts Decoratifs, Paris, France/Archives Charmet/Bridgeman Images

Un mot sur la culture

Jeu de paume

Tennis is a popular spectator sport in France where it is also widely practiced. It is a British adaptation of an old French sport called **jeu de paume** that dates back to the 14th century. Following the Battle of Azincourt (1415), the French Duke of Orleans was imprisoned in England. During this period, he introduced the game to his English captors. Originally players used the palm of their hand. Gloves were soon worn and then bats were added. Early in the 16th century, wooden rackets were introduced. In England, the game evolved into tennis and then spread to France in the 19th century. **Jeu de paume** is still played in France, but it is nowhere near as popular as tennis.

• Do you know any other modern-day sports that have historical origins?

Pour parler des activités et poser des questions

Le verbe **faire** / L'inversion

DU FILM *LIAISONS*

Un coup d'œil sur la grammaire

Look at this photo from the film *Liaisons* and its caption.

MME SIMONE GAGNER Qu'est-ce que tu **fais** là-bas? Viens jouer avec moi.

You have seen the verb **fais** from the infinitive **faire** many times. Do you remember what this verb means?

Le verbe *faire*

⁖ **Faire** *(to do, to make)* is another irregular verb in French.

The present tense of **faire** *(to do, to make)*	
je **fais**	nous **faisons**
tu **fais**	vous **faites**
il/elle/on **fait**	ils/elles **font**

⁖ **Faire** may be used with or without an object and may be used in questions as well as in general statements.

—Qu'est-ce que **tu fais**?   —*What **are you doing**?*

—**Je fais** mes devoirs.   —*I am doing my homework.*

—Qu'est-ce qu'**il fait** à manger?   —*What is he making to eat?*

—**Il fait** des pâtes.   —*He's making pasta.*

⁖ The questions **Qu'est-ce que tu fais?, Qu'est-ce qu'ils font?,** etc. may be answered with verbs other than **faire.**

—Qu'est-ce qu'ils **font**?   —*What are they doing?*

—Ils **cherchent** un appartement.   —*They are looking for an apartment.*

—Qu'est-ce que tu **vas faire** ce soir?   —*What are you going to do this evening?*

—Je **vais jouer** au tennis avec un ami. —*I am going to play tennis with a friend.*

⁖ As you learned in **Chapitre 1**, indefinite articles (**un, une, des**) are replaced by **de/d'** in negative sentences. The partitive articles that make up some expressions used with **faire** (**du, de la, de l', des**) also become **de/d'** in negative sentences.

—Je fais **de la** gym tous les jours.   —*I work out everyday.*

—Je **ne** fais **pas de** gym tous les jours. —*I don't work out everyday.*

Note de grammaire

Recall that definite articles (**le, la, l', les**) do not change in negative sentences.

Samira **ne** fait **pas les** devoirs de français. *Samira is not doing French homework.*

Elle fait **les** devoirs de biologie. *She is doing biology homework.*

L'inversion

•••› You have already learned two ways to ask questions in French: **est-ce que (Est-ce que tu as un stylo?)** and intonation **(Ça va?).** Another way to ask questions is to use inversion which means inverting the subject pronoun and the conjugated verb. Generally speaking, inversion is considered more formal and is more often used in writing or more formal and polite conversation.

Parlez-vous français?	***Do you speak*** French?
Claire et Abia **sont-elles** amies?	***Are*** Claire and Abia friends?

•••› If the verb ends in a vowel and the subject pronoun is **il, elle,** or **on,** a **-t-** is added to facilitate pronunciation.

Comment **va-t-elle**?	*How's she doing*?
Y a-t-il un examen aujourd'hui?	*Is there an exam today*?

•••› In a negative question with inversion, **ne… pas** goes around the inversion.

Ne mangent-ils pas avec nous?	*Are they not eating with us*?

ACTIVITÉ K Activités populaires Finish these sentences by choosing the correct subject. Then, indicate if people typically practice these activities or watch them, or both.

			On pratique cette activité.	On regarde cette activité.
1. _____ **faisons** du cheval.	a. Nous	b. Vous	☐	☐
2. _____ **faites** du vélo.	a. Nous	b. Vous	☐	☐
3. _____ **faisons** de la natation.	a. Nous	b. Vous	☐	☐
4. _____ **faisons** de l'aérobic.	a. Nous	b. Vous	☐	☐
5. _____ **faites** du patinage.	a. Nous	b. Vous	☐	☐
6. _____ **faites** de la marche.	a. Nous	b. Vous	☐	☐

•••› **Et vous?** Which of the above activities do you like? **Moi, j'aime…**

ACTIVITÉ L En été ou en hiver? Finish these sentences by choosing the correct subject. Then, indicate if each activity is typically done during the summer or the winter, or during both seasons.

			en été	en hiver
1. _____ **fait** de la marche.	a. Je	b. Pierre	☐	☐
2. _____ **fait** du ski nautique.	a. Tu	b. Elle	☐	☐
3. _____ **fais** du ski alpin.	a. Tu	b. Hélène	☐	☐
4. _____ **fait** de la planche à voile.	a. Je	b. Marc	☐	☐
5. _____ **fais** du ski de fond.	a. Je	b. Monique	☐	☐
6. _____ **fais** de la gym.	a. Tu	b. Il	☐	☐

ACTIVITÉ M Qui fait… ? Which classmates are most likely to do the following activities? Do you remember how they responded earlier in activities in **Vocabulaire 2**? Use the name of your classmates (and even your instructor) to complete these sentences. Finish the last item with an activity of your choosing.

1. _____ **fait** du vélo.

2. _____ **font** de la marche.

3. _____ ne **font** pas de yoga.

4. _____ **fait** souvent de la gym.

5. _____ ne **fait** pas de jogging.

6. _____ **font** _____.

ACTIVITÉ N Qu'est-ce qu'ils font? What activities are the following people most likely to do? Complete each statement with a form of the verb **faire** and the most logical activity.

1. Michael Phelps

2. Bruce Irons

3. Forrest Gump

4. Moi

5. Mon/Ma colocataire et moi, nous

6. Mes amis

Michael Phelps, nageur américain

© Mitch Gunn/Shutterstock.com

ACTIVITÉ O Oui ou non? With a partner, answer these trivia questions.

	Oui	Non
1. Tom Cruise **parle-t-il** français?	☐	☐
2. Justine Henin **joue-t-elle** au tennis?	☐	☐
3. Les Français **mangent-ils** du fromage?	☐	☐
4. Les Américains **sont-ils** fans de rugby?	☐	☐
5. Martha Stewart **aime-t-elle** la cuisine française?	☐	☐
6. Maria Sharapova **fait-elle** du vélo?	☐	☐
7. Luc Besson et Steven Spielberg **sont-ils** réalisateurs?	☐	☐
8. Joël Robuchon et Emeril Lagasse **cuisinent-ils** bien?	☐	☐
9. Faudel **chante-t-il** en français?	☐	☐
10. Le Cirque du Soleil **est-il** américain?	☐	☐

"Logo of The Ohio State University Department of French and Italian's Cercle français" With permission of the designer, Rebecca H. Bias, Ph.D.

ACTIVITÉ P **Les activités pour un Cercle français**

Étape 1. Ask your classmates if they do these activities. If someone answers yes, note his/her name. Remember that **du, de la, de l'** and **des** become **de** in negative sentences.

Modèles: faire du ski   **Faites-vous du ski?**

1. cuisiner des repas (meals) français
2. chanter des chansons françaises
3. regarder des films français
4. écouter de la musique francophone
5. faire du cheval
6. jouer au tennis de table
7. jouer au bowling
8. danser des danses folkloriques françaises

Étape 2. What three activities are most popular? Who does these activities? Who doesn't do these activities?

Modèle: Darla, Kim et David cuisinent des repas français. Ils ne jouent pas au tennis de table et ils ne regardent pas de films français.

Pour aller plus loin

Les mots utiles: *avec, mais* et *pour*

Avec *(with),* **mais** *(but),* and **pour** *(for)* are useful **mots utiles** in communication.

Essayez! Complete these sentences with the correct **mots utiles**.

1. J'ai un livre _____ toi.
2. Nous mangeons _____ le professeur.
3. Je parle français _____ je ne parle pas italien.
4. Je joue au tennis _____ Marc.

Liaisons musicales

JEANNEAU/SIPA/Newscom

A French icon, Serge Gainsbourg (1928–1991) was a singer, songwriter, actor, and director. His music mixed a variety of styles including jazz, ballads, pop, Afro-Caribbean, and **chanson française.** Find three of Gainsbourg's songs on the Internet. List their titles and their musical styles.

OUI, JE PEUX!   Here are two "can do statements" for you to check your progress so far. Look at each statement and rate yourself on how well you think you can perform the task. Then verify your ability with a partner. How did you do?

1. **"I can say two sports that I play and ask others what sports they play."**

   I can perform this function
   ☐ with ease
   ☐ with some difficulty
   ☐ not at all

2. **"I can ask someone else what he/she is going to do today, tonight, tomorrow, this weekend, and so on."**

   I can perform this function
   ☐ with ease
   ☐ with some difficulty
   ☐ not at all

iLrn™

Are you looking for more practice? You can find it in **iLrn**.

🔊 # Les **loisirs**

Pastimes

faire du camping

faire un
pique-nique

faire un barbecue

jouer de la batterie

jouer du violon

jouer du violoncelle

jouer du piano

jouer de la guitare

jouer de la musique

faire de
la danse
classique

faire de
la photo

faire de
la danse
moderne

jouer aux
cartes *(f. pl.)*

faire la sieste

faire du
jardinage

Les activités de loisir

Vocabulaire complémentaire

aller au spa *to go to the spa*
commander une pizza *to order a pizza*
dessiner *to draw, to sketch*
écrire des lettres *to write letters*
écrire des textos *to write text messages*

faire du bricolage *to do home improvement, DIY*
faire des courses *to run errands*
faire la cuisine *to cook*
faire la fête *to party*
faire la grasse matinée *to sleep in*

faire une promenade *to take a walk*
faire du shopping *to shop*
faire un voyage *to take a trip*
jouer aux jeux de société *(m. pl.) to play board games*

lire les courriels *to read e-mails*
lire le journal *to read the newspaper*
lire un roman *to read a novel*

un loisir *a leisure activity*
un passe-temps *a pastime, a hobby*

> **Note de vocabulaire**
> You will learn the conjugations of **écrire** and **lire** in **Grammaire 3**.

ACTIVITÉ A Où fait-on ces activités? You will hear a series of activities.
2-5 Where are they typically conducted: **a)** à l'intérieur *(inside)*, **b)** à l'extérieur *(outside)*, or **c) les deux** *(both)*?

1. _____
2. _____
3. _____
4. _____
5. _____

6. _____
7. _____
8. _____
9. _____
10. _____

ACTIVITÉ B Qui fait l'activité? You will hear another series of activities.
2-6 Which of these people are famous for them?

1. a. Carlos Santana   b. Mick Jagger   c. Mickey Hart
2. a. Johann Sebastian Bach b. Bill Gates   c. Jay Leno
3. a. Andrew Lloyd Webber   b. Louis Armstrong   c. John Mayer
4. a. Anne Geddes   b. Jim Carrey   c. Stephen Colbert

ACTIVITÉ **C** **Plaisirs ou obligations?**

Étape 1. Decide if each activity is **un plaisir** or **une obligation**.

	un plaisir	une obligation		un plaisir	une obligation
1. faire la cuisine	☐	☐	5. faire des courses	☐	☐
2. faire du jardinage	☐	☐	6. faire la sieste	☐	☐
3. lire les courriels	☐	☐	7. lire un roman	☐	☐
4. faire du shopping	☐	☐	8. lire le journal	☐	☐

Étape 2. Share your answers with a partner to see if you have similar ideas, and be ready to report back to the class.

Modèle: **Faire la cuisine est un plaisir pour moi mais une obligation pour mon/ma partenaire.**

ACTIVITÉ **D** **Vos préférences**

Étape 1. Use the preposition and articles to finish these sentences.

1. On aime **jouer aux**   a. piano   b. jardinage   c. cartes
2. On aime **jouer du**   a. violoncelle   b. guitare   c. musique
3. On aime **faire du**   a. bricolage   b. fête   c. cuisine
4. On aime **jouer aux**   a. musique   b. violoncelle   c. jeux de société
5. On aime **commander une**   a. pizza   b. danse classique   c. loisir
6. On aime **faire un**   a. fête   b. pique-nique   c. promenade
7. On aime **faire la**   a. voyage   b. grasse matinée   c. batterie
8. On va **au**   a. spa   b. piano   c. sieste

Étape 2. Finish each sentence with a recreational activity that you like to do.

1. J'aime **faire** _____.   2. J'aime **jouer** _____.   3. J'aime _____.

Étape 3. Do you remember which activity Claire's mother likes to do at the hospital?

Madame Gagner aime **jouer** _____.

ACTIVITÉ **E** **Qu'est-ce qu'on fait ici?** What kinds of activities do you generally do in these locations?

Modèle: dans une salle de répétition (*rehearsal room*)
　　　　　　On joue du piano.

1. dans un bar   5. au conservatoire de danse
2. au conservatoire de musique   6. à l'université
3. dans une boîte de nuit (*nightclub*) 7. dans un parc
4. dans une pizzeria   8. à la maison (*at home*)

Liaisons musicales

Fabien KLOTCHKOFF/VISUAL Press/Photoshot

Quebecoise cellist Jorane (1975–) is known in Quebec and in Europe for her alternative musical style and for her haunting voice as she sings and plays cello at the same time. Jorane's musical style and cello playing is sometimes compared to Tori Amos and her piano. Go to Jorane's official website to listen for yourself.

ACTIVITÉ F **Qui a un talent secret?** Ask the following questions to different classmates to see if they have hidden talents. When you find someone who says yes, note his/her name next to the activity. Don't forget that **un, une, du, de la, de l'** and **des** become **de/d'** in negative sentences.

Modèle: jouer de la guitare   **Est-ce que tu joues de la guitare?**

Qui a un talent pour...

1. dessiner?
2. faire du bricolage?
3. bien faire la cuisine?
4. bien jouer aux cartes?
5. faire de la photographie?
6. faire la fête?
7. bien faire du jardinage?
8. jouer de la guitare?

© Diego Cervo/Shutterstock.com

ACTIVITÉ G **Les professeurs ou les étudiants?**

Étape 1. Make a list of four activities that you typically associate with students and four that you associate with professors at your university.

Modèle: **Généralement, les étudiants jouent de la batterie.**
Généralement, les professeurs font du jardinage.

Étape 2. Read your list to a partner and tell him/her whether you agree (**Je suis d'accord.**) or do not agree (**Je ne suis pas d'accord.**) with his/her statements.

Modèle: É1: **Typiquement les professeurs font du jardinage.**
É2: **Oui, je suis d'accord. / Je ne suis pas d'accord. Les professeurs et les étudiants jouent de la batterie.**

ACTIVITÉ H **Itinéraire** Plan an itinerary for an exchange student with at least two activities you will do together **le matin, l'après-midi,** and **le soir.** Be prepared to share your itinerary with the class so it can decide whose activities are the most interesting.

Modèle: **Le matin, nous allons faire une promenade.**

ACTIVITÉ I **Le plus grand plaisir dans la vie** What do students in your class think is the biggest pleasure in life? Select your top three activities from those presented in **Vocabulaire 3** in order of preference. Your instructor will take a poll to see which activity is the greatest pleasure for your class.

Modèle: **Mes plus grands plaisirs sont 1) aller au spa, 2) commander une pizza et 3) faire de la photo(graphie).**

Pour aller plus loin
Depuis combien de temps

If you would like to ask someone in French how long he/she has been doing something or going somewhere, use the construction **depuis combien de temps** plus the present tense of the verb. To answer the question, recycle **depuis** and give the length of time.

—**Depuis combien de temps joue-t-il de la guitare?**

—*How long has he been playing guitar?*

—**Depuis quatre semaines.**

—*For four weeks.*

—**Depuis combien de temps fais-tu de la danse classique?**

—*How long have you been doing classical dance?*

—**Depuis cinq ans.**

—*For five years.*

Essayez! Answer the following questions with **depuis.**

Modèle: Depuis combien de temps est-ce que tu fais la sieste?
Depuis vingt minutes.

1. Depuis combien de temps est-ce que tu étudies le français?
2. Depuis combien de temps est-ce que tu es étudiant(e) à l'université?
3. Depuis combien de temps est-ce que tu habites dans cette *(this)* ville?
4. Depuis combien de temps est-ce que tu écoutes ton professeur aujourd'hui?

Un mot sur la culture

Regarder les gens passer: passe-temps populaire

According to France's Ministry of Culture French households spend about €1,400 (1,400 euros) a year on culture, leisure activities, sports, and games. One of the most popular past-times, however, is free. This activity is **regarder les gens passer** *(people-watching)*. It is so popular that cafés are designed to promote people-watching by having all their café chairs face the street. The wait staff also helps promote this activity by not rushing to bring you your check right away so you can enjoy a leisurely coffee or meal while watching the world go by.

- Aimez-vous regarder les gens passer?
- Où sont les meilleurs endroits *(best places)* pour regarder les gens passer?

© Peter Frank Edwards/Redux

🔊 **Liaisons avec les mots et les sons**

2-7

Les consonnes finales muettes

In general, final consonants in French are silent.

salut	nous	stylos	allemand	concert	chocolat

However, there are some final consonant letters that are generally pronounced: **q, k, b, c, r, f,** and **l.** To help you remember these consonants, think of the consonants in the phrase **QuiCK—Be CaReFuL!**

cinq	public	anorak	club	chic	loisir	neuf	journal

An exception is **r** in words ending in **-ier** and **-er.**

cahier	papier	regarder	travailler	parler

If a word ends in an unaccented **e** or in **es**, the preceding consonant is always pronounced, but the **e / es** remains silent.

porte	allemand / allemande	petit / petite	grand / grande

You learned a major exception in **Chapitre 1:** Some final consonants that are normally silent will be pronounced if there is **une liaison** (for example, between an article and a noun).

les étudiants	les hallucinations	les années	les optimistes

Pratique A. Listen to and repeat these pairs of words.

1. chez / chef
2. français / française
3. c'est / cinq
4. intéressant / intéressante
5. publie / public
6. étudiant / étudiante

Pratique B. Listen to and repeat these statements about **les loisirs.** Which words have pronounced final consonants? Don't forget the **liaison.**

Quand il fait beau, on fait du cheval et on joue au golf. Mais quand il fait mauvais, on fait de l'aérobic ou on joue aux cartes.

🔊 **À vos stylos!** **C'est l'heure de la dictée!**

2-8
You will hear three sentences from the film *Liaisons*. Listen closely to them. You will then hear the sentences a second time. Write the three sentences you hear.

Sujet Claire parle de sa mère.

PARTIE 3 GRAMMAIRE 3

Pour parler de la communication

Les verbes **lire, écrire, dire** / Les adverbes

DU FILM *LIAISONS*

Un coup d'œil sur la grammaire

Do you remember this opening scene from the prologue of the film *Liaisons*? Read the following sentence.

Une femme **écrit lentement** sur une feuille de papier.

1. What does the verb **écrit** mean?
2. **Lentement** is an adverb. Which adjective does it come from?

Les verbes *lire, écrire, dire*

Lire, écrire, and dire are three useful verbs of communication. They share a similar conjugation pattern. Here are their present tense forms.

lire *(to read)*	
je **lis**	nous **lisons**
tu **lis**	vous **lisez**
il/elle/on **lit**	ils/elles **lisent**

dire *(to say)*	
je **dis**	nous **disons**
tu **dis**	vous **dites**
il/elle/on **dit**	ils/elles **disent**

écrire *(to write)*	
j'**écris**	nous **écrivons**
tu **écris**	vous **écrivez**
il/elle/on **écrit**	ils/elles **écrivent**

Nous **lisons** le journal.

Qu'est-ce que vous **dites**?

Je **lis** le texte rapidement.

Elle **écrit** un courriel à son amie.

*We **are reading** the newspaper.*

*What **are you saying**?*

*I **am reading** the text rapidly.*

*She **is writing** an e-mail to her friend.*

Les adverbes

Adverbs allow you to be more precise in your descriptions. They modify verbs, adjectives, and other adverbs. You already saw some adverbs like **beaucoup, souvent, trop,** and **très** in **Chapitre 1.**

✈ **Si vous y allez**

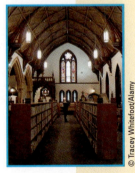

© Tracey Whitefoot/Alamy

Si vous allez à Québec, allez à la Bibliothèque Saint Jean-Baptiste. In the **Quartier Saint Jean-Baptiste** of Quebec City on **rue Saint Jean,** this library is inside the old Anglican Church of St. Matthew, a historical landmark in Quebec. On the grounds of this church / library is a cemetery that houses the remains of British soldiers from the battle of 1759 when New France was lost to the British.

• Most adverbs are formed by adding -**ment** to the feminine form of an adjective.

Feminine Adjective	Adverb
active	**activement** *actively*
sérieuse	**sérieusement** *seriously*

• If the masculine form of the adjective ends in a vowel, add -**ment** to it.

Masculine Adjective	Adverb
absolu	**absolument** *absolutely*
poli	**poliment** *politely*
vrai	**vraiment** *really, truly*

• If the masculine form of the adjective ends in -**ent** or -**ant,** replace the ending with -**emment** and -**amment,** respectively. Both endings have the same pronunciation.

Masculine Adjective	Adverb
évident	**évidemment** *evidently*
patient	**patiemment** *patiently*
constant	**constamment** *constantly*
courant	**couramment** *fluently*

• Some adverbs are irregular.

Adjective	Adverb
bon/bonne	**bien** *well*
mauvais/mauvaise	**mal** *badly*
gentil/gentille	**gentiment** *nicely*

• **Vite** means *quickly* or *fast* and can also be used as an exclamation to mean *hurry*.

Il mange trop **vite.**	*He eats too **fast**.*
Vite! Vite!	***Hurry! Hurry!***

• When adverbs modify adjectives or other adverbs, they usually precede them.

Anne est **très** intelligente.	*Anne is **very** intelligent.*
Tom regarde **trop souvent** la télé.	*Tom watches TV **too often**.*

• When an adverb modifies a verb, it usually goes after the verb.

Je mange **rapidement.**	*I eat **quickly**.*
On travaille **bien** ensemble.	*We work **well** together.*

• In a negative construction, the adverb comes after **pas.**

Je ne parle pas **bien** le français.	*I don't speak French **well**.*
Je ne fais pas **rapidement** les courses.	*I don't run errands **quickly**.*

© Elena Elisseeva/Shutterstock.com

ACTIVITÉ **J** **Activités d'aujourd'hui ou d'autrefois?** How have forms of communication changed? Finish the sentences below by choosing the correct subject. Afterwards, indicate if this is an activity of today (**aujourd'hui**), an activity of the past (**autrefois**), or both (**les deux**).

			Aujourd'hui	Autrefois	Les deux
1. … **écrivons** des lettres à la main (hand).			☐	☐	☐
a. Je b. Elle c. Nous					
2. … **écrivent** des courriels.			☐	☐	☐
a. Tu b. Ils c. Vous					
3. … **lis** les infos (news) sur Internet.			☐	☐	☐
a. Il b. Je c. Elles					
4. … **lisez** des romans.			☐	☐	☐
a. Vous b. On c. Nous					
5. … **écrit** des textos.			☐	☐	☐
a. Je b. Ils c. Il					
6. … **lisons** des poèmes.			☐	☐	☐
a. Tu b. Nous c. On					
7. … **dis** «bonjour» à Maman au téléphone.			☐	☐	☐
a. Je b. Nous c. Vous					
8. … **dites** «salut» par message instantané.			☐	☐	☐
a. Tu b. Elles c. Vous					

Conclusion Est-ce que la communication d'aujourd'hui est très différente de la communication d'autrefois?　　oui / non

ACTIVITÉ **K** **Est-ce que vous dites la vérité?**

Étape 1. Read each situation with a partner and tell each other if you say the truth: **Oui, je dis la vérité. / Non, je ne dis pas la vérité.**

Est-ce que vous dites la vérité si…

1. un(e) ami(e) a une coupe de cheveux (haircut) horrible. Il/Elle vous demande: «Est-ce que tu aimes ma coupe de cheveux?»

2. le café de votre ami(e) est très mauvais. Il/Elle vous demande: «Est-ce que tu aimes mon café?»

3. la robe (dress) de votre amie est très belle. Elle vous demande: «Est-ce que tu aimes ma robe?»

4. un(e) ami(e) impoli(e) vous demande: «Est-ce que je suis impoli(e)?»

5. un(e) colocataire a un(e) petit(e) ami(e) méchant(e). Il/Elle vous demande: «Est-ce que tu aimes mon/ma petit(e) ami(e)?»

Étape 2. Est-ce que votre camarade de classe et vous êtes similaires ou différent(e)s? Est-ce que vous êtes honnêtes?

ACTIVITÉ **L** **Les activités de communication** How often do you do the following activities? Answer with **rarement, constamment,** or **trop souvent.**

Modèle: écrire des lettres à la main   **J'écris rarement des lettres à la main.**

1. écrire des lettres à la main
2. écrire des courriels
3. écrire des textos
4. écrire des lettres d'amour
5. lire les courriels
6. lire les infos sur Internet
7. lire le journal papier
8. lire l'horoscope
9. dire «bonjour» au professeur
10. dire la vérité *(truth)*

ACTIVITÉ **M** **Un(e) bon(ne) ou mauvais(e) étudiant(e)?**

Étape 1. Read the following descriptions about student activities and decide if each statement describes **un(e) bon(ne) étudiant(e)** or **un(e) mauvais(e) étudiant(e).**

	bon(ne) étudiant(e)	mauvais(e) étudiant(e)
1. Il/Elle fait **patiemment** les devoirs.	☐	☐
2. Il/Elle n'écrit pas **intelligemment**.	☐	☐
3. Il/Elle réussit *(succeeds)* **brillamment** aux examens.	☐	☐
4. Il/Elle répond *(answers)* **intelligemment** aux questions.	☐	☐
5. Il/Elle ne va pas **fréquemment** aux cours.	☐	☐
6. Il/Elle étudie **sérieusement**.	☐	☐
7. Il/Elle parle **méchamment** aux professeurs.	☐	☐
8. Il/Elle est **rarement** en retard pour les cours.	☐	☐

 Étape 2. Now ask a classmate if he/she does these activities to determine if he/she is **un(e) bon(ne) étudiant(e)** or **un(e) mauvais(e) étudiant(e).**

Modèle: É1: **Est-ce que tu fais patiemment les devoirs?**
    É2: **Non, je ne fais pas patiemment les devoirs. Je fais rapidement les devoirs.**
    É1: **Est-ce que tu écris intelligemment?**
    É2: **Oui, j'écris intelligemment.**

Étape 3. Based on you and your partner's responses in **Étape 2,** indicate whether the two of you are **bon(ne)s** or **mauvais(e)s étudiant(e)s.**

ACTIVITÉ N **Comment font-ils?** With a classmate, decide how or how frequently you think the following celebrities do these activities.

Modèles: John Meyer / écrire de la musique rock acoustique
John Meyer écrit brillamment de la musique rock acoustique.

Paris Hilton / faire les courses
Paris Hilton fait rarement les courses.

1. Bette Midler et Céline Dion / donner des concerts
2. Ben Affleck / jouer aux cartes
3. Beyoncé / faire de la danse classique
4. Wolfgang Puck / faire la cuisine
5. Jim Carrey et Will Ferrell / jouer des rôles sérieux au cinéma
6. Jackie Chan / jouer au football américain
7. Taylor Swift / écrire des poèmes
8. Gwyneth Paltrow et Bradley Cooper / parler français

ACTIVITÉ O **Vos tendances**

Étape 1. Answer these questions using an adverb.

LEXIQUE

attentivement	élégamment	mal	sérieusement
bien	fréquemment	prudemment	souvent
brillamment	(im)patiemment	rapidement	toujours
constamment	horriblement	rarement	vite

Modèles: Comment écrivez-vous les courriels?
J'écris impatiemment les courriels.

À quelle fréquence *(With what frequency)* écrivez-vous des textos?
J'écris presque *(almost)* constamment des textos.

Comment...

1. faites-vous vos devoirs?
2. écrivez-vous les compositions?
3. dînez-vous?
4. faites-vous les courses?
5. faites-vous la cuisine?

À quelle fréquence…

6. lisez-vous vos courriels?
7. dites-vous la vérité?
8. faites-vous de la gym?
9. faites-vous du sport?
10. allez-vous au spa?

Étape 2. Ask a partner the questions and note his/her answers. Based on your partner's answers, which adjective would you use to describe him/her?

LEXIQUE

équilibré(e)	paresseux/paresseuse	stressé(e) *(stressed)*
farfelu(e) *(scatter-brained)*	sérieux/sérieuse	travailleur/travailleuse

ACTIVITÉ P Sondage

Étape 1. Ask questions to different classmates to try to find someone who engages in these activities at the frequency or in the manner indicated. When you find someone, make note of his/her name, and be ready to share your answers with the class.

Modèle: Trouvez quelqu'un qui fait constamment la fête.

Est-ce que tu fais constamment la fête?

Trouvez quelqu'un qui…

1. écrit tous les jours sur Facebook.
2. compose élégamment de la poésie (*poetry*).
3. dit rarement des mensonges (*lies*).
4. fait constamment la fête.
5. joue sérieusement aux jeux de société.
6. écoute attentivement du jazz.
7. lit un roman en ce moment.
8. commande fréquemment des pizzas.

Étape 2. Based on what you found out in this activity, how do you think your class appears in the eyes of the instructor? **Bizarre? Excessive? Normale? Chanceuse** (*Lucky*)? **Malchanceuse? Gâtée** (*Spoiled*)?

OUI, JE PEUX! Here are two "can do statements" for you to check your progress so far. Look at each statement and rate yourself on how well you think you can perform the task. Then verify your ability with a partner. How did you do?

1. **"I can say two activities that I do during my leisure time and ask others if they like the same or different activities."**

   I can perform this function
   ☐ with ease
   ☐ with some difficulty
   ☐ not at all

2. **"I can describe how I do different activities (patiently, quickly, seriously, well, badly, and so on)."**

   I can perform this function
   ☐ with ease
   ☐ with some difficulty
   ☐ not at all

iLrn™

Are you looking for more practice? You can find it in **iLrn**.

Avant de visionner

ACTIVITÉ A **Qui l'a dit?** Do you remember who said these lines in **Séquence 1**?

	Claire	Abia	Alexis
1. «Elle mange, elle joue aux cartes, elle lit et elle dort.»	☐	☐	☐
2. «Qu'est-ce qu'il y a?»	☐	☐	☐
3. «Elle a des moments de lucidité mais…»	☐	☐	☐
4. «Et les hallucinations?»	☐	☐	☐
5. «Vous êtes Claire… ?»	☐	☐	☐
6. «J'ai oublié ma brosse à dents chez moi.»	☐	☐	☐

ACTIVITÉ B **Vous rappelez-vous?** In **Séquence 1,** Claire met a man named Alexis Prévost at the hotel. With a classmate, fill in the missing words from part of their encounter. You will check your answers later.

ALEXIS Claire. C'est votre (1) _____, n'est-ce pas?

CLAIRE Oui. Je (2) _____ Claire. Claire Gagner.

ALEXIS (3) _____, Claire Gagner.

CLAIRE Enchantée.

ALEXIS C'est joli.

CLAIRE Pardon?

ALEXIS Votre prénom. C'est un (4) _____ prénom, Claire.

CLAIRE Merci. Euh, vous (5) _____ client de (6) _____, monsieur?

ALEXIS Oui. Excusez-moi, mademoiselle. Je m'appelle (7) _____.

▶ **Regarder la séquence**

You will now watch **Séquence 1.** Verify your answers to **Activité B.**

Après le visionnage

ACTIVITÉ **C** **Les deux hommes**

In **Séquence 1,** Claire meets two men at the hotel: a man who hands her an envelope and a man who needs a toothbrush. Decide if the following adjectives describe **l'homme avec l'enveloppe, Alexis, les deux** *(both)* or **ni l'un ni l'autre** *(neither)*.

1. Il est sérieux.   2. Il est sociable.   3. Il est beau.   4. Il est mystérieux.

ACTIVITÉ **D** **Résumé de la Séquence 1** Complete the summary of **Séquence 1** by supplying the missing words. Not all the words listed will be used, so be careful!

avec   depuis   enveloppe   mère   nous   parle   psychiatrique   vous

Claire travaille à l'hôtel (1) _____ son amie Abia. Claire (2) _____ avec Abia de sa (3) _____ qui est à l'hôpital (4) _____. Simone Gagner est à l'hôpital (5) _____ plus de *(more than)* six ans. À l'hôtel, un homme mystérieux donne à Claire une (6) _____ et il disparaît *(disappears)*.

a   l'hôtel   Il   ont   Prévost   sympathique

Claire rencontre un homme qui (7) _____ besoin d'une brosse à dents. (8) _____ est client de (9) _____ et il s'appelle Alexis (10) _____. Claire trouve cet homme (11) _____ et très beau.

© Sebastian Rich / Corbis

Dans les coulisses

In **Séquence 1,** Claire meets two somewhat mysterious men. One gives her an envelope. The other asks for a toothbrush, claiming he is a guest of the hotel. What makes these men mysterious? Which of the two might have an important role in the film? What are your reasons for thinking this? As you ponder these questions, consider time on screen, information exchanged during conversations, and Claire's actions. All of these are tools that writers and directors use to indicate relationships among people and to suggest what might appear later in the story.

À DÉCOUVRIR: La France et le rugby à Toulouse

À DÉCOUVRIR:
La France

Pays: La France
Géographie: En Europe de l'Ouest, entre la Belgique et l'Espagne (France métropolitaine)
Climat: Hivers frais et étés doux mais hivers doux et étés chauds dans le sud (France métropolitaine)
Population: 63,9 millions (France métropolitaine)
Capitale: Paris

À DÉCOUVRIR:
La ville de Toulouse

Région: Midi-Pyrénées
Département: Haute-Garonne
Population: Plus de 400 000
Réputation: Une technopole européenne pour les industries aéronautique, de l'espace (aérospatiale) et de l'information
Climat: Tempéré océanique à influences méditerranéenne et continentale

Avant de lire

France is a relatively diverse country with different climates, cuisines, regional identities, traditions, and favorite pastimes. In the upcoming reading, you will discover a popular pastime in the city of Toulouse.

Que savez-vous déjà?

1. Est-ce que vous connaissez quelque chose de *(something)* célèbre à Toulouse?

2. Quelles industries ou entreprises se trouvent *(are found)* à Toulouse?

OUTILS DE LECTURE
Using glosses

Glosses are translations of words whose meanings may be more challenging to guess from context. To develop good reading skills, it is best to try to guess the meanings of unfamiliar words from context first and then use the glosses to confirm your guesses. As you read **Découvrir le rugby à Toulouse,** try to guess the meaning of unfamiliar words and then use the glosses to check your predictions.

Découvrir le rugby à Toulouse

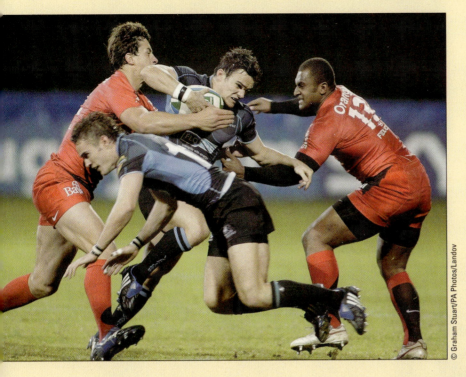

© Graham Stuart/PA Photos/Landov

Alors que° le football est de loin° le sport le plus populaire en France et à travers le monde°, le rugby est particulièrement populaire dans le sud-ouest de la France. Le Championnat de France est régulièrement dominé par les clubs des villes du sud-ouest: Bordeaux, Montpellier, Narbonne, Pau, Perpignan, Tarbes... et Toulouse, qui a remporté° dix-sept titres de Champion de France. Au niveau° international, la France participe au Tournoi annuel° des Six Nations (avec l'Angleterre°, l'Écosse°, l'Irlande, l'Italie, le Pays de Galles°) et à la Coupe du Monde, une compétition qui a lieu° tous les quatre ans.

Toulouse, qui est un des grands centres technologiques en France (le siège° du constructeur aéronautique Airbus), est aussi célèbre pour son club de rugby, le Stade Toulousain, qui est un grand club professionnel. Au niveau sportif, les supporters du Stade Toulousain sont passionnés par leur équipe, dont° les joueurs portent des maillots° rouge et noir.

Clément Poitrenaud est un des joueurs les plus célèbres de l'équipe de rugby de Toulouse. Il joue généralement en poste d'arrière°. Il est connu° pour son jeu spectaculaire, pour son goût du° risque, mais aussi pour ses blessures°.

Alors que *While* **de loin** *by far* **à travers le monde** *throughout the world* **a remporté** *won* **niveau** *level* **Tournoi annuel** *yearly tournament* **l'Angleterre** *England* **l'Écosse** *Scotland* **le Pays de Galles** *Wales* **qui a lieu** *which is held* **le siège** *corporate headquarters* **dont** *whose (of which)* **maillots** *jerseys* **en poste d'arrière** *in the position of fullback* **est connu** *is known* **goût du** *taste for* **blessures** *injuries*

Après avoir lu

Compréhension

1. Est-ce que le rugby est le sport le plus (*most*) populaire en France?   Oui / Non
2. Est-ce que le club de Toulouse a eu (*has had*) beaucoup de succès en France?   Oui / Non
3. Est-ce que Toulouse est seulement une ville de rugby?   Oui / Non
4. Est-ce que Clément Poitrenaud est connu pour son jeu médiocre?   Oui / Non

Et vous?

1. Est-ce que tu joues au rugby?
2. Est-ce que tu portes parfois le maillot de ton équipe de sport préférée?
3. Est-ce qu'il y a un(e) athlète professionnel(le) que tu aimes regarder?

Share It!

Use **Share It!** in **iLrn**™ to express your reactions to the reading and to find out what your classmates think.

LIAISONS AVEC LA LECTURE ET L'ÉCRITURE Le portrait

Here is a **portrait** for rugby player Clément Poitrenaud.

Clément Poitrenaud (1m88, 91 kilos *[approx. 6ft 2in, 200 lbs.]*) est un joueur très célèbre de l'équipe de rugby de Toulouse. Né le 20 mai 1982 à Castres dans le sud-ouest de la France, Poitrenaud joue aussi en équipe nationale de France. Il joue généralement en poste d'arrière mais quelquefois il joue aussi au centre. À la suite d'une fracture du tibia en février 2008, il ne participe pas au Tournoi des Six Nations pour affronter l'Angleterre. Mais il revient en pleine forme en 2009. Les autres joueurs du club de Toulouse pensent que Poitrenaud est très fidèle au sport et à l'équipe. Ils aiment beaucoup jouer avec lui au Stade Toulousain.

Adapted from: http://www.lequipe.fr/Rugby/RugbyFichejoueur2472.htm

© Jean-Paul Pelissier /Reuters /Landov

Avant d'écrire

1. List the kinds of information that appear in Poitrenaud's **portrait.**

2. Answer the following questions to help you write your own **portrait.**

   a. Qui es-tu? Tu es étudiant(e)? Parent? Athlète?

   b. Tu es de quelle ville? De New York? De Columbus?

   c. Quelles sont tes caractéristiques personnelles? Tu es sociable? Travailleur (Travailleuse)?

   d. As-tu des talents particuliers? Tu joues de la guitare?

   e. Qu'est-ce que tu vas faire après tes études *(studies)*? Tu vas être professeur?

Écrire

Using information from **Avant d'écrire**, write your own portrait of 6–8 sentences in French.

Après avoir écrit

Exchange your **portrait** with a partner. 1) Circle all the descriptors and verify that all the adjectives agree in number and gender. 2) Underline all the adverbs and verify that your partner correctly conjugated all of the verbs. 3) Put a * next to the sentence that best communicates your partner's personal information. 4) How would you characterize your partner's portrait: **unique, banal, stéréotypé, original, intéressant, amusant, drôle, sarcastique, vantard** *(boastful)*, **modeste**, etc.? Discuss your reactions together and then write a second version of your **portrait**, taking into account your partner's comments and corrections.

RÉSUMÉ DE VOCABULAIRE

PARTIE 1 2–9

LES MOIS DE L'ANNÉE

janvier	*January*
février	*February*
mars	*March*
avril	*April*
mai	*May*
juin	*June*
juillet	*July*
août	*August*
septembre	*September*
octobre	*October*
novembre	*November*
décembre	*December*
un an / une année	*year*
un mois	*month*
une saison	*season*

LES SAISONS

l'automne (*m.*)	*fall*
l'été (*m.*)	*summer*
l'hiver (*m.*)	*winter*
le printemps	*spring*

LE TEMPS / LA MÉTÉO

Quelle température fait-il?	*What's the temperature?*
Il fait 20 degrés.	*It's 20 degrees Celsius. / It's 68° Fahrenheit.*
Quel temps fait-il?	*What's the weather like?*
Il fait beau.	*The weather is nice.*
Il fait chaud.	*It's hot.*
Il fait frais.	*It's cool.*
Il fait froid.	*It's cold.*
Il fait gris.	*It's dreary.*
Il fait lourd.	*It's hot and muggy.*
Il fait mauvais.	*The weather is bad.*
Il fait (du) soleil.	*It's sunny.*
Il fait du vent.	*It's windy.*
Il neige.	*It's snowing.*
Il pleut.	*It's raining.*
Le ciel est couvert.	*It's cloudy / overcast.*
l'étoile (*f.*)	*star*
la lune	*moon*
la météo	*weather forecast*
la neige	*snow*
des nuages (*m.*)	*(some) clouds*
la pluie	*rain*
le soleil	*sun*
la tornade	*tornado*

LA DATE

Quelle est la date (aujourd'hui)?	*What's the date (today)?*
C'est le premier (1er) mai.	*It's May first.*
C'est / On est / Nous sommes le 10 novembre.	*It's the 10th of November.*
C'est quand ton / votre anniversaire?	*When is your birthday?*
C'est quand l'anniversaire de Samir?	*When is Samir's birthday?*

VERBES

aller	*to go*
annoncer	*to forecast*

DIVERS

depuis combien de temps	*for how long*
pour	*for*

PARTIE 2 2–10

LES SPORTS ET LES ACTIVITÉS SPORTIVES

le baseball	*baseball*
le basket-ball / le basket	*basketball*
le football / le foot	*soccer*
le football américain	*football*
le golf	*golf*
le hockey	*hockey*
le rugby	*rugby*
le tennis	*tennis*
le tennis de table	*ping-pong, table tennis*
le volley-ball	*volleyball*
faire	*to do, to make*
faire de l'aérobic	*to do aerobics*
faire du bowling	*to go bowling*
faire du cheval	*to go horseback riding*
faire de la gym	*to work out, to exercise*
faire du jogging	*to go jogging*
faire de la marche	*to walk (for exercise)*
faire de la natation	*to swim (for exercise)*
faire du patinage	*to ice skate, to go iceskating*
faire de la planche à voile	*to go wind-surfing*
faire du ski (alpin)	*to go (downhill) skiing*
faire du ski de fond	*to go cross-country skiing*
faire du ski nautique	*to water-ski*
faire du sport	*to work out, to exercise*
faire du surf	*to surf*
faire du vélo	*to go bike riding*
faire du yoga	*to do yoga*

jouer (à + sport)	*to play (a sport)*
pratiquer	*to play / to do (a sport)*
une équipe	*a team*
un joueur / une joueuse	*a player*
un match (de + sport)	*a match, a game (of a sport)*

PARTIE 3 2–11

LES ACTIVITÉS DE LOISIR

aller au spa	*to go to the spa*
commander une pizza	*to order a pizza*
dessiner	*to draw, to sketch*
écrire des lettres	*to write letters*
écrire des textos	*to write text messages*
faire un barbecue	*to have a BBQ*
faire du bricolage	*to tinker, to do odd jobs, to act the handyman/woman*
faire du camping	*to go camping*
faire les courses	*to run some errands*
faire la cuisine	*to cook*
faire de la danse classique	*to do classical dance*
faire de la danse moderne	*to do modern dance*
faire la fête	*to party*
faire la grasse matinée	*to sleep in*
faire du jardinage	*to garden*
faire de la photo(graphie)	*to practice photography*
faire un pique-nique	*to (have/go on a) picnic*
faire une promenade (en ville)	*to take a walk (in town)*
faire du shopping	*to shop, to go shopping*
faire la sieste	*to take a nap*
faire un voyage	*to take a trip*
jouer aux cartes (f. pl.)	*to play cards*
jouer aux jeux de société (m. pl.)	*to play board games*

jouer de la batterie	*to play the drums*
jouer de la guitare	*to play the guitar*
jouer de la musique	*to play, to listen to music*
jouer du piano	*to play the piano*
jouer du violon	*to play violin*
jouer du violoncelle	*to play cello*
lire les courriels	*to read e-mail*
lire le journal	*to read the newspaper*
lire un roman	*to read a novel*
un loisir	*a leisure activity*
un passe-temps	*a pastime, a hobby*
un plaisir	*a pleasure*

VERBES

dire	*to say*
écrire	*to write*
lire	*to read*

DIVERS

la vie	*life*

ADVERBES

absolument	*absolutely*
activement	*actively*
constamment	*constantly*
couramment	*fluently*
évidemment	*evidently*
gentiment	*nicely*
lentement	*slowly*
patiemment	*patiently*
poliment	*politely*
sérieusement	*seriously*
vraiment	*really, truly*
bien	*well*
mal	*badly*
vite, rapidement	*fast, quickly, hurry!*

Nos **origines**

En bref In this chapter, you will:

- learn nationalities and countries
- learn prepositions to express geographical locations
- learn the verbs **venir** and **devenir**
- learn possessive and demonstrative adjectives
- learn adjective placement to talk about physical traits and colors

- learn **-ir** verbs like **sortir, partir, dormir,** and **sentir**
- learn about oral vowels
- read about the origins of family names, of linguistic and cultural differences, and of people in France and the Francophone world

 You will also watch **SÉQUENCE 2: La décision** of the movie *Liaisons*.

Ressources

 audio   video   Share It!   iLrn™   http://www.cengagebrain.com

© Lise Gagne/iStockphoto.com

L'origine **culturelle**

Cultural origins

Les nationalités

les Allemand(e)s

les Anglais(es)

les Américain(e)s

les Belges

les Brésiliens / Brésiliennes

les Canadiens / Canadiennes

les Chinois(es)

les Espagnol(e)s

les Français(es)

les Irlandais(es)

les Italiens / Italiennes

les Ivoiriens / Ivoiriennes

les Japonais(es)

les Marocain(e)s

les Mexicain(e)s

les Québécois(es)

les Roumain(e)s

les Russes

les Sénégalais(es)

les Suisses

les Tunisiens / Tunisiennes

les Vietnamiens /
     Vietnamiennes

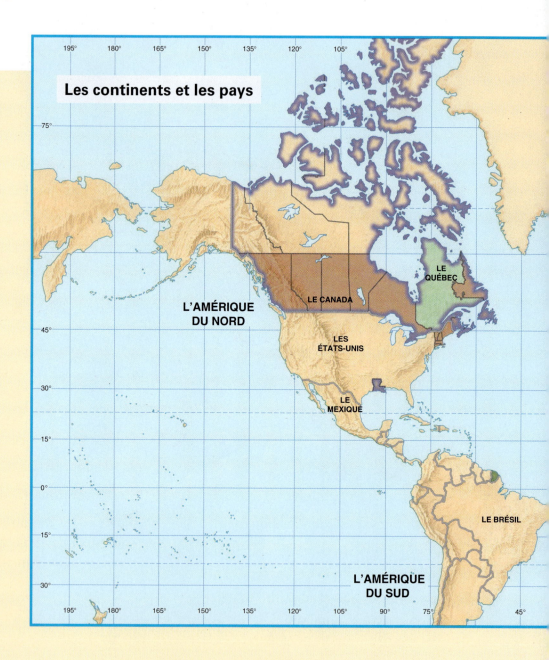

Les continents et les pays

LE QUÉBEC

L'AMÉRIQUE DU NORD

LE CANADA

LES ÉTATS-UNIS

LE MEXIQUE

LE BRÉSIL

L'AMÉRIQUE DU SUD

Pour aller plus loin
C'est vs. Il/Elle est

C'est is followed by the name of a person or place or by an article and a noun. It is primarily used to identify. Il/Elle est is usually followed by an adjective and is used to describe.

C'est Gérard Depardieu.
That's Gérard Depardieu.

Il est français.
He is French.

C'est une Italienne.
That's an Italian (woman).

Elle est italienne.
She's Italian.

Essayez! Complétez chaque phrase avec **C'est** ou **Il/Elle est** et identifiez une personne de cette nationalité.

Modèle: Elle est espagnole.
C'est Penelope Cruz.

1. _____ américain.

2. _____ une Québécoise.

3. _____ anglaise.

4. _____ un Italien.

ACTIVITÉ A Quelle région? Vous allez entendre *(hear)* le nom d'un pays. Le pays se trouve *(is found)* sur quel continent ou dans quelle région?

1. a. l'Amérique du Sud b. l'Afrique du Nord c. l'Asie
2. a. l'Afrique de l'Est b. l'Asie c. l'Europe de l'Est
3. a. l'Afrique du Nord b. l'Europe de l'Ouest c. l'Amérique du Nord
4. a. l'Amérique du Sud b. l'Asie c. l'Amérique du Nord
5. a. l'Asie b. l'Amérique du Sud c. l'Afrique du Nord
6. a. l'Afrique de l'Ouest b. l'Europe de l'Ouest c. l'Amérique du Nord
7. a. l'Amérique du Sud b. l'Afrique de l'Ouest c. l'Europe de l'Ouest
8. a. l'Afrique du Nord b. l'Asie c. l'Europe de l'Est

ACTIVITÉ B Les pays et leurs produits ou activités Vous allez entendre *(hear)* une série de pays. Associez le pays que vous entendez à un produit ou à une activité.

1. a. le baseball b. le football
2. a. le Coca-cola b. le sushi
3. a. le saké b. la tequila
4. a. *Les Misérables* b. *Don Quichotte*
5. a. Toyota b. Volkswagen
6. a. le chocolat b. la pizza

ACTIVITÉ C La Francophonie Quels pays sont dans l'Organisation Internationale de la Francophonie? Cherchez les pays sur Internet si nécessaire.

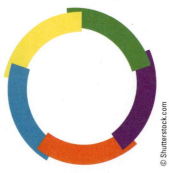

© Shutterstock.com

ACTIVITÉ D Les nationalités et les pays Vous allez entendre *(hear)* une série de nationalités. Associez la nationalité que vous entendez à un pays.

1. 2. 3. 4. 5. 6. 7. 8. 9. 10.

ACTIVITÉ E Associations Quelles nationalités associez-vous aux choses suivantes?

1. le Château Frontenac 5. la Grande Muraille de Chine
2. Mercedes-Benz 6. le TGV
3. la Maison Blanche *(White House)* 7. la Tour de Pise
4. Astérix 8. le chocolat Nestlé

Courtesy Le Colonial San Francisco

Si vous y allez

Si vous allez à Chicago ou à San Francisco, allez au restaurant Le Colonial pour goûter la cuisine franco-vietnamienne.

ACTIVITÉ F L'origine nationale / La nationalité Identifiez leur origine nationale.

Modèles: George Washington / américain **Il est américain.**

Hillary Clinton / américain **Elle est américaine.**

1. Saint Patrick
2. Heidi Klum
3. Léopold Sédar Senghor
4. Marie-Antoinette
5. Ludwig van Beethoven
6. Frida Kahlo

ACTIVITÉ G L'origine / La nationalité / La culture Abia, le personnage du film *Liaisons,* est de culture québécoise et de nationalité canadienne. Mais les ancêtres d'Abia sont d'origine ivoirienne. Et vous?

Étape 1. Quelle est votre nationalité? Quelle est votre origine culturelle?

1. Je suis de nationalité _____.
2. Je suis d'origine culturelle _____.

Étape 2. Trouvez la nationalité et l'origine culturelle de trois personnes dans la classe et complétez la grille *(fill in the grid)*. Posez les questions suivantes:

1. Quelle est ta nationalité?
2. Quelle est ton origine culturelle?

Nom	La nationalité	L'origine culturelle
_____	_____	_____
_____	_____	_____
_____	_____	_____

Étape 3. Faites une liste de toutes les nationalités et origines culturelles de la classe. Soyez prêt(e)s à partager *(Be ready to share)* vos réponses. Ensuite, regardez vos listes et répondez aux questions suivantes:

1. Est-ce qu'il y a plusieurs *(several)* nationalités dans votre classe?
2. Est-ce qu'il y a plusieurs origines culturelles dans votre classe?

Un mot sur la culture
Ying Chen

Ying Chen (1961–) est une écrivaine québécoise qui habite à Montréal. Elle est née° à Shanghai en Chine, elle est donc d'origine chinoise. Son livre *L'Ingratitude* (1995) a obtenu le Prix Paris-Québec. Ce livre est publié aux États-Unis en anglais sous le titre *Ingratitude.* Ying Chen écrit en français mais elle parle aussi le chinois, le russe, l'italien et l'anglais.

née *born*

• Connaissez-vous l'origine culturelle de ces personnes?

1. Carla Bruni-Sarkozy
2. Zinédine Zidane
3. Édith Piaf
4. Julia Child

© Ulf Andersen/Getty Images Entertainment/Getty Images

Pour parler des pays, des villes et de nos origines

Les prépositions et les lieux géographiques / Les verbes **venir** et **devenir**

DU FILM *LIAISONS*

Un coup d'œil sur la grammaire

Look at these photos from the film *Liaisons* and their captions. Note the different prepositions used in French to express that one is *in* a geographical location.

Claire habite **au** Canada, **à** Montréal.
L'oncle Michel habite **en** France, **à** Paris.

Abia habite **au** Canada, **à** Montréal.
La famille d'Abia habite **en** Côte d'Ivoire.

Unlike English, the use of prepositions with geographical locations in French depends on whether the place is a country or city and whether a country is masculine or feminine. Answer these questions based on the photo captions.

1. Is the preposition **à** used with cities or countries?   a. cities   b. countries
2. Is the preposition **en** used with cities or countries?   a. cities   b. countries
3. Is the preposition **au** used with cities or countries?   a. cities   b. countries

Countries and Continents

••• To say that you are *in* or going *to* a country, use the preposition **au** with masculine countries and **en** with feminine countries.

J'étudie **au** Canada.	*I am studying **in** Canada.*
Nous allons **au** Maroc.	*We are going **to** Morocco.*
Pierre habite **en** France.	*Pierre lives **in** France.*
Anne va **en** Espagne.	*Anne is going **to** Spain.*

••• Use the preposition **aux** to express *in* or *to* with countries that have plural grammatical gender like **les États-Unis.**

Les Tremblay habitent **aux** États-Unis.	*The Tremblays live **in** the United States.*
Nous retournons **aux** États-Unis.	*We are returning **to** the United States.*

- Use the preposition **en** to express *in* or *to* with continents because they are feminine.

  Le Canada est **en** Amérique du Nord.   *Canada is **in** North America.*

  Nous allons **en** Europe.   *We are going **to** Europe.*

- To express *from* a country or continent, use the prepositions **du** *(m.)*, **de** *(f.)*, **d'** (before a vowel sound) or **des** *(pl.)*, depending on the location's grammatical gender.

Maria est **du** Brésil.   *Maria is **from** Brazil.*

Abia est **de** Côte d'Ivoire.   *Abia is **from** the Ivory Coast.*

Je suis **d'**Asie.   *I am **from** Asia.*

Nous rentrons **des** États-Unis.   *We are returning **from** the United States.*

Note de vocabulaire
See the vocabulary list at the end of this chapter for a list of U.S. states in French.

States and Provinces

- States and provinces follow the same rules as countries and continents.

  Sarah habite **en** Californie *(f.)*.   *Sarah lives **in** California.*

  Elle étudie **au** Québec *(m.)*.   *She is studying **in** Quebec [province].*

  Jean va **en** Provence *(f.)*.   *Jean is going **to** Provence.*

  Tom est **du** Colorado *(m.)*.   *Tom is **from** Colorado.*

  Marie est **de** Lorraine *(f.)*.   *Marie is **from** Lorraine.*

  Je suis **d'**Ohio.   *I am **from** Ohio.*

- To express *in* with states, **dans** plus the definite article may also be used.

  La maison de Frank Llyod Wright est **dans** l'Illinois.   *Frank Llyod Wright's house is in Illinois.*

  Les arbres sont beaux **dans le** Maine.   *The trees are beautiful in Maine.*

Liaisons musicales

© Heinz Ruckemann/UPI/ Landov

Daniel Lavoie est un chanteur du Manitoba (au Canada) qui a obtenu de nombreux prix et distinctions. Sa chanson *Je voudrais voir* (I would like to see) *New York* (1986) parle des villes et des pays qu'il aimerait voir. Cherchez les paroles *(lyrics)* de cette chanson. Nommez les villes et les pays mentionnés.

Cities

- To express *in* or *to* a city, use the preposition **à**. To express *from* a city, use the preposition **de.**

  Nous allons **à** Paris.   *We are going **to** Paris.*

  Claire est **à** Québec.   *Claire is **in** Quebec City.*

  Luciano est **de** Rome.   *Luciano is **from** Rome.*

Les verbes *venir* et *devenir*

- The verbs **venir** (*to come*) and **devenir** (*to become*) are another class of -**ir** verbs and take the following conjugations.

venir *(to come)*		devenir *(to become)*	
je **viens**	nous **venons**	je **deviens**	nous **devenons**
tu **viens**	vous **venez**	tu **deviens**	vous **devenez**
il/elle/on **vient**	ils/elles **viennent**	il/elle/on **devient**	ils/elles **deviennent**

Elsa **vient** du Maroc.	*Elsa **comes** from Morocco.*
Vous **venez** dîner ce soir?	***Are** you **coming** to dinner this evening?*
Lise **devient** citoyenne américaine.	*Lise **is becoming** an American citizen.*

Venir de + infinitive

- When **venir de** is followed by a verb in the infinitive, the meaning changes from *to come from* to *to have just done something a few moments ago.*

Nous **venons de terminer** nos devoirs.	*We **just finished** our homework.*
Il **vient de rentrer** du Maroc.	*He **just returned** from Morocco.*

ACTIVITÉ **H** **Où vont-ils?** Des étudiants parlent de leurs projets de vacances. Utilisez les prépositions pour déterminer où va chaque étudiant(e).

1. Je vais **au…**   a. Maroc   b. Paris   c. Espagne
2. Je prends des cours **en…**   a. Marseille   b. Italie   c. Canada
3. Nous allons **à…**   a. Sénégal   b. New York   c. Brésil
4. Je prends mes vacances **en…** a. Rome   b. Mexique   c. Tunisie
5. Nous allons **à…**   a. Montréal   b. France   c. Belgique
6. Je vais **au…**   a. Tokyo   b. Texas   c. Los Angeles
7. Mon ami va **en…**   a. Suisse   b. Maroc   c. Québec
8. Nous allons **au…**   a. Irlande   b. Viêt-Nam   c. Berlin

- **Et vous?** Où est-ce que vous aimeriez aller en vacances?

ACTIVITÉ **I** D'où viennent-ils?

Étape 1. Le directeur d'une auberge de jeunesse *(youth hostel)* vous présente ses clients. Utilisez les prépositions pour déterminer d'où vient chaque personne.

1. Je vous présente Coralie. Elle vient **de…**
   a. Mexique   b. Montréal   c. Irlande

2. Voici Anna. Elle vient **du…**
   a. Japon   b. Tokyo   c. Chine

3. Nicoleta vient **de…**
   a. Viêt-Nam   b. Roumanie   c. Allemagne

4. Laura vient **des…**
   a. Brésil   b. Italie   c. États-Unis

5. Bernard vient **d'…**
   a. Allemagne   b. Russie   c. France

6. Gabrielle et Caroline viennent **de…**
   a. Ohio   b. Californie   c. Canada

Étape 2. Répondez à ces *(these)* questions.

1. D'où venez-vous? _____

2. D'où vient un(e) de vos camarades de classe? _____

ACTIVITÉ **J** **Dans quelle ville?** Dans quelle ville peut-on *(can one)* trouver les choses suivantes?

Modèle: On trouve le meilleur *(best)* café **à Seattle.**

1. On trouve la meilleure pizza _____.
2. On trouve la meilleure équipe de baseball _____.
3. On trouve les meilleurs restaurants _____.
4. On trouve les meilleurs parcs _____.
5. On trouve le meilleur shopping _____.
6. On trouve les meilleurs musées _____.

ACTIVITÉ **K** **Dans quels pays?**

Étape 1. Lisez ces descriptions. Complétez chaque phrase avec une préposition et un pays.

Modèle: Les femmes sont très élégantes **en France.**

1. Il y a beaucoup d'écologistes _____.
2. Les femmes ont beaucoup de liberté _____.
3. Les habitants ont beaucoup d'enfants _____.
4. On trouve le meilleur *(best)* système de soins médicaux *(healthcare)* _____.
5. On trouve le meilleur système de transport public _____.
6. On trouve la meilleure qualité de vie _____.

Si vous y allez

Si vous allez à Québec, allez au restaurant Chez Victor pour les meilleurs hamburgers et les meilleures frites en Amérique du Nord. Visitez le site officiel du restaurant sur Internet.

© Wynne Wong

Étape 2. Partagez *(Share)* vos réponses de l'Étape 1 avec un(e) camarade de classe. Avez-vous écrit les mêmes choses? Voulez-vous changer vos réponses?

> **Modèle:** É1: **Je pense qu'il y a beaucoup d'écologistes aux États-Unis. Et toi?**
> É2: **Moi, je pense qu'il y a beaucoup d'écologistes au Canada.**
> É1: **Ah oui! Je suis d'accord** *(I agree)* **avec toi. Il y a beaucoup d'écologistes au Canada. / Non, je ne suis pas d'accord.**

Étape 3. Partagez vos réponses et celles *(those)* de votre partenaire avec la classe. Ensuite, faites un résumé des opinions de votre classe.

La classe pense…

1. qu'il y a beaucoup d'écologistes **au Canada, en France et aux États-Unis.**

2. que les femmes ont beaucoup de liberté _____.

3. que les habitants ont beaucoup d'enfants _____.

4. qu'on trouve le meilleur système de soins médicaux _____.

5. qu'on trouve le meilleur système de transport public _____.

6. qu'on trouve la meilleure qualité de vie _____.

ACTIVITÉ L D'où viennent…?

Répondez à chaque question avec un pays et une phrase complète.

> **Modèle:** D'où viennent les meilleurs hot-dogs?
> **Les meilleurs hot-dogs viennent des États-Unis.**

© Kiselev Andrey Valerevich / Shutterstock.com

1. les meilleurs films? 3. les meilleurs artistes?

2. les meilleurs athlètes? 4. les meilleures voitures *(cars)*?

ACTIVITÉ M «Sur Twitter» Une personne célèbre est un client à l'hôtel Frontenac. Un journaliste décrit toutes ses activités sur Twitter. Indiquez si chaque activité se passe **maintenant** *(now)* ou vient de se passer **à l'instant** *(a few moments ago)*.

	maintenant	à l'instant
1. Il vient de manger un hot-dog.	☐	☐
2. Il parle avec le serveur.	☐	☐
3. Il lit le journal *La Gazette*.	☐	☐
4. Il vient de lire un texto intéressant.	☐	☐

© Bruno Morandi/Robert Harding World Imagery/ Passage/Corbis

ACTIVITÉ **N** **Qu'est-ce qu'ils viennent de faire?** Regardez ces images du film *Liaisons.* Qu'est-ce que les personnages viennent de faire? Complétez les phrases en utilisant les verbes entre parenthèses.

1. (rencontrer) _____   **2.** (lire) _____

ACTIVITÉ **O** **Dans un monde idéal** Dans un monde *(world)* idéal, tout le monde a des qualités. Qu'est-ce que les gens peuvent *(can)* devenir?

Modèles: Les gens stupides **deviennent intelligents.**
Une femme méchante **devient gentille.**

1. Un étudiant paresseux _____.
2. Une étudiante timide _____.
3. Un enfant *(child)* triste _____.
4. Les professeurs ennuyeux _____.
5. Les étudiants impatients _____.

6. Les professeurs pauvres _____.
7. Les gens pessimistes _____.
8. Les gens embêtants _____.
9. Les gens difficiles _____.
10. La classe de français et moi, nous _____.

OUI, JE PEUX! Here are two "can do statements" for you to check your progress so far. Look at each statement and rate yourself on how well you think you can perform the task. Then verify your ability with a partner. How did you do?

1. **"I can tell someone where I am from and find out where he/she is from."**

   I can perform this function
   ☐ with ease
   ☐ with some difficulty
   ☐ not at all

2. **"I can tell someone three countries I am going to go to one day and find out which countries he/she is going to go to."**

   I can perform this function
   ☐ with ease
   ☐ with some difficulty
   ☐ not at all

iLrn™
Are you looking for more practice? You can find it in **iLrn**.

🔊 L'origine **familiale**

Family heritage

Adelai

Bisa

FATIMA

Fatima   Xavier   Abia   Nadia   François

Patrick   Aude   Fifi

La famille d'Abia Ndono

Note de **vocabulaire**
Remember that in French ownership and relationship can be indicated by a phrase with **de: Owen Wilson est le frère de Luke Wilson. C'est le livre de Pierre.** Remember the following contractions when using **de** with a definite article: **de + le = du (Ce sont les enfants du président.), de + les = des (Voici les amis des enfants.).** There is no contraction with **la** or **l': La mère de la fille s'appelle Annie. Mona est l'amie de l'oncle de Sonia.**

La famille proche *(Immediate family)*

Adelai est **le père** d'Abia.

Bisa est **la mère** d'Abia.

Adelai et Bisa sont **les parents** d'Abia.

Abia est **la fille** d'Adelai et de Bisa.

Xavier est **le fils** d'Adelai et de Bisa.

La femme de Xavier, Fatima, est **décédée.**

Abia, Nadia et Xavier sont **les enfants** d'Adelai et de Bisa.

Adelai est **le mari** de Bisa.

Bisa est **la femme** d'Adelai.

Xavier est **le frère** d'Abia.

Nadia est **la sœur** d'Abia.

Patrick est **le neveu** d'Abia et **le petit-fils** d'Adelai et de Bisa.

Aude est **la nièce** d'Abia et **la petite-fille** d'Adelai et de Bisa.

Fifi est **le chat** de Patrick et Aude.

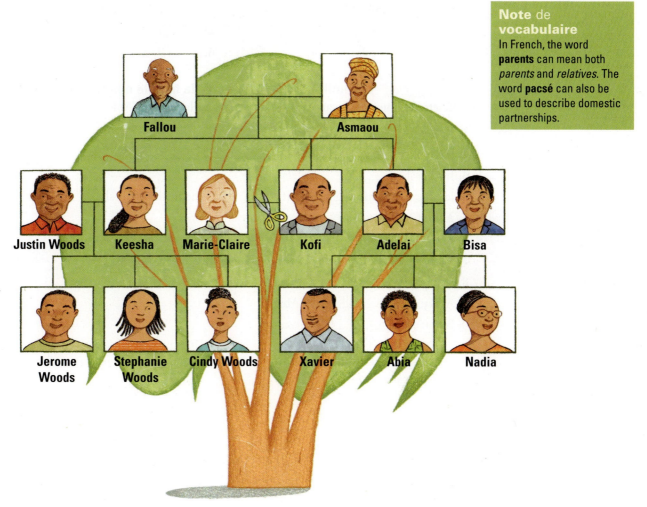

La famille d'Adelai Ndono (le père d'Abia)

Note de vocabulaire

In French, the word **parents** can mean both *parents* and *relatives*. The word **pacsé** can also be used to describe domestic partnerships.

La famille élargie *(Extended family)*

Fallou est **le grand-père** d'Abia.

Asmaou est **la grand-mère** d'Abia.

Fallou et Asmaou sont **les grands-parents** d'Abia.

Keesha est **la tante** d'Abia.

Kofi est **l'oncle** d'Abia.

Justin Woods est **le beau-frère** d'Adelai.

Bisa est **la belle-sœur** de Keesha.

Jerome est **le cousin** d'Abia.

Stephanie et Cindy sont **les cousines** d'Abia.

Fallou est **le beau-père** de Justin Woods.

Asmaou est **la belle-mère** de Justin Woods.

Vocabulaire complémentaire

le/la conjoint(e) / partenaire *significant other / domestic partner*

la famille proche *immediate family*

la famille élargie *extended family*

le beau-fils *stepson, son-in-law*

la belle-fille *stepdaughter, daughter-in-law*

l'animal *(m.)* **domestique** *pet*

le chien *dog*

le chat *cat*

---

célibataire *single*

marié(e) *married*

divorcé(e) *divorced*

décédé(e) *deceased*

veuf / veuve *widower / widow*

ACTIVITÉ A **La famille d'Abia—la famille proche** Regardez le dessin *(drawing)* de la famille d'Abia. Vous allez entendre des descriptions. Pour chaque description, indiquez si c'est vrai ou faux et corrigez les phrases fausses.

3-4

1.   2.   3.   4.   5.   6.   7.   8.

ACTIVITÉ B **La famille d'Adelai Ndono—la famille élargie d'Abia**
Complétez les phrases suivantes à propos de la famille élargie d'Abia.

1. Xavier est _____ d'Adelai.

2. Bisa est _____ de Keesha.

3. Justin est _____ d'Adelai.

4. Jerome, Stephanie et Cindy sont _____ de Justin et Keesha.

5. Abia et Nadia sont _____ d'Adelai et de Bisa.

6. Kofi et Adelai sont _____ de Jerome, Stephanie et Cindy.

7. Bisa est _____ de Jerome, Stephanie et Cindy.

8. Jerome est _____ d'Abia.

9. Asmaou est _____ d'Abia.

10. Fallou est _____ de Bisa.

ACTIVITÉ C **Qui dans la famille d'Abia...?** Répondez à chaque *(each)* question avec une phrase complète.

Qui dans la famille d'Abia est / sont...

1. divorcé(s)?

2. célibataire(s)?

3. décédé(s)?

4. veuf(s)?

5. marié(s)?

6. un animal domestique?

ACTIVITÉ D **La famille d'Abia**
Préparez un paragraphe de 5 à 6 phrases pour décrire la famille d'Abia. **SUGGESTIONS:** D'où vient sa famille? Combien d'enfants est-ce qu'il y a dans sa famille? Combien de frères et sœurs est-ce qu'Abia a? Et combien de cousin(e)s? Quels membres de la famille sont mariés? Divorcés?

ACTIVITÉ E **Votre famille**

Étape 1. Parlez de votre famille avec un(e) camarade de classe. Vous pouvez utiliser l'Activité D comme modèle.

Étape 2. Posez des questions à votre camarade pour en savoir plus *(to find out more)* sur sa famille.

Questions possibles		
Comment s'appelle X?	X est marié(e)?	X est célibataire?
X a des enfants?	Il/Elle a des animaux domestiques?	

ACTIVITÉ F Familles célèbres

Étape 1. Connaissez-vous *(Do you know)* des familles célèbres? Créez des phrases pour décrire la famille des personnes suivantes.

Modèle: Marge Simpson

**Marge Simpson est la femme de Homer Simpson.
C'est la mère de Bart et Lisa.**

1. le Prince Charles
2. Jeb Bush
3. Jenna et Barbara Bush
4. Arnold Schwarzenegger
5. Pippa Middleton
6. Hillary Clinton
7. Janet et LaToya Jackson
8. Bart et Lisa Simpson

Étape 2. Choisissez *(Choose)* une personne célèbre et écrivez un portrait de cette *(this)* personne. **SUGGESTIONS:** Cette personne est de quel pays? Où habite cette personne? Qui sont ses parents et ses frères et sœurs? Il/Elle est marié(e), célibataire ou divorcé(e)? Il/Elle a des enfants?

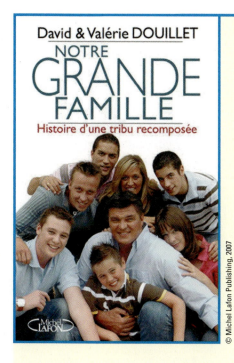

David & Valérie DOUILLET
NOTRE GRANDE FAMILLE
Histoire d'une tribu recomposée

© Michel Lafon Publishing, 2007

Un mot sur la culture

La famille recomposée

Les familles recomposées sont devenues ordinaires et acceptées en France. Le terme désigne une famille dans laquelle° des enfants viennent d'une union précédente des parents. Une autre expression pour «famille recomposée» est «famille patchwork». Dans une famille patchwork, il est normal d'avoir un demi-frère ou une demi-sœur et un beau-père ou une belle-mère. David Douillet, un judoka français qui a obtenu la médaille d'or aux jeux Olympiques (en 1996 et 2000), est un exemple. Il a écrit un livre avec sa femme Valérie à propos de leur famille.

dans laquelle *in which*

À noter | Ces termes ont deux sens: beau-père *(stepfather* or *father-in-law)* et belle-mère *(stepmother* or *mother-in-law)*.

• Est-ce que les familles recomposées sont acceptées dans votre culture?

• Vous connaissez des familles recomposées célèbres?

Pour parler des familles

Les adjectifs possessifs / Les adjectifs démonstratifs

DU FILM *LIAISONS* ....

Un coup d'œil sur la grammaire

Look at these photos from the film **Liaisons** and their captions. Note the words used to express ownership.

CLAIRE Et elle? Comment va-t-elle?

INFIRMIÈRE (NURSE) Elle va mieux ces jours-ci. Elle est dans **sa** chambre. Allez la voir.

SIMONE C'est toi, Claire? Ce n'est pas une de **mes** hallucinations?

What do you think the following expressions mean?

1. **sa** chambre

    a. my room   b. your room   c. her room

2. **mes** hallucinations

    a. my hallucinations   b. your hallucinations   c. her hallucinations

Les adjectifs possessifs

❖ In French, possessive adjectives must agree both in gender and number with the nouns they modify, *not* with the person(s) who own(s) the nouns.

Voici **mon** père et **ma** mère.   *Here are **my** father and **my** mother.*

Mes parents vivent en France.   ***My** parents live in France.*

masculine singular	feminine singular	plural	
mon	ma	mes	*my*
ton	ta	tes	*your (fam. & sing.)*
son	sa	ses	*his/her/its*
notre	notre	nos	*our*
votre	votre	vos	*your (form. or pl.)*
leur	leur	leurs	*their*

- The masculine singular forms **mon, ton,** and **son** are also used with feminine singular nouns if those nouns begin with a vowel sound.

Mon amie va à Québec.	***My*** *friend is going to Quebec.*
Ton étudiante est ici.	***Your*** *student is here.*
Son école est fermée.	***His/Her*** *school is closed.*

- **Notre, votre,** and **leur** are used for both masculine and feminine singular nouns.

Notre mère s'appelle Aline.	***Our*** *mother's name is Aline.*
Votre père est beau.	***Your*** *father is handsome.*
Leur voiture est belle.	***Their*** *car is beautiful.*

- Note that **sa, son,** and **ses** can mean either *his, her,* or *its.* The context usually makes the meaning clear.

Tom adore **son** frère.	*Tom loves **his** brother.*
Anne adore **son** frère aussi.	*Anne loves **her** brother too.*
Sarah vient avec **sa** sœur.	*Sarah is coming with **her** sister.*
Pierre vient avec **sa** cousine.	*Pierre is coming with **his** cousin.*
Salima adore **ses** amis.	*Salima loves **her** friends.*
Marc adore **ses** amis.	*Marc loves **his** friends.*

Les adjectifs démonstratifs

- Demonstrative adjectives *(this, that, those, these)* allow you to be more specific when you identify or describe things. Like possessive adjectives, demonstrative adjectives in French must agree in gender and number with the nouns they modify.

masc. sing.	masc. sing. before a vowel sound	fem. sing.	masc./fem. plural
ce livre	**cet** étudiant	**cette** fille	**ces** enfants
		cette étudiante	

Ce garçon est mon neveu.	***This*** *boy is my nephew.*
Cet homme est mon oncle.	***This*** *man is my uncle.*
Cette étudiante est ma nièce.	***This*** *student is my niece.*
Ces filles sont mes cousines.	***These/Those*** *girls are my cousins.*

- To be more precise, **-ci** and **-là** may be added to the noun to indicate *here* (close by) and *there* (farther away), respectively.

Cette fille-**ci** est ma nièce.	***This*** *girl (**over here**) is my niece.*
Ce garçon-**là** est mon neveu.	***That*** *boy (**over there**) is my nephew.*
J'aime **cette** photo-**ci**.	*I like **this** photo (**here**).*
Il préfère **ces** stylos-**là**.	*He prefers **those** pens (**over there**).*

Liaisons musicales

© Vittorio Zunino Celotto/ Getty Images Entertainment/ Getty Images

Carla Bruni-Sarkozy est une chanteuse française. Sa chanson, *L'amoureuse* (2008) est dédiée *(dedicated)* à son mari, Nicolas Sarkozy, l'ancien président de la France. Trouvez une vidéo de la chanson sur Internet.

ACTIVITÉ G **Les photos de famille** Un étudiant à l'Université McGill vous montre *(shows)* ses photos de famille. Complétez ses descriptions.

1. Voici **ma…**	a. mère	b. père	c. parents
2. Et voici **mon…**	a. mère	b. père	c. parents
3. Ici, ce sont **mes…**	a. tante	b. sœur	c. frères
4. Ils aiment bien **leurs…**	a. sœur	b. oncle	c. parents
5. Je n'aime pas **cette…**	a. oncle	b. fille	c. garçon
6. C'est **notre…**	a. cousins	b. cousine	c. oncles
7. J'aime bien **ces…**	a. enfants	b. garçon	c. fille
8. Ce sont **nos…**	a. neveux	b. nièce	c. cousin

ACTIVITÉ H **Qui le dit? Un professeur ou un(e) étudiant(e)?** Qui dit ces phrases? Un professeur? Un(e) étudiant(e)? Les deux *(Both)*? Personne *(Nobody)*?

1. J'aime bien **cette** université.   **3.** J'aime bien **ce** cours de français.

2. J'aime bien **cette** salle de classe-**ci**.   **4.** J'aime bien **ces** étudiant(e)s-**là**.

ACTIVITÉ I **Claire ou Alexis?**

Étape 1. Décidez si ces descriptions des personnages du film *Liaisons* décrivent *(describe)* Claire, Alexis ou les deux.

	Claire	Alexis	Les deux
1. Ses cheveux sont courts.	☐	☐	☐
2. Sa langue maternelle, c'est le français.	☐	☐	☐
3. Sa meilleure amie est Abia.	☐	☐	☐
4. Son accent est français.	☐	☐	☐
5. Son nom de famille est Gagner.	☐	☐	☐
6. Ses cours sont à l'Université McGill.	☐	☐	☐

Étape 2. Et toi? Répondez aux questions.

1. Tes cheveux sont courts ou longs?

2. Quelle est **ta** langue maternelle?

3. Qui est **ton/ta** meilleur(e) ami(e)?

4. Quel est **ton** nom de famille?

Connaissez-vous bien l'Université McGill?

Étape 1. Voici des phrases sur les étudiants ou les professeurs de l'Université McGill. Est-ce que chaque phrase est vraie ou fausse? Corrigez les phrases fausses.

	Vrai	Faux
1. **Leur** université est grande. McGill a environ 31 000 étudiants.	☐	☐
2. **Leur** campus est dans le centre-ville de Québec.	☐	☐
3. **Leurs** étudiants parlent anglais et français.	☐	☐
4. 20% de **leurs** étudiants sont francophones.	☐	☐

Étape 2. Avec un(e) camarade, préparez des phrases pour décrire **votre** université.

Modèle: Notre université est grande aussi...

ACTIVITÉ **K** **Vos préférences**

Étape 1. Répondez aux questions et écrivez vos réponses dans la colonne **Moi**. Ensuite, trouvez un(e) partenaire. Posez ces questions à votre partenaire. Écrivez ses réponses.

	Moi	Mon/Ma partenaire
1. Quel est **ton** cours préféré?	_____	_____
2. Quel est **ton** film préféré?	_____	_____
3. Quelle est **ta** voiture préférée?	_____	_____
4. Quelle est **ta** boisson *(drink)* préférée?	_____	_____
5. Quels sont **tes** restaurants préférés?	_____	_____
6. Quelles sont **tes** villes préférées?	_____	_____

Étape 2. Préparez 3 à 4 phrases pour décrire les préférences de votre camarade et partagez-les *(share them)* avec la classe.

Liaisons musicales

Dans les années soixante-dix, le chanteur québécois Richard Séguin a formé avec sa sœur jumelle *(twin)* Marie-Claire le duo Les Séguin. Leur premier album *Séguin* (1973) est un mélange *(mix)* de folk-rock et d'influences amérindiennes. Aujourd'hui, Richard et Marie-Claire sont deux artistes solos très populaires au Québec. Visitez le site officiel de Richard Séguin sur Internet.

OUI, JE PEUX! Here are two "can do statements" for you to check your progress so far. Look at each statement and rate yourself on how well you think you can perform the task. Then verify your ability with a partner. How did you do?

1. **"I can say who is in my family and where these family members live."**

   I can perform this function
   ☐ with ease
   ☐ with some difficulty
   ☐ not at all

2. **"I can ask someone else about his/her family and where these family members live."**

   I can perform this function
   ☐ with ease
   ☐ with some difficulty
   ☐ not at all

iLrn™

Are you looking for more practice? You can find it in **iLrn**.

🔊 # Les traits **physiques**

Physical traits

les cheveux frisés / bouclés

les cheveux courts

un grand nez

les cheveux blonds

les yeux *(m.)* bleus

les yeux *(m.)* marron

les cheveux gris

une barbe

grand

les yeux verts

les cheveux *(m.)* gris

grande

les cheveux longs et raides

petit

petite

gros

grosse

Mimi   Paul   Marie   Stéphane   Mathieu   Caroline

La famille Dubois

Vocabulaire complémentaire

les cheveux noirs *black hair*	**chauve** *bald*
les cheveux ondulés *wavy hair*	**laid(e)** *ugly*
les cheveux roux *red hair*	**mince** *thin, slender, slim*
un(e) blond(e) *a blond*	**musclé(e)** *muscular*
un roux / une rousse *a redhead*	

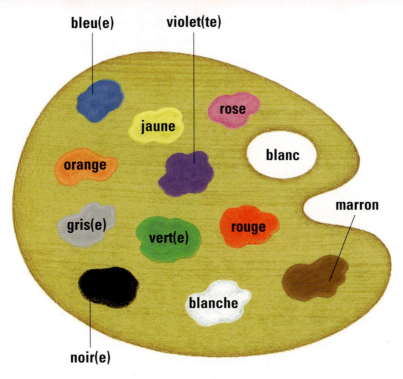

bleu(e) violet(te)

rose

jaune

orange

blanc

marron

gris(e)

vert(e) rouge

blanche

noir(e)

Les couleurs

🔊 **ACTIVITÉ A** **C'est qui?** Regardez bien la photo de la famille Dubois et
3-5 répondez aux questions que vous entendez *(hear)*.

   1.   **2.**   **3.**   **4.**   **5.**   **6.**   **7.**   **8.**

🔊 **ACTIVITÉ B** **Claire ou Abia?** Indiquez
3-6 si chaque phrase que vous entendez décrit
a) Claire du film *Liaisons* ou **b) Abia**.

   1.   **2.**   **3.**   **4.**

ACTIVITÉ C **Les traits physiques et les nationalités** À quelles
nationalités associez-vous ces traits physiques?

1. Ils sont très **grands**.	a. les Japonais	b. les Allemands
2. Ils ont les **cheveux roux**.	a. les Irlandais	b. les Chinois
3. Elles sont très **minces**.	a. les Françaises	b. les Américaines
4. Elles ont les **cheveux blonds**.	a. les Suisses	b. les Sénégalaises
5. Ils ont les **yeux bleus**.	a. les Américains	b. les Vietnamiens

🔊 **ACTIVITÉ D Connaissez-vous bien les drapeaux du monde?** Vous
3-7   allez entendre *(hear)* une série de couleurs. Avec quel drapeau *(flag)* associez-vous
ces couleurs?

1. a. le drapeau québécois
   b. le drapeau français
2. a. le drapeau chinois
   b. le drapeau ivoirien
3. a. le drapeau italien
   b. le drapeau canadien
4. a. le drapeau américain
   b. le drapeau belge

© Tetra Images/Getty Images

ACTIVITÉ E Dans la classe: C'est qui? Vous allez écrire une description
d'un(e) de vos camarades de classe. Ensuite *(Then)*, vos camarades vont deviner
(guess) qui c'est. Si vos camarades ne peuvent pas *(cannot)* deviner qui c'est, ils vont
vous poser *(ask you)* des questions.

Modèle: É1: **Il a les yeux verts. Il a les cheveux courts et bruns. C'est qui?**
  É2: **Je ne sais pas. Il est petit ou grand?**
  É1: **Il est grand.**
  É3: **C'est Mark?**
  É1: **Oui, c'est Mark.**

ACTIVITÉ F À qui ressemblez-vous dans votre famille?

Étape 1. Regardez votre partenaire et faites une liste de ses traits physiques.
Écrivez ces traits dans la première colonne.

Modèle: les yeux bleus

Les traits physiques de mon/ma partenaire	mère	père	les deux	autre parent	personne
1. _____	☐	☐	☐	☐	☐
2. _____	☐	☐	☐	☐	☐
3. _____	☐	☐	☐	☐	☐
4. _____	☐	☐	☐	☐	☐

Étape 2. Interviewez votre partenaire pour déterminer si les traits physiques sur
votre liste semblent *(seem)* venir de sa mère, de son père, des deux, d'un autre parent
ou de personne *(nobody)* dans sa famille. Cochez (✔) ses réponses.

Étape 3. D'après les réponses à l'Étape 2, comment décririez-vous *(would you
describe)* votre partenaire?

Mon/Ma partenaire…

- ressemble plus à sa mère.
- ressemble plus à son père.
- ressemble à sa mère et à son père.
- ressemble à un autre parent.
- ne ressemble à personne dans sa famille.

Un mot sur la culture

Cyrano de Bergerac

© Douglas Pearson/Latitude/Corbis

Voici un célèbre trait physique dans la culture française: le grand et long nez de Cyrano, le personnage principal dans *Cyrano de Bergerac* (pièce de théâtre d'Edmond Rostand, 1897). Cyrano a peur de déclarer son amour à Roxane parce qu'il est laid. Cyrano aime beaucoup jouer avec la langue française comme dans cette citation: «Tous les mots° sont fins° quand la moustache est fine°»*. Il y a beaucoup d'expressions en français qui mentionnent des traits physiques.

mots *words* **fins** *witty* **fine** *thin*

* Citation dans *Cyrano de Bergerac*, par Edmond Rostand, Acte II, scène 6.
Source: http://www.babelio.com/auteur/Edmond-Rostand/5207/citations

- Que veulent dire ces expressions?

1. «mon œil»	a. *under someone's very nose*
2. «au nez et à la barbe de quelqu'un»	b. *by word of mouth*
3. «de bouche à oreille»	c. *no way*

🔊 Liaisons avec les mots et les sons

3-8

Les voyelles orales et les voyelles nasales

French vowel sounds mainly fall into two categories: oral and nasal vowels. When forming oral vowels, air escapes through the mouth. When forming nasal vowels, air is concentrated in the nose and the **n** and **m** sounds are not pronounced. Put your hand under your nose and notice the sensations when you pronounce these words.

Oral Vowels	Nasal Vowels	Oral Vowels	Nasal Vowels
beau	bon	mot	mon
leur	lent	ta	temps
vie	vin	fait	fin
vous	vont	nos	nom

An oral vowel sound that does not exist in English is the French **u** sound. To make this sound, place the tip of your tongue behind your lower teeth, round your lips like you are going to whistle and say *ee*.

d**u**	ét**u**des	m**u**sclé	ond**u**lé	t**u**	**u**ne

Pratique A. Écoutez bien et encerclez le mot *(word)* que vous entendez *(hear)*.

1. les / lent   2. mot / mon   3. vos / vont   4. allez / allons   5. tes / temps

Pratique B. Écoutez et répétez ces répliques du film *Liaisons* à haute voix *(aloud)*. Encerclez toutes les voyelles nasales et soulignez *(underline)* toutes les voyelles orales.

CLAIRE Ça va, mon chat? Tu as faim?

CLAIRE Vous avez une réservation à mon nom?

🔊 À vos stylos! C'est l'heure de la dictée!

3-9

Vous allez entendre quatre phrases. Écoutez bien. Vous allez entendre les phrases une deuxième fois. Écrivez les phrases.

Sujet Une scène de la Séquence 2 du film *Liaisons*

Pour parler de nos familles et de nos traits physiques

La position des adjectifs / Les verbes **sortir**, **partir**, **dormir** et **sentir**

DU FILM *LIAISONS*

Un coup d'œil sur la grammaire

À l'Hôtel Delta, Claire rencontre un client **intéressant**: un **bel** homme **charmant** aux cheveux **blonds.** Il s'appelle Alexis Prévost.

Look at this photo from the film **Liaisons** and its caption, paying special attention to the adjectives.

Now answer these questions about the position of the adjectives.

1. Which adjectives follow the nouns they modify?
2. Which adjective precedes the noun it modifies?

Les adjectifs prénominaux

In **Chapitre préliminaire** and **Chapitre 1,** you learned that adjectives in French agree in gender and number with the nouns they modify and that they are usually placed after the noun.

Claire est une femme **intelligente.**   Abia a les cheveux **noirs.**

There are several adjectives used to describe people or things that are usually placed *before* the noun. Because they go before the noun, these adjectives are called prenominal adjectives or **adjectifs prénominaux** in French.

Les adjectifs prénominaux		
Masculine	**Feminine**	
C'est un **petit** quartier *(neighborhood)*.	C'est une **petite** ville.	*small*
C'est un **grand** quartier.	C'est une **grande** ville.	*big, tall, great*
C'est un **joli** quartier.	C'est une **jolie** ville.	*pretty*
C'est un **bon** quartier.	C'est une **bonne** ville.	*good*
C'est un **mauvais** quartier.	C'est une **mauvaise** ville.	*bad*
C'est un **jeune** homme.	C'est une **jeune** femme.	*young*

Note de **grammaire**
Note that **jeune** is used with both masculine and feminine nouns.

Grand can mean *big, tall,* or *honorable* depending on its placement.

C'est un homme **grand.**   *That's a **tall** man.*

C'est un **grand** homme.   *That's a **great** man.*

→ Three prenominal adjectives have different masculine singular forms when they precede consonants and vowels or a mute *h* (*h* **muet**).

Masculine before a consonant	Masculine before a vowel or *h* muet	Feminine	
un **beau** quartier	un **bel** appartement	une **belle** ville	*beautiful*
	un **bel** homme		*handsome*
un **nouveau** quartier	un **nouvel** appartement	une **nouvelle** ville	*new*
un **vieux** quartier	un **vieil** appartement	une **vieille** ville	*old*
	un **vieil** homme		

→ When prenominal adjectives precede a plural noun, the plural indefinite article **des** usually becomes **de.** Note that some prenominal adjectives have irregular plural forms.

Masculine plural before a consonant	Masculine plural before a vowel or *h* muet	Feminine plural
de **beaux** quartiers	de **beaux** appartements	de **belles** villes
	de **beaux** hommes	
de **nouveaux** quartiers	de **nouveaux** appartements	de **nouvelles** villes
de **vieux** quartiers	de **vieux** hommes	de **vieilles** villes

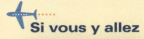
Si vous y allez

Si vous allez à Paris, visitez le quartier asiatique pour ses bons restaurants chinois, surtout pendant le nouvel an chinois.

Il y a **des** quartiers **intéressants** à Montréal.   *but*

Il y a **de beaux** quartiers à Montréal.

Il y a **de vieux** appartements dans mon quartier.

J'ai **de nouvelles** lampes dans mon nouvel appartement.

La bibliothèque a **de nouveaux** livres.

→ Adjectives may also immediately follow the verb **être.**

Les quartiers à Montréal **sont beaux.**

Les appartements **sont vieux.**

L'homme aux yeux bleus **est beau,** n'est-ce pas?

Les verbes *dormir, partir, sentir* et *sortir*

→ You have already studied several classes of verbs in French. There is a subset of verbs ending in **-ir.** These **-ir** verbs follow the same pattern.

dormir *(to sleep)*	
je **dors**	nous **dormons**
tu **dors**	vous **dormez**
il/elle/on **dort**	ils/elles **dorment**

partir *(to leave)*	
je **pars**	nous **partons**
tu **pars**	vous **partez**
il/elle/on **part**	ils/elles **partent**

sentir *(to smell)*	
je **sens**	nous **sentons**
tu **sens**	vous **sentez**
il/elle/on **sent**	ils/elles **sentent**

sortir *(to go out)*	
je **sors**	nous **sortons**
tu **sors**	vous **sortez**
il/elle/on **sort**	ils/elles **sortent**

Mon frère **dort** beaucoup.

Papa, tu **pars** déjà?

Les cheveux de maman **sentent** bon.

Nous **sortons** souvent le samedi.

*My brother **sleeps** a lot.*

*Dad, you're **leaving** already?*

*Mom's hair **smells** good.*

*We often **go out** on Saturdays.*

ACTIVITÉ G Quel dessin?

3-10

Étape 1. Vous allez entendre une description d'un dessin. Écoutez bien la description et choisissez le bon dessin.

1.

a.   b.

2.

a.   b.

3.

a.   b.

4.

a.   b.

5.

a.   b.

6.

a.   b.

Étape 2. Voici encore des descriptions de dessins. Regardez bien les adjectifs pour déterminer le bon objet dans le dessin.

1. Il y a **une vieille…**
   a. appartement
   b. maison *(house)*
   c. quartier

2. Ce sont **de nouvelles…**
   a. fenêtres
   b. quartiers
   c. instruments de musique

3. C'est **un nouvel…**
   a. professeur
   b. appartement
   c. maison

4. Ce sont **de beaux…**
   a. femmes
   b. hommes
   c. homme

5. C'est **un vieux…**
   a. tableau
   b. ordinateur
   c. homme

6. C'est **un vieil…**
   a. stylo
   b. table
   c. ordinateur

7. Ce sont **de vieux…**
   a. amis
   b. amies
   c. dames

8. Ce sont **de nouveaux…**
   a. étudiantes
   b. chaises
   c. amis

ACTIVITÉ H Dans la maison de ma famille

Étape 1. Dans la maison de votre famille, les objets sont-ils pour la plupart *(mostly)* vieux ou nouveaux? Complétez les phrases suivantes avec la forme appropriée de l'adjectif **nouveau** ou **vieux**.

Dans la maison de _____ [membre de la famille], il y a…

1. un _____ téléviseur.
2. de _____ chaises.
3. un _____ ordinateur.
4. un _____ bureau.
5. de _____ lampes *(f.)*.
6. un _____ réfrigérateur.
7. de _____ assiettes *(f.) (plates)*.
8. une _____ table.

© Peter Horree / Alamy

Étape 2. Qu'avez-vous dans votre maison ou appartement? Complétez les phrases suivantes avec la forme appropriée de l'adjectif **nouveau** ou **vieux**.

1. J'ai un _____ téléviseur.
2. J'ai de _____ chaises.
3. J'ai un _____ ordinateur.
4. J'ai un _____ bureau.
5. J'ai de _____ lampes.
6. J'ai un _____ réfrigérateur.
7. J'ai de _____ assiettes.
8. J'ai une _____ table.

Conclusion En général, préférez-vous les objets dans votre maison ou appartement ou les objets dans la maison de votre famille?

ACTIVITÉ **I** **Portrait d'un membre de votre famille**

Étape 1. Vous allez faire une description d'un membre de votre famille pour un(e) artiste qui va faire son portrait. Choisissez la personne, notez son âge et faites une liste d'adjectifs pour décrire ses traits physiques.

Membre de ma famille: _____ **Son âge:** _____

Les traits	Les adjectifs
les yeux	_____
le nez	_____
les oreilles *(f.) (ears)*	_____
les cheveux	_____
la bouche *(mouth)*	_____
le corps *(body)*	_____

Étape 2. Écrivez un paragraphe pour décrire ce membre de votre famille. Puis, lisez le paragraphe à un(e) camarade. Votre camarade est l'artiste qui va faire le portrait!

Modèle: **C'est mon grand-père. Il est vieux. Il a les yeux noirs et un petit nez,** etc.

Étape 3. Est-ce que le portrait ressemble au membre de la famille que vous avez décrit?

ACTIVITÉ **J** **Les odeurs**

Étape 1. Un article dans la revue *Châtelaine* dit que les odeurs peuvent évoquer des sentiments *(feelings)* différents pour des personnes différentes. Décrivez l'odeur des choses *(things)* suivantes. Complétez les phrases avec l'adverbe **bon** ou **mauvais.**

Modèle: Les fleurs sentent **bon.**

© Courtesy of Wynne Wong

1. Les roses **sentent** _____.
2. La campagne **sent** _____.
3. Le café **sent** _____.
4. La bière **sent** _____.
5. Les hôpitaux *(m.)* **sentent** _____.
6. Les bébés **sentent** _____.

Étape 2. Comparez vos réponses avec celles *(those)* d'un(e) camarade. Avez-vous écrit les mêmes choses ou avez-vous des réponses différentes? Est-ce que l'article avait raison?

Modèle: É1: **Comment sentent les roses?**
É2: **D'après moi, les roses sentent mauvais. Et toi?**
É1: **D'après moi, les roses sentent bon.**

ACTIVITÉ (K) **La famille: stéréotype des années 1950 ou du 21ᵉ siècle?**

Étape 1. Les familles et les adolescents des séries télévisées *(TV shows)* sont souvent stéréotypés. Lisez chaque description et cochez (✓) la période à laquelle elle correspond.

	Les années 1950	Le 21ᵉ siècle *(century)*
1. Les enfants **partent** pour l'école ensemble.	☐	☐
2. Les enfants **dorment** jusqu'à midi le week-end.	☐	☐
3. Les enfants **sortent** dans les bars le week-end.	☐	☐
4. La famille **sort** ensemble le vendredi soir.	☐	☐
5. Les garçons préfèrent les **jolies** filles **minces** aux **cheveux longs**.	☐	☐
6. Les filles préfèrent les **beaux** garçons **musclés**.	☐	☐

Quelle famille! (What a Family!) est une série télévisée québécoise des années 1950.

 Étape 2. Posez ces questions à un(e) camarade pour savoir s'il/si elle est plutôt comme un(e) enfant des années 1950 ou un(e) enfant du 21ᵉ siècle.

1. Tu pars à l'université avec ton frère ou ta sœur?
2. Combien d'heures dors-tu chaque nuit?
3. Tu sors dans les bars le week-end?
4. Tu sors avec ta famille le week-end?
5. Penses-tu que les garçons préfèrent les jolies filles minces aux cheveux longs?
6. Penses-tu que les filles préfèrent les beaux garçons musclés?

Conclusion Mon/Ma camarade est plus comme un(e) enfant des années 1950 / du 21ᵉ siècle.

OUI, JE PEUX!

Here are two "can do statements" for you to check your progress so far. Look at each statement and rate yourself on how well you think you can perform the task. Then verify your ability with a partner. How did you do?

1. **"I can describe the physical traits of two of my family members, including their size, height, hair, and eye color."**

   I can perform this function
   ☐ with ease
   ☐ with some difficulty
   ☐ not at all

2. **"I can ask someone else about the physical appearance of his/her family members (size, height, hair, and eye color)."**

   I can perform this function
   ☐ with ease
   ☐ with some difficulty
   ☐ not at all

iLrn™

Are you looking for more practice? You can find it in **iLrn**.

Avant de visionner

ACTIVITÉ A **Vous rappelez-vous?**

Vous rappelez-vous *(Do you remember)* ce qui s'est passé *(what happened)* dans la Séquence 1 du film *Liaisons*? Pour chaque phrase, indiquez si c'est vrai ou faux.

	Vrai	Faux
1. Claire a reçu une enveloppe d'un homme mystérieux.	☐	☐
2. L'amie de Claire s'appelle Simone.	☐	☐
3. Claire trouve Alexis Prévost très beau.	☐	☐
4. Alexis Prévost avait besoin d'une brosse à dents *(toothbrush)*.	☐	☐

ACTIVITÉ B **Un coup d'œil sur une scène** Voici une scène de la Séquence 2 du film *Liaisons* que vous allez regarder. Claire reçoit un appel *(phone call)* de son oncle. Choisissez *(Choose)* la lettre du mot qui correspond à chaque blanc *(blank)* dans le dialogue. Vous allez vérifier vos réponses plus tard.

MICHEL (OFF) C'est (1) _____
oncle Michel.

CLAIRE Michel! (2) _____ Je
dormais. Je n'ai pas reconnu ta voix
(voice)...

MICHEL (OFF) Claire, (3) _____.
Tu dois aller à Québec.

CLAIRE Comment?

> **Note de vocabulaire**
> OFF veut dire *(means)* **voix off** *(voice off screen)*.

1. a. ta	b. ton	3. a. écoute	b. s'il te plaît
2. a. Ça va?	b. Pardon.		

> ▶ **Regarder la séquence**
> Vous allez regarder la Séquence 2 du film *Liaisons*. Utilisez le contexte pour comprendre les dialogues.

Après le visionnage

ACTIVITÉ C **Vérifiez votre compréhension**

1. Qui a payé la réservation à l'hôtel Frontenac pour Claire?
2. L'oncle Michel a téléphoné à quelle heure?
3. Est-ce qu'Abia est contente que Claire veuille *(wants)* aller à Québec?
4. Qui est-ce que Claire voit *(sees)* à la fin de la Séquence 2?

ACTIVITÉ **D** **Avez-vous compris?** Relisez vos réponses dans l'Activité B. Avez-vous choisi *(choose)* les bons mots? Si nécessaire, regardez la scène encore une fois *(again)* pour vérifier vos réponses.

ACTIVITÉ **E** **Utilisez le contexte** Claire dit à Abia qu'elle va aller à Québec. Regardez bien les mots **en gras** *(bold)* et répondez aux questions.

ABIA Claire, cet homme qui te fait la réservation… c'est peut-être **(1) un meurtrier,** un psychopathe!

CLAIRE **(2) Ne dramatise pas,** Abi. […]

ABIA Et tu ne vas pas changer d'avis?

CLAIRE Non. Tu veux bien **(3) garder** Émile pour moi cette **(4) fin de semaine**?

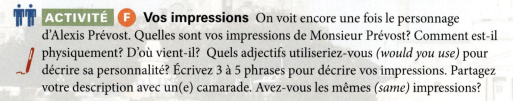

1. Que veut dire le mot **meurtrier**?

2. **Dramatiser** veut dire *to dramatize*. Que veut dire l'expression **Ne dramatise pas**?

3. Le verbe **garder** veut normalement dire *to keep* en anglais. Mais dans le contexte de ce dialogue, **garder** a un sens différent. Dans ce contexte, que veut dire **garder**?

4. **Fin de semaine** est une expression québécoise. Que veut dire **fin de semaine**?

ACTIVITÉ **F** **Vos impressions** On voit encore une fois le personnage d'Alexis Prévost. Quelles sont vos impressions de Monsieur Prévost? Comment est-il physiquement? D'où vient-il? Quels adjectifs utiliseriez-vous *(would you use)* pour décrire sa personnalité? Écrivez 3 à 5 phrases pour décrire vos impressions. Partagez votre description avec un(e) camarade. Avez-vous les mêmes *(same)* impressions?

© Courtesy of Wynne Wong

Liaisons avec la culture

La ville de Québec

La ville de Québec est la capitale nationale de la province du Québec, située sur les rives du fleuve Saint-Laurent. On dit **à Québec** et **de Québec** pour parler de la ville et **au Québec** et **du Québec** pour parler de la province. La ville est fondée en 1608 par l'explorateur français Samuel de Champlain et reste l'un des plus anciens territoires européens en Amérique du Nord. Elle est également la seule ville fortifiée en Amérique du Nord. Depuis 1985, elle figure sur la liste du patrimoine mondial établie par l'UNESCO. 95% de la population de Québec parle français comme langue maternelle. Chaque année, les touristes viennent à Québec pour profiter de son caractère européen et de son patrimoine français.

LIAISONS
CULTURELLES

Le monde francophone et ses origines

OUTILS DE LECTURE
Guessing temporal reference

The temporal reference of a sentence is not limited to verb forms alone. You can often guess it by considering other elements in the text such as the context or other words that indicate whether the action or description is taking place in the present, past, or future. For example, in **L'origine des noms de famille québécois**, you see the verb **a été** in the sentence **Avant 1960, la religion catholique a été très importante dans la société québécoise**.

1. Does **a été** refer to the past, present or future?
2. What information in the sentence provides the clue?

L'origine des noms de famille québécois

Saviez-vous que certains noms de famille sont particulièrement fréquents au Québec: Tremblay, Gagnon, Roy, Côté, Bouchard? Il y a des raisons historiques: ce sont les descendants des premiers Français qui ont émigré en Nouvelle-France. En 1540, l'explorateur Jacques Cartier a essayé° de fonder une colonie française en Amérique du Nord. Ces premières familles d'origine française ont eu beaucoup d'enfants. Avant 1960, la religion catholique a été très importante dans la société québécoise. Sous l'influence de l'Église catholique, les femmes avaient 8 à 12 enfants. Leurs patronymes ou noms de famille sont aujourd'hui les plus répandus° au Québec.

essayer *to try* **répandus** *widespread*

© Bettmann/Corbis

Vrai ou faux?

1. Tremblay, Gagnon, Roy, Côté et Bouchard sont les noms des familles riches au Québec.   V / F
2. Ces noms sont les noms des premiers Français qui sont arrivés en Nouvelle-France.   V / F
3. Avant 1960, la religion protestante était très importante.   V / F
4. Avant 1960, les femmes avaient beaucoup d'enfants.   V / F

© Pathé Films/Courtesy Everett Collection

L'origine des différences linguistiques et culturelles en France

Bienvenue chez les Ch'tis (2008), réalisé par Dany Boon, est un grand succès commercial en France. Philippe Abrams, un habitant du sud de la France déménage dans le nord et habite avec les *Ch'tis*, les habitants de la région Nord-Pas-de-Calais qui parlent un dialecte français qui s'appelle le «ch'ti». Philippe trouve les Ch'tis froids, incultes° et arriérés° mais, petit à petit, il apprécie ses nouveaux amis du nord. Ces différences linguistiques et culturelles trouvent leurs origines dans les différentes régions de la France. La France est divisée en beaucoup de régions différentes, chacune° avec sa cuisine, son histoire, son climat, son dialecte et parfois sa langue distincte.

incultes *uneducated* **arriérés** *backwards* **chacune** *each*

Adapted from: http://www.musicme.com/Bienvenue-Chez-les-Ch'tis/biographie

Vrai ou faux?

1. Les Ch'tis sont les habitants du sud de la France.   V / F

2. Le ch'ti est un dialecte français.   V / F

3. La France a beaucoup de régions, chacune avec sa culture distincte.   V / F

Les origines littéraires aux Antilles

La littérature francophone aux Antilles a connu un grand développement après la Seconde Guerre mondiale°. Elle trouve ses origines dans les traditions littéraires françaises, dans les cultures locales et dans la langue française et les langues créoles. Deux thèmes principaux de cette littérature sont l'héritage culturel et la recherche° de l'identité. Une écrivaine de littérature antillaise très importante—que l'on appelle parfois «la Grande Dame de la littérature antillaise»—s'appelle Maryse Condé. Elle vient de Pointe-à-Pitre en Guadeloupe. Dans ses écrits, elle explore la question du panafricanisme ou de l'unification des Africains et de leurs descendants en dehors de l'Afrique.

la Seconde Guerre mondiale *WWII* **la recherche** *the search*

© Eric Fougere/Corbis Entertainment/VIP Images/Corbis

Vrai ou faux?

1. La littérature antillaise a ses origines dans la littérature française.   V / F

2. Maryse Condé vient de Martinique.   V / F

3. Un thème important pour Condé est l'unification des Africains en Afrique.   V / F

© Sandro Campardo/Corbis Wire/epa/Corbis

Un humoriste d'origine franco-maghrébine

Il y a beaucoup de Français aujourd'hui qui ont un héritage franco-maghrébin. Ils ont des racines dans la culture française et dans la culture d'un pays du Maghreb, c'est-à-dire le Maroc, l'Algérie ou la Tunisie. Ils ont des parents ou des grands-parents qui sont immigrés ou ils sont eux-mêmes° immigrés. Un homme très fier de ses origines franco-maghrébines est l'humoriste Jamel Debbouze. Il est né à Paris en 1975 de parents d'origine marocaine. Debbouze est humoriste, acteur et producteur. Dans ses sketches, il aime se moquer des° différences culturelles entre les Français, les Nord-Africains et les Français nés de parents immigrés du Maghreb. Par exemple, il plaisante° souvent sur le sujet des différences culinaires, musicales, linguistiques et religieuses entre la France et le Maroc.

eux-mêmes *themselves* **se moquer des** *to make fun of*
plaisante *jokes*

Compréhension

1. Nommez un pays du Maghreb.

2. Les parents de Jamel Debbouze sont originaires de quel pays?

3. Qu'est-ce que Debbouze fait comme métier *(job)*?

4. De quels sujets est-ce que Debbouze aime se moquer dans ses sketches?

▷ LIAISONS CULTURELLES
....

La Polynésie française

Use **iLrn**™ to access the video **Le monde francophone** to learn more about the French-speaking world. Be prepared to answer the question **Et vous? Où souhaitez-vous aller en premier pour pratiquer votre français?** Share your responses with your classmates in **Share It!**

PARTIE 1   3–11

LES CONTINENTS ET LES PAYS

le continent	*continent*
le pays	*country*
l'Afrique *(f.)* du Nord	*North Africa*
l'Afrique de l'Ouest	*West Africa*
l'Allemagne *(f.)*	*Germany*
l'Amérique *(f.)* du Nord	*North America*
l'Amérique du Sud	*South America*
l'Angleterre *(f.)*	*England*
l'Asie *(f.)*	*Asia*
la Belgique	*Belgium*
le Brésil	*Brazil*
le Canada	*Canada*
la Chine	*China*
la Côte d'Ivoire	*Ivory Coast*
l'Espagne *(f.)*	*Spain*
les États-Unis *(m. pl.)*	*United States*
l'Europe *(f.)* de l'Est	*Eastern Europe*
l'Europe de l'Ouest	*Western Europe*
la France	*France*
l'Irlande *(f.)*	*Ireland*
l'Italie *(f.)*	*Italy*
le Japon	*Japan*
le Maroc	*Morocco*
le Mexique	*Mexico*
le Québec	*Quebec*
la Roumanie	*Romania*
la Russie	*Russia*
le Sénégal	*Senegal*
la Suisse	*Switzerland*
la Tunisie	*Tunisia*
le Viêt-Nam	*Vietnam*

LES ÉTATS DES ÉTATS-UNIS

l'Alabama *(m.)*	l'Iowa *(m.)*
l'Alaska *(m.)*	le Kansas
l'Arizona *(m.)*	le Kentucky
l'Arkansas *(m.)*	la Louisiane
la Californie	le Maine
la Caroline du Nord	le Maryland
la Caroline du Sud	le Massachusetts
le Colorado	le Michigan
le Connecticut	le Minnesota
le Dakota du Nord	le Mississippi
le Dakota du Sud	le Missouri
le Delaware	le Montana
l'état *(m.)* de New York	le Nebraska
l'état *(m.)* de Washington	le Nevada
la Floride	le New Hampshire
la Géorgie	le New Jersey
Hawaii (Hawaï)	le Nouveau-Mexique
l'Idaho *(m.)*	l'Ohio *(m.)*
l'Illinois *(m.)*	l'Oklahoma *(m.)*
l'Indiana *(m.)*	l'Oregon *(m.)*
la Pennsylvanie	
le Rhode Island	
le Tennessee	
le Texas	
l'Utah *(m.)*	
le Vermont	
la Virginie	
la Virginie Occidentale	
le Wisconsin	
le Wyoming	

LES NATIONALITÉS

les Allemand(e)s	*Germans*
les Américain(e)s	*Americans*
les Anglais(es)	*British*
les Belges	*Belgians*
les Brésiliens / Brésiliennes	*Brazilians*
les Canadiens / Canadiennes	*Canadians*
les Chinois(es)	*Chinese*
les Espagnol(e)s	*Spaniards*
les Français(es)	*French*
les Irlandais(es)	*Irish*
les Italiens / Italiennes	*Italians*
les Ivoiriens / Ivoiriennes	*of the Ivory Coast*
les Japonais(es)	*Japanese*
les Marocain(e)s	*Moroccans*
les Mexicain(e)s	*Mexicans*
les Québécois(es)	*Quebeckers*
les Roumain(e)s	*Romanians*
les Russes	*Russians*
les Sénégalais(es)	*Senegalese*
les Suisses	*Swiss*
les Tunisiens / Tunisiennes	*Tunisians*
les Vietnamiens / Vietnamiennes	*Vietnamese*

VERBES

devenir	*to become*
venir / venir de	*to come / to have just done something*

LES PRÉPOSITIONS

à	*to, in*
au(x)	*to, in*
de / du	*from*
en	*to, in*

PARTIE 2   3–12

LA FAMILLE

le beau-fils	*stepson, son-in-law*
le beau-frère	*brother-in-law, stepbrother*
le beau-père	*father-in-law, stepfather*
la belle-fille	*stepdaughter, daughter-in-law*

la belle-mère	mother-in-law, stepmother
la belle-sœur	sister-in-law, stepsister
le / la conjoint(e), partenaire	significant other, (domestic) partner
le / la cousin(e)	cousin
les enfants (m.)	children
la famille élargie	extended family
la famille proche	immediate family
la femme	wife, woman
la fille	daughter, girl
le fils	son
le frère	brother
la grand-mère	grandmother
les grands-parents (m.)	grandparents
le grand-père	grandfather
le mari	husband
la mère	mother
le neveu	nephew
la nièce	niece
l'oncle (m.)	uncle
les parents (m.)	parents, relatives
le père	father
la petite-fille	granddaughter
le petit-fils	grandson
la sœur	sister
la tante	aunt
l'animal (m.) domestique	pet
le chat	cat
le chien	dog
célibataire	single
décédé(e)	deceased
divorcé(e)	divorced
marié(e)	married
veuf / veuve	widower / widow

LES ADJECTIFS POSSESSIFS

ma/mon/mes	my
ta/ton/tes (fam. & sing.)	your
sa/son/ses	his/her/its
notre/nos	our
votre/vos (formal sing. or pl.)	your
leur/leurs	their

LES ADJECTIFS DÉMONSTRATIFS

ce (m. sing.)	this
cet (m. sing. before vowel sound)	this
cette (f. sing.)	this
ces	these, those

PARTIE 3   3–13

LES TRAITS PHYSIQUES

une barbe	beard
un(e) blond(e)	a blond
les cheveux (m.) blonds	blond hair
les cheveux bouclés / frisés	curly hair
les cheveux bruns	brown hair
les cheveux courts	short hair
les cheveux longs et raides	long straight hair
les cheveux noirs	black hair
les cheveux ondulés	wavy hair
les cheveux roux	red hair
un grand nez	a big nose
un roux / une rousse	a redhead
les yeux (m.) bleus	blue eyes
les yeux marron	brown eyes
les yeux verts	green eyes
chauve	bald
gros / grosse	fat
laid(e)	ugly
mince	slim, lean, slender
musclé(e)	muscular

LES COULEURS

blanc / blanche	white
bleu(e)	blue
gris(e)	grey
jaune	yellow
marron	brown
noir(e)	black
orange	orange
rose	pink
rouge	red
vert(e)	green
violet(te)	violet, purple

VERBES

dormir	to sleep
partir	to leave
sentir	to smell
sortir	to go out

LES ADJECTIFS

beau / bel / belle	handsome, beautiful
bon / bonne	good
grand(e)	big, tall
jeune	young
joli(e)	pretty
mauvais(e)	bad
nouveau / nouvel / nouvelle	new
petit(e)	small, short
vieux / vieil / vieille	old

La littérature dans la francophonie

Victor Hugo

Né à Besançon, Victor Hugo (1802–1885) est un poète, écrivain, dramaturge°, homme politique, académicien et intellectuel engagé français. Hugo occupe une place importante dans l'histoire des lettres françaises et est considéré comme l'un des plus° importants écrivains romantiques de la langue française. Cet écrivain est aussi un romancier° du peuple. Ses succès mondiaux° *Notre-Dame de Paris* (1831) et *Les Misérables* (1862) restent encore populaires aujourd'hui.

Adapted from: http://www.lespoetes.net/poete-91-Victor-HUGO.html

dramaturge *playwright* **l'un des plus** *one of the most* **romancier** *novelist* **mondiaux** *worldwide*

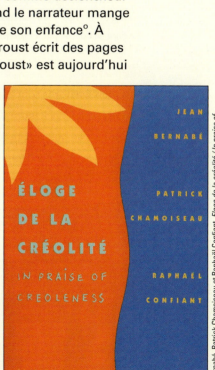

© Danny Martindale/WireImage/Getty Images

© Ginet -Drin/SoFood Collection/Photolibrary

La «madeleine de Proust»

Une madeleine est un petit gâteau° traditionnel lorrain en forme de coquillage°. Ces gâteaux sont très populaires en France en partie° parce que dans son œuvre° de sept volumes *À la recherche du temps perdu* (1913–1927), Marcel Proust utilise une madeleine comme déclencheur° de souvenirs°. Dans ce roman, quand le narrateur mange une madeleine, il revit° une scène de son enfance°. À partir de° cette simple madeleine, Proust écrit des pages et des pages… La «madeleine de Proust» est aujourd'hui une métaphore pour parler des souvenirs du passé.

petit gâteau *cookie* **coquillage** *seashell* **en partie** *in part* **œuvre** *work* **déclencheur** *trigger*
souvenirs *memories* **revit** *relives* **enfance** *childhood* **À partir de** *From*

Un mouvement littéraire et culturel: la créolité

En 1989, trois écrivains martiniquais—Jean Bernabé, Raphaël Confiant et Patrick Chamoiseau—ont publié l'*Éloge de la créolité*. Le but° de ce mouvement littéraire est de reconnaître° l'hybridité ou le métissage culturel° des Antilles, dont la population est d'origine africaine, asiatique et européenne. La créolité a eu une influence considérable dans le monde francophone. Ce mouvement constitue un reflet de la diversité ethnique, culturelle et linguistique de la Martinique et de la Guadeloupe, deux départements français d'outre-mer°.

but *purpose* **reconnaître** *recognize* **métissage culturel** *cultural cross-fertilization*
d'outre-mer *overseas*

Jean Bernabé, Patrick Chamoiseau et Raphaël Confiant, *Eloge de la créolité / In praise of Creolness* ("Hors série Littérature"). Traduit de l'anglais (Martinique) par M. B. Taleb-Khyar. © Éditions GALLIMARD

© Louis MONIER/Getty Images

Marguerite Yourcenar

D'origine belge, Marguerite Yourcenar (1903–1987) a vécu° pendant longtemps aux États-Unis. Cette écrivaine française a été poète, traductrice° et critique. Célèbre pour ses romans historiques et ses mémoires autobiographiques, Yourcenar est une des meilleures° romancières du vingtième siècle. Son roman *Mémoires d'Hadrien* a connu un succès mondial°. En 1980, elle est devenue° la première femme élue° à l'Académie française.

a vécu *lived* **traductrice** *translator* **meilleures** *best* **mondial** *worldwide* **est devenue** *became* **élue** *elected*

Ken Bugul

Née° Mariétou Biléoma Mbaye en 1947, cette romancière sénégalaise écrit sous son nom de plume°, Ken Bugul. Ironiquement, Ken Bugul signifie en wolof «personne n'en veut°». Dans *Rue Félix-Faure* (2005) et *La pièce d'or* (2006), elle critique son pays natal, le Sénégal. Elle vit° à Porto-Novo au Bénin où elle dirige° Collection d'Afrique, un centre de promotion des œuvres° culturelles et des objets d'art. Elle a obtenu le Grand Prix Littéraire d'Afrique Noire en 1999.

© Elise Fitte-Duval/Maxppp/Landov

Adapted from: http://www.lesfrancophonies.com/maison-des-auteurs/bugul-ken

Née *Born* **le nom de plume** *pen name* **personne n'en veut** *no one wants any* **vit** *lives* **dirige** *directs* **œuvres** *works*

Révision

1. Quels écrivains sont associés au mouvement de la créolité?
2. Qui écrit sous le nom Ken Bugul?
3. Qui est associé aux madeleines?
4. Qui a écrit *Notre-Dame de Paris*?
5. Qui a été *(was)* la première femme élue à l'Académie française?

▶ LIAISONS CULTURELLES

Alors, quel est votre auteur français préféré?

Use **iLrn**™ to access the video **La littérature** to learn more about the literature of the French-speaking world. Be prepared to answer the question **Alors, quel est votre auteur français préféré?** Share your responses with your classmates in **Share It!**

Les **espaces**

En bref   In this chapter, you will:

- talk about your house, furniture, and household chores

- learn the present tense of **-ir** verbs like **choisir, obéir,** and **finir**

- learn places in the city, on campus, and in the great outdoors

- learn commands to give orders and directions

- learn vocabulary for expressing the sequence of events

- learn prepositions of location and the numbers 100 and above

- learn more about question words and nasal vowels

- read about **Côte d'Ivoire** and the city of Abidjan

- write a brief description of a city

You will also re-watch **SÉQUENCE 2: La décision** of the film *Liaisons.*

Ressources

 audio   video   Share It!   iLrn™   http://www.cengagebrain.com

© Plush Studios/Vetta/Getty Images

VOCABULAIRE 1

Les espaces personnels

Personal spaces

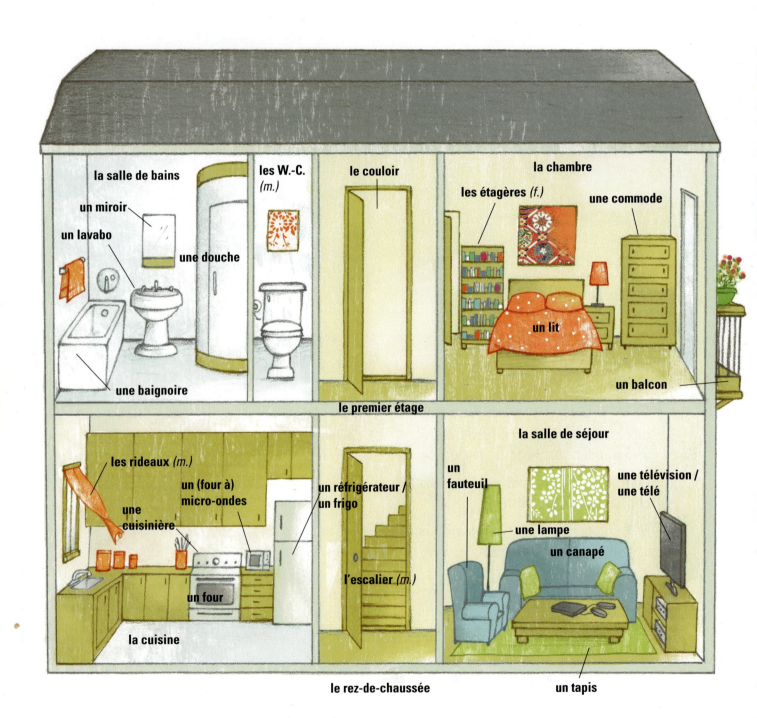

la salle de bains

un miroir

un lavabo

une douche

une baignoire

les W.-C. (m.)

le couloir

la chambre

les étagères (f.)

une commode

un lit

un balcon

le premier étage

les rideaux (m.)

un (four à) micro-ondes

une cuisinière

un four

la cuisine

un réfrigérateur / un frigo

l'escalier (m.)

la salle de séjour

un fauteuil

une lampe

un canapé

une télévision / une télé

un tapis

le rez-de-chaussée

Les pièces et les objets de la maison

Vocabulaire complémentaire

les affaires *(f.) things, stuff*

un appareil électroménager *household appliance*

un appartement *apartment*

le garage *garage*

un loyer *rent*

un meuble *piece of furniture*

une pièce *room*

un placard *closet*

la salle à manger *dining room*

le salon *formal living / sitting room*

le sous-sol *basement*

les tâches *(f.)* ménagères *chores, housekeeping tasks*

un(e) voisin(e) *neighbor*

louer *to rent*

partager *to share*

passer l'aspirateur *(m.) to vacuum*

ranger (la maison) *to pick up (the house), to put things away*

sortir la poubelle *to take out the garbage, trash*

faire la lessive *to do the laundry*

faire le ménage *to do the housework*

faire la poussière *to dust*

faire la vaisselle *to do the dishes*

équipé(e) *equipped*

propre *clean*

sale *dirty*

Note de **grammaire**
Remember that verbs ending in **-ger** like **manger**, **ranger**, and **partager** have a spelling change in the **nous** form (**nous rangeons, nous partageons**).

✈······
Si vous y allez

© Peter Horree/Alamy

Si vous allez à Paris, allez au marché aux puces *(flea market)* de Saint-Ouen pour voir de vieux objets pour la maison et de vieux meubles.

© Elizabeth Whiting & Associates/Alamy

Un mot sur la langue

Les toilettes ou les W.-C.?

En France, on a des expressions différentes pour parler de l'endroit° où on trouve la cuvette des W.-C.° On appelle cette petite pièce **les toilettes** ou les **W.-C.** *(water closet).* Il y a aussi des expressions imagées. On dit aussi **les cabinets, le nécessaire** et **le petit coin°**. Dans tous les cas°, dans les résidences, les toilettes sont généralement séparées de la salle de bains; on n'y trouve donc pas de baignoire et pas de douche!

l'endroit *place* **la cuvette des W.-C.** *toilet bowl* **coin** *corner* **cas** *cases*

• Est-ce que cette séparation des toilettes et de la salle de bains est pratique ou problématique, à votre avis *(in your opinion)*?

ACTIVITÉ A **Où se trouve-t-il?** Dans quelle(s) pièce(s) se trouve chaque
4-1 objet mentionné?

1. a. le garage	b. le salon	**5.** a. la salle de séjour	b. les W.-C.
2. a. la chambre	b. le balcon	**6.** a. la chambre	b. la salle de bains
3. a. la salle de bains	b. le couloir	**7.** a. la cuisine	b. la chambre
4. a. l'escalier	b. la chambre	**8.** a. le balcon	b. le couloir

ACTIVITÉ B **Quel objet?** Trouvez l'intrus *(the one that doesn't belong)*.

1. a. un lavabo b. une cuisinière c. un micro-ondes d. un four

2. a. des étagères b. un lit c. une baignoire d. les rideaux

3. a. une douche b. une baignoire c. un miroir d. un fauteuil

4. a. un fauteuil b. un tapis c. une cuisinière d. un canapé

5. a. un colocataire b. un voisin c. un escalier d. une meilleure amie

6. a. un appartement b. une maison c. une chambre d. les tâches ménagères

ACTIVITÉ C **Dans quelle pièce?** Où est-ce que vous aimez faire ces activités?

Modèle: parler au téléphone **J'aime parler au téléphone dans ma chambre.**

1. manger	**4.** regarder la télé	**7.** parler au téléphone
2. étudier	**5.** faire une sieste	**8.** écouter de la musique
3. lire	**6.** jouer aux jeux vidéo	**9.** naviguer sur Internet

ACTIVITÉ D **Un appartement typique d'étudiant**

Étape 1. Est-ce qu'un appartement typique d'étudiant a ces objets ou ces pièces?

Modèle: un four **Oui, il y a un four. / Non, il n'y a pas de four.**

1. un balcon	**5.** une baignoire	**9.** des étagères
2. un micro-ondes	**6.** un canapé	**10.** un miroir
3. une salle à manger	**7.** une télé	**11.** un salon
4. un frigo	**8.** une commode	**12.** un lavabo

Étape 2. Quels objets ou quelles pièces sont dans l'appartement de Claire Gagner?

Étape 3. Demandez à un(e) camarade de classe s'il/si elle a les pièces ou les objets présentés dans l'Étape 1.

Modèle: É1: **Est-ce que tu as un garage?**

É2: **Oui, j'ai un garage. / Non, je n'ai pas de garage.**

Conclusion Est-ce que l'appartement de votre camarade de classe est bien équipé?

ACTIVITÉ **E** **Qui suis-je?** Quel appareil ou objet est décrit *(described)* par chaque phrase?

1. Je suis un appareil électroménager que tu passes pour rendre propre le tapis.

2. Je suis quelque chose que tu paies *(pay)* chaque mois pour louer un logement.

3. Je suis la personne qui habite à côté de *(next to)* vous.

ACTIVITÉ **F** **Dans quelle pièce ou partie de la maison?** Dans quelle pièce ou partie de la maison fait-on chaque activité que vous allez entendre?

4-2

1.   **2.**   **3.**   **4.**   **5.**   **6.**

ACTIVITÉ **G** **Le ménage**

Étape 1. Indiquez la fréquence à laquelle *(how often)* vous faites ces activités ménagères: **tous les jours, une fois** *(one time)* **par semaine, une fois toutes les deux semaines** *(every other week),* **une fois par mois** ou **jamais.**

1. Je fais la vaisselle…

2. Je passe l'aspirateur…

3. Je fais la lessive…

4. Je fais le ménage…

5. Je sors la poubelle…

6. Je fais la poussière…

7. Je range la vaisselle…

8. Je range la lessive…

Étape 2. Montrez vos réponses à un(e) partenaire. Est-ce qu'il/elle a une maison plutôt **sale** ou bien **propre**?

ACTIVITÉ **H** **Qui fait quoi?** Indiquez qui fait normalement ces tâches ménagères chez vous.

Modèle: **Ma sœur et moi faisons la vaisselle.**

1. faire la vaisselle

2. faire la lessive

3. passer l'aspirateur

4. sortir la poubelle

5. ranger la salle de séjour

6. ranger la lessive

ACTIVITÉ I **Un(e) colocataire potentiel(le)?** Posez ces questions à un(e) camarade de classe. Décidez s'il/si elle est un(e) colocataire potentiel(le) pour vous.

1. Quel est le loyer que tu veux *(want)* payer?
2. Tu as des meubles?
3. Partager la salle de bains est facile pour toi?
4. Tu aimes mieux un appartement ou une maison?
5. Tu es poli(e) avec tes voisins?
6. Tu as des appareils électroménagers?
7. Tu fais le ménage?
8. Tu ranges tes affaires?

ACTIVITÉ J **Mon logement pour la prochaine année scolaire** Quels critères vont être **(a) non négociables, (b) préférables** et **(c) peu importants** pour vous quand vous allez chercher un logement pour l'année prochaine? Préparez trois à quatre phrases.

Modèle: Pour mon logement pour l'année prochaine, je vais préférer louer une maison avec deux amies avec un loyer de 600 dollars par mois. Comme critères, deux salles de bains vont être non négociables et trois chambres vont être préférables. On va avoir besoin d'une cuisine propre et équipée avec une cuisinière, un four et un frigo. Les meubles de la salle de séjour vont être peu importants parce que nous avons déjà un canapé et deux fauteuils très confortables.

ACTIVITÉ K **L'Hôtel Château Frontenac**

Étape 1. Dans le film *Liaisons,* Claire va visiter le Château Frontenac, un hôtel quatre étoiles *(stars)* au Québec. Faites la description **des pièces, des objets, des meubles** et **de l'état de propreté** *(cleanliness)* que vous imaginez pour chaque type de chambre.

1. une chambre standard
2. une suite

© Chris Cheadle/All Canada Photos/Canopy/Corbis

Étape 2. Cherchez le site officiel de l'Hôtel Château Frontenac sur Internet et trouvez des photos et descriptions des chambres. Comparez vos descriptions aux informations que vous trouvez sur le site. Avez-vous besoin de modifier vos réponses?

ACTIVITÉ **L** **Petite annonce** Préparez une petite annonce dans laquelle vous décrivez votre appartement ou maison, votre personnalité, vos activités et le genre *(kind)* de colocataire que vous recherchez.

Modèle: **Je suis une étudiante de 20 ans et je recherche une colocataire. J'ai un appartement de quatre pièces: deux chambres, un W.-C., une salle de bains, une cuisine équipée, une salle de séjour et une salle à manger avec meubles. Je suis calme et polie. Je suis une étudiante sérieuse. Je recherche une jeune femme célibataire. Elle a besoin de partager le ménage. Le loyer est $560 par mois avec $100 de charges.**

ACTIVITÉ **M** **Sondage: Le logement idéal** Faites un sondage pour déterminer les préférences de vos camarades de classe en matière de logement. Posez chaque question à au moins trois étudiants différents et notez leurs réponses.

Questions	É1	É2	É3
1. Quelles pièces sont essentielles?	_____	_____	_____
2. Quel est le bon nombre de colocataires?	_____	_____	_____
3. Quels appareils électroménagers sont nécessaires?	_____	_____	_____
4. Quelles tâches ménagères sont importantes?	_____	_____	_____
5. Quels meubles sont indispensables?	_____	_____	_____

© Imagehit Inc./Alamy

Un mot sur la culture

Où faire la lessive?

Si vous avez besoin de faire la lessive dans une maison française, vous allez sans doute trouver la machine à laver° et le sèche-linge° dans un endroit différent de celui où vous les trouvez dans votre maison. Aux États-Unis et au Québec, les maisons ont tendance à avoir une lingerie° au sous-sol, à côté de° la cuisine ou près des° chambres. Mais en France, les buanderies° sont assez rares dans les résidences privées. On trouve le plus souvent les appareils ménagers pour le linge° dans la salle de bains ou dans la cuisine parce que c'est dans ces deux endroits qu'on trouve la plomberie° nécessaire à leur installation. C'est aussi assez commun en France pour une famille de ne pas avoir de séchoir°. En général, les Français préfèrent faire sécher° leurs vêtements à l'extérieur (dans le jardin° ou sur le balcon) ou bien à l'intérieur dans la salle de bains.

une machine à laver *washing machine* **un sèche-linge** *clothes dryer* **une lingerie** *laundry room* **à côté de** *next to* **près de** *near* **les buanderies** *laundry rooms* **le linge** *laundry* **la plomberie** *plumbing* **séchoir** *dryer* **faire sécher** *to allow to dry* **le jardin** *yard*

• Comment préférez-vous faire sécher vos vêtements: naturellement (dans le jardin, sur un balcon ou dans la salle de bains) ou bien dans un séchoir?

Pour parler de nos maisons et de notre vie

Les verbes choisir, finir et obéir

DU FILM *LIAISONS*

Un coup d'œil sur la grammaire

Look at these photos from the film **Liaisons** and their captions. Note the verbs used to communicate the actions that are taking place.

Claire vient de **finir** son cours de psychologie.

Émile, le chat de Claire, n'**obéit** pas toujours.

What do you think these verbs mean?

1. **finir**   a. to begin   b. to obey   c. to finish
2. **obéir**   a. to finish   b. to obey   c. to choose

❖ **Choisir, finir,** and **obéir** are another class of regular -**ir** verbs that follow a set pattern of endings in the present tense.

finir *(to finish)*	choisir *(to choose)*	obéir (à) *(to obey)*
je fin**is**	je chois**is**	j'obé**is**
tu fin**is**	tu chois**is**	tu obé**is**
il/elle/on fin**it**	il/elle/on chois**it**	il/elle/on obé**it**
nous fin**issons**	nous chois**issons**	nous obé**issons**
vous fin**issez**	vous chois**issez**	vous obé**issez**
ils/elles fin**issent**	ils/elles chois**issent**	ils/elles obé**issent**

Je **finis** toujours mes devoirs avant 20h.   *I always **finish** my homework before 8 pm.*

Elle **choisit** ses cours aujourd'hui.   *She **is choosing** her classes today.*

❖ Common expressions used with the verb **obéir (à)** are: **obéir aux règles** *(to obey the rules)*, **obéir à la loi** *(to obey the law)*, and **obéir aux parents.**

Nous **obéissons** toujours à la loi.   *We always **obey** the law.*

Here are other regular **-ir** verbs that follow the same pattern: **grossir** *(to gain weight)*, **maigrir** *(to lose weight)*, **grandir** *(to grow up)*, **réussir (à)** *(to succeed at/in)*, **réfléchir (à)** *(to reflect upon, to consider)*, and **salir** *(to dirty)*.

Les êtres humains **grossissent** s'ils mangent tout le temps.
*Humans **gain weight** if they eat all the time.*

Nous **maigrissons** si nous faisons du sport.
*We **lose weight** if we exercise.*

De nos jours, les enfants **grandissent** dans une société matérialiste.
*These days, children **grow up** in a materialistic society.*

Est-ce que tu **réussis** toujours **à** tes examens?
*Do you always **pass** your exams?*

Je **réfléchis au** sujet que le professeur propose pour cette rédaction.
*I **am thinking about** the topic that the professor is proposing for this essay.*

Liaisons musicales

© Alex Anger /Visual Press Agency/Photoshot

Gage (né Pierre Gage) est un chanteur québécois de Montréal. Sa musique est influencée par Bob Marley, Stevie Wonder et Marvin Gaye. Dans sa chanson *Tu peux choisir*, il chante avec une chanteuse française qui s'appelle Vitaa (née Charlotte Gonin). Cherchez les paroles de la chanson. Qu'est-ce qu'ils essaient *(try)* de choisir avant la fin de la chanson?

Pour aller plus loin
La préposition *chez*

Chez is a preposition that means *at one's place* or *at the home of someone.*

Je finis mes devoirs **chez** Claire.	*I am finishing my homework at Claire's (house).*
Les enfants vont grandir **chez** nous.	*The children will grow up at our house / place.*
Je travaille **chez** moi.	*I'm working at home (my place).*

Essayez! Chez qui aimez-vous faire ces activités?

1. étudier   **2.** manger   **3.** regarder un film   **4.** faire la fête

---

ACTIVITÉ N **Choisir des meubles et des objets de décoration**
Choisissez les sujets appropriés.

1. _____ chois**is** des meubles pour l'appartement.   a. Je   b. Il   c. Nous

2. _____ chois**issons** un miroir pour la salle de bains.   a. Nous   b. Vous   c. Elle

3. _____ chois**is** une table pour la salle à manger.   a. Tu   b. On   c. Ils

4. _____ chois**issent** les rideaux pour les chambres.   a. Vous   b. Je   c. Elles

5. _____ chois**issez** un fauteuil pour la salle de séjour.   a. Tu   b. Vous   c. Nous

6. _____ chois**it** un tapis pour le salon.   a. On   b. Elles   c. Tu

Et vous? Aimez-vous choisir des meubles et des objets de décoration?

ACTIVITÉ O **La vie aujourd'hui** Choisissez le sujet approprié pour chaque phrase que vous allez entendre.

4-3

1. a. L'enfant   b. Les enfants   **4.** a. La fille   b. Les filles

2. a. Le garçon   b. Les garçons   **5.** a. L'étudiant   b. Les étudiants

3. a. La femme   b. Les femmes   **6.** a. Le professeur   b. Les professeurs

ACTIVITÉ P La vie des personnages de *Liaisons*

Étape 1. Complétez les phrases avec un verbe qui convient: **maigrir, finir, grossir, réfléchir, salir, obéir, grandir** ou **choisir.**

1. Claire _____ au message dans l'enveloppe mystérieuse et va au Québec.
2. Abia et Claire _____ leur journée de travail à l'hôtel à 18h.
3. Le chat de Claire _____ parce qu'il mange beaucoup.
4. Mme Gagner _____ parce qu'elle n'aime pas la cuisine de l'hôpital.
5. La femme de ménage de l'hôtel n'aime pas les clients qui _____ leur chambre.
6. Robert _____ toujours avant de parler aux clients de l'hôtel.

Étape 2. Et vous? Répondez à ces questions.

1. À quelle heure est-ce que vous finissez vos cours?
2. Est-ce que vous grossissez quand vous mangez beaucoup?
3. Est-ce que vos colocataires salissent votre appartement?
4. Est-ce que vous réfléchissez avant de parler avec vos profs?

ACTIVITÉ Q Est-ce que vous êtes un(e) bon(ne) colocataire? Posez ces questions à un(e) partenaire.

Modèle: réfléchir longtemps avant de choisir un appartement
É1: **Tu réfléchis longtemps avant de choisir un appartement?**
É2: **Oui / Non, je (ne) réfléchis (pas) longtemps avant de choisir un appartement.**

1. réfléchir avant d'inviter des amis
2. réussir à payer le loyer chaque mois
3. obéir aux règles
4. finir les tâches ménagères
5. choisir des objets de décoration de bon goût (*taste*)
6. salir les meubles et les tapis

ACTIVITÉ R Trouvez quelqu'un qui... Posez chaque question à un(e) étudiant(e) différent(e). Quand vous trouvez quelqu'un qui correspond à chaque action, notez son prénom.

Trouvez quelqu'un qui...	Prénom de l'étudiant(e)
1. **finit** toujours ses devoirs avant le cours.	_____
2. n'**obéit** pas toujours à la loi.	_____
3. **choisit** de prendre l'autobus.	_____
4. **réussit à** tous ses cours.	_____
5. **maigrit** à cause du stress.	_____
6. **grossit** pendant les vacances.	_____
7. **réfléchit** souvent **à** son avenir (*future*).	_____
8. ne **réussit** pas toujours **aux** examens.	_____

Pour aller plus loin
Il faut…

When you want to express something that you or someone else must do, use **Il faut** + *infinitive.* Context will determine the precise meaning.

Il faut ranger la chambre.

You have to pick up the bedroom. / I must pick up the bedroom. / We have got to pick up the bedroom. / It is necessary to pick up the bedroom.

Essayez! Avec quelles phrases êtes-vous d'accord? Préparez deux phrases de votre invention pour les numéros 9 et 10.

1. Il faut étudier tous les jours pour réussir à l'école.
2. Il faut toujours obéir aux règles de l'université.
3. Il faut réfléchir avant de parler en classe.
4. Il faut louer un logement près de *(near)* l'université.
5. Il faut souvent faire le ménage.
6. Il faut choisir de bons/bonnes colocataires.
7. Il ne faut pas salir les salles de cours.
8. Il ne faut pas payer son loyer en retard.
9. Il faut…
10. Il ne faut pas…

OUI, JE PEUX!

Here are two "can do statements" for you to check your progress so far. Look at each statement and rate yourself on how well you think you can perform the task. Then verify your ability with a partner. How did you do?

iLrn™

Are you looking for more practice? You can find it in **iLrn**.

1. **"I can describe my house, apartment, or room and find out what someone else's living space is like."**

   I can perform this function
   ☐ with ease
   ☐ with some difficulty
   ☐ not at all

2. **"I can say what tasks and household chore(s) I do each week and ask someone else if he/she does these chores or tasks as well."**

   I can perform this function
   ☐ with ease
   ☐ with some difficulty
   ☐ not at all

🔊 Les **espaces urbains**

Urban spaces

une banque

une boutique / un magasin

le bureau de poste

le cinéma

une église

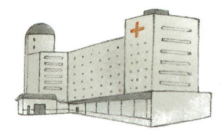

un hôpital

un institut de beauté

un kiosque à journaux

une librairie

un musée

une laverie automatique

une piscine municipale

Les endroits en ville

Vocabulaire complémentaire

un amphithéâtre *lecture hall*
une banlieue *suburbs*
un bâtiment *building*
un centre commercial *shopping center / district*
un centre sportif *recreation center*
le centre-ville *downtown*
un endroit *location, place*
un laboratoire *laboratory*
un lycée *high school*
un parking *parking lot*

un plan *map (of a city)*
un quartier (résidentiel) *(residential) neighborhood*
une résidence universitaire *residence hall*
un restaurant universitaire *campus cafeteria*
une rue *street*
un stade *stadium*
une ville *a city, a town*

Note de **vocabulaire**
You learned previously that **les W.-C.** is used in the home for *bathroom*. In public settings, **les W.-C. (publics)** or **les toilettes (publiques)** is used for *restrooms*.

Les prépositions

à côté (de)	*next (to)*	en face (de)	*across (from)*
au coin (de)	*on the corner (of)*	entre	*between*
à droite (de)	*to/on the right (of)*	loin (de)	*far (from)*
à gauche (de)	*to/on the left (of)*	près (de)	*near*
derrière	*behind*	tout droit	*straight ahead*
devant	*in front (of)*		

- Recall that **de** contracts with **le** and **les**: **de** + **le** = **du**; **de** + **les** = **des**. There is no contraction with **la** and **l'**: **de la, de l'**.

La librairie est **en face du** stade.	*The bookstore is **across from the** stadium.*
Le stade est **loin des** W.-C. publics.	*The stadium is **far from the** public restrooms.*
Le musée est **près de la** piscine.	*The museum is **near the** pool.*
Le lycée est **à côté de l'**église.	*The high school is **next to the** church.*

Un mot sur la langue

Une laverie automatique ou un Lavomatique?

En France, on a tendance à appeler certains objets populaires d'usage courant par le nom de la marque° qui les fabrique° au lieu d°'utiliser le mot de vocabulaire qui leur correspond. C'est ce qu'on appelle des noms de marque générique°. Le terme **un Lavomatique**, par exemple, est souvent utilisé pour désigner une laverie automatique. **Lavomatique** est en fait le nom d'une société° de laveries automatiques française. Les noms de marque générique commencent toujours par une majuscule°. On fait la même chose en anglais, par exemple, on dit *Coke* pour *soda*.

marque *brand* **fabrique** *makes, manufactures* **au lieu d'** *instead of* **générique** *generic* **une société** *company* **majuscule** *capital letter*

- Connaissez-vous ces exemples: **un Kleenex, du Vicks, du Nutella, une Barbie, un Bic, un Frigidaire, un Jacuzzi, une Jeep, un Stetson, un Tupperware, une Vespa** et **un Zippo**?

ACTIVITÉ A Notre campus

4-4

Étape 1. Comment s'appellent ces bâtiments sur votre campus?

Modèle: un laboratoire **McQuigg Hall**

1. 2. 3. 4. 5. 6. 7. 8. 9. 10. 11.

Étape 2. Les cours de psychologie de Claire Gagner sont dans le Pavillon Stewart sur le campus de McGill University. Dans quels bâtiments sont vos cours?

ACTIVITÉ B La ville et le campus

Étape 1. Quel nom associez-vous à chaque lieu?

Modèle: un musée   **le Louvre**

1. un musée
2. une église
3. un café

4. un lycée
5. une pharmacie
6. un centre commercial

7. un hôpital
8. un cinéma
9. un institut de beauté

 Étape 2. Demandez à un(e) partenaire si on trouve ces endroits dans son quartier. Décidez s'il/si elle habite dans un quartier intéressant.

Modèle: É1: **Est-ce qu'il y a un musée dans ton quartier?**
É2: **Oui, il y a un musée dans mon quartier: le Columbus Art Museum. /**
Non, il n'y a pas de musée dans mon quartier.

 ACTIVITÉ C Où faut-il aller? Vous allez entendre des débuts de phrase. Où

4-5 est-ce qu'on fait chaque activité?

1. 2. 3. 4. 5. 6. 7. 8. 9. 10.

ACTIVITÉ D Quel bâtiment? Choisissez cinq bâtiments sur votre campus et complétez les phrases. Ensuite, échangez vos phrases avec un(e) partenaire et devinez *(guess)* de quels bâtiments votre partenaire parle.

Modèle: É1: **Ce bâtiment se trouve derrière le stade.**
É2: **C'est le *French Field House.***

1. Ce bâtiment se trouve **en face de** _____ et **à côté de** _____.
2. Ce bâtiment se trouve **devant** _____ et **entre** _____ et _____.
3. Ce bâtiment se trouve **près de** _____ et **à gauche de** _____.
4. Ce bâtiment se trouve **derrière** _____ et **à droite de** _____.
5. Ce bâtiment est **au coin de** _____. Il est **loin de** _____.

Si vous y allez

© Erwan Le Prunnec/
Iconotec/Glow Images

Si vous allez à Plombières-les-Bains en Lorraine (France), allez aux Thermes Napoléon—un institut de beauté et des bains publics romains.

ACTIVITÉ **E** **Énigmes** Identifiez ces mots de vocabulaire.

1. C'est un établissement d'enseignement du second degré.
2. C'est un endroit où on achète (buys) des médicaments (medications).
3. C'est un commerce où on vend (sells) des marchandises.
4. C'est un établissement où on trouve des lettres et des paquets.
5. C'est une partie d'une ville avec certaines caractéristiques ou une certaine unité.
6. C'est la représentation graphique d'une ville, d'une banlieue, d'une région.
7. C'est un endroit où les spectateurs regardent du sport.

 ACTIVITÉ **F** **Quel endroit?** Où aimez-vous faire ces activités? Notez vos réponses. Puis, demandez à votre partenaire où il/elle aime faire ces activités. Qu'est-ce que vous allez peut-être faire ensemble?

Modèle: prendre le déjeuner
　　　　É1: **Où est-ce que tu aimes prendre le déjeuner?**
　　　　É2: **J'aime prendre le déjeuner au restaurant universitaire.**

	Moi	Mon/Ma partenaire
1. étudier?	_____	_____
2. faire la lessive?	_____	_____
3. voir (see) un film?	_____	_____
4. dîner?	_____	_____
5. faire du sport?	_____	_____
6. aller le week-end?	_____	_____

Un mot sur la culture

Les arrondissements de Paris

Paris est la capitale de la France mais c'est aussi une métropole°. C'est-à-dire que c'est une grande ville qui comprend° de nombreux quartiers et des banlieues. La ville de Paris est divisée en vingt arrondissements° et compte au moins quinze quartiers distincts et différents. Certains quartiers couvrent deux ou trois arrondissements. On dit souvent que chaque quartier parisien a son propre° caractère ou sa propre personnalité.

métropole metropolis **comprend** includes **arrondissements** districts, sections **propre** own

• Y a-t-il des arrondissements ou quartiers différents dans votre ville?

Pour donner des ordres et des indications

L'impératif

DU FILM *LIAISONS*

Un coup d'œil sur la grammaire

Look at these photos from the film *Liaisons* and their captions, paying special attention to the words used to express orders.

MICHEL Va à Québec.

CLAIRE Et n'**oublie** pas que mon oncle a téléphoné ce matin…

What do you think these expressions mean?

1. **Va** à Québec. 2. N'**oublie** pas.

❖ The imperative (**l'impératif**) is used to make suggestions and to give commands. For regular verbs and most irregular verbs, the imperative forms are identical to the present tense forms. To form the **tu** form of -**er** verbs and **aller,** however, you drop the final -**s** from the present tense form. You do not use subject pronouns with the imperative.

❖ The verbs **avoir** and **être** have irregular command forms.

	-er *verbs*	-ir *verbs*	aller	avoir	être
(tu)	mange	finis	va	aie	sois
(nous)	mangeons	finissons	allons	ayons	soyons
(vous)	mangez	finissez	allez	ayez	soyez
	faire	**partir**	**sortir**	**lire**	**dire**
(tu)	**fais**	pars	sors	lis	dis
(nous)	**faisons**	partons	sortons	lisons	disons
(vous)	**faites**	partez	sortez	lisez	**dites**

Note de grammaire
In spoken French, the **nous** form of commands is less common than **tu** and **vous** commands. The pronoun **on** + the present tense is often used in a question instead of the **nous** command: **On va au restaurant ce soir?** *Let's go to the restaurant tonight.*

Parlez français!	***Speak*** *French!*
Écoutons le professeur.	***Let's listen*** *to the professor.*
Allez à la bibliothèque pour étudier.	***Go*** *to the library to study.*
Fais le ménage, s'il te plaît.	***Do*** *the housework, please.*

In negative commands, put **ne... pas** around the verb.

N'aie pas peur.   *Don't be afraid.*

Ne parlons pas de politique, s'il vous plaît.   *Let's not talk about politics, please.*

Use the imperative to give directions (**des indications**) in French. Here are some common expressions that you will hear and can use.

tourner à droite / à gauche	*to turn right / left*
traverser la rue / la place	*to cross the street / town square*
aller / continuer tout droit	*to go / to continue straight ahead*
aller / continuer jusqu'à	*to go / to continue until*
aller jusqu'au bout	*to go to the end*
aller vers	*to go towards*
Tourne à droite après le stade.	***Turn right*** *after the stadium.*
Traversons la rue ensemble.	***Let's cross the street*** *together.*

Liaisons musicales

© RA/Lebrecht Music & Arts

Ne me quitte pas (1959) est une chanson très connue en France et dans tout le monde francophone. Jacques Brel, un chanteur belge, est l'auteur et l'interprète de cette chanson. Les chansons de Brel ont souvent un message socio-politique. Cherchez les paroles de cette chanson sur Internet.

Pour aller plus loin
L'ordre des événements

The following expressions are useful in sequencing series of events or activities.

d'abord	*first*	**plus tard**	*later*
puis / ensuite	*then, next*	**enfin**	*finally*

Essayez! Voici une recette *(recipe)* pour un plat *(dish)* québécois très populaire, la poutine. Mettez *(Put)* les instructions dans le bon ordre.

_____ **Ensuite,** mettez le fromage et la sauce sur les frites.

_____ **Enfin,** dévorez le plat!

_____ **Puis,** faites cuire *(cook)* les frites et réchauffer *(heat up)* la sauce.

_____ **D'abord,** achetez des frites, du fromage en grains et de la sauce.

ACTIVITÉ G **À Québec** D'abord, trouvez ces endroits sur le plan de la ville de Québec. Ensuite, vous allez entendre une série de phrases sur ces endroits. Est-ce que les phrases sont vraies ou fausses?

4-6

1. _____ le Château Frontenac

2. _____ le Parc des Gouverneurs

3. _____ la Place de l'Hôtel-de-Ville

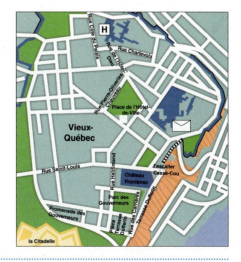

ACTIVITÉ H Dans le cours de français Vous allez entendre une série
4-7 d'ordres. À qui chaque ordre est-il destiné (intended): a) un étudiant ou b) tous les
étudiants?

1.   2.   3.   4.   5.   6.

ACTIVITÉ I À qui parle-t-on? Qu'est-ce que vous diriez (would say) à
chaque personne? Quelle suggestion est la meilleure (best) à votre avis?

1. au professeur de français
   a. Ne **donne** pas de devoirs.
   b. Ne **donnons** pas de devoirs.
   c. Ne **donnez** pas de devoirs.

2. à votre meilleur(e) ami(e)
   a. **Réfléchis** avant de parler.
   b. **Réfléchissons** avant de parler.
   c. **Réfléchissez** avant de parler.

3. à votre colocataire
   a. **Sois** sérieux. On a besoin
      d'étudier.
   b. **Soyons** sérieux. On a besoin
      d'étudier.
   c. **Soyez** sérieux. On a besoin d'étudier.

4. à vous et vos amis
   a. Ne **sors** pas après minuit.
   b. Ne **sortons** pas après minuit.
   c. Ne **sortez** pas après minuit.

5. à vos camarades de classe
   a. **Étudie** tous les jours.
   b. **Étudions** tous les jours.
   c. **Étudiez** tous les jours.

6. à vous et vos camarades de classe
   a. **Fais** les devoirs ensemble au café.
   b. **Faisons** les devoirs ensemble
      au café.
   c. **Faites** les devoirs ensemble
      au café.

ACTIVITÉ J Des ordres ou des conseils à suivre Quels ordres ou
conseils est-ce qu'il faut suivre (follow) dans ces différents endroits? Suivez-vous
normalement chaque ordre ou conseil?

Modèle: **À la bibliothèque, ne parle pas avec ton voisin.**
À la bibliothèque, fais attention aux livres.

Possibilités					
aller	recopier (to copy)	demander	être	manger	oublier
avoir	critiquer	écrire	lire	obéir	parler

1. Dans la salle informatique, _____ près des ordinateurs.

2. Dans le parking, _____ tes clés (keys) de voiture.

3. Dans la salle de cours, _____ les devoirs de tes camarades de classe.

4. Dans un restaurant, _____ attentivement la carte (menu).

5. À l'église, _____ respectueux.

6. Dans un cinéma, _____ avec tes voisins pendant le film.

7. Dans le bureau d'un professeur, _____ les autres étudiants de la classe.

8. Dans la queue (check-out line) de la librairie universitaire, _____ de la patience.

ACTIVITÉ K Qu'est-ce qu'il faut faire?

Étape 1. Dites à un(e) ami(e) les activités qu'il faut faire dans chaque ville.

Modèle: à Pittsburgh, PA

Visite le Heinz History Center, va à un match de hockey de l'équipe des Pittsburgh Penguins et mange un sandwich au restaurant Primanti Brothers.

1. à New York, NY
2. à Washington D.C.
3. à La Nouvelle-Orléans, LA
4. à Chicago, IL
5. à Seattle, WA
6. à Las Vegas, NV
7. à Los Angeles, CA
8. à Miami, FL
9. à ???

Étape 2. Et chez vous? Préparez une liste de trois choses *(things)* qu'il faut faire et une liste de trois choses qu'il ne faut pas faire dans votre ville ou sur votre campus. Ensuite, partagez vos listes avec un(e) partenaire. Avez-vous les mêmes idées?

ACTIVITÉ L **Suggestions** Faites des suggestions aux différents camarades de classe. Parlez avec plusieurs *(several)* étudiants. Quelles suggestions est-ce que vous allez essayer *(try)*?

Modèle: É1: **Je ne sais pas toujours quoi faire le vendredi soir.**
É2: **Va à un restaurant Applebee's avec tes amis.**

1. Je ne sais pas où faire du sport.
2. Je grossis.
3. Je maigris.
4. Je ne sais pas quoi faire dans le quartier.
5. J'ai besoin d'une coupe de cheveux *(haircut)*.
6. Je ne réussis pas à mon cours de français.
7. Je ne sais pas où louer un appartement.
8. Mon colocataire ne range pas ses affaires.

ACTIVITÉ M **Erreurs à éviter** Quelles sont les erreurs à éviter dans ces différents endroits, à votre avis *(in your opinion)*?

Modèle: à la banque   **Ne soyez pas impatient(e)!**

1. au centre-ville
2. dans le cours de français
3. dans un hôpital
4. chez vous
5. dans la rue
6. dans un amphithéâtre
7. au restaurant universitaire
8. dans un parking
9. dans un stade
10. dans une résidence universitaire

ACTIVITÉ N **Boîte à commentaires** Préparez quatre suggestions d'activités pour votre cours de français.

Modèle: **Allons dans un restaurant français.**

ACTIVITÉ O **Le plan du campus de l'Université Laval**

Étape 1. À l'aide du *(With the help of the)* plan du campus de l'Université Laval (Québec), trouvez la destination pour chaque série d'indications suivantes.

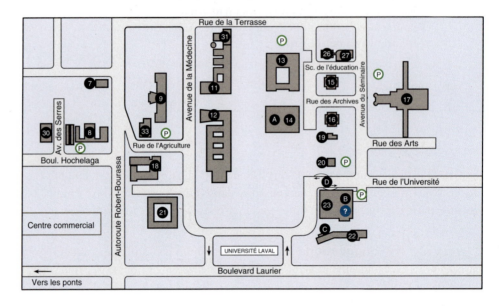

Pavillons

7 Maison Omer-Gingras	19 Maison Eugène Roberge
8 Pavillon des Services	20 Maison Marie-Sirois
9 Pavillon Ferdinand-Vandry	21 Pavillon Agathe-Laserte
11 Pavillon Alexandre-Vachon	22 Pavillon Ernest-Lemieux
12 Pavillon Adrien-Pouliot	23 Pavillon Alphonse-Desjardins
13 Pavillon Charles-de-Korinck	26 Pavillon J.-A.-De Sève
14 Pavillon Jean-Charles-Bonenfant	27 Pavillon La Laurentienne
15 Pavillon des Sciences de l'éducation	30 Pavillon de l'Envirotron
16 Pavillon Félix-Antoine-Savard	31 Pavillon d'Optique Photonique
17 Pavillon Louis-Jacques-Casault	33 Édifice logeant Héma Québec
18 Pavillon Paul-Comtois	

Services

A Bibliothèque	D Arrêt Métrobus
B Caisse populaire Desjardins	P Parking
C Sécurité	? Information

1. Quittez *(Leave)* le parking par la rue de l'Agriculture. Tournez à droite et puis suivez la rue de l'Agriculture jusqu'au bout. Ensuite, traversez l'autoroute Robert-Bourassa et c'est le bâtiment juste en face.

2. Quittez la bibliothèque. D'abord, tournez à droite dans la rue des Archives. Suivez la rue des Archives et passez le Pavillon Félix-Antoine-Savard. Ensuite, au coin, tournez à gauche sur l'avenue du Séminaire et enfin, allez jusqu'au premier bâtiment à gauche.

Étape 2. Choisissez une destination sur ce campus et écrivez des indications pour arriver à cette destination. Vous quittez l'arrêt Métrobus.

Étape 3. Lisez vos indications à un(e) partenaire. Il/Elle va deviner (*guess*) la destination.

ACTIVITÉ P Donnez des indications Choisissez un lieu sur le campus ou en ville et écrivez une série d'indications. Ensuite, échangez vos indications avec un(e) partenaire et essayez de deviner le lieu de votre partenaire.

Modèle: D'abord, quitte la bibliothèque. Ensuite, tourne à droite et va jusqu'au parking. Puis, tourne à gauche et continue tout droit. C'est à côté du restaurant universitaire, à gauche. On arrive où?

ACTIVITÉ Q Quelques projets pour le professeur Avec un(e) partenaire, suggérez quatre projets pour votre professeur ce week-end.

Modèle: D'abord, cherchez un bon livre à la bibliothèque. Puis, allez au café pour lire.

1. D'abord, _____.
2. Puis, _____.
3. Ensuite, _____.
4. Enfin, _____.

OUI, JE PEUX! Here are two "can do statements" for you to check your progress so far. Look at each statement and rate yourself on how well you think you can perform the task. Then verify your ability with a partner. How did you do?

1. "I can say what buildings and facilities are in my neighborhood and I can give directions to one of them."

   I can perform this function
   ☐ with ease
   ☐ with some difficulty
   ☐ not at all

2. "I can ask someone else if he/she has certain facilities in his/her neighborhood to determine whose neighborhood has more resources."

   I can perform this function
   ☐ with ease
   ☐ with some difficulty
   ☐ not at all

iLrn™

Are you looking for more practice? You can find it in **iLrn**.

Les **espaces verts**

Green spaces

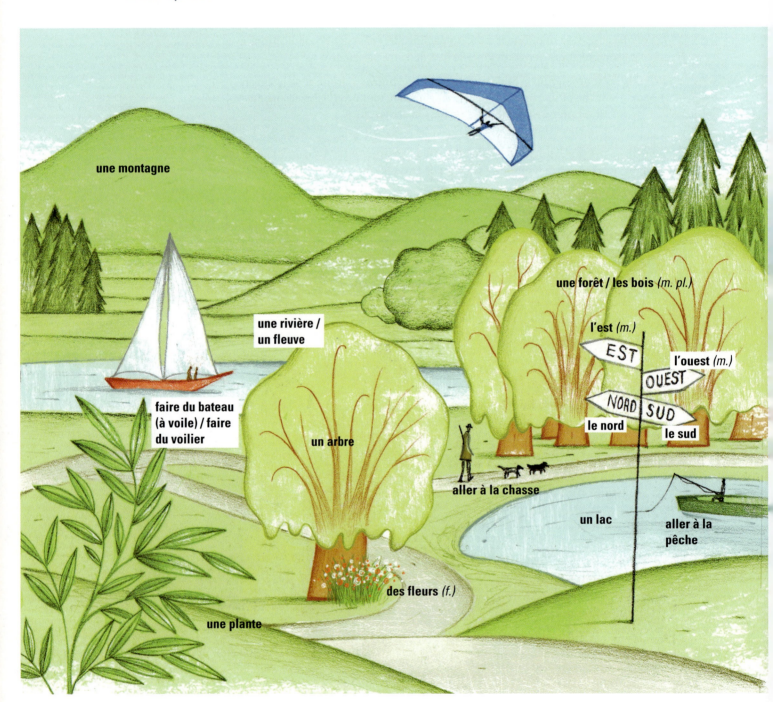

une montagne

une forêt / les bois (m. pl.)

une rivière /
un fleuve

l'est (m.)

EST

l'ouest (m.)

OUEST

NORD SUD

le nord

le sud

faire du bateau
(à voile) / faire
du voilier

un arbre

aller à la chasse

un lac

aller à la
pêche

des fleurs (f.)

une plante

Un après-midi à la campagne

Vocabulaire complémentaire

la campagne *the country(side)*
une ferme *farm*
un jardin *garden, lawn*

la mer *the sea*
la plage *the beach*

faire de la randonnée *to go hiking*

Les numéros plus grands que 100

100	**cent**	1 100	**mille cent**
105	**cent cinq**	1 300	**mille trois cents**
135	**cent trente-cinq**	1 550	**mille cinq cent cinquante**
200	**deux cents**	1 999	**mille neuf cent quatre-vingt-dix-neuf**
250	**deux cent cinquante**	2 000	**deux mille**
300	**trois cents**	2 780	**deux mille sept cent quatre-vingts**
375	**trois cent soixante-quinze**	1 000 000	**un million**
400	**quatre cents**	1 500 000	**un million cinq cent mille**
500	**cinq cents**	2 000 000	**deux millions**
600	**six cents**	2 555 000	**deux millions cinq cent cinquante-cinq mille**
700	**sept cents**	1 000 000 000	**un milliard**
800	**huit cents**	2 000 000 000	**deux milliards**
900	**neuf cents**		
1000	**mille**		

- **Cent** and **vingt** take an **s** if preceded by a number greater than one, but do not take an **s** if another number follows. **Cent** is never preceded by **un** to mean *one/a hundred*.

  deux cents   **cinq cents**   **sept cent trente**
  quatre-vingts   **quatre-vingt-un**

- **Mille** never takes an **s** and is never preceded by **un** to mean *one/a thousand*.

  mille étoiles   **mille huit cents personnes**   **quatre mille personnes**

- The number **un** is used before **million** to express *one/a million*. **Million(s)** is followed by **de/d'** before a noun.

  un million de personnes   **trois millions de fleurs**   **dix millions d'arbres**

- In French, commas are used to denote decimals, and periods or a space are used after thousands, millions, etc. Read a comma as **virgule** and a period as **point.**

  12,98 euros   Il y a **10 000 (10.000)** étudiants sur le campus.

🔊 4-8 **ACTIVITÉ A Qu'est-ce que c'est?** Associez chaque élément de la nature que vous allez entendre à son site naturel.

1. a. le Grand Canyon   b. le mont Everest
2. a. le Mississippi   b. la vallée de la Mort *(Death Valley)*
3. a. Sherwood   b. les chutes du Niagara
4. a. l'Hudson   b. l'Érié
5. a. le Rio Grande   b. la Méditerranée
6. a. Daytona   b. les Rocheuses *(the Rockies)*

🔊 4-9 **ACTIVITÉ B Où va-t-on?** Où est-ce qu'on fait chaque activité que vous allez entendre?

1. a. dans un arbre   b. sur un lac   3. a. dans une ferme   b. sur une rivière
2. a. à la montagne   b. à la mer   4. a. dans les bois   b. au soleil

🔊 4-10 **ACTIVITÉ C Nombre de visiteurs approximatif** Vous allez entendre des phrases sur le nombre de visiteurs de sites touristiques en France. Choisissez le nombre correct.

1. la région naturelle de la Camargue (par mois)   a. 245 000   b. 1 245 000
2. le lac de Gérardmer (par an)   a. 2 000   b. 200 000
3. les jardins du château de Versailles (par an)   a. 1 000 000   b. 10 000 000
4. la vallée de la Loire (par an)   a. 400 000   b. 4 000 000

🔊 4-11 **ACTIVITÉ D Moments historiques**

Note de grammaire
You will learn how to say historical dates and years in **Chapitre 8**.

Étape 1. Choisissez la date historique que vous entendez.

1. a. 1799   b. 1789   5. a. 1066   b. 1166
2. a. 1944   b. 1844   6. a. 1271   b. 1211
3. a. 1929   b. 1829   7. a. 1940   b. 1914
4. a. 1669   b. 1609   8. a. 1777   b. 1767

Étape 2. Associez les six dates appropriées de l'Étape 1 aux événements historiques suivants.

1. _____ Les premières batailles de la Première Guerre mondiale *(WWI)* commencent dans les montagnes d'Alsace.
2. _____ René de La Salle, explorateur-voyageur français, explore le fleuve Mississippi.
3. _____ Les forces alliées attaquent les plages de Normandie.
4. _____ La fleur de lys devient le symbole de la noblesse *(nobility)* française.
5. _____ La conquête de la campagne anglaise par Guillaume, duc de Normandie.
6. _____ Le Marquis de Lafayette traverse la mer atlantique pour soutenir *(support)* les rebelles américains et leur révolution.

Étape 3. Écrivez les dates de l'Étape 2 en toutes lettres.

Modèle: (496) **quatre cent quatre-vingt-seize**

ACTIVITÉ E Et si Abia… ? Abia apprécie beaucoup les espaces verts. Complétez chaque phrase avec le mot de vocabulaire qui convient.

1. Et si Abia désire dire: «Je suis désolée» à quelqu'un, elle envoie *(sends)* _____.

2. Et si Abia a un(e) ami(e) avec une nouvelle maison, elle offre souvent _____.

3. Et si Abia fête *(celebrates)* le Jour de la Terre *(Earth)*, elle plante souvent _____.

4. Et si Abia a envie de trouver des fruits bien frais *(fresh)*, elle va dans _____.

5. Et si Abia désire aller à la pêche, elle passe beaucoup de temps sur _____.

6. Et si Abia fait du jardinage, elle passe du temps dans _____.

Et vous? Est-ce que vous aimez mieux *(better)* les espaces verts ou la ville?

ACTIVITÉ F Les activités et les espaces verts Dans quel espace vert est-ce qu'on fait normalement ces activités?

Modèle: faire un pique-nique

On fait un pique-nique à la campagne.

1. aller à la chasse
2. faire du bateau à voile
3. faire de la randonnée
4. aller à la pêche

ACTIVITÉ G Dans quelle partie des États-Unis? Complétez chaque phrase avec deux ou trois activités populaires dans la région.

Modèle Dans le nord des États-Unis en été, on **va à la chasse.**

1. Dans le nord des États-Unis au printemps, on…

2. Dans le nord-est des États-Unis en automne, on…

3. Dans l'ouest des États-Unis en été, on…

4. Dans le sud des États-Unis en hiver, on…

5. Dans le Midwest des États-Unis en hiver, on…

6. Dans le sud-ouest des États-Unis en été, on…

Et vous? Vous êtes de quelle région? Quelles activités faites-vous en été et en hiver dans cette région?

Si vous y allez

Si vous allez dans les Hautes-Vosges—la chaîne de montagnes en Lorraine et en Alsace (France)— allez à la ferme-auberge du Kastelberg pour goûter *(taste)* la cuisine fermière traditionnelle de la région.

ACTIVITÉ **H** **Qu'est-ce que c'est?**

Étape 1. Avec un(e) partenaire, décrivez chaque site naturel suivant en une phrase.

Modèle: Le Rio Grande est un fleuve entre le Mexique et les États-Unis.

1. le lac Huron
2. les Alpes
3. la Seine
4. la jungle amazonienne
5. la Méditerranée

6. Venice (en Californie)
7. le Saint-Laurent
8. le Mississippi
9. le lac Supérieur

Étape 2. Toujours avec votre partenaire, préparez une liste de tous les sites naturels dans votre région qui valent le détour *(worth the trip)*.

 ACTIVITÉ **I** **Un hôtel de rêves**

Étape 1. Préparez une description de quatre ou cinq phrases dans laquelle vous décrivez le bel hôtel *(resort)* et le forfait-vacances *(vacation package)* de vos rêves *(dreams)*. N'oubliez pas de mentionner en détail: le lieu *(setting)*, les activités et le prix *(price)*!

Modèle: **Pour l'hôtel et le forfait-vacances de mes rêves, je suis à la plage. Ma chambre d'hôtel est face à l'océan et il y a des fleurs et des plantes aux belles couleurs partout. Il y a beaucoup d'activités possibles: faire du bateau à voile, faire une promenade sur la plage la nuit et faire de la randonnée dans les montagnes toutes proches. Il y a un spa et des cocktails exceptionnels. Le prix est mille trois cents dollars par personne.**

 Étape 2. Montrez vos descriptions à un(e) partenaire. Désirez-vous aller à l'hôtel de votre partenaire? Quel bel hôtel est-ce que votre prof va préférer?

Un mot sur la culture

Sépaq du Québec

On dit souvent des Canadiens en général, et des Québécois en particulier, qu'ils sont de grands amateurs de la nature et des espaces verts. En fait, on appelle le Québec «la Belle Province» à cause de sa beauté naturelle. Au Québec, il existe la Société des établissements de plein air du Québec (Sépaq) qui a pour mission la conservation des espaces verts canadiens et la protection de ses territoires naturels pour en assurer le bénéfice° aux Québécois, générations futures y comprises, et aux touristes qui visitent «la Belle Province».

le bénéfice *the benefit*

Courtesy of Wynne Wong

• Est-ce que les espaces verts sont un sujet sérieux chez vous?

Liaisons avec les mots et les sons

4-12

Les voyelles nasales

You were introduced to nasal vowels in **Chapitre 3.** Nasal vowels usually end in **m** or **n** in a single syllable. There are three basic nasal vowel sounds in French as illustrated by these words.

vin	**vent**	**vont**	**bain**	**banc**	**bon**

Nasal vowel sounds may have different spellings. The sound **bon** may be spelled **on** or **om.**

bl**on**d	mais**on**	sal**on**	micro-**on**des	b**om**be

The nasal sound in **fin** may be spelled **ien, ain, aim, in,** or **im.**

b**ien**	**in**vitation	f**aim**	**im**portant	mexic**ain**

The nasal sound in **an** may be spelled **an, am, en,** or **em.**

qu**an**d	b**an**que	restaur**an**t	comm**en**t	t**em**ps

Pratique A. Écoutez et répétez ces mots.

1. la chambre
2. la salle de bains
3. une lampe
4. les plantes
5. un voisin
6. l'arrondissement
7. la banlieue
8. un amphithéâtre
9. un jardin
10. un centre sportif
11. au coin de
12. devant

Pratique B. Écoutez et répétez ces répliques de la Séquence 2 du film *Liaisons.* Ensuite, relisez et écoutez les répliques. Encerclez toutes les voyelles nasales.

CLAIRE Oui. Je m'appelle Claire Gagner. Vous avez une réservation à mon nom?... Cette fin de semaine... Oui, samedi et dimanche... Ah, bon. Qui a fait la réservation, s'il vous plaît?... OK. Merci.

 À vos stylos! C'est l'heure de la dictée!

4-13 Vous allez entendre trois phrases deux fois. La première fois, écoutez bien. La deuxième fois, écrivez les phrases.

 Sujet Citations célèbres

Pour poser des questions

Les mots d'interrogation

DU FILM LIAISONS

Un coup d'œil sur la grammaire

Look at this photo from the film *Liaisons* and its caption, paying special attention to the question words.

CLAIRE Qui ferait *(would make)* une réservation pour moi? Et pourquoi?

What two question words do you recognize?

❖ The following words are commonly used in French to ask questions (**poser des questions**) aimed at obtaining specific information. These question words may be used with **est-ce que** or with inversion.

où *where*	**combien de** *how many, how much*
quand *when*	**comment** *how*
que / qu' *what*	**pourquoi** *why*
qui *who(m)*	**quel(le)(s)** *which*

Combien de vélos est-ce que vous avez? *How many bikes do you have?*

Que faites-vous ici? *What are you doing here?*

❖ When **qui** is the subject of a question, it is immediately followed by a singular verb. When **qui** is the direct object, it may be used with **est-ce que** or inversion.

Qui va à la campagne? *Who is going to the countryside?*

Qui est-ce que tu regardes? *Whom are you looking at?*

Qui aimez-vous? *Who do you like?*

❖ **Qui** may also be the object of prepositions like **à, avec, de,** and **pour.** In these cases, **qui** is equivalent to the English *whom.*

Avec qui est-ce que tu parles? *With whom are you speaking?*

De qui parlez-vous? *About whom are you speaking?*

❖ Informational question words (except **que**) may also be used alone.

—J'ai envie d'aller au lac.	—*I feel like going to the lake.*
—**Quand?**	—***When?***
—J'ai envie d'aller quelque part.	—*I feel like going somewhere.*
—**Où?**	—***Where?***

❖ Both **quand** and **à quelle heure** can mean *when*. Use **quand** to inquire about a day, date, season, or year. Use **à quelle heure** to inquire about a particular time or hour of day.

—**Quand** allez-vous faire du ski cette année?	—***When*** *are you going skiing this year?*
—Nous allons faire du ski en février.	—*We're going skiing in February.*
—**À quelle heure** est-ce que nous partons?	—***At what time*** *are we leaving?*
—À dix heures du matin.	—*At ten o'clock in the morning.*

❖ You answer questions asked with **pourquoi** with **parce que/qu'**.

—Je vais téléphoner à ma mère.	—*I am going to call my mother.*
—**Pourquoi?**	—***Why?***
—**Parce que** c'est son anniversaire.	—***Because*** *it's her birthday.*

❖ You have already seen and used **quel/quelle/quels/quelles** in previous chapters. It is an adjective that agrees in number and gender with the noun it modifies. It can also appear in front of the verb **être**.

Quel âge as-tu?	*How old are you?*
Quelle est ta spécialisation?	*What is your major?*
Quels sont tes cours favoris?	*What are your favorite courses?*
Quelles sont les bonnes plages?	*Which are the good beaches?*

Pour aller plus loin
Quoi?!

To ask *What?* in French, you have a few options: **Quoi?**, **Comment?**, or **Pardon?** It is acceptable to use **Quoi?** with family and friends, but it is considered impolite in more formal contexts. In those instances, you want to use **Comment?** or **Pardon?**

Essayez! Dites-vous **Quoi?**, **Comment?** ou **Pardon?** dans ces situations?

1. Ton/Ta colocataire te demande *(asks you)* si tu as un stylo.
2. Ton professeur te pose une question.

🔊
4-14

ACTIVITÉ J Comment répond-on? Vous allez entendre une série de questions. Choisissez la réponse logique.

1. a. Je sors avec mon frère et ma sœur.　　b. J'ai un frère et une sœur.
2. a. Parce que j'adore la langue.　　b. Avec mes collègues français.
3. a. Je travaille dans mon bureau.　　b. Je travaille huit heures par jour.
4. a. Mon cours est dans le laboratoire.　　b. Mon professeur est Mme Simard.
5. a. J'arrive sur le campus en voiture.　　b. J'arrive sur le campus vers 7h30 du matin.
6. a. Parce que j'adore sortir le soir.　　b. Je vais souvent au cinéma.

ACTIVITÉ K Questions-Réponses Faites correspondre les questions et leurs réponses.

1. _____ Quand parlez-vous au téléphone?　　a. Avec ma famille.
2. _____ Combien d'heures travaillez-vous par jour?　　b. Avec mes camarades du cours de français.
3. _____ Avec qui sortez-vous?　　c. Huit heures par jour.
4. _____ Pourquoi n'êtes-vous pas à la maison le vendredi soir?　　d. Le soir.
5. _____ Avec qui parlez-vous français?　　e. Vers 7h30 du matin.
6. _____ À quelle heure arrivez-vous sur le campus?　　f. Parce que j'adore sortir.

© Diego Cervo / Shutterstock.com

ACTIVITÉ L La préparation du cours Complétez chaque question et puis posez les questions à deux étudiants différents. N'oubliez pas de jouer les deux rôles. Avez-vous les mêmes habitudes de travail?

1. _____ étudiez-vous: dans le silence, devant la télé, sérieusement, avec des amis, etc.?
   a. Comment　　b. Combien de　　c. Quoi
2. _____ faites-vous vos devoirs: l'après-midi, le soir, etc.?
   a. Pourquoi　　b. Qui　　c. Quand
3. _____ temps passez-vous à faire vos devoirs: trente minutes par jour, une heure par jour, deux heures par jour, plus de *(more than)* trois heures par jour, etc.?
   a. Quoi　　b. Combien de　　c. Où
4. _____ finissez-vous vos devoirs: avant 19h, vers 20h, vers 22h, après minuit, etc.?
   a. Quand　　b. Comment　　c. Pourquoi

ACTIVITÉ M Détecteur de mensonges Répondez aux questions. Mais **une** des réponses doit être **fausse.** Vous allez partager vos réponses en petits groupes et votre groupe va détecter le mensonge *(lie)*.

1. **Combien de** colocataires avez-vous?
2. **Que** pensez-vous du restaurant universitaire sur votre campus?
3. **Avec qui** aimez-vous sortir?
4. **Où** allez-vous normalement le week-end?
5. **Quel** est votre film préféré?

ACTIVITÉ N Êtes-vous fans de quiz? Complétez chaque phrase et puis essayez *(try)* de répondre à toutes les questions.

1. Sur _____ ferme de fiction est-ce qu'on trouve Fern, Charlotte et Wilbur?
   a. quel   b. quelle   c. quels   d. quelles

2. Dans _____ lac légendaire habite Viviane, la Dame du Lac?
   a. quel   b. quelle   c. quels   d. quelles

3. Dans _____ bois habitent Robin des Bois et ses hommes?
   a. quel   b. quelle   c. quels   d. quelles

4. Dans _____ mer le dieu *(god)* grec Poséidon habite-t-il?
   a. quel   b. quelle   c. quels   d. quelles

5. _____ montagnes sont le lieu de naissance *(birthplace)* de Davy Crockett?
   a. Quel   b. Quelle   c. Quels   d. Quelles

6. Dans _____ forêt est-il interdit *(forbidden)* de pénétrer pour les étudiants de Poudlard *(Hogwarts)*?
   a. quel   b. quelle   c. quels   d. quelles

ACTIVITÉ O Personnages célèbres Complétez chaque phrase et puis essayez *(try)* de deviner *(guess)* qui sont les personnages *(characters)*.

1. _____ qui est-ce que les gens de la Vallée endormie *(Sleepy Hollow)* ont peur?
   a. De   b. Pour

2. _____ qui est-ce que le père cueille *(picks)* une rose du jardin de la Bête *(Beast)*?
   a. À   b. Pour

3. _____ qui est-ce que la pionnière *(pioneer)* Laura habite dans la prairie américaine?
   a. Avec   b. Selon

4. _____ qui est-ce que Hansel et Gretel mangent des bonbons?
   a. Chez   b. Après

5. _____ qui est-il obligatoire que des jeunes participent chaque année au jeu télévisé *Hunger Games*?
   a. À   b. Selon

ACTIVITÉ P Meneurs de jeu *(Quiz Masters)* C'est votre tour *(turn)* maintenant de préparer un quiz! Utilisez le vocabulaire de ce chapitre et préparez quatre questions que vous allez poser à vos camarades de classe.

Modèle: **Quel fleuve traverse la ville de Paris? (la Seine)**
Combien de pièces la Maison Blanche a-t-elle? (132 pièces)
Combien de bureaux de poste y a-t-il aux États-Unis? (26 000+)

1. _____

2. _____

3. _____

4. _____

ACTIVITÉ Q Chiche! Chiche! est une association française de «jeunes écologistes alternatifs solidaires». Ils ont comme but *(goal)* la protection de l'environnement et des espaces verts. Voici l'extrait d'une interview d'un membre. Quelles sont les questions probablement posées pendant l'interview?

Modèle: Question: **Combien de membres avez-vous?**

Réponse: Nous avons au moins 200 membres.

1. Question: _____

   Réponse: Nous désirons organiser des actions de sensibilisation à la protection de l'environnement et de critique de la société de consommation.

2. Question: _____

   Réponse: Notre slogan est: «Tu crois que tu vas changer le monde? Chiche!»

3. Question: _____

   Réponse: Nous avons des groupes locaux à Amiens, à Bordeaux, à Lille, à Rennes et à Toulouse.

4. Question: _____

   Réponse: On travaille souvent avec des membres de la fédération politique Jeunes Verts.

ACTIVITÉ R Enthousiastes de la nature? Vous allez faire un sondage *(survey)* pour trouver des enthousiastes de la nature dans le cours. Préparez au moins trois questions et puis posez vos questions aux étudiants.

Modèle: **Combien de fois par an est-ce que tu fais des randonnées?**
Quelle(s) plage(s) est-ce que tu fréquentes et à quelle fréquence?
Quand est-ce que tu vas à la campagne et pour faire quoi?

ACTIVITÉ S Artistes de paysages

Étape 1. Dessinez un paysage *(landscape)*, sans le montrer à votre partenaire.

Étape 2. Posez des questions à votre partenaire sur son paysage et essayez de *(try to)* le dessiner. Utilisez les prépositions que vous avez apprises *(you learned)* dans le **Vocabulaire 2.**

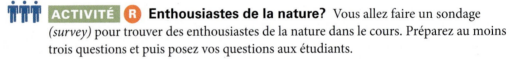

D'AUTRES EXPRESSIONS UTILES

au centre *in the middle, center*   **en bas** *on bottom*   **en haut** *on top*

Modèle: É1 (artiste): **Qu'est-ce qu'on trouve dans ton image?**
É2: **Des fleurs, une rivière, quelques nuages et un arbre.**
É1: **Où sont les fleurs?**
É2: **À côté de la rivière. À droite.**
É1: **Combien de nuages est-ce qu'il y a?**
É2: **Trois gros nuages.**
É1: **Comment est l'arbre?**
É2: **Petit.**

© Eric Cabanis/AFP/Getty Images

Pour aller plus loin
Que / Qu' vs. Quoi

Choosing between **que/qu'** and **quoi** depends on the structure of the question and sometimes the verb. Compare the differences.

Qu'est-ce que nous mangeons?	*What are we eating?*
On mange **quoi**?	*We are eating what?*
Que mangeons-nous?	*What are we eating?*
De quoi est-ce que vous parlez?	*What are you talking about?*
Vous parlez **de quoi**?	*You are talking about what?*
De quoi parlez-vous?	*What are you talking about?*

Qu'est-ce que is commonly used in spoken French. When used in written French, it is less formal than **que** used with inversion.

Que is used with inversion in both written and oral forms. In oral French, **que** plus inversion is more common in Quebec than in France.

Quoi is used with intonation and prepositions. With intonation, it is considered very informal and is used when speaking with friends. It is seldom written.

Essayez! Complétez chaque phrase avec **que/qu'** ou **quoi**.

1. _____ est-ce que tu penses de la langue française?
2. _____ fais-tu normalement après le cours de français?
3. De _____ est-ce que tu as besoin pour réussir dans le cours de français?

Liaisons musicales

© Pierre Guibert/Visual Press Agency/Photoshot

La musique d'Alister mélange *(mixes)* la chanson française avec le rock. Sa célèbre chanson, *Qu'est-ce qu'on va faire de toi?* (2008), est la première chanson de son premier album. Cherchez les paroles de cette chanson. Quelle action choisissez-vous parmi *(among)* les possibilités présentées dans la chanson?

OUI, JE PEUX!

Here are two "can do statements" for you to check your progress so far. Look at each statement and rate yourself on how well you think you can perform the task. Then verify your ability with a partner. How did you do?

1. **"I can describe my favorite green spaces and state the types of activities I like to do there."**

   I can perform this function
   ☐ with ease
   ☐ with some difficulty
   ☐ not at all

2. **"I can ask someone else three information questions (for example, where, what, how many, which) about the types of green spaces in his/her hometown."**

   I can perform this function
   ☐ with ease
   ☐ with some difficulty
   ☐ not at all

iLrn™

Are you looking for more practice? You can find it in **iLrn**.

DEUXIÈME
PROJECTION

Avant de visionner

ACTIVITÉ **A** **Vous rappelez-vous?** Vous rappelez-vous *(Do you remember)* qui a dit ces phrases dans la Séquence 2 du film *Liaisons*?

	Claire	Abia	Michel
1. Émile? Où es-tu?	☐	☐	☐
2. Qui a fait la réservation, s'il vous plaît?	☐	☐	☐
3. Va à Québec, Claire. Pour la famille…	☐	☐	☐
4. … cet homme qui t'a fait la réservation, c'est peut-être un meurtrier, un psychopathe…	☐	☐	☐
5. Tu es sûre de ta décision?	☐	☐	☐
6. Il était là, près de la sortie *(exit)*.	☐	☐	☐

ACTIVITÉ **B** **Une scène du film** Vous rappelez-vous cette scène? Claire dit à Abia qu'elle veut aller au Château Frontenac. Complétez les phrases avec les mots qui manquent *(are missing)*.

ABIA Tu es (1) _____?

CLAIRE Abia, c'est peut-être une (2) _____.

ABIA Aventure? Un homme (3) _____—un homme que tu ne connais pas—il te fait une (4) _____ pour le Frontenac (5) _____ Québec, et tu ne sais pas qui a payé (6) _____.

▶ **Regarder la séquence**

Vous allez regarder la Séquence 2 du film *Liaisons* deux fois. La première fois, vérifiez vos réponses à l'Activité A et à l'Activité B. La deuxième fois, faites attention à l'appartement de Claire et prenez des notes.

SUGGESTIONS: Son appartement est petit ou grand? Quels meubles y a-t-il dans l'appartement? Comment est la décoration: moderne, traditionnelle? L'appartement est propre, rangé, en désordre?

Après le visionnage

ACTIVITÉ **C** **L'appartement de Claire**

1. Faites une description de l'appartement de Claire à l'aide de vos notes.

2. Décrivez la personnalité de Claire avec trois adjectifs.

3. On dit que notre espace personnel reflète notre personnalité. Voyez-vous *(Do you see)* des liaisons entre l'appartement de Claire et sa personnalité?

ACTIVITÉ **D** **Claire et Abia**

Étape 1. Notez des similarités et des différences entre Claire et Abia. Pensez à leurs traits physiques et à leurs personnalités.

Similarités	Différences
_____	_____
_____	_____
_____	_____
_____	_____
_____	

Étape 2. Partagez vos notes avec un(e) camarade. Avec lui/elle, écrivez un profil de Claire et d'Abia pour la classe.

ACTIVITÉ **E** **Résumé de la Séquence 2** Voici un résumé de la Séquence 2 du film. Choisissez les mots qui manquent.

aller	Château Frontenac	famille	quart	en
appel	Hôtel Mont Royal	mystérieuse	Québec	son

Claire reçoit une enveloppe (1) _____. C'est une réservation anonyme pour deux nuits au (2) _____ à (3) _____. À trois heures et (4) _____ du matin, elle reçoit un (5) _____ de son oncle Michel (6) _____ France. Il dit qu'elle doit (7) _____ à Québec pour la (8) _____.

Abia **amie** **bonne** **cette** **homme** **mauvaise**

Claire parle avec Abia au sujet de (9) _____ réservation. Elle dit à (10) _____ qu'elle va aller à Québec. Abia pense que c'est une (11) _____ idée. Abia a peur pour son (12) _____.

Dans les coulisses

You compared physical and personality profiles of Claire and Abia in **Activité D**. Abia comes from a large family and maintains close relationships with her relatives. Claire's family background is less clear. Her mother is in a psychiatric hospital, and her only other relative appears to be an uncle in France. Why do you think Claire and Abia are friends? What role does Abia play in Claire's life? What roles do secondary characters typically play in movies?

À DÉCOUVRIR: La Côte d'Ivoire et la ville d'Abidjan

À DÉCOUVRIR: La Côte d'Ivoire

Pays: La Côte d'Ivoire
Géographie: En Afrique occidentale sub-saharienne
Climat: Tropical sur la côte et semi-aride dans le nord; trois saisons: chaud et sec (novembre-mars), très chaud et sec (mars-mai), très chaud et pluvieux (juin-octobre).
Population: Plus de 20 millions
Capitale: Yamoussoukro

À DÉCOUVRIR: La ville d'Abidjan

Structure: Une mégalopole moderne
Région: Région des lagunes
Population: Plus de 3,5 millions
Réputation: La capitale économique de la Côte d'Ivoire; le carrefour culturel ouest-africain

Avant de lire

You will discover in this reading the city of Abidjan, the economic capital of **Côte d'Ivoire.**

Que savez-vous déjà?

1. Quels bâtiments sont normalement associés aux grandes villes?
2. Quelles activités est-ce qu'on fait normalement dans les grandes villes?
3. Quand vous voyez le mot **mégalopole**, qu'est-ce que vous imaginez?

OUTILS DE LECTURE
Using context to learn new nouns
Knowing the main idea of a text can help you guess what some unfamiliar nouns are. For example, if you know that the city of Abidjan is the economic capital of **Côte d'Ivoire,** what do you think the following words in bold mean in English?

1. Abidjan est un important **carrefour** commercial et culturel de l'Afrique de l'Ouest.
2. **le quartier des affaires**

Découvrir une mégalopole africaine

© Craig Pershouse/Getty images

Une des plus grandes villes francophones, Abidjan, avec 6,8 millions d'habitants dans l'agglomération°, est la capitale économique de la Côte d'Ivoire (Yamoussoukro est la capitale politique). Le français est la langue officielle. Parmi° les autres langues, on trouve le dioula, le bété et le baoulé (il y a une soixantaine° de langues en Côte d'Ivoire).

Abidjan est un important carrefour° commercial et culturel de l'Afrique de l'Ouest. Le Plateau, le quartier des affaires, qui compte de nombreux immeubles° modernes, est quelquefois appelé «le Manhattan des tropiques»[1]. La ville est divisée en deux parties: Abidjan sud (au bord du° Golfe de Guinée) et Abidjan nord (de l'autre côté des° lagunes).

Cette ville tropicale au bord de l'océan possède aussi des plages avec des palmiers et des cocotiers.

Comme beaucoup de villes africaines, elle a des quartiers d'habitation° «à l'européenne» (Cocody) et des quartiers traditionnels (Marcory ou Treichville) avec plusieurs logements construits autour de° cours collectives. Avec ses nombreuses discothèques et une vie nocturne particulièrement animée, Abidjan est un des centres de la musique africaine. Parmi les genres musicaux d'origine ivoirienne, il y a le zouglou et le mapouka. Avec des musiciens comme Alpha Blondy et Tiken Jah Fakoly, Abidjan est aussi le centre du reggae en Afrique.

[1]http://www.abidjan.net/cotedivoire/presentation/abidjan.htm

agglomération *greater urban area* **Parmi** *Among* **soixantaine** *approximately sixty* **carrefour** *crossroads* **immeubles** *buildings* **au bord du** *at the edge of* **de l'autre côté des** *on the other side of* **quartiers d'habitation** *residential neighborhoods* **autour de** *around*

Après avoir lu

Compréhension

	Vrai	Faux
1. Abidjan n'est pas une grande ville francophone.	☐	☐
2. Le français est la langue officielle de la ville.	☐	☐
3. C'est une ville tropicale au bord de l'océan.	☐	☐
4. Il n'y a pas de vie nocturne à Abidjan.	☐	☐

Et vous?

1. Est-ce que tu viens d'une mégalopole?
2. Est-ce que le commerce est un aspect important de ta ville d'origine?
3. Est-ce qu'il y a une vie nocturne d'où tu viens? Qu'est-ce que les gens font?
4. Est-ce que la musique a une importance culturelle chez toi?

Share It!

Use **Share It!** in iLrn™ to express your reactions to the reading and to find out what your classmates think.

LIAISONS AVEC LA LECTURE ET L'ÉCRITURE
La description d'une ville

Descriptions of cities appear in many kinds of publications such as novels, magazines, travel guides, and study abroad brochures. Here is a description of the city of Abidjan in **Côte d'Ivoire,** Africa.

Abidjan, très grande ville francophone, compte 6,8 millions d'habitants avec le centre-ville et les banlieues. C'est la capitale économique de la Côte d'Ivoire. On trouve à Abidjan une importante industrialisation avec des industries diverses et une urbanisation rapide avec un nombre constant de personnes qui viennent vivre dans la région. Abidjan est à l'origine un petit village de pêcheurs mais aujourd'hui, avec son grand port, Abidjan est un carrefour commercial important pour tout le continent.

© Kambou Sia/AFP/Getty Images

Avant d'écrire

1. List the kinds of observations that appear in the description of Abidjan.

2. Answer the following questions to help you write your own **description d'une ville**.

   a. De quelle ville voulez-vous faire une description?

   b. Qu'est-ce que vous appréciez et/ou n'appréciez pas dans votre ville?

   c. La ville a-t-elle certains traits physiques importants et/ou certaines activités préférées?

   d. Comment décrivez-vous le caractère ou la personnalité de cette ville?

   e. Cette ville change-t-elle selon les saisons, l'heure, le temps ou le jour de la semaine?

Écrire

Using information from **Avant d'écrire**, write your own description of 6–8 sentences in French.

Après avoir écrit

Exchange your **description d'une ville** with a partner. 1) Circle all the prepositions used with geographical location and verify that they are all correct. 2) Underline all verbs and verify that your partner correctly conjugated them. 3) Double-check that your partner made all of the adjectives agree in number and gender. 4) Put a * next to the key phrase or key idea that best communicates your partner's description. 5) How would you characterize your partner's description: **créative, amusante, banale, objective, imaginative, drôle, inspirante, neutre, ennuyeuse,** etc.? Discuss your reactions together and then write a second version of your **description d'une ville** taking into account your partner's comments and corrections.

PARTIE 1 4–15

LES LOGEMENTS

un appartement	apartment
le loyer	rent
une maison	house, home
le premier étage	second floor (USA)
le rez-de-chaussée	ground floor, first floor (USA)
les tâches ménagères (f.)	household chores
un(e) voisin(e)	neighbor

LES PIÈCES DE LA MAISON

la chambre	bedroom
le couloir	hallway
la cuisine	kitchen
le garage	garage
une pièce	room
la salle de bains	bathroom
la salle à manger	dining room
la salle de séjour	living room, family room
le salon	salon, formal living room
les W.-C. (m.)	toilet (room), water closet

DANS LA MAISON

les affaires (f.)	things, stuff
un appareil électroménager	household appliance
une baignoire	bathtub
un balcon	balcony
un canapé	couch
une commode	chest of drawers
une cuisinière	stove
une douche	shower
l'escalier (m.)	staircase
les étagères (f.)	bookshelves
un fauteuil	armchair
un four	oven
une lampe	lamp
un lavabo	bathroom sink
un lit	bed
un meuble	piece of furniture
un (four à) micro-ondes	microwave
un miroir	mirror
un objet	object
un placard	closet
un réfrigérateur / un frigo	refrigerator / fridge
les rideaux (m.)	curtains
le sous-sol	basement
un tapis	rug
une télévision / une télé	TV

VERBES

choisir	to choose
faire la lessive	to do the laundry
faire le ménage	to do the housework
faire la poussière	to dust
faire la vaisselle	to do the dishes
finir	to finish
grandir	to grow up
grossir	to gain weight
louer	to rent
maigrir	to lose weight
obéir (à)	to obey
partager	to share
passer l'aspirateur (m.)	to vacuum
ranger	to pick up (the house), to put things away
réfléchir (à)	to reflect (upon), to consider
réussir (à)	to succeed (at, in)
salir	to dirty
sortir la poubelle	to take out the garbage, trash

ADJECTIFS

équipé(e)	equipped
propre	clean
sale	dirty

DIVERS

chez	at the home / place of
Il faut + *infinitive*	It is necessary . . . / One must . . . / to have to . . .
la loi	law
les règles (f.)	rules

PARTIE 2 4–16

LES LIEUX / ENDROITS

un amphithéâtre	lecture hall
la banlieue	suburbs
une banque	bank
un bâtiment	building
une boutique	store, boutique
un bureau de poste	post office
le centre commercial	shopping center / district
un centre sportif	recreation center
le centre-ville	downtown
le cinéma	movie theater
une église	church
un endroit	location, place
un hôpital	hospital
un institut de beauté	spa, beauty parlor
un kiosque à journaux	newsstand
un laboratoire	laboratory
une laverie automatique	laundromat
une librairie	bookstore
un lycée	high school
un magasin	store
un musée	museum
un parking	parking lot
une pharmacie	pharmacy
la piscine (municipale)	(public) swimming pool
un quartier (résidentiel)	a (residential) neighborhood
une résidence universitaire	university / college residence hall
un restaurant universitaire	campus cafeteria
la rue	street
un stade	stadium
une ville	a city, a town

RÉSUMÉ DE VOCABULAIRE

L'ORDRE DES ÉVÉNEMENTS

d'abord	*first*
ensuite / puis	*next, then*
plus tard	*later*
enfin	*finally*

PRÉPOSITIONS

à côté (de)	*next (to)*
au coin (de)	*on the corner (of)*
à droite (de)	*to/on the right (of)*
à gauche (de)	*to/on the left (of)*
derrière	*behind*
devant	*in front (of)*
en face (de)	*across (from)*
en ville	*in town, in the city*
entre	*between*
loin (de)	*far (from)*
près (de)	*near*
tout droit	*straight ahead*

LES INDICATIONS

un plan	*map (of a city)*
tourner à droite / à gauche	*to turn right / left*
traverser la rue	*to cross the street*
aller / continuer tout droit	*to go / to continue straight ahead*
aller / continuer jusqu'à	*to go / to continue until*
aller jusqu'au bout	*to go to the end*
aller vers	*to go towards*

PARTIE 3 4–17

LES ESPACES VERTS

un arbre	*tree*
les bois *(m. pl.)*	*woods*
la campagne	*the country(side)*
une ferme	*farm*
une fleur	*flower*
une forêt	*forest*
un jardin	*garden, lawn*
un lac	*lake*
la mer	*the sea*
une montagne	*mountain*
la plage	*the beach*
une plante	*plant*
une rivière / un fleuve	*river*

LES ACTIVITÉS

aller à la chasse	*to go hunting, to hunt*
aller à la pêche	*to go fishing*
faire du bateau (à voile) / faire du voilier	*to go (sail)boating*
faire de la randonnée	*to go hiking, to hike*

LES DIRECTIONS

l'est *(m.)*	*east*
le nord	*north*
l'ouest *(m.)*	*west*
le sud	*south*

LES NOMBRES

100	cent	1 550	mille cinq cent cinquante
105	cent cinq	1 999	mille neuf cent quatre-vingt-dix-neuf
135	cent trente-cinq		
200	deux cents		
250	deux cent cinquante	2 000	deux mille
300	trois cents	2 780	deux mille sept cent quatre-vingts
375	trois cent soixante-quinze	1 000 000	un million
400	quatre cents	1 500 000	un million cinq cent mille
500	cinq cents		
600	six cents	2 000 000	deux millions
700	sept cents	2 555 000	deux millions cinq cent cinquante-cinq mille
800	huit cents		
900	neuf cents		
1 000	mille	1 000 000 000	un milliard
1 100	mille cent	2 000 000 000	deux milliards
1 300	mille trois cents		

LES MOTS D'INTERROGATION

combien de	*how many, how much*
comment	*how*
où	*where*
pourquoi	*why*
quand	*when*
que / qu'	*what*
quel(le)(s)	*which*
qui	*who(m)*
quoi (informal)	*what*
parce que/qu'	*because*
poser des questions	*to ask questions*

DIVERS

un point	*period/point*
une virgule	*comma*

Les **plaisirs** de **la table**

En bref   In this chapter, you will:

- learn about food, beverages, meals, and nutrition
- learn the verbs **prendre, apprendre,** and **comprendre**
- learn partitive articles
- learn the verb **boire**

- learn vocabulary to discuss tastes and flavors, and learn expressions of quantity
- learn the **passé composé** with **avoir**
- learn the /r/ sound
- read about food, diet, and health in France and the Francophone world

 You will also watch **SÉQUENCE 3: À Québec** of the film *Liaisons*.

Ressources

 audio   ▶ video   Share It!   iLrn™   🌐 http://www.cengagebrain.com

Les **repas**

Meals

Note de **prononciation**
The **f** in the singular form **un œuf** is pronounced, but it is not pronounced in the plural **des œufs.**

la confiture

le beurre

le café

un croissant

Le petit déjeuner français

le pain le jus d'orange le sucre

la crème

les œufs (m.)

les saucisses (f.)

Le (petit) déjeuner québécois

le poulet

la soupe à la tomate

l'eau minérale (f.)

une salade

les pâtes (f.)

Le déjeuner

un gâteau au chocolat

le vin

les haricots verts (m.)

une pomme de terre

le steak

Le dîner

les plats (m.) *courses*

  un hors-d'œuvre / une entrée *starter / appetizer*

  un plat principal *main course, dish (kind of food)*

  un dessert *dessert*

  le goûter *snack*

la nourriture *food*

  un aliment *a particular food*

  les biscuits (m.) *cookies*

  des céréales (f.) *cereal*

  les chips (f.) *chips*

  les frites (f.) *French fries*

  le fromage *cheese*

  la glace *ice cream*

  une omelette *omelet*

  la pizza *pizza*

  le poisson *fish*

  le riz *rice*

  un sandwich (au fromage) *(cheese) sandwich*

  le yaourt *yogurt*

les boissons (f.) *drinks/beverages*

  la bière *beer*

  le citron pressé *lemonade*

  le Coca *Coca-Cola*

  le lait *milk*

  le thé *tea*

les fruits (m.) *fruits*

  une banane *banana*

  une orange *orange*

  une pomme *apple*

les légumes (m.) *vegetables*

  les carottes (f.) *carrots*

  les épinards (m.) *spinach*

la viande *meat*

  le bœuf *beef*

  le jambon *ham*

  un rôti (de porc) *(pork) roast*

ACTIVITÉ A (Petit) déjeuner français ou québécois? Vous allez entendre le nom d'un aliment. Indiquez si l'aliment est associé **(a) au petit déjeuner français**, **(b) au déjeuner québécois** ou **(c) aux deux** (*both*).

1.   2.   3.   4.   5.   6.   7.   8.

Un mot sur la langue

Petit déjeuner ou déjeuner?

Est-ce qu'il y a une différence entre *dinner* et *supper* en anglais? La signification de ces mots varie selon la région ou le pays. En France, on prend **le petit déjeuner** le matin, **le déjeuner** à midi et **le dîner** le soir. Mais au Québec, en Belgique et en Suisse, **le déjeuner** est le repas du matin, **le dîner** le repas du midi et **le souper** le repas du soir.

- Complétez avec **le déjeuner, le dîner, le petit déjeuner** ou **le souper.**

  1. À 18h00 au Québec, on prend (*have, eat*)...

  2. À 9h00 en France, on prend...

  3. À midi en Belgique, on prend...

  4. À 20h00 en France, on prend...

ACTIVITÉ **B** **Les plats** Vous allez entendre le nom d'un aliment. Quels plats associez-vous à chaque aliment: **(a) apéritif**, **(b) entrée / hors d'œuvre**, **(c) plat principal** ou **(d) dessert**?

5-2

1.   2.   3.   4.   5.   6.   7.   8.   9.   10.

ACTIVITÉ **C** **Associations**

5-3

Étape 1. Vous allez entendre le nom de plusieurs aliments. Quelle couleur associez-vous à chaque aliment?

1.   2.   3.   4.   5.   6.   7.   8.   9.   10.

Étape 2. Quels autres aliments associez-vous à ces couleurs?

1. rose   **2.** blanc   **3.** vert   **4.** jaune   **5.** rouge   **6.** orange

ACTIVITÉ **D** **Les marques** Pour chaque aliment, donnez une marque (*brand name*) populaire.

Modèle: le poulet   **Tysons / Kentucky's**

1. la glace
2. le citron pressé
3. les pommes de terre
4. les pâtes
5. la confiture
6. le jambon
7. la soupe
8. le thé
9. les biscuits
10. les céréales
11. le bœuf
12. l'eau minérale

© Raphael Demaret/REA/Redux

© Courtesy of Wynne Wong

✈ Si vous y allez

Si vous allez à Québec, allez au Café Krieghoff pour un bon (petit) déjeuner québécois. Le café-bistro est également un gîte du passant* *(bed and breakfast)* bon marché pour les touristes. Cherchez le site officiel sur Internet pour voir les tarifs *(rates)*.

*The term **gîte du passant** is used in Quebec. In France, one would hear **chambre d'hôtes**.

ACTIVITÉ **E** **Dans votre culture, quel aliment est bon pour... ?** Créez des phrases selon *(according to)* le modèle.

Modèle: pour les cheveux   **Les œufs sont bons pour les cheveux.**

1. pour les yeux
2. pour l'estomac *(stomach)*
3. pour les muscles
4. pour le cerveau *(brain)*
5. pour les os *(bones)*
6. contre *(against)* le rhume *(cold)*

ACTIVITÉ **F** **Votre opinion**

Étape 1. Indiquez ce que vous pensez de chaque aliment avec les adjectifs suivants ou d'autres: **délicieux, succulent, bon, mauvais, dégoûtant.**

Modèle: la confiture   **La confiture est délicieuse.**

1. les céréales   4. le steak
2. le poisson   5. la pizza
3. le yaourt   6. les pâtes

Étape 2. Demandez à un(e) camarade de classe s'il/si elle aime ces aliments.

Modèle: É1: **Aimes-tu les céréales?**
            É2: **Oui, les céréales sont délicieuses. / Non, les céréales sont mauvaises.**

ACTIVITÉ **G** **Pour le goûter** Quels aliments est-ce que la classe aime pour le goûter? Demandez à vos camarades s'ils aiment les aliments suivants et écrivez leurs noms et leurs réponses.

Modèle: É1: **Est-ce que tu aimes le Coca?**
            É2: **Oui, j'aime le Coca.**

1. le lait   5. les biscuits
2. le citron pressé   6. le Coca
3. les frites   7. le fromage
4. les chips   8. l'eau minérale

ACTIVITÉ **H** **Un dîner élégant** Avec deux ou trois camarades de classe, préparez un menu pour un dîner élégant chez votre professeur. Qu'est-ce que vous allez servir *(serve)* en **entrée**, pour le **plat principal** et au **dessert**?

Modèle: **Entrée: soupe et pain**

© Lauri Patterson/iStockphoto.com

Un mot sur la culture

De la frite belge à la poutine québécoise

Comme les Français, les Belges adorent les frites. Les Belges sont très fiers d'être les inventeurs de ce plat célèbre! En Belgique, on mange souvent des frites avec des moules°. En France, le steak-frites est un plat typique. Les Québécois ont aussi inventé un plat avec des frites: la poutine. On prépare la poutine avec des frites, du fromage en grains° et une sauce brune.

moules *mussels* **fromage en grains** *cheese curds*

• Qu'est-ce que vous aimez manger avec les frites?

GRAMMAIRE 1

Pour parler de la nourriture

Le verbe **prendre** / Les articles partitifs

DU FILM *LIAISONS*

Un coup d'œil sur la grammaire

Look at this photo from the film *Liaisons* and its caption.

Claire **prend une petite salade** et **du café** dans **un** restaurant à Trois-Rivières.

1. What does **prend** mean?
   a. *to drink*   b. *to have*
2. Which article is used with nouns that are countable?
   a. **du**   b. **un/une**
3. Which article is used with mass nouns that are normally not counted?
   a. **du**   b. **un/une**

Le verbe *prendre*

The verb **prendre** *(to take)* is commonly used with food to mean *to have (food)*. It is irregular in the present tense.

prendre	
je **prends**	nous **prenons**
tu **prends**	vous **prenez**
il/elle/on **prend**	ils/elles **prennent**

—Qu'est-ce que vous **prenez**?   —*What are you having?*

—Je **prends** du pain.   —*I am having (some) bread.*

Some common expressions with **prendre** include **prendre le déjeuner / le dîner** *(to have lunch / dinner)*, **prendre un verre** *(to have a drink)*, and **prendre son temps** *(to take one's time)*.

Other verbs conjugated like **prendre** are **apprendre** *(to learn)* and **comprendre** *(to understand)*.

Marc et Lisa **apprennent** l'italien.   Nous **comprenons** le français.

When an infinitive follows **apprendre**, the preposition **à** must be used.

Il **apprend à** faire la cuisine.   *He is learning (how) to cook.*

Les articles partitifs

In addition to definite and indefinite articles, French has partitive articles. Roughly equivalent to *some* or *any* in English, the **partitif** is used with mass nouns or things that are normally not counted and that you only take a part of like bread, cake, milk, butter, meat, fish, and sugar.

(m. sing.)	du	Vous prenez **du** pain?	Are you having any/some bread?
(f. sing.)	de la	**de la** viande?	any/some meat?
(m. / f. + vowel sound)	de l'	**de l'**eau?	any/some water?

Tu prends **de la** crème dans ton café?	*Do you take (any) cream in your coffee?*
Nous mangeons **du** poulet ce soir.	*We are eating (some) chicken tonight.*

With countable nouns, meaning those that are easily made plural and can be used with numbers (**un œuf, trois œufs**), the indefinite article (**un, une, des**) is used.

Je vais préparer **une** omelette.	*I am going to make an omelet.*
Je vais acheter **des** œufs.	*I am going to buy some eggs.*
Je vais faire **un** gâteau.	*I am going to make a cake.*

Un, une, and numbers may be used with mass nouns such as coffee and ice cream when referring to a fixed quantity. When the quantity is undetermined, use the **partitif.**

Nous prenons **du** café.	*We are having (some) coffee.*
Je prends **un** café.	*I'm having a coffee (a cup).*
Trois cafés, s'il vous plaît.	*Three coffees, please.*
On prend **de la** glace comme dessert.	*We're having (some) ice cream for dessert.*
Je prends **une** glace.	*I'm having an ice cream (a cone).*

As you learned in **Chapitre 1** and **Chapitre 2,** with negation, the partitive and indefinite articles become **de** or **d'.**

Tu ne manges pas **de** porc?	*You don't eat pork?*
Je n'ai pas **d'**œufs.	*I don't have any eggs.*
Elle ne prend pas **de** glace.	*She isn't having ice cream.*

Un mot sur la langue

La glace et la crème glacée

Au Québec on dit **la crème glacée** au lieu de *(instead of)* **la glace.** C'est parce que le Québec est en Amérique du Nord et donc influencé par les mots anglais *(ice cream)*.

- Où trouve-t-on la meilleure *(best)* crème glacée dans votre ville?

ACTIVITÉ I Au gîte du passant

Étape 1. Les clients d'un gîte du passant *(bed and breakfast)* ont beaucoup d'activités. Utilisez les verbes pour déterminer le sujet de chaque phrase.

1. _____ **prennent** le goûter à 15h.   a. Émile   b. Émile et son frère

2. _____ **comprend** le russe.   a. Julie   b. Julie et Pierre

3. _____ **apprends à** jouer du piano.   a. J(e)   b. Claire

4. _____ **comprennent** le chinois.   a. Marthe   b. Marthe et Sarah

5. _____ **comprenons** l'allemand.   a. J(e)   b. Nous

6. _____ **apprenons à** jouer au rugby.   a. J(e)   b. Nous

7. _____ **prenez** du vin.   a. Nous   b. Vous

Étape 2. Et vous? Complétez les phrases.

1. Je comprends _____.   **2.** J'apprends (à) _____.

ACTIVITÉ J **Qui prend… ?** Est-ce que vous connaissez les préférences alimentaires de vos camarades de classe? Devinez qui prend ces aliments régulièrement.

> **SUGGESTIONS**
>
> Je   Le professeur   Nous   Mon/Ma camarade de classe _____

Modèle: _____ des escargots.   **Paul et Ben prennent** des escargots.

1. _____ des pâtes.   **5.** _____ de la glace.

2. _____ du café.   **6.** _____ du Coca.

3. _____ du fromage.   **7.** _____ une pomme.

4. _____ un sandwich.   **8.** _____ des croissants.

ACTIVITÉ K Qu'est-ce que ce touriste prend au petit déjeuner?
Utilisez les articles pour déterminer ce que le touriste prend au petit déjeuner.

1. Je prends **un…**   a. pain   b. croissant

2. Je prends **des…**   a. saucisses   b. pain

3. Je prends du café avec **de la…**   a. crème   b. lait

4. Je prends **un…**   a. biscuit   b. beurre

5. Je prends **une…**   a. confiture   b. omelette

6. Je prends **du…**   a. jus d'orange   b. œuf

7. Je prends **de l'…**   a. eau   b. œuf

8. Je prends **une…**   a. crème   b. petite baguette

Conclusion Pensez-vous que le touriste est en France ou au Québec?

ACTIVITÉ **L** **Qu'est-ce qu'elle prend?** Choisissez l'image qui correspond à chaque phrase.

1. Elle prend **du** thé.

a.  b.

2. Elle prend **un** Coca.

a.  b.

3. Elle prend **un** yaourt.

a. b.

4. Elle prend **de la** glace.

a.  b.

5. Elle prend **un** café.

a.  b.

6. Elle prend **du** gâteau.

a.  b.

ACTIVITÉ **M** **Robert mange bien?** Dites si Robert prend ou ne prend pas les aliments suivants. Complétez avec **(a) Il prend** ou **(b) Il ne prend pas.** Attention aux articles!

Robert Levesque, gérant *(manager)* de l'hôtel dans le film *Liaisons*

1. _____ **de** beurre.

2. _____ **de** crème.

3. _____ **des** pommes

4. _____ **de** l'eau minérale.

5. _____ **de** sucre.

6. _____ **du** poisson.

7. _____ **une** salade.

8. _____ **de** biscuits.

9. _____ **des** haricots verts.

10. _____ **du** riz complet *(brown rice)*.

11. _____ **de** bière.

12. _____ **de** chips.

Conclusion Est-ce que Robert mange bien? Pourquoi ou pourquoi pas?

Et vous? Prenez-vous ces aliments? Vous êtes comme Robert?

ACTIVITÉ N **Que mettez-vous sur la pizza?**

Étape 1. Choisissez les ingrédients que vous mettez *(put)* sur la pizza.

- ☐ **du** fromage
- ☐ **du** bœuf
- ☐ **du** jambon
- ☐ **du** poulet
- ☐ **des** saucisses
- ☐ **de la** sauce tomate

- ☐ **des** oignons
- ☐ **des** olives
- ☐ **des** champignons *(mushrooms)*
- ☐ **de l'**ananas *(pineapple)*
- ☐ **des** anchois *(anchovies)*
- ☐ **???**

Étape 2. Demandez à un(e) camarade de classe s'il/si elle prend ces ingrédients pour décider si vous allez partager *(share)* une pizza avec lui/elle.

Modèle: É1: **Est-ce que tu prends du fromage?**
É2: **Oui, je prends du fromage. / Non, je ne prends pas de fromage.**

Conclusion Allez-vous partager une pizza avec lui/elle?

ACTIVITÉ O **Mangez-vous bien?**

Étape 1. Indiquez si vous prenez ou si vous ne prenez pas les aliments suivants.

Modèle: le beurre **Je prends du beurre. / Je ne prends pas de beurre.**

1. le bœuf
2. le lait
3. l'eau
4. les frites
5. les épinards
6. les chips

7. le Coca
8. les biscuits
9. le riz
10. le yaourt
11. le poisson
12. la bière

Étape 2. Montrez *(Show)* vos réponses à un(e) camarade de classe. Est-ce que votre camarade mange bien? Est-ce que vous mangez bien?

Liaisons musicales

Le chanteur-rappeur turc Lil' Maaz a eu beaucoup de succès avec *Mange du kebab* (2007). Cherchez les paroles *(lyrics)* et/ou un vidéo-clip de cette chanson sur Internet et identifiez les termes liés à *(related to)* la nourriture.

ACTIVITÉ P **Un brunch**

Étape 1. Qu'est-ce que vous prenez normalement au brunch?

Étape 2. Montrez votre réponse à un(e) camarade de classe. Quelle description est appropriée *(appropriate)* pour lui/elle? (Une personne qui apprécie la bonne nourriture ou qui aime manger est **gourmande.**)

Tu es raisonnable *(sensible)*.

Tu es un peu gourmand(e).

Tu es très gourmand(e).

Pour aller plus loin
Les expressions avec *avoir*

You already learned some expressions with **avoir** in **Chapitre 1**. Other expressions that use **avoir** include **avoir faim** *(to be hungry)* and **avoir soif** *(to be thirsty)*.

Quand est-ce qu'on mange? J'**ai faim**.	*When are we eating? I'm hungry.*
Maman **a soif**. As-tu de l'eau?	*Mom is thirsty. Do you have some water?*

The adjectives **chaud** and **froid** are also used with **avoir** if you want to say that a person is hot or cold in the sense of temperature.

Anne **a chaud**. Elle va à la piscine.	*Anne is hot. She's going to the pool.*
Il neige et les filles **ont froid**.	*It's snowing and the girls are cold.*

When **faim, soif, chaud,** and **froid** refer to people and are used with **avoir**, agreement is not necessary. However, when **chaud** and **froid** do not refer to people and are used with **être**, agreement is necessary: **La soupe est froide**.

Essayez! Complétez les phrases avec **avoir chaud, avoir faim, avoir froid** ou **avoir soif**.

1. Mes amis mangent un steak. Ils…
2. Il fait 98° F (37° C). Laura…
3. Guy prend trois Coca. Il…
4. Il fait 12° F (–11° C). Jean et Yves…

OUI, JE PEUX!

Here are two "can do statements" for you to check your progress so far. Look at each statement and rate yourself on how well you think you can perform the task. Then verify your ability with a partner. How did you do?

1. **"I can tell someone what I typically eat for each meal during the week."**

   I can perform this function
   ☐ with ease
   ☐ with some difficulty
   ☐ not at all

2. **"I can ask someone else what he/she typically eats at each meal during the week and determine if we have similar eating habits."**

   I can perform this function
   ☐ with ease
   ☐ with some difficulty
   ☐ not at all

iLrn™

Are you looking for more practice? You can find it in **iLrn**.

🔊 Une **alimentation** équilibrée

A balanced diet

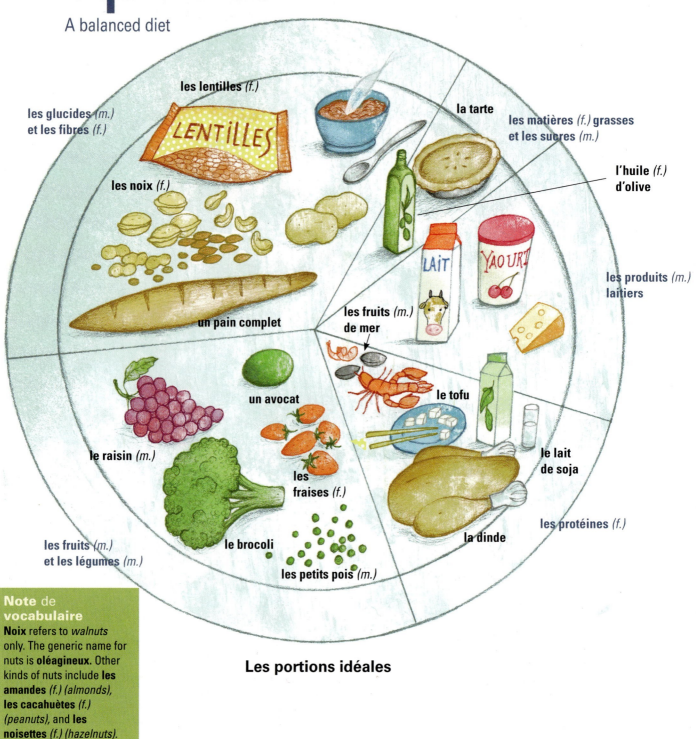

les **lentilles** (f.)

les **glucides** (m.)
et les **fibres** (f.)

LENTILLES

la **tarte**

les **matières** (f.) grasses
et les **sucres** (m.)

l'**huile** (f.)
d'olive

les **noix** (f.)

LAIT

YAOURT

les **produits** (m.)
laitiers

un pain complet

les **fruits** (m.)
de mer

un avocat

le tofu

le raisin (m.)

**le lait
de soja**

les
fraises (f.)

les **protéines** (f.)

les **fruits** (m.)
et les **légumes** (m.)

le brocoli

les **petits pois** (m.)

la dinde

Les portions idéales

Note de
vocabulaire
Noix refers to *walnuts*
only. The generic name for
nuts is **oléagineux.** Other
kinds of nuts include **les
amandes** (f.) (almonds),
les cacahuètes (f.)
(peanuts), and **les
noisettes** (f.) (hazelnuts).

Vocabulaire complémentaire

les bleuets *(m.)* *blueberries*
les framboises *(f.)* *raspberries*

les aliments industriels *(m.)* *processed foods*
un bonbon *candy*
le fast-food *fast food*
un hamburger *(ham)burger*

l'agneau *(m.)* *lamb*
le canard *duck*
le veau *veal*
la volaille *poultry*

être au régime *to be on a diet*
éviter (de + *infinitive*) *to avoid (doing something)*
faire attention (à) *to pay attention (to)*
fumer *to smoke*

alcoolisé(e) *alcoholic*
frais / fraîche *fresh, cool*
frit(e) *fried*
sain(e) *healthy*
la santé *health*
un(e) végétalien(ne) *vegan*
un(e) végétarien(ne) *vegetarian*

Note de vocabulaire
Not typically found in France, **les bleuets** of North America are a specialty of Quebec. In France, similar berries are called **les myrtilles** *(f.),* and they are not typically found in North America.

5-4

ACTIVITÉ **A** **Une protéine ou un fruit?** Dites si chaque aliment mentionné est **(a)** une protéine ou **(b)** un fruit.

1.   2.   3.   4.   5.   6.
7.   8.   9.   10.   11.   12.

Un mot sur la langue

Les mots étrangers au Québec

Dans la province du Québec, qui est située dans un pays principalement anglophone, il est courant° de franciser les mots° étrangers (c'est-à-dire de substituer un mot français à un mot d'origine étrangère), surtout les mots liés à la nourriture. En France, par contre, cette tendance est peu répandue° parce que le français dans l'Hexagone est moins menacé° par la langue anglaise. Par exemple, en France, on dit **hotdog** pour *hot dog* mais, au Québec, on dit souvent **chien chaud**. En France, Kentucky Fried Chicken est **KFC** mais, au Québec, c'est **PFK** qui signifie **Poulet frit du Kentucky**.

courant *common* un mot *word* répandue *widespread* menacé *threatened*

• Associez les mots étrangers utilisés en France aux mots étrangers utilisés au Québec.

En France	Au Québec
1. _____ chips	a. beignet
2. _____ sandwich	b. croustilles
3. _____ riz cantonais	c. riz frit chinois
4. _____ donut	d. sandwich sous-marin

ACTIVITÉ B Les catégories Quel aliment ne va pas avec les autres?

1. a. le brocoli   b. l'avocat   c. les noix   d. les petits pois

2. a. la dinde   b. le riz complet   c. le pain complet   d. les pâtes

3. a. le poulet   b. le canard   c. le steak   d. la dinde

4. a. l'agneau   b. le veau   c. les œufs   d. les bonbons

5. a. le lait   b. le lait de soja   c. le yaourt   d. la crème

6. a. l'huile   b. les aliments frits   c. le tofu   d. le beurre

ACTIVITÉ C Associations Associez les éléments de la première colonne aux éléments de la deuxième colonne.

1. _____ la volaille   a. le fromage

2. _____ fumer   b. grossir

3. _____ être au régime   c. MacDo

4. _____ un produit laitier   d. maigrir

5. _____ un aliment industriel   e. le canard

6. _____ le fast-food   f. le tabac

           g. la viande Spam

ACTIVITÉ D Nommez-le!

5-5

Étape 1. Nommez un aliment pour chaque catégorie que vous entendez.

    1.   **2.**   **3.**   **4.**   **5.**   **6.**
    7.   **8.**   **9.**   **10.**   **11.**

Étape 2. Aimez-vous la pizza? La pizza représente *(represents)* quels groupes alimentaires?

© Denis Nata/Shutterstock.com

ACTIVITÉ E Quiz santé Quel aliment est meilleur pour la santé?

1. a. le poulet au four   b. le poulet frit

2. a. un hamburger MacDo   b. un hamburger végétarien

3. a. le pain blanc   b. le pain complet

4. a. les noix   b. les chips

5. a. la volaille   b. la viande rouge

6. a. le tofu   b. le veau

7. a. l'agneau   b. les fruits de mer

8. a. le beurre   b. l'huile d'olive

9. a. le riz blanc   b. le riz complet

10. a. le Coca   b. le jus d'orange

11. a. les lentilles   b. les frites

12. a. les pâtes au blé complet   b. la pizza au fromage

ACTIVITÉ **F** **Faites-vous attention à votre santé?** Prenez-vous les aliments suivants chaque jour? Qu'est-ce que vous prenez?

Modèle: **Oui, je prends des épinards et des fraises.**

1. des fruits et des légumes?
2. des glucides?
3. des protéines?
4. des produits laitiers?

 ACTIVITÉ **G** **Les produits à éviter** Demandez à un(e) partenaire combien de fois par semaine il/elle prend ces produits.

Modèle: **É1: Combien de fois par semaine est-ce que tu manges des aliments industriels?**

É2: Je mange des aliments industriels une fois par semaine. / Jamais!

1. manger des aliments industriels
2. prendre des boissons alcoolisées
3. prendre du tabac
4. manger de la viande rouge
5. manger du fast-food

Conclusion Est-ce que ton/ta partenaire fait attention à sa santé?

ACTIVITÉ **H** **Les menus** Avec un(e) partenaire, préparez un menu équilibré pour quelqu'un qui est…

1. au régime
2. végétarien(ne)
3. végétalien(ne)
4. gourmand(e)

Si vous y allez

Si vous allez à Paris, allez au restaurant Cojean pour sa cuisine rapide et saine. Allez sur le site officiel du restaurant pour voir le menu.

© Directphoto Collection/Alamy

©Pascal Sittler/REA/Redux

Un mot sur la culture
Le fast-food en France

Le fast-food ou la restauration rapide, une invention américaine, a réussi à s'implanter en France et en Europe. On peut° trouver en France des chaînes déjà bien connues aux États-Unis comme McDo, KFC, Subway, Pizza Hut. Cependant, au cours des dernières années, ce mode de restauration a évolué avec un menu plus sain, des bars à salades et des jus de fruits naturels. Aujourd'hui en France, on peut trouver des restaurants qui servent de la nourriture rapide et plus saine. Le magasin Monoprix, par exemple, propose une gamme° de produits alimentaires plus sains en self-service. Les supermarchés vendent des repas préparés qu'on réchauffe° à la maison.

peut *can* **une gamme** *product line* **réchauffer** *to reheat*

• Avez-vous une chaîne de restauration rapide préférée?

Pour parler des boissons et exprimer ses préférences

Le verbe **boire** / Les articles définis et les articles partitifs

DU FILM *LIAISONS*

Un coup d'œil sur la grammaire

Look at these photos from the film *Liaisons* and their captions.

SERVEUSE Vous préférez **les** tartes peut-être? J'ai **la** tarte au sucre, **la** tarte aux bleuets...

CLAIRE Vous prenez quelque chose? Quelque chose à **boire**?

1. Why does the server use definite articles instead of indefinite or partitive articles with the food items?

   a. One typically only eats part of a pie.
   b. She is referring to pies in a general sense.
   c. She is referring to preferences.

   d. b and c
   e. a and c
   f. All of the above

2. What do you think **boire** means?

   a. *to drink*   b. *to eat*   c. *to take*

Le verbe *boire*

The verb **boire** *(to drink)* is irregular in the present tense.

boire	
je **bois**	nous **buvons**
tu **bois**	vous **buvez**
il/elle/on **boit**	ils/elles **boivent**

Because liquids are typically mass nouns and not countable, **boire** is often used with partitive articles.

—Vous **buvez du** lait?   —*Do you drink milk?*

—Oui, je **bois du** lait.   —*Yes, I drink milk.*

—Non, nous **buvons du** vin.   —*No, we are drinking wine.*

- As with **prendre**, indefinite articles (**un, une, des**) may be used with **boire** if referring to a fixed quantity of a liquid.

—Qu'est-ce que Luc **boit**?	—*What is Luc drinking?*
—Il **boit un** thé vert.	—*He is drinking a (a cup of) green tea.*

- In negative statements with **boire,** partitive and indefinite articles become **de/d'**.

—Tu **bois du** vin rouge?	—*Do you drink red wine?*
—Non, je **ne bois pas de** vin rouge.	—*No, I don't drink red wine.*
—Vous **buvez de** l'eau minérale?	—*Do you drink mineral water?*
—Non, je **ne bois pas d'**eau minérale.	—*No, I don't drink mineral water.*

Les préférences et l'article défini

- Because definite articles refer to nouns in a general sense, they are used to express (dis)likes with verbs like **aimer mieux, aimer bien, adorer,** and **détester**.

J'adore **les** biscuits!	*I adore cookies!*
Aimez-vous **la** viande rouge?	*Do you like red meat?*
Nous aimons mieux **le** poisson.	*We prefer fish.*
J'aime beaucoup **le** tofu et **les** lentilles.	*I like tofu and lentils a lot.*
Moi, je déteste **le** tofu.	*Me, I hate tofu.*

- Remember that, in negative sentences, the definite article does not change.

Je n'aime pas **les** aliments industriels.	*I don't like processed foods.*
Pierre n'aime pas **la** viande rouge.	*Pierre does not like red meat.*

ACTIVITÉ ❶ **Qui boit quoi?** Quand on fait la fête, on sert une variété de boissons. Trouvez le sujet de chaque phrase.

1. _____ **buvons** de l'eau minérale.	a. Je	b. Vous	c. Nous
2. _____ **bois** du vin rouge.	a. Tu	b. Il	c. Elles
3. _____ **boit** un Coca.	a. Elle	b. Tu	c. Ils
4. _____ **buvez** du jus d'orange.	a. Nous	b. Vous	c. Elles
5. _____ **boivent** du thé glacé *(iced)*.	a. Je	b. Il	c. Ils
6. _____ **bois** de la bière.	a. Je	b. Elle	c. Vous
7. _____ **buvons** du citron pressé.	a. Vous	b. Nous	c. On
8. _____ **buvez** du chocolat chaud.	a. Nous	b. Tu	c. Vous

Conclusion Que buvez-vous normalement aux fêtes?

ACTIVITÉ **J** **Les boissons**

Étape 1. Qui boit ces boissons? Regardez bien les verbes et complétez les phrases avec **(a) Le professeur** ou **(b) Les étudiants.**

1. _____ **boit** du thé vert.
2. _____ **boivent** du Coca.
3. _____ **boivent** du lait.
4. _____ **boit** du café.
5. _____ **boivent** de la bière.
6. _____ **boit** du champagne.

Étape 2. Et à votre université? Qui boit normalement ces boissons?

Modèle: À mon université, les étudiants boivent du thé vert.

ACTIVITÉ **K** **Les boissons et la santé** Utilisez les articles pour déterminer si ces étudiants boivent ou ne boivent pas ces boissons. Complétez les phrases avec **(a) Nous buvons** ou **(b) Nous ne buvons pas.**

1. _____ **de** l'eau minérale.
2. _____ **de** café.
3. _____ **du** jus d'orange.
4. _____ **de** Mountain Dew.
5. _____ **du** thé vert.
6. _____ **de** bière.
7. _____ **de** Coca.
8. _____ **du** vin rouge.
9. _____ **du** lait du soja.
10. _____ **d'**espresso.

Conclusion Analysez *(Review)* les réponses. Est-ce que ces étudiants font attention à leur santé?

•:• **Et vous?** Qu'est-ce que vous buvez et qu'est-ce que vous ne buvez pas? Est-ce que vous faites attention à votre santé?

ACTIVITÉ **L** **Qu'est-ce que vous buvez?**

Étape 1. Indiquez ce que vous buvez dans chaque situation suivante dans la colonne **Moi.**

	Moi	Mon/Ma partenaire
1. Quand il fait chaud	Je bois un Coca.	Il/Elle boit de l'eau.
2. Quand il fait froid		
3. Quand tu as sommeil		
4. Quand tu as très très soif		
5. Quand tu es nerveux(-euse)		
6. Quand tu es malade *(sick)*		

Étape 2. Posez les questions à un(e) partenaire. Notez ses réponses dans la colonne **Mon/Ma partenaire.**

Modèle: É1: Qu'est-ce que tu bois quand il fait chaud?
É2: Je bois de l'eau.

Pour aller plus loin

À ou *de*?

To say that juice is of a certain kind of fruit, the preposition **de** or **d'** is used followed by the fruit.

le jus **d'orange**   le jus **de framboise**   le jus **de pomme**

To say that a dessert is made with a certain kind of fruit, the preposition **à** is usually used and contracted with the plural form of the fruit.

une tarte **aux pommes**   une tarte **aux bleuets**   un gâteau **aux fraises**

With mass nouns such as chocolate and cheese, the preposition **à** is contracted with the singular form of the noun.

les biscuits **au chocolat**   le gâteau **au chocolat**   le gâteau **au fromage**

Essayez! Donnez les noms de ces boissons et de ces desserts en français?

1. grape juice

2. strawberry juice

3. a raspberry pie

4. a chocolate pie

5. a strawberry cake

6. a banana cake

ACTIVITÉ Ⓜ **Proposer un restaurant**

Étape 1. Complétez les phrases avec **Je déteste, Je n'aime pas, J'aime bien, J'aime beaucoup** ou **J'adore**.

1. _____ **les** fruits de mer.

2. _____ **les** pâtes.

3. _____ **la** nourriture chinoise.

4. _____ **la** pizza.

5. _____ **le** sushi.

6. _____ **la** cuisine végétarienne.

7. _____ **la** cuisine végétalienne.

8. _____ **le** fast-food.

 Étape 2. Comparez vos réponses avec un(e) partenaire.

Modèle: É1: **Je n'aime pas les fruits de mer. Et toi?**
  É2: **Moi, j'adore les fruits de mer. J'aime beaucoup les pâtes. Et toi?**
  É1: **Moi aussi. J'aime beaucoup les pâtes.**

 Étape 3. Proposez trois restaurants à votre partenaire.

Modèle: **Pour toi, je propose les restaurants Red Lobster, Olive Garden et MacDo.**

Liaisons musicales

© RA/Lebrecht Music & Arts

Les cornichons (1966) de Nino Ferrer est une chanson sur un pique-nique en famille. Cherchez les paroles *(lyrics)* et/ou un vidéo-clip de la chanson sur Internet. Des articles partitifs et des articles indéfinis sont utilisés dans la première partie de la chanson et des articles définis dans la deuxième partie. Pourquoi? Et comment dit-on **un cornichon** en anglais?

ACTIVITÉ **N** **Aimer ou prendre?**

Étape 1. Utilisez les articles pour déterminer si cet étudiant **aime** ou s'il **prend** les aliments suivants. Complétez les phrases avec **(a) J'aime** ou **(b) Je prends.**

1. _____ **les** chips.
2. _____ **du** tofu.
3. _____ **des** haricots noirs.
4. _____ **le** steak.
5. _____ **le** poisson frit.
6. _____ **un** hamburger végétarien.

Étape 2. Et toi? Est-ce qu'il y a des aliments que **tu aimes** mais que **tu ne prends pas** parce qu'ils sont mauvais pour la santé? Donne des exemples.

Modèle: **J'aime le Coca mais je ne prends pas de Coca.**

ACTIVITÉ **O** **Sont-ils difficiles?** Utilisez les articles pour déterminer le verbe approprié pour chaque phrase.

1. _____ **les** oranges.
   a. Édouard n'aime pas
   b. Édouard prend
2. _____ **du** jus d'orange.
   a. Bill boit
   b. Bill ne boit pas
3. _____ **d'**agneau.
   a. Stacey ne mange pas
   b. Stacey n'aime pas
4. _____ **le** poulet frit.
   a. Wynne ne prend pas
   b. Wynne adore
5. _____ **le** fromage.
   a. Édouard déteste
   b. Édouard prend
6. _____ **du** gâteau au fromage.
   a. Bill prend
   b. Bill ne prend pas
7. _____ **le** café.
   a. Stacey prend
   b. Stacey adore
8. _____ **de** bière.
   a. Édouard boit
   b. Édouard ne boit pas

ACTIVITÉ **P** **Êtes-vous difficile en ce qui concerne la nourriture?**

Étape 1. Complétez les phrases suivantes à propos de vos préférences alimentaires. Vous devez mentionner au moins trois aliments pour chaque phrase.

Modèle: **Je n'aime pas l'huile d'olive, le pain complet et le sushi.**
Je prends souvent de la viande rouge, du riz et des légumes verts.

1. J'aime _____.
2. Je n'aime pas _____.
3. Je prends souvent _____.
4. Je ne prends pas _____.
5. Je ne mangerais (*would eat*) jamais _____.
6. Je mangerais _____ tous les jours.

Étape 2. Lisez vos phrases à un(e) partenaire. Votre partenaire va déterminer si vous êtes **très difficile, difficile, un peu difficile** ou **pas difficile.**

Étape 3. Préparez des questions pour votre professeur pour voir s'il/si elle est difficile.

Modèle: **Est-ce que vous aimez le poisson? Est-ce que vous prenez du fromage?**

ACTIVITÉ Q Repas équilibrés

Étape 1. Avec un(e) partenaire, décidez si les repas suivants sont des repas équilibrés. Si un repas n'est pas équilibré, expliquez pourquoi.

1. Repas A: yaourt, bleuets, œufs, pain complet, noix, jus d'orange
2. Repas B: banane, fraises, haricots verts, carottes, raisin, jus de pomme
3. Repas C: veau, épinards, agneau, avocat, poisson, vin
4. Repas D: tarte, frites, œufs, steak, gâteau, chocolat chaud
5. Repas E: dinde, petits pois, framboises, riz, gâteau, lait
6. Repas F: tofu, lentilles, avocat, fromage, pain, jus de pomme

Étape 2. Écrivez ce que *(what)* vous avez mangé *(ate)* ce matin. Avec votre partenaire, décidez si votre petit déjeuner est équilibré ou pas équilibré.

© Ekaterina Pokrovsky / Shutterstock.com

ACTIVITÉ R Les étudiants de votre université

Étape 1. Avec un(e) partenaire, décrivez les habitudes alimentaires des étudiants typiques de votre université. Qu'est-ce qu'ils aiment? Qu'est-ce qu'ils n'aiment pas? Qu'est-ce qu'ils prennent au petit déjeuner? Qu'est-ce qu'ils prennent au dîner? Qu'est-ce qu'ils boivent le week-end? En général, est-ce que leurs repas sont équilibrés?

Étape 2. Proposez un menu équilibré pour **le petit déjeuner**, **le déjeuner** et **le dîner** pour ces étudiants.

OUI, JE PEUX!

Here are two "can do statements" for you to check your progress so far. Look at each statement and rate yourself on how well you think you can perform the task. Then verify your ability with a partner. How did you do?

1. **"I can say what I like and do not like to eat and drink."**

   I can perform this function
   ☐ with ease
   ☐ with some difficulty
   ☐ not at all

2. **"I can ask someone else what he/she likes to eat and drink and determine if he/she eats well overall."**

   I can perform this function
   ☐ with ease
   ☐ with some difficulty
   ☐ not at all

iLrn™

Are you looking for more practice? You can find it in **iLrn**.

La cuisine

Cooking

le vinaigre

la farine

la mayonnaise

la moutarde

des poivrons *(m.)*

un citron vert

un citron

l'ail *(m.)*

un oignon

le sel   le poivre

Faire la cuisine

Vocabulaire complémentaire

un ingrédient *ingredient*	**aigre** *sour*
une recette *recipe*	**amer / amère** *bitter*
(un steak) à point *medium-cooked (steak)*	**épicé(e)** *spicy*
bien cuit *well-done*	**grillé(e)** *grilled*
saignant *medium rare*	**piquant(e)** *hot*
bleu *rare*	**salé(e)** *salty*
	sucré(e) *sweet*
à la vapeur *steamed*	
au four *baked*	

Les expressions de quantité

une cuillère (de/d') *a spoon (of)*
une tasse (de/d') *a cup (of)*

une boîte (de/d') *a box (of)*
une bouteille (de/d') *a bottle (of)*
un sac (de/d') *a bag (of)*
un verre (de/d') *a glass (of)*

un kilo (de/d') *a kilogram (of)*
une livre (de/d') *a pound (of)*

Note de vocabulaire
Note that **une livre** means *a pound* while **un livre** means *a book*. While *pound* is typically used in the U.S., **kilo** is more commonly used in the Francophone world.

- After expressions of quantity and before a noun, **de/d'** is used instead of **du, de la, de l'** or **des.**

  Je prends **un verre de** lait.   *I'm having **a glass of** milk.*
  Elle a **un kilo d'**oranges.   *She has **a kilogram of** oranges.*

- Expressions of quantity you already know are **assez (de/d'), beaucoup (de/d'), (un) peu (de/d'),** and **trop (de/d').**

  J'ai **beaucoup de** citrons.   *I have **a lot of** lemons.*
  Nous avons mangé **trop d'**ail.   *We ate **too much** garlic.*

Pour aller plus loin
Quelque chose de sucré

Quelque chose means *something* in French. To say *something sweet, something salty, something spicy* and so forth, use the construction **quelque chose + de/d'** + the masculine form of the adjective.

quelque chose de sucré
 something sweet

quelque chose d'épicé
 something spicy

quelque chose de salé
 something salty

quelque chose de délicieux
 something delicious

Essayez! Quel est l'équivalent de ces expressions en français?

1. something cold
2. something hot
3. something good
4. something bad
5. something interesting
6. something cool (fresh)

ACTIVITÉ A **Les saveurs** Choisissez l'aliment qui va avec la description que vous entendez.

5-6

1. a. la moutarde   b. un biscuit
2. a. les oignons verts   b. le vinaigre
3. a. le sel   b. un citron vert
4. a. la mayonnaise   b. la moutarde
5. a. le chocolat noir   b. le sucre
6. a. le poivre   b. la farine

ACTIVITÉ B **Quiz culinaire**

Étape 1. Quel ingrédient n'appartient pas *(doesn't belong)* à la recette?

1. un gâteau	a. les œufs	b. la farine	c. l'ail
2. le steak-frites	a. les pommes de terre	b. le poulet	c. le bœuf
3. un sandwich	a. le pain	b. le fromage	c. les citrons
4. une omelette	a. la mayonnaise	b. les poivrons	c. les oignons
5. la sauce tomate	a. les tomates	b. l'ail	c. la moutarde
6. la vinaigrette	a. la farine	b. l'huile	c. le vinaigre
7. les pâtes	a. le fromage	b. la crème	c. la confiture
8. le coq au vin	a. la mayonnaise	b. le poulet	c. le vin

 Étape 2. Vous allez entendre le nom d'un ingrédient et une quantité. Quel aliment associez-vous à la quantité de chaque ingrédient?

5-7

9. a. une salade aux œufs   b. un hamburger
10. a. un sandwich   b. des macaronis au fromage
11. a. un gâteau   b. une tasse de café
12. a. une sangria   b. une fondue

✈ ······
Si vous y allez

© Berti Hanna/REA/Redux

Si vous allez à Fresnoy-Le-Grand (France), visitez le dépôt d'usine *(factory outlet)* Le Creuset. Le Creuset fabrique des articles de cuisine d'une qualité exceptionnelle depuis 1925. Visitez le site officiel de Le Creuset pour voir la gamme des produits et des recettes.

Résultats du quiz

12: Bravo! Vous êtes le prochain Jacques Pépin!

9–11: Pas mal. Continuez.

6–8: Des cours de cuisine vous seraient *(would be)* utiles.

3–5: Attention! Vous êtes un peu dangereux/dangereuse dans la cuisine.

1–2: Quelle horreur! Vous êtes nul/nulle *(hopeless)* en cuisine!

ACTIVITÉ **C** **Les recettes** Vous allez entendre des extraits de recettes. Quel aliment associez-vous à chaque phrase?

1. a. un gâteau   b. une salade
2. a. les frites   b. une pomme de terre au four
3. a. la soupe   b. la glace
4. a. le thé glacé   b. la soupe
5. a. une tarte   b. une pizza
6. a. un sandwich   b. la glace

ACTIVITÉ **D** **Votre viande, comment l'aimez-vous?** Quand vous commandez (order) un steak au restaurant, comment le commandez-vous: **bien cuit, à point, saignant** ou **bleu?**

Modèle: le steak   **J'aime mon steak bien cuit.**

1. le steak   2. le hamburger   3. l'agneau   4. la dinde   5. le porc

ACTIVITÉ **E** **Quelle préparation?**

Étape 1. Indiquez la préparation que vous aimez pour chaque aliment.

Modèle: le poulet   **J'aime le poulet rôti.**

1. le poulet   5. le steak
2. le poisson   6. le porc
3. le canard   7. les pommes de terre
4. l'agneau   8. les légumes

Étape 2. Montrez vos réponses à un(e) partenaire. Est-ce que vous avez des préférences semblables? Qui a une alimentation plus saine?

ACTIVITÉ **F** **Qu'est-ce que Claire Gagner prépare ce soir?** Utilisez les articles pour déterminer si la première partie de chaque phrase est **(a) Elle prend…** ou **(b) Elle prend un kilo…**

1. _____ **de l'**emmental.   4. _____ **de** pommes vertes.
2. _____ **du** pain.   5. _____ **de l'**ail.
3. _____ **de** gruyère.   6. _____ **de** farine.

Conclusion Est-ce que Claire prépare **une tarte** ou **une fondue** avec ces ingrédients?

ACTIVITÉ G **Mme Saxton** Vous avez rencontré Madame Saxton dans la Séquence 1 du film *Liaisons.* Que prend Madame Saxton pour le goûter? Complétez chaque aliment avec une expression de quantité logique.

Modèle: _____ bonbons   **Madame Saxton prend un sac de** bonbons.

1. _____ lait   **2.** _____ Coca   **3.** _____ chips   **4.** _____ biscuits

ACTIVITÉ H **Vos habitudes alimentaires**

Étape 1. Complétez les phrases avec une expression de quantité: **jamais de/d'**, **un peu de/d'**, **assez de/d'**, **beaucoup de/d'** ou **trop de/d'**.

Normalement, je (ne) prends…

1. _____ fruits et légumes
2. _____ glucides
3. _____ produits laitiers
4. _____ eau

5. _____ matières grasses
6. _____ produits sucrés
7. _____ alcool
8. _____ tabac

Étape 2. Comparez vos habitudes *(habits)* alimentaires avec un(e) partenaire. Qui a une alimentation plus saine?

Un mot sur la culture

La fondue suisse

Ingrédients: ½ kilo de gruyère, ½ kilo d'emmental, 1 ½ tasse de vin blanc, une gousse d'ail, 3 cuillères à soupe de Kirsch, du sel et du poivre

La fondue suisse est une fondue au fromage. Traditionnellement, on sert cette fondue avec des petits morceaux de pain piqués sur une fourchette°. Selon la tradition, la personne qui laisse tomber° son morceau de pain dans la casserole *(pot)* doit embrasser° son voisin de gauche ou lui payer une bouteille de vin!

fourchette *fork* **laisse tomber** *drops* **doit embrasser** *must kiss*

- Quels sont les ingrédients de ces autres types de fondue?

1. la fondue bourguignonne   2. la fondue au chocolat

Liaisons avec les mots et les sons

5-9
Le /r/ français

The French /r/ is a sound unique to French and is nothing like the English *r* or the Spanish *r*. Because the sound is made in the back of the throat, it is sometimes equated with the sound that one makes when you are about to gargle. The French /r/ is actually closer to an English *h* sound. To make the French /r/ sound, try replacing it with the English *h* sound and then push the air out gently as if you are about to gargle. Try practicing with the following words that have a similar sound.

Loch (Ness monster)	Bach (the composer)

Pratique A. Écoutez et répétez ces mots qui se terminent *(end)* par le son /r/.

1. beurre
2. verre
3. porc
4. boire
5. yaourt
6. canard

Pratique B. Écoutez et répétez ces mots qui commencent par le son /r/.

1. repas
2. rôti
3. raisin
4. riz
5. rester
6. Roger

Pratique C. Une voyelle précède le son /r/ dans ces mots. Écoutez et répétez les mots.

1. céréales
2. carotte
3. nourriture
4. hamburger
5. orange
6. haricots

Pratique D. Une consonne précède le son /r/ dans ces mots. Écoutez et répétez les mots.

1. fromage
2. croissant
3. grillé
4. brocoli
5. prendre
6. citron

Pratique E. Écoutez et répétez ces répliques de la Séquence 3 du film *Liaisons.*

CLAIRE Pardon. Asseyez-vous, je vous en prie. Vous prenez quelque chose? Quelque chose à boire?

 À vos stylos! C'est l'heure de la dictée!

5-10
Vous allez entendre quatre phrases deux fois. La première fois, écoutez bien. La deuxième fois, écrivez les phrases.

Sujet Une serveuse *(waitress)* parle à Claire dans un café.

Pour parler du passé

Le passé composé

DU FILM *LIAISONS*

Un coup d'œil sur la grammaire

Look at these photos from the film *Liaisons* and their captions.

CLAIRE ... j'**ai cherché** votre nom dans le registre... mais je ne l'**ai pas trouvé.**

CLAIRE Alors, vous **avez fait** ma connaissance, Monsieur Prévost. Mission accomplie!

1. What four verbs do you recognize?
2. The verbs in bold are in the past tense. What verb is used to form the past tense?

Note de grammaire
Some verbs are also conjugated with **être** in the **passé composé.** You will learn these verbs in **Chapitre 6.**

To indicate that an event or an action has been completed in the past, French uses the **passé composé.** The **passé composé** of most verbs is formed with the present tense of **avoir** (the auxiliary verb) plus a past participle.

passé composé du verbe *manger*	
j' **ai mangé**	nous **avons mangé**
tu **as mangé**	vous **avez mangé**
il/elle/on **a mangé**	ils/elles **ont mangé**

The **passé composé** can express three meanings in English. For example, **j'ai mangé** can mean *I ate, I have eaten,* or *I did eat,* depending on the context.

The past participle of **-er** verbs is formed by dropping the **-er** and replacing it with **é.**

J'**ai acheté** des fraises hier.	I *bought* some strawberries yesterday.
Nous **avons mangé** un gâteau au chocolat.	We *have eaten* a chocolate cake.
Il **a cuisiné** un poulet hier soir.	He *cooked* a chicken last night.
Vous **avez parlé** avec le cuisinier?	*Did* you *speak* with the cook?

- To form the past participle of regular -**ir** verbs, drop the **r**.

J'**ai fini** mes devoirs la semaine passée.	*I **finished** my homework last week.*
Il **a choisi** une pomme verte.	*He **chose** a green apple.*
Nous **avons obéi** à la loi.	*We **have obeyed** the law.*
Tu **as réussi** à faire une omelette!	*You **succeeded** in making an omelette!*

- The past participle of **prendre, apprendre,** and **comprendre** are **pris, appris,** and **compris.**

Vous **avez pris** des légumes hier?	*Did you **have** any vegetables yesterday?*
J'**ai appris** le français l'année dernière.	*I **learned** French last year.*

- The following verbs have irregular past participles.

avoir	**eu**	dire	**dit**	être	**été**
boire	**bu**	écrire	**écrit**	faire	**fait**
				lire	**lu**

Note de **grammaire**
The **passé composé** of **il y a** is **il y a eu**; that of **il faut** is **il a fallu.**

J'**ai eu** des cours difficiles.	*I **have had** difficult courses.*
Ils **ont bu** du thé vert.	*They **drank** (some) green tea.*
Qu'est-ce que vous **avez dit**?	*What **did you say**?*
Nous **avons été** malades.	*We **have been** sick.*
Vous **avez fait** cette tarte?	*You **made** this pie?*
Tu **as lu** la recette?	*Did you **read** the recipe?*

- In negative sentences, **ne/n'… pas** and **ne/n'… jamais** go around the auxiliary verb **avoir.**

Je **n'ai pas bu** de café hier matin.	*I **didn't drink** any coffee yesterday morning.*
Nous **n'avons jamais pris** de vin.	*We **have never had** any wine.*

- In questions with inversion, the subject pronoun and the conjugated form of **avoir** are inverted.

Avez-vous fini vos devoirs?	***Did you finish** your homework?*
Luc **a-t-il travaillé** hier?	***Did Luc work** yesterday?*
Les filles **ont-elles dansé** hier soir?	***Did the girls dance** last night?*

- Short adverbs are placed between **avoir** and the past participle.

Il **a bien fait** ses devoirs.	*He **did** his homework **well**.*

- These expressions are often used with the **passé composé.**

avant-hier	*the day before yesterday*	l'année dernière / passée	*last year*
		le mois dernier / passé	*last month*
hier	*yesterday*	la semaine dernière / passée	*last week*
hier soir	*last night*		

ACTIVITÉ I **Aujourd'hui ou hier?** Écoutez les activités des étudiants.
5-11 Indiquez s'ils font les activités **(a) aujourd'hui** ou s'ils ont fait les activités **(b) hier.**

Modèle: Vous entendez: Nous avons fait nos devoirs.

Vous répondez: **hier**

1. **2.** **3.** **4.** **5.** **6.** **7.** **8.** **9.** **10.**

ACTIVITÉ J **Ce soir ou la semaine dernière?** Utilisez les verbes pour déterminer si Abia fait ces activités ce soir ou si elle a fait ces activités la semaine passée. Complétez les phrases avec **(a) Ce soir** ou **(b) La semaine dernière.**

1. _____, j'**ai fait** un gâteau au fromage.

2. _____, j'**ai mangé** un steak.

3. _____, je **prends** du poulet rôti.

4. _____, j'**ai bu** un Coca.

5. _____, j'**ai** un cours de cuisine.

6. _____, j'**ai pris** des frites.

7. _____, je **prépare** du riz complet.

8. _____, j'**écris** à ma mère.

Conclusion Est-ce qu'Abia a été raisonnable *(sensible)* la semaine dernière? Et ce soir?

ACTIVITÉ K **Céline Dion** Utilisez les verbes pour déterminer si Céline a fait ces activités **(a) l'année dernière** ou si elle fait ces activités **(b) aujourd'hui.**

1. _____ elle **chante** pour son mari.

2. _____ elle **fait** du shopping.

3. _____ elle **a dit** bonjour à ses fans.

4. _____ elle **finit** une tournée *(tour).*

5. _____ elle **a chanté** à Paris.

6. _____ elle **a lu** sa biographie.

7. _____ elle **a appris** une nouvelle langue.

8. _____ elle **mange** avec son fils René-Charles.

Conclusion Est-ce que la vie de Céline est plus calme aujourd'hui ou l'année passée?

ACTIVITÉ L **Messagerie instantanée** Quelqu'un vous écrit par messagerie instantanée pour savoir si vous aimez la cuisine française. Répondez aux questions avec des phrases complètes.

Modèle: Avez-vous pris un steak-frites?

Non, je n'ai pas pris de steak-frites.

1. Avez-vous visité la France?

2. Avez-vous lu un livre de recettes en français?

3. Avez-vous appris à faire la cuisine française?

4. Avez-vous mangé des escargots?

5. Avez-vous bu du vin français?

6. Avez-vous fait un steak-frites?

7. Avez-vous pris du fromage français?

8. Avez-vous écrit à un chef français?

ACTIVITÉ **M** **Connaissez-vous bien vos camarades de classe?**

Étape 1. Qu'est-ce que vous avez fait hier? Écrivez cinq phrases complètes avec cinq verbes différents de la liste.

Modèle: J'ai étudié à la bibliothèque.

boire	être	naviguer
choisir	faire	parler
cuisiner	finir	prendre
danser	jouer	regarder
écouter	lire	
écrire	manger	

Étape 2. Devinez *(Guess)* ce que votre partenaire a fait hier. Écrivez cinq phrases.

Modèle: Il/Elle a lu le journal.

Étape 3. Demandez à votre partenaire s'il/si elle a fait les activités.

Modèle: É1: Est-ce que tu as lu le journal hier?
   É2: Oui, j'ai lu le journal. / Non, je n'ai pas lu le journal.

Liaisons musicales

© Francois Durand/Getty Images Entertainment/Getty Images

Benjamin Biolay (1973–) est un chanteur français et aussi l'ex-mari de Chiara Mastroianni, la fille de Catherine Deneuve. Sa chanson *Brandt rhapsodie* contient une petite recette. Cherchez les paroles *(lyrics)* et/ou un vidéo-clip de cette chanson sur Internet. Identifiez les termes liés à *(related to)* la nourriture et les verbes au passé composé.

OUI, JE PEUX! Here are two "can do statements" for you to check your progress so far. Look at each statement and rate yourself on how well you think you can perform the task. Then verify your ability with a partner. How did you do?

1. **"I can say what I ate and drank for dinner last night."**

   I can perform this function
   ☐ with ease
   ☐ with some difficulty
   ☐ not at all

2. **"I can ask someone else what he/she ate and drank for dinner last night and determine who had a better dinner."**

   I can perform this function
   ☐ with ease
   ☐ with some difficulty
   ☐ not at all

iLrn™

Are you looking for more practice? You can find it in **iLrn**.

PREMIÈRE PROJECTION

Avant de visionner

ACTIVITÉ Ⓐ **Vous rappelez-vous?** Vous rappelez-vous *(Do you remember)* ce qui s'est passé dans la Séquence 2 du film *Liaisons*? Pour chaque phrase, indiquez si c'est vrai ou faux.

	Vrai	Faux
1. Claire a téléphoné au Château Frontenac pour vérifier la réservation.	☐	☐
2. Claire a reçu un coup de téléphone de sa tante.	☐	☐
3. Claire a décidé d'aller à Québec.	☐	☐
4. Abia a eu peur pour Claire.	☐	☐
5. Claire a pensé avoir vu *(saw)* sa mère à l'hôtel.	☐	☐

ACTIVITÉ Ⓑ **Mettez-les en ordre** Mettez ces répliques entre Claire et Alexis en ordre (1-8). Vous allez vérifier vos réponses plus tard.

a. _____ A: Alexis Prévost. C'est un plaisir de vous revoir.

b. _____ A: Bonjour, mademoiselle! Excusez-moi. Je vous ai surprise.

c. _____ C: Je vais à Québec et je me suis arrêtée *(stopped)* pour manger quelque chose. Et vous?

d. _____ A: Moi aussi. Oui. Je viens de goûter la tarte aux bleuets d'ailleurs *(moreover)*. Ici, elle est délicieuse. Puis-je?

e. _____ C: Monsieur Prévost, n'est-ce pas?

f. _____ C: Oui. Pardon. Asseyez-vous *(Sit down)*. Je vous en prie.

g. _____ C: Pour moi aussi.

h. _____ A: Que faites-vous à Trois-Rivières?

ACTIVITÉ Ⓒ **Devinez** Devinez *(Guess)* qui dit les phrases suivantes dans la Séquence 3: Claire **(C)** ou Alexis **(A)**? Vous allez vérifier vos réponses plus tard.

1. _____ Vous pouvez me demander ce que *(what)* vous voulez, sauf *(except)* mon âge et mon poids *(weight)*.

2. _____ … j'ai cherché votre nom dans le registre… mais je ne l'ai pas trouvé.

3. _____ … je n'étais pas un des clients de l'hôtel.

4. _____ Je voulais juste faire votre connaissance.

▶ **Regarder la séquence**

Vous allez regarder la Séquence 3 du film *Liaisons*. Vérifiez vos réponses de l'Activité B et de l'Activité C.

Après le visionnage

ACTIVITÉ **D** **Avez-vous compris?**

1. D'où vient Alexis Prévost?
2. Pourquoi Alexis Prévost va-t-il à Québec?
3. Claire va loger dans quel hôtel à Québec?
4. Qui est-ce que Claire voit *(sees)* passer par la fenêtre du café?

ACTIVITÉ **E** **Utilisez le contexte** Regardez bien les mots en caractères gras *(boldface)* et répondez aux questions.

CLAIRE Alors, vous avez fait ma connaissance, Monsieur Prévost. Mission accomplie! Et maintenant? Que faites-vous ici? Vous me (1) **suivez**?

PRÉVOST Mademoiselle. (2) **Ce n'est pas mon genre**. ... Je ne suis pas un psychopathe. Non, c'est juste une belle coïncidence de vous rencontrer ici.

CLAIRE Hmmm... est-ce que je devrais *(should)* vous (3) **croire**?

1. Le mot **suivez** vient du verbe **suivre**. Que veut dire ce verbe?
   a. *to suggest*   b. *to follow*

2. Le mot **genre** veut dire *(means) kind, sort* ou *type*. Quand M. Prévost dit à Claire «Ce n'est pas mon genre», qu'est-ce qu'il veut dire?
   a. *I'm not that kind of person.*   c. *That's not my style.*
   b. *I'm not into that.*   d. a, b, c

3. Que veut dire le verbe **croire**?
   a. *to believe*   b. *to think*

La tarte au sucre

Liaisons avec la culture

La cuisine traditionnelle du Québec

Les premiers colons° français sont arrivés au Canada avec des traditions culinaires de la France, mais ils les ont vite adaptées à leur nouvel environnement. La cuisine traditionnelle québécoise est souvent riche en calories, avec de grandes quantités de graisse animale dans sa préparation pour affronter° le climat rude de l'hiver et avoir l'énergie nécessaire pour pouvoir travailler dehors, malgré le froid. Dans cette cuisine, on trouve surtout des produits du terroir, comme par exemple le sirop d'érable°, la viande, le poisson et les pommes de terre. Parmi les spécialités les plus connues, on peut citer la soupe aux pois, les tourtières, la tarte au sucre, la tarte aux bleuets, le pouding chômeur et le pâté chinois.

colons *colonists* **affronter** *to face* **sirop d'érable** *maple syrup*

LIAISONS
CULTURELLES

La nourriture et la santé

OUTILS DE LECTURE

Learning adjectives by recognizing past participles

The past participle forms of verbs are not only used to form the **passé composé**. They may also function as adjectives. The following are taken from the texts you will read.

a. [...] le dîner **pris** en commun est un facteur d'équilibre du cercle familial.

b. Il est **adapté** aux grandes villes [...].

c. Le filet de poisson [...] est **mariné** pendant trente minutes [...].

d. D'autres plats sont **influencés** par la cuisine chinoise [...].

1. What do the adjectives in bold mean?

2. What verbs do the adjectives come from?

L'importance des repas en famille au Maghreb

Dans trois pays arabophones du Maghreb (l'Algérie, le Maroc, la Tunisie), le français est une deuxième langue importante. Comme dans la plupart des° pays francophones, le repas reste un moment convivial privilégié. Manger ensemble, en famille ou avec des amis, c'est le moment de se détendre°, se retrouver° et discuter des événements de la journée. Rituel quotidien°, le déjeuner ou le dîner pris en commun est un facteur d'équilibre du cercle familial. La fonction sociale du repas est donc aussi importante ou même plus que la nourriture.

© Thierry Tronnel/Corbis

la plupart des *most of* **se détendre** *relax* **se retrouver** *get together* **quotidien** *daily*

Vrai ou faux?

1. Le français est la première langue du Maroc.   V / F

2. La fonction sociale du repas est plus importante que la nourriture.   V / F

3. Dans les pays du Maghreb, chaque membre de la famille mange séparément.   V / F

4. Le moment du repas n'a pas beaucoup d'importance dans la structure familiale.   V/ F

Courtesy of Larry Wong

Le fast-food et l'obésité en France

À la surprise générale, les entreprises américaines de restauration rapide ont réussi à s'implanter° en France. Les raisons de ce succès relatif sont connues: ce type de nourriture est économique et rapide. Il est adapté aux grandes villes et aux situations où on n'a pas le temps de faire la cuisine et on doit manger «sur le pouce»°. Cependant, comme aux États-Unis, ces changements d'habitudes alimentaires°, associés au manque° d'exercice physique, mènent° souvent à des conséquences semblables: les cas d'obésité augmentent chez les adultes. On peut même observer un nouveau phénomène d'obésité chez certains enfants. L'obésité en France est donc devenue un sujet de préoccupation ces dernières années.

Adapted from: http://obesitefastfood.over-blog.com/article-18446848.html

s'implanter *establish* **manger «sur le pouce»** *eat in a hurry* **habitudes alimentaires** *eating patterns / customs* **manque** *lack* **mènent** *lead to*

Vrai ou faux?

1. Les entreprises de restauration rapide ont réussi à s'implanter en France.   V / F
2. Les mauvaises habitudes alimentaires contribuent à l'augmentation de l'exercice physique.   V / F
3. L'obésité chez les enfants est un problème en France.   V / F

Les traditions culinaires et les nouvelles tendances en Polynésie

Tahiti est la plus connue° des îles° de la Polynésie française et, pour un grand nombre de Français, cette île est le paradis tropical par excellence. La cuisine polynésienne, principalement à base de poissons, de crustacés° et de légumes et végétaux locaux, tels que le taro et la patate douce, reflète parfaitement cette image d'exotisme. Un des plats les plus connus est le poisson cru° à la tahitienne. Le filet de poisson (généralement du thon°) est mariné dans du jus de citron pendant trente minutes avant d'être servi accompagné de lait de noix de coco. D'autres plats dans la cuisine polynésienne sont influencés par la cuisine chinoise ou par celle de° la Métropole°.

© Douglas Peebles/Stock Connection/Aurora

connue *known* **une île** *island* **crustacés** *shellfish* **cru** *raw* **thon** *tuna* **celle de / celui de** *that of* **la Métropole** *the European part of France (roughly equivalent to the concept of the 48 contiguous states)*

Vrai ou faux?

1. Beaucoup de plats tahitiens sont influencés par la cuisine mexicaine.   V / F
2. Beaucoup de Français sont attirés par le climat tropical de la Polynésie.   V / F
3. La cuisine polynésienne est à base de viande rouge (du bœuf, de l'agneau).   V / F

Les végétariens et les végétaliens en France et au Québec

Pour les anglophones, le terme **végétarien** est facile à comprendre. Mais, quand on est **végétalien,** on ne mange ni œufs ni° produits laitiers. Les Américains qui voyagent beaucoup à l'étranger° remarquent° souvent qu'il est relativement plus facile de trouver des plats végétariens ou végétaliens au Québec, qui est plus directement influencé par les habitudes alimentaires provenant des° États-Unis. Par contre, il est encore° rare de trouver des restaurants (ou des plats préparés) végétariens en France. Quant à° la cuisine végétalienne, c'est un phénomène récent et minoritaire en France.

ni... ni... *neither . . . nor . . .*   **à l'étranger** *abroad*   **remarquent** *notice*   **provenant des** *originating from*   **encore** *still*   **Quant à** *As for*

Compréhension

1. Les végétaliens ne mangent pas de _____.
   a. fruits   b. produits laitiers

2. La cuisine _____ est un phénomène récent en France.
   a. végétalienne   b. végétarienne

3. Les Québécois sont influencés par les habitudes alimentaires des _____.
   a. Russes   b. Américains

LIAISONS CULTURELLES

spécialités régionales

Use **iLrn™** to access the video **La cuisine** to learn more about the cuisine of the French-speaking world. Be prepared to answer the question **Et vous? Quel type de nourriture aimez-vous manger?** Share your responses with your classmates in **Share It!**

PARTIE 1   5–12

LES REPAS

le repas	*meal*
le petit déjeuner	*breakfast*
le déjeuner	*lunch*
le goûter	*snack*
le dîner	*dinner*

LES PLATS

le dessert	*dessert*
le hors-d'œuvre (*m.*) / l'entrée (*f.*)	*starter / appetizer*
le plat principal	*main course, dish (kind of food)*
les plats (*m.*)	*courses (meals)*

LA NOURRITURE

l'aliment (*m.*)	*a particular food*
la nourriture	*food*
le beurre	*butter*
la confiture	*jam*
la crème	*cream*
le sucre	*sugar*
les fruits (*m.*)	*fruits*
une banane	*banana*
une orange	*orange*
une pomme	*apple*
les légumes (*m.*)	*vegetables*
les carottes (*f.*)	*carrots*
les épinards (*m.*)	*spinach*
les haricots verts (*m.*)	*green beans*
une pomme de terre (*f.*)	*potato*
la viande	*meat*
le bœuf	*beef*
le jambon	*ham*
le poulet	*chicken*
un rôti (de porc)	*(pork) roast*
un biscuit	*cookie*
les céréales (*f.*)	*cereal*
les chips (*f.*)	*chips*
un croissant	*croissant*
les frites (*f.*)	*fries*
le fromage	*cheese*
un gâteau	*cake*
la glace	*ice cream*
les œufs (*m.*)	*eggs*
une omelette	*omelet*
le pain	*bread*
les pâtes (*f.*)	*pasta*
la pizza	*pizza*
le riz	*rice*
le poisson	*fish*
la salade	*salad*

un sandwich (au fromage)	*(cheese) sandwich*
les saucisses (*f.*)	*sausages*
la soupe (à la tomate)	*(tomato) soup*
le steak	*steak*
le yaourt	*yogurt*

LES BOISSONS

la bière	*beer*
le café	*coffee*
le citron pressé	*lemonade*
le Coca	*Coca-Cola*
l'eau minérale (*f.*)	*mineral water*
le jus d'orange	*orange juice*
le lait	*milk*
le thé	*tea*
le vin	*wine*

VERBES

avoir chaud	*to be hot*
avoir faim	*to be hungry*
avoid froid	*to be cold*
avoir soif	*to be thirsty*
apprendre (à)	*to learn*
comprendre	*to understand*
prendre	*to take; to have food*
prendre le déjeuner / le dîner	*to have lunch / dinner*
prendre un verre	*to have a drink*
prendre son temps	*to take one's time*

PARTIE 2   5–13

UNE ALIMENTATION ÉQUILIBRÉE

les fibres (*f.*)	*fibers*
les glucides (*m.*)	*carbohydrates*
les matières grasses (*f.*)	*fats*
les produits laitiers (*m.*)	*dairy products*
les protéines (*f.*)	*proteins*
les sucres (*m.*)	*sugars*

LA NOURRITURE

l'avocat (*m.*)	*avocado*
les bleuets (*m.*)	*blueberries*
les fraises (*f.*)	*strawberries*
les framboises (*f.*)	*raspberries*
le raisin (*m.*)	*grapes*
le brocoli	*broccoli*
les petits pois (*m.*)	*peas*
l'agneau (*m.*)	*lamb*
le canard	*duck*
la dinde	*turkey*
le veau	*veal*
la volaille	*poultry*

les aliments industriels (m.)	processed foods
les bonbons (m.)	candies
le fast-food	fast food
les fruits (m.) de mer	shellfish
un hamburger	hamburger
l'huile (f.) (d'olive)	(olive) oil
les lentilles (f.)	lentils
les noix (f.)	walnuts
le pain complet	whole grain bread
la tarte	pie
le tofu	tofu

LA BOISSON

le lait de soja	soy milk

ADJECTIFS

alcoolisé(e)	alcoholic
frais / fraîche	fresh, cool
frit(e)	fried
sain(e)	healthy
végétalien(ne)	vegan
végétarien(ne)	vegetarian

VERBES

boire	to drink
être au régime	to be on a diet
éviter (de + infinitive)	to avoid (doing something)
faire attention (à)	to pay attention (to)
fumer	to smoke

DIVERS

la santé	health

PARTIE 3   5–14

LES INGRÉDIENTS ET LES RECETTES

l'ail (m.)	garlic
un citron	lemon
un citron vert	lime
la farine	flour
un ingrédient	ingredient
la mayonnaise	mayonnaise
la moutarde	mustard
un oignon	onion
le poivre	pepper

un poivron rouge / vert	red / green pepper
le sel	salt
une tomate	tomato
le vinaigre	vinegar

une recette	recipe

à point	medium
bien cuit	well-done
saignant	medium rare
bleu	rare

au four	baked
grillé(e)	grilled
à la vapeur	steamed

aigre	sour
amer / amère	bitter
épicé(e)	spicy
piquant(e)	hot
salé(e)	salty
sucré(e)	sweet

quelque chose de/d' + adjective	something + adjective

LES EXPRESSIONS DE QUANTITÉ

une cuillère (de/d')	a spoon (of)
une tasse (de/d')	a cup (of)
un verre (de/d')	a glass (of)

une boîte (de/d')	a box (of)
une bouteille (de/d')	a bottle (of)
un sac (de/d')	a bag (of)

un kilo (de/d')	a kilogram (of)
une livre (de/d')	a pound (of)

EXPRESSIONS AVEC LE PASSÉ

l'année (f.) dernière / passée	last year
avant-hier	the day before yesterday
hier	yesterday
hier soir	last night
le mois dernier / passé	last month
la semaine dernière / passée	last week

Du **marché** à la **table**

En bref   In this chapter, you will:

- learn about types of grocery and food stores

- learn vocabulary related to restaurants and learn how to order food

- learn the verb **vendre** and other regular -**re** verbs

- learn the **passé composé** with the verb **être**

- learn direct object pronouns

- learn about final consonants that are pronounced

- read about the **marché de Belleville** in Paris

- write about a food establishment that you visited

You will also re-watch **SÉQUENCE 3: À Québec** of the film *Liaisons*.

Ressources

 audio   video   Share It!   iLrn™   http://www.cengagebrain.com

VOCABULAIRE 1

Les **grandes surfaces**

Large stores, shopping places

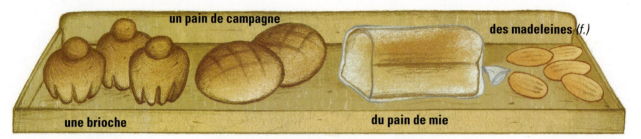

un pain de campagne

des madeleines *(f.)*

une brioche

du pain de mie

Le rayon boulangerie-pâtisserie

le saucisson

le rosbif

Le rayon charcuterie

le homard

les crevettes *(f.)*

les moules *(f.)*

le saumon

Le rayon poissons et fruits de mer

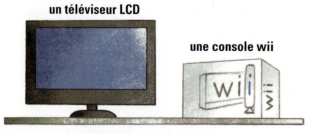

un téléviseur LCD

une console wii

Le rayon audiovisuel

Dans un hypermarché

Vocabulaire complémentaire

le rayon boucherie *meat counter*
  le bœuf haché *ground beef*
  une côtelette d'agneau / de porc
    lamb / pork chop
le rayon surgelés *frozen food aisle*
  les surgelés *(m. pl.) frozen foods*

l'argent *(m.) money*
une boîte (de conserves) *box, can*
  (canned goods)
un centime *cent*
un chariot *shopping cart*

un panier *basket*
le prix *price*
un supermarché *supermarket*

coûter *to cost*

Ça fait combien? *How much is it?*
Ça fait... euros. *That makes*
  (It costs) . . . euros.
C'est combien? *How much is it?*
Combien coûte(nt)...? *How much*
  is/are . . . ?

🔊 **ACTIVITÉ** Ⓐ **Les rayons** Indiquez le rayon qui est associé à chaque produit
6-1 mentionné: **(a) boulangerie-pâtisserie, (b) boucherie, (c) charcuterie, (d) poissons
et fruits de mer, (e) audiovisuel.**

  1.   2.   3.   4.   5.   6.   7.   8.
  9. 10. 11. 12. 13. 14.

❖ **Et vous?** Quel rayon préférez-vous?

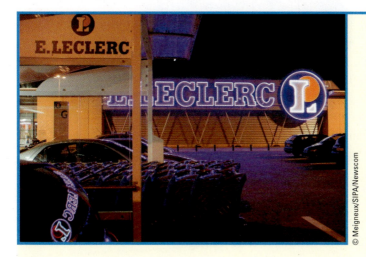

Un mot sur la langue

L'hypermarché et le supermarché

Un **supermarché** est un établissement qui vend *(sells)* des produits alimentaires. Un **hypermarché** est plus grand qu'un supermarché et vend des produits alimentaires et non-alimentaires comme les articles de maison et de jardin. On trouve souvent de bons prix et de bonnes promotions *(sales)* dans les hypermarchés.

- Quel est votre supermarché préféré?
- Avez-vous un hypermarché dans votre quartier?

© Meigneux/SIPA/Newscom

ACTIVITÉ B Associations Associez les éléments de la première colonne avec les éléments de la deuxième colonne.

1. _____ le rayon surgelés   a. les haricots verts Green Giant
2. _____ les centimes   b. la glace
3. _____ une boîte de conserves   c. un panier
4. _____ un chariot   d. l'argent
5. _____ le rayon produits laitiers   e. le lait

 ACTIVITÉ C Ça fait combien? Quel produit associez-vous à chaque prix que vous entendez?

6-2

1. a. un homard   b. du pain de mie
2. a. une côtelette de porc   b. un téléviseur LCD
3. a. un micro-ondes   b. 2 livres de moules
4. a. une brioche   b. un ordinateur
5. a. une pizza surgelée   b. une console wii
6. a. une livre de bœuf haché b. un frigo

ACTIVITÉ D À l'hypermarché

> **Note de vocabulaire**
> You will learn more about the verb **acheter** *(to buy)* in **Vocabulaire 2.**

Étape 1. Indiquez à quel rayon Claire doit *(must)* aller pour acheter *(to buy)* ces produits.

Modèle: Elle va acheter des pommes et du bœuf haché.
Il faut aller au rayon fruits et légumes et au rayon boucherie.

1. Elle va acheter du pain de mie, du rosbif et du porc haché.
2. Elle va acheter des fraises surgelées et un lecteur DVD.
3. Elle va acheter du rosbif, des moules et des madeleines.
4. Elle va acheter une pizza surgelée, des haricots verts et du lait.
5. Elle va acheter un pain de campagne et du fromage.

Étape 2. Qu'est-ce que vous allez acheter? Dans quels rayons faut-il aller?

Modèle: **Je vais acheter des pommes, du pain de mie et du saumon. Il faut aller au rayon fruits et légumes, au rayon boulangerie-pâtisserie et au rayon poissons et fruits de mer.**

ACTIVITÉ E **Faire les courses** Pour préparer un déjeuner, vous avez 25 € pour faire les courses au supermarché. Indiquez ce que vous allez acheter et combien ça vous coûte.

Modèle: J'achète un homard, un kilo de pommes de terre et une madeleine.
Ça coûte 24,59 €.

1,49 €

20 €

1kg 10,25 €

1 kg 15,50 €

1 kg 16,50 €

5,29 €

1kg 3,59 €

1,00 €

Si vous y allez

Si vous allez en France, allez à l'hypermarché Carrefour pour acheter des cadeaux *(gifts)* ou des produits alimentaires. Visitez la boutique virtuelle sur le site officiel de Carrefour pour voir le choix de produits et les prix.

Un mot sur la culture

Les hypermarchés en France

Les Français ont créé leur premier hypermarché, Carrefour, en 1963 à Sainte-Geneviève-des-Bois, une banlieue parisienne. Les principales caractéristiques de l'hypermarché sont le libre-service°, l'usage des chariots, un vaste choix° de produits alimentaires et non-alimentaires à bas° prix et la présence d'un parking et d'une station-service°. Le nombre d'hypermarchés a beaucoup augmenté° depuis les années soixante. En 1966, il y avait seulement deux hypermarchés en France. Aujourd'hui, on compte plus de 2000 hypermarchés en France, dont les principaux sont Carrefour, Leclerc, Casino, Cora et Hyper U.

libre-service *self-service* **choix** *choice* **bas** *low* **station-service** *gas station* **augmenté** *increased*

Adapted from: http://www.carrefour.com/fr/content/les-hypermarch%C3%A9s

- Aimez-vous faire les courses dans les hypermarchés? Lesquels *(Which ones)*?

Pour parler des activités

Les verbes comme **vendre** / Le verbe **mettre**

DU FILM *LIAISONS*
···

Un coup d'œil sur la grammaire

Look at these photos from the film *Liaisons* and their captions.

Le café vend de très bons sandwichs et d'excellents desserts.

Elle met un verre d'eau sur la table.

1. Which word in the left photo caption is a verb? What does this verb mean?

2. Which word in the right photo caption is a verb? What does this verb mean?

Vendre et les verbes réguliers en *-re*

Note de **prononciation**
The **d** is not pronounced in the **je**, **tu** or **il/elle/on** forms of regular **-re** verbs in the present tense, but it is pronounced in the **nous**, **vous**, and **ils/elles** forms.

❖ The verb **vendre** is a regular **-re** verb that means *to sell*. It and other regular **-re** verbs like it follow a set pattern of endings in the present tense.

vendre		
je **vends**	nous **vendons**	
tu **vends**	vous **vendez**	PAST PARTICIPLE: **vendu**
il/elle/on **vend**	ils/elles **vendent**	

—Qu'est-ce que les supermarchés **vendent**?   —*What do supermarkets **sell**?*

—Ils **vendent** des produits alimentaires.   —*They **sell** food products.*

—Vous **vendez** des fleurs?   —*Do you **sell** flowers?*

—Oui, nous **vendons** des roses.   —*Yes, we **sell** roses.*

❖ The past participle of regular **-re** verbs is formed by dropping the **-re** from the infinitive and adding an **u.**

J'ai vendu mes livres.   *I **sold** my books.*

••• Here are some other verbs conjugated like **vendre.**

attendre *to wait, to wait for*	**rendre** *to give back, to return*
descendre *to go down (to), to get off*	**rendre visite à** *to visit (someone)*
entendre *to hear*	**répondre à** *to answer*
perdre *to lose*	

Elle **attend** Pierre à l'hypermarché.	She **is waiting for** Pierre at the hypermarket.
Ils **descendent** l'escalier.	They **are going down** the stairs.
Vous **entendez** la musique?	**Do** you **hear** the music?
Elle **rend** le livre à la bibliothèque.	She **is returning** the book at the library.
Nous **rendons visite à** notre mère.	We **are visiting** our mother.
J'**ai perdu** 25 centimes.	I **lost** 25 cents.
Il **a répondu** à la question.	He **answered** the question.

••• To express *to visit people,* use the expression **rendre visite à,** not **visiter. Visiter** is only used with places or things.

À Québec, il **a visité** l'Université Laval et il **a rendu visite à** sa tante.

••• As you encountered in **Séquence 3** of the film *Liaisons,* the expression **descendre à l'hôtel** means *to stay at the hotel (a specific hotel).* You can also say **descendre dans un hôtel** when you are not referring to any specific hotel.

Je **descends** toujours **à l'Hôtel Delta.**	I always **stay at the Delta Hotel.**
Luc **descend dans un hôtel** de luxe.	Luc **stays at a luxury hotel.**

Le verb *mettre*

••• The verb **mettre** is an irregular **-re** verb that means *to place* or *to put.* It does not follow the same pattern as **vendre** in the present tense.

mettre		
je **mets**	nous **mettons**	
tu **mets**	vous **mettez**	PAST PARTICIPLE: **mis**
il/elle/on **met**	ils/elles **mettent**	

Je **mets** une brioche dans mon panier.	I **put** a brioche in my shopping basket.
Elle **a mis** du saumon dans son chariot.	She **placed** some salmon in her shopping cart.
Mettez les pommes dans le panier.	**Put** the apples in the basket.

••• **Mettre la table** is an idiomatic expression that means *to set the table.*

Jacques **met la table** pour sa mère.	Jacques **is setting the table** for his mother.

Note de prononciation

Note de prononciation: The **t** is not pronounced in the **je, tu** or **il/elle/on** forms of **mettre** in the present tense, but it is pronounced in the **nous, vous,** and **ils/elles** forms.

🔊 6-3 **ACTIVITÉ** **F** **eBay** Écoutez les verbes pour déterminer si c'est **Robert** qui **vend** ces choses (things) sur eBay ou si ce sont **Robert et Abia** qui les **vendent.**

Modèle: Il vend des stylos.   **Robert**

1.   2.   3.   4.   5.   6.   7.   8.

⋯⋅ **Et vous?** Est-ce que vous vendez des choses sur eBay? Quels produits?

🔊 6-4 **ACTIVITÉ** **G** **Il faut attendre** Utilisez les verbes pour déterminer si le sujet de chaque phrase est (a) **Nous** ou (b) **Vous.**

Modèle: ... attendez vos parents. **b (Vous)**

1.   2.   3.   4.   5.   6.   7.   8.

⋯⋅ **Et vous?** Qui est-ce que vous attendez souvent?

ACTIVITÉ **H** **Les activités de la famille d'Abia** Abia parle avec sa sœur Nadia à propos de leurs activités et des activités de leur famille. Utilisez les verbes pour déterminer le sujet de chaque phrase.

1. _____ descend**s** dans un hôtel.   a. Je   b. Maman et moi
2. _____ attend**ez** Maman.   a. Vous   b. Ils
3. _____ rend**s** visite à une amie.   a. Keesha   b. Je
4. _____ répond**ent** à mes questions.   a. Patrick et Aude   b. Aude
5. _____ entend**ons** la radio de Patrick.   a. Justin   b. Nous
6. _____ perd ses amis.   a. Xavier   b. Xavier et Patrick

ACTIVITÉ **I** **L'argent pour le Cercle français** Votre classe va vendre des choses pour avoir de l'argent pour le Cercle français. Décidez qui va vendre les choses suivantes.

SUGGESTIONS			
Je	**Le professeur**	**Nous**	**Noms des étudiants _____**

Modèle: _____ des éclairs   **Paul et Ben vendent** des éclairs.

1. _____ des madeleines.   4. _____ de la confiture.
2. _____ du camembert (fromage). 5. _____ des baguettes.
3. _____ des croissants.   6. _____ des biscuits.

Liaisons musicales

© Serge Dion/Agence Quebec Presse/Newscom

Plume LaTraverse est un chanteur-compositeur-artiste-écrivain de Montréal. Ses chansons, comme par exemple J'ai vendu ma chèvre (goat), racontent (tell) souvent des situations drôles. Trouvez les paroles de cette chanson sur Internet pour savoir (to know) pourquoi il a vendu sa chèvre.

ACTIVITÉ **J** Les étudiants du passé et d'aujourd'hui

Étape 1. Ces phrases décrivent-elles les étudiants des années soixante-dix, du 21ᵉ siècle ou les deux à la fois?

	années soixante-dix	21ᵉ siècle
1. ... rendent leurs livres à la bibliothèque.	☐	☐
2. ... attendent des lettres de leurs parents.	☐	☐
3. ... répondent aux courriels de leurs amis.	☐	☐
4. ... rendent visite à leur famille le week-end.	☐	☐
5. ... vendent leurs livres à la librairie.	☐	☐
6. ... perdent souvent leurs devoirs.	☐	☐
7. ... descendent dans un hôtel pendant les vacances.	☐	☐

Conclusion Les étudiants d'aujourd'hui sont-ils très différents des étudiants des années soixante-dix?

Étape 2. Demandez à votre partenaire s'il/si elle fait ces activités.

> **Modèle:** É1: **Est-ce que tu rends tes livres à la bibliothèque?**
> É2: **Non, je ne rends pas mes livres à la bibliothèque.**

Conclusion Votre partenaire et vous, êtes-vous similaires ou différent(e)s?

ACTIVITÉ **K** Qu'est-ce que vous perdez?

Étape 1. Répondez aux questions avec des phrases complètes. Est-ce que vous perdez souvent...

1. vos stylos?
2. vos devoirs?
3. vos livres?
4. vos clés *(keys)*?
5. votre portable?

Étape 2. Partagez vos réponses avec un(e) partenaire. Qui est plus distrait(e) *(absent-minded)*?

ACTIVITÉ **L** *Rendre visite à* ou *visiter*? Complétez chaque phrase avec **rendre visite à** ou **visiter** au présent.

1. Je _____ mes cousins à Paris.
2. Ma sœur _____ le Louvre ce matin.
3. Mes parents _____ leurs amis.
4. Mon frère _____ notre tante.
5. Nous _____ le Quartier latin à 13h00.
6. Nous _____ notre tante Marie ce soir.
7. Je vais _____ la tour Eiffel demain.
8. Nous allons _____ Marseille demain soir.

❖ **Et vous?** Qu'est-ce que vous avez fait le mois dernier? À qui est-ce que vous avez rendu visite? Qu'est-ce que vous avez visité? Préparez des phrases au passé composé.

ACTIVITÉ 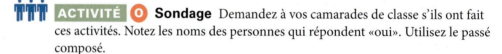 **M** **Qu'est-ce qu'ils mettent dans leurs sandwichs?**

Étape 1. Utilisez les verbes pour déterminer le sujet de chaque phrase.

1. ... met des oignons.	a. Je	b. Mustapha	c. Claire et Anne
2. ... met**ez** du jambon.	a. Luc et Paul	b. Nicole	c. Vous
3. ... met**s** de la mayonnaise.	a. Je	b. Vous	c. Alex
4. ... mett**ons** du rosbif.	a. Tu	b. Nous	c. Vous
5. ... mett**ent** des poivrons rouges.	a. Léon	b. Léon et Yves	c. Vous
6. ... met**s** de la dinde.	a. Tu	b. Michelle	c. On

Étape 2. Inventez un sandwich original. Quel est le nom de votre sandwich? Qu'est-ce que vous mettez dans le sandwich?

Modèle: **Mon sandwich s'appelle** *le club français.* **Je mets de la dinde, du brie, de la moutarde, des œufs et des oignons dans une baguette.**

Étape 3. Demandez à votre partenaire le nom de son sandwich et quels *(which)* ingrédients on met dans ce sandwich.

Modèle: **Comment s'appelle ton sandwich? Qu'est-ce que tu mets dans ton sandwich?**

ACTIVITÉ **N** **Les sandwichs et les pizzas célèbres** Qu'est-ce qu'on met dans ces sandwichs et ces pizzas célèbres?

Modèle: un croque-madame   **On met du jambon, du fromage et un œuf.**

1. un croque-monsieur   **3.** une pizza Margherita

2. un Philly cheesesteak   **4.** un burrito

ACTIVITÉ **O** **Sondage** Demandez à vos camarades de classe s'ils ont fait ces activités. Notez les noms des personnes qui répondent «oui». Utilisez le passé composé.

Modèle: **Est-ce que tu as déjà** *(ever)* **attendu le bus plus de trente minutes?**

1. (attendre) le bus plus de trente minutes

2. (entendre) les nouvelles *(news)* à la télé

3. (rendre) les DVD au club vidéo en retard

4. (rendre) visite à la famille de son (sa) petit(e) ami(e)

5. (vendre) des choses sur eBay

6. (vendre) son chien ou son chat

7. (répondre) à une petite annonce *(ad)* pour un appartement

8. (répondre) à une petite annonce pour trouver un(e) petit(e) ami(e)

9. (mettre) des posters dans son appartement

10. (mettre) des anchois *(anchovies)* sur une pizza

Pour aller plus loin

Il y a + expression de temps

You learned that **il y a** + *noun* means *there is* or *there are:* **Il y a des crevettes dans mon chariot.** However, when **il y a** is followed by a time expression, it conveys that something happened at a time *ago* in the past.

—Quand avez-vous fini vos devoirs? —*When did you finish your homework?*

—**Il y a trente minutes.** —***Thirty minutes ago.***

Il a vendu ses livres **il y a deux semaines.** *He sold his books **two weeks ago.***

Nous avons rendu visite à papa **il y a trois mois.** *We visited Dad **three months ago.***

Il y a un an, j'ai perdu mon chat. ***A year ago,** I lost my cat.*

Essayez! Utilisez **il y a** pour répondre à ces questions.

1. Quand avez-vous parlé avec votre colocataire?
2. Quand avez-vous mangé au restaurant?
3. Quand avez-vous rendu visite à votre famille?
4. Quand avez-vous fait la cuisine?
5. Quand avez-vous pris du café?
6. Quand avez-vous regardé un film?

OUI, JE PEUX!

Here are two "can do statements" for you to check your progress so far. Look at each statement and rate yourself on how well you think you can perform the task. Then verify your ability with a partner. How did you do?

1. **"I can tell someone what my favorite grocery store is and some unique or great things the store sells."**

   I can perform this function
   ☐ with ease
   ☐ with some difficulty
   ☐ not at all

2. **"I can ask someone else what his/her favorite grocery store is and what that store sells."**

   I can perform this function
   ☐ with ease
   ☐ with some difficulty
   ☐ not at all

iLrn™

Are you looking for more practice? You can find it in **iLrn**.

Les **petits magasins** d'alimentation

Small food stores

les potirons *(m.)*

les pamplemousses *(m.)*   les cerises *(f.)*

les poires *(f.)*   les pêches *(f.)*

les mangues *(f.)*   les melons *(m.)*   la laitue

les aubergines *(f.)*

les pastèques *(f.)*

les radis *(m.)*

les asperges *(f.)*

le maïs

les concombres *(m.)*

les champignons *(m.)*

Au marché

Note de **vocabulaire**
In Quebec, you can say **un melon d'eau** for **une pastèque.**

Vocabulaire complémentaire

une boucherie *butcher's shop*
une boulangerie *bread shop*
une charcuterie *deli shop*
une épicerie *small grocery store*
un magasin (de produits) bio *health /
organic food store*
un marché (en plein air) *(open air)
market*
une pâtisserie *pastry shop / pastry*
une poissonnerie *fish and seafood
shop*

un éclair *éclair*
un pain au chocolat *croissant-type
pastry filled with chocolate*

acheter *to buy*
amener *to bring someone*
apporter *to bring something*
préférer *to prefer*

biologique(s) / bio *organic*

Note de vocabulaire
Une **épicerie** is a small neighborhood grocery store that is usually family-owned.

Note de vocabulaire
To say *to bring something*, use **apporter**. To express *to bring someone*, use **amener**: Nous apportons un gâteau à la fête. Nous amenons les enfants.

Les verbes comme *acheter* et *préférer*

- Some regular -**er** verbs have spelling changes in their verb stems (that is, what remains when the final -**er** is dropped). For infinitives whose next-to-last syllable contains an **e** that has no accent, the **e** changes to **è** in all but the **nous** and **vous** forms of the present tense. **Acheter** and **amener** are verbs of this type.

acheter	
j'ach**è**te	nous achetons
tu ach**è**tes	vous achetez
il/elle/on ach**è**te	ils/elles ach**è**tent

amener	
j'am**è**ne	nous amenons
tu am**è**nes	vous amenez
il/elle/on am**è**ne	ils/elles am**è**nent

- For infinitives whose next-to-last syllable contains an **é,** the **é** changes to **è** in all but the **nous** and **vous** forms of the present tense. Verbs of this type are **célébrer** (*to celebrate*), **espérer** (*to hope*), **préférer** (*to prefer*), and **répéter** (*to repeat*).

espérer	
j'esp**è**re	nous espérons
tu esp**è**res	vous espérez
il/elle/on esp**è**re	ils/elles esp**è**rent

préférer	
je préf**è**re	nous préférons
tu préf**è**res	vous préférez
il/elle/on préf**è**re	ils/elles préf**è**rent

Note de vocabulaire
Célébrer is generally used in a religious or ceremonial context. The more common equivalent of *to celebrate* is **fêter** or **faire la fête**.

J'**amène** mon mari Luc chez mes parents.

Nous **célébrons** la première communion de ma sœur.

Luc **achète** une bouteille de vin.

J'**espère** être à l'heure chez mes parents.

🔊 6-5 **ACTIVITÉ A** **Qu'est-ce qu'on achète?** Vous allez entendre une série de petits magasins. Qu'est-ce qu'on achète dans ces magasins?

1. a. du bœuf haché   b. un pain au chocolat
2. a. un pain de campagne   b. un saucisson
3. a. des crevettes   b. une côtelette de porc
4. a. un homard   b. un steak
5. a. une brioche   b. des asperges
6. a. du poisson frit   b. des fruits biologiques
7. a. des fraises fraîches   b. des fraises congelées
8. a. des céréales   b. un téléviseur LCD

ACTIVITÉ B **Les catégories** Quel (Which) aliment ne va pas avec les autres?

1. a. la laitue   b. les asperges   c. les mangues   d. les concombres
2. a. les pêches   b. le maïs   c. les pamplemousses   d. les cerises
3. a. une tarte   b. une madeleine   c. du pain de mie   d. un éclair
4. a. un potiron   b. une pastèque   c. une aubergine   d. un radis
5. a. les champignons   b. les melons   c. les poires   d. les framboises

🔊 6-6 **ACTIVITÉ C** **Les fruits, les légumes et leurs couleurs** Nommez un aliment qui correspond aux descriptions que vous allez entendre.

Modèle: un fruit rouge   **une pomme**

1.   2.   3.   4.   5.   6.   7.   8.   9.   10.   11.   12.

ACTIVITÉ D **Où va Claire?** Où est-ce que Claire doit (must) aller pour acheter les aliments suivants?

Modèle: Elle achète des crevettes.   **Elle va à la poissonnerie.**

1. Elle achète des pains au chocolat.
2. Elle achète une baguette.
3. Elle achète des côtelettes d'agneau.
4. Elle achète un saucisson.
5. Elle achète des œufs biologiques.
6. Elle achète des boîtes de conserves.
7. Elle achète des fruits et des légumes.
8. Elle achète des moules.

✈ ······
Si vous y allez

© Courtesy of Wynne Wong

Si vous allez à Québec, allez à l'épicerie J.A. Moisan, la plus vieille épicerie en Amérique du Nord. Allez sur son site officiel pour voir la sélection de produits.

ACTIVITÉ E **Qu'est-ce qu'il faut acheter à l'épicerie?** Nommez trois ingrédients qu'il faut acheter pour préparer les plats suivants.

Modèle: un gâteau au chocolat   **On achète des œufs, de la farine et du chocolat.**

1. une tarte au potiron   2. une salade de fruits   3. une pizza

ACTIVITÉ **F** **Visites en famille** Déterminez la personne ou la chose qu'Abia amène ou apporte.

1. Abia **amène** _____ chez ses parents.
   a. du chocolat   b. Claire

2. Elle **apporte** _____ chez sa grand-mère.
   a. des éclairs   b. sa sœur

3. Elle **apporte** _____ chez sa nièce.
   a. Claire   b. des madeleines

4. Finalement, elle **amène** _____ chez sa tante.
   a. Claire   b. une pastèque

ACTIVITÉ **G** **Les occasions spéciales** Pour chaque occasion, indiquez qui vous amenez et ce que *(what)* vous apportez.

Modèle: le repas de Noël   **J'amène ma sœur. J'apporte des éclairs et du champagne.**

1. une fête d'anniversaire
2. un pique-nique pour le 4 juillet
3. un dîner de Thanksgiving
4. un déjeuner à la bonne franquette *(potluck)*

ACTIVITÉ **H** **Au buffet de salades**

Étape 1. Dites à un(e) partenaire ce que vous mettez normalement dans votre salade.

Modèle: É1: **Qu'est-ce que tu mets dans ta salade quand tu es au buffet de salades?**
É2: **Je mets de la laitue, des radis, des champignons, du jambon et des œufs.**

Étape 2. Avec votre partenaire, inventez une salade originale.

Modèle: **Notre salade s'appelle** *la salade César française.* **On met de la laitue, des œufs, du brie, de l'huile d'olive, des croûtons et des olives niçoises.**

© Tyler Olson/Shutterstock.com

Un mot sur la culture

La religion et la nourriture au Québec

L'Église catholique a eu une influence considérable dans la société québécoise avant les années soixante. Cette influence se reflète dans le français parlé au Québec par la présence de mots liés° à la religion catholique. Par exemple, une pâtisserie populaire qu'on trouve dans les épiceries québécoises s'appelle **les pets° de sœurs** ou **les pets de nonnes**°. Les Québécois apprécient aussi **les oreilles de crisse,** un plat constitué de lard salé frit qu'on mange avec du sirop d'érable°. Le mot **crisse** signifie **Christ.**

liés *tied* **pets** *farts* **nonnes** *nuns* **sirop d'érable** *maple syrup*

- Avez-vous envie de manger des pets de sœurs ou des oreilles de crisse?

Pour parler du passé

Le passé composé avec **être**

DU FILM *LIAISONS*

Un coup d'œil sur la grammaire

Look at these photos from the film *Liaisons* and their captions.

CLAIRE [...] quand **vous êtes parti,** **j'ai cherché** votre nom dans le registre *(registry)*...

ALEXIS J'habite à Paris. **Je suis arrivé** au Canada il y a une semaine.

In the captions, **partir, chercher,** and **arriver** are all in the past tense. What auxiliary verb do these verbs use to form the **passé composé**?

1. chercher **2.** partir **3.** arriver

You learned in **Chapitre 5, Grammaire 3** that most verbs form the **passé composé** with the auxiliary verb **avoir**. Some verbs, however, form the **passé composé** with être. You already know three of them: **aller, partir,** and **sortir**.

Passé composé of *aller*	
je **suis allé(e)**	nous **sommes allé(e)s**
tu **es allé(e)**	vous **êtes allé(e)(s)**
il/elle/on **est allé(e)**	ils/elles **sont allé(e)s**

Note de grammaire
It is also accepted to use a plural past participle with **on** when it is meant as plural: **On est allés au restaurant** (*We went to the restaurant.*).

In the **passé composé** with **être**, the past participle must agree with the subject in gender and number.

Monique **est partie** hier après le déjeuner. *Monique **left** yesterday after lunch.*

Pierre et Guy **sont partis** il y a deux heures. *Pierre and Guy **left** two hours ago.*

In negative sentences, **ne/n'... pas** goes around the auxiliary verb **être**.

Il **n'est pas allé** au marché. *He did not go to the market.*

Elles **ne sont pas sorties** hier. *They did not go out yesterday.*

In questions with inversion, the subject pronoun and the conjugated form of **être** are inverted.

Êtes-vous allés à l'épicerie? ***Did you go** to the grocery store?*

Julie **est-elle partie** à 6h00? ***Did Julie leave** at 6:00?*

Many of the verbs that take **être** in the **passé composé** deal with motion.

Infinitive	Past participle	English equivalent
aller	allé	*to go*
arriver	arrivé	*to arrive*
descendre	descendu	*to go down, to get off*
devenir	devenu	*to become*
entrer	entré	*to enter*
monter	monté	*to go up, to climb, to get on*
mourir	mort	*to die*
naître	né	*to be born*
partir	parti	*to leave*
passer (par)	passé	*to pass, to go by*
rentrer	rentré	*to return, to go home*
rester	resté	*to stay*
retourner	retourné	*to return, to go back*
revenir	revenu	*to come back*
sortir	sorti	*to go out*
tomber	tombé	*to fall*
venir	venu	*to come*

•❖ Note that **passer** can take either **avoir** or **être** depending on the intended meaning. To express *to pass by*, use **être.** To say *to pass / spend time*, use **avoir.**

Sara **est passée** par la bibliothèque ce matin.	*Sara **passed** by the library this morning.*
Sara **a passé** trois heures à la bibliothèque.	*Sara **spent** three hours at the library.*

•❖ **Partir** and **quitter** both mean *to leave.* **Partir** means *to leave* in a general sense (opposite of **arriver**) and cannot take a direct object. It may, however, be followed by a preposition, day, date, or time. **Quitter** means *to leave something or someone.* It takes **avoir** as its auxiliary verb and it must have a direct object.

Nous **sommes parti(e)s** jeudi matin.	*We **left** Thursday morning.*
Claire **est partie** pour Québec.	*Claire **left** for Quebec.*
Vous **avez quitté** la maison à 8h.	*You **left** the house at 8:00.*
Luc **a quitté** sa femme.	*Luc **left** his wife.*

•❖ If **descendre, monter,** and **sortir** are followed by a direct object, **avoir** is used in the **passé composé** instead of **être.**

Heidi **est descendue** de la montagne.	*Heidi **came down** from the mountain.*
Heidi **a descendu** l'horloge de sa chambre.	*Heidi **took** the clock **down** from her room.*
Les copains **sont sortis** hier soir.	*The friends **went out** last night.*
Ils **ont sorti** leur argent.	*They **took out** their money.*

ACTIVITÉ I Abia ou Robert?
Utilisez les participes passés pour déterminer quel(le) employé(e) de l'Hôtel Delta a dit les phrases suivantes: **(a) Abia** ou **(b) Robert, son patron** *(boss).*

1. Je suis arrivée à l'hôtel à 7h00 ce matin.
2. Je suis allé au salon de beauté hier.
3. Je suis descendue à l'Hôtel Reine-Elizabeth.
4. Je suis retourné en Europe trois fois.
5. Je suis passé par le parc Lafontaine.
6. Je suis restée ici tout l'après midi.
7. Je suis passée vous voir à 15h00.
8. Je suis entrée dans le bar à 17h00.
9. Je suis sorti avec un client à 18h30.
10. Je suis partie avec un ami à 19h00.

ACTIVITÉ J Qui a fait quoi? Utilisez les participes passés pour déterminer qui a fait ces activités.

1. _____ est tombée à l'hypermarché hier. a. Ève   b. Luc   c. Ève et Luc
2. _____ sont allés à la pâtisserie.   a. Yves   b. Tom et Yves   c. Anne et Alice
3. _____ est resté dans sa chambre.   a. Roger   b. Rose   c. Roger et Rose
4. _____ sont passées par un café.   a. Marc   b. Marc et Guy   c. Kim et Diane
5. _____ sont revenus du supermarché.   a. Frank   b. Lise et Anne   c. Frank et Anne
6. _____ est devenue célèbre.   a. Laura   b. Koffi   c. Laura et Joël

ACTIVITÉ K Où sont-ils nés? Quand sont-ils morts? Utilisez le participe passé pour déterminer le sujet de chaque phrase.

1. _____ sont nées en Suisse.   a. Colette   b. Colette et Luc   c. Colette et Sara
2. _____ est né au Canada.   a. Ahmed   b. Candice   c. Victor et Candice
3. _____ est morte en 2001.   a. Clara   b. Antoine   c. Clara et Antoine
4. _____ sont morts en 2002.   a. Georges   b. Georges et Luc   c. Anne et Clara

⁘ **Et vous?** Où êtes-vous né(e)?

ACTIVITÉ L Personnes célèbres Où et quand est-ce que ces personnes sont nées? Quand est-ce qu'elles sont mortes?

Modèle: Jackie Kennedy est née à Southhampton en 1929. Elle est morte en 1994.

POSSIBILITÉS
Joal, Sénégal (1906–2001)   Tampico, IL (1911–2004)
Dallas (1981–)   Vienne (1755–1793)

1. Marie-Antoinette
2. Léopold Sédar Senghor
3. Barbara et Jenna Bush
4. Ronald Reagan

Liaisons musicales

Les Français et les Québécois admirent beaucoup James Dean. *Mourir comme lui* est une chanson de l'opéra rock de Michel Berger et Luc Plamondon *La légende de Jimmy,* un opéra sur la vie de James Dean. Écoutez la chanson sur un site Internet.

© Terence/Shutterstock.com

ACTIVITÉ

ACTIVITÉ M *Qu'est-ce qu'ils sont devenus?* Qu'est-ce que ces personnes célèbres sont devenues?

Modèle: Marion Cotillard **Elle est devenue une actrice célèbre.**

1. Donald Trump et Bill Gates
2. Julia Child
3. Barack Obama
4. Justine Henin
5. Madonna et Céline Dion
6. Jennifer Lawrence

ACTIVITÉ N **Vos activités d'hier**

Étape 1. Est-ce que vous avez fait ces activités hier?

Modèle: Êtes-vous parti(e) de chez vous tôt?
Oui, je suis parti(e) de chez moi tôt.

1. Êtes-vous parti(e) pour l'université le matin?
2. Êtes-vous allé(e) au restaurant pour manger?
3. Êtes-vous sorti(e) avec un(e) ami(e)?
4. Êtes-vous passé(e) par un supermarché ou une épicerie?
5. Êtes-vous rentré(e) chez vous très tard?
6. Est-ce que vos amis sont venus manger chez vous?

© John James / Shutterstock.com

Étape 2. Posez les questions de l'Étape 1 à un(e) camarade de classe. Avez-vous fait des activités similaires?

Modèle: **Mon/Ma partenaire et moi, nous sommes parti(e)s pour l'université le matin et nous sommes sorti(e)s avec une amie.**

ACTIVITÉ O *Avoir* ou *être*?

Étape 1. Utilisez les verbes pour compléter les phrases qui décrivent une journée de Claire Gagner.

1. Claire **est partie**   a. à 8h00.   b. son appartement à 8h00.
2. Claire **a sorti**   a. son livre.   b. avec Abia.
3. Claire **est descendue**   a. du métro.   b. une lampe.
4. Claire **a monté**   a. avec Robert.   b. l'escalier.
5. Claire **est sortie**   a. avec Abia.   b. ses livres de psychologie.
6. Claire **a descendu**   a. du train.   b. le fleuve Saint-Laurent en bateau.
7. Claire **est montée**   a. dans le train.   b. la colline à bicyclette.
8. Claire **a quitté**   a. l'hôtel à 17h00.   b. à 17h00.

Étape 2. Mettez les verbes au passé composé pour décrire une journée d'Abia.

1. Abia _____ (sortir) son argent.
2. Abia _____ (sortir) avec sa sœur.
3. Abia _____ (descendre) une photo de sa mère.
4. Abia _____ (monter) dans le métro.

ACTIVITÉ P **Le week-end dernier** Complétez les phrases avec **(a) Nous avons** ou **(b) Nous sommes**.

1. _____ **partis** à 11h.
2. _____ **allés** au supermarché.
3. _____ **acheté** des fruits biologiques.
4. _____ **passés** par un parc.
5. _____ **fait** un pique-nique.
6. _____ **mangé** des fruits et du fromage.
7. _____ **bu** de l'eau minérale
8. _____ **rentrés** chez nous à 16h.

ACTIVITÉ Q **La famille Kardashian** Devinez *(Guess)* ce que les membres de la famille ont fait hier en utilisant les phrases suivantes.

POSSIBILITÉS

aller au cinéma	parler au téléphone	rendre visite à leurs amis
danser à la discothèque	partir pour l'Europe	sortir avec un intello *(nerd)*
faire la cuisine	prendre du vin	

Modèle: **Kris a fait la cuisine.**

1. Kim _____
2. Kim et Khloé _____
3. Kim et Rob _____
4. Rob _____
5. Bruce Jenner _____
6. Kris et Bruce Jenner _____

ACTIVITÉ R **Avez-vous l'esprit jeune?** C'est quand la dernière fois *(time)* que vous avez fait ces activités? Répondez aux questions pour voir si vous avez l'esprit jeune *(young at heart)*.

Modèle: acheter du chewing-gum **J'ai acheté du chewing-gum il y a un mois.**

1. aller à Disneyland
2. faire un bonhomme de neige *(snowman)*
3. sortir pour prendre une glace
4. entrer dans une maison hantée
5. jouer à la marelle *(hopscotch)*
6. regarder un dessin animé *(cartoon)*

ACTIVITÉ S **Avons-nous une vie intéressante?** Posez ces questions à vos camarades de classe. Utilisez le passé composé.

Modèle: loger dans une auberge de jeunesse
    É1: **Est-ce que tu as logé dans une auberge de jeunesse?**
    É2: **Non, je n'ai jamais logé dans une auberge de jeunesse.**
    É3: **Moi, si. J'ai logé dans une auberge de jeunesse.**

1. arriver en classe en pyjama
2. rencontrer quelqu'un de célèbre
3. tomber d'un arbre
4. retourner à ton lycée pour une fête
5. aller à la campagne
6. visiter une ville francophone
7. boire du champagne
8. rentrer chez toi après minuit

Pour aller plus loin
Pendant et depuis

Pendant + *a period of time* is used to say that something happened for a specific period of time that has ended. The verb in such sentences is usually in the **passé composé**.

J'ai travaillé **pendant huit heures**.	*I worked **for eight hours**.*
Elle est restée chez elle **pendant deux jours**.	*She stayed at home **for two days**.*

To ask for how long something happened, use **pendant combien de temps**.

—**Pendant combien de temps** avez-vous étudié hier?	—***(For) how long** did you study yesterday?*
—**Pendant cinq heures**.	—***For five hours**.*

Remember from **Chapitre 2, Grammaire 3** that, if an event or action has not ended and continues into the present, **depuis** is used with a verb in the present tense.

—**Depuis quand** étudiez-vous?	—***(For) how long** have you been studying?*
—J'étudie **depuis deux heures**.	—*I have been studying **for two hours**.*

Essayez! Complétez les phrases avec **(a) pendant** ou **(b) depuis**.

1. Alexis **a habité** en France _____ vingt ans.
2. Il **visite** le Québec _____ une semaine.
3. Claire **étudie** à McGill _____ deux ans.
4. Elle **travaille** à l'hôtel _____ trois ans.
5. Abia **a étudié** à Montréal _____ quatre ans.
6. Elle **a travaillé** dans un café _____ deux mois.

OUI, JE PEUX!

Here are two "can do statements" for you to check your progress so far. Look at each statement and rate yourself on how well you think you can perform the task. Then verify your ability with a partner. How did you do?

1. **"I can say when I last went to an outdoor market and what I bought there."**

   I can perform this function
   ☐ with ease
   ☐ with some difficulty
   ☐ not at all

2. **"I can ask someone else when he/she last went to an outdoor market and what he/she bought there."**

   I can perform this function
   ☐ with ease
   ☐ with some difficulty
   ☐ not at all

iLrn™

Are you looking for more practice? You can find it in **iLrn**.

VOCABULAIRE 3

Les **arts** de la **table**

The art of the table

une serveuse

un serveur

un bol

une assiette

une tasse

l'addition (f.)

un menu

un verre

un couteau

une fourchette

un verre à vin

une cuillère

une serviette

Samedi soir au restaurant

Vocabulaire complémentaire

les couverts (m.) *cutlery*
les doigts (m.) *fingers*
une réservation *reservation*

au milieu (de) *in the middle (of)*
au-dessous (de) *below*
au-dessus (de) *above*

commander *to order*
laisser (un pourboire) *to leave (a tip)*
payer (en liquide / par carte de crédit) *to pay (in cash / with credit card)*
payer chacun sa part *to go Dutch*
réserver (une table) *to reserve (a table)*

Qu'est-ce que vous voulez prendre? *What are you going to have?*

Vous désirez? *What would you like?*
Je vais prendre... *I am going to have . . .*
Je voudrais... *I would like . . .*
Pour moi..., s'il vous plaît. *For me . . . , please.*
Autre chose? *Anything else?*
C'est tout! *That's all!*
C'est servi avec quoi? *What does this come with?*
C'est à votre goût? *Is it to your liking / taste?*
À table! *Let's eat! / The food is ready!*
À votre santé! *To your health!*
Bon appétit! *Enjoy (the meal)!*
Le service est compris. *The tip is included.*

Les verbes comme *payer*

- **Payer** *(to pay)* is an **-er** verb that has an optional spelling change in its verb stem (the **y** can change to **i**) in all forms of the present tense except the **nous** and **vous** forms. Another verb of this type is **essayer (de)** *(to try)*.

payer	
je pa**y**e (pa**i**e)	nous **payons**
tu pa**y**es (pa**i**es)	vous **payez**
il/elle/on pa**y**e (pa**i**e)	ils/elles pa**y**ent (pa**i**ent)

essayer	
j'essa**y**e (essa**i**e)	nous **essayons**
tu essa**y**es (essa**i**es)	vous **essayez**
il/elle/on essa**y**e (essa**i**e)	ils/elles essa**y**ent (essa**i**ent)

Je **paie** en liquide.
Ils **essaient** les desserts.
Elle **a payé** par carte de crédit.
Il **n'a pas essayé** ce restaurant.

*I **am paying** in cash.*
*They **are trying** the desserts.*
*She **paid** with her credit card.*
*He **didn't try** this restaurant.*

ACTIVITÉ A **Qu'est-ce qu'on utilise?** Qu'est-ce qu'on utilise normalement pour manger chaque aliment mentionné?

6-7

1. a. une cuillère   b. une fourchette   c. un verre
2. a. un couteau   b. une fourchette   c. un bol
3. a. une tasse   b. une assiette   c. une fourchette
4. a. un bol   b. une fourchette   c. une cuillère
5. a. un bol   b. les doigts   c. un couteau
6. a. un verre   b. une assiette   c. une fourchette

ACTIVITÉ B **Associations** Associez les éléments de la première colonne aux éléments de la deuxième colonne.

1. _____ un client   a. l'addition
2. _____ laisser un pourboire   b. commander
3. _____ payer   c. mettre la table
4. _____ une fourchette et un couteau   d. les couverts
5. _____ un serveur   e. Le service n'est pas compris.

ACTIVITÉ C **Expressions** Choisissez la bonne réponse pour chaque question ou phrase que vous entendez.

6-8

1. a. À votre santé!   b. Je voudrais le steak-frites.
2. a. Avec des légumes.   b. Le service est compris.
3. a. Non, merci. C'est tout.   b. À table!
4. a. Bon appétit!   b. Oui, merci.
5. a. Je voudrais une omelette.   b. En liquide.
6. a. Oui, au nom de Tremblay.   b. Pour moi, un verre d'eau.
7. a. Une tarte, s'il vous plaît.   b. Un café, s'il vous plaît.
8. a. Bon appétit!   b. On paie chacun sa part.

✈ Si vous y allez

©Ludovic/REA/Redux

Si vous allez à Paris, à New York ou à Las Vegas, visitez L'Atelier de Joël Robuchon, le restaurant du célèbre cuisinier français Joël Robuchon. Cherchez le site Web de son restaurant et regardez le menu. Qu'est-ce que vous avez envie de commander?

ACTIVITÉ D **Les pourboires** Avec un(e) partenaire, discutez du pourboire que vous donnez aux personnes dans les situations suivantes aux États-Unis.

Modèle: un chauffeur de taxi
       É1: **Combien donnes-tu au chauffeur de taxi?**
       É2: **Je laisse 15 pour cent. / Je ne laisse pas de pourboire.**

1. au serveur quand le service est satisfaisant
2. au serveur quand le service n'est pas satisfaisant
3. au serveur dans un resto-rapide ou fast-food
4. au coiffeur (*hairdresser*)
5. au toiletteur (*dog groomer*)
6. au livreur (*delivery person*) de fleurs
7. au livreur de pizza
8. à la femme de chambre dans un hôtel

ACTIVITÉ **E** **Chez vous** Quand vous mangez chez vous, quels couverts utilisez-vous pour les aliments suivants?

Modèle: le poulet frit   **J'utilise une assiette et mes doigts.**

1. les pâtes   3. la pizza   5. une côtelette de porc
2. le poulet rôti   4. les frites   6. la glace

Conclusion Avez-vous de bonnes manières *(manners)* chez vous?

ACTIVITÉ **F** **Mettez la table** Regardez le dessin et répondez aux questions.

1. Où est le couteau?   a. à gauche de l'assiette   b. à droite de l'assiette
2. Où est la fourchette?   a. à gauche de l'assiette   b. à droite de l'assiette
3. Où est la cuillère?   a. à côté de la fourchette   b. à côté du couteau
4. Où est l'assiette?   a. entre la fourchette et   b. à côté du bol
                                le couteau
5. Où est la serviette?   a. sous la fourchette   b. sur la fourchette
6. Où est la bouteille?   a. au-dessous du verre   b. au milieu de la table
7. Où est le bol?   a. au-dessus de la tasse   b. au-dessous de la tasse
8. Où est le verre?   a. à côté de la bouteille   b. entre le vase et la bouteille

ACTIVITÉ **G** **Les restaurants et les couverts** Avec deux camarades de classe, décidez où on met les choses suivantes dans ces situations.

Modèle: à un pique-nique   **On met la fourchette et la cuillère sur l'assiette.**

1. dans un restaurant comme Denny's: cuillère, couteau, fourchette, serviette

2. au dîner chez vous: assiette, fourchette, couteau, cuillère, serviette, verre

3. dans un restaurant chic: assiette à salade, assiette pour le plat principal, serviette, verre à vin, verre à eau, fourchette principale, fourchette à salade, cuillère à café, cuillère à soupe, couteau, assiette à pain

L'art de mettre la table

© aboikis/Shutterstock.com

ACTIVITÉ H **Les situations**

 Étape 1. Dans quelles situations est-ce qu'on peut faire les choses suivantes? Discutez-en avec un(e) camarade de classe.

un rendez-vous romantique **un dîner avec des amis** **un entretien** *(interview)*

1. On arrive au restaurant en retard.
2. On paie chacun sa part.
3. On commande du vin.
4. On mange des frites avec les doigts.
5. On demande un *doggybag*.
6. On partage une assiette.

 Étape 2. Choisissez une des situations de l'Étape 1 et préparez un sketch avec vos camarades de classe.

ACTIVITÉ I **Questions personnelles** Posez ces questions à un(e) ou deux camarade(s) de classe.

1. Chez vous, qui met la table? Qui fait la cuisine et la vaisselle?
2. Vous laissez toujours un pourboire au restaurant? Combien?
3. Si le service est compris, vous laissez aussi un pourboire? Combien?
4. Vous préférez payer en liquide ou par carte de crédit?
5. Quel est votre restaurant préféré pour fêter une occasion spéciale?

Note de **vocabulaire**
La merguez est une saucisse épicée d'Afrique du Nord à base de viande de bœuf et d'agneau.

Un mot sur la culture

Les restaurants nord-africains en France

La cuisine nord-africaine est très populaire en France. Parmi° les spécialités de la cuisine nord-africaine, on trouve les merguez (des saucisses), le couscous, le tajine et le thé à la menthe°. Un détail intéressant à noter est que les Nord-Africains mangent souvent avec les doigts. Par exemple, au lieu d'°une fourchette, on peut° utiliser un morceau de pain pour manger la viande dans un tajine. Les restaurants tunisiens et marocains sont nombreux, pas uniquement en France, mais aussi dans le monde francophone et même en Amérique du Nord.

Parmi *Among* **menthe** *mint* **au lieu d'** *instead of* **peut** *can*

- Avez-vous déjà mangé dans un restaurant nord-africain? Qu'avez-vous pris?

© Elzbieta Sekowska/Shutterstock.com

Un tajine d'agneau

🔊 Liaisons avec les mots et les sons

Les consonnes finales

As you know from **Chapitre 2,** final consonants, except for **q, k, b, c, r, f,** and **l,** are usually silent in French. However, some words borrowed from other languages may have final consonants besides **q, k, b, c, r, f,** and **l** that are pronounced.

l'inde**x**	le foo**t**	le week-en**d**	le bu**s**

Numbers and geographical directions may have final consonants that are pronounced.

si**x**	sep**t**	su**d**	es**t**

Proper names are also some exceptions.

Agnè**s**	Anaï**s**	Maghre**b**	Viêt-N**am**

Remember that a **liaison** occurs when a word that normally ends in a silent consonant (**s, t, x,** or **n**) is followed by a word that begins with a vowel sound.

Nous‿adorons ce restaurant.	Ils‿ont deux‿enfants.

There are also some cases where final consonants that are usually pronounced are not pronounced.

le dîne~~r~~	le pain blan~~c~~	le por~~c~~	le taba~~c~~

Pratique A. Écoutez bien et répétez ces mots dont les consonnes finales sont prononcées.

1. chic
2. lac
3. serveur
4. hiver
5. hôtel
6. bel
7. soif
8. huit
9. dix
10. ouest
11. Alfred
12. iPod

🔊 À vos stylos! C'est l'heure de la dictée!

6-10

Voici un extrait d'une petite conversation entre Claire et Alexis Prévost de la Séquence 3 du film *Liaisons.* Vous allez entendre les phrases de cette conversation deux fois. Écoutez bien et complétez les phrases. Ensuite, encerclez toutes les consonnes finales qui sont prononcées.

CLAIRE (1) Vous _____. (2) Votre accent... _____?

ALEXIS (3) _____. (4) _____. (5) _____ des affaires _____

qui exigent _____.

Pour parler des objets et des gens

Les pronoms compléments d'objet direct

DU FILM *LIAISONS*

Un coup d'œil sur la grammaire

Look at this photo from the film *Liaisons* and its caption.

ALEXIS J'ai vu une jeune femme
charmante, avec un beau sourire *(smile)*...
et j'ai voulu *(wanted)* **la** rencontrer.

1. What does **la** refer to in the photo caption?

a. une jeune femme   b. un beau sourire

❖❖❖ Direct object pronouns allow you to substitute pronouns for direct object nouns.
They may replace nouns that refer to people, places, objects, or situations.

J'aime **ces biscuits.** Je **les** achète.	*I like **these cookies.** I am buying **them.***
Il adore **le musée.** On **le** visite aujourd'hui.	*He loves **the museum.** We are visiting **it** today.*
Il a **une sœur.** Il **la** garde aujourd'hui.	*He has **a sister.** He is looking after **her** today.*

Direct object pronouns			
Singular		Plural	
me/m'	*me*	**nous**	*us*
te/t'	*you*	**vous**	*you*
le/la/l'	*him/her/it*	**les**	*them*

❖❖❖ Direct object pronouns go before the conjugated verb. Note that **me, te, le,** and **la** become **m', t,'** and **l'** if they appear before a vowel or a vowel sound.

Nous **vous** entendons.	*We hear **you.***
Est-ce que tu **m'**aimes?	*Do you love **me?***
Je **t'**aime beaucoup.	*I love **you** very much.*
Je **l'**aime bien.	*I like **it.***

- **Ne... pas** goes around the direct object pronoun and the conjugated verb.

Tu sors avec Luc? Je **ne l'aime pas.**	*You're going out with Luc? I **don't like him.***
Ses livres? Elle **ne les lit pas.**	*Her books? She **is not reading them.***

- When an infinitive follows a conjugated verb, the direct object pronoun goes before the infinitive. In negative statements, **ne... pas** goes around the conjugated verb.

Les livres? Nicole va **les** acheter.	*The books? Nicole is going to buy **them.***
La télévision? J'aime **la** regarder.	*TV? I love to watch **it.***
J'aime **te** regarder danser.	*I like to watch **you** dance.*
Son vélo? Il **ne va pas le vendre.**	*His bike? He **is not going to sell it.***

- When a direct object pronoun is used with the **passé composé,** the past participle agrees in gender and number with the direct object. In negative statements, **ne... pas** goes around the direct object pronoun and the conjugated auxiliary verb.

—Tu as mis **la fourchette** sur la serviette?	—*You placed **the fork** on the napkin?*
—Oui, je **l'ai mise** sur la serviette.	—*Yes, I **placed it** on the napkin.*
—Vous avez regardé **les films** hier?	—*Did you watch **the movies** yesterday?*
—Non, nous **ne les avons pas regardés** hier.	—*No, we **did not watch them** yesterday.*
—Yves a écrit **les lettres?**	—*Did Yves write **the letters?***
—Non, il **ne les a pas écrites.**	—*No, he **didn't write them.***

Pour aller plus loin
L'impératif et les pronoms compléments d'objet direct

Direct object pronouns are added to the end of affirmative commands separated by a hyphen. For the first and second persons, **moi** and **toi** are used.

Lisez **le journal.** Lisez-**le.**	*Read **the paper.** Read **it.***
Regardons **les films.** Regardons-**les.**	*Let's watch **the movies.** Let's watch **them.***
Regarde-**moi.**	*Look at **me.***

In negative commands, the pronoun precedes the verb. **Me** and **te** are used for the first and second persons. **Ne... pas** goes around the object pronoun and the verb.

Ne me regarde **pas.**	***Don't** look at **me.***
Ne le lisez **pas.**	***Don't** read **it.***

Essayez! Dites à un enfant de 5 ans de faire ou de ne pas faire ces activités.

Modèle: (lire) une lettre personnelle   **Ne la lis pas.**

1. (regarder) le film *Le Roi Lion*
2. (regarder) le film *Poltergeist*
3. (faire) tes devoirs
4. (lire) les livres de Stephen King

ACTIVITÉ **J** **Qu'est-ce qu'elle vend?**

Étape 1. Stéphanie, la cousine d'Abia, déménage *(is moving)* et elle vend des choses sur eBay. Regardez les pronoms pour déterminer les choses qu'elle vend.

Modèle: Elle le vend.   **son lit**

1. Elle **la** vend.	a. son téléviseur LCD	b. sa table	c. ses rideaux
2. Elle **les** vend.	a. ses livres	b. sa poêle	c. sa lampe
3. Elle **le** vend.	a. son ordinateur	b. sa poubelle	c. ses tapis
4. Elle **les** vend.	a. sa table	b. sa console wii	c. ses assiettes
5. Elle **le** vend.	a. son micro-ondes	b. ses verres à vin	c. sa chaise
6. Elle **la** vend.	a. son frigo	b. sa maison	c. ses affiches

Étape 2. Et vous? Indiquez si vous vendez les choses suivantes.

Modèle: votre lit   **Oui, je le vends. / Non, je ne le vends pas.**

1. vos livres   **2.** votre iPod   **3.** vos affiches   **4.** votre maison

ACTIVITÉ **K** **À l'hypermarché hier** Utilisez les participes passés pour déterminer ce que Robert Levesque a acheté.

1. Il **l'**a acheté.	a. la glace Good Humor	b. le yaourt Yoplait
2. Il **l'**a achetée.	a. l'eau minérale Évian	b. le punch Kool-Aid
3. Il **l'**a achetée.	a. la moutarde Maille	b. le ketchup Walmart
4. Il **les** a achetées.	a. les pâtes fraîches	b. les macaronis au fromage Kraft
5. Il **l'**a acheté.	a. la crème à 35%	b. le lait à 2%
6. Il **les** a achetés.	a. les fruits biologiques	b. les pizzas surgelées
7. Il **les** a achetées	a. les fromages Philadelphia	b. les fraises Natural Choice
8. Il **l'**a acheté.	a. les hamburgers de Macdo	b. le poulet rôti de St. Hubert
9. Il **l'**a achetée.	a. la glace au lait de soja	b. les pets de sœurs de Tim Horton
10. Il **les** a achetés.	a. les bières Budweiser	b. les jus biologiques POM

Conclusion Est-ce que Robert a acheté les produits qui sont bons pour la santé ou les produits qui sont mauvais pour la santé?

Étape 2. Demandez à un(e) camarade de classe s'il/si elle a acheté les produits de l'Étape 1.

Modèle: É1: **Est-ce que tu as acheté la glace Good Humor?**
É2: **Oui, je l'ai achetée.**
É1: **Est-ce que tu as acheté le yaourt Yoplait?**
É2: **Non, je ne l'ai jamais acheté.**

ACTIVITÉ L Questions personnelles Répondez aux questions avec les pronoms compléments d'objet direct.

Modèle: Vous avez attendu <u>votre camarade</u>?

Oui, je l'ai attendu(e). / Non, je ne l'ai pas attendu(e).

1. Vous avez regardé <u>la télévision</u> hier?
2. Vous avez fait <u>vos devoirs</u> hier soir?
3. Vous avez mis <u>la table</u> hier soir?
4. Vous avez fait <u>la vaisselle</u> hier soir?
5. Vous avez lu <u>le journal</u> hier?
6. Vos amis <u>vous</u> ont invité chez eux?

ACTIVITÉ M Avez-vous envie de les goûter? Demandez à vos camarades de classe s'ils ont envie de goûter *(to try)* les aliments suivants. Notez les noms des personnes qui répondent «oui».

Modèle: **Est-ce que tu as envie de goûter le poulet frit?**

Oui, j'ai envie de le goûter. / Non, je n'ai pas envie de le goûter.

1. le couscous
2. le tajine
3. les merguez
4. les oreilles de crisse
5. les pets de sœurs
6. la poutine
7. la fondue au chocolat
8. les cuisses *(f.)* de grenouilles *(frog legs)*

Liaisons musicales

Françoise Hardy (1944–) est une actrice et chanteuse française et aussi une icône culturelle depuis longtemps en France. Elle a écrit la chanson *Je te cherche* en 1974. Trouvez les paroles de cette chanson sur Internet. À votre avis *(opinion)*, qui est «te» dans la chanson?

OUI, JE PEUX! Here are two "can do statements" for you to check your progress so far. Look at each statement and rate yourself on how well you think you can perform the task. Then verify your ability with a partner. How did you do?

1. **"I can say what my favorite restaurant is, what my favorite thing to order is, and when I last ordered this item."**

   I can perform this function
   ☐ with ease
   ☐ with some difficulty
   ☐ not at all

2. **"I can ask someone else what his/her favorite restaurant is, what his/her favorite thing is to order, and when the last time was that he/she ordered this item."**

   I can perform this function
   ☐ with ease
   ☐ with some difficulty
   ☐ not at all

iLrn™

Are you looking for more practice? You can find it in **iLrn**.

DEUXIÈME PROJECTION

Avant de visionner

ACTIVITÉ **A** **Vous rappelez-vous?** Vous rappelez-vous *(Do you remember)* qui a dit ces phrases dans la Séquence 3 du film *Liaisons?*

	Claire	Alexis	La serveuse
1. … encore du café, madame?	☐	☐	☐
2. … j'ai cherché votre nom dans le registre… mais je ne l'ai pas trouvé.	☐	☐	☐
3. Non, je n'étais pas un des clients de l'hôtel.	☐	☐	☐
4. J'ai vu une jeune femme charmante… avec un beau sourire… et j'ai voulu la rencontrer.	☐	☐	☐
5. J'habite à Paris. Je suis arrivé au Canada il y a une semaine.	☐	☐	☐
6. … attendez. Monsieur! S'il vous plaît.	☐	☐	☐

ACTIVITÉ **B** **Une scène du film** Vous rappelez-vous cette scène? Claire demande à Alexis s'il la suit *(follows)*. Écrivez les mots qui manquent *(are missing)*.

CLAIRE Alors, vous avez fait ma
(1) _____, Monsieur Prévost.
(2) _____ accomplie! Et maintenant?
Que faites-vous (3) _____? Vous
(4) _____ suivez?

ALEXIS (5) _____, ce n'est pas
mon (6) _____. Je ne suis pas un
psychopathe. Non, c'est juste une
belle (7) _____ de vous rencontrer.

▶ **Regarder la séquence**

Vous allez regarder la Séquence 3 du film *Liaisons*. Vérifiez vos réponses à l'Activité A et à l'Activité B.

Après le visionnage

ACTIVITÉ **C** **Alexis Prévost**

Étape 1. Quelles nouvelles informations est-ce que Claire apprend sur Alexis Prévost au café à Trois-Rivières? Faites une liste d'au moins *(at least)* trois nouvelles informations.

Étape 2. Comparez votre liste avec la liste d'un(e) partenaire. Avez-vous écrit les mêmes choses?

ACTIVITÉ **D** **Est-ce que vous le croyez?** Pour chaque phrase, indiquez si vous croyez *(believe)* Alexis ou si vous ne le croyez pas.

Modèle: Alexis dit qu'il n'est pas descendu à l'hôtel. **Je le crois. / Je ne le crois pas.**

1. Il dit qu'il ne suit *(follows)* pas Claire.
2. Il dit qu'il avait besoin d'une brosse à dents.
3. Il dit qu'il est français.
4. Il dit qu'il n'est pas un homme dangereux.
5. Il dit qu'il est arrivé au Canada il y a trois semaines.
6. Il dit que sa famille a des affaires à Québec.

Conclusion Est-ce qu'Alexis Prévost est un homme honnête?

ACTIVITÉ **E** **Résumé de la séquence** Voici un résumé de la Séquence 3 du film. Choisissez les mots qui manquent.

la tarte   un croque-monsieur   manger   Québec   Trois-Rivières

En route pour (1) _____, Claire prend quelque chose à (2) _____ dans un café à (3) _____. Quand la serveuse apporte (4) _____, elle revoit Alexis Prévost.

aussi   café   famille   l'hôtel   mystérieux   Paris   pas   sa   salade

Claire apprend qu'Alexis n'est (5) _____ un client de (6) _____. Il voulait simplement faire (7) _____ connaissance. Alexis dit qu'il est de (8) _____ et qu'il va à Québec (9) _____ parce qu'il a des affaires de (10) _____. Après sa conversation avec Alexis au (11) _____, Claire voit l'homme (12) _____ qui lui a donné l'enveloppe par la fenêtre.

Dans les coulisses

In a **shot-reverse shot,** the director films one character looking at another, who is often off-screen, and then cuts to that second character who is shown looking back at the first character. This technique establishes a character's point of view and is effective for filming conversations and exchanges of looks between two or more characters. A **shot-reverse shot** may have the following functions: a) to establish relationships between characters; b) to draw comparisons; or c) to make associations between characters.

In which scenes can you observe this technique in **Séquence 3** and what do you think the function(s) was (were) in using a **shot-reverse shot?**

À DÉCOUVRIR: La ville de Paris et son marché de Belleville

© Thomas Samson/Getty Images

À DÉCOUVRIR: La ville de Paris

Importance: La ville la plus peuplée et la capitale de la France

Région: Île-de-France

Population: Plus de 2,2 millions à Paris intra-muros *(inner-Paris)*; plus de 10 millions à Paris métropole

Réputation: La capitale économique et commerciale de la France; la ville lumière *(light)*; la plus belle ville romantique du monde *(world)*; la capitale mondiale de l'industrie de la mode *(fashion)*

Climat: Un climat de type océanique avec des étés relativement frais, des hivers doux avec des pluies fréquentes en toute saison et un temps changeant

Avant de lire

You will discover in this reading the vibrant and dynamic outdoor market of Belleville.

Que savez-vous déjà?

1. Quels genres d'articles est-ce qu'on trouve typiquement dans un marché en plein air?

2. Quelles sont quelques différences entre un marché en plein air et un supermarché?

OUTILS DE LECTURE

Using adverbs and conjunctions to predict content

Some adverbs and conjunctions will help you predict what kind of information is in a sentence. When you see the conjunction **comme** *(like, as)*, expect to read about some kind of comparison. If you come across **pourtant** *(however)*, it is likely that the previously stated idea is being challenged. When you see **donc** *(thus, therefore)*, expect to read an example or idea that supports an earlier idea. If you see **mais**, expect to read an idea that may contradict an earlier statement. Guess what the rest of this French sentence might be about based on the beginning of the sentence.

1. **Comme** toutes les grandes villes... a. a small city b. a large city

---

Découvrir le marché de Belleville

© Gerald Haenel/laif/Redux

À Paris, on trouve beaucoup de marchés en plein air, comme par exemple le marché du boulevard de Belleville, qui est un des plus connus, et qui a aussi la réputation d'être un des moins chers°.

Paris, comme beaucoup de grandes villes, est divisé en quartiers, qu'on appelle des arrondissements. Le marché de Belleville se trouve dans le onzième arrondissement, un quartier avec une histoire très riche. En effet, le onzième arrondissement était le cœur° du Paris révolutionnaire au dix-huitième siècle et le site de plusieurs grandes révoltes ouvrières° du dix-neuvième siècle. Aujourd'hui, la vie est plus calme dans ce quartier, mais il est toujours dynamique. En effet°, c'est un quartier multiculturel avec une grande diversité ethnique. On y trouve donc une grande variété de denrées° alimentaires au marché.

Le marché de Belleville est ouvert deux fois par semaine, le mardi et le vendredi. C'est principalement un marché alimentaire: on y trouve des fruits, des légumes, de la viande... On y vend aussi des fleurs, des tissus°, des couverts et des ustensiles de cuisine. Belleville est aussi un centre touristique où on trouve beaucoup de cafés, de boulangeries-pâtisseries et de restaurants. En raison du multiculturalisme du quartier, on y trouve également une boucherie halal°, une pâtisserie casher°, un restaurant chinois et même un hammam°.

chers *expensive* **cœur** *heart* **ouvrières** *working class* **En effet** *In fact* **denrées** *food and food-related items* **tissus** *fabrics* **halal** *food deemed appropriate for Muslims* **casher** *kosher* **hammam** *Turkish bath*

Après avoir lu

Compréhension

1. Qu'est-ce qu'on peut acheter au marché de Belleville?
2. Nommez trois choses intéressantes à propos du onzième arrondissement de Paris.
3. Est-ce que les produits du marché coûtent cher ou est-ce qu'ils ne coûtent pas cher?
4. Donnez un exemple du multiculturalisme qu'on trouve dans le quartier.

Et vous?

1. Est-ce qu'il y a un marché en plein air dans votre quartier ou dans votre ville?
2. Avez-vous déjà acheté des produits dans un marché en plein air? Quels produits?
3. Préférez-vous faire vos courses au marché en plein air ou dans un supermarché?
4. Avez-vous envie de visiter le marché de Belleville?

Share It!

Use **Share It!** in iLrn™ to express your reactions to the reading and to find out what your classmates think.

La description d'un établissement d'alimentation

People often write descriptions of places that have impressed them and that they recommend others see. Here is a tourist's description of her visit to the **marché de Belleville.**

Il y a deux semaines, je suis allée au marché de Belleville dans le onzième arrondissement de Paris. Ce marché m'a impressionnée parce qu'il est dans un quartier multiculturel avec beaucoup de diversité ethnique. J'ai acheté beaucoup de choses intéressantes: de la confiture pour ma mère, des tissus pour ma grand-mère, des pâtisseries tunisiennes et des couverts pour la maison. J'ai aussi mangé dans un excellent restaurant marocain. J'ai pris des merguez, du couscous et du thé à la menthe. Si vous avez envie d'acheter des produits d'alimentation provenant de cultures différentes et de manger dans de bons restaurants, allez au marché et dans le quartier de Belleville.

© Regis Duvignau/Reuters/Landov

Avant d'écrire

The chart displays information the tourist used in her description. Complete it with information that you would like to include in your description.

	La touriste	Vous
Nom de l'établissement	le marché de Belleville	_____
Où est cet établissement?	le onzième arrondissement de Paris	_____
Quand l'avez-vous visité?	il y a deux semaines	_____
Pourquoi l'aimez-vous?	C'est un marché multiculturel.	_____
Qu'est-ce que vous avez acheté ou mangé?	de la confiture, des tissus, des pâtisseries tunisiennes, des couverts, des merguez, du couscous, du thé à la menthe	_____ _____ _____

Écrire

Using information from **Avant d'écrire,** write your own description of a **supermarché, hypermarché, marché en plein air, restaurant,** or **café.** Write 6–8 sentences in French.

Après avoir écrit

Exchange your description with a partner. 1) Circle all the adjectives and verify that they all agree in number and gender. 2) Underline all of the verbs and verify that your partner correctly conjugated them, especially the verbs in the past tense. Did he/she use the correct auxiliary verb? Is past participle agreement correctly made if needed? 3) Put a * next to the sentence(s) that you think is (are) most interesting and explain why. 4) Does your partner's description make you want to go visit this place? Discuss your reactions together and then write a second version of your description, taking into account your partner's feedback.

PARTIE 1 6–11

À L'HYPERMARCHÉ

un hypermarché	*hypermarket*
un supermarché	*supermarket*
le rayon boucherie	*meat counter*
du bœuf haché (*m.*)	*ground beef*
une côtelette d'agneau / de porc	*lamb / pork chop*
le rayon boulangerie-pâtisserie	*bakery-pastry aisle*
une brioche	*round egg bread*
des madeleines (*f.*)	*madeleine cakes*
un pain de campagne	*country-style bread*
du pain de mie	*loaf of sliced bread*
le rayon charcuterie	*deli aisle*
le rosbif	*roast beef*
un saucisson	*dry salami type sausage*
le rayon poissons et fruits de mer	*fish and seafood aisle*
les crevettes (*f.*)	*shrimp*
le homard	*lobster*
les moules (*f.*)	*mussels*
le saumon	*salmon*
le rayon surgelés	*frozen food aisle*
les surgelés (*m.*)	*frozen foods*
le rayon audiovisuel	*audio visual equipment aisle*
une console wii	*wii game box*
un téléviseur LCD	*flat screen tv*
l'argent (*m.*)	*money*
une boîte (de conserves)	*can (canned goods)*
un centime	*cent*
un chariot	*shopping cart*
un panier	*basket*
le prix	*price*

EXPRESSIONS

Ça fait combien?	*How much is it?*
Ça fait... euros.	*That makes (It costs) . . . euros.*
C'est combien?	*How much is it?*
Combien coûte(nt)... ?	*How much is/are . . . ?*

VERBES

attendre	*to wait (for)*
coûter	*to cost*
descendre	*to go down (to), to get off*
entendre	*to hear*
mettre (la table)	*to place, to put, to set (the table)*
perdre	*to lose*
rendre	*to give back, to return*
rendre visite à	*to visit (someone)*
répondre à	*to answer*
vendre	*to sell*
visiter	*to visit (something)*

DIVERS

il y a + *period of time*	*ago*

PARTIE 2 6–12

LES PETITS MAGASINS

une boucherie	*butcher's shop*
une boulangerie	*bread shop*
une charcuterie	*deli shop*
une épicerie	*small grocery store*
un magasin (de produits) bio	*health / organic food store*
un marché (en plein air)	*(open air) market*
une pâtisserie	*pastry shop / pastry*
un éclair	*eclair*
un pain au chocolat	*croissant-type pastry filled with chocolate*
une poissonnerie	*fish and seafood shop*

LES FRUITS

les cerises (*f.*)	*cherries*
les mangues (*f.*)	*mangos*
les melons (*m.*)	*cantelopes*
les pamplemousses (*m.*)	*grapefruits*
les pastèques (*f.*)	*watermelons*
les pêches (*f.*)	*peaches*
les poires (*f.*)	*pears*

LES LÉGUMES

les asperges (*f.*)	*asparagus*
les aubergines (*f.*)	*eggplants*
les champignons (*m.*)	*mushrooms*
les concombres (*m.*)	*cucumbers*
la laitue	*lettuces*
le maïs	*corn*
les potirons (*m.*)	*pumpkins*
les radis (*m.*)	*radishes*

ADJECTIF

biologique (bio)	*organic*

VERBES

acheter	*to buy*
amener	*to bring someone*
apporter	*to bring something*
célébrer	*to celebrate*
espérer	*to hope*
préférer	*to prefer*
quitter	*to leave (a place / a person)*
répéter	*to repeat*

LES VERBES AU PASSÉ COMPOSÉ AVEC *ÊTRE*

aller	*to go*
arriver	*to arrive*
descendre	*to go down, to get off*
devenir	*to become*
entrer	*to enter*
monter	*to go up, to climb, to get on*
mourir	*to die*
naître	*to be born*
partir	*to leave*
passer (par)	*to pass (by), to go by*
rentrer	*to return, to go home*
rester	*to stay*
retourner	*to return, to go back*
revenir	*to come back*
sortir	*to go out*
tomber	*to fall*
venir	*to come*

DIVERS

depuis quand + *period of time*	*how long, since when*
pendant + *period of time*	*for*

PARTIE 3   6–13

AU RESTAURANT

l'addition (*f.*)	*check*
une assiette	*plate*
un bol	*bowl*
un couteau	*knife*
les couverts (*m.*)	*cutlery*
une cuillère	*spoon*
les doigts (*m.*)	*fingers*
une fourchette	*fork*
un menu	*menu*
un pourboire	*tip*

une réservation	*reservation*
un serveur / une serveuse	*waiter / waitress*
une serviette	*napkin*
un verre	*glass*
un verre à vin	*wine glass*

PRÉPOSITIONS

au-dessous (de)	*below*
au-dessus (de)	*above*
au milieu (de)	*in the middle (of)*

EXPRESSIONS

Qu'est-ce que vous voulez prendre?	*What are you going to have?*
Vous désirez?	*What would you like?*
Je vais prendre...	*I am going to have . . .*
Je voudrais...	*I would like . . .*
Pour moi..., s'il vous plaît.	*For me . . . please.*
Autre chose?	*Anything else?*
C'est tout!	*That's all.*
C'est servi avec quoi?	*What does this come with?*
C'est à votre goût?	*Is it to your liking / taste?*
À table!	*Let's eat! / The food is ready!*
À votre santé!	*To your health!*
Bon appétit!	*Enjoy (the meal)!*
Le service est compris.	*The tip is included.*

VERBES

commander	*to order*
essayer (de)	*to try (to)*
goûter	*to taste*
laisser un pourboire	*to leave a tip*
payer	*to pay*
chacun sa part	*to go Dutch*
en liquide	*in cash*
par carte de crédit	*with a credit card*
réserver	*to reserve*

L'art et l'architecture en France et dans la francophonie

Le Louvre: au cœur de l'art européen

Il y a beaucoup de musées à Paris. Le plus important et le plus grand, c'est évidemment le Louvre, avec 60 000 mètres carrés° consacrés aux expositions. Musée universaliste, avec des collections d'art égyptien, grec et romain, le Louvre contient plus de 30 000 œuvres°, qui vont de la préhistoire au dix-neuvième siècle°. Les pièces les plus célèbres sont sans doute *La Vénus de Milo, La Victoire de Samothrace, La Joconde* de Léonard de Vinci et *La Liberté guidant le peuple* d'Eugène Delacroix.

© Laurie Chamberlain/Latitude/Corbis

mètre carré *square meter* **œuvres** *works* **siècle** *century*

La tour Eiffel: symbole de Paris et de la France

© Denis Pepin/Shutterstock.com

Symbole de la capitale française, la tour Eiffel, surnommée° «la dame de fer°», est l'un des monuments les plus célèbres et les plus reconnus° au monde. Initialement nommée «tour de 300 mètres», la tour Eiffel est une tour de fer puddlé° construite par Gustave Eiffel et ses collaborateurs pour l'Exposition universelle de Paris de 1889. Ce monument est situé à l'extrémité du parc du Champ-de-Mars en bordure de la Seine. D'une hauteur de 312 mètres à l'origine, la tour Eiffel est restée le monument le plus élevé du monde pendant 41 ans, et attire près de 7 millions de visiteurs chaque année.

surnommée *nicknamed* **fer** *iron* **reconnus** *recognized* **fer puddlé** *puddled iron, form of wrought iron*

Adapted from: http://tpe-tour-eiffel.e-monsite.com/pages/iii-la-tour-eiffel-une-utilisation-qui-evolue/c-une-tour-symbole.html

Marc Chagall: peintre français d'origine russe

Né en 1887 en Russie, Marc Chagall part pour la France en 1910 pour y étudier les arts plastiques. Il devient° très vite l'un des artistes français les plus célèbres du vingtième siècle. Son œuvre présente des caractéristiques du surréalisme ainsi que du néo-primitivisme. Chagall s'inspire de la tradition juive° et du folklore russe et élabore° une iconographie très particulière. La richesse poétique de son œuvre lui vaut° beaucoup de commandes° comme par exemple la décoration de l'Opéra de Paris. Le Musée national Marc Chagall de Nice est consacré à cet artiste.

© 2014 Artists Rights Society (ARS), New York/Bildrecht, Vienna. Erich Lessing/Art Resource, NY

devient *becomes* **juive** *Jewish* **élabore** *develops* **lui vaut** *earned him*
commandes *commissions*

© AISA/World Illustrated/Photoshot

Paul Gauguin: de la France à la Polynésie

Paul Gauguin est né à Paris en 1848. Son œuvre constitue une transition entre la fin de l'impressionnisme et les différents mouvements qui caractérisent le modernisme du début du vingtième siècle, en particulier le fauvisme et le cubisme. Il a influencé les peintres° Picasso et Matisse. Il est particulièrement célèbre pour les tableaux qu'il a peints° pendant qu'il vivait° en Polynésie. Dans ces tableaux, il a produit des représentations idéalisées de la nature tropicale et de la culture polynésienne.

peintres *painters* **peints** *painted* **vivait** *was living*

Les Automatistes

Ce groupe d'artistes, fondé en 1942, a été actif à Montréal pendant les années quarante et cinquante. Influencé par la psychanalyse et par le mouvement surréaliste, et en particulier par la théorie de l'écriture automatique, les Automatistes ont tenté de développer une forme de peinture° intuitive, qui puisse° refléter les profondeurs° des sentiments inconscients, sans° passer par le filtre des processus intellectuels conscients. Le fondateur de ce groupe était Paul-Émile Borduas, surtout connu pour ses œuvres abstraites.

© 2014 Artists Rights Society (ARS), New York/SODRAC, Montreal. Painting, 1956 (acrylic on canvas), Borduas, Paul-Emile (1905-60)/Private Collection/Bridgeman Images

peinture *painting* **puisse** *can* **profondeurs** *profoundness* **sans** *without*
Adapted from: http://www.le-surrealisme.com/automatistes.html

Révision

1. Quel artiste a été influencé par la culture polynésienne?
2. Quel monument est le symbole de la France?
3. Quel musée est le plus célèbre au monde?
4. Quel groupe d'artistes a été influencé par le surréalisme?
5. Quel artiste est associé à la décoration de l'Opéra de Paris?

▶ LIAISONS CULTURELLES

Notre-Dame de Paris

Use **iLrn™** to access the video **L'architecture** to learn more about the architecture of the French-speaking world. Be prepared to answer the question **Et vous? Quel est votre monument préféré dans le monde francophone?** Share your responses with your classmates in **Share It!**

La **vie professionnelle**

En bref   In this chapter, you will:

- learn vocabulary related to professions, jobs, schools, and degrees

- learn indirect object pronouns and the pronouns **y** and **en**

- learn the verbs **vouloir, pouvoir,** and **devoir**

- learn vocabulary for talking about personalities and abilities

- learn vocabulary related to banking and expenses

- learn how to make statements using comparisons and superlatives

- learn more about the vowel sound **o**

- read about work and school in France, Quebec, and Louisiana

 You will also watch **SÉQUENCE 4: La clé** of the film *Liaisons.*

Ressources

 audio   video   Share It!   iLrn™   http://www.cengagebrain.com

🔊 # Les professions

Professions

un(e) agent(e)
de police

un avocat
(une avocate)

une chanteuse
(un chanteur)

un coiffeur
(une coiffeuse)

un comptable
(une comptable)

un cuisinier
(une cuisinière)

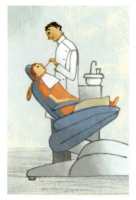

un dentiste
(une dentiste)

une enseignante
(un enseignant)

une infirmière
(un infirmier)

une femme médecin
(un médecin)

un musicien
(une musicienne)

un plombier
(une femme plombier)

un pompier
(une femme pompier)

Quelques professions

Note de
vocabulaire
Un(e) enseignant(e) is a
general term for *teacher*
and may apply to any
education level.

un acteur / une actrice *actor, actress*
un(e) assistant(e) social(e) *social worker*
un(e) employé(e) *employee*
un(e) gérant(e) *manager*
un homme / une femme d'affaires *businessman / businesswoman*
un(e) informaticien(ne) *computer specialist*
un ingénieur / une femme ingénieur *engineer*
un(e) journaliste *journalist*
un ouvrier / une ouvrière *(factory) worker*
un(e) patron(ne) *boss*
un(e) psychologue *psychologist*
un(e) secrétaire *secretary*
un vendeur / une vendeuse *salesperson*

une carrière *career*
un emploi *job*
une entreprise *company*
un poste *position*
une profession *profession*
un salaire *salary, pay, wages*
le travail *work*

gagner de l'argent *to earn money*
gagner sa vie *to earn a living*

> **Note de vocabulaire**
> In informal contexts, French speakers often use the slang term **un boulot** in place of **un emploi**.

Un mot sur la langue

La féminisation des professions en français

Pendant longtemps, beaucoup de professions ont été réservées aux hommes en France. Par conséquent, les noms de ces professions avaient uniquement une forme masculine; par exemple, **un médecin**. Quand les femmes ont commencé à obtenir des diplômes et à exercer ces professions, on a d'abord ajouté le préfixe **femme** aux noms des professions et plus tard, on leur a donné une forme féminine. Cette pratique est encore plus courante° au Québec où on utilise, par exemple, des **professeurs** et des **professeures** à l'université.

courante *widespread*

- Est-ce qu'il y a des exemples de la féminisation des professions en anglais?

🔊 **ACTIVITÉ A Quel secteur d'activité?** À quel secteur d'activité associez-
7-1 vous chaque profession mentionnée: **(a) médical**, **(b) technologie / bâtiment**,
(c) arts et spectacles ou **(d) commerce**?

1.   2.   3.   4.   5.   6.   7.   8.   9.   10.   11.   12.

ACTIVITÉ B Carrières correspondantes Quelle carrière ne correspond pas
au même secteur d'activité que les deux autres?

1. a. une enseignante	b. une cuisinière	c. un assistant social
2. a. une journaliste	b. une femme médecin	c. une infirmière
3. a. un vendeur	b. une femme d'affaires	c. un avocat
4. a. un musicien	b. un comptable	c. une chanteuse
5. a. une coiffeuse	b. une femme ingénieur	c. une plombière
6. a. un pompier	b. un agent de police	c. une secrétaire

🔊 **ACTIVITÉ C Homme ou femme?** Qui exerce chaque profession mentionnée:
7-2 **(a) un homme** ou **(b) une femme**?

1.   2.   3.   4.   5.   6.   7.   8.   9.   10.   11.   12.

ACTIVITÉ D Les objets et les emplois Quel emploi associez-vous aux
choses suivantes?

1. un évier	**4.** le feu *(fire)*	**7.** un revolver	**10.** un divan
2. une calculatrice	**5.** une poêle *(pan)*	**8.** l'addition	**11.** les cheveux
3. un ordinateur	**6.** les dents *(teeth)*	**9.** un hôpital	**12.** un manuel *(textbook)* de français

ACTIVITÉ E Les personnes et les carrières Quelle profession associez-
vous aux personnes ou aux personnages suivants?

1. Anderson Cooper	**4.** Yo Yo Ma	**7.** Audrey Tautou
2. Homer Simpson	**5.** Donald Trump	**8.** Adele
3. Robert Pattinson	**6.** Dr. Phil	**9.** Robert du film *Liaisons*

ACTIVITÉ F Les emplois et les salaires

1. Nommez trois emplois qui rapportent *(bring in)* beaucoup d'argent.

2. Nommez trois emplois qui ne rapportent pas beaucoup d'argent.

3. Nommez un emploi qui est très satisfaisant mais qui ne rapporte pas beaucoup
d'argent.

4. En général, les enfants aiment quels emplois?

ACTIVITÉ G Les professions et la classe Quelle profession suggérez-vous à chaque étudiant(e)?

Modèle: un étudiant doué *(gifted)* en mathématiques

comptable ou ingénieur

1. un étudiant doué en musique
2. une étudiante douée en biologie
3. un étudiant doué en informatique
4. une étudiante douée en communication
5. une étudiante douée en commerce
6. un étudiant doué pour l'accueil *(hospitality)*
7. une étudiante douée en droit *(law)*
8. un étudiant doué en bricolage *(maintenance)*

Si vous y allez

Si vous allez à Lyon (France), allez au Musée des métiers *(vocations)* et des sciences pour des expositions sur l'histoire de quelques vieilles professions et vieux métiers en France.

© Lucas Dolega/epa/Corbis

ACTIVITÉ H Pour quelle profession êtes-vous fait(e)?

Étape 1. Complétez chaque phrase avec votre réponse personnelle.

	important	peu important	à éviter
1. Travailler pour une grande entreprise, c'est…	_____	_____	_____
2. Trouver facilement un emploi, c'est…	_____	_____	_____
3. Garder longtemps un poste, c'est…	_____	_____	_____
4. Avoir un bon patron, c'est…	_____	_____	_____
5. Avoir un gros salaire, c'est…	_____	_____	_____
6. Gagner suffisamment *(sufficiently)* bien sa vie, c'est…	_____	_____	_____

Étape 2. Échangez vos réponses avec un(e) camarade de classe. Quelles professions ou quels emplois lui suggérez-vous? Pourquoi?

Un mot sur la culture

Le travail comme thème littéraire ou poétique

LE LABOUREUR ET SES ENFANTS

© Lebrecht Music & Arts

Le travail est un des thèmes importants de la littérature française. Un exemple bien connu, qui traite° du sujet, est la célèbre fable *Le laboureur et ses enfants* (1679) de Jean de La Fontaine. Les fables sont de petites histoires qui ont souvent des animaux comme personnages et qui se terminent toujours par une leçon de morale. Dans *Le laboureur et ses enfants,* un fermier° sait que ses fils sont obsédés par l'argent et il utilise leur obsession pour leur faire travailler la terre°; il leur dit qu'un trésor est caché dans leur champ°. La leçon de morale dans cette fable est que la richesse n'est pas forcément° matérielle; c'est le fruit du travail des fils qui va être leur trésor.

traite *treats* **fermier** *farmer* **terre** *earth, ground* **champ** *field* **forcément** *necessarily*

• Êtes-vous d'accord avec la morale de cette fable?

Pour décrire qui fait quoi à qui

Les pronoms compléments d'objet indirect

DU FILM *LIAISONS*

Un coup d'œil sur la grammaire

Look at these photos from the film *Liaisons* and their captions.

CLAIRE Je t'expliquerai tout ça plus tard...

ABIA D'accord. J'ai hâte que tu **me** racontes tout.

1. What does **t'** mean in the left caption? To whom does **t'** refer?
2. What does **me** mean in the right caption? To whom does **me** refer?

❖ Indirect object pronouns replace indirect object nouns. Indirect objects answer the questions *to whom* or *for whom*.

—À qui Paul demande-t-il de l'argent?   —*Whom does Paul ask for money?*

—Il **me** demande de l'argent.   —*He asks **me** for money.*

❖ Indirect object pronouns are identical in form to direct object pronouns except for the third-person forms **lui** and **leur**.

<table>
<tr><td colspan="4" align="center">**Indirect object pronouns**</td></tr>
<tr><td colspan="2" align="center">**Singular**</td><td colspan="2" align="center">**Plural**</td></tr>
<tr><td>**me/m'**</td><td>*(to / for) me*</td><td>**nous**</td><td>*(to / for) us*</td></tr>
<tr><td>**te/t'**</td><td>*(to / for) you*</td><td>**vous**</td><td>*(to / for) you*</td></tr>
<tr><td>**lui**</td><td>*(to / for) him/her*</td><td>**leur**</td><td>*(to / for) them*</td></tr>
</table>

Note de **grammaire**
Me and **te** become **m'** and **t'** when they appear before a vowel or a vowel sound.

❖ The placement of indirect object pronouns is identical to the placement of direct object pronouns. They usually precede the conjugated verb.

Je donne mon CV **à la secrétaire**.   Je **lui** donne mon CV.

Karim parle **à son patron**.   Il **lui** parle.

Guy donne des bonbons **à ses amis**.   Guy **leur** donne des bonbons.

··› In negative statements, **ne… pas** goes around the indirect object pronoun and the conjugated verb.

—Tu téléphones souvent à ta mère?   —*You call your mother often?*

—Non, je **ne lui téléphone pas** souvent.   —*No, I **don't call her** often.*

—Il me donne le travail?   —*He is giving me the job?*

—Non, il **ne te donne pas** le travail.   —*No, he **is not giving you** the job.*

··› When an infinitive follows a conjugated verb, the indirect object pronoun goes before the infinitive. In negative statements, **ne… pas** goes around the conjugated verb.

—Nicole **va me donner** ses livres?   —*Nicole **is going to give me** her books?*

—Oui, elle **va te donner** ses livres.   —*Yes, **she is going to give you** her books.*

—Elle désire parler à l'infirmière?   —*Does she want to speak to the nurse?*

—Non, elle **ne désire pas lui parler.**   —*No, she **does not want to speak to her.***

··› Unlike direct object pronouns, when an indirect object pronoun is used with the **passé composé,** the past participle does *not* agree in gender and number with the indirect object.

Je **leur ai parlé** hier.   *I **spoke to them** yesterday.*

Ils **nous ont téléphoné** hier soir.   *They **called us** last night.*

··› When statements in the **passé composé** are negative, **ne… pas** goes around the indirect object pronoun and the conjugated auxiliary verb.

Je **ne leur ai pas** parlé hier.   *I **didn't speak to them** yesterday.*

Ils **ne nous ont pas téléphoné** hier soir.   *They **didn't call us** last night.*

··› If a sentence has an indirect object, it often also has a direct object. Verbs that often have both indirect and direct objects include:

demander à *to ask*	**montrer à** *to show to*
donner à *to give to*	**poser une question à** *to ask a question to*
écrire à *to write to*	**prêter à** *to lend to*
envoyer à *to send to*	**vendre à** *to sell to*

> **Note de grammaire**
> For infinitives that end in **-yer**, like **envoyer**, the **y** becomes an **i** in all forms of the present tense except the **nous** and **vous** forms: **j'envoie, tu envoies, il/elle/on envoie, ils/elles envoient,** but **nous envoyons, vous envoyez.**

Je lui écris une lettre.   *I am writing him/her a letter.*

Elle me prête son livre.   *She is lending me her book.*

Ils nous ont montré la maison.   *They showed us the house.*

Il m'a vendu son vélo.   *He sold me his bike.*

··› **Parler à**, **téléphoner à**, and **répondre à** are always used with indirect objects.

Le patron **va leur répondre** demain.   *The boss **is going to answer them** tomorrow.*

ACTIVITÉ I À qui est-ce qu'elle téléphone? Abia parle souvent au téléphone. Écoutez bien les pronoms compléments d'objet indirect pour déterminer à qui elle téléphone.

7-3

Modèle: Elle leur téléphone.   **à Antoine et David**

1. a. à Sarah et Marie   b. à Marie   c. à toi

2. a. à Karine   b. à moi   c. à Karine et David

3. a. à nous   b. à Éric   c. à Éric et Jean

4. a. à Luc   b. à toi   c. à nous

5. a. à moi   b. à nous   c. à toi

6. a. à Marc   b. à toi   c. à Tom et Damien

7. a. à Chloé   b. à Luc et Guy   c. à vous

8. a. à Maurice   b. à Hugo et Carole   c. à toi

Et vous? À qui téléphonez-vous souvent?

ACTIVITÉ J À qui est-ce qu'il ne parle pas souvent? Utilisez les pronoms compléments d'objet indirect pour déterminer à qui Robert Levesque du film *Liaisons* ne parle pas souvent.

1. Il ne **lui** parle pas souvent.   a. à Frank   b. à nous   c. à Frank et Paul

2. Il ne **me** parle pas souvent.   a. à Julien   b. à moi   c. à nous

3. Il ne **leur** parle pas souvent.   a. à Céline   b. à toi   c. à Paul et Céline

4. Il ne **te** parle pas souvent.   a. à Stéphanie   b. à toi   c. à Anne et Paul

5. Il ne **nous** parle pas souvent.   a. à Carole   b. à moi   c. à nous

6. Il ne **lui** parle pas souvent.   a. à Véronique   b. à vous   c. à Sara et Nicole

Et vous? À qui est-ce que vous ne parlez pas souvent?

ACTIVITÉ K La communication Répondez aux questions avec un pronom complément d'objet indirect.

Modèle: Est-ce que vous envoyez des textos <u>à votre sœur</u>?

         Oui, je lui envoie des textos. / Non, je ne lui envoie pas de textos.

1. Est-ce que vous envoyez des courriels <u>à votre professeur</u>?

2. Est-ce que vous envoyez des lettres <u>à vos parents</u>?

3. Est-ce que vous envoyez des textos <u>à votre meilleur(e) ami(e)</u>?

4. Est-ce que vous envoyez des messages instantanés <u>à vos camarades de classe</u>?

ACTIVITÉ ⬤ **L** **Complément d'objet direct ou indirect?**

Étape 1. Utilisez les pronoms pour compléter les phrases.

1. M. Dupont **lui**…   a. parle tous les jours.   b. regarde tous les jours.
2. Carole **le**…   a. parle le matin.   b. lit le matin.
3. Michel **la**…   a. regarde souvent.   b. téléphone souvent.
4. Antoine **leur**…   a. étudie souvent   b. téléphone souvent.
5. Marc **les**…   a. fait le soir.   b. parle le soir.

Étape 2. Répondez aux questions en remplaçant les mots soulignés (*underlined*) par un pronom complément d'objet direct ou indirect.

Modèle: Lisez-vous souvent <u>vos courriels</u>?

Oui, je les lis souvent. / Non, je ne les lis pas souvent.

1. Prêtez-vous vos livres <u>à vos camarades de classe</u>?
2. Regardez-vous souvent <u>les films de François Truffaut</u>?
3. Demandez-vous de l'argent <u>à votre colocataire</u>?
4. Posez-vous des questions <u>à votre professeur</u>?
5. Faites-vous souvent <u>la cuisine</u>?
6. Lisez-vous souvent <u>le journal</u>?

ACTIVITÉ ⬤ **M** **Les cadeaux et les professionnels** Avez-vous des idées de cadeaux (*gifts*) pour les personnes suivantes?

Modèle: des journalistes   **On leur achète un portable.**

Idées			
argent liquide	calculatrice	fleurs	fruits
biscuits	chocolat	fromage	vin

1. une dentiste   3. des cuisiniers   5. des comptables
2. un secrétaire   4. une infirmière   6. un professeur de français

❖ **Et vous?** Quels cadeaux aimez-vous recevoir?

ACTIVITÉ ⬤ **N** **L'année dernière et l'année prochaine**

Étape 1. Qu'avez-vous acheté à ces personnes comme cadeaux l'année dernière? Discutez avec un(e) partenaire.

Modèle: à votre mère   É1: **Qu'est-ce que tu lui as acheté?**
                             É2: **Je lui ai acheté du chocolat.**

1. à votre (vos) colocataire(s)   4. à votre frère ou votre sœur
2. à votre meilleur(e) ami(e)   5. à votre mère ou votre père
3. à votre petit(e) ami(e)   6. à votre cousin(e)

Étape 2. À partir des réactions des personnes de l'Étape 1 aux cadeaux offerts l'année dernière, qu'est-ce que vous allez leur acheter l'année prochaine? Discutez avec votre partenaire.

Modèle: à votre mère **Elle n'a pas aimé le chocolat alors l'année prochaine, je vais lui acheter des fleurs.**

 ACTIVITÉ O **Êtes-vous gentil(le)?** Est-ce que vous allez prêter ces choses aux personnes suivantes?

Modèle: vos stylos <u>à votre sœur</u>   **Je (ne) vais (pas) lui prêter mes stylos.**

1. votre iPod <u>aux enfants</u>

2. votre ordinateur <u>à votre colocataire</u>

3. votre vélo <u>à vos parents</u>

4. votre argent <u>à votre voisin(e)</u>

5. votre livre <u>à vos colocataires</u>

6. votre brosse à dents *(toothbrush)* <u>à votre colocataire</u>

 ACTIVITÉ P **Des gestes généreux** Par groupes de trois, dites qui s'est montré(e) généreux (généreuse) envers vous. Parlez de trois à cinq choses que quelqu'un a faites pour vous.

Modèle: É1: **Mon colocataire m'a prêté son livre.**
　　　　　 É2: **Mes parents m'ont donné de l'argent pour mon loyer.**
　　　　　 É3: **Mon petit ami m'a préparé un dîner romantique.**

Suggestions			
acheter	faire	argent	dîner
apporter	montrer	cadeaux	livres
donner	parler	chocolat	loyer
écrire	préparer	gâteau	ordinateur
envoyer	prêter	devoirs	soupe

ACTIVITÉ Q **Encore des gestes généreux** Avec un(e) partenaire, décidez quels gestes vous allez faire pour ces personnes.

Modèle: Un enfant est très triste.   **Nous allons lui acheter des bonbons.**

1. Une vieille femme est au marché. Il fait chaud et elle a soif.

2. La mère de votre ami(e) est à l'hôpital.

3. Un homme sans abri *(homeless)* a très faim.

4. Votre colocataire est très triste.

5. Votre petit(e) ami(e) est malade *(sick)*.

6. Les parents de votre ami(e) vous invitent à dîner chez eux.

7. Votre voisin(e) est déprimé(e) *(depressed)*.

8. Les enfants ont perdu *(lost)* leur chien.

Pour aller plus loin
L'impératif et les pronoms compléments d'objet indirect

Indirect object pronouns are added to the end of affirmative imperative commands separated by a hyphen. For the first and second person, **moi** and **toi** are used.

Donnez-moi dix minutes.	**Give me** ten minutes.
Achète-toi un ordinateur.	**Buy yourself** a computer.
Téléphonons-lui aujourd'hui.	**Let's phone him/her** today.

In negative commands, the pronouns precede the verb. Use **me** and **te** in negative commands. **Ne… pas** goes around the object pronoun and the verb.

Ne me posez pas de questions.	**Don't ask me** any questions.
Ne lui téléphonons pas aujourd'hui.	**Let's not phone him/her** today.
Ne lui donne pas plus de dix minutes.	**Don't give him/her** more than ten minutes.

Essayez! Indiquez trois choses qu'on donne et trois choses qu'on ne donne pas à un enfant de 3 ans.

Modèle: Donne-lui du lait.
Ne lui donne pas de couteau.

Liaisons musicales

Henri Salvador a écrit une chanson comique sur l'obsession du travail: *Le travail, c'est la santé* (1965). Cherchez les paroles de cette chanson sur Internet et identifiez les termes liés au *(related to)* travail.

OUI, JE PEUX!

Here are two "can do statements" for you to check your progress so far. Look at each statement and rate yourself on how well you think you can perform the task. Then verify your ability with a partner. How did you do?

1. **"I can state the profession I would like to have and explain why."**

   I can perform this function
   ☐ with ease
   ☐ with some difficulty
   ☐ not at all

2. **"I can say two things that I loan or give to people and to whom I loan or give these things."**

   I can perform this function
   ☐ with ease
   ☐ with some difficulty
   ☐ not at all

iLrn™

Are you looking for more practice? You can find it in **iLrn**.

🔊 # Les **atouts professionnels**

Professional skills

1. Avez-vous de bonnes capacités de communication?

oui   **non**

☐   ☐

2. Êtes-vous bon(ne) avec les chiffres?

oui   **non**

☐   ☐

3. Êtes-vous créatif (créative)?

oui   **non**

☐   ☐

4. Êtes-vous souvent de bonne humeur?

oui   **non**

☐   ☐

5. Êtes-vous souvent de mauvaise humeur?

oui   **non**

☐   ☐

6. Êtes-vous organisé(e)?

oui   **non**

☐   ☐

7. Êtes-vous jaloux (jalouse)?

oui   **non**

☐   ☐

8. Êtes-vous du matin?

oui   **non**

☐   ☐

9. Êtes-vous du soir?

oui   **non**

☐   ☐

Test de personnalité et de caractère

Vocabulaire complémentaire

acharné(e) *competitive, cutthroat*
coincé(e) *uptight*
déloyal(e) *disloyal*
drôle *funny, odd*
excentrique *eccentric*
exigeant(e) *demanding*
extraverti(e) *extroverted, extrovert*
farfelu(e) *scatter-brained*
flexible *flexible*
inflexible *inflexible*
introverti(e) *introverted, introvert*
loyal(e) *loyal, faithful*

professionnel(le) *professional*
sensible *sensitive*
têtu(e) *stubborn*

---

avoir le goût du travail *to have a good work ethic*
avoir le sens de l'humour *to have a sense of humor*
être précis(e) *to be good with details*

---

les atouts *(m.)* **professionnels** *professional skills*

Note de **vocabulaire**
Acharné(e) through **têtu(e)** are adjectives but **acharné(e), excentrique, extraverti(e), farfelu(e), introverti(e)**, and **professionnel(le)** can also be used as nouns.

Pour aller plus loin
Quelqu'un de...

To say *someone interesting, someone sensitive, someone funny* and so forth, use the construction **quelqu'un + de/d'** + the masculine form of the adjective.

Il y a **quelqu'un d'intéressant** dans la salle.

*There is **someone interesting** in the room.*

Il y a **quelqu'un de sensible** dans ma classe.

*There is **someone sensitive** in my class.*

J'ai rencontré **quelqu'un de drôle** à la fête.

*I met **someone funny** at the party.*

Essayez! Dites si vous voulez rencontrer ces types de personnes à une fête.

Modèle: quelqu'un d'exigeant   **Je (ne) veux (pas) rencontrer quelqu'un d'exigeant.**

1. quelqu'un d'acharné
2. quelqu'un d'extraverti
3. quelqu'un de coincé
4. quelqu'un d'excentrique
5. quelqu'un de farfelu
6. quelqu'un de têtu

🔊 **ACTIVITÉ A Descriptions** Choisissez le mot qui complète le mieux *(the best)*
7-4 chaque phrase que vous entendez.

1. a. déloyal   b. inflexible   c. farfelu   d. précis

2. a. têtu   b. flexible   c. sensible   d. exigeant

3. a. créatif   b. coincé   c. drôle   d. fidèle

4. a. introverti   b. acharné   c. professionnel   d. extraverti

ACTIVITÉ B Traits de caractère et qualités Qui a ces traits de caractère
ou ces qualités?

Modèle: drôle   **Margaret Cho et ma colocataire sont drôles.**

1. sensible

2. être du soir

3. coincé(e)

4. créatif / créative

5. têtu(e)

6. être bon(ne) avec les chiffres

7. farfelu(e)

8. être de mauvaise humeur

9. jaloux / jalouse

10. être du soir

ACTIVITÉ C Les patrons agréables et détestables

Étape 1. Décidez si les phrases décrivent un(e) patron(ne) agréable ou détestable.
Puis partagez vos réponses avec un(e) partenaire. Avez-vous les mêmes opinions?

	Agréable	Détestable
1. Il/Elle a le sens de l'humour.	_____	_____
2. Il/Elle est exigeant(e) et inflexible.	_____	_____
3. Il/Elle a le goût du travail.	_____	_____
4. Il/Elle est du matin et souvent de bonne humeur.	_____	_____
5. Il/Elle est farfelu(e) et pas précis(e).	_____	_____
6. Il/Elle a de bonnes capacités de communication.	_____	_____

Étape 2. Robert est le patron de Claire et
d'Abia. À votre avis, quelles phrases de
l'Étape 1 décrivent Robert?

Étape 3. Avec votre partenaire, décrivez
votre patron(ne) idéal(e).

ACTIVITÉ D Et vous?

Étape 1. Complétez le test de personnalité et de caractère à la page 278.

Étape 2. Partagez vos réponses avec un(e) camarade de classe. Lisez ses réponses.
Quelle profession lui recommandez-vous? Pourquoi?

ACTIVITÉ **E** **Employés de l'entreprise** Complétez les évaluations de ces employés avec le mot qui convient.

Modèle: Cet employé travaille tout le temps pour les promotions personnelles.

Il est **acharné.** / C'est **un acharné.**

1. Cet employé ne parle pas beaucoup avec les autres. C'est _____.

2. Cette employée est très originale et même un peu bizarre. C'est _____.

3. Cet employé n'est pas très honnête. Il est _____.

4. Cette employée est très compétente et respectueuse. Elle est _____.

5. Cet employé travaille depuis longtemps pour cette entreprise. Il est

_____.

 ACTIVITÉ **F** **Annonces d'emploi** Préparez une annonce d'emploi *(job ad)* de trois à quatre phrases pour les emplois suivants. Identifiez le profil idéal et les traits à éviter.

Modèle: un(e) comptable

Nous cherchons un(e) comptable. Il faut être bon avec les chiffres et bien organisé. Nous désirons un(e) employé(e) extraverti(e). Cette personne doit avoir le goût du travail. Nous ne désirons pas quelqu'un d'inflexible.

1. un infirmier / une infirmière

2. un vendeur / une vendeuse

3. un(e) journaliste

4. un(e) secrétaire

Si vous y allez

Si vous allez à Avernes-Saint-Gourgon en Normandie, prenez un des cours de savoir-vivre et de bonnes manières de la Baronne Hargitay-Gran. Elle offre des cours sur la communication et le savoir-vivre en public et sur beaucoup d'autres thèmes similaires.

Un mot sur la culture

Le savoir-vivre

En français, il existe une expression très importante qu'on utilise aussi parfois en anglais: **le savoir-vivre°**. Le sens de cette expression est, en effet, un peu philosophique. Il ne s'agit pas uniquement° de connaître, suivre et respecter «les règles de vie» (l'étiquette, la courtoisie et la politesse) mais aussi de bien vivre, c'est-à-dire avoir une vie équilibrée tout en profitant aussi de la vie°. Par exemple, même si le travail joue un rôle important dans la vie des Français, ceux-ci font aussi tout leur possible pour garder° le travail et ses obligations en harmonie avec «les plaisirs de la vie» comme la famille et les amis, les vacances et les loisirs, et bien sûr la bonne cuisine.

savoir-vivre *to know how to live* **Il ne s'agit pas uniquement** *It's not only about* **profitant de la vie** *taking advantage of life* **garder** *to keep*

• Et vous? Quel rôle le travail joue-t-il dans votre vie? Avez-vous du savoir-vivre?

Pour parler des désirs, des capacités et des obligations

Les verbes **vouloir, pouvoir, devoir** / Les pronoms **y** et **en**

DU FILM *LIAISONS*

Un coup d'œil sur la grammaire

Look at these photos from the film *Liaisons* and their captions.

CLAIRE Je ne sais pas qui m'a offert ce séjour *(stay)*.

RÉCEPTIONNISTE Si vous **voulez**, je **peux** demander à mon superviseur.

Claire a une clé pour un coffre-fort *(safety deposit box)*. Mais c'est samedi et la banque est fermée. Donc, Claire ne peut pas **y** aller aujourd'hui.

1. In the left photo caption, which verb means *can*? Which verb means *want*?
2. In the right photo caption, what does the pronoun **y** refer to?

Les verbes *vouloir, pouvoir, devoir*

⚬➤ The verbs **vouloir** *(to want)*, **pouvoir** *(to be able to, can)*, and **devoir** *(to have to, must, to owe)* are irregular. They often appear with infinitives, and they are conjugated with **avoir** in the **passé composé**.

vouloir	pouvoir	devoir
je **veux**	je **peux**	je **dois**
tu **veux**	tu **peux**	tu **dois**
il/elle/on **veut**	il/elle/on **peut**	il/elle/on **doit**
nous **voulons**	nous **pouvons**	nous **devons**
vous **voulez**	vous **pouvez**	vous **devez**
ils/elles **veulent**	ils/elles **peuvent**	ils/elles **doivent**
PAST PARTICIPLE: **voulu**	PAST PARTICIPLE: **pu**	PAST PARTICIPLE: **dû**

Voulez-vous voir la patronne?	*Do you **want** to see the boss?*
Pouvons-nous parler avec le gérant?	*Can we speak to the manager?*
Je **dois** travailler très tôt demain.	*I **have to** work very early tomorrow.*
Il **a pu terminer** son travail.	*He **was able to** / **managed to** finish his work.*

⚬➤ **Devoir** means *to owe* when used with a noun.

Je **dois six euros** à mon patron.	*I owe my boss **six euros**.*

Les pronoms *y* et *en*

⋯ The pronouns **y** and **en** replace phrases that contain previously mentioned ideas. **Y** replaces phrases that begin with a preposition (**à, chez, dans, en,** or **sur**), and **en** replaces phrases that begin with a partitive or indefinite article or phrases that begin with the preposition **de**.

Claire étudie **à l'Université McGill.**	*Claire studies **at McGill University.***
Claire **y** étudie.	*Claire studies **there.***
Marc prend **du sucre** dans son café.	*Marc takes **sugar** in his coffee.*
Marc **en** prend dans son café.	*Marc takes **some** in his coffee.*

⋯ Verbs used with **à** include **penser à, réussir à,** and **répondre à.** Verbs used with **de** include **penser de, parler de, avoir besoin de, avoir envie de,** and **avoir peur de.**

Karim pense **à son travail.** Il **y** pense.	*Karim thinks **about his work.** He thinks **about it.***
Il a peur **des chiens.** Il **en** a peur.	*He is afraid **of dogs.** He is afraid **of them.***

⋯ The placement of **y** and **en** is identical to that of other object pronouns. In the **passé composé,** the past participle does not agree with **y** and **en.**

—Il a répondu **à la question**?	*—He answered **the question**?*
—Oui, il **y** a répondu.	*—Yes, he answered **it.***
—Il a mis **de la** crème dans la soupe?	*—Did he put **any** cream in the soup?*
—Non, il n'**en** a pas mis.	*—No, he did not put **any.***
—Tu vas manger **dans ton bureau**?	*—Are you going to eat **in your office**?*
—Oui, je vais **y** manger.	*—Yes, I am going to eat **there.***
—Avez-vous besoin **de papier**?	*—Do you need **some paper**?*
—Non, nous n'**en** avons pas besoin.	*—No, we don't need **any.***

⋯ **En** is also used to replace a noun that is modified by a number or by an expression of quantity.

—Combien de biscuits allez-vous manger?	*—How many cookies are you going to eat?*
—Je vais **en** manger **trois.**	*—I am going to eat **three (of them).***
—Vous avez **beaucoup de** devoirs?	*—Do you have **a lot of** homework?*
—Non, je n'**en** ai pas **beaucoup.**	*—No, I don't have **much (a lot of it).***

⋯ With some verbs, **y** and **en** cannot replace people. When referring to people, use a disjunctive pronoun after the preposition.

Je pense souvent **à Marc.**	Je pense souvent **à lui.**
Il parle **de Luc et de Marie.**	Il parle **d'eux.**

⋯ In the imperative, add an **s** to the **tu** form of any -**er** verb before adding **y** or **en.**

Va **au bureau.**	Va**s**-y.	*Go **there.***
Mange **du chocolat.**	Mange**s**-en.	*Eat **some.***

ACTIVITÉ G **Qui le dit?** Qui dit les phrases suivantes?

1. Je **dois** mettre la table.   a. un client   b. un serveur
2. Je **veux** un nouveau look.   a. un client   b. un coiffeur
3. Je **ne peux pas** faire la cuisine.   a. un cuisinier   b. un enfant
4. Je **peux** travailler avec mes mains. a. un psychologue   b. un plombier
5. Je **dois** de l'argent à mes parents. a. un étudiant   b. un patron
6. Je **ne veux pas** travailler avec les chiffres. a. un comptable b. un acteur
7. Je **veux** vendre un gâteau.   a. un client   b. une vendeuse
8. Je **dois** faire mes devoirs.   a. un étudiant   b. un professeur

ACTIVITÉ H **Désirs, compétences et obligations** Des gens parlent des désirs, des compétences et des obligations dans le monde du travail. Choisissez le sujet approprié pour chaque phrase.

1. _____ **veut** trouver un bon poste.   a. Je   b. Frank   c. Nous
2. _____ **veux** un bon salaire.   a. Marie   b. Marie et Luc   c. Je
3. _____ **veulent** un travail flexible. a. Yin et Tran   b. Vous   c. Nous
4. _____ **pouvez** travailler le week-end. a. Nous   b. Vous   c. Luc
5. _____ **peux** être organisée.   a. Je   b. Marie   c. Nous
6. _____ **pouvons** voyager souvent.   a. Vous   b. Pierre   c. Nous
7. _____ **dois** 10 euros au patron.   a. Tu   b. Michel   c. Vous
8. _____ **devez** être sociables.   a. Marc et Luc   b. Nous   c. Vous
9. _____ **doivent** travailler tard.   a. Sara et Anne b. Mustapha   c. Tu
10. _____ **devons** être du matin.   a. Vous   b. Luc et Yves   c. Nous

Et vous? Complétez les phrases.

1. Je veux _____.   2. Je peux _____.   3. Je dois _____.

ACTIVITÉ I **Votre professeur** Devinez si chaque activité est un désir, une compétence ou une obligation pour votre professeur. Complétez chaque phrase avec **veut, peut** ou **doit.**

Mon professeur…

1. _____ parler français.   5. _____ manger dans un café français.
2. _____ regarder des films français. 6. _____ faire du shopping.
3. _____ travailler le soir.   7. _____ lire des courriels.
4. _____ faire la cuisine.   8. _____ rendre visite à sa famille.

Et vous? Refaites l'activité avec **Je veux, Je peux** ou **Je dois.** Est-ce que vous êtes comme votre professeur?

ACTIVITÉ **J** **Les personnalités, les compétences et les carrières**

Étape 1. Quelles compétences est-ce que ces personnes doivent avoir?

Modèle: Marc veut être professeur de français.   **Il doit parler français.**

1. Jean veut être comptable.
2. Marie veut être baby-sitter.
3. Benoît et Ali veulent être artistes.
4. Émilie et Sara veulent être journalistes.

Étape 2. Quelle carrière est-ce que ces personnes peuvent avoir?

Modèle: Marie aime faire du shopping.   **Elle peut devenir vendeuse.**

1. Claire Gagner aime la psychologie.
2. Antoine joue de la guitare.
3. Luc et Lise aiment faire la cuisine.
4. Nicole et Luce sont excentriques.

ACTIVITÉ **K** **Les talents** Demandez à un(e) partenaire s'il/si elle **peut** faire ces activités. Si votre partenaire répond «non», demandez s'il/si elle **veut** faire ces activités.

Modèle: É1: **Est-ce que tu peux jouer du piano?**
   É2: **Non, je ne peux pas jouer du piano.**
   É1: **Est-ce que tu veux jouer du piano?**
   É2: **Oui, je veux jouer du piano.**

1. jouer de la guitare
2. chanter bien
3. faire du karaoké
4. dessiner bien
5. danser bien
6. écrire des poèmes
7. préparer un repas français
8. parler français

Conclusion Avez-vous les mêmes *(same)* talents? Voulez-vous faire les mêmes activités?

Modèle: **Nous pouvons parler français. Nous voulons bien chanter et danser.**

ACTIVITÉ **L** **Les contes de fées** Lisez-vous des contes de fées *(fairytales)*? Complétez chaque phrase avec les éléments suivants au passé composé.

(devoir) dormir pendant 100 ans	(ne pas pouvoir) dire des mensonges *(lies)*
(devoir) travailler dans la forêt	(ne pas vouloir) grandir
(ne pas pouvoir) aller au bal *(ball)*	(vouloir) être humain(e)

1. La petite sirène Arielle _____.
2. La Belle au bois dormant _____.
3. Cendrillon _____.
4. Peter Pan _____.
5. Pinocchio _____.
6. Les sept nains *(dwarfs)* _____.

Liaisons musicales

En 1991, Céline Dion a enregistré une chanson de Luc Plamondon, *Le blues du businessman.* Dans la chanson, un homme d'affaires veut être artiste. Cherchez les paroles de cette chanson sur Internet. Identifiez toutes les choses que le businessman veut et peut faire s'il est artiste.

ACTIVITÉ M Les activités de Patrick, le neveu d'Abia Utilisez les pronoms pour déterminer de quoi Patrick parle.

1. J'**y** joue. a. au tennis b. du violon
2. J'**en** joue. a. au football b. de la guitare
3. J'**en** prends. a. au café b. du thé
4. J'**y** mange. a. au bistro b. du pain
5. J'**y** ai réussi. a. à mon examen b. de ses devoirs
6. J'**y** ai pensé. a. à Abia b. à la fête

ACTIVITÉ N Êtes-vous un(e) bon(ne) employé(e)? Répondez aux questions en remplaçant les mots soulignés avec les pronoms **y** ou **en**.

Modèle: Avez-vous peur <u>de la compétition</u>? **Non, je n'en ai pas peur.**

1. Avez-vous besoin <u>d'un travail flexible</u>?
2. Travaillez-vous souvent <u>chez vous</u>?
3. Avez-vous <u>des enfants</u>?
4. Buvez-vous souvent <u>de l'alcool</u>?
5. Allez-vous souvent <u>aux toilettes</u>?
6. Répondez-vous rapidement <u>aux courriels</u>?
7. Avez-vous envie <u>de travailler le week-end</u>?
8. Pensez-vous constamment <u>à votre travail</u>?

- Quelles questions sont normalement interdites *(forbidden)* dans un entretien d'embauche?

ACTIVITÉ O Vous êtes bien équipé(e)? Posez ces questions à un(e) partenaire. Est-ce qu'il/elle est bien équipé(e)?

Modèle: É1: **Tu as combien de calculatrices?**
　　　　É2: **J'en ai trois.**

1. Tu as combien de télés?
2. Tu as combien de téléphones?
3. Tu as combien d'iPods?
4. Tu as combien d'ordinateurs?

ACTIVITÉ P Les activités de Claire Gagner Claire a-t-elle fait les activités suivantes dans le film *Liaisons*? Avec un(e) partenaire, répondez aux questions pour voir si vous avez une bonne mémoire.

Modèle: Claire a lu <u>son livre de psychologie</u>? **Oui, elle l'a lu.**

1. Claire a mangé <u>des oranges</u> au café?
2. Claire a regardé <u>la télé</u> chez elle?
3. L'oncle Michel a téléphoné <u>à Claire</u>?
4. Claire est allée <u>à Québec</u>?
5. Elle a répondu <u>aux questions des clients</u>?
6. Claire a pensé <u>à Alexis Prévost</u>?
7. Claire a fait <u>ses devoirs</u>?
8. Claire a bu beaucoup <u>de bières</u>?

Pour aller plus loin

L'ordre des pronoms compléments d'objet

Use this sequence when a sentence contains two object pronouns.

me te nous vous	*before*	le la les	*before*	lui leur	*before*	y / en

Double object pronouns occupy the same position in sentences as single object pronouns.

Mon père (ne) m'achète (pas) les livres.	→	Il (ne) **me les** achète (pas).
Les voisins (ne) lui ont (pas) donné du (de) sucre.	→	Ils (ne) **lui en** ont (pas) donné.
Luc (ne) leur a (pas) montré les maisons.	→	Luc (ne) **les leur** a (pas) montr**ées**.
Ne lui donne pas le couteau.	→	Ne **le lui** donne pas.

In affirmative commands, the direct object pronoun precedes the indirect object pronoun. Remember that **moi** and **toi** are used instead of **me** and **te**.

Montrez-moi les assiettes.	→	Montrez-**les-moi**.

Essayez! Répondez aux questions avec deux pronoms.

1. Vous montrez <u>les films</u> d'horreur de Wes Craven <u>aux enfants</u>?
2. L'an dernier, vous avez donné <u>des cadeaux</u> <u>à votre voisin</u>?
3. L'année prochaine, vous allez acheter <u>vos livres</u> <u>à la librairie universitaire</u>?

OUI, JE PEUX!

Here are two "can do statements" for you to check your progress so far. Look at each statement and rate yourself on how well you think you can perform the task. Then verify your ability with a partner. How did you do?

1. **"I can name three professional skills or personality traits I have and find out if others have the same or different ones."**

   I can perform this function
   ☐ with ease
   ☐ with some difficulty
   ☐ not at all

2. **"I can state one thing I want to do, one thing I can do, and one thing I must do this week."**

   I can perform this function
   ☐ with ease
   ☐ with some difficulty
   ☐ not at all

iLrn™
Are you looking for more practice? You can find it in **iLrn**.

La **formation** et les **dépenses**

Training and expenses

une école de commerce

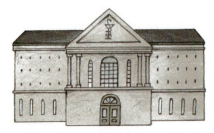

une faculté de médecine

Note de **vocabulaire**
In France, **une faculté de sciences et de technologie** may also be called **une école polytechnique.**

une faculté de droit

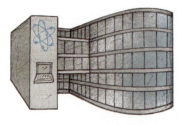

une faculté de sciences et de technologie

une faculté de lettres et de sciences humaines

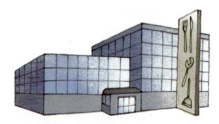

une école professionnelle

La formation

Vocabulaire complémentaire

le baccalauréat *end-of-high-school exam*
un collège *junior high / middle school*
un diplôme (universitaire) *(university) diploma*
un doctorat *doctorate, Ph.D.*
les études supérieures *(f.) higher education*
une formation *training*
une licence *equivalent of a bachelor's degree*

un lycée *high school*
un master *master's degree*
un MBA *MBA*
un stage de formation *internship*

une bourse d'études *scholarship*
une carte bancaire *debit card*
un compte-chèques *checking account*
les frais de scolarité *(m.) tuition*
un prêt étudiant *student loan*

une carte de crédit

un distributeur automatique

les pièces de monnaie (f.)

les billets (m.)

Les dépenses

Vocabulaire complémentaire

dépenser (de l'argent) *to spend (money)*   **payer en liquide** *to pay cash*
déposer (de l'argent) *to deposit (money)*   **payer par chèque** *to pay by check*
emprunter *to borrow*   **rembourser** *to pay back*
faire des économies *to save money*   **retirer de l'argent** *to withdraw money*

Un mot sur la langue

Différences lexicales: faculté vs U.F.R.

Il y a eu une évolution dans l'utilisation du mot **faculté** en France. En effet, avec la loi Savary de 1984, le terme **faculté** a été remplacé° par l'expression **unité de formation et de recherche** (U.F.R.). Cependant, par tradition, certaines universités ont gardé l'ancienne appellation° **faculté** et la plupart des° Français continuent d'utiliser le nom **faculté**. Il existe aussi des différences entre le français et le québécois en ce qui concerne le nom des établissements universitaires.

remplacé *replaced* **l'appellation** *the name* **la plupart des** *the majority of*

- Essayez de trouver les équivalents de ces deux expressions québécoises dans la liste de vocabulaire de cette leçon.

    1. l'école secondaire   2. un diplôme d'études secondaires

🔊 7-5 **ACTIVITÉ A** **Les écoles et leurs diplômes** Dans quelle institution obtient-on les diplômes mentionnés?

1. a. au lycée   b. dans une faculté de médecine
2. a. dans une école professionnelle   b. dans une faculté de sciences et technologie
3. a. au collège   b. dans une faculté de mathématiques
4. a. dans une faculté de lettres   b. au lycée
5. a. dans une école de commerce   b. dans une faculté de médecine
6. a. dans une faculté de lettres   b. dans une école professionnelle

🔊 7-6 **ACTIVITÉ B** **Les professions et la formation** Quelle école ou faculté associez-vous aux professions mentionnées?

1. a. une école de commerce   b. une faculté de sciences et technologie
2. a. une faculté de médecine   b. une faculté de lettres et de sciences humaines
3. a. une faculté de droit   b. une école polytechnique
4. a. une école professionnelle   b. une faculté de sciences humaines et sociales

ACTIVITÉ C **Où ont-ils étudié?** Où est-ce que ces personnes ont étudié?

Modèle: un comptable   **dans une école de commerce**

1. un médecin   3. une assistante sociale   5. un avocat
2. un plombier   4. un ingénieur   6. un cuisinier

ACTIVITÉ D **Qualifications nécessaires** Quels diplômes sont nécessaires pour ces professions et ces emplois?

Modèle: une assistante sociale   **Il faut une licence.**

1. une infirmière   3. un gérant   5. un enseignant
2. un agent de police   4. un professeur   6. un ouvrier

ACTIVITÉ E **Claire Gagner** Claire étudie la psychologie. Répondez à ces questions au sujet de Claire.

1. Quelle profession Claire a-t-elle choisie?
2. Dans quelle école ou faculté est-ce que Claire étudie?
3. Claire prépare un MBA ou un doctorat à l'Université McGill?

ACTIVITÉ **F** **L'argent** Complétez chaque phrase logiquement.

1. Si tu paies avec **des billets** et **des pièces de monnaie,** tu…
   a. paies en liquide.
   b. paies par chèque.

2. Si tu **retires de l'argent** de ton compte, tu…
   a. soustrais *(subtract)* de l'argent.
   b. ajoutes *(add)* de l'argent.

3. Au **distributeur automatique,** il faut insérer *(insert)*…
   a. ta carte de crédit.
   b. ta carte bancaire.

4. Si tu **paies par chèque,** la banque soustrait la somme d'argent de…
   a. ton compte-chèques.
   b. ton prêt étudiant.

5. Si tu **déposes de l'argent** sur ton compte, tu…
   a. fais des économies.
   b. dépenses ton argent.

6. On paie typiquement les **frais de scolarité…**
   a. en liquide.
   b. par chèque.

7. Il faut **rembourser…**
   a. un prêt étudiant.
   b. une bourse d'études.

8. On **n'a pas besoin de rembourser…**
   a. un prêt étudiant.
   b. une bourse d'études.

ACTIVITÉ **G** **Vos études**

Étape 1. Répondez aux questions.

1. Quelle est votre spécialisation à l'université? Quelle profession avez-vous choisie?

2. Dans quelle école ou faculté est-ce que vous étudiez?

3. Vous voulez obtenir *(to get)* un master? un doctorat? un MBA?

4. Qui paie vos frais de scolarité? Comment payez-vous vos frais? Avez-vous un prêt étudiant? une bourse d'études?

Étape 2. Posez les questions ci-dessus à un(e) partenaire. Préparez un résumé de ses réponses.

Modèle: **La spécialisation de Luc est la comptabilité. Il veut être comptable…**

ACTIVITÉ **H** **Votre partenaire et son argent** Posez ces questions à un(e) partenaire. Est-ce qu'il/elle gère *(manage)* bien son argent?

1. Tu préfères dépenser ton argent ou faire des économies?

2. Tu aimes payer en liquide, avec ta carte bancaire ou avec ta carte de crédit?

3. As-tu un crédit en cours *(credit card/active loan)*?

Si vous y allez

Fondation Alliance française

Si vous allez à Paris, prenez des cours de français à l'Alliance Française Paris Île-de-France pour obtenir un Diplôme de Français Professionnel (en affaires) si ça vous intéresse!

ACTIVITÉ I **Descriptions de professions** Complétez le tableau pour chaque profession selon le système universitaire américain. Utilisez les **Vocabulaires 1, 2 et 3.**

Profession	Institution	Diplômes et années d'études	Compétences nécessaires
1. un(e) journaliste	une faculté de lettres	une licence, 4 années	intelligent, acharné, créatif, précis, extraverti
2. un(e) avocat(e)	_____	_____	_____
3. un(e) comptable	_____	_____	_____
4. un(e) musicien(ne)	_____	_____	_____
5. un homme / une femme d'affaires	_____	_____	_____

ACTIVITÉ J **À la recherche** Posez des questions à des étudiants différents. Quand vous trouvez quelqu'un qui correspond à chaque action, notez son prénom.

Trouvez quelqu'un qui…

1. emprunte de l'argent de temps en temps.
2. a fait un stage de formation.
3. désire étudier dans une faculté de droit.
4. va obtenir un master.
5. n'a pas d'argent sur son compte-chèques.
6. a besoin de rembourser ses parents.
7. fait des économies.
8. a utilisé sa carte bancaire hier.
9. a envie d'obtenir un MBA.
10. a reçu une bourse d'études.

Un mot sur la culture

Après le bac

Comme le montre la phrase «Passe ton bac d'abord», souvent répétée par les parents, le baccalauréat est une étape très importante dans la vie des lycéens en France. Cependant, même si le bac ouvre les portes de l'université, tous les lycéens ne choisissent pas de poursuivre des études universitaires. En effet, certains préfèrent entrer directement dans le monde du travail. Pour ceux qui choisissent l'université, il est important de noter qu'en France, il n'y a pas de *major / minor*. Les cours généraux que les étudiants américains suivent la première année sont en fait l'équivalent du baccalauréat que les lycéens français passent à la fin du lycée. Par conséquent, dès que° les étudiants français entrent à l'université, ils choisissent leur spécialisation.

© Christophe Morin / Maxppp / Landov

dès que *as soon as*

• Quels examens sont importants pour les lycéens aux États-Unis?

Liaisons avec les mots et les sons

 ### Les voyelles ouvertes et fermées: o / au / eau

7-7
You have already seen how the **o** vowel sound can be written in different ways in French (**o / au / eau**). It is important to learn now that two sounds are associated with **o**.

The first sound is called an open **o**. This sound is often found in a syllable that ends with a pronounced consonant. This sound is more frequent in French.

sp**o**rt	pr**o**f	ad**o**re	**o**ffre	n**o**tre	téléph**o**ne	b**o**l	h**o**rloge

The second sound is called a closed **o**. This sound is usually, but not always, the last sound of the syllable. It can be spelled **o, ô, au,** or **eau**.

h**ô**tel	bat**eau**	f**au**te	bur**eau**	g**au**che	m**o**t	vél**o**	gr**o**s

However, when the **o** is followed by the pronounced consonant **s,** which creates the **z** sound, it is pronounced as a closed **o**.

ch**o**se	r**o**se	prop**o**se	dép**o**se	p**o**ser	philo**o**phie	prépo**o**itions

Pratique A. Écoutez et répétez ces mots de vocabulaire.

Les voyelles ouvertes		Les voyelles fermées	
1. un compte-chèques	**4.** une informaticienne	**7.** un diplôme	**10.** un agent de police
2. un collège	**5.** un doctorat	**8.** déposer de l'argent	**11.** une profession
3. un homme d'affaires	**6.** la formation	**9.** un assistant social	**12.** composé

Pratique B. Écoutez ces répliques de la Séquence 4 du film *Liaisons.* Soulignez *(Underline)* les mots avec des voyelles ouvertes et encerclez *(circle)* les mots avec des voyelles fermées.

CLAIRE Cet hôtel est un vrai château.

CLAIRE Oui. Je vous attendrai au rez-de-chaussée…

ALEXIS Bon après-midi…

 À vos stylos! C'est l'heure de la dictée!

7-8
Vous allez entendre trois phrases deux fois. La première fois, écoutez bien. La deuxième fois, écrivez les phrases.

Sujet Citations célèbres

Pour faire des comparaisons

Les expressions de comparaison et les superlatifs

DU FILM *LIAISONS*

Un coup d'œil sur la grammaire

Look at these photos from the film *Liaisons* and their captions.

CLAIRE Cet hôtel est un vrai château. Il est encore **plus beau que** je l'avais imaginé.

RÉCEPTIONNISTE C'est **le plus célèbre** du Québec.

1. How do you say *more beautiful than* in French?
2. How do you say *the most famous* in French?

❖ To compare adverbs and adjectives in French, use **plus** *(more)*, **moins** *(less)*, and **aussi** *(as)* before the adverb or adjective and **que** *(than, as)* after them.

adverb
↓

Les Français parlent **plus** vite **que** les Américains.
The French speak faster than Americans.

adjective
↓

Les professeurs américains sont **moins** sévères **que** les professeurs français.
American professors are less strict than French professors.

adjective
↓

Les diplômes universitaires sont **aussi** importants en France **qu'**au Québec.
University diplomas are as important in France as in Quebec.

❖ The superlative form of adjectives is formed by adding the appropriate definite article (**le, la, les**) to the comparative form and placing it after the noun (when the noun is expressed). The preposition **de** is used to express *in* or *of.*

Les médecins sont les gens **les plus riches.**	*Doctors are the richest people.*
C'est l'hôtel **le plus cher de la ville.**	*It's the most expensive hotel in the city.*
Anne est **la moins payée** dans l'entreprise.	*Anne is the least paid in the company.*

- Adjectives that precede the noun such as **beau, grand, petit,** and **nouveau** may precede or follow the nouns they modify in the superlative form.

Paris, c'est **la plus belle** ville.	*Paris is the most beautiful city.*
Paris, c'est la ville **la plus belle.**	*Paris is the most beautiful city.*

- The article **le** is always used in the superlative of adverbs because adverbs do not have gender or number.

Les Français parlent **le plus vite.**	*The French speak **the fastest.***
Cette calculatrice coûte **le moins cher.**	*This calculator costs **the least.***

- Some adverbs and adjectives have irregular comparative and superlative forms.

Adjectif	Comparatif	Superlatif
bon(ne)(s)	meilleur(e)(s)	le/la/les meilleur(e)(s)
mauvais(e)(es)	pire(s) *or*	le/la/les pire(s) *or*
	plus mauvais(e)(es)	le/la/les plus mauvais(e)(es)

Adverbe	Comparatif	Superlatif
bien	mieux	le mieux
mal	plus mal	le plus mal

Note de **vocabulaire**
In spoken French, you may also hear **pire** used instead of **plus mal.**

Les oranges sont **meilleures que** les pommes.	*The oranges are **better than** the apples.*
Les examens sont **pires que** les devoirs.	*Exams are **worse than** homework.*
Tu chantes **mieux que** moi.	*You sing **better than** me.*
Luc danse **plus mal que** Marc.	*Luc dances **worse than** Marc.*
C'est **la meilleure** profession du monde!	*That's **the best** profession in the world!*
C'est **la plus mauvaise** histoire.	*That's **the worst** story.*
Il chante **le plus mal** dans le groupe.	*He sings **the worst** in the group.*

- To compare nouns or quantities of things, use the following expressions.

plus de/d'	+ *noun*	+ **que**	*(more . . . than)*
moins de/d'	+ *noun*	+ **que**	*(less . . . than)*
autant de/d'	+ *noun*	+ **que**	*(as much / many . . . as)*

Anne a **plus de** livres **que** Luc.	*Anne has **more books than** Luc.*
Koffi a moins d'enfants **que** Luc.	*Koffi has **fewer children than** Luc.*
J'ai **autant** d'argent que toi.	*I have as **much money as** you.*

- To compare quantities that do not involve nouns, there is no **de.**

Je travaille **plus que** toi.	*I work more than you.*
Ils dorment **moins que** moi.	*They sleep less than I.*
Nous mangeons **autant qu'**elles.	*We eat as much as they.*

🔊 **ACTIVITÉ** Ⓚ **Vrai ou faux?** Vous allez entendre des phrases sur la
7-9 géographie. Sont-elles vraies ou fausses?

1.   2.   3.   4.   5.   6.   7.   8.   9.   10.

ACTIVITÉ Ⓛ **Le monde du travail** Complétez les phrases suivantes et puis
indiquez si vous êtes d'accord ou pas d'accord.

1. Les secrétaires sont _____ riches que leurs patrons.
a. moins de   b. moins

2. Les infirmières travaillent _____ que les médecins.
a. autant   b. autant de

3. Les comptables sont _____ bons avec les chiffres que les ingénieurs.
a. autant de   b. aussi

4. Les chanteurs gagnent _____ argent que les acteurs.
a. autant d'   b. aussi

ACTIVITÉ Ⓜ **Votre opinion** Donnez votre opinion sur les sujets suivants avec
les éléments donnés.

Modèle: médecin / cuisinier (gagner / argent)
Un médecin gagne plus d'argent qu'un cuisinier.

1. étudiants / professeurs (être / riche)

2. les Français / les Anglais (cuisiner / bien)

3. pompier / enseignant (être / courageux)

4. Big Mac / pizza (avoir / calories)

5. Garfield / Bart Simpson (chanter / mal)

6. chocolat belge / chocolat suisse (être / bon)

ACTIVITÉ Ⓝ **Comparaisons**

Étape 1. Posez ces questions à deux camarades de classe. Notez leurs réponses.

	É1	É2
1. Tu as quel âge?	_____	_____
2. Tu as combien d'argent sur toi en ce moment?	_____	_____
3. Tu étudies pendant combien d'heures le week-end?	_____	_____
4. Tu as combien de frères et de sœurs?	_____	_____
5. Tu as combien de colocataires?	_____	_____

Étape 2. À partir des informations de l'Étape 1, écrivez quatre à cinq phrases pour
comparer vos deux camarades de classe.

Modèle: **Paul est plus jeune que Marc. Marc a moins de frères que Paul.**

ACTIVITÉ O Êtes-vous d'accord? Êtes-vous d'accord avec les phrases suivantes?

1. Andy Warhol est l'artiste le plus créatif.
2. Tom Cruise est l'acteur le moins beau.
3. Rachael Ray cuisine le moins bien.
4. Martha Stewart cuisine le mieux.

ACTIVITÉ P Les personnes célèbres et nos opinions

Étape 1. Répondez aux questions et écrivez vos réponses dans la colonne 1.

	Moi	É1	É2
1. Qui est l'actrice la plus belle?	_____	_____	_____
2. Qui est la chanteuse la plus farfelue?	_____	_____	_____
3. Qui est le chanteur le plus excentrique?	_____	_____	_____
4. Qui est l'acteur le plus drôle?	_____	_____	_____
5. Qui chante le mieux?	_____	_____	_____
6. Qui chante le plus mal?	_____	_____	_____

 Étape 2. Posez les questions à deux personnes. Écrivez leurs réponses dans la colonne 2 et la colonne 3.

 Étape 3. Faites un résumé de vos opinions et des opinions de vos camarades de classe.

Modèle: Pour mes camarades de classe, les actrices les plus belles sont Natalie Portman et Keira Knightley. Pour moi, l'actrice la plus belle est Emma Watson.

Liaisons musicales

© Guibbaud Christophe/MCT/Newscom

Laure Milan, chanteuse française de musique R&B et hip-hop, vient de Toulouse. Dans sa chanson *La meilleure* (2006), son petit ami l'a quittée. Est-ce qu'elle veut de nouveau être en couple? Cherchez les paroles de cette chanson pour trouver la réponse à la question.

OUI, JE PEUX! Here are two "can do statements" for you to check your progress so far. Look at each statement and rate yourself on how well you think you can perform the task. Then verify your ability with a partner. How did you do?

1. **"I can name the type of institution in which I am studying and explain how I pay for my tuition."**

   I can perform this function
   ☐ with ease
   ☐ with some difficulty
   ☐ not at all

2. **"I can say if I study more, less or as much as another classmate and I can say who studies the most in the class."**

   I can perform this function
   ☐ with ease
   ☐ with some difficulty
   ☐ not at all

iLrn™

Are you looking for more practice? You can find it in **iLrn**.

PREMIÈRE PROJECTION

LIAISONS
SÉQUENCE 4: La clé

Avant de visionner

ACTIVITÉ A **Vous rappelez-vous?** Vous rappelez-vous *(Do you remember)* ce qui s'est passé dans la Séquence 3 du film *Liaisons*? Pour chaque phrase, indiquez si c'est vrai ou faux.

	Vrai	Faux
1. Claire est partie pour la ville de Québec.	☐	☐
2. Claire a pris quelque chose à manger dans un café.	☐	☐
3. Claire a appris qu'Alexis Prévost est de Trois-Rivières.	☐	☐
4. Claire a un rendez-vous avec M. Prévost à Montréal.	☐	☐

ACTIVITÉ B **Devinez** Devinez ce qui va se passer dans la Séquence 4 du film *Liaisons*. Pour chaque phrase, indiquez si c'est vrai ou faux. Vous allez vérifier vos réponses plus tard.

	Vrai	Faux
1. Claire va arriver à Québec.	☐	☐
2. Claire va apprendre qui a fait la réservation pour elle.	☐	☐
3. Claire va revoir *(is going to see again)* Alexis Prévost.	☐	☐
4. Claire va revoir l'homme mystérieux qui lui a donné l'enveloppe.	☐	☐
5. Un nouveau mystère va attendre Claire.	☐	☐

ACTIVITÉ C **Un coup d'œil sur une scène** Voici une scène de la Séquence 4 du film *Liaisons*. Claire est au Château Frontenac. Elle parle avec la réceptionniste de l'hôtel. Choisissez la lettre du mot qui correspond à chaque espace *(space)* dans le dialogue. Vous allez vérifier vos réponses plus tard.

RÉCEPTIONNISTE Voici votre
(1) _____. La (2) _____ 315. [...] Les
(3) _____ sont à votre gauche. Avez-
vous (4) _____ d'aide *(help)* avec vos
(5) _____?

CLAIRE Non, ça va. Je n'en ai qu(e)
(6) _____.

Note de grammaire

Ne… que/qu' means *only*. You will learn this construction in **Chapitre 10, Grammaire 3**.

1. a. chambre   b. clé *(key)*
2. a. chambre   b. clé
3. a. ascenseurs *(elevators)*   b. escaliers
4. a. besoin   b. envie
5. a. sacs   b. valises *(suitcases)*
6. a. deux   b. une

▶ **Regarder la séquence**

Vous allez regarder la Séquence 4 du film *Liaisons*. Vérifiez vos réponses à l'Activité B et à l'Activité C.

Après le visionnage

ACTIVITÉ **D** **Avez-vous compris?** Complétez les phrases.

1. Quelqu'un a remis _____ à la chambre de Claire.
   a. une clé dans une enveloppe   b. des fleurs et du chocolat

2. Claire parle avec _____ avant de sortir de l'hôtel.
   a. le concierge   b. sa mère

3. Claire prend une tasse de thé dans un café et lit un livre sur _____.
   a. la psychose   b. la ville de Québec

4. Claire apprend qu'Alexis Prévost va _____.
   a. rester à Québec pendant une semaine   b. partir pour la France lundi

Note de **grammaire**
The verb **remettre** *(to deliver)* is conjugated like **mettre**.

ACTIVITÉ **E** **Utilisez le contexte**

Regardez bien les mots en caractères gras *(boldface)* et répondez aux questions.

CONCIERGE C'est une clé de (1) **coffre-fort**.

CLAIRE Comme dans une banque?

CONCIERGE Oui, c'est ça. [...] [Ma mère] avait une clé (2) **semblable**. Elle avait un **coffre-fort** à la Banque Nationale.

1. Le mot **coffre-fort** veut dire *(means)*...   a. safety deposit box.   b. jewelry box.

2. Le mot **semblable** veut dire...   a. différent.   b. similaire.

ACTIVITÉ **F** **Les personnages du film** Répondez aux questions sur **Abia, Claire, Alexis Prévost** et **Simone Gagner**. Puis, posez ces questions à un(e) partenaire pour voir si vous avez les mêmes opinions.

1. Qui est le/la plus drôle dans le film?
2. Qui est le/la plus sensible dans le film?
3. Qui est le/la plus loyal(e)?
4. Qui est le/la plus mystérieux (mystérieuse)?

Liaisons avec la culture

Le Château Frontenac

Le Château Frontenac, situé dans le quartier du Vieux-Québec, est l'une des attractions les plus populaires de la ville. Son architecture est inspirée des châteaux français de l'époque de la Renaissance. On lui a donné le nom Frontenac en l'honneur de Louis de Buade, comte de Frontenac, qui a été gouverneur de la Nouvelle-France de 1672 à 1682 et de 1689 à 1698. Selon le journal *Le Soleil*, le Château Frontenac est l'hôtel le plus photographié au monde et le monument le plus associé à la ville de Québec.

© AP Images/Robert F. Bukaty

LIAISONS
CULTURELLES

Au travail!

OUTILS DE LECTURE

Using content words to predict meaning

Content words—which include nouns, verbs, adjectives, and adverbs—are words that tend to carry the most meaning in a text. Content words usually carry a lot more meaning than function words. When you recognize lots of content words when you read, you can use them to predict the meaning of a text.

1. Skim the text **Les universités et les grandes écoles** and make a list of the content words you recognize.

2. Look at your list and brainstorm in English what ideas may be in this text.

Les universités et les grandes écoles

Contrairement à la plupart des pays comparables, la France a un double système d'études supérieures: les universités et les grandes écoles. Les grandes écoles sont des instituts d'études spécialisées: les affaires, l'administration, le génie, etc. Pour s'inscrire à l'université, il faut réussir aux examens du baccalauréat. Par contre°, pour entrer dans une grande école, il faut non seulement avoir son bac, mais aussi faire des études préparatoires (2 ou 3 ans) et passer un examen de sélection.

© Loïc Venance/AFP/Getty Images

Par contre *By contrast*

Vrai ou faux?

1. Il faut avoir le baccalauréat pour entrer à l'université.   V / F
2. Les universités sont généralistes, mais les grandes écoles sont spécialisées.   V / F
3. Il est plus facile d'entrer à l'université que dans une grande école.   V / F

CODOFIL and Department of Culture, Recreation & Tourism, Louisiana

Conseil pour le développement du français en Louisiane

D'après le dernier recensement°, il y a plus de 200 000 francophones en Louisiane. Le Conseil pour le développement du français en Louisiane (CODOFIL) a été créé en 1968 pour promouvoir° le français dans les écoles et dans la société louisianaises. Aujourd'hui, plus de 17 000 élèves apprennent le français en Louisiane. De nombreuses bourses d'études sont financées par cette fondation. Il y a plus de 127 enseignants, non seulement de Louisiane et des autres états des États-Unis, mais aussi de France, de Belgique, du Canada, de plusieurs pays africains francophones et de Haïti.

recensement *census* **promouvoir** *promote*

Vrai ou faux?

1. Il n'y a pas beaucoup de francophones en Louisiane.   V / F

2. CODOFIL donne des bourses aux étudiants pour étudier le français.   V / F

3. Tous les enseignants de français en Louisiane sont de France.   V / F

Ressources humaines: film de Laurent Cantet

La particularité du film réalisé par Laurent Cantet en 1999, *Ressources humaines,* c'est que l'essentiel de l'intrigue° est situé dans le monde du travail. Le personnage° principal, Franck, est un brillant étudiant dans une grande école de commerce à Paris. Avant de terminer ses études, il fait un stage de formation° au service des ressources humaines à l'usine° où son père est ouvrier depuis trente ans. Quand il y a un conflit du travail entre les employés et la direction° de l'entreprise, Franck doit décider s'il va soutenir° les ouvriers en grève° ou les cadres°.

intrigue *plot* **personnage** *character* **un stage de formation** *internship* **usine** *factory* **la direction** *the management* **soutenir** *support* **en grève** *on strike* **cadres** *executives*

Courtesy Everett Collection

Compréhension

1. *Ressources humaines* est un film _____.
   a. romantique   b. réaliste

2. Franck, le personnage principal, est le fils d'un _____.
   a. cadre   b. ouvrier

3. Les ouvriers sont en grève à cause d'un conflit _____.
   a. amoureux   b. du travail

© Patrick Rodrigue

Les CÉGEP au Québec

Après leurs études secondaires, les étudiants québécois doivent aller au CÉGEP (collège d'enseignement général et professionnel). Ces collèges offrent deux types de programmes. Les programmes techniques durent trois ans et mènent° au marché du travail et à certains programmes universitaires. Les programmes pré-universitaires durent deux ans et mènent à l'université. Ce système a été créé° pour faciliter l'accès à l'université et au marché du travail ainsi que° la transition entre l'école secondaire et l'université. Le Québec est la seule° province au Canada à posséder le système de CÉGEP.

mènent *lead* **créé** *created* **ainsi que** *as well as* **seule** *only*

Vrai ou faux?

1. Les étudiants vont au CÉGEP après l'université.   V / F
2. Les CÉGEP facilitent l'accès à l'université.   V / F
3. Les programmes techniques mènent au marché du travail.   V / F
4. La province d'Alberta a aussi le système de CÉGEP.   V / F

▶ **LIAISONS CULTURELLES** ....

Use **iLrn**™ to access the video **L'université** to learn more about the different types of universities and university experiences in France. Be prepared to answer the question **Et vous? Est-ce que votre expérience à l'université peut vous aider à vous préparer à la vraie vie?** Share your responses with your classmates in **Share It!**

PARTIE 1 7–10

LES PROFESSIONS

un acteur / une actrice	actor, actress
un(e) agent(e) de police	police officer
un(e) assistant(e) social(e)	social worker
un(e) avocat(e)	lawyer
un chanteur / une chanteuse	singer
un coiffeur / une coiffeuse	hairdresser
un(e) comptable	accountant
un cuisinier / une cuisinière	cook
un(e) dentiste	dentist
un(e) employé(e)	employee
un(e) enseignant(e)	instructor, teacher
un(e) gérant(e)	manager
un homme / une femme d'affaires	businessman / businesswoman
un infirmier / une infirmière	nurse
un(e) informaticien(ne)	computer specialist
un ingénieur / une femme ingénieur	engineer
un(e) journaliste	journalist
un médecin / une femme médecin	doctor
un(e) musicien(ne)	musician
un ouvrier / une ouvrière	(factory) worker
un(e) patron(ne)	boss
un plombier / une femme plombier	plumber
un pompier / une femme pompier	firefighter
un(e) psychologue	psychologist
un(e) secrétaire	secretary
un vendeur / une vendeuse	salesperson

NOMS

une carrière	career
un emploi	job
une entreprise	company
un poste	position
une profession	profession
un salaire	salary, pay, wages
le travail	work

VERBES

demander (à)	to ask
donner (à)	to give
envoyer (à)	to send
gagner de l'argent	to earn money
gagner sa vie	to earn a living
montrer (à)	to show
poser (une question) (à)	to ask (a question)
prêter (à)	to lend

PRONOMS COMPLÉMENTS D'OBJET INDIRECT

me/m'	(to / for) me
te/t'	(to / for) you
lui	(to / for) him, her
nous	(to / for) us
vous	(to / for) you
leur	(to / for) them

PARTIE 2 7–11

ADJECTIFS

coincé(e)	uptight
créatif / créative	creative
déloyal(e)	disloyal
drôle	funny, odd
exigeant(e)	demanding
flexible	flexible
inflexible	inflexible
jaloux / jalouse	jealous
loyal(e)	loyal, faithful
organisé(e)	organized
sensible	sensitive
têtu(e)	stubborn

ADJECTIFS OU NOMS

acharné(e)	competitive, cutthroat
excentrique	eccentric
extraverti(e)	extroverted, extrovert
farfelu(e)	scatter-brained
introverti(e)	introverted, introvert
professionnel(le)	professional

EXPRESSIONS

avoir de bonnes capacités de communication	to have good communication skills
avoir le goût du travail	to have a good work ethic
avoir le sens de l'humour	to have a sense of humor
être bon / bonne avec les chiffres	to be good with numbers
être de bonne humeur	to be in a good mood
être de mauvaise humeur	to be in a bad mood
être du matin	to be a morning person
être précis(e)	to be good with details
être du soir	to be a night person

VERBES

devoir	to have to, must, to owe
pouvoir	to be able, can
vouloir	to want

RÉSUMÉ DE VOCABULAIRE

PRONOMS

en	*of them/it, some*
y	*there, of / about it*

DIVERS

quelqu'un de/d' + adjectif	*someone + adjective*

PARTIE 3   7–12

LES DIPLÔMES ET LES ÉTUDES

le baccalauréat	*end-of-high-school exam*
un collège	*junior high / middle school*
un diplôme (universitaire)	*(university) diploma*
un doctorat	*doctorate, Ph.D.*
les études supérieures *(f.)*	*higher education*
une licence	*equivalent of a bachelor's degree*
un lycée	*high school*
un master	*master's degree*
un MBA	*MBA*
un stage de formation	*internship*

LES INSTITUTIONS

une école de commerce	*business school*
une école professionnelle	*professional / vocational school*
une faculté de droit	*law school*
une faculté de lettres et de sciences humaines	*liberal arts college*
une faculté de médecine	*medical school*
une faculté de sciences et de technologie	*science and technology college*

LES FINANCES

les billets *(m.)*	*bills, banknotes*
une bourse d'études	*scholarship*
une carte bancaire	*debit card*
une carte de crédit	*credit card*
un compte-chèques	*checking account*
un distributeur automatique	*ATM*
les frais de scolarité *(m.)*	*tuition*
les pièces de monnaie *(f.)*	*coins*
un prêt étudiant	*student loan*

VERBES

dépenser (de l'argent)	*to spend (money)*
déposer (de l'argent)	*to deposit (money)*
emprunter	*to borrow*
faire des économies	*to save money*
payer en liquide	*to pay cash*
payer par chèque	*to pay by check*
rembourser	*to pay back*
retirer de l'argent	*to withdraw money*

COMPARATIFS

aussi… que	*as . . . as*
autant de… que	*as many, as much . . . as*
meilleur(e)(s) *(adj.)*	*better*
mieux *(adv.)*	*better*
moins (de)… que	*less, fewer . . . than*
pire *(adj.)*	*worse*
plus (de)… que	*more . . . than*
plus mal *(adv.)*	*worse*
plus mauvais *(adj.)*	*worse*

SUPERLATIFS

le/la/les meilleur(e)(s) *(adj.)*	*the best*
le mieux *(adv.)*	*the best*
le/la/les moins	*the least*
le/la/les pire(s) *(adj.)*	*the worst*
le/la/les plus	*the most*
le plus mal *(adv.)*	*the worst*
le/la/les plus mauvais(e)(es) *(adj.)*	*the worst*

Les **événements marquants**

En bref In this chapter, you will:

- talk about parties, holidays, personal events, and historical events

- learn the imperfect past tense

- learn vocabulary to talk about the different stages of life

- learn when to use the **passé composé** and the **imparfait**

- learn about important historical events in the Francophone world

- learn more about the vowel sound **eu**

- read about Canada and **les Fêtes de la Nouvelle-France**

- write about a memorable holiday or party

 You will also re-watch **SÉQUENCE 4:** **La clé** of the film *Liaisons*.

Ressources

 audio   video   Share It!   iLrn™ 🌐 http://www.cengagebrain.com

© Michael Blann/Photodisc/Getty Images

Les événements historiques

Historical events

Célébrez le patrimoine français et francophone!

Hommage à douze personnes qui ont influencé la France et le monde francophone

Charlemagne (768–814) est devenu **Roi** des Francs en 768 et **Empereur** d'Occident en 800.

Jeanne d'Arc (1412–1431), **une héroïne** nationale dans la culture française, **a aidé** l'armée française à **gagner la guerre contre** l'Angleterre.

Jacques Cartier (1497–1557), **un explorateur** français, a pris possession du Canada (la Nouvelle-France) au nom de la France en 1534.

Samuel de Champlain (1580–1635), **un soldat** et un explorateur français, **a fondé** la ville de Québec le 3 juillet 1608.

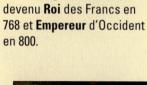

Louis XIV (1654–1715), appelé *le Roi-Soleil,* a imposé la grandeur de la langue française et sa culture en Europe.

Napoléon 1er (1769–1821), **un général** ambitieux, est devenu *Empereur des Français* en 1804 et a organisé beaucoup de **réformes** de la société française.

Charles de Gaulle (1890–1970), militaire et **homme politique français,** a été **Président** de la République.

Léopold Senghor (1906–2001), homme politique et **écrivain** sénégalais, est le symbole de la coopération entre la France et ses anciennes **colonies.**

Félix Leclerc (1914–1988), **poète,** chanteur et **écrivain,** est le «père» de la *chanson québécoise* et un symbole important du **nationalisme** québécois.

René Lévesque (1922–1987), **Premier Ministre** du Québec de 1976 à 1985, a encouragé le désir d'**indépendance** du Québec par des efforts **pacifiques.**

Assia Djebar (1936–2015), **une écrivaine** algérienne d'expression française, traite souvent des thèmes de **la guerre** et de **la liberté humaine.**

Patrick Chamoiseau (1953–), **écrivain** français originaire de la Martinique et associé au **mouvement** de la *Créolité,* écrit aussi pour le théâtre et le cinéma.

Pour parler de l'affiche

un empereur / une impératrice *emperor / empress*

un explorateur / une exploratrice *explorer*

un général *general (military)*

un héros / une héroïne *hero / heroine*

un homme / une femme politique *politician*

un poète / une femme poète *poet*

(Madame / Monsieur) le Premier Ministre *Prime Minister*

(Madame / Monsieur) le Président *President (of a country)*

le roi / la reine *king / queen*

un soldat / une femme soldat *soldier*

la colonie *colony*

la guerre (contre) *war (against)*

l'indépendance (f.) *independence*

la liberté *freedom*

le mouvement *(political) movement*

le nationalisme *nationalism*

la réforme *reform*

aider *to help*

fonder *to found, to constitute*

gagner *to win*

pacifique *peaceful*

Note de vocabulaire
Un général has no feminine form.

Note de vocabulaire
Madame le Président is the President of a country.
Madame la Présidente is the wife of the President.

Vocabulaire complémentaire

la colonisation *colonization*

la décolonisation *decolonization*

l'époque contemporaine (f.) *contemporary time*

la monarchie *monarchy*

la paix *peace*

une révolution *revolution*

la tolérance *tolerance*

marquant(e) (adj.) *memorable, important*

- There are three ways to say the date in French. There is no real difference in meaning among the three.

  C'est le 28 avril 2010.   **On est le 28 avril 2010.**   **Nous sommes le 28 avril 2010.**

- There are two ways to say years before 2000 and one way for years after 2000.

  1999 **mille neuf cent quatre-vingt-dix-neuf / dix-neuf cent quatre-vingt-dix-neuf**

  2001 **deux mille un**   2010 **deux mille dix**   2050 **deux mille cinquante**

- To express the sixties, the seventies, and so forth, use **les années** with the decade.

  Les années 60 marquent la Révolution tranquille au Québec.

Un mot sur la culture

Quelques événements historiques importants

Les événements suivants ont déterminé l'histoire de la France et du Québec.

1759: La France a perdu la Nouvelle-France dans une bataille sur Les Plaines d'Abraham.

1789: La Révolution française (la fin de la monarchie française)

1830: La France a commencé à établir son empire colonial en Afrique.

1960: La Révolution tranquille au Québec (la séparation de l'Église catholique et de l'État)

1977: Le français est devenu la seule langue officielle du Québec avec la Loi 101.

🔊 **ACTIVITÉ A Qui c'est?**

8-1
Étape 1. Quel(s) personnage(s) correspond(ent) aux mots que vous entendez?

1. a. Jacques Cartier   b. Patrick Chamoiseau
2. a. Léopold Senghor   b. René Lévesque
3. a. Jeanne d'Arc   b. Félix Leclerc
4. a. Napoléon 1er   b. Charles de Gaulle
5. a. Samuel de Champlain   b. Louis XIV
6. a. Charles de Gaulle   b. Charlemagne
7. a. Jeanne d'Arc   b. Assia Djebar
8. a. Jeanne d'Arc   b. Assia Djebar

Étape 2. Nommez une personne qui correspond aux mots que vous entendez.

Modèle: Vous entendez: un homme politique
         Vous dites: **Léopold Senghor**

1.   2.   3.   4.   5.   6.

🔊 **ACTIVITÉ B Associations** Quelle(s) association(s) faites-vous avec chaque

8-2 nom de personnage historique que vous allez entendre?

1. a. la guerre contre l'Angleterre   b. la fondation du Québec
2. a. la grandeur de la culture française b. le mouvement de la Créolité
3. a. l'indépendance du Québec   b. la Révolution française
4. a. la décolonisation   b. la Nouvelle-France
5. a. les réformes égalitaires   b. le Roi-Soleil
6. a. la colonisation   b. le père de la chanson québécoise

ACTIVITÉ C Personnages célèbres Identifiez ces personnages célèbres.

Modèle: Colin Powell: **un homme politique**

1. Winston Churchill: _____
2. Elizabeth II d'Angleterre: _____
3. Louis XIV: _____
4. Hillary Clinton: _____
5. Christophe Colomb: _____
6. Maya Angelou: _____

🔊 **ACTIVITÉ D Quelle année dans l'histoire de la France?** Complétez

8-3 chaque phrase avec l'année que vous entendez.

Modèle: Vous entendez: La ville de Québec a été fondée en **mille six cent huit.**
         Vous écrivez: La ville de Québec a été fondée en __1608.__

1. Clovis, premier roi chrétien de France, est baptisé à Reims en _____.
2. La Réforme protestante provoque des guerres de religions qui commencent en _____.
3. Napoléon 1er vend la Louisiane aux États-Unis en _____.
4. La Révolution tranquille au Québec a commencé en _____.

ACTIVITÉ E **Les anniversaires** Quand est-ce que ces personnes sont nées?

Modèle: R. Lévesque: 24/08/22

Il est né le vingt-quatre août mille neuf (dix-neuf) cent vingt-deux.

1. Assia Djebar: 30/06/36
2. Patrick Chamoiseau: 03/12/53
3. Félix Leclerc: 02/08/14
4. Malala Yousafzai: 12/07/97
5. Maya Angelou: 04/04/28
6. Martin Luther King, Jr.: 15/01/29
7. La reine Elizabeth: 21/04/26
8. Le prince Georges: 22/07/13

ACTIVITÉ F **Événements marquants**

Étape 1. Écrivez le premier exemple qui vient à l'esprit *(comes to mind)* pour chaque événement mentionné. Écrivez aussi la date et l'année si possible.

Modèle: une exploration **Christophe Colomb en 1492**

1. une élection
2. une guerre
3. une révolution
4. un attentat terroriste *(terrorist attack)*
5. un ouragan
6. un tremblement de terre *(earthquake)*

Étape 2. Comparez vos exemples avec deux camarades de classe. Est-ce qu'il y a des exemples qui sont les mêmes *(same)* pour tout le monde? Si oui, expliquez pourquoi ces exemples sont marquants pour tout le monde.

Étape 3. Comparez vos exemples avec la classe. Quels événements sont les plus marquants pour votre classe?

Si vous y allez

Si vous allez à Québec, allez au Parc-des-Champs-de-Bataille, l'endroit où la France a perdu la Nouvelle-France dans la bataille de 1759.

© Parti Libéral du Québec

Un mot sur la culture

La Révolution tranquille au Québec

Au Québec, les années 60, ou années de la Révolution tranquille, ont été marquées par la séparation entre l'Église catholique et l'État et par la construction d'une véritable identité québécoise. Cette rupture avec la tradition marque l'entrée du Québec dans la modernité. C'est une révolution «tranquille», car elle s'est faite sans violence. À la suite de la Révolution tranquille, «les Canadiens-Français» sont officiellement appelés «les Québécois» et deviennent maîtres° de leur destin.

maîtres *masters*

• Pouvez-vous nommer d'autres révolutions dans l'histoire?

Pour décrire et parler des événements habituels

L'imparfait

DU FILM *LIAISONS*
··
Un coup d'œil sur la grammaire

Look at these photos from the film *Liaisons* and their captions.

CLAIRE Cet hôtel est un vrai château. [...] Quand j'**étais** petite fille, je **voulais** toujours descendre au Château Frontenac.

CONCIERGE [Ma mère] **avait** une clé semblable. Elle **avait** un coffre à la Banque Nationale.

1. What are the infinitive forms of the verbs **étais, voulais,** and **avait**?

2. What do the verbs **étais, voulais,** and **avait** mean?

The **passé composé** is used to talk about actions that occurred at a specific time in the past such as yesterday, last week, and last year. To talk about repeated, habitual, or ongoing events or activities in the past or to express how things used to be, French uses the **imparfait** *(imperfect)*. The **imparfait** has several equivalents in English: **je dansais** *(I danced, I was dancing, I used to dance,* or *I would dance).*

Quand j'**étais** petit, je **chantais** à l'église le dimanche.

*When I **was** a child, I **used to sing** at church on Sundays.*

Mustapha **sortait** avec sa grand-mère le samedi soir.

*Mustapha **would go out** with his grandmother Saturday evenings.*

With the exception of **être**, the **imparfait** of all verbs is formed by dropping the **-ons** from the **nous** form of the present tense and adding the **imparfait** endings.

Note de **prononciation**
The imperfect endings of the singular forms and the **ils/elles** forms are all pronounced alike. The **nous** and **vous** forms, **-ions** and **-iez**, are distinguished from the present tense forms by the **i** sound in their endings.

avoir	parler	prendre
av~~ons~~ → av-	parl~~ons~~ → parl-	pren~~ons~~ → pren-
j'**avais**	je **parlais**	je **prenais**
tu **avais**	tu **parlais**	tu **prenais**
il/elle/on **avait**	il/elle/on **parlait**	il/elle/on **prenait**
nous **avions**	nous **parlions**	nous **prenions**
vous **aviez**	vous **parliez**	vous **preniez**
ils/elles **avaient**	ils/elles **parlaient**	ils/elles **prenaient**

- The imperfect stem of **être** is **ét-**: j'**étais**, tu **étais**, il/elle/on **était**, nous **étions**, vous **étiez**, ils/elles **étaient**.

- Verbs like **étudier**, which have an imperfect stem that ends in **i** (**étudi-**), have a double **i** in the first- and second-person plural forms of the **imparfait: nous étudiions, vous étudiiez.**

- Verbs whose infinitives end in -**ger** add an **e** before all endings of the **imparfait** except the **nous** and **vous** forms. Verbs whose infinitives end in -**cer** change **c** to **ç** before all endings except the **nous** and **vous** forms.

tu **mangeais**	*but*	nous **mangions**
elles **commençaient**	*but*	vous **commenciez**

- Here are some words and expressions associated with habitual or recurring events.

à cette époque-là	*at that time, in those days*	**le lundi, le samedi...**
autrefois	*in the past, long ago*	**souvent**
chaque année / mois	*each year / month*	**toujours**
d'habitude	*usually*	**tous les jours**

Le dimanche, nous **prenions** l'apéritif à 18h00.

*Every Sunday we **would have** a drink at 6:00 pm.*

Quand j'**étais** jeune, je **n'allais pas** toujours à mes cours.

*When I **was** young, I **did not** always **go** to my classes.*

- The **imparfait** is also often used to talk about age and states of mind or to provide descriptions in the past.

Guy **était** mince quand il **avait** 5 ans.

*Guy **was** thin when he **was** five years old.*

Il **faisait** du soleil pendant nos vacances.

*It **was** sunny during our vacation.*

Il y **avait** un étudiant français dans mon cours.

*There **was** a French student in my class.*

- **Devoir, pouvoir,** and **vouloir** are often used in the **imparfait** to talk about the past.

Tu **voulais** être pompier?

*You **wanted** to be a fireman?*

Je **devais** faire mes devoirs.

*I **had to do** my homework.*

Nous ne **pouvions** pas dormir.

*We **could** not sleep.*

- The following expressions are also helpful to learn in the **imparfait**.

Il pleuvait et **il neigeait.**

It was raining and snowing. / It rained and snowed.

Il fallait rendre les livres.

It was necessary to return the books.

ACTIVITÉ G Aujourd'hui ou quand nous étions plus jeunes? Les cousins d'Abia parlent de leurs activités. Utilisez les verbes pour déterminer s'ils font ces activités aujourd'hui ou s'ils faisaient ces activités quand ils étaient plus jeunes.

	Aujourd'hui	Quand ils étaient plus jeunes
1. Nous **regardons** *Les Simpson*.	☐	☐
2. Nous **faisions** la vaisselle.	☐	☐
3. Nous **lisions** le journal.	☐	☐
4. Nous **dansons** dans les fêtes.	☐	☐
5. Nous **allions** à l'église.	☐	☐
6. Nous **jouons** aux cartes.	☐	☐
7. Nous **étudiions** tous les jours.	☐	☐
8. Nous **n'étudions** jamais.	☐	☐

Conclusion Sont-ils plus sérieux aujourd'hui ou quand ils étaient plus jeunes?

🔊 8-4 **ACTIVITÉ H Aujourd'hui ou dans leur enfance?** Écoutez bien les verbes pour déterminer si les étudiants font ces activités **(a) aujourd'hui** ou s'ils faisaient ces activités **(b) dans leur enfance** *(childhood)*.

1.   2.   3.   4.   5.   6.   7.   8.

ACTIVITÉ I Quand Madame Gagner était petite

Étape 1. Simone Gagner, la mère de Claire Gagner, est à l'hôpital psychiatrique. Comment imaginez-vous sa vie quand elle était petite? Complétez les phrases.

1. Elle **habitait** _____.
2. Elle **allait** _____ le dimanche.
3. Elle **pouvait** _____.
4. Elle **était** souvent _____.
5. Elle **parlait** toujours avec _____.
6. Elle **désirait** _____.

Étape 2. Comment imaginez-vous la vie de Claire et d'Abia quand elles étaient plus jeunes? Complétez les phrases.

1. Elles **étudiaient** _____.
2. Elles **faisaient** _____.
3. Elles **devaient** _____.
4. Elles **buvaient** _____.
5. Elles **sortaient** _____.
6. Elles **réussissaient** _____.

Étape 3. Et quand vous étiez jeune?

1. Je **regardais** _____.
2. Je **dormais** _____.
3. Je **lisais** _____.
4. Je **finissais** _____.
5. Je **jouais** _____.
6. Je **voulais** _____.

ACTIVITÉ J Quand vous étiez petit(e)

Étape 1. Répondez à ces questions sur votre enfance (*childhood*).

Quand vous étiez petit(e), vous...

1. **jouiez** aux Lego?
2. **buviez** du lait?
3. **aviez** peur des orages?
4. **dormiez** avec un animal en peluche (*stuffed animal*)?
5. **aimiez** les épinards?
6. **regardiez** *Sesame Street*?
7. **étiez** scout / éclaireuse (*boy scout / girl scout*)?
8. **faisiez** du camping?

Étape 2. Posez les questions de l'Étape 1 à un(e) partenaire.

Modèle: É1: **Quand tu étais petit(e), tu jouais aux Lego?**

É2: **Oui, je jouais aux Lego. / Non, je ne jouais pas aux Lego.**

Conclusion Votre enfance et l'enfance de votre partenaire étaient typiques?

ACTIVITÉ K Quand votre professeur était petit(e) Que faisait votre professeur quand il/elle était petit(e)? Préparez cinq questions avec les éléments suivants. Posez les questions à votre professeur.

Modèle: **Quand vous étiez petit(e), vous regardiez des films français?**

aimer chanter en français

écouter des chansons françaises

étudier le français à l'école

lire des livres français

manger des pets de sœurs

pouvoir parler français

regarder des films français

vouloir être professeur de français

voyager dans un pays francophone

????

Conclusion Votre professeur(e) était destiné(e) à être professeur(e) de français?

Et vous? Quelle profession aimiez-vous quand vous étiez petit(e)?

ACTIVITÉ L Quel âge aviez-vous? Quel âge aviez-vous quand vous avez fait ces activités pour la première fois? Vous pouvez répondre **jamais** si vous n'avez jamais fait ces activités.

Modèle: boire un Coca   J'avais 5 ans.

1. faire la cuisine
2. aller au lycée
3. faire du vélo
4. pouvoir parler
5. pouvoir marcher
6. boire du champagne

ACTIVITÉ **M** **Quel temps faisait-il?** Quel temps faisait-il pendant ces journées? Répondez aux questions.

Modèle: la fête du Travail   **Il pleuvait.**

1. Noël dernier
2. Halloween dernier
3. votre dernier anniversaire

4. votre dernier pique-nique ou barbecue
5. lundi dernier
6. hier

ACTIVITÉ **N** **Au lycée** Quand vous étiez au lycée, que faisiez-vous…

1. tous les jours?
2. le week-end?
3. le samedi matin?

4. le lundi soir?
5. chaque Noël ou Hanoukka?
6. pendant les vacances de printemps?

Conclusion Est-ce que vos activités aujourd'hui sont différentes de vos activités au lycée?

ACTIVITÉ **O** **La première scène du film *Liaisons***

Étape 1. Écrivez une description de cette scène en répondant aux questions suivantes. Utilisez votre imagination.

C'était quelle année? Quel temps faisait-il? Quels meubles étaient dans la chambre?

Qui était dans la chambre? Qui écrivait? Qu'est-ce que la personne écrivait?

Étape 2. Montrez votre description à un(e) partenaire. Avez-vous écrit les mêmes détails?

ACTIVITÉ **P** **La société québécoise d'autrefois**

Étape 1. Choisissez le verbe et complétez chaque phrase à l'imparfait.

La vie au Québec (1) _____ (avoir / être) très différente avant les années 60.

L'Église catholique (2) _____ (avoir / être) une influence considérable sur la

société québécoise. Les femmes (3) _____ (devoir / faire) avoir beaucoup d'enfants,

parfois douze enfants. Les filles (4) _____ (aller / faire) rarement à l'école parce

qu'elles (5) _____ (faire / rester) les tâches ménagères à la maison. Les fils

(6) _____ (étudier / vouloir) pour devenir prêtres (*priests*). Les hommes

(7) _____ (étudier / travailler) souvent dans les forêts ou dans les bois. Ils ne

(8) _____ (devenir / pouvoir) pas avoir de bons emplois parce qu'ils ne

(9) _____ (faire / parler) pas anglais, la langue dominante au Québec avant la Loi 101.

Étape 2. Écrivez trois à quatre phrases pour décrire votre société avant les années 60. Comment était la vie? Que faisaient les femmes? Que faisaient les hommes? Qu'est-ce qu'ils ne pouvaient pas faire?

ACTIVITÉ Q La vie avant les ordinateurs

Étape 1. Pouvez-vous imaginer votre vie sans (*without*) ordinateur? Notre société n'avait pas d'ordinateurs avant 1975. Écrivez un paragraphe de cinq à six phrases pour parler de ce que (*what*) les gens faisaient quand il n'y avait pas d'ordinateurs.

> **Questions possibles à discuter**
> - Comment est-ce que les étudiants faisaient leurs devoirs?
> - Que faisaient les étudiants s'ils devaient trouver la définition d'un mot?
> - Comment est-ce que les étudiants communiquaient avec leurs professeurs? Avec leurs amis? Avec leur famille?
> - Que faisaient les gens s'ils avaient besoin d'une recette ou d'une réservation?
> - Que faisaient les gens s'ils voulaient retirer de l'argent de leur compte-chèques?
> - Que faisaient les gens s'ils voulaient regarder un film?
> - Que faisaient les gens s'ils voulaient trouver un(e) petit(e) ami(e)?

Étape 2. Montrez vos phrases à un(e) partenaire. Avez-vous écrit des phrases similaires? Voulez-vous modifier vos phrases? Voulez-vous ajouter (*add*) des phrases?

Étape 3. Vous préférez la vie d'aujourd'hui ou la vie d'autrefois? Est-ce qu'il y a des avantages associés à une vie sans ordinateur?

Liaisons musicales

Avec la Loi 101, le français est devenu langue officielle du Québec. Michel Rivard (1951–) a écrit *Le cœur de ma vie* pour célébrer la langue française des Québécois. Il chante: *C'est une langue de France aux accents d'Amérique.* Cherchez les paroles de cette chanson sur Internet. Quelles sont d'autres caractéristiques de la langue française au Québec?

OUI, JE PEUX! Here are two "can do statements" for you to check your progress so far. Look at each statement and rate yourself on how well you think you can perform the task. Then verify your ability with a partner. How did you do?

1. **"I can say three things that I did regularly when I was a child."**

   I can perform this function
   ☐ with ease
   ☐ with some difficulty
   ☐ not at all

2. **"I can ask someone else what he/she did regularly when he/she was a child to find out if we did similar activities when we were children."**

   I can perform this function
   ☐ with ease
   ☐ with some difficulty
   ☐ not at all

iLrn™

Are you looking for more practice? You can find it in **iLrn**.

🔊 Les **occasions spéciales**

Special occasions

l'anniversaire

la fête des Mères

la fête des Pères

la fête nationale

Hanoukka

Pâques

le 1er avril / le poisson d'avril

Mardi gras

la Saint-Valentin

le jour de l'Action de Grâce

Noël

le jour de l'An

Note de vocabulaire

L'Action de Grâce is used in Quebec. Because this holiday is not celebrated in France, the French call it **Thanksgiving.**

Quelques grands jours de festivités

Vocabulaire complémentaire

l'anniversaire (m.) de mariage *wedding anniversary*

la fête du Travail *Labor Day*

la Saint-Sylvestre *New Year's Eve*

la veille de Noël *Christmas Eve*

un jour férié *legal holiday*

un cadeau *gift*

une carte de vœux *greeting card*

une fête *holiday, party, celebration*

une soirée *(evening) party*

Bon / Joyeux anniversaire! *Happy birthday!*

Bonne année! *Happy New Year!*

Félicitations! *Congratulations!*

Meilleurs vœux! *Best wishes!*

fêter *to celebrate*

organiser une fête *to throw / organize a party*

Les nombres ordinaux

premier (1er) / première (1ère) *first (1st)*

quatrième (4e) *fourth (4th)*

cinquième (5e) *fifth (5th)*

neuvième (9e) *ninth (9th)*

vingt-et-unième (21e) *twenty-first (21st)*

trente-et-unième (31e) *thirty-first (31st)*

soixante-quinzième (75e) *seventy-fifth (75th)*

centième (100e) *hundredth (100th)*

- Used to rank people or things, ordinal numbers are formed by adding **-ième** to a cardinal number. If a number ends in **e,** the final **e** is dropped before adding **-ième.** The exception is **un** whose ordinal numbers are **premier / première.**

- **Cinq** and **neuf** have spelling changes in their ordinal forms: **cinquième, neuvième.**

- Ordinal numbers have two possible abbreviations.

    3e / 3ème   12e / 12ème   51e / 51ème   80e / 80ème

- To say the century in French, use **au** + ordinal number + **siècle** *(century).*

    Nous sommes au vingt-et-unième siècle. / Nous sommes au 21e siècle.

ACTIVITÉ A Fête ou jour férié?

Les fêtes suivantes sont quel genre de fête: **(a) une fête religieuse, (b) une fête laïque** *(secular)*, **(c) un jour férié, (d) une combinaison d'une fête et d'un jour férié?**

1. la fête nationale
2. Mardi gras
3. Hanoukka
4. la fête du Travail
5. le poisson d'avril
6. Noël
7. le jour du Nouvel An
8. la fête des Mères

ACTIVITÉ B Traditions

Étape 1. Nommez au moins *(at least)* une fête qui correspond à chaque tradition suivante.

Modèle: On mange des latkes. ➔ **Hanoukka**

1. On donne des cadeaux.
2. On porte un costume.
3. On envoie une carte de vœux.
4. On mange des œufs au chocolat.
5. On dit «Bonne année!»
6. On mange du gâteau.
7. On décore la maison avec des cœurs *(hearts)* rouges.
8. On boit du champagne.
9. On fait des farces *(tricks / pranks)* à quelqu'un.
10. On fait la fête avec des feux d'artifice *(fireworks)*.

 Étape 2. Demandez à un(e) partenaire comment il/elle fête…

1. Halloween
2. l'Action de Grâce
3. la Saint-Sylvestre
4. son anniversaire

ACTIVITÉ C Quel anniversaire est mémorable? Notez les anniversaires mentionnés. Et pour vous, quel anniversaire est mémorable?

8-5

Modèle: Vous entendez: Mon troisième anniversaire.
          Vous écrivez: _____3ᵉ_____

1.   2.   3.   4.   5.   6.   7.   8.   9.   10.   11.   12.

 ACTIVITÉ D Personnages historiques

Étape 1. Avec un(e) partenaire, décidez à quel siècle ces personnes sont nées.

Modèle: George Washington   **Il est né au dix-huitième siècle.**

1. Assia Djebar
2. le prince Georges
3. Marco Polo
4. Louis XIV
5. Napoléon 1ᵉʳ
6. Jeanne d'Arc
7. Charlemagne
8. Charles de Gaulle

Étape 2. À quel siècle les personnages du film *Liaisons* sont-ils nés?

1.

Claire Gagner

2.

Alexis Prévost

ACTIVITÉ **E** **Les traditions d'autrefois et d'aujourd'hui**

Étape 1. Avec un(e) partenaire, décidez si les phrases suivantes décrivent une tradition d'**autrefois**, d'**aujourd'hui** ou **les deux** (both).

1. On préfère dire «meilleurs vœux» et pas «joyeux Noël».
2. Il faut aller à la messe (mass) de minuit la veille de Noël.
3. Il faut échanger des cadeaux le jour de l'An.
4. Il ne faut pas porter (wear) de blanc après la fête du Travail.
5. Il ne faut pas porter de noir à un mariage (wedding).
6. Les hommes ne peuvent pas voir (see) la robe de mariée (bride) avant la cérémonie du mariage.

Étape 2. Discutez avec votre partenaire des traditions de l'Étape 1 que vous respectez. Est-ce qu'il y a d'autres (other) traditions que vous respectez?

ACTIVITÉ **F** **Une fête nationale mémorable**

 Étape 1. Écrivez un petit paragraphe pour décrire une fête nationale mémorable. Utilisez l'imparfait.

Questions à discuter		
Vous aviez quel âge?	Vous étiez avec qui?	Que buviez-vous?
Quel temps faisait-il?	Que mangiez-vous?	Que faisiez-vous?

Étape 2. Lisez votre description à un(e) partenaire. Qui a passé une meilleure fête nationale?

© Jacques Morell/Kipa/Corbis

Liaisons musicales

La chanson *Gens du pays* de Gilles Vigneault est l'hymne national du Québec: *Gens du pays // c'est à ton tour* (turn) *// de te laisser parler d'amour.* Pour fêter l'anniversaire de quelqu'un, on chante cette chanson aussi mais on remplace *gens du pays* avec *mon/ma cher/ chère ami(e).* Trouvez cette chanson sur Internet pour découvrir sa mélodie.

© Dimitrios Papadopoulos/The Quebec Press/Newscom

Un mot sur la culture

Variations autour de la fête nationale

En France, on appelle le 14 juillet «le jour de la prise de la Bastille»; cette fête commémore le 14 juillet 1789, jour où le peuple de Paris a pris la Bastille. La fête du Canada est le 1er juillet. Cette fête commémore l'indépendance du Canada du Royaume-Uni en 1867. La fête nationale au Québec, «la Saint-Jean», est le 24 juin; c'est la fête du saint patron du Québec, Saint-Jean Baptiste.

Aux États-Unis, on appelle la fête nationale américaine «le jour de l'Indépendance»; cette fête commémore la déclaration d'indépendance des États-Unis par rapport à l'Angleterre en 1776.

Même s'il y a des différences d'un pays à l'autre, la fête nationale représente toujours la naissance de son pays ou de sa communauté.

- Est-ce que vous fêtez les fêtes nationales des autres pays?

Pour parler du passé

L'imparfait et le passé composé

DU FILM *LIAISONS*

Un coup d'œil sur la grammaire

Look at these photos from the film *Liaisons* and their captions.

RÉCEPTIONNISTE L'hôtel **a ouvert** ses portes en 1893.

CONCIERGE Quand ma mère **est morte**, il **fallait** qu'on s'occupe *(take care)* de ses affaires. Elle **avait** une clé semblable.

1. Identify the verb(s) in the **passé composé** and the verb(s) in the **imparfait**.
2. Which verb tense is used to talk about events that have been completed at a specific point in time in the past? Which one describes continuous actions or states in the past?

❖ As you know from **Grammaire 1,** the **imparfait** is used to express how things used to be and to describe repeated or habitual actions that do not have a beginning or end. If an event began or ended at a specific time in the past, the **passé composé** is used. Expressions like **hier, la semaine dernière, il y a trois ans,** and **à 14h00** are often used with the **passé composé.**

Je **lisais** un livre chaque semaine.	*I read (was reading) a book each week.*
Hier, j'**ai lu** ce livre.	*Yesterday I read this book.*
Avant les ordinateurs, on **écrivait** des lettres.	*Before computers, we used to write letters.*
La semaine dernière, Luc **a écrit** une lettre.	*Last week Luc wrote a letter.*

❖ In **Grammaire 1,** you also learned that the **imparfait** is used to give background information, to describe a scene, weather, physical or mental states, and to express age in the past. To describe a sequence of events, however, the **passé composé** is used.

Imparfait

Claire **avait** 8 ans. Il **neigeait** mais il **faisait** du soleil. Claire **était** heureuse parce que c'**était** son anniversaire.
Claire was eight. It was snowing, but it was sunny. Claire was happy because it was her birthday.

Passé composé

Claire **a préparé** le déjeuner. Puis, elle **a fait** la vaisselle et elle **a sorti** la poubelle.
Claire prepared lunch. Then she did the dishes and took out the trash.

•••❖ The **imparfait** and the **passé composé** may also be used together. In fact, it is often difficult to tell a story in the past without using both. The **imparfait** describes an activity or condition that was in progress (background information) while the **passé composé** expresses an interruption of that activity or condition to move the story along in time.

Quand je **suis entré** dans le bar, Guy **chantait.**	*When I entered the bar, Guy was singing.*
J'**écoutais** Guy quand le serveur **est arrivé.**	*I was listening to Guy when the waiter arrived.*
Guy **était** content parce que je **suis venu** à son spectacle.	*Guy was happy because I came to his show.*

•••❖ To indicate a change of state in a narration, the **passé composé** is used. Words like **soudain** (*suddenly*), **tout d'un coup** (*all of a sudden*), **une fois** (*once*), **un jour,** and **un matin** often denote a change of state.

Je **dormais** quand **tout d'un coup** j'**ai entendu** le tonnerre.	*I was sleeping when all of a sudden I heard the thunder.*
Carole **buvait toujours** du café américain. **Un jour**, elle **a essayé** le café français et elle l'**a adoré**! Aujourd'hui, elle boit toujours du café français.	*Carole always drank American coffee. One day she tried French coffee and she loved it! Today she always drinks French coffee.*

•••❖ The chart summarizes the basic uses of the **imparfait** and the **passé composé.**

Uses of *imparfait*	Uses of *passé composé*
1. To communicate that an event occurred repeatedly in the past (how things used to be) • Events without reference to a beginning or end • Habitual or continuous actions of unspecified duration	1. Events that happened at a particular point in time • Events that are confined by time limits • Completed actions of specific duration
2. To describe or provide background information in the past • Scene or setting • Weather, age, and mental or physical states	2. Sequence of actions in the past
3. To communicate that an event was in progress	3. To communicate actions interrupting something in progress or changes in states

🔊 **ACTIVITÉ G** **Les activités de Nadia, la sœur d'Abia** Écoutez bien les verbes pour déterminer si Nadia faisait l'activité **(a)** souvent (imparfait) ou si elle a fait l'activité **(b)** la semaine dernière (passé composé).

8-6

1.   2.   3.   4.   5.   6.   7.   8.   9.   10.

ACTIVITÉ H **Le père d'Abia**

Étape 1. Adelai Ndono, le père d'Abia, parle de ses activités. Décidez s'il faisait l'activité quand il était jeune ou s'il a fait l'activité hier.

	quand j'étais jeune	hier
1. J'**écoutais** la radio.	☐	☐
2. Je **jouais** aux jeux de société.	☐	☐
3. J'**ai fait** du jogging.	☐	☐
4. Je **lisais** des livres d'histoire.	☐	☐
5. J'**ai joué** au tennis.	☐	☐
6. Je **faisais** la grasse matinée	☐	☐
7. J'**ai dansé** le tango.	☐	☐
8. Je **suis allé** au centre sportif.	☐	☐

Conclusion Adelai était plus actif quand il était jeune ou hier?

Étape 2. Et vous?

1. Écrivez trois activités que vous faisiez quand vous étiez plus jeune.

2. Écrivez trois activités que vous avez faites hier.

Conclusion Vous étiez plus actif (active) hier ou quand vous étiez plus jeune?

ACTIVITÉ I **Nos activités du passé** Complétez les phrases avec l'imparfait ou le passé composé.

1. **La semaine dernière,** je _____.

2. **Halloween passé,** mes amis _____.

3. **D'habitude,** mes camarades et moi, nous _____.

4. **Pendant la dernière classe,** nous _____.

5. Je _____ **tous les jours.**

6. Mon/Ma colocataire _____ **tous les soirs.**

ACTIVITÉ J **Une Saint-Sylvestre mémorable**

Étape 1. Décrivez une Saint-Sylvestre mémorable en répondant aux questions.

1. C'était en quelle année? Vous aviez quel âge? Quel temps faisait-il?

2. Quelles sont trois activités que vous avez faites ce soir-là?

Étape 2. Écrivez un petit paragraphe avec les informations de l'Étape 1.

ACTIVITÉ **K** **Les séquences du film** *Liaisons*

Étape 1. Choisissez les bonnes réponses.

1. Dans le Prologue, Claire **attendait** le bus et elle…
   a. **lisait** un livre de psychologie.
   b. **lisait** un journal.

2. Dans la Séquence 1, quand l'oncle Michel **a téléphoné**, Claire…
   a. **mangeait**.
   b. **dormait**.

3. Dans la Séquence 2, quand Claire **a dit** à Abia qu'elle **allait** à Québec, Abia…
   a. **était** contente.
   b. **était** surprise.

4. Dans un café à Trois-Rivières, Claire **lisait** son livre quand…
   a. Abia **est entrée** dans le café.
   b. Alexis Prévost **est passé** devant la fenêtre.

Étape 2. Décrivez ces scènes du film *Liaisons* avec les éléments donnés.

Modèle: parler / poser

Claire parlait au téléphone quand Mme Saxton lui a posé une question.

1.

arriver / parler

3.

donner une enveloppe / travailler

2.

entrer / jouer

4.

travailler / demander une brosse à dents

Liaisons musicales

© Alexandra Boulat/VII/Corbis

Un événement tragique qui a beaucoup affecté la société américaine est l'acte terroriste du 11 septembre 2001. Médine Zaouiche, un rappeur français d'origine algérienne, a écrit une chanson à propos de cet événement tragique intitulée *11 septembre*. Écoutez et regardez le clip de cette chanson sur Internet.

ACTIVITÉ L Des événements historiques

Étape 1. Associez les situations de la colonne A avec les événements de la colonne B.

A	B
1. La France **était** une monarchie quand...	a. un groupe de terroristes **a attaqué** New York le 11 septembre 2001.
2. Autrefois, le Canada **était** un territoire français mais...	b. les Français **ont perdu** ce territoire pendant la guerre de Sept Ans en 1763.
3. Autrefois, la Louisiane **était** un territoire français mais...	c. le peuple de Paris **a pris** la Bastille en 1789.
4. Abraham Lincoln **était** au théâtre *Ford* quand...	d. l'ouragan Katrina **est arrivé** le 28 août 2008.
5. Les gens de La Nouvelle-Orléans **avaient** peur quand...	e. la France **a perdu** ce territoire face aux Britanniques après la bataille de 1759.
6. George W. Bush **lisait** un livre aux enfants quand...	f. un assassin l'**a tué** *(killed)* le 15 avril 1865.

Étape 2. Répondez aux questions à propos d'un événement marquant.

1. Quel événement du passé a été le plus marquant *(memorable)* pour vous?
2. Quelle est la date de cet événement? Qu'est-ce qui s'est passé *(What happened)*?
3. Vous étiez où? Vous étiez avec qui?
4. Qu'est-ce que vous faisiez?
5. Quelles étaient vos émotions?

 Étape 3. Posez les questions de l'Étape 2 à un(e) partenaire pour savoir quel événement était le plus marquant pour lui/elle.

ACTIVITÉ M Les histoires à suspense

Étape 1. Aimez-vous les films à suspense ou les films d'horreur? Créez des situations avec du suspense avec les éléments donnés.

> **Mots utiles**
>
> | | | |
> |---|---|---|
> | **un assassin** *assassin, killer* | **frapper** *to knock* | **une sorcière** *witch* |
> | **attaquer** *to attack* | **hurler** *to howl, to yell* | **un vampire** *vampire* |
> | **attentat** *attack* | **un loup-garou** *werewolf* | **un voleur** *robber* |
> | **crier** *to scream* | **un monstre** *monster* | |
> | **un extraterrestre** *alien* | **pleurer** *to cry* | |

Modèle: Une fille _____ quand **soudain** _____.

   Une fille regardait un film quand soudain son voisin a crié.

1. Les enfants _____ quand **soudain** _____.
2. Une princesse _____ quand **tout d'un coup** _____.
3. La baby-sitter _____. **Soudain,** _____.
4. L'homme _____. **Tout d'un coup,** _____.

Étape 2. Montrez vos situations à un(e) partenaire. Qui est le/la meilleur(e) scénariste *(screen writer)*? Vous ou votre partenaire?

Étape 3. Choisissez une situation de votre partenaire et continuez son histoire avec deux autres phrases.

🔊 **ACTIVITÉ** Ⓝ **L'histoire d'une rencontre**

8-7

Étape 1. Vous allez écouter une histoire qui raconte comment Nadia, la sœur d'Abia, a rencontré son conjoint. Vous allez entendre l'histoire deux fois. Pendant que vous écoutez l'histoire, prenez notes des détails de l'histoire mais n'écrivez pas de phrases complètes. Vous allez comparer vos notes avec vos camarades de classe plus tard.

Étape 2. Montrez vos notes à deux camarades de classe. Avec toutes vos notes, essayez de raconter l'histoire que vous avez écoutée.

Étape 3. Lisez votre histoire à la classe. Écoutez les histoires de vos camarades de classe. Est-ce qu'il vous manque *(missing)* des détails?

Étape 4. Et vous? Est-ce que quelqu'un dans votre famille a rencontré l'âme sœur *(soulmate)*? Comment? Avez-vous rencontré l'âme sœur? Comment?

OUI, JE PEUX! Here are two "can do statements" for you to check your progress so far. Look at each statement and rate yourself on how well you think you can perform the task. Then verify your ability with a partner. How did you do?

1. **"I can describe a holiday from my past and say three things that happened on this day that made it memorable."**

   I can perform this function
   ☐ with ease
   ☐ with some difficulty
   ☐ not at all

2. **"I can ask someone else what holiday was memorable for him/her and why it was memorable."**

   I can perform this function
   ☐ with ease
   ☐ with some difficulty
   ☐ not at all

iLrn™

Are you looking for more practice? You can find it in **iLrn**.

🔊 Les événements personnels

Personal events

la naissance de Luce

le baptême

Luce à l'âge de 5 ans
l'enfance *(f.)*

Luce à l'âge de 13 ans
l'adolescence *(f.)*

Luce à l'âge de 16 ans
la jeunesse

Luce à l'âge de 18 ans
la cérémonie de remise
des diplômes

Luce à l'âge de 22 ans
l'âge adulte *(m.)*

Luce à l'âge de 24 ans
les fiançailles *(f.)*

Luce à l'âge de 25 ans
le mariage

Luce à l'âge de 65 ans
la retraite

Luce à l'âge de 75 ans
le troisième âge / la vieillesse

Luce à l'âge de 84 ans
l'enterrement *(m.)*

Les étapes de la vie de Luce

Vocabulaire complémentaire

un banquet *banquet*
un coup de foudre *love at first sight*
un décès *death*
un divorce *divorce*
une étape (de la vie) *stage (of life)*
une réception *(formal) reception*
un voyage de noces *honeymoon*

un(e) adolescent(e) *adolescent*
un(e) adulte *adult*
un couple *couple*
un époux / une épouse *spouse*
des nouveaux mariés *newly weds*
une relation *relationship*
un rendez-vous *date, appointment*

Bonne chance! *Good luck!*
Au bonheur de (qqn)! *To the happiness of (someone)!*
Mes condoléances. *My condolences.*
Bonne retraite! *Happy retirement!*
À la réussite de (qqn, qqch)! *To the success of (someone, something)!*

prendre sa retraite *to retire (from a job)*
rêver (de) *to dream (of, about)*
tomber amoureux / amoureuse (de) *to fall in love (with)*

> **Note de vocabulaire**
> Note that **qqn** and **qqch** are abbreviations for **quelqu'un** and **quelque chose**.

ACTIVITÉ A **Les étapes de la vie** À quelle(s) étape(s) de la vie ces grands événements arrivent-ils *(do they happen)* typiquement à une personne? Indiquez vos réponses. Anticipez-vous un grand événement personnel cette année?

a. pendant l'enfance   **b. pendant l'adolescence**   **c. à l'âge adulte**   **d. au troisième âge**

1. la retraite
2. un divorce
3. un rendez-vous
4. un baptême

5. les fiançailles
6. un coup de foudre
7. un décès
8. un mariage

9. une naissance
10. la remise des diplômes
11. un voyage de noces
12. tomber amoureux

Un mot sur la langue

Laissez les bons temps rouler!

En Louisiane, surtout à La Nouvelle-Orléans, on entend souvent dire **Laissez les bons temps rouler!** Les Français, eux, ne comprennent pas toujours cette phrase parce qu'elle est calquée° sur l'anglais *Let the good times roll*. En France, on dit plutôt **Que la fête commence!** *(Let the party begin!)* Le français de Louisiane, appelé aussi le cajun, a des caractéristiques particulières parce que la langue française y a évolué différemment quand la France a perdu la Louisiane au dix-neuvième siècle.

calquée *calqued, directly and literally translated*

- Est-ce qu'il y a des mots ou des expressions que les anglophones utilisent qui sont calqués sur le français?

ACTIVITÉ B **Ça fait penser à... ?** À quelle étape de la vie est-ce que chaque phrase vous fait penser?

1. On joue à la marelle *(hopscotch)*.
2. On a une relation romantique.
3. On a peur de perdre son époux / épouse.
4. On est des nouveaux mariés.
5. On rêve du coup de foudre.
6. On habite avec ses parents.
7. On rêve de devenir pompier.
8. On prend sa retraite.

ACTIVITÉ C **Les gens célèbres**

Étape 1. Donnez un exemple pour chaque description.

Modèle: Nommez le couple le plus célèbre aux États-Unis.

Brad Pitt et Angelina Jolie

Nommez…

1. le couple le plus célèbre du monde francophone
2. le mariage le plus célèbre d'Hollywood
3. le décès le plus tragique
4. le divorce le plus scandaleux
5. l'adolescent(e) le/la plus célèbre
6. la retraite la plus méritée *(deserved)*
7. l'époux / l'épouse le/la plus fidèle
8. un couple du troisième âge célèbre

 Étape 2. Montrez vos réponses à un(e) partenaire. Avez-vous les mêmes opinions? Voulez-vous modifier vos réponses?

ACTIVITÉ D **Les grands événements personnels** À quel grand événement personnel est-ce que chaque phrase vous fait penser?

1. On entend «Mes condoléances».
2. Il y a une séparation du couple.
3. On dit «Oui» *(I do)*.
4. Quelqu'un vous dit «Bonne chance!»
5. On dit «C'est une fille!»
6. Un bébé crie.
7. On dit «Bonne retraite!»
8. Un homme présente une bague *(ring)*.
9. Quelqu'un vous dit «À ta réussite!»
10. On entend «Au bonheur des nouveaux mariés!»

ACTIVITÉ **E** **Les endroits pour des événements exceptionnels**

Étape 1. Répondez aux questions.

Où est le meilleur endroit pour…

Modèle: **Un parc est le meilleur endroit pour un premier rendez-vous.**

1. un premier rendez-vous?   3. un voyage de noces?   5. des fiançailles?

2. un mariage?   4. une réception?   6. un banquet?

Étape 2. Posez les questions à un(e) partenaire. Notez ses réponses.

Étape 3. Regardez vos réponses et les réponses de votre partenaire.

1. Qui est plus romantique?   2. Qui est plus extravagant(e)?   3. Qui est plus pratique?

ACTIVITÉ **F** **Comment fêter?**

Étape 1. Comment aimez-vous fêter les événements suivants? Avec un banquet? une réception? Avez-vous d'autres suggestions?

1. un mariage   3. une retraite

2. une cérémonie de remise de diplômes   4. une naissance

Étape 2. Posez les questions à un(e) partenaire pour savoir *(know)* ses préférences.

ACTIVITÉ **G** **Les endroits pour quels événements?**

Étape 1. Les endroits suivants sont bons pour quels événements? Notez vos réponses.

Étape 2. Posez des questions à deux camarades de classe et notez leurs réponses. Ensuite, décidez si vous êtes plus comme l'Étudiant(e) 1 ou comme l'Étudiant(e) 2.

Modèle: Vous: **Un stade est un bon endroit pour quel événement?**
         É1: **Un stade est un bon endroit pour les fiançailles.**
         É2: **Pour moi, un stade est un bon endroit pour un anniversaire.**

	Moi	É1	É2
1. un stade	_____	_____	_____
2. une église	_____	_____	_____
3. un parc	_____	_____	_____
4. le restaurant *Chucky Cheese*	_____	_____	_____
5. l'hôtel Ritz Carlton	_____	_____	_____
6. une maison	_____	_____	_____
7. un cimetière *(cemetery)*	_____	_____	_____
8. une école	_____	_____	_____

Étape 3. Dans le film *Liaisons,* Claire descend au Château Frontenac. À votre avis, cet hôtel est idéal pour quels événements?

ACTIVITÉ **H** **On est un groupe de romantiques?** Faites un sondage *(poll)* pour savoir combien d'étudiant(e)s dans votre classe…

Noms des étudiant(e)s

1. ont un rendez-vous ce week-end. _____

2. sont tombé(e)s amoureux / amoureuses de quelqu'un. _____

3. pensent que le coup de foudre existe. _____

✈ ········
Si vous y allez

Si vous allez dans le Val de Loire en France, cherchez des couples américains qui se marient dans cette région. La France et ses châteaux sont un choix très populaire!

Pour aller plus loin
Depuis quand… ?

As you know, to ask *how long* someone has been doing something, you ask **depuis combien de temps** and you answer with **depuis** + the length of time. To ask *since when* someone has been doing something, form your question with **depuis quand** and answer with **depuis** + a precise moment, for example, a day, a month, a date, or a year.

Depuis combien de temps habitez-vous à Paris?   **Depuis** trois ans.
(For) how long have you been living in Paris?   *For three years.*

Depuis quand habitez-vous à Paris?   **Depuis** 2010.
Since when have you been living in Paris?   *Since 2010.*

········

Essayez! Répondez à ces questions.

1. **Depuis combien de temps** étudiez-vous le français? Depuis _____.
2. **Depuis quand** étudiez-vous à cette université? Depuis _____.

Un mot sur la culture

Les unions en France

Les couples français ont plusieurs options quand ils veulent former une union. Tout d'abord, il y a le mariage, qui est considéré comme un acte civil et religieux. Les couples doivent d'abord se présenter à la mairie° pour être mariés par un officier d'état civil°. En effet, seul le mariage civil est reconnu par l'État français. Après la mairie, le couple peut également faire un mariage religieux, s'il le désire. Une autre option d'union civile en France est le Pacte civil de solidarité (PACS). Le PACS est un partenariat contractuel entre deux personnes qui veulent organiser leur vie ensemble. Le mariage pour deux personnes du même sexe ou «mariage pour tous» est autorisé en France depuis le 17 mai 2013.

mairie *city / town hall* **officier d'état civil** *civil officer*

• Quelles sont les options pour les couples qui veulent former une union dans votre culture?

Liaisons avec les mots et les sons

 ### Les voyelles ouvertes et fermées: eu

8-8

You were introduced to open and closed vowels in **Chapitre 7** through the **o** vowel sound. French also has the **eu** vowel sound that can be open or closed.

If the last sound of a syllable is **eu** or if **eu** is followed by a **z** sound, it is closed.

séri**eu**x	mi**eu**x	vend**eu**se	serv**eu**se	d**eu**x	p**eu**	heur**eu**x

If a pronounced consonant follows **eu,** it is open.

b**eu**rre	project**eu**r	j**eu**ne	ordinat**eu**r	chant**eu**r	déj**eu**ner

The vowel combination **œu** is also typically pronounced as an open **eu** sound.

belle-s**œu**r	**œu**f	b**œu**f	c**œu**r

Pratique A. Écoutez et répétez ces mots de vocabulaire.

Les voyelles ouvertes | | **Les voyelles fermées** |
---|---|---|---
1. un explorateur | **4.** un chanteur | **7.** tu peux | **10.** eux
2. un empereur | **5.** ils peuvent | **8.** deuxième | **11.** une chanteuse
3. la grandeur | **6.** meilleurs | **9.** je veux | **12.** curieux

Pratique B. Écoutez ces répliques de la Séquence 4 du film *Liaisons*. Ensuite, encerclez toutes les voyelles **eu** ouvertes et soulignez *(underline)* toutes les voyelles **eu** fermées.

RÉCEPTIONNISTE Ah voilà. Claire Gagner. C'est pour deux nuits?

RÉCEPTIONNISTE Voici votre clé. La chambre 315. Les ascenseurs sont à votre gauche.

  À vos stylos! C'est l'heure de la dictée!

8-9

Vous allez entendre trois phrases deux fois. La première fois, écoutez bien. La deuxième fois, écrivez les phrases. Ensuite, encerclez toutes les voyelles **eu** ouvertes et soulignez toutes les voyelles **eu** fermées.

Sujet Citations célèbres

GRAMMAIRE 3

Pour parler des gens et des informations

Les verbes **connaître** et **savoir**

DU FILM *LIAISONS*

Un coup d'œil sur la grammaire

Look at these photos from the film *Liaisons* and their captions.

CLAIRE Je ne **sais** pas qui m'a offert ce séjour.

CLAIRE [...] je ne **connais** pas très bien la ville.

1. Which verb means *to know* or *to be familiar with a place*?
2. Which verb means *to know information*?

❖ Both **connaître** and **savoir** mean *to know,* but they are used differently.

connaître		savoir	
je **connais**	nous **connaissons**	je **sais**	nous **savons**
tu **connais**	vous **connaissez**	tu **sais**	vous **savez**
il/elle/on **connaît**	ils/elles **connaissent**	il/elle/on **sait**	ils/elles **savent**
PAST PARTICIPLE: **connu**		PAST PARTICIPLE: **su**	

❖ **Connaître** means *to know* or *to be familiar with people, places, or things* and is followed by a direct object.

Je **connais** très bien Abia Ndono.	*I know Abia Ndono very well.*
Nous ne **connaissons** pas cet adolescent.	*We don't know this adolescent.*
Claire **connaît** bien Montréal.	*Claire knows Montreal well.*
Vous **connaissez** cette chanson?	***Do you know / Are you familiar with** this song?*

❖ **Savoir** means *to know facts, information,* or *how to do something* and may be followed by:

- an infinitive

Nous **savons parler** français.	*We **know how to speak** French.*
Nicole **sait jouer** du piano.	*Nicole **knows how to play** the piano.*

- a clause introduced by **que**

Je **sais qu**'il est tombé amoureux d'elle.	*I know (that) he fell in love with her.*
Elles **savent que** Pierre est beau.	*They know (that) Pierre is handsome.*

- a clause introduced by a question word or **si**

Tu **sais pourquoi** Anouk est triste?	*Do you know why Anouk is sad?*
Savez-vous **si** Sadia est jolie?	*Do you know if Sadia is pretty?*

•••> To talk about the past, **connaître** and **savoir** are usually used in the **imparfait**.

Tu **connaissais** Madame Leclerc?	***Did you know*** *Madame Leclerc?*
Il **savait** jouer de la flûte.	***He knew*** *how to play the flute.*

•••> When used in the **passé composé**, **connaître** means *to have met someone*, and **savoir** means *to have found out* or *discovered*.

J'**ai connu** ma femme à une fête.	*I **met** / **came to know** my wife at a party.*
Claire **a su** qu'Alexis n'était pas un client.	*Claire **found out** that Alexis was not a client.*

Pour aller plus loin
Connaître ou *savoir* un poème?

To talk about things that can be known, either **connaître** or **savoir** may be used, but there is a subtle difference in meaning. **Savoir** implies you know something by heart. **Connaître** suggests you are familiar with something, but do not necessarily know it by heart.

Je **sais** la chanson.	*(You can sing or recite the song by heart.)*
Je **connais** la chanson.	*(You've heard of the song before but can't necessarily recite it.)*
Je **sais** son adresse.	*(You know the address by heart).*
Je **connais** son adresse.	*(You know the address but not necessarily by heart.)*

Essayez! Complétez les phrases avec **Je connais** ou **Je sais**.

1. _____ le courriel de mon professeur.
2. _____ mon numéro de téléphone.
3. _____ l'hymne *(anthem)* national.
4. _____ la chanson *Jingle Bells*.

ACTIVITÉ **I** **Les personnes et les événements dans nos vies**

Répondez à chaque question avec «oui» ou «non».

1. Connaissez-vous quelqu'un qui a pris sa retraite?
2. Connaissez-vous des nouveaux mariés?
3. Savez-vous qui va être votre époux ou épouse?
4. Savez-vous quand est votre cérémonie de remise des diplômes?

ACTIVITÉ J À l'hôtel Delta Les clients de l'hôtel Delta parlent avec Abia et Claire. Choisissez le sujet.

1. _____ **connaissez** la rue Sainte-Catherine? a. Nous b. Vous c. Ils

2. _____ **sais** que le café ferme à minuit. a. Ils b. Je c. Elle

3. _____ **savons** parler anglais. a. Nous b. Ils c. Vous

4. _____ **connaissent** bien la ville. a. Elles b. Vous c. Je

5. _____ **savez** parler français? a. Ils b. Nous c. Vous

6. _____ **connais** ce client? a. Tu b. Elle c. Ils

7. _____ **savent** où est la boutique? a. Je b. On c. Elles

8. _____ **connaît** le parc La Fontaine? a. Il b. Tu c. Elles

Et vous? Vous connaissez l'hôtel Delta? Vous savez où sont les hôtels Delta aux États-Unis?

ACTIVITÉ K Claire et Abia

Étape 1. Décidez si Claire et Abia du film *Liaisons* connaissent ou savent les choses suivantes. Complétez les phrases avec **(a) Elles connaissent** ou **(b) Elles savent.**

1. _____ les poèmes de Félix Leclerc. 5. _____ qu'on parle français en Louisiane.

2. _____ parler anglais. 6. _____ faire la fête.

3. _____ quelqu'un d'excentrique. 7. _____ la ville de Montréal.

4. _____ les livres de Victor Hugo. 8. _____ où est le Château Frontenac.

Étape 2. Refaites l'Étape 1 avec **Je (ne) connais (pas)** ou **Je (ne) sais (pas).**

ACTIVITÉ L Les choses en commun

Étape 1. Vous savez / connaissez les choses et les informations suivantes?

Modèle: les films *Twilight*   **Je ne connais pas les films *Twilight*.**

1. les films *Harry Potter*

2. qui était le/la *American Idol* l'année dernière

3. Paris

4. les chansons de Lady Gaga

5. faire la cuisine

6. les livres de *Stephen King*

7. qui est l'épouse du prince William

8. étudier le français

Étape 2. Posez les questions à un(e) partenaire.

Étape 3. Indiquez ce que vous et votre partenaire avez en commun *(in common)*.

Modèle: **Nous connaissons Paris. Nous savons qui est l'époux de Beyoncé.**

Liaisons musicales

© Richard Melloul/Sygma/Corbis

Félix Leclerc (1914–1988) est connu comme le père de la chanson québécoise. Poète engagé pour la souveraineté du Québec et pour la langue française, il avait une influence considérable sur la culture québécoise. Sa chanson *Le petit bonheur* parle de la situation des Canadiens-Français avant la Révolution tranquille. Écoutez la chanson sur Internet.

Étape 1. Écrivez cinq informations que vous avez apprises de la télévision, d'Internet ou du journal de votre ville ou de votre campus.

Modèle: **La mort de Whitney Houston. L'ouragan** *(hurricane)* **à Miami. La visite du président sur notre campus.**

Étape 2. Demandez à deux camarades de classe s'ils/si elles savaient les informations que vous avez écrites.

Modèle: É1: **Saviez-vous que Whitney Houston était morte?**
É2: **Oui, je le savais.**

Étape 3. Répondez aux questions de vos camarades de classe. Indiquez trois à cinq choses que vous avez apprises d'eux.

Modèle: **J'ai appris qu'il allait neiger. J'ai appris que Lupita Nyong'o avait un nouveau film.**

ACTIVITÉ **N** **Une personne que vous admirez** Décrivez quelqu'un que vous connaissez et que vous admirez mais qui n'est pas un membre de votre famille. Traitez *(Treat)* des questions suivantes.

- Qui est cette personne?
- Comment avez-vous rencontré cette personne?
- Depuis quand / combien de temps le/la connaissez-vous?
- Pourquoi l'admirez-vous?
- Est-ce que cette personne a des talents spéciaux?
- Qu'est-ce qu'il/elle sait faire?

OUI, JE PEUX! Here are two "can do statements" for you to check your progress so far. Look at each statement and rate yourself on how well you think you can perform the task. Then verify your ability with a partner. How did you do?

1. **"I can say two things one knows how to do during adolescence and during adulthood, and ask someone if he/she knows how to do some of these things."**

   I can perform this function
   ☐ with ease
   ☐ with some difficulty
   ☐ not at all

2. **"I can say that I know or do not know brilliant people and ask someone else if he/she knows brilliant people. "**

   I can perform this function
   ☐ with ease
   ☐ with some difficulty
   ☐ not at all

iLrn™

Are you looking for more practice? You can find it in **iLrn**.

DEUXIÈME
PROJECTION

Avant de visionner

ACTIVITÉ A Qu'est-ce qui s'est passé? Qu'est-ce qui s'est passé *(What happened)* dans la Séquence 4 du film *Liaisons*? Mettez les événements en ordre.

a. _____ Claire a trouvé une clé.

b. _____ Claire lisait un livre dans un café.

c. _____ Claire savait que des clients célèbres étaient descendus au Château Frontenac.

d. _____ Claire a trouvé une enveloppe dans sa chambre.

e. _____ Claire a téléphoné à Abia.

f. _____ Claire savait que la clé était pour un coffre-fort.

g. _____ Claire admirait un tableau d'art.

h. _____ Claire a vu *(saw)* Alexis Prévost.

ACTIVITÉ B Une scène du film Vous rappelez-vous *(Do you remember)* cette scène? Claire téléphone à Abia dans sa chambre. Écrivez les mots qui manquent *(are missing)*.

CLAIRE Oh (1) _____, aujourd'hui j'ai reçu une (2) _____ pour un coffre-fort.

ABIA (3) _____?

CLAIRE C'est (4) _____. Je t'expliquerai tout ça plus tard, mais je (5) _____ aller à la Banque Nationale (6) _____. Donc, je ne (7) _____ pas si je serai (8) _____ pour le travail...

▶ **Regarder la séquence**

Vous allez regarder la Séquence 4 du film *Liaisons*. Vérifiez vos réponses à l'Activité A et à l'Activité B.

Après le visionnage

ACTIVITÉ C Qu'est-ce qu'on sait?

Étape 1. On a regardé quatre séquences du film *Liaisons*. Avec deux camarades de classe, décidez si on a maintenant les informations suivantes à propos du film.

1. On sait pourquoi la mère de Claire est à l'hôpital psychiatrique?
2. On sait qui est l'homme qui a donné à Claire l'enveloppe avec la réservation?
3. On sait pourquoi quelqu'un a payé une réservation pour Claire au Château Frontenac?
4. On sait qui est Alexis Prévost?
5. On sait pourquoi Alexis Prévost est au Québec?
6. On sait qui a mis une enveloppe dans la chambre de Claire à l'hôtel?
7. On sait ce qui *(what)* était dans l'enveloppe que Claire a trouvée dans sa chambre?
8. On sait ce qui est dans le coffre-fort à la Banque Nationale?

Étape 2. Avec vos deux camarades, faites une liste des choses de l'Étape 1 qu'on ne sait pas encore. Spéculez sur ce que les réponses pourraient *(could)* être.

Modèle: On ne sait pas qui sont les deux personnes dans le Prologue.

É1: L'homme est peut-être la personne qui a donné l'enveloppe à Claire.
É2: Oui. Il écrivait quelque chose. Peut-être que c'était la réservation?
É3: Ou peut-être que c'était l'oncle Michel?

ACTIVITÉ D **Résumé de la Séquence 4** Si vous deviez raconter la Séquence 4 à quelqu'un, qu'est-ce que vous diriez *(would say)*? Complétez le résumé.

Claire est arrivée à Québec. Elle est allée au Château Frontenac et elle a demandé la clé de sa chambre. Claire était dans la salle de bains quand quelqu'un a remis…

Dans les coulisses

After Claire leaves the concierge, the camera shows her strolling through different streets and sights of Old Quebec without dialogue. The scene ends with Claire stopping to admire an artist's painting. When a filmmaker includes city or scenery shots without dialogue, he/she may want to draw a parallel between the character and scenery in some way. The places can comment on the character's psychology: inner thoughts, fears, dreams, and so forth. What do you think these scenes reveal about Claire?

À DÉCOUVRIR: Le Canada et ses Fêtes de la Nouvelle-France

À DÉCOUVRIR: Le Canada

Pays: Le Canada
Géographie: L'Amérique du Nord
Climat: Varié: tempéré dans le sud, subarctique et arctique dans le nord
Population: Plus de 33 millions
Capitale: Ottawa

À DÉCOUVRIR: La ville de Québec

Structure: La ville capitale de la province du Québec
Région: Capitale-Nationale
Population: Plus de 700 000
Réputation: «La Vieille Capitale»; la communauté métropolitaine de Québec

Avant de lire

You will discover in this reading the summer Festival of New France in Old Quebec.

Que savez-vous déjà?

1. Quels genres d'activités est-ce qu'on fait typiquement dans une fête d'été?
2. Quels genres de spectacles ou d'attractions font partie d'une fête d'été?
3. Quels sont plusieurs thèmes populaires pour les fêtes d'été en général?
4. Pourquoi aime-t-on souvent faire revivre *(relive)* l'histoire sous forme de fêtes?

OUTILS DE LECTURE
Visualizing a text as you read

Visualizing a text as you read can help you better understand the various pieces of information and better "see" how they fit together. Read the following sentence about the Festival of New France and try to picture the details in your mind. Share and compare your visualizations with a partner. What do you see in your "mind's eye?"

> **Pendant les Fêtes, les rues du Vieux-Québec sont pleines d'acteurs, de musiciens, d'artisans et de touristes portant des costumes des dix-septième et dix-huitième siècles.**

Découvrir les Fêtes de la Nouvelle-France

Les premières Fêtes de la Nouvelle-France ont été organisées en 1997, mais ce que les Québécois fêtent pendant cet événement qui a lieu tous les ans au début du mois d'août remonte à beaucoup plus loin. Ces fêtes célèbrent l'histoire du Québec, et en particulier les débuts de la présence française en Amérique du Nord. Elles fournissent° une occasion aux participants de faire revivre quelques événements historiques et de réanimer de vieilles traditions culinaires, culturelles et festives.

Les premiers colons travaillaient la terre, organisaient les marchés, tressaient° des paniers et forgeaient des objets en métal°. Et pendant les fêtes, ils dansaient, jouaient de la musique et préparaient un cochon au feu de bois°. Aujourd'hui, les visiteurs des Fêtes de la Nouvelle-France peuvent découvrir des mises en scène de toutes ces activités.

Pendant les Fêtes, les rues du Vieux-Québec sont pleines d'acteurs, de musiciens, d'artisans et de touristes en costumes des dix-septième et dix-huitième siècles. On peut aussi admirer plusieurs «géants», des statues ambulantes°, qui sont portées° à travers la ville. Chacun de ces géants représente un personnage historique ou un aspect de l'histoire du Québec. Cette tradition remonte au Moyen Âge° en France. Le défilé° de ces géants, de quatre ou cinq mètres, constitue un spectacle impressionnant.

fournissent *provide* **tressaient** *wove* **forgeaient des objets en métal** *worked metal* **préparaient un cochon au feu de bois** *roasted a pig* **statues ambulantes** *parading statues* **portées** *carried* **remonte au Moyen Âge** *dates back to the Middle Ages* **défilé** *parade*

Après avoir lu

Compréhension

	Vrai	Faux
1. Les Fêtes de la Nouvelle-France ont lieu à Montréal.	☐	☐
2. Les débuts de la présence française sont fêtés.	☐	☐
3. La tradition des «géants» remonte au Moyen Âge en France.	☐	☐

Et vous?

1. Est-ce qu'il y a des fêtes intéressantes ou amusantes dans votre région?

2. Est-ce que votre ville d'origine est connue pour une certaine tradition festive?

3. Est-ce qu'il y a quelque chose que vous voudriez voir fêté l'été?

Share It!

Use **Share It!** in **iLrn**™ to express your reactions to the reading and to find out what your classmates think.

People often write about memorable occasions from their childhood. Here is an example of **une fête mémorable.**

© Britt Erlanson/Stockbyte/Getty Images

J'avais 11 ou 12 ans et ma famille et moi, nous sommes allés chez mes grands-parents maternels un samedi soir pour le dîner. Toutes mes tantes et tous mes oncles et cousins étaient aussi invités. Nous étions vingt personnes. Après le dîner (tous les adultes dans la salle à manger et tous les enfants dans la cuisine), ma sœur, mes six cousins et moi avions envie de faire quelque chose d'amusant. Comme c'était le mois d'octobre et que nous avions la fête d'Halloween à l'esprit, on a décidé d'organiser «un château hanté» au sous-sol pour nos parents et grands-parents. On a emprunté des vêtements de nos grands-parents pour faire des déguisements et on a utilisé des décorations d'Halloween pour décorer le sous-sol. On a créé des «scènes monstrueuses»! C'était une fête mémorable chez nos grands-parents.

Avant d'écrire

Complete the chart with information about a memorable occasion you experienced.

	L'auteur	Vous
Âge du narrateur	11 ou 12 ans	_____
Endroit de la fête	Chez ses grands-parents	_____
Invités à la fête	Parents, sœur, tantes, oncles, cousins	_____
Saison ou raison pour la fête	Dîner chez grand-mère un samedi soir juste avant Halloween	_____
Événement(s) mémorable(s)	Les enfants ont organisé «un château hanté».	_____

Écrire

Using information from **Avant d'écrire,** write your own description of **une fête mémorable** in 6–8 French sentences.

Après avoir écrit

Exchange your memorable holiday or party story with a partner. (1) Underline all the adjectives and verify that they all agree in number and gender. (2) Circle all of the verbs in the **imparfait** and verify that your partner correctly conjugated them. Did he/she correctly use the **imparfait**? (3) Put a * next to the sentence(s) that you think create(s) the best visualization or image of the story and explain why. (4) Are you able to picture the entire story clearly in your mind's eye? Discuss your reactions together and then write a second version of your description, taking into account your partner's feedback.

PARTIE 1 8–10

LES TITRES

un écrivain / une écrivaine	*writer*
un empereur / une impératrice	*emperor / empress*
un explorateur / une exploratrice	*explorer*
un général	*general*
un héros / une héroïne	*hero / heroine*
un homme / une femme politique	*politician*
un poète / une femme poète	*poet*
(Madame / Monsieur) le Premier Ministre	*Prime Minister*
(Madame / Monsieur) le Président	*President (country)*
un roi / une reine	*king / queen*
un soldat / une femme soldat	*soldier*

NOMS

la colonie	*colony*
un empire	*empire*
une guerre (contre)	*war (against)*
l'indépendance *(f.)*	*independence*
la liberté	*freedom*
une monarchie	*monarchy*
un mouvement	*(political) movement*
le nationalisme	*nationalism*
la paix	*peace*
des réformes *(f.)*	*reforms*
une révolution	*revolution*
la tolérance	*tolerance*

LES MOMENTS HISTORIQUES

la colonisation	*colonization*
la décolonisation	*decolonization*
l'époque contemporaine *(f.)*	*contemporary time*

VERBES

aider	*to help*
fonder	*to found*
gagner	*to win*

DIVERS

à cette époque-là	*at that time, in those days*
autrefois	*in the past, long ago*
chaque	*each*
d'habitude	*usually*
marquant(e)	*memorable, important*
pacifique	*peaceful*

PARTIE 2 8–11

LES FÊTES

l'anniversaire *(m.)*	*birthday*
l'anniversaire de mariage	*wedding anniversary*
la fête des Mères	*Mother's Day*
la fête des Pères	*Father's Day*
la fête du Travail	*Labor Day*
la fête nationale	*National Holiday*
Hanoukka	*Hanukah*
le jour de l'Action de Grâce	*Thanksgiving*
le jour de l'An	*New Year's Day*
Mardi gras	*Mardi Gras*
Noël	*Christmas*
Pâques	*Easter*
le 1er avril / le poisson d'avril	*April 1st / April Fools' Day*
la Saint-Sylvestre	*New Year's Eve*
la Saint-Valentin	*St. Valentine's Day*
la veille de Noël	*Christmas Eve*

NOMS

un cadeau	*gift*
une carte de vœux	*greeting card*
une fête	*holiday, party, celebration*
un jour férié	*legal holiday*
une soirée	*(evening) party*

EXPRESSIONS

Bon / Joyeux anniversaire!	*Happy birthday!*
Bonne année!	*Happy New Year!*
Félicitations!	*Congratulations!*
Meilleurs vœux!	*Best wishes!*

VERBES

fêter	*to celebrate*
organiser une fête	*to throw / organize a party*

LES NOMBRES ORDINAUX

premier (1er) / première (1ère)	*first (1st)*
quatrième (4e)	*fourth (4th)*
cinquième (5e)	*fifth (5th)*
neuvième (9e)	*ninth (9th)*
vingt-et-unième (21e)	*twenty-first (21st)*
trente-et-unième (31e)	*thirty-first (31st)*
soixante-quinzième (75e)	*seventy-fifth (75th)*
centième (100e)	*hundredth (100th)*

DIVERS

une fois	*once*
soudain	*suddenly*
tout d'un coup	*all of a sudden*

LES ÉTAPES DE LA VIE

l'adolescence *(f.)*	*adolescence*
l'âge adulte *(m.)*	*adulthood*
l'enfance *(f.)*	*childhood*
une étape (de la vie)	*stage (of life)*
la jeunesse	*youth*
la vieillesse / le troisième âge	*old age, the elderly*

LES ÉVÉNEMENTS PERSONNELS

un baptême	*baptism*
la cérémonie de remise des diplômes	*graduation ceremony*
un décès	*death*
le divorce	*divorce*
un enterrement	*burial, funeral*
les fiançailles *(f.)*	*engagement*
le mariage	*marriage*
une naissance	*birth*
la retraite	*retirement*
un voyage de noces	*honeymoon*
un(e) adolescent(e)	*adolescent*
un(e) adulte	*adult*
le coup de foudre	*love at first sight*
un couple	*couple*

un époux / une épouse	*spouse*
les nouveaux mariés	*newly weds*
une relation	*relationship*
un rendez-vous	*date, appointment*

LES FÊTES

un banquet	*banquet*
une réception	*(formal) reception*

EXPRESSIONS

Bonne chance!	*Good luck!*
Au bonheur de (qqn)!	*To the happiness of (someone)!*
Mes condoléances.	*My condolences.*
Bonne retraite!	*Happy retirement!*
À la réussite de (qqn, qqch)!	*To the success of (someone, something)!*

VERBES

connaître	*to know, to be familiar with*
prendre sa retraite	*to retire (from a job)*
rêver (de)	*to dream (of, about)*
savoir	*to know, to know how to, to know by heart*
tomber amoureux / amoureuse (de)	*to fall in love (with)*

Les **arts** et les **médias**

En bref In this chapter, you will:

- learn about visual arts, literature, film, and television

- learn the present conditional tense

- talk about possibilities, expectations, and hypothetical situations

- learn the demonstrative pronouns **celui, celle, ceux, celles**

- learn about the sounds **qu / ph / th / gn / ch**

- read about visual arts and popular media in France and the Francophone world

 You will also watch SÉQUENCE **5**: **Une rencontre** of the film *Liaisons.*

Ressources

 audio   video   Share It! iLrn™   http://www.cengagebrain.com

🔊 Les **arts visuels**

Visual arts

faire de la sculpture (Elle fait de la sculpture.)

une tapisserie

un sculpteur / une sculptrice

une sculpture

faire de la peinture (Il fait de la peinture.)

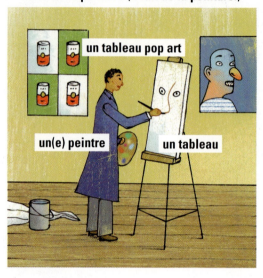

un tableau pop art

un(e) peintre

un tableau

faire un portrait (Elle fait un portrait.)

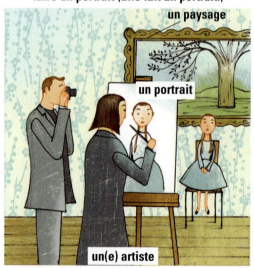

un paysage

un portrait

un(e) artiste

photographier (Il photographie.)

une nature morte

un(e) photographe

Les artistes au travail

Note de vocabulaire

A painting is usually referred to as **un tableau,** but it can also mean any other kind of framed art that hangs on a wall. The plural is **des tableaux.**

La peinture can also mean *paint* as in the *paint* on an artist's palette or *painting* as in the art form an artist practices.

The verb **photographier** means *to photograph* in the artistic sense. **Faire de la photo** and **prendre une (des) photo(s)** are commonly used in everyday speech to express *to take a photo (photos).*

Vocabulaire complémentaire

les beaux-arts (m.) *fine arts*

un chef-d'œuvre *a masterpiece*

un dessin *a drawing*

une exposition *an exhibition*

une galerie d'art *an art gallery*

une œuvre d'art *a work of art*

une photographie / une photo *a photograph*

le style *the style*

le sujet *the subject*

abstrait(e) *abstract*

cubiste *cubist*

impressionniste *impressionist*

sombre *somber, dark*

surréaliste *surrealist*

vif / vive *bright, lively, colorful*

  ACTIVITÉ A Qui fait quoi? Quelle œuvre peut produire chaque artiste mentionné?

9-1

1. a. une nature morte   c. une photographie
   b. un dessin   d. une sculpture

2. a. un tableau   c. un paysage
   b. une sculpture   d. un portrait

3. a. une sculpture   c. un tableau
   b. une photographie   d. une tapisserie

4. a. un paysage   c. une nature morte
   b. une sculpture   d. un portrait

Sculpture de l'artiste américain Jeff Koons au Château de Versailles (2008)

© Benoit Tessier/Reuters/Landov

Un mot sur la langue

Le sens culturel du mot artiste

On peut distinguer deux sens culturels au terme **«artiste»** en français. Le premier sens décrit une personne qui pratique un des beaux-arts (peinture, architecture, etc.). Le deuxième sens désigne une personne qui pratique à un niveau supérieur un des arts appliqués. Par conséquent, les personnes qui dessinent des espaces (architecture d'intérieur), des articles de mode (vêtements, accessoires), des objets (industriels ou autres) et les personnes qui travaillent dans la communication (multimédia, publicité) sont considérées comme des artistes.

- Les gens qui pratiquent ces professions sont aussi considérés comme des **artistes** en France. Êtes-vous d'accord?

  1. acteur
  2. architecte
  3. cinéaste
  4. créateur *(designer)*
  5. danseur
  6. écrivain
  7. jongleur *(juggler)*
  8. musicien

ACTIVITÉ **B** **Découvrir trois musées importants à Paris** Il y a beaucoup de musées à Paris mais les trois principaux sont: **le musée du Louvre** (un musée universaliste des œuvres d'art de la préhistoire jusqu'au 19ᵉ siècle), **le musée d'Orsay** (qui rassemble la peinture et la sculpture occidentale de 1848 à 1914) et **le Centre Pompidou** (qui possède une des plus importantes collections d'art moderne et contemporain au monde). Dans lequel de ces trois musées trouveriez-vous *(would you find)* les œuvres d'art suivantes?

© Jorge Felix Costa / Shutterstock.com

1. des tableaux pop art
2. des tableaux impressionnistes
3. des antiquités gréco-romaines
4. des sculptures classiques
5. des tableaux cubistes
6. des tableaux de la Renaissance

Et vous? Quels genres d'œuvres d'art pouvez-vous trouver sur votre campus?

ACTIVITÉ **C** **Des artistes et des chefs-d'œuvre célèbres**

9-2

Étape 1. Vous allez entendre des phrases qui parlent de genres artistiques ou qui mentionnent les noms d'œuvres d'art. Quelle œuvre d'art ou quel(le) artiste associez-vous à chaque genre ou œuvre mentionné(e)?

Modèle: Vous entendez: une photographie
Vous dites: **Anne Geddes**

1.   2.   3.   4.   5.   6.   7.   8   9.

Étape 2. Dans la Séquence 4 du film *Liaisons,* Claire parle avec un artiste à propos d'un tableau. Quel est le genre, le sujet et le style de ce tableau?

ACTIVITÉ **D** **Pensées et préférences** Nommez quelque chose ou quelqu'un qui correspond à chaque description.

1. un tableau sombre
2. un artiste cubiste célèbre
3. un chef-d'œuvre impressionniste
4. un sculpteur bien connu
5. une exposition d'art intéressante
6. votre musée préféré
7. votre peintre préféré
8. votre genre de tableau préféré
9. votre style d'art préféré
10. votre sujet d'art préféré

ACTIVITÉ **E** **Quelques outils nécessaires** Quels genres d'œuvres d'art peuvent être créés avec les outils *(tools)* suivants?

1. des crayons
2. de la pierre *(stone)*
3. de la peinture
4. un stylo
5. du tissu *(fabric)*
6. un appareil photo

Et vous? Travaillez-vous avec ces outils pour créer des œuvres d'art?

ACTIVITÉ **F** **Chez Christie's** Christie's est une société de commissaires-priseurs *(auction company)*. La société a organisé des enchères *(auctions)* à Paris. Notez les informations que vous allez entendre pour décrire ces trois chefs-d'œuvre de l'art français.

9-3

1. *Femme accroupie* (squatting) de Henri Laurens (1885–1954)

   a. Genre: _____   c. Sujet: _____
   b. Style: _____   d. Prix: _____

2. *La montagne Sainte-Victoire vue des Lauves* de Paul Cézanne (1838–1906)

   a. Genre: _____   c. Sujet: _____
   b. Style: _____   d. Prix: _____

3. *Composition, dans l'usine* (factory) de Fernand Léger (1881–1955)

   a. Genre: _____   c. Sujet: _____
   b. Style: _____   d. Prix: _____

ACTIVITÉ **G** **Catalogue d'une galerie d'art**

Étape 1. Complétez ces descriptions selon vos impressions de chaque œuvre d'art.

© Courtesy of Patrick Rodrigue

Sous un œil bienveillant (2008) de Patrick Rodrigue

© Wynne Wong

La tour Eiffel, Paris (2010) de Neal Turner

1. a. Genre: _____
   b. Style: _____
   c. Sujet: _____
   d. Couleurs: _____
   e. Valeur *(Value)*: _____

2. a. Genre: _____
   b. Style: _____
   c. Sujet: _____
   d. Couleurs: _____
   e. Valeur: _____

© Courtesy of Julie M. Nagaro

✈ ·····
Si vous y allez

Si vous allez à Baie-Saint Paul à Charlevoix, allez à la Galerie Clarence Gagnon pour voir des tableaux d'artistes québécois tels que Patrick Rodrigue. Charlevoix est une région pittoresque du Québec qui fascine beaucoup d'artistes.

Étape 2. Parlez de vos réponses aux questions suivantes avec deux étudiants.

1. Est-ce qu'il y a une galerie d'art sur votre campus ou dans votre ville? Si oui, quels genres d'œuvres d'art est-ce qu'on y trouve?

2. Est-ce qu'il y a une exposition d'art sur votre campus ou dans votre ville en ce moment? Si oui, quel(s) est (sont) le(s) sujet(s) de l'exposition?

ACTIVITÉ 🅷 **Quatre artistes contemporains à découvrir**

🔊 **Étape 1.** Écoutez ces descriptions de quatre artistes contemporains québécois et 9-4 français et décidez quel artiste a créé chaque tableau: **M.A.J. Fortier, Denis Nolet, Patrick Rodrigue** ou **Neal Turner.**

a.

© 2015 Artists Rights Society (ARS), New York/SODRAC, Montreal

_____

c.

© Wynne Wong

_____

b.
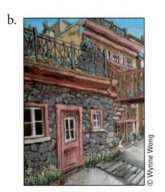

© Wynne Wong

_____

d.

© Bill VanPatten

_____

✏ **Étape 2.** Regardez bien les quatre tableaux. Écrivez une petite description de chaque tableau, puis inventez et donnez un titre à chaque tableau.

Modèle: C'est un paysage. Il y a une maison. Le style est un peu abstrait. Il y a beaucoup de couleurs sombres. Le titre est *Souvenirs de Québec.*

Étape 3. Montrez vos descriptions et vos titres à un(e) partenaire.

1. Qui a les descriptions et les titres les plus intéressants, vous ou votre partenaire?

2. Qui ferait un(e) meilleur(e) rédacteur / rédactrice *(writer)* de catalogues d'art?

3. Lequel *(Which one)* de ces tableaux préférez-vous? Et votre partenaire?

Étape 4. Notez le nom de l'artiste et le titre de chaque tableau de l'Étape 1. Vérifiez vos réponses. Préférez-vous les vrais titres ou vos titres inventés?

ACTIVITÉ I Qu'est-ce que l'art?

Étape 1. Est-ce que ces objets sont des œuvres d'art pour vous? Indiquez oui ou non.

1. un tableau de Claude Monet
2. un dessin d'un enfant de 10 ans
3. un pastel d'Edgar Degas
4. une sculpture en neige de l'Arc de Triomphe
5. une sculpture en Spam de la tour Eiffel
6. une photographie d'Ansel Adams
7. une photographie d'un arbre prise par votre mère
8. un vase de Christian Dior
9. un vase en papier mâché qu'un enfant a fait
10. des graffitis

Étape 2. Demandez à deux camarades de classe ce qu'*(what)* ils pensent.

Modèle: Un tableau de Claude Monet est une œuvre d'art pour toi?

Conclusion Qui a une définition de l'art plus rigide? Qui a une définition de l'art plus flexible?

Si vous allez à Miami, allez au musée *Haitian Heritage Museum* pour voir des spectacles de danse et de musique et des œuvres d'art haïtiennes.

ACTIVITÉ J **Votre premier projet d'art** Décrivez l'un de vos premiers projets d'art. Considérez les questions suivantes.

- C'était quoi: un dessin, une sculpture, une peinture faite avec les doigts?
- Quel était le sujet?
- Quels matériaux avez-vous utilisés: de la peinture, du papier, des bâtonnets en bois *(popsicle sticks)*, de la céramique, de la pâte à modeler *(modeling clay)*?
- Qu'est-ce que vous avez fait de votre projet d'art?

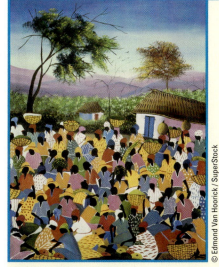

***Market Scene* de André Pierre, 1977**

Un mot sur la culture

L'art haïtien

Haïti est célèbre pour son art distinctif, notamment sa peinture, aux couleurs très vives, et sa sculpture. La nourriture et les paysages luxuriants sont deux des thèmes préférés des artistes haïtiens. Le marché est aussi un sujet très populaire. La peinture haïtienne s'inspire aussi de l'environnement et de la spiritualité. Elle a été une source d'inspiration pour plusieurs écrivains et poètes français, tels que° André Breton et André Malraux.

tels que *such as*

- Savez-vous quelle forme d'art populaire ces artistes haïtiens pratiquent?

1. Raoul Peck
2. Jacques Roumain
3. Wyclef Jean
4. Emeline Michel

Pour parler des désirs, des possibilités et des suggestions

Le conditionnel

DU FILM *LIAISONS*

Un coup d'œil sur la grammaire

Look at these photos from the film *Liaisons* and their captions.

ALEXIS Il y a des choses que j'**aimerais** vous dire, *[pause]* mais...

CLAIRE **Pourriez**-vous me donner les indications pour retourner à l'hôtel Frontenac s'il vous plaît?

Aimerais and **pourriez** are verb forms that make requests and suggestions sound more polite.

1. In the left photo caption, what do you think **aimerais** means?
2. What do you think **pourriez** in the right photo caption means?

❖ The conditional form is used to express wishes and possibilities, to give advice, and to make polite requests and suggestions.

J'**aimerais** aller en France cet été.	I **would like** to go to France this summer.
Nous **pourrions** voir l'exposition en ville.	We **could see** the exhibition in town.
Ils **devraient** faire leurs devoirs.	They **should do** their homework.
Voudriez-vous faire une promenade?	**Would** you **like** to take a walk?
Est-ce que je **pourrais** avoir un verre d'eau?	**Could** I **have** a glass of water?

❖ To form the conditional of regular verbs, add the **imparfait** endings to the infinitive. If the infinitive ends in -**e**, drop the -**e** before adding the endings.

manger	partir	dire
je manger**ais**	je partir**ais**	je dir**ais**
tu manger**ais**	tu partir**ais**	tu dir**ais**
il/elle/on manger**ait**	il/elle/on partir**ait**	il/elle/on dir**ait**
nous manger**ions**	nous partir**ions**	nous dir**ions**
vous manger**iez**	vous partir**iez**	vous dir**iez**
ils/elles manger**aient**	ils/elles partir**aient**	ils/elles dir**aient**

Tu **préférerais** ce dessin?	*Would you prefer this drawing?*	
Vous **diriez** toujours la vérité.	*You would always tell the truth.*	
Je **sortirais** avec toi.	*I would go out with you.*	
L'artiste **vendrait**-il ce tableau?	*Would the artist sell this painting?*	

••• For irregular verbs, add the **imparfait** endings to the irregular stems.

aller	ir-	devoir	devr-	savoir	saur-
avoir	aur-	faire	fer-	venir	viendr-
envoyer	enverr-	mourir	mourr-	vouloir	voudr-
être	ser-	pouvoir	pourr-		

À ta place, j'**irais** chez le dentiste.	*In your place, I would go to the dentist's.*
Auriez-vous assez de patience?	*Would you have enough patience?*

••• Verbs conjugated in the present like **venir** (**devenir** and **revenir**) have similar stems in the conditional.

Ils **deviendraient** artistes.	*They would become artists.*
Il a dit qu'il **reviendrait** aujourd'hui.	*He said he would come back today.*

••• Some verbs have a spelling change in the stems of the conditional.

appeler	acheter	essayer
j'**appellerais**	j'**achèterais**	j'**essaierais**
tu **appellerais**	tu **achèterais**	tu **essaierais**
il/elle/on **appellerait**	il/elle/on **achèterait**	il/elle/on **essaierait**
nous **appellerions**	nous **achèterions**	nous **essaierions**
vous **appelleriez**	vous **achèteriez**	vous **essaieriez**
ils/elles **appelleraient**	ils/elles **achèteraient**	ils/elles **essaieraient**

Liaisons musicales

Stephane Cardinale/People Avenue/Corbis Entertainment/ Corbis

Indochine est un groupe de rock français de style *new wave*. Leur chanson *J'ai demandé à la Lune* (2002) est un mélange de métal industriel et de musique pop électronique. Cherchez les paroles de la chanson dans laquelle ils parlent d'une aventure. Pourquoi cette aventure ne durerait-elle pas?

••• Verbs with **é** in the stem like **préférer** and **répéter** are regular in the conditional. They do not change spelling.

Je **préférerais** une pizza.	*I would prefer a pizza.*
On **espérerait** qu'il a étudié.	*One would hope that he studied.*
Est-ce que tu le **répéterais**?	*Would you repeat it?*

••• To say that one *should* do something, use the conditional of **devoir** + infinitive.

Je **devrais** faire plus de sport.	*I should exercise more.*
Elle **devrait** écouter le professeur.	*She should listen to the professor.*
Nous **devrions** partir tout de suite.	*We should leave right away.*

••• To say that one *could* do something, use the conditional of **pouvoir** + infinitive.

Tu **pourrais** me faire un dessin.	*You could draw me a picture.*
Nous **pourrions** aller au musée.	*We could go the museum.*
Je **pourrais** prendre un café.	*I could have a coffee.*

ACTIVITÉ K Les personnages du film *Liaisons*

Étape 1. Claire du film *Liaisons* parle des goûts artistiques des personnages. Utilisez les verbes pour déterminer le sujet de chaque phrase.

1. ____ **aimerait** avoir un tableau. a. Ma mère b. Les clients
2. ____ **choisirait** un tableau cubiste pour le restaurant. a. Je/J' b. Robert
3. ____ **préféreraient** un tableau impressionniste. a. Abia b. Les clients
4. ____ **choisirions** un portrait. a. Alexis b. Abia et moi
5. ____ **achèterais** une nature morte. a. Je/J' b. Vous

Et vous? Quel genre de tableau aimeriez-vous avoir?

Étape 2. Qu'est-ce que les clients de l'hôtel Delta devraient dire pour être plus polis?

Modèle: Je veux du lait!
            J'aimerais avoir du lait, s'il vous plaît. / Pourriez-vous m'apporter du lait?

1. Je veux un verre d'eau.
2. Nous avons besoin de plus d'eau minérale.
3. Vous devez fermer la fenêtre.
4. Nous voulons écouter de la musique.

ACTIVITÉ L Actions variées

Étape 1. Que feraient-ils? Complétez les phrases avec des noms de célébrité(s).

1. Entre Los Angeles ou New York, _____ et _____ **travailleraient** à New York.
2. Entre faire un film ou un album, _____ et _____ **feraient** un film.
3. Entre chanter de la pop ou du rap, _____ **chanterait** de la pop.
4. Entre adopter un bébé ou un chien, _____ **adopterait** un chien.

Étape 2. Que feriez-vous? Que feraient les gens que vous connaissez?

Modèle: Entre Détroit et Chicago, ma colocataire (habiter) **habiterait à Chicago.**

1. Entre New York et Paris, ma/mon colocataire (habiter) _____.
2. Entre Toronto et Québec, mes camarades de classe (aller) _____.
3. Entre le fromage français et le fromage américain, j(e) (acheter) _____.
4. Entre le vin californien et le vin français, mon professeur (prendre) _____.
5. Entre une pizza ou des escargots, mes amis et moi, nous (choisir) _____.
6. Entre un Coca et un Perrier, mon/ma colocataire (boire) _____.

Étape 3. Posez les questions de l'Étape 2 à un(e) partenaire pour savoir ce qu'il/elle ferait.

Modèle: É1: **Est-ce que tu habiterais à New York ou à Paris?**
            É2: **J'habiterais à New York.**

Conclusion Est-ce que votre partenaire est francophile?

ACTIVITÉ Ⓜ **Suggestions** Quelques étudiants ont besoin de conseils. Qu'est-ce qu'on pourrait suggérer?

Modèle: Je suis en retard.

Tu devrais marcher plus vite. / Tu pourrais partir plus tôt.

1. J'étais absent(e) le jour d'un examen.
2. Mon ami a perdu son livre.
3. Mes amis veulent voir un film.
4. Nous avons faim.

ACTIVITÉ Ⓝ **Êtes-vous audacieux / audacieuse?**

Étape 1. Indiquez votre réponse à chaque question pour savoir si vous êtes quelqu'un d'audacieux *(daring)*.

	Oui	Non
1. Seriez-vous un(e) modèle nu(e) pour un cours d'art?	☐	☐
2. Feriez-vous du saut en parachute *(skydiving)*?	☐	☐
3. Mangeriez-vous des insectes?	☐	☐
4. Prendriez-vous un repas dans un restaurant tout(e) seul(e) *(alone)*?	☐	☐
5. Iriez-vous à une plage nudiste?	☐	☐
6. Sortiriez-vous avec quelqu'un que vous rencontrez sur Internet?	☐	☐
7. Loueriez-vous une maison hantée?	☐	☐
8. ???	☐	☐

Étape 2. Posez les questions de l'Étape 1 à un(e) partenaire. Préparez une question pour le numéro 8.

OUI, JE PEUX! Here are two "can do statements" for you to check your progress so far. Look at each statement and rate yourself on how well you think you can perform the task. Then verify your ability with a partner. How did you do?

1. **"I can say the type of artist I would like to be and explain why."**

   I can perform this function
   ☐ with ease
   ☐ with some difficulty
   ☐ not at all

2. **"I can say three things that I should do this week and find out if others should also do these things or not this week."**

   I can perform this function
   ☐ with ease
   ☐ with some difficulty
   ☐ not at all

iLrn™

Are you looking for more practice? You can find it in **iLrn**.

VOCABULAIRE 2

🔊 La **littérature** et les **spectacles**

Literature and shows, performances

un orchestre   un concert

un ballet

une danseuse / un danseur

un auteur / une femme auteur

une pièce de théâtre

un opéra

un chœur

un compositeur / une femme compositeur / une compositrice

Célébrons l'art théâtral et les arts du spectacle

Note de **vocabulaire**

Un auteur / Une femme auteur can also suggest more generally an author of any type of written text; yet **un(e) dramaturge** *(a playwright, dramatist)* and **un poète / une femme poète** exist as well. In Quebec, **une auteure** is used instead of **une femme auteur.**

Vocabulaire complémentaire

une **chanson** *a song*

une **comédie musicale** *a musical (stage, film)*

un **conte (de fées)** *a tale (fairytale)*

un(e) **critique** *a reviewer, critic*

une **critique** *a review, critique*

le **début** *the beginning*

la **fin** *the end, ending*

un **genre** *a genre*

────────────

littéraire *literary*

poétique *poetic*

récent(e) *recent*

────────────

applaudir *to applaud*

publier *to publish*

La musique

le **blues** / le **R'n'B**

le **hip-hop**

le **jazz**

la **musique alternative**

la **musique classique**

la **(musique) country**

les **musiques du monde**

la **musique folk (contemporaine)** / le **folk**

la **musique new age**

la **pop**

le **rap**

le **rock**

© Yellowj/Shutterstock.com

Un mot sur la langue

Mon coup de cœur

(Avoir un) coup de cœur est une expression idiomatique qu'on utilise pour exprimer une passion personnelle ou une admiration pour quelque chose ou quelqu'un. Cette expression n'existe pas en anglais mais elle est semblable à *favorite pick, personal favorite, heart stopper* et *falling in love with something*. Quand on tombe amoureux d'un livre, d'un film, d'un acteur, d'une nourriture ou d'une autre chose, on peut dire **J'ai eu un coup de cœur!** ou **C'est mon coup de cœur du moment!** Regardez ces exemples.

En littérature, mes **coups de cœur** sont *L'étranger* d'Albert Camus et *Gigi* de Colette.

Bénabar, c'est mon **coup de cœur** de l'année!

J'ai eu un **coup de cœur** pour la chanson *L'amour existe encore* de Céline Dion.

Mes parents ont eu un **coup de cœur** pour cette maison.

• Quels sont vos coups de cœur actuels dans les catégories suivantes?

1. art   2. musique   3. cinéma

ACTIVITÉ A **Qui écrit quoi?** Qui écrit chaque genre de texte mentionné?

9-5

1. a. un critique   b. un auteur   c. un compositeur
2. a. un compositeur   b. un poète   c. un journaliste
3. a. un poète   b. un auteur   c. un critique
4. a. une femme auteur b. une femme compositeur c. une femme poète
5. a. une critique   b. une femme auteur   c. une compositrice
6. a. un musicien   b. un auteur   c. un critique

ACTIVITÉ B **Associations artistiques** Associez les mots de la première colonne aux mots de la deuxième colonne.

1. _____ *Roméo et Juliette* de Shakespeare   a. un opéra
2. _____ *Cats* d'Andrew Lloyd Webber   b. une pièce de théâtre
3. _____ *Le Corbeau (The Raven)* d'Edgar Allen Poe c. un roman
4. _____ *Cendrillon* de Charles Perrault   d. un poème
5. _____ *Carmen* de Georges Bizet   e. une chanson
6. _____ *Happy* de Pharrell Williams   f. une comédie musicale
7. _____ le Philharmonique de Londres   g. un orchestre
8. _____ *Divergent* de Veronica Roth   h. un conte de fées
9. _____ *Le Lac des Cygnes (Swan Lake)* de Tchaïkovski i. un ballet

Si vous y allez

Si vous allez à New York, trouvez La Comédie-Française New York qui propose des cours de comédie *(acting)* en français.

ACTIVITÉ C **Les artistes célèbres**

Étape 1. Quelle(s) personne(s) célèbre(s) est-ce que vous associez aux mots suivants?

1. un chœur   3. un orchestre   5. un auteur de pièces de théâtre
2. un auteur   4. un compositeur   6. une critique

Étape 2. Quel(le) artiste (musique, littérature, théâtre ou poésie) aimeriez-vous être?

Modèle: chanteur / chanteuse   **J'aimerais être Taylor Swift.**

1. chanteur / chanteuse   2. auteur / femme auteur   3. danseur / danseuse

ACTIVITÉ D **Les spectacles** Dans la Séquence 5 du film *Liaisons* que vous allez regarder, Claire a un rendez-vous avec Alexis Prévost. À votre avis, quel type de spectacle de l'Activité B Claire préférerait-elle? Quel type de spectacle préférerait Alexis Prévost?

Et vous? Quels types de spectacles est-ce que vous aimez et n'aimez pas?

ACTIVITÉ E Caractéristiques importantes Donnez les titres des œuvres qui correspondent à chaque caractéristique mentionnée.

1. **2.** **3.** **4.** **5.** **6.** **7.** **8.**

Et vous? Quels genres d'histoire *(stories)* ou quelles caractéristiques appréciez-vous dans les œuvres?

ACTIVITÉ F Testez vos connaissances

Étape 1. Avec un(e) partenaire, complétez les phrases avec les mots qui manquent *(missing)*.

Modèle: Émile Nelligan est **un poète québécois.**

1. Claude Debussy est _____.
2. Félix Leclerc est _____.
3. Charles Baudelaire est _____.
4. Simone de Beauvoir est _____.

5. *Chant d'automne* est _____.
6. *Notre-Dame de Paris* est _____.
7. *Le Roi Soleil* est _____.
8. *Le Misanthrope* et *Tartuffe* sont _____.

Étape 2. Votre professeur va vous donner les réponses. Avez-vous bien réussi au quiz?

ACTIVITÉ G Résister à l'épreuve du temps

Étape 1. Parlez avec un(e) partenaire des œuvres ou des personnes qui ont résisté à l'épreuve du temps *(withstood the test of time)*. Notez vos réponses.

	Nous	**Autre paire**
1. un écrivain français	_____	_____
2. une pièce de théâtre américaine	_____	_____
3. un conte de fées allemand	_____	_____
4. un opéra italien	_____	_____
5. une écrivaine anglaise	_____	_____

Étape 2. Interviewez une autre paire d'étudiants et notez leurs réponses.

Modèle: É1: **À votre avis, quel écrivain français a résisté à l'épreuve du temps?**
É2: **Nous avons dit Jean-Paul Sartre.**

Étape 3. Est-ce que les œuvres suivantes vont résister à l'épreuve du temps, à votre avis?

1. la série *Harry Potter*
2. les romans de Stephen King
3. les comédies musicales d'Andrew Lloyd Webber
4. les chansons de Britney Spears
5. les poèmes de Maya Angelou
6. les romans de la saga *Twilight*

Étape 4. Défendez vos prédictions de l'Étape 3 dans votre petit groupe.

ACTIVITÉ H Associations musicales

Étape 1. Quel artiste associez-vous aux mots suivants?

1. le blues / le R'n'B
2. le jazz
3. le hip-hop
4. la musique classique
5. le folk contemporain
6. la musique alternative

7. le rock
8. la pop
9. les musiques du monde
10. la country
11. le rap
12. la musique new age

 Étape 2. Montrez vos réponses de l'Étape 1 à deux camarades de classe. Connaissez-vous les artistes ou compositeurs que vos camarades ont mentionnés?

Modèle: É1: **Pour le blues, j'ai mis John Lee Hooker. Et vous?**
É2: **Moi, je ne connais pas bien le blues mais j'ai mis Usher pour le R'n'B.**
É3: **Moi, j'ai mis Billie Holiday.**

Étape 3. Quels sont vos coups de cœur en musique? Nommez-en trois.

 Étape 4. Partagez vos coups de cœur avec deux autres camarades de classe.

Modèle: **Mes coups de cœur sont Taylor Swift, Norah Jones et Lady Gaga. Taylor Swift est une chanteuse de musique country. Norah Jones fait de la musique jazz. Lady Gaga est une chanteuse de musique pop.**

ACTIVITÉ I Goûts musicaux Quels genres musicaux est-ce que les personnes suivantes écoutent? Que pensez-vous de leurs goûts musicaux? C'est cool? C'est nul? C'est moyen? C'est bien?

1. votre colocataire
2. vos grands-parents
3. votre meilleur(e) ami(e)
4. vos parents

5. votre prof de français
6. vos amis
7. votre frère / votre sœur
8. vos voisins

Et vous? Quel(s) genre(s) musical (musicaux) écoutez-vous?

ACTIVITÉ J La musique et nos activités

Étape 1. Quel genre de musique aimez-vous écouter quand vous faites ces activités?

Modèle: étudier   **Quand j'étudie, j'aime écouter du jazz.**

1. étudier
2. faire le ménage
3. faire la fête

4. faire un pique-nique
5. aller à un dîner élégant
6. faire de la gym

Étape 2. Posez les questions à un(e) partenaire. Êtes-vous similaires ou différent(e)s?

ACTIVITÉ Ⓚ **Une île déserte**

Étape 1. Imaginez que vous êtes naufragé(e) *(marooned)* sur une île déserte. Posez ces questions à un(e) partenaire et notez ses réponses.

1. Quels cinq romans est-ce que tu voudrais avoir avec toi?
2. Quels cinq albums musicaux est-ce que tu voudrais avoir avec toi?

Étape 2. Aimez-vous les choix de votre partenaire? Voudriez-vous être naufragé(e) sur la même île que votre partenaire ou préféreriez-vous être naufragé(e) sur votre propre *(own)* île déserte?

Étape 3. Avec votre partenaire, devinez *(guess)* les réponses de votre professeur. Quels romans ou albums musicaux votre professeur aimerait avoir avec lui/elle s'il/elle était naufragé(e) sur une île déserte? Ensuite, demandez à votre professeur ses réponses.

ACTIVITÉ Ⓛ **Ou peut-être une critique?** Préparez une critique de cinq ou six phrases d'un roman récent que vous avez lu, d'une pièce de théâtre que vous avez vue *(seen)*, d'une nouvelle chanson que vous avez entendue ou d'un concert auquel *(which)* vous avez assisté *(attended)*.

Modèle: Je viens de terminer le dernier roman de Stephenie Meyer, *Révélation*. C'est le quatrième roman de sa série *Twilight*. Je dois dire que je n'ai pas du tout aimé ses personnages. Meyer a écrit avec le même style de langue captivant et j'applaudis ses efforts pour essayer de développer les personnages mais la fin est mauvaise. J'ai envie de donner le livre au magasin Goodwill.

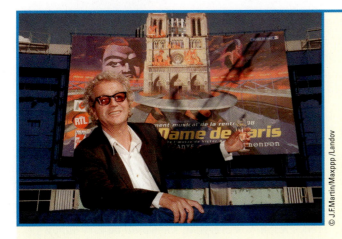
© J.F.Martin/Maxppp /Landov

Un mot sur la culture

Les comédies musicales

La comédie musicale est un genre de spectacle qui combine la comédie ou la tragédie, le chant et généralement la danse. On a tendance à associer ce genre à la culture américaine mais, en fait, elle a une longue histoire européenne aussi. En Europe, le théâtre musical date du temps des Grecs anciens. Shakespeare a plusieurs scènes chantées dans beaucoup de ses pièces de théâtre et Molière a ajouté des chansons et des danses à plusieurs de ses farces. Dans le monde francophone aujourd'hui, c'est à Montréal (Québec) et à Paris (France) qu'on a le plus de chance de voir une comédie musicale française, telle que *Notre-Dame de Paris*, *Le Roi Soleil*, *Les Dix Commandements*, *Roméo et Juliette* et *Mozart: l'opéra rock*.

- Avez-vous déjà vu *(seen)* une comédie musicale?
- Avez-vous peut-être joué dans une comédie musicale? Quel(s) rôle(s)?
- Est-ce que vous aimeriez jouer dans une comédie musicale? Laquelle?

Pour parler des situations hypothétiques

Le conditionnel dans les phrases avec *si*

DU FILM *LIAISONS*

Un coup d'œil sur la grammaire

Look at these photos from the film *Liaisons* and their captions.

Si Alexis Prévost **n'avait pas besoin** de retourner à Paris, il **pourrait** passer plus de temps avec Claire.

Si Abia **n'avait pas besoin** de travailler, elle **irait** à Québec pour rejoindre *(to join)* Claire.

Sentences that express hypothetical situations often begin with **si** *(if)*.

1. What two verb tenses or moods are in boldface in the captions?
2. Which tense or mood is used with **si** to express a hypothetical situation?

⋯⟫ In addition to conveying possibilities, offering suggestions, and making requests more polite, the present conditional is also used to express ideal or hypothetical, contrary-to-fact situations. In this usage, the **conditionnel présent** is used to express what *would happen* if a hypothetical situation in a **si** clause *were to occur*. The verb in the **si** clause is in the **imparfait**.

Si j'**avais** plus d'argent, j'**achèterais** une nouvelle voiture.
*If I **had** more money, I **would buy** a new car.*

Nous **réussirions** notre examen **si** nous **faisions** attention pendant le cours.
*We **would pass** our exam **if** we **paid** attention in class.*

Si Anne **pouvait** manger dans un restaurant français tous les jours, elle **serait** très contente.
*If Anne **could eat** at a French restaurant everyday, she **would be** very happy.*

⋯⟫ Notice that **si** + **il/ils** contract to become **s'il** and **s'ils**.

S'ils **voulaient** parler avec le professeur, ils **iraient** le voir dans son bureau.
*If they **wanted** to speak with the professor, they **would go** see him in his office.*

❖❖❖ The **si** clause can begin the sentence or appear in the second half. Note that if the **si** clause begins the sentence, it is followed by a comma. If the **si** clause occurs in the second half of the sentence, there is no comma.

> **Si** elle **prenait** son temps, elle **ferait** mieux ses devoirs.
> *If she **took** her time, she **would do** her homework better.*

> Vous **auriez** plus de chance dans la vie **si** vous **travailliez** plus dur.
> *You **would have** more luck in life **if** you **worked** harder.*

❖❖❖ A **si** clause may be used alone with the **imparfait** to express a wish or to make a suggestion.

> **Si** on **allait** au cinéma?
> *How about going to the movies?*

> **Si** seulement il y **avait** moins de monde ici!
> *If only there were fewer people here!*

Pour aller plus loin
Le verbe *vivre*

Like the verb **habiter**, the verb **vivre** means *to live*. Its present tense forms are **je vis, tu vis, il/elle/on vit, nous vivons, vous vivez, ils/elles vivent.** Its past participle is **vécu.**

Habiter and **vivre** can be used interchangeably to express *to reside in / at a place.*

Si je pouvais, j'**habiterais** à Paris.	*If I could, I **would live** in Paris.*
Si je pouvais, je **vivrais** à Paris.	*If I could, I **would live** in Paris.*

To express *a moment in time when you have lived or are living*, a *lifestyle* or *to live for someone / something*, use **vivre.**

Ils **vivent** pour l'art et la musique.	*They **live** for art and music.*
Je **vivais** sans meubles quand j'étais petit.	*I **lived** without furniture when I was little.*
Elle veut **vivre** jusqu'à l'âge de 100 ans.	*She wants **to live** till she's 100.*
Mes grands-parents **ont vécu** la guerre.	*My grandparents **lived** through the war.*

Vivre is also used idiomatically to mean *long live.*

Vive la France!	*Long live France!*

Essayez! Complétez les phrases avec le nom de personnes que vous connaissez.

Modèle: _____ vit au Canada.   **Ma tante vit au Canada.**

1. _____ **vit** pour les livres.
2. _____ **vivent** dans une petite ville.
3. _____ **vivait** simplement.
4. _____ **ont vécu** une situation difficile.

ACTIVITÉ **M** **Que feriez-vous?**

Étape 1. Indiquez ce que vous feriez dans chaque situation.

1. **Si** je **pouvais** acheter un tableau d'art d'un musée, j'…
   a. **achèterais** *La Joconde (Mona Lisa).*
   b. **achèterais** un tableau surréaliste de Salvador Dali.
   c. **achèterais** un portrait d'Elvis Presley.
   d. ???

2. **Si** je **devais** lire un roman, je…
   a. **lirais** *Les Misérables* de Victor Hugo.
   b. **lirais** *Crime et Châtiment* de Fiodor Dostoïevski.
   c. **lirais** *Harry Potter* de J.K. Rowling.
   d. ???

3. **Si** je **voulais** écouter de la musique, j'…
   a. **écouterais** des chansons d'artistes français ou francophones.
   b. **écouterais** de la musique classique.
   c. **écouterais** de la musique country.
   d. ???

4. **Si** j'**avais** envie d'aller à un spectacle, j'…
   a. **irais** à un opéra.
   b. **irais** à une comédie musicale.
   c. **irais** à un concert de blues.
   d. ???

5. **Si** je **pouvais** vivre dans un autre pays, je…
   a. **vivrais** en France.
   b. **vivrais** en Angleterre.
   c. **vivrais** au Canada.
   d. ???

Liaisons musicales

© ZICH/SIPA/Newscom

Willy Denzey est un chanteur / rappeur français d'origine laotienne qui est inspiré par la musique R'n'B et la soul. Cherchez les paroles de sa chanson *Et si tu n'existais pas* et trouvez une *suite (ending)* pour Willy à «si tu n'existais pas».

 Étape 2. Montrez vos réponses à un(e) partenaire. Dans quelles situations avez-vous les mêmes réponses?

 Étape 3. Avec votre partenaire, devinez *(guess)* comment votre professeur répondrait.

Modèle: Si notre professeur pouvait acheter un tableau d'art d'un musée, il/elle achèterait *La Joconde.*

ACTIVITÉ **N** **Connaissez-vous bien votre famille et vos amis?** Complétez les conditions et situations suivantes.

1. Si mon/ma colocataire devait étudier une langue étrangère, il/elle _____.

2. Mes parents seraient très contents si _____.

3. Si mon ami(e) et moi avions beaucoup d'argent, nous _____.

4. Le petit ami de mon amie irait à un opéra si _____.

5. Si mon ami(e) et moi trouvions une grosse somme d'argent dans la rue, nous _____.

Étape 1. Que feriez-vous si les cours étaient annulés *(cancelled)*? Notez vos réponses.

1. réviser pour un autre cours ou regarder la télé?
2. chatter sur Internet ou lire la prochaine leçon du livre de français?
3. terminer les devoirs ou envoyer des textos?
4. lire un roman ou faire du shopping sur Internet?
5. dormir ou faire le ménage?

Étape 2. Posez les questions à un(e) partenaire. Qui profiterait *(would take advantage)* davantage *(more)* des cours annulés? Vous ou votre partenaire?

ACTIVITÉ **P** Des situations hypothétiques

Étape 1. Répondez aux questions. Inventez une situation hypothétique pour le numéro 6.

1. Si vous n'étudiiez pas à cette université, où étudieriez-vous?
2. Si le français n'était pas proposé, quelle langue choisiriez-vous?
3. Si vous pouviez vivre dans une ville francophone, où vivriez-vous?
4. Si vous pouviez rencontrer une personne célèbre, qui aimeriez-vous rencontrer?
5. Si vous vouliez avoir des enfants, combien d'enfants auriez-vous?
6. ???

Étape 2. Posez ces questions à deux camarades de classe. Est-ce que leurs réponses sont similaires ou différentes?

OUI, JE PEUX! Here are two "can do statements" for you to check your progress so far. Look at each statement and rate yourself on how well you think you can perform the task. Then verify your ability with a partner. How did you do?

iLrn™
Are you looking for more practice? You can find it in **iLrn**.

1. **"I can say the type of show or performance I would go to if I had the money and find out if others would do the same."**

   I can perform this function
   ☐ with ease
   ☐ with some difficulty
   ☐ not at all

2. **"I can say the type(s) of music I would listen to if I were happy and sad."**

   I can perform this function
   ☐ with ease
   ☐ with some difficulty
   ☐ not at all

La **télévision** et le **cinéma**

Television and movies

un film d'horreur

un film de science-fiction

un western

un policier

Au ciné

un match télévisé

BBC AMERICA

les informations / les infos *(f.)*

une émission de téléachat

1-888-555-6781

un jeu télévisé

À la télé

Vocabulaire complémentaire

une émission *a broadcast, TV show*
les nouvelles *(f.)* *news, news items*
un personnage *a character*
une publicité / une pub *a commercial*
un réalisateur / une réalisatrice *a director (TV or movie)*
un rôle *a role*

D'autres genres de films

une comédie *comedy*
un documentaire *documentary*
un drame (psychologique) *(psychological) drama*
un film d'action *action film*
un film romantique *romance film*
un film à suspense *suspense film*

D'autres émissions de télé

une causerie *talk show*
un dessin animé / un film d'animation *(animated) cartoon / animated film*
une émission de téléréalité *reality TV show*
une émission de variétés *variety show*
un feuilleton *soap opera*
une série *a serial sitcom or TV drama*

> **Note de vocabulaire**
> **Un dessin animé** may also refer to an animated film.

Un mot sur la langue

Prépositions avec la radio et la télé

In French, you can use the prepositions **à** and **sur** with both television and radio, but the meanings are very different. Compare the differences.

J'ai vu un chat tout mignon *à* la télé.	*I saw a really cute cat **on** TV.*
J'ai vu un chat tout mignon *sur* la télé.	*I saw a really cute cat **on (top)** of the TV.*

• Répondez aux questions avec des informations personnelles.

1. Quelle émission regardez-vous souvent **à la télé**?
2. Avez-vous quelque chose **sur la télé** chez vous?

🔊 **ACTIVITÉ** Ⓐ **Émissions de télé** Écoutez les genres d'émission de télé et
9-7 donnez un titre d'une émission correspondante.

1. _____   5. _____
2. _____   6. _____
3. _____   7. _____
4. _____   8. _____

🔊 **ACTIVITÉ** Ⓑ **Quel genre de film?** Quel film appartient *(belongs)* au genre
9-8 cinématographique mentionné?

a. _____ *Halloween* de John Carpenter
b. _____ *The Godfather* de Francis Ford Coppola
c. _____ *Capitalism: A Love Story* de Michael Moore
d. _____ *Pirates of the Caribbean* de Gore Verbinski
e. _____ *Shrek* de Andrew Adamson et Vicky Jenson
f. _____ *Star Trek Into Darkness* de J. J. Abrams
g. _____ *A Fistful of Dollars* de Sergio Leone
h. _____ *Psycho* d'Alfred Hitchcock

👥 **ACTIVITÉ** Ⓒ **Vos préférences personnelles**

Étape 1. Parlez avec un(e) partenaire des films ou des émissions de télé que vous
adorez et que vous **détestez** pour chaque genre mentionné ici. Donnez deux ou trois
titres pour chaque numéro.

1. un film d'action   **4.** une émission de téléréalité   **7.** une comédie
2. un film à suspense   **5.** un dessin animé   **8.** un jeu télévisé
3. un feuilleton   **6.** un film romantique   **9.** une série

Étape 2. Vous connaissez un peu les personnalités de Claire et d'Abia du film
Liaisons. Quels genres de films ou d'émissions de télé imaginez-vous qu'elles
aimeraient et détesteraient? Pourquoi?

ACTIVITÉ Ⓓ **Cinéphile du cinéma français?** Faites correspondre les
phrases suivantes.

1. L'œuvre du réalisateur François
Truffaut est...

2. *Les Enfants du paradis* (Carné, 1945)
a été voté...

3. On compare souvent les films de
Jean Renoir...

4. Jean Reno est une star française...

5. Comparé souvent à Hitchcock,...

a. aux tableaux de son père Auguste
Renoir.

b. Claude Chabrol est réputé *(known)*
pour ses films à suspense.

c. caractérisée par des personnages
intéressants.

d. connue pour ses films d'action et ses
policiers.

e. «Meilleur film du siècle» par des
critiques français.

⋮ **Et vous?** Connaissez-vous les réalisateurs, le film ou l'acteur mentionnés ici?

ACTIVITÉ **E** **Films et personnages classiques**

Étape 1. Nommez un personnage, un acteur ou une actrice classique qui, selon vous *(according to you),* est typique pour chaque genre de film.

1. un policier
2. un film d'horreur
3. un film de science-fiction
4. un western
5. un drame psychologique
6. un film romantique
7. un film à suspense
8. une comédie musicale
9. un film d'action
10. une comédie

Étape 2. Quel est le genre de ces films? Quels films sont de grands classiques?

1. *Superman*
2. *Star Wars*
3. *Friday the 13th*
4. *Gone with the Wind*
5. *The Notebook*
6. *Ace Ventura*
7. *High Noon*
8. *West Side Story*
9. *The Sixth Sense*
10. *Usual Suspects*

 Étape 3. Comparez vos réponses de l'Étape 1 et de l'Étape 2 avec celles *(those)* d'un(e) autre camarade de classe. Êtes-vous d'accord avec toutes ses réponses? Qui est plus cinéphile *(film enthusiast)?*

> **Note** de **vocabulaire**
>
> **Un programme** in French refers to a TV program guide and not an actual TV show, which is **une émission (de télé)**.

ACTIVITÉ **F** **Le programme de télé** Quelles émissions passent *(air)* typiquement à la télé à ces moments de la journée?

Modèle: à 10h   des causeries

1. le samedi matin
2. tous les après-midi
3. à midi
4. après l'école
5. le vendredi soir
6. tous les soirs
7. le samedi après-midi
8. à 18h
9. le dimanche soir
10. le dimanche après-midi
11. tard la nuit
12. à 21h

Et vous? Quelles émissions de télé regardez-vous et à quelles heures?

ACTIVITÉ **G** **Petit quiz!**

Étape 1. Utilisez un mot de chaque colonne ou d'autres mots pour préparer une petite description d'un film ou d'une émission de télé. Ne donnez pas le titre!

Modèle: **C'est une série télévisée. Les personnages sont un groupe d'amis et une famille qui habitent à Point Place dans l'état du Wisconsin.**

un dessin animé	les spectateurs	montrer
une émission de téléréalité	les personnages	raconter *(to tell)*
une série télévisée	les participants	jouer
un film de science-fiction	les rôles	être sur
un film romantique	l'histoire *(story)*	avoir pour vedette *(to star)*
???	???	???

Étape 2. Échangez votre description avec un(e) partenaire. Essayez de deviner le titre.

Modèle: C'est *That 70s Show.*

 ACTIVITÉ H **Si tu pouvais…**

 Étape 1. À tour de rôle *(Taking turns)*, posez les questions à un(e) partenaire et notez ses réponses.

Modèle: jouer un rôle de série de télé

É1: **Si tu pouvais jouer un rôle de série de télé, quel rôle est-ce que tu aimerais jouer?**

É2: **J'aimerais jouer le rôle de Jack Bauer de la série *24*. Et toi?**

1. faire un numéro *(number, act)* pour une émission de variétés
2. être l'animateur / l'animatrice *(host)* d'un jeu télévisé ou d'une causerie
3. commenter un match sportif
4. dessiner pour un dessin animé
5. être un(e) participant(e) dans une émission de téléréalité

Étape 2. Discutez de vos réponses à ces questions avec votre partenaire.

1. Quelles réponses vous ont surpris(e)?
2. Avez-vous maintenant une nouvelle impression de votre camarade de classe?
3. Qui pourrait jouer votre personnage si un réalisateur voulait tourner *(to make)* un film sur vous?

Si vous y allez

© Stefan Ataman/Shutterstock.com

Si vous allez à Paris, allez au Musée de Radio-France pour visiter les premiers studios de radio et de télévision en France et pour voir *(to see)* une belle collection de «machines à son et images» de 1898 à aujourd'hui.

Un mot sur la culture
Les émissions de variétés

En général, les Français sont fous de° leurs émissions de variétés. Il y en a normalement au moins une par semaine. Ces émissions accueillent typiquement des artistes de spectacles de tous les coins du monde. Il y a des acrobates, des magiciens, des transformistes°, des illusionnistes, des humoristes, des chanteurs et des danseurs. Les numéros de musique sont souvent nostalgiques avec des reprises contemporaines de vieilles chansons françaises. Les spectateurs participent très souvent et chantent avec les artistes qui sont sur scène°.

fous de *crazy about / for* **transformistes** *quick-change artists* **en scène** *on stage*

© Jean-Marc Haedrich/Visual Press/Photoshot

• La culture française a une longue tradition des arts du spectacle dans la rue, au théâtre, dans les cabarets, aux music-halls et à la télé. Est-ce que c'est similaire dans votre culture?

Liaisons avec les mots et les sons

9-9

qu / ph / th / gn / ch

Some consonant combinations have a relatively constant pronunciation in French.

The combination **qu** is pronounced like the English *k* and the combination **th** like *t*.

criti**que**	cho**que**	**qu**and	**th**éâtre	**th**é	sympathi**que**

The combination **ph** is pronounced like the English *f* and the combination **gn** like the *n* sound in *onion*.

photogra**ph**ie	télé**ph**one	cinématogra**ph**ie	compa**gn**e	ga**gn**er	Espa**gn**e

The combination **ch** is usually pronounced like the English *sh*, as in *shush*. When the **ch** appears in a word that is borrowed from another language, pronounce it like *k*.

Examples of the *sh* sound:	blan**ch**e	**ch**ose	**ch**anson
Examples of the *k* sound:	psy**ch**ologie	**ch**œur	or**ch**estre

Pratique A. Écoutez et répétez ces mots de vocabulaire.

1. **qu**el
2. **qu**oi
3. une **ph**oto
4. la **ph**ilosophie
5. une pièce de **th**éâtre
6. les ma**th**s
7. l'Allema**gn**e
8. l'espa**gn**ol
9. une **ch**anson
10. une dou**ch**e
11. un psy**ch**ologue
12. la te**ch**nologie

Pratique B. Écoutez ces répliques du film *Liaisons*. Ensuite, encerclez toutes les combinaisons de consonnes de cette leçon.

CLAIRE Ne dramatise pas Abi. […] mon oncle a téléphoné ce matin…

CLAIRE Bon, quand vous êtes parti, j'ai cherché votre nom dans le registre… mais je ne l'ai pas trouvé.

ALEXIS Claire Gagner. Vous attendez quelqu'un? À une prochaine fois, j'espère.

À vos stylos! C'est l'heure de la dictée!

Vous allez entendre deux citations *(quotations)* deux fois. La première fois, écoutez bien. La deuxième fois, écrivez les phrases.

9-10 **Sujet** Citations célèbres

Pour parler de nos observations et nos sentiments

Les verbes **croire, recevoir** et **voir** / Les pronoms démonstratifs

DU FILM *LIAISONS*

Un coup d'œil sur la grammaire

Look at these photos from the film *Liaisons* and their captions.

Claire **voit** encore une fois l'homme mystérieux qui lui a donné l'enveloppe.

Abia dit à Claire qu'elle **a reçu** un message d'une femme de France.

1. What do you think **voit** means in the left caption?
2. What do you think **a reçu** means in the right caption?

Les verbes *croire, voir* et *recevoir*

Croire *(to believe)*, **voir** *(to see)*, and **recevoir** *(to receive)* are irregular verbs. They take **avoir** in the **passé composé,** and they have irregular conditional stems.

<aside>
Note de **grammaire**
The verb **revoir** *(to see again)* is conjugated like **voir: Ils ont revu leurs amis.** *They saw their friends again.*
</aside>

croire *(to believe)*	voir *(to see)*	recevoir *(to receive)*
je **crois**	je **vois**	je **reçois**
tu **crois**	tu **vois**	tu **reçois**
il/elle/on **croit**	il/elle/on **voit**	il/elle/on **reçoit**
nous **croyons**	nous **voyons**	nous **recevons**
vous **croyez**	vous **voyez**	vous **recevez**
ils/elles **croient**	ils/elles **voient**	ils/elles **reçoivent**
PAST PARTICIPLE: **cru**	PAST PARTICIPLE: **vu**	PAST PARTICIPLE: **reçu**
CONDITIONAL STEM: **croir-**	CONDITIONAL STEM: **verr-**	CONDITIONAL STEM: **recevr-**

S'il pouvait, il **verrait** l'opéra *Carmen.* *If he could, he **would see** the opera* Carmen.
Je **n'ai pas reçu** votre message. *I **didn't receive** your message.*

To express *to believe in something or someone*, use **croire à.** To express *to believe someone or something*, **à** is not used.

Les enfants **croient au** Père Noël.	*Children **believe in** Santa Claus.*
Il **croit** Anne.	*He **believes** Anne.*
Nous ne **croyons** pas les hommes politiques.	*We **do not believe** politicians.*

Note de **vocabulaire**
To express *to believe in God,* use **croire en:** Ma famille croit en Dieu.

Les pronoms démonstratifs

Demonstrative pronouns are used to refer to a person, thing, or idea that has already been mentioned. They agree in gender and number with the noun to which they refer.

	Singular	Plural
Masculine	celui	ceux
Feminine	celle	celles

Demonstrative pronouns are often used with prepositional phrases.

Quelles pommes voulez-vous? **Celles de** Provigo ou **celles du** marché?
*Which apples do you want? **The ones from** Provigo or **the ones from** the market?*

Est-ce que nous suivons les conseils de Marc ou **ceux du** professeur?
*Are we following Marc's advice or **the professor's**?*

Quel film voyons-nous? **Celui avec** Gérard Depardieu ou **celui avec** Beyoncé?
*Which film are we seeing? **The one with** Gérard Depardieu or **the one with** Beyoncé?*

Est-ce que tu préfères l'émission sur le Québec ou **celle sur** la Guadeloupe?
*Do you prefer the program on Quebec or **the one on** Guadeloupe?*

ACTIVITÉ I Les choix

Étape 1. Répondez aux questions.

1. **Quel concert** aimeriez-vous **voir**? **Celui** de Carrie Underwood ou **celui** de Sarah McLaughlin. J'aimerais **voir celui** de _____.

2. **Quel livre** aimeriez-vous **recevoir**? **Celui** de Victor Hugo ou **celui** de Kurt Vonnegut? J'aimerais **recevoir celui** de _____.

3. **Quelle sculpture** aimeriez-vous **recevoir**? **Celle** de Rodin ou **celle** de Picasso? J'aimerais **recevoir celle** de _____.

4. **Quels films** aimeriez-vous **voir**? **Ceux** de Steven Spielberg ou **ceux** de Quentin Tarantino? J'aimerais **voir ceux** de _____.

5. **À quelles** promesses *(promises)* **croyez**-vous? **À celles** de votre patron ou **à celles** de votre professeur? Je crois **à celles** de _____.

6. **Quels films** aimeriez-vous **revoir**? J'aimerais **revoir ceux** de _____.

7. **Quel CD** aimeriez-vous **recevoir**? J'aimerais **recevoir celui** de _____.

8. **À quel** discours *(speech)* présidentiel **croyez**-vous? Je **crois à celui** de _____.

Étape 2. Posez les questions à un(e) partenaire. Avez-vous les mêmes réponses?

ACTIVITÉ J De quoi parle-t-on? Choisissez la bonne réponse pour chacune des questions suivantes.

1. Préféreriez-vous voir **celui** sur les pingouins ou **celui** sur la nourriture biologique?
   a. l'émission culturelle   b. le documentaire

2. Aimeriez-vous **celle** avec Kiefer Sutherland ou **celle** avec Patrick Dempsey?
   a. la série   b. le feuilleton

3. Verriez-vous **ceux** de Tim Burton ou **ceux** de Steven Spielberg?
   a. les films   b. le film

4. Choisiriez-vous **celles** sur NBC ou **celles** sur ABC?
   a. la série télévisée   b. les séries télévisées

ACTIVITÉ K Vos chaînes de télé préférées?

Étape 1. Complétez chaque phrase avec le pronom démonstratif approprié et votre chaîne de télé *(TV channel)* préférée pour chaque genre d'émission de télévision suivant.

Modèle: Pour les dessins animés, je préfère **ceux de la chaîne Fox.**

1. Pour les informations, je préfère _____ de _____.
2. Pour les jeux télévisés, je préfère _____ de _____.
3. Pour les séries, je préfère _____ de _____.
4. Pour les causeries, je préfère _____ de _____.
5. Pour les émissions de téléréalité, je préfère _____ de _____.
6. Pour les feuilletons, je préfère _____ de _____.
7. Pour les dessins animés, je préfère _____ de _____.

Étape 2. Montrez vos réponses à un(e) partenaire. Pouvez-vous regarder la télé ensemble?

ACTIVITÉ L Moments mémorables Formulez des phrases avec un mot de chaque colonne ou d'autres mots pour raconter *(to tell about)* quelques moments mémorables que vous et des gens que vous connaissez avez vécus.

Modèle: É1: **J'ai reçu mon premier vélo comme cadeau de Noël quand j'avais 8 ans.**
          É2: **Mes parents m'ont vu danser une fois à la télé.**

je	voir	cadeau(x)
mon/ma meilleur(e) ami(e)	croire	à la télé
nous	recevoir	dans un film / dans un match
mes amis	revoir	le mensonge *(lie)*
???	???	???

ACTIVITÉ M **Croyez-vous toujours?** Posez des questions à un(e) partenaire. Inventez un sujet pour le numéro 8.

Modèle: É1: **Est-ce que tu crois tes parents?**
É2: **Oui, je crois mes parents. / Oui, je les crois.**
É1: **Est-ce que tu crois aux promesses de ton/ta colocataire?**
É2: **Oui, je crois à ses promesses. / Oui, j'y crois.**

1. aux promesses du président
2. tes professeurs
3. au Père Noël
4. au karma
5. tes amis
6. ton/ta colocataire
7. au coup de foudre
8. ???

 ACTIVITÉ N **Fanatiques** Posez ces questions à trois étudiants différents. Notez leurs réponses.

Modèle: É1: **Quelles comédies est-ce que tu verrais si tu étais triste?**
É2: **Je verrais celles de Will Ferrell.**

1. Quelle musique est-ce que tu écouterais si tu avais envie de danser?
2. Quelles publicités te donnent envie d'acheter le(s) produit(s) présenté(s)?
3. Quelles œuvres d'art t'impressionnent beaucoup?
4. Quels films est-ce que tu verrais si tu étais de mauvaise humeur?

OUI, JE PEUX!

Here are two "can do statements" for you to check your progress so far. Look at each statement and rate yourself on how well you think you can perform the task. Then verify your ability with a partner. How did you do?

1. **"I can name my three favorite types of TV shows and explain why they are my favorites."**

   I can perform this function
   ☐ with ease
   ☐ with some difficulty
   ☐ not at all

2. **"I can list the film genre(s) that I usually see in movie theaters and find out if others typically see the same or different genres of film."**

   I can perform this function
   ☐ with ease
   ☐ with some difficulty
   ☐ not at all

iLrn™

Are you looking for more practice? You can find it in **iLrn**.

Avant de visionner

ACTIVITÉ A **Vous rappelez-vous?** Vous rappelez-vous *(Do you remember)* qui a dit ces phrases dans la Séquence 4 du film *Liaisons*?

	Claire	Alexis	Abia
1. […] quelqu'un a déposé une enveloppe pour moi à ma chambre.	☐	☐	☐
2. Oui, c'est dommage mais mon pays m'attend.	☐	☐	☐
3. C'est simplement une coïncidence.	☐	☐	☐
4. Ne t'en fais pas *(Don't worry)*. Je m'occuperai *(will take care)* de Robert.	☐	☐	☐
5. J'ai hâte *(look forward)* que tu me racontes tout…	☐	☐	☐
6. […] j'ai reçu une clé pour un coffre-fort.	☐	☐	☐

ACTIVITÉ B **Devinez** Devinez *(Guess)* ce qui va se passer dans la Séquence 5 du film *Liaisons*. Pour chaque phrase, indiquez si c'est vrai ou faux. Vous allez vérifier vos réponses plus tard.

	Vrai	Faux
1. Claire et Alexis visitent la ville de Québec.	☐	☐
2. Claire découvre ce qui est dans le coffre-fort.	☐	☐
3. Alexis Prévost dit un grand secret à Claire.	☐	☐
4. Claire revoit l'homme mystérieux qui lui a donné l'enveloppe.	☐	☐
5. Claire fait un voyage en France.	☐	☐

ACTIVITÉ C **Un coup d'œil sur une scène** Voici une scène de la Séquence 5 du film *Liaisons*. Claire parle au téléphone avec une femme, Mme Papillon. Avec un(e) partenaire, devinez le mot qui correspond à chaque espace *(space)* dans le dialogue. Vous allez vérifier vos réponses plus tard.

MME PAPILLON Oui, Mademoiselle Gagner. C'est (1) _____. Une (2) _____. (3) _____ était encore jeune.

CLAIRE Pardon? Mais qu'est-ce qui s'est passé *(happened)*?

MME PAPILLON Ah, ma pauvre petite. J'ai une (4) _____ nouvelle à vous annoncer. Votre (5) _____ est (6) _____.

1. a. merveilleux	b. terrible		**4.** a. bonnes	b. mauvaise	
2. a. comédie	b. tragédie		**5.** a. oncle	b. mère	
3. a. Il	b. Elle		**6.** a. mort	b. morte	

▶ **Regarder la séquence**

Vous allez regarder la Séquence 5 du film *Liaisons*. Vérifiez vos réponses à l'Activité B et à l'Activité C.

Après le visionnage

ACTIVITÉ **D** **L'avez-vous compris?** Complétez les phrases.

1. Alexis dit à Claire qu'il espère qu'elle pourra *(will be able to)* _____ quelqu'un.
   a. aimer   b. pardonner à

2. Dans l'église, Claire voit _____ qui pleurait.
   a. une petite fille   b. une vieille dame

3. Mme Papillon dit à Claire qu'elle a trouvé son oncle dans _____.
   a. un restaurant vers 3h00   b. son appartement vers 3h00.

> **Note** de **grammaire**
> **Pleurer** *(to cry)* is a regular -**er** verb.

ACTIVITÉ **E** **Utilisez le contexte** Regardez bien les mots en caractères gras *(boldface)* et répondez aux questions.

AGENT DE POLICE Ça va, madame? Vous êtes **blessée**?

CLAIRE Non. Ça va.

AGENT DE POLICE Vous êtes sûre? Je vous **emmène** à l'hôpital?

1. L'adjectif **blessée** veut dire *(means)...*   a. *blessed*   b. *hurt*
2. Le verbe **emmener** veut dire...   a. *to take (someone) somewhere*   b. *to emulate*

ACTIVITÉ **F** **Une scène mystérieuse**

Étape 1. Dans cette séquence, il y avait une scène mystérieuse dans une église. Faites une liste des détails de cette scène dont *(that)* vous vous souvenez *(you remember)*.

 Étape 2. Montrez votre liste à un(e) partenaire. Avez-vous écrit les mêmes choses? Quelles questions est-ce qu'on peut poser à propos de cette scène?

Wynne Wong

Liaisons avec la culture

Les plaines d'Abraham: parc historique

Le 13 septembre 1759, l'armée française menée par le Général Montcalm a perdu la Nouvelle-France face à l'armée anglaise sur *Les plaines d'Abraham*. Cette bataille marque le début de la conquête britannique et la fin du régime français en Nouvelle-France. Aujourd'hui, *Les plaines d'Abraham* est un parc d'une valeur inestimable au cœur de la ville de Québec.

LIAISONS
CULTURELLES

L'expression culturelle

OUTILS DE LECTURE
Reading first without stopping

It can be helpful to read a text once through first without stopping, especially if it's a shorter text. Reading without stopping can allow you to isolate key vocabulary and help you identify main ideas. Rather than concentrating on what you're missing, keep reading until the end. Then, think about the text as a whole before reading it a second time.

1. Read the text **La bande dessinée franco-belge** once through without stopping. Then make a list of any repeating key vocabulary you notice and any main ideas you gather.

2. Share your list with a partner. Based on what he/she noticed, what other key vocabulary and main ideas will you look for the second time you read the text?

La bande dessinée franco-belge

La bande dessinée est souvent appelée le «neuvième art» en Belgique et à travers le monde francophone. C'est une forme d'expression artistique populaire, tout comme le cinéma ou la chanson. La bande dessinée (la «BD» ou «bédé») a acquis° dans le monde francophone un statut culturel qui lui est spécifique et qui est différent de celui des *comics strips* aux États-Unis. Les albums de BD sont souvent appréciés des adultes, et certains auteurs de BD sont même plus connus que les romanciers°. Les BD sont donc similaires aux *graphic novels*, qui peuvent être l'objet de critiques comme les romans. La BD franco-belge est sans aucun doute la BD la plus célèbre avec des personnages mondialement connus, comme Tintin ou Astérix.

a acquis *has acquired, taken on* **romanciers** *novelists*

© David Crausby / Alamy

Vrai ou faux?

1. La bande dessinée est une forme d'art en France et en Belgique. V / F

2. Ce sont seulement les enfants qui lisent les BD. V / F

3. Quelques personnages de la BD franco-belge sont mondialement connus. V / F

© Caroline Penn/Historical/Corbis

Un cinéaste sénégalais: Ousmane Sembène

Voici un des plus grands cinéastes° du cinéma africain. Ousmane Sembène (1923–2007) a acquis à travers ses films et ses romans un statut exceptionnel dans le patrimoine° culturel du Sénégal moderne. En 1966, il a réalisé le premier long-métrage° de l'Afrique sub-saharienne, un film qui s'appelle *La Noire de...* Dans son œuvre cinématographique, il traite souvent de sujets difficiles, comme la critique de la colonisation française, certains aspects de la société sénégalaise et la condition des femmes au Sénégal.

cinéastes *filmmakers* **patrimoine** *heritage*
long-métrage *full-length film*

Compréhension

1. Ousmane Sembène est un réalisateur _____.
   a. typique   b. important

2. *La Noire de...* est le _____ long-métrage de l'Afrique sub-saharienne.
   a. premier   b. dernier

3. Dans son œuvre, Sembène traite de sujets _____.
   a. comiques   b. sérieux

La Comédie-Française

En France, la Comédie-Française, fondée en 1680 à Paris, est le théâtre national le plus ancien et le seul° avec une troupe° permanente de comédiens°. C'est pourquoi on l'appelle aussi le Théâtre-Français ou le théâtre de la République. La Comédie-Française est le plus souvent associée au dramaturge° français Molière (1622–1673). Même si on a tendance à considérer la Comédie-Française comme «la maison de Molière»,

© Philippe Lavieille/Maxppp/Landov

la troupe d'aujourd'hui monte° beaucoup de pièces de théâtre variées. Située dans le 1er arrondissement dans la salle Richelieu à côté du Palais Royal, la troupe a un répertoire de plus de 3 000 pièces de théâtre à sa disposition.

le seul *the only one* **troupe** *theater company, troop* **comédiens** *stage actors* **dramaturge** *playwright* **monte** *puts on*

Vrai ou faux?

1. La Comédie-Française est une nouvelle salle de théâtre à Paris. V / F
2. La troupe de la Comédie-Française est composée d'acteurs intérimaires. V / F
3. La Comédie-Française a un répertoire de pièces de théâtre très limité. V / F

© Toby Adamson/ZUMApress/Newscom

Un héritage culturel: la Louisiane et sa musique

La Louisiane est célèbre pour beaucoup de choses mais c'est peut-être sa musique qu'on apprécie le plus. La musique de la Louisiane est très variée. Dans le sud, il y a la musique cadienne°, la musique créole, le *swamp blues* et le zydeco. Dans le nord, on entend beaucoup de musique du style country ou country rock. Mais, c'est à La Nouvelle-Orléans qu'on trouve la plus grande variété de musique louisianaise. On peut y entendre du jazz *Dixieland* et du blues aux influences afroantillaises mais aussi de la musique *gospel*, du rap et du *heavy metal*. On note aussi toujours la présence de la langue française dans la musique louisianaise, comme par exemple dans la musique du groupe Beausoleil.

cadienne *Cajun*

Vrai ou faux?

1. La musique de la Louisiane est très diverse. V / F
2. C'est dans le nord qu'on entend du zydeco. V / F
3. On peut entendre du *heavy metal* à La Nouvelle-Orléans. V / F
4. Toutes les chansons louisianaises sont en anglais. V / F

▶ LIAISONS CULTURELLES

les années 80

Use **iLrn** to access the video **La musique** to learn more about traditional and modern French music. Be prepared to answer the question **Que pensez-vous de la musique francophone?** Share your responses with your classmates in **Share It!**

PARTIE 1 9–11

LES ARTS VISUELS

les beaux-arts *(m.)*	*fine arts*
un chef-d'œuvre	*masterpiece*
un dessin	*drawing*
une nature morte	*still life*
une œuvre d'art	*work of art*
un paysage	*landscape*
une photographie / une photo	*photograph*
le pop art	*pop art*
un portrait	*portrait*
une sculpture	*sculpture*
un tableau	*painting*
une tapisserie	*tapestry*

LES ARTISTES

un(e) artiste	*artist*
un(e) peintre	*painter*
un(e) photographe	*photographer*
un sculpteur / une sculptrice	*sculptor*

NOMS

une exposition	*exhibition*
une galerie d'art	*art gallery*
le sujet	*subject*
le style	*style*

VERBES

faire de la peinture	*to paint*
faire de la sculpture	*to sculpt*
photographier	*to photograph*

ADJECTIFS

abstrait(e)	*abstract*
cubiste	*cubist*
impressionniste	*impressionist*
moderne	*modern*
sombre	*somber, dark*
surréaliste	*surrealist*
vif / vive	*bright, lively, colorful*

PARTIE 2 9–12

LES ARTS DU THÉÂTRE ET DU SPECTACLE

un ballet	*ballet*
une chanson	*song*
un chœur, une chorale	*choir*
une comédie musicale	*musical (stage, film)*
un compositeur / une femme compositeur / une compositrice	*composer*
un concert	*concert*
un danseur / une danseuse	*dancer*
un opéra	*opera*
un orchestre	*orchestra*
une pièce de théâtre	*play*
un spectacle	*show, performance*

LES ARTS DE LA PAGE

un auteur / une femme auteur	*author*
un conte (de fées)	*tale (fairytale)*
un(e) critique	*reviewer, critic*
une critique	*review, critique*
le début	*beginning*
la fin	*end, ending*
un genre	*genre*

LES GENRES DE MUSIQUE

le blues / le R'n'B	*blues, R&B*
le hip-hop	*hip-hop*
le jazz	*jazz*
la musique alternative	*alternative*
la musique classique	*classical*
la (musique) country	*country*
la musique folk (contemporaine) / le folk	*folk*
les musiques du monde	*world music*
la musique new age	*new age music*
la pop	*pop*
le rap	*rap*
le rock	*rock*

ADJECTIFS

littéraire	*literary*
poétique	*poetic*
récent(e)	*recent*

VERBES

applaudir	*to applaud*
publier	*to publish*
vivre	*to live*

PARTIE 3 9–13

LE CINÉMA

une comédie	*comedy*
un documentaire	*documentary*
un drame (psychologique)	*(psychological) drama*
un film d'action	*action film*
un film d'horreur	*horror film*
un film romantique	*romance film*
un film à suspense	*suspense film*
un film de science-fiction	*sci-fi film*
un policier	*crime / detective film*
un western	*western*

LA TÉLÉVISION

une causerie	*talk show*
un dessin animé / un film d'animation	*(animated) cartoon / animated film*
une émission	*broadcast; TV show*
une émission de téléachat	*shopping network show*
une émission de téléréalité	*reality TV show*
une émission de variétés	*variety show*
un feuilleton	*soap opera*
les informations / les infos (f.)	*news broadcast*
un jeu télévisé	*game show*
un match télévisé	*televised game*
les nouvelles (f.)	*news, news items*
une publicité / une pub	*commercial*
une série	*serial sitcom or TV drama*

NOMS

un personnage	*character*
un réalisateur / une réalisatrice	*director (TV or movie)*
un rôle	*role*

VERBES

croire	*to believe*
recevoir	*to receive*
revoir	*to see again*
voir	*to see*

LES PRONOMS DÉMONSTRATIFS

celui (m.)	*this one, that one*
ceux (m. pl.)	*these (ones), those (ones)*
celle (f.)	*this one, that one*
celles (f. pl.)	*these (ones), those (ones)*

Le cinéma francophone

Denys Arcand

Un des réalisateurs québécois les plus connus, Denys Arcand, a obtenu deux grands succès critiques et commerciaux avec *Le déclin de l'empire américain* (1986) et sa suite, filmée dix-huit ans plus tard, *Les invasions barbares* (2003). Ses autres films sont en général très enracinés° dans la réalité sociale du Québec moderne. L'œuvre° d'Arcand est un bon exemple de la réussite du cinéma québécois, le second cinéma francophone par le nombre de films produits. Il a travaillé avec beaucoup d'acteurs et d'actrices célèbres tels que Johanne Marie Tremblay (Simone Gagner) du film **Liaisons.**

© AP Images/Patrick Gardin

enracinés *rooted* **œuvre** *(artistic) work*

© Archives du 7eme Art/Photos 12/Alamy

Madame Brouette

Ce film sénégalais contemporain mais classique a été réalisé en 2002 par Moussa Sène Absa. L'histoire est située dans un quartier populaire de Dakar, la capitale. Construit autour d'une enquête policière sur un meurtre°, le film décrit la lutte quotidienne de Mati, une commerçante° qu'on appelle «Madame Brouette», pour gagner sa vie et assurer un avenir° à sa fille. Accompagné d'une très belle musique et d'images aux couleurs vives qui mélangent humour et critique sociale, ce film nous rappelle que le cinéma sénégalais ne se limite pas à l'œuvre d'Ousmane Sembène (1923–2007) et que c'est un cinéma riche et divers.

une enquête policière sur un meurtre *police murder investigation* **une commerçante** *shopkeeper* **un avenir** *future*

Les origines du cinéma

Il existe, depuis longtemps, un grand débat sur les origines du cinéma. Un groupe de spécialistes du cinéma dit que c'est Thomas Edison, aux États-Unis, qui a inventé le cinéma et un autre groupe dit que ce sont les frères Lumière, en France. En réalité, l'invention du cinéma doit ses origines à plusieurs bricoleurs° en Europe et aux États-Unis. Edison a été le premier à inventer *le kinétoscope*, une machine permettant le visionnement d'une œuvre photographique qui donne l'illusion du mouvement, mais ce sont les frères Lumière qui ont inventé *le cinématographe*, une caméra qui était aussi un projecteur. De plus, les frères Lumière ont été les premiers à penser à la projection de la pellicule photographique° (qu'ils ont aussi inventée) sur un écran devant un public.

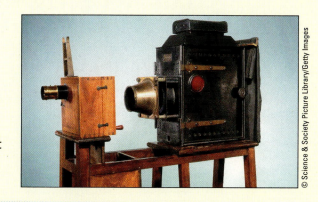

© Science & Society Picture Library/Getty Images

bricoleurs *tinkerers* **pellicule photographique** *film roll*

Les frères Dardenne

Les frères Jean-Pierre et Luc Dardenne ont largement contribué à faire connaître le cinéma franco-belge, qui a connu de grands succès au niveau international. Les deux frères belges travaillent toujours ensemble sur un film. Ils ont renouvelé le cinéma social, qui était autrefois° un élément caractéristique du cinéma français. Leurs films ont obtenu plusieurs prix au Festival de Cannes, le grand festival de cinéma qui a lieu en France chaque année en mai.

autrefois *formerly, in the past*

Merzak Allouache

Célèbre réalisateur émigré° d'origine algérienne qui tourne des films en France et en Algérie, Merzak Allouache a produit une œuvre variée (*Bab El-Oued City, Salut Cousin!, Chouchou, Bab el web*), avec des films aux dialogues à la fois° en arabe et en français. Observateur critique de la société algérienne et de la société française, Allouache a surtout réalisé des comédies acides qui jouent parfois sur les conflits et les influences réciproques entre les réalités culturelles en Algérie et en France.

émigré *emigrant* **à la fois** *at the same time*

Révision

1. Quel est le second cinéma francophone par le nombre de films produits?
2. Quel réalisateur est connu pour ses images aux couleurs vives?
3. Quels réalisateurs travaillent toujours ensemble sur un film?
4. Qui a inventé le cinématographe?
5. Quelles langues est-ce que Merzak Allouache utilise dans ses films?

▶ LIAISONS CULTURELLES

200 films produits par an

Use **iLrn™** to access the video **Le cinéma** to learn more about the Lumière brothers and cinema in France. Be prepared to answer the question **Alors, ce soir, vous regardez quoi?** Share your responses with your classmates in **Share It!**

Les **relations interpersonnelles**

En bref   In this chapter, you will:

- learn how to express how you feel

- learn negative and affirmative adverbs and pronouns

- talk about values, lifestyles, relationships, and personal characteristics

- learn about reflexive verbs like **s'aimer, se marier, se respecter,** and **se rappeler**

- learn about semi-vowels

- read about changing family structures and relationships in Togo

- write about relationships

You will also re-watch **SÉQUENCE 5: Une rencontre** of the film *Liaisons*.

Ressources

 audio   ▶ video   Share It!   iLrn™   http://www.cengagebrain.com

© Burke/Triolo Productions/Photolibrary/Getty Images

Les caractéristiques personnelles

Personal characteristics

une femme au foyer

un homme au foyer

les fanas de la santé

les retraités

les bourreaux de travail

les écologistes / les écolos

les membres de la jet-set

les accros du shopping

les babas cool / les hippies

Les modes *(m.)* **de vie**

Vocabulaire complémentaire

les célibataires *(m., f.) single people*
une mère active / un père actif *a working mom / a working dad*
une mère célibataire / un père célibataire *a single mother / a single father*

l'amitié *(f.) friendship*
l'amour *(m.) love*
le bonheur *happiness*
l'environnement *(m.) environment*
la fidélité / l'infidélité *(f.) loyalty / disloyalty*
la moralité *morality*
le prestige *prestige*
la spiritualité *spirituality*
le succès *success*

avare *miserly, stingy*
bavard(e) *talkative, gossipy*
bête *stupid, idiotic*
bien habillé(e) / mal habillé(e) *well-dressed / poorly-dressed*
égoïste *selfish*
fidèle / infidèle *loyal / disloyal*
gracieux / gracieuse *graceful, gracious*
jaloux / jalouse *jealous*
maladroit(e) *clumsy*
prétentieux / prétentieuse *pretentious*
simple *simple*

être bien dans sa peau *to have confidence in / to feel good about oneself*

10-1

ACTIVITÉ **A** **Antonymes** Choisissez l'antonyme de chaque adjectif mentionné.

1. a. beau
b. gracieux
c. difficile
d. égoïste

2. a. infidèle
b. prétentieux
c. grand
d. avare

3. a. intelligent
b. jaloux
c. idiot
d. vieux

4. a. jeune
b. bavard
c. difficile
d. fidèle

5. a. nouveau
b. facile
c. avare
d. mal habillé

6. a. fière
b. maladroite
c. meilleure
d. célèbre

7. a. brillant
b. nerveux
c. jaloux
d. délicieux

8. a. nombreuse
b. pessimiste
c. silencieuse
d. active

🔊 **ACTIVITÉ B** **Quelles valeurs?** Quelle valeur associez-vous à chaque mode
10-2 de vie mentionné?

Modèle: les babas cool   **l'amour, la paix, le bonheur**

1.   **2.**   **3.**   **4.**   **5.**   **6.**   **7.**   **8.**   **9.**   **10.**

👥 **ACTIVITÉ C** **À qui cela vous fait penser?**

Étape 1. À quelle personne connue est-ce que chaque mot de vocabulaire vous fait
penser? Partagez vos idées avec un(e) partenaire. Pensez-vous de la même manière?

1. intelligent	**7.** bête
2. prétentieuse	**8.** gracieux
3. infidèle	**9.** avoir beaucoup de succès
4. bavard	**10.** être bien habillé
5. jalouse	**11.** être bien dans sa peau
6. égoïste	**12.** avoir beaucoup de prestige

Étape 2. Quelles caractéristiques utiliseriez-vous pour décrire ces personnages du
film *Liaisons*?

1. Claire Gagner   **2.** Abia Ndono   **3.** Alexis Prévost

ACTIVITÉ D **Les priorités**

Étape 1. Classez (*Classify*) ces valeurs par ordre d'importance pour les personnes
suivantes.

l'amour	l'environnement	la famille	la spiritualité	le succès

Modèle: les fanas de la santé
**Pour les fanas de la santé, la spiritualité vient en premier, l'environnement
en deuxième, l'amour en troisième, la famille en quatrième et le succès en
cinquième.**

1. les pères actifs	**5.** les femmes au foyer
2. les mères célibataires	**6.** les bourreaux de travail
3. les retraités	**7.** les écologistes
4. les accros du shopping	**8.** les hommes au foyer

Étape 2. Classez les valeurs de l'Étape 1 par ordre d'importance pour vous. Y a-t-il
d'autres valeurs que vous voudriez ajouter (*add*)?

👥 **Étape 3.** Montrez vos réponses de l'Étape 1 et de l'Étape 2 à un(e) partenaire.
Décidez pour quel mode de vie votre partenaire est fait(e).

ACTIVITÉ E **Les stéréotypes** Quels sont les stéréotypes pour chacun *(each one)* de ces modes de vie?

Modèle: Les célébrités sont **prétentieuses et bien habillées. Elles apprécient la liberté.**

1. Les hommes au foyer sont _____.
2. Les membres de la jet-set sont _____.
3. Les mères actives sont _____.
4. Les écologistes sont _____.
5. Les célibataires sont _____.
6. Les pères célibataires sont _____.

ACTIVITÉ F **La question des caractéristiques** Comment considéreriez-vous ces caractéristiques?

	Toujours positif	Toujours négatif	Ça dépend.
1. être simple	_____	_____	_____
2. être bavard(e)	_____	_____	_____
3. être avare	_____	_____	_____
4. être bien dans sa peau	_____	_____	_____
5. être prétentieux / prétentieuse	_____	_____	_____

Si vous y allez

Si vous allez à Saint-Tropez en France, allez au Café Le Sénéquier sur le port pour regarder les gens passer, surtout des célébrités ou des membres de la jet-set!

ACTIVITÉ G **Les pages de Facebook** Préparez une description pour votre page d'accueil de Facebook.

Modèle: Je suis un jeune homme célibataire de 23 ans et un grand joueur de foot. L'amitié est très importante pour moi et je cherche des amis aussi passionnés par le foot que moi. Je déteste les gens prétentieux et je préfère vivre une vie active.

Les supermamans

Un mot sur la culture

Les modes de vie en transformation

En France, comme ailleurs, il y a une transformation constante des modes de vie. Prenons le cas *des femmes actives / des hommes actifs*. Dans le passé, les Français ne croyaient pas forcément à la possibilité d'avoir à la fois° une carrière professionnelle et une vie familiale. Aujourd'hui, on constate° une transformation dans le développement du mode de vie «actif»: on souhaite à la fois avoir une famille heureuse et une carrière réussie. Les médias en parlent assez souvent et on trouve de plus en plus de produits et de magazines qui expliquent comment réussir sa vie familiale et professionnelle.

à la fois *at the same time* **constate** *observes*

- Quelles transformations constatez-vous dans les modes de vie de votre culture?

Pour parler de nos rapports

Les verbes réfléchis

DU FILM *LIAISONS*

Un coup d'œil sur la grammaire

Claire et Alexis **se parlent** après leur rendez-vous.

Claire **se parle** après le départ d'Alexis.

1. What do you think the verb **se parlent** means in the left caption?
2. What do you think the verb **se parle** means in the right caption?

❖ A reflexive construction is one in which the subject and object of a verb are the same. In English, this is generally rendered with *-self / -selves.* Compare the following.

> I know myself. (*I* am both the subject and the object of *know.*)
> I know him. (*I* am the subject but someone else—a male—is the object.)

> They know themselves. (*They* is both the subject and the object of *know.*)
> They know him. (*They* is the subject but someone else is the object of *know.*)

❖ French uses reflexive pronouns for this kind of construction.

Je **me connais.**	*I know myself.*
Je le connais.	*I know him.*
Ils **se connaissent.**	*They know themselves.*
Ils le connaissent.	*They know him.*

❖ The reflexive pronouns are the same as direct object pronouns with the exception of the third-person which uses **se.**

je **me connais**	nous **nous connaissons**
tu **te connais**	vous **vous connaissez**
il/elle/on **se connaît**	ils/elles **se connaissent**

❖ Just about any verb that can take a direct object can be reflexive, including **aimer / s'aimer, connaître / se connaître, détester / se détester, parler / se parler, regarder / se regarder,** and **voir / se voir.**

When the subject and object of a verb are plural and are the same, the English equivalent can be *-selves* or *each other*. Context determines which is meant.

Ils **se voient** (dans le miroir).	*They **see themselves** (in the mirror).*
Ils **se voient** tous les jours.	*They **see each other** everyday.*
Elles **se connaissent** bien.	*They **know themselves** well.*
Elles sont amies et **se connaissent** bien.	*They are friends and **know each other** well.*

Some verbs in French use reflexive pronouns, but do not normally translate into English as *-self / -selves* or *each other*. One group deals with emotions and psychological states. When used reflexively, the English translation often uses *get / become* + adjective.

s'amuser	*to have a good time*	**se fâcher**	*to get angry*
s'ennuyer	*to get bored*	**s'inquiéter**	*to worry*
s'énerver	*to get upset*	**se sentir**	*to feel*

Note de **grammaire**
S'ennuyer is a spelling-changing verb like **payer**: je m'ennuie, nous nous ennuyons. **S'inquiéter** is like **espérer**: je m'inquiète, nous nous inquiétons.

Another group of verbs almost never occurs without the reflexive pronoun. You have to memorize their meanings and their typical English translations.

se disputer	*to argue*	**se rendre compte** (**que / de**)	*to realize*
se marier	*to get married*	**se souvenir de**	*to remember*

Jean et Luce **se marient**.	*Jean and Luce **are getting married**.*
Je **me marie** aujourd'hui.	*I'm **getting married** today.*
Est-ce que Yves et Guy **se disputent** souvent?	*Do Yves and Guy **argue** often?*
Nous **nous disputons** avec nos voisins.	*We **argue** with our neighbors.*

Note de **grammaire**
Se souvenir is conjugated like **venir** (je me souviens, nous nous souvenons, ils se souviennent).

The English equivalent of some French verbs may change depending on whether the verb uses a reflexive pronoun or not. This is because English does not have this construction.

aller / s'en aller	*to go / to leave, to go away*
demander / se demander	*to ask / to wonder*
entendre / s'entendre	*to hear / to get along*
mettre / se mettre (à)	*to put / to begin (to)*
quitter / se quitter	*to leave / to break up*
trouver / se trouver	*to find / to be located*

Je **m'en vais** ce soir.	*I'm **going away** tonight.*
Est-ce que tu **te demandes** pourquoi il est triste?	*Are you **wondering** why he is sad?*

Note de **grammaire**
You will learn more reflexive verbs in **Vocabulaire 2**.

In the infinitive, the reflexive pronoun precedes the infinitive and agrees with the subject of the verb. Place **ne** before the reflexive pronoun and **pas** after the verb in negative constructions.

Nous allons **nous marier** demain.	*We are getting married tomorrow.*
Ils aimeraient bien **s'entendre**.	*They would like to get along (with each other).*
Vous **ne vous détestez pas**.	*You don't hate each other.*

ACTIVITÉ H Les couples À votre avis, les phrases suivantes décrivent quels types de couple?

1. Ils ne **se voient** pas souvent.
   a. une femme au foyer et un bourreau de travail
   b. un mari et une femme retraités

2. Ils **se connaissent** bien.
   a. des jeunes mariés
   b. un mari et une femme retraités

3. Ils **se parlent** souvent.
   a. un homme au foyer et une femme jet-set
   b. un homme et une femme au foyer

4. Ils **se disputent** souvent.
   a. une femme jet-set et un baba cool
   b. un baba cool et une écologiste

ACTIVITÉ I Les valeurs et les modes de vie Choisissez un verbe pour chaque phrase.

1. Les gens bavards ____ constamment.	a. se connaissent	b. se parlent
2. Je ____ quand je suis avec des gens infidèles.	a. m'amuse	b. me fâche
3. Un bourreau de travail ____ sans *(without)* travail.	a. se sent	b. s'ennuie
4. Les parents ____ les anniversaires de leurs enfants.	a. se rappellent	b. se sentent
5. Je ____ que la famille est importante.	a. me rends compte	b. m'énerve
6. Un bourreau de travail ____ à travailler à 7h00.	a. se met	b. met
7. Les hommes célibataires ____ ma fille belle.	a. se trouvent	b. trouvent
8. Les couples infidèles ____ souvent.	a. se quittent	b. quittent
9. Les couples fidèles ____ bien.	a. s'entendent	b. entendent
10. On ____ aux employés d'être bien habillés.	a. se demande	b. demande

ACTIVITÉ J Les gens bavards au Château Frontenac Les clients du Château Frontenac se parlent au bar. Choisissez le sujet de chaque verbe.

1. ____ **me souviens de** son premier mari.	a. Je	b. Caroline
2. ____ **se voient** souvent.	a. Mon copain	b. Mes enfants
3. ____ **nous disputons** parfois.	a. Mon mari et moi, nous	b. Mes voisins
4. ____ **s'amuse** avec sa copine.	a. Nous	b. Mon neveu
5. ____ **te maries** avec Mustapha?	a. Caroline	b. Tu
6. ____ ne **vous sentez** pas bien? Buvez du thé.	a. Vous	b. Vos enfants
7. ____ **me demande** si mon voisin est infidèle.	a. Je	b. Mes amis
8. ____ **s'énerve** parce que son copain est jaloux.	a. Tu	b. Ma fille

❖ **Et vous?** Vous êtes bavard(e)?

Liaisons musicales

© Michel krakowski/Afp/Getty Images

Ancien participant de l'émission de télé *Star Academy,* Patxi Garat est un auteur-compositeur-interprète *(singer-songwriter)* du pays basque français. Connu maintenant sous le nom de Patxi, il a sorti la chanson *S'embrasser* en 2006. Cherchez les paroles de cette chanson. Qu'est-ce qu'ils pourraient faire ensemble?

ACTIVITÉ K Abia et Nadia Abia du film *Liaisons* et sa sœur Nadia se parlent. Complétez les phrases avec la forme appropriée du verbe qui convient.

NADIA Abia, est-il difficile d'être célibataire? Je (1) _____ souvent pour toi.

    a. s'énerver   b. s'inquiéter   c. se disputer   d. se souvenir

NADIA Est-ce que tu (2) _____ seule *(lonely)*, Abia?

    a. s'ennuyer   b. se fâcher   c. se sentir   d. s'entendre

ABIA Mais non! J'ai de bons amis comme Claire et nous (3) _____ souvent.

    a. s'amuser   b. s'ennuyer   c. s'énerver   d. se fâcher

NADIA Mais tu ne veux pas trouver un copain? Est-ce que tu veux (4) _____ un jour?

    a. s'aimer   b. se disputer   c. se quitter   d. se marier

ABIA Si, mais c'est difficile. Je (5) _____ quand je parle avec des hommes égoïstes.

    a. se fâcher   b. se sentir   c. se trouver   d. s'en aller

NADIA Je comprends. Ce n'est pas toujours facile de (6) _____ la bonne personne.

    a. trouver   b. se trouver   c. entendre   d. s'entendre

ABIA C'est vrai que parfois je (7) _____ le week-end quand je ne sors pas.

    a. s'en aller   b. s'ennuyer   c. se trouver   d. se souvenir

ABIA Mais je (8) _____ aujourd'hui qu'il est plus important d'être bien dans sa peau.

    a. se sentir   b. s'énerver   c. s'inquiéter   d. se rendre compte

ABIA Et toi Nadia, est-ce que tu (9) _____ parfois si tu préférerais être célibataire?

    a. demander   b. se demander   c. aller   d. s'en aller

NADIA Non, jamais. François et moi, nous (10) _____ très bien. Je l'adore.

    a. mettre   b. se mettre   c. entendre   d. s'entendre

NADIA Je (11) _____ de la naissance de Patrick. Ma famille est ma vie.

    a. se souvenir   b. se sentir   c. se fâcher   d. se demander

ABIA Bon! Je vais (12) _____ à chercher l'homme de ma vie aujourd'hui!

    a. mettre   b. se mettre   c. demander   d. se demander

Et vous? Préférez-vous être célibataire ou en couple?

ACTIVITÉ L Vos sentiments

Étape 1. Comment compléteriez-vous les phrases suivantes?

Modèle: Je m'amuse quand **je joue avec mon chien.**

1. Je m'amuse quand _____.
2. Je m'ennuie quand _____.
3. Je m'énerve quand _____.
4. Je me fâche quand _____.
5. Je m'inquiète quand _____.
6. Je me sens triste quand _____.

Étape 2. Posez les questions à un(e) partenaire.

Modèle: É1: **Quand est-ce que tu t'amuses?**
É2: **Je m'amuse quand je joue avec mon chien. Et toi?**
É1: **Moi, je m'amuse quand mes parents me rendent visite.**

Étape 3. Est-ce que vous et votre partenaire avez des réponses qui sont similaires? Si oui, lesquelles?

Modèle: **Mon partenaire et moi, nous nous fâchons quand nous parlons avec des gens bêtes.**

ACTIVITÉ M Les célébrités

Étape 1. Quelle personne célèbre associez-vous à chaque description suivante?

Modèle: Il/Elle s'aime beaucoup. **Paris Hilton s'aime beaucoup.**

1. Il/Elle se regarde souvent dans le miroir.
2. Il/Elle se connaît bien.
3. Il/Elle s'aime beaucoup.
4. Il/Elle ne s'aime pas.
5. Il/Elle ne se connaît pas bien.
6. Il/Elle se parle parfois.

Étape 2. Quelles descriptions de l'Étape 1 vous décrivent aussi?

Modèle: **Je me regarde souvent dans le miroir aussi. Je me connais bien.**

Étape 3. Demandez à un(e) partenaire si les descriptions de l'Étape 1 le/la décrivent.

Modèle: É1: **Est-ce que tu te regardes souvent dans le miroir?**
É2: **Non, je ne me regarde pas souvent dans le miroir.**

Conclusion Est-ce que votre partenaire et vous êtes similaires ou différent(e)s?

ACTIVITÉ N Dans votre famille

Étape 1. Répondez aux questions au sujet des membres de votre famille.

Modèle: Quelles personnes s'aiment? **Mon frère et moi, nous nous aimons beaucoup.**

1. Quelles personnes s'aiment beaucoup?
2. ... se disputent souvent?
3. ... se voient souvent?
4. ... se connaissent bien?
5. ... se parlent souvent?
6. ... s'entendent bien?
7. ... se fâchent parfois?
8. ... se détestent parfois?
9. ... ne se parlent pas souvent?
10. ... se voient rarement?

Étape 2. Posez les questions à un(e) partenaire.

Modèle: É1: **Quelles personnes dans ta famille s'aiment beaucoup?**
É2: **Mes grands-parents s'aiment beaucoup.**

Étape 3. Écrivez trois choses que vous avez apprises au sujet de *(about)* votre partenaire.

Modèle: **Ses sœurs s'aiment beaucoup. Sa tante et sa mère se disputent souvent. Elles ne s'entendent pas bien.**

Pour aller plus loin
Les verbes réfléchis et les questions

To ask a question using inversion with a reflexive verb, invert the verb and the subject pronoun and place the reflexive pronoun before it.

Nicole **se marie-t-elle** bientôt?	*Is Nicole getting married soon?*
Pourquoi **vous fâchez-vous**?	*Why are you getting angry?*

However, in spoken French, **est-ce que** and intonation are more frequently used.

Nicole **se marie** bientôt?	Pourquoi **est-ce que** vous **vous fâchez**?

Essayez! Posez les questions suivantes à votre professeur avec l'inversion.

Modèle: (se disputer) avec les voisins **Vous disputez-vous avec vos voisins?**

1. (s'amuser) en cours de français
2. (s'entendre) bien avec les voisins

OUI, JE PEUX!
Here are two "can do statements" for you to check your progress so far. Look at each statement and rate yourself on how well you think you can perform the task. Then verify your ability with a partner. How did you do?

1. **"I can say what lifestyle best characterizes me and explain why, and I can ask someone else to explain what lifestyle best characterizes him/her."**

   I can perform this function
   ☐ with ease
   ☐ with some difficulty
   ☐ not at all

2. **"I can say in what situations I have a good time and when I get bored, and I can ask someone else when he/she has a good time and gets bored to find out if we are similar."**

   I can perform this function
   ☐ with ease
   ☐ with some difficulty
   ☐ not at all

iLrn™

Are you looking for more practice? You can find it in **iLrn**.

VOCABULAIRE 2

Les **rapports personnels**

Personal relationships

Un couple s'installe dans sa nouvelle maison. (s'installer dans / à)

Ils se détendent dans le salon. (se détendre)

Elle se dépêche parce qu'elle est en retard. (se dépêcher)

Il se promène avec son chien dans le parc. (se promener)

Ils s'arrêtent. (s'arrêter)

Ils s'embrassent. (s'embrasser)

Ils se perdent parce que l'homme ne veut pas regarder le plan. (se perdre)

Je suis désolé.

Non, je suis désolée.

Ils s'excusent. (s'excuser)

Ils se réconcilient. (se réconcilier)

La vie d'un jeune couple

Vocabulaire complémentaire

s'appeler *to be named / called*

se fiancer *to get engaged*

s'intéresser (à) *to be interested (in)*

se méfier (de) *to be suspicious (of)*

s'occuper (de) *to take care (of)*

se passer *to happen*

se rappeler *to remember*

se reposer *to rest*

se téléphoner *to téléphone*

se tromper (de) *to be mistaken (about)*

À mon (votre) avis *In my (your) opinion*

- **S'appeler, se rappeler,** and **se promener** are spelling-change verbs.

s'appeler	je m'appelle, nous nous appelons
se rappeler (like **s'appeler**)	je me rappelle, nous nous rappelons
se promener (like **acheter**)	je me promène, nous nous promenons

- **Se rappeler** means approximately the same thing as **se souvenir,** and many people use them interchangeably in everyday speech. However, **se rappeler** can be used more often with facts that one recalls and **se souvenir** with memories one remembers. The important difference is grammatical: **on se rappelle quelque chose** *but* **on se souvient <u>de</u> quelque chose.**

- Note the meaning of these verbs when they are used reflexively and non-reflexively.

s'appeler	*to be named / called*
se rappeler	*to remember*
se tromper (de)	*to be mistaken (about)*
appeler	*to call*
rappeler	*to call back*
tromper	*to cheat on (someone)*

Si vous y allez

© Robert Chiasson/All Canada Photos/Getty Images

Si vous allez à Québec, visitez la promenade des Gouverneurs. La construction de ces planches *(boardwalk)* a débuté en 1958 pour commémorer le 350e anniversaire de la fondation de Québec par Samuel de Champlain en 1608. 200 000 personnes empruntent chaque année la promenade des Gouverneurs. La vue est vraiment spectaculaire!

Un mot sur la langue

Mon chum et ma blonde

Dans le français parlé au Québec, on peut aussi dire **mon chum** pour **mon petit ami/mon copain** et **ma blonde** pour **ma petite amie/ma copine.**

Luc se promène avec **sa blonde.**

Carole se fiance avec **son chum.**

- Comment s'appelle votre chum ou votre blonde?

ACTIVITÉ A Qui l'a dit? Vous vous rappelez qui a dit les phrases suivantes dans le film *Liaisons*?

1. De temps en temps, il **s'occupe** des réservations spéciales.
    a. Abia   b. Claire   c. Alexis   d. Réceptionniste

2. La chambre 315, c'est la suite présidentielle. Elle **se trouve** au 14ᵉ étage…
    a. Abia   b. Claire   c. Alexis   d. Réceptionniste

3. Quand ma mère est morte, il fallait qu'on **s'occupe de** ses affaires.
    a. Abia   b. Claire   c. Alexis   d. Concierge

4. Vous êtes à Québec pour **vous occuper d'**affaires de famille.
    a. Abia   b. Claire   c. Alexis   d. Concierge

5. C'est l'homme qui m'a donné l'enveloppe avec la réservation au Frontenac. Il **s'appelle** Tremblay.
    a. Abia   b. Claire   c. Alexis   d. Robert

6. Je dois **m'en aller**. J'ai beaucoup de choses à faire très tôt demain.
    a. Abia   b. Claire   c. Alexis   d. Concierge

7. Pas de problème. Je vais **m'occuper** de Robert.
    a. Abia   b. Claire   c. Alexis   d. Concierge

8. Je **me rappelle** quand Michel parlait de vous.
    a. Abia   b. Claire   c. Alexis   d. Mme Papillon

ACTIVITÉ B Quelqu'un qui est… Choisissez un verbe pour chaque phrase.

1. Quelqu'un qui est fana de la santé _____ les conseils de son entraîneur *(trainer)*.
    a. se promène   b. se rappelle   c. se fiance   d. se trompe

2. Quelqu'un qui est bourreau de travail ne _____ pas assez.
    a. se passe   b. se réconcilie   c. s'intéresse   d. se détend

3. Quelqu'un qui est célèbre _____ souvent des paparazzi.
    a. se dépêche   b. se promène   c. se méfie   d. se passe

4. Une mère célibataire _____ de ses enfants.
    a. s'occupe   b. s'arrête   c. se téléphone   d. se repose

5. Les retraités _____ plus que les bourreaux de travail.
    a. se trompent   b. se reposent   c. s'installent   d. se passent

6. Les écologistes _____ à l'environnement.
    a. s'intéressent   b. s'embrassent   c. s'appellent   d. se détendent

7. Les gens bavards ne _____ jamais de bavarder *(to gossip)*.
    a. se méfient   b. se rappellent   c. s'arrêtent   d. se réconcilient

8. Les membres de la jet-set _____ toujours dans une suite d'un bel hôtel en vacances.
    a. s'installent   b. s'occupent   c. se méfient   d. se trompent

ACTIVITÉ C La famille d'Abia

Étape 1. Abia décrit ce que les membres de sa famille font ou disent pendant la fête d'anniversaire de sa nièce Aude. Choisissez un verbe pour chaque phrase.

1. Aude _____ son chat Fifi.
   a. appelle   b. s'appelle

2. Xavier _____ en route pour la fête.
   a. perd   b. se perd

3. Papa et l'oncle Kofi _____ leurs clés *(keys)*.
   a. perdent   b. se perdent

4. Aude demande à Patrick «Qu'est-ce qui _____?»
   a. passe   b. se passe

5. Keesha annonce que Jerome va nous _____ plus tard.
   a. rappeler   b. se rappeler

6. Adelai dit qu'il pense que son voisin _____ sa femme.
   a. trompe   b. se trompe

7. Abia pense que son père _____ parce que le voisin est un homme fidèle.
   a. trompe   b. se trompe

Étape 2. Et vous? Complétez les phrases.

1. Je m'appelle _____.
2. Je perds souvent _____.
3. Je me perds parfois _____.
4. Je me rappelle _____.

ACTIVITÉ D L'ami de Robert Levesque Robert, le patron de Claire dans le film *Liaisons* parle de son ami Yves. Complétez les phrases avec la forme appropriée des verbes qui conviennent.

1. Mon ami Yves _____ à Montréal. Il est vendeur dans une boutique.
   a. se passer   b. se dépêcher   c. se rappeler   d. s'installer

2. Nous sommes de bons amis. Nous _____ au parc Lafontaine le week-end.
   a. se promener   b. se tromper   c. se dépêcher   d. se passer

3. Yves _____ de sa sœur Sarah qui a 15 ans.
   a. s'occuper   b. se téléphoner   c. s'arrêter   d. se reposer

4. Ce soir, nous _____ parce que nous allons à un concert.
   a. s'intéresser   b. se passer   c. s'occuper   d. se dépêcher

5. Je _____ souvent donc il faut partir très tôt.
   a. se fiancer   b. se méfier   c. se perdre   d. s'excuser

6. Yves _____ souvent d'adresse aussi.
   a. s'appeler   b. s'intéresser   c. s'embrasser   d. se tromper

7. Mais ce soir on n'a pas besoin de _____ pour demander notre chemin *(to ask for directions)*.
   a. se méfier   b. s'arrêter   c. se tromper   d. se passer

8. Nous arrivons au concert. Nous _____ en écoutant *(while listening)* la musique.
   a. se détendre   b. se fiancer   c. s'excuser   d. s'installer

❖ **Et vous?** Est-ce que vous vous perdez facilement?

PARTIE 2 VOCABULAIRE 2

ACTIVITÉ E Questionnaire: Mode de vie

Étape 1. Répondez aux questions suivantes.

	Oui	Non
1. Est-ce que vous vous méfiez de l'amitié ou de l'amour?	_____	_____
2. Est-ce que vous vous occupez de votre santé?	_____	_____
3. Est-ce que vous vous intéressez plus au travail qu'aux vacances?	_____	_____
4. Est-ce que vous vous rappelez toujours qu'il faut économiser de l'énergie?	_____	_____
5. Est-ce que vous vous intéressez à l'amour?	_____	_____
6. Est-ce que vous vous reposez souvent?	_____	_____

Étape 2. Posez les questions de l'Étape 1 à un(e) partenaire. Notez ses réponses.

Modèle: **Est-ce que tu te méfies de l'amitié ou de l'amour?**

Étape 3. À partir de vos réponses aux questions de l'Étape 1 et des réponses de votre partenaire aux questions de l'Étape 2, pour quel(s) mode(s) de vie êtes-vous fait(e)s?

ACTIVITÉ F Interview avec Michel Cymes et Marina Carrère d'Encausse Michel Cymes et Marina Carrère d'Encausse sont les présentateurs du *Magazine de la santé* sur la chaîne *(channel)* de télévision France 5. Voici un extrait d'une interview avec Audrey Aveaux, fana de la santé, diététicienne et auteur célèbre de livres de cuisine. Inventez une réponse logique pour chaque question.

Modèle: Question: À votre avis, on doit se méfier des matières grasses?
Réponse: **Oui, il faut arrêter de manger des matières grasses et du sucre.**

1. Question: Selon vous, il faut manger des produits bio. Est-ce que vous vous méfiez des produits non biologiques?

Réponse: _____

2. Question: À votre avis, est-ce qu'on peut trop se reposer?

Réponse: _____

3. Question: Est-ce que vos ami(e)s s'occupent de leur santé comme vous?

Réponse: _____

4. Question: À quoi est-ce que vous allez vous intéresser l'année prochaine?

Réponse: _____

Et vous? Répondez aux questions.

1. Est-ce que vous vous méfiez des produits non biologiques?

Réponse: _____

2. Est-ce que vous vous reposez assez?

Réponse: _____

3. Est-ce que vous vous occupez bien de votre santé?

Réponse: _____

ACTIVITÉ G **Sondage: À propos de la communication en public**

Posez les questions suivantes à trois étudiants pour découvrir leurs opinions.

1. Que pensez-vous des gens qui s'embrassent en public?

2. Que pensez-vous des gens qui se fiancent en public?

3. Que pensez-vous des gens qui se disputent en public?

4. Selon vous, est-ce qu'on devrait s'excuser en public?

5. À votre avis, est-ce qu'on devrait se réconcilier en public?

Un mot sur la langue

C'est le fun!

Une expression populaire qu'on entend souvent au Québec est **C'est le fun!** En français standard, cette expression veut dire **C'est amusant!** ou **C'est génial!** *(That's great!)* Les Québécois disent parfois aussi **J'ai du fun** pour **Je m'amuse bien.** Donc, **avoir du fun** est un peu comme le verbe **s'amuser** en français standard.

J'ai du fun chez toi!	Je **m'amuse** chez toi!
On va **avoir du fun** ce soir!	On va **s'amuser** ce soir!
C'est le fun d'avoir vos amis ici.	**C'est amusant** d'avoir vos amis ici.
Le Carnaval de Québec, **c'est le fun**!	Le Carnaval de Québec, **c'est amusant**!

• Êtes-vous d'accord avec cette phrase? **Apprendre le français, c'est le fun!**

Un mot sur la culture

L'espace privé et l'espace public en France

En Amérique du Nord, quand on rencontre une personne pour la première fois, on a l'habitude de lui poser des questions telles que «Comment vous appelez-vous?» ou «Qu'est-ce que vous faites dans la vie?». Cependant, si vous posez ces mêmes° questions en France, on va vous trouver impoli(e). Les Français ont une conception de l'espace° privé et de l'espace public qui est différente de celle des Américains. En France, le nom de quelqu'un ainsi que° sa profession appartiennent° à l'espace privé. Les Français se demandent souvent pourquoi les Américains s'intéressent tellement° à la vie privée des gens, surtout la vie privée des hommes et des femmes politiques. Par contre°, c'est tout à fait° normal pour les Français d'exprimer° leurs sentiments ou de se montrer affectueux en public. On peut aussi voir les Français se disputer et s'embrasser en public.

mêmes *same* **l'espace** *space* **ainsi que** *as well as* **appartiennent** *belong* **tellement** *so much* **Par contre** *On the contrary* **tout à fait** *entirely* **exprimer** *to express*

• Posez-vous souvent la question suivante?: «Qu'est-ce que vous faites dans la vie?»

Pour parler du passé

Les verbes réfléchis au passé composé

DU FILM *LIAISONS*

Un coup d'œil sur la grammaire

Look at these photos from the film *Liaisons* and their captions.

CLAIRE Merci, Alexis. Je **me suis bien amusée** aujourd'hui.

CLAIRE Pardon? Mais qu'est-ce qui **s'est passé**?

1. What two reflexive verbs do you recognize in the two photo captions?
2. Is the auxiliary verb **avoir** or **être** used in the photo captions?
3. Why is there an **e** at the end of **amusée** in the left caption?

❖ Reflexive verbs always take **être** in the **passé composé.** The reflexive pronoun goes before the verb **être** and there is usually agreement between the past participle and the subject pronoun.

Ils **se sont excusés.**	*They apologized.*
Nous **nous sommes occupés** du problème.	*We took care of the problem.*
Vous **vous êtes mariés** en 2002.	*You got married in 2002.*
Elle **s'est mise à** faire ses devoirs.	*She began to do her homework.*

❖ The past participle *does not* agree with the subject pronoun when the reflexive pronoun is an indirect object. If the non-reflexive form of the verb takes **à** + *indirect object*, the reflexive pronoun is an indirect object.

téléphoner à quelqu'un: Ils **se sont téléphoné** hier.	*They **called each other** yesterday.*
parler à quelqu'un: Elles **se sont parlé** hier.	*They **spoke to each other** yesterday.*

❖ The past participle of **se rendre compte** also never agrees with its subject pronoun.

Elles **se sont rendu compte** de l'heure.	*They realized the time.*

Note de **grammaire**
The **conditionnel** and **imparfait** of reflexive verbs are formed just like for non-reflexive verbs: **je me perdrais, on s'amusait.**

To form negative statements with reflexive verbs in the **passé composé**, put **ne** before the reflexive pronouns and **pas** after the conjugated auxiliary verb **être**.

Ils **ne se sont pas disputés** hier soir.   They **didn't fight with each other** last night.

Elle **ne s'est pas installée** dans la maison.   She **didn't move** into the house.

To ask a question using inversion with a reflexive verb in the **passé composé**, invert the auxiliary verb **être** and the subject pronoun. Place the reflexive pronoun before the auxiliary verb.

Luc **s'est-il perdu** à Montréal?   *Did Luc get lost in Montreal?*

In spoken French, intonation and **est-ce que** are more frequently used to ask questions with reflexive verbs than inversion.

Est-ce que tu t'es fâché avec lui?   *Did you get angry with him?*
Vous vous êtes mis à travailler à 20h00?   *You began to work at 8 pm?*

Liaisons musicales

© POL Emile/SIPA/Newscom

Richard Anthony est un chanteur français connu pour ses reprises *(covers)* françaises des chansons étrangères des années 60, surtout de style twist et rock. Cherchez les paroles de sa chanson *Je me suis souvent demandé* (1965) et trouvez ce qu'il s'est souvent demandé.

ACTIVITÉ **H** **Couples célèbres** Complétez ces phrases avec la (les) célébrité(s) qui rend(ent) chaque phrase vraie.

Possibilités: le prince Andrew/Charles/William; S. Ferguson, K. Middleton

1. _____ se sont rencontrés à l'Université Saint Andrews.
2. _____ se sont mariés en 1986.
3. _____ s'est marié avec son amoureuse en 1981.
4. _____ se sont quittés en 1996.

ACTIVITÉ **I** **Comment sont ces étudiants?** Complétez ces phrases avec le participe passé qui convient.

1. Ils ne se sont pas _____.   a. excusé   b. excusés.
2. Elles ne se sont pas _____.   a. réconcilié   b. réconciliées
3. Nous ne nous sommes pas _____ aux études.   a. intéressé   b. intéressés
4. Elles se sont _____ à causer des problèmes au prof.   a. mis   b. mises
5. Nous nous sommes _____ pendant le cours.   a. disputé   b. disputés
6. Ils se sont _____ pendant que le prof parlait.   a. parlé   b. parlés

Conclusion Ces étudiants sont-ils de bons ou de mauvais étudiants?

ACTIVITÉ **J** **Les cousins d'Abia**

Étape 1. Les cousins d'Abia parlent de leurs activités. Indiquez qui a dit chaque phrase: **(a) Jerome** ou **(b) Cindy.**

Jerome   Cindy

1. Je me suis détendu chez moi.
2. Je me suis détendue chez Stéphanie.
3. Je ne me suis pas occupé de mon chien.
4. Je me suis promenée dans le parc.
5. Je me suis amusée avec mes amis.
6. Je ne me suis pas occupée de Fifi.
7. Je me suis disputée avec Nadia.
8. Je me suis amusé avec Patrick.

Étape 2. Et vous? Répondez aux questions avec des phrases complètes.

Modèle: Est-ce que vous vous êtes amusé(e) avec votre voisin hier?
Non, je ne me suis pas amusé(e) avec mon voisin hier.

1. Est-ce que vous vous êtes amusé(e) avec vos amis hier?
2. Est-ce que vous vous êtes occupé(e) de votre linge *(laundry)* hier?
3. Est-ce que vous vous êtes disputé(e) avec un professeur hier?
4. Est-ce que vous vous êtes détendu(e) devant la télévision hier?

Étape 3. Posez les questions à un(e) partenaire. Avez-vous fait les mêmes choses hier?

Modèle: **Est-ce que tu t'es amusé(e) avec tes amis hier?**

ACTIVITÉ K Quand ils étaient petits Que faisaient régulièrement vos camarades de classe quand ils étaient petits? Posez ces questions à deux camarades de classe.

1. Comment est-ce que vous vous amusiez le samedi matin?
2. Vous vous entendiez bien avec qui?
3. Vous vous méfiiez de qui?
4. Vous vous disputiez souvent avec qui?
5. Qu'est-ce que vous faisiez quand vous vous ennuyiez?

Conclusion Les deux camarades de classe étaient-ils similaires ou différents quand ils étaient petits?

ACTIVITÉ L Des rêves bizarres Faites-vous parfois des rêves bizarres sur des célébrités ou sur des gens que vous connaissez? Inventez des rêves (au passé composé).

Modèle: **Angelina Jolie s'est rendu compte que Brad Pitt n'est pas un bon mari.**

Suggestions			
s'amuser	s'embrasser	s'intéresser à	(se) quitter
(se) demander	se fâcher	se marier	se réconcilier
se détester	se fiancer	se méfier de	se rendre compte de / que
se disputer	s'installer	se parler	(se) tromper

1. Johnny Depp…
2. Beyoncé…
3. Miley Cyrus…
4. Les clowns du Cirque du Soleil…
5. Will Smith et Jada P. Smith…
6. Venus et Serena Williams…
7. Justin Timberlake et _____…
8. Mon professeur…
9. Moi, je…
10. _____ et moi, nous…

Les verbes réfléchis à l'impératif

The imperative of reflexive verbs is formed as it is for non-reflexive verbs. In affirmative commands, the reflexive pronoun follows the verb with a hyphen; **toi** is used instead of **te/t'**. In negative commands, the reflexive pronoun precedes the verb.

Amuse-**toi** bien!	*Have a good time!*
Dépêchez-**vous**!	*Hurry up!*
Téléphonons-**nous** ce soir.	*Let's phone each other tonight.*
Ne **t'**inquiète pas.	*Don't worry.*
Ne **vous** sentez pas mal.	*Don't feel bad.*
Ne **nous** téléphonons pas.	*Let's not phone each other.*

Essayez! Que diriez-vous aux personnes suivantes?

Modèle: (s'inquiéter) Un ami a perdu son emploi. **Ne t'inquiète pas.**

1. (se reposer) Votre ami est très fatigué aujourd'hui. _____
2. (se dépêcher) Votre ami est en retard pour son cours de français. _____
3. (se perdre) Votre ami doit aller dans une ville qu'il ne connaît pas bien. _____
4. (s'amuser) Vos amis vont aller à une fête ce soir. _____
5. (s'inquiéter) Vos amis ont un examen et ils sont nerveux. _____
6. (se disputer) Vous devez étudier mais vos colocataires se disputent. _____

OUI, JE PEUX!

Here are two "can do statements" for you to check your progress so far. Look at each statement and rate yourself on how well you think you can perform the task. Then verify your ability with a partner. How did you do?

1. **"I can say three things that I did and three things that I did not do last week using reflexive verbs."**

   I can perform this function
   ☐ with ease
   ☐ with some difficulty
   ☐ not at all

2. **"I can ask someone else if he/she also did these activities last week to see if we did similar things."**

   I can perform this function
   ☐ with ease
   ☐ with some difficulty
   ☐ not at all

iLrn™

Are you looking for more practice? You can find it in **iLrn**.

L'expression personnelle

Personal expression

Les médias

Vocabulaire complémentaire

un article *article*

un hebdomadaire / un hebdo *a weekly (magazine, newspaper) publication*

un (magazine) mensuel *a monthly (magazine) publication*

un (journal) quotidien *a daily (newspaper) publication*

un réseau social *a social network*

un site Web *a website*

une pensée *a thought*

les potins / un potin *a gossip / a piece of gossip*

un sentiment *a feeling*

déranger *to bother, to upset*

exprimer *to express*

faire plaisir à quelqu'un *to please someone*

pleurer *to cry*

raconter *to tell (about), to narrate*

regretter *to regret, to be sorry about*

rendre quelqu'un (heureux) *to make someone (happy)*

ressentir *to feel (emotion—sadness)*

toucher *to touch, to deeply move*

C'est dommage! *That's too bad!*

Enfin! *Finally!*

Formidable! / Génial! *Great! / Awesome!*

Je regrette. / Je suis désolé(e). *I'm sorry.*

Merveilleux! / Super! *Marvelous! Wonderful! / Super!*

de temps en temps *from time to time*

parfois / quelquefois *sometimes, at times*

la plupart du temps *most of the time*

Note de vocabulaire

Note that **s'ennuyer** means *to be bored,* but **ennuyer** means *to bore:*
Je m'ennuie. *(I am bored.)*
Les potins m'ennuient. *(Gossip bores me.)*

Pour aller plus loin
Les adjectifs à partir des verbes

You can make adjectives out of most regular and irregular verbs in French by dropping the **-ons** ending from the **nous** form of the verb conjugated in the present tense and adding **-ant(e)(s)**.

Anne est vraiment **énervante** aujourd'hui.	*Anne is really irritating today.*
C'est **bouleversant**.	*That's overwhelming.*
Les deux lettres sont très **touchantes**.	*The two letters are very touching.*

Essayez! Qu'est-ce que vous pensez des sujets suivants? Sont-ils **inquiétants, ennuyants, troublants, amusants, dérangeants, reposants**, etc.?

1. la politique
2. le climat économique
3. les films de Ron Howard
4. Fox News

Si vous y allez

© Ekaterina Pokrovsky / Shutterstock.com

Si vous allez à Paris, allez voir les bouquinistes *(booksellers)* sur le bord de la Seine entre le pont Marie et le quai du Louvre.

🔊 10-3 **ACTIVITÉ A** **C'est quelle publication?** Identifiez le genre de publication pour chaque exemple mentionné.

1. a. un journal intime   b. un quotidien   c. un hebdomadaire
2. a. un quotidien   b. un blog   c. une revue
3. a. un microblogging   b. un magazine   c. un blog
4. a. un quotidien   b. un journal intime   c. un magazine de mode
5. a. un article   b. un mensuel   c. un hebdomadaire
6. a. un blog   b. un réseau social   c. un site Web
7. a. un réseau social   b. une revue   c. un journal intime
8. a. un article   b. un microblogging   c. un hebdomadaire

🔊 10-4 **ACTIVITÉ B** **Exclamations** Quelle phrase déclenche *(elicits)* logiquement chaque exclamation que vous entendez?

1. a. Tu me déranges là.   b. Ça me rend très heureux.
2. a. C'est bouleversant.   b. Comment tu te sens?
3. a. J'ai perdu mon chien.   b. Je me sens très bien.
4. a. Tu m'énerves!   b. Ça me fait très plaisir.
5. a. Ça me rend triste.   b. Je ressens de la joie.
6. a. C'est dommage.   b. Ça me touche beaucoup.

ACTIVITÉ C **Vous êtes discrets / discrètes?**

Étape 1. Indiquez les publications dans lesquelles vous exprimeriez les choses ci-dessous *(below)*: **dans un blog, dans un microblog, dans un journal intime, sur un réseau social** ou **dans un courriel.**

1. raconter votre journée   4. exprimer vos pensées intimes
2. raconter vos projets   5. exprimer vos sentiments personnels
3. raconter des potins   6. exprimer vos idées *(ideas)* sur la vie

Étape 2. Formulez et posez des questions à un(e) partenaire. Est-ce que vous êtes discret / discrète?

Modèle: **Dans quel genre de publication est-ce que tu raconterais ta journée?**

ACTIVITÉ D **Langue des textos** Faites correspondre les abréviations avec leur signification.

1. _____ A+   a. Mort de rire
2. _____ MDR   b. À plus tard
3. _____ mr6   c. Merci
4. _____ SQZ   d. Occupé
5. _____ OQP   e. Énervé
6. _____ NRV   f. Excuse-moi!

ACTIVITÉ **E** **État d'esprit**

10-5

Étape 1. Indiquez votre état d'esprit *(state of mind)* pour chaque activité mentionnée.

	Ça me dérange.	Ça m'ennuie.	Ça me fait plaisir.	Ça m'énerve.
1.	_____	_____	_____	_____
2.	_____	_____	_____	_____
3.	_____	_____	_____	_____
4.	_____	_____	_____	_____

Étape 2. Répondez à ces questions et puis montrez vos réponses à un(e) camarade de classe. Avez-vous des tendances similaires ou bien différentes?

1. Qui ou qu'est-ce qui *(What)* vous dérange le plus dans la vie?
2. Qui ou qu'est-ce qui vous plaît le plus dans la vie?
3. Qui ou qu'est-ce qui vous touche le plus dans la vie?
4. Qui ou qu'est-ce qui vous fait pleurer?

ACTIVITÉ **F** **Émoticônes** Indiquez *le smiley* qui correspond à chaque émotion suivante.

Possibilités

a. :-)   b. :-(c. :-| d. :'-)   e. xP   f. :-<

1. _____ Ça me rend heureux / heureuse.
2. _____ Je m'ennuie.
3. _____ Ça ne me fait pas plaisir.
4. _____ Je veux pleurer.
5. _____ Ça me touche vraiment.
6. _____ Ça me dérange beaucoup.

Et vous? Quels *smileys* utilisez-vous pour exprimer vos émotions?

ACTIVITÉ **G** **Moyens de communication et d'expression** Indiquez les moyens de communication d'**il y a 20 ans** et ceux d'**aujourd'hui** pour ces besoins.

	Il y a 20 ans	Aujourd'hui
1. Pour rester en contact avec des amis	_____	_____
2. Pour parler des activités de la journée	_____	_____
3. Pour poser une question à un collègue	_____	_____
4. Pour exprimer ses pensées intimes	_____	_____
5. Pour se renseigner sur *(To become informed about)* l'actualité	_____	_____
6. Pour apprendre ce qui s'est passé dans un cours qu'on a séché *(skipped)*	_____	_____
7. Pour se renseigner sur les nouvelles tendances de la mode	_____	_____
8. Pour rencontrer des gens	_____	_____

Conclusion Est-ce que les moyens de communication ont changé pour le meilleur ou le pire?

ACTIVITÉ H Répliques attendues

Quelles expressions est-ce que Claire utiliserait pour répondre si Abia lui disait ces phrases?

Modèle: J'ai réussi à mon examen. **Formidable!**

1. La pizza m'a rendue malade hier.

2. Je me suis beaucoup dérangée pour venir.

3. Je me sentais mieux ce matin.

4. Je m'ennuie. Et si on allait au cinéma?

Et vous? Comment répondriez-vous à votre meilleur(e) ami(e)?

ACTIVITÉ I Vos télécommunications

Étape 1. Faites trois ou quatre phrases qui expriment vos expériences et/ou pratiques de télécommunication.

Modèle: **Parfois, j'exprime mes sentiments dans un blog. La plupart du temps, je fais du microblogging. De temps en temps, je mets des photos sur un réseau social.**

Possibilités			
parfois	exprimer	des faits	un Smartphone
souvent	lire / écrire	des sentiments	un texto
de temps en temps	mettre	des pensées	le microblogging
la plupart du temps	publier	des photos	un réseau social
toujours	regretter	des potins	un site Web / un blog

Étape 2. Lisez vos phrases à deux ou trois camarades de classe. Demandez-leur si vous faites preuve de «bon sens» sur Internet ou pas! Si c'est non, ont-ils/elles des conseils pour vous?

Un mot sur la culture

Les réseaux sociaux en France

Les réseaux sociaux sont tellement populaires en France qu'il y a plusieurs classements°. On compte des réseaux sociaux *pro* (à but° professionnel: trouver des postes), *perso* (à but personnel: rester en contact avec des amis ou la famille) et *fun* (à but récréatif: partager des informations sur les loisirs). Voici des réseaux sociaux populaires parmi les internautes° français: Facebook, Youtube, Google +, LinkedIn, Twitter, Instagram et Copainsdavant.

© Marlene Awaad/Maxppp / Landov

classements *classifications* **but** *goal* **internautes** *Internet users*

Liaisons avec les mots et les sons

10-6
Les semi-voyelles

French has three semi-vowels, which are letter combinations that sound like vowels that glide from or into an accompanying vowel sound.

A semi-vowel sound occurs with **u** when it is pronounced like the vowel sound in **tu.** The sound then glides into the following vowel.

| intellect**u**el | s**u**is | biling**ui**sme | l**ui** | spirit**u**alité | mens**u**el |

A semi-vowel sound occurs with **y, i,** or **ill** when they are pronounced like the English *ee.* The sound then glides into the following sound.

| fam**ille** | national | b**i**en | ch**i**en | pa**y**er | br**ill**ant | b**ill**ets |

A semi-vowel sound occurs with **o** or **ou** when they are pronounced like the English *w* as in **soif.** The sound then glides into the following sound.

| **ou**i | m**o**i | b**oî**te | framb**o**ise | b**o**ire | L**ou**is XIV | b**o**is |

Pratique A. Écoutez et répétez ces mots. Soulignez (*Underline*) les semi-voyelles **u.** Encerclez (*Circle*) les semi-voyelles **y, i, ill.** Cochez (*Check*) les semi-voyelles **o** et **ou.**

1. fois
2. parfois
3. se voir
4. merveilleux

5. se payer
6. gentille
7. ennuyer
8. intellectuel

9. juin
10. fiançailles
11. juillet
12. mois

Pratique B. Écoutez et répétez ces répliques de la Séquence 5 du film *Liaisons*. Soulignez (*Underline*) les mots avec des semi-voyelles.

ALEXIS […] cette fois-ci, ce n'est pas une coïncidence. Nous avons rendez-vous.

CLAIRE Oui. Allons-y!

ALEXIS Allons voir ce que cette belle capitale nous propose.

 À vos stylos! C'est l'heure de la dictée!

10-7
Vous allez entendre trois phrases deux fois. La première fois, écoutez bien. La deuxième fois, écrivez les phrases.

Sujet Citations célèbres

Pour exprimer la négation

Les expressions négatives

DU FILM *LIAISONS*

Un coup d'œil sur la grammaire

Look at these photos from the film *Liaisons* and their captions, focusing on the negative expressions.

RÉCEPTIONNISTE Avez-vous besoin d'aide avec vos valises *(suitcases)*?

CLAIRE Non. Ça va. Je **n'**en ai **qu'**une.

CLAIRE Mon oncle Michel? Et la personne qui a téléphoné, c'était qui?

ABIA Je n'ai **aucune** idée.

1. In the left caption, what does **Je n'en ai qu'une** mean?
2. In the right caption, what do you think **Je n'ai aucune idée** means?

❖ You already know how to make sentences negative using **ne... pas.** Here are some other common negative expressions and their affirmative counterparts. The placement of these negative expressions is the same as **ne… pas.**

AFFIRMATIVE	NEGATIVE
toujours *always*	**ne… jamais** *never*
encore *still*	**ne… plus** *no longer, no more*
déjà *already*	**ne… pas encore** *not yet*

Je suis **toujours** en retard.	*I am **always** late.*
Je **ne** suis **jamais** en retard.	*I am **never** late.*
Guy parle **encore** avec ses amis de lycée.	*Guy **still** speaks with his high school friends.*
Marie **ne** parle **plus** avec ses amis.	*Marie **no longer** speaks to her friends.*

❖ The following are additional useful negative expressions.

ne… aucun(e)	*none, not any*	**ne… pas du tout**	*not at all*
ne… personne	*nobody, no one*	**ne… que**	*only*
ne… rien	*nothing, not anything*	**ne… ni… ni**	*neither . . . nor*

Je **ne** vois **personne.**	*I don't see **anyone.***
Il **n'**y a **rien** dans le frigo!	*There's **nothing** in the fridge!*
Elle **n'**aime **pas du tout** étudier.	*She does not like to study **at all.***
Ils **n'**ont **que** trois euros.	*They **only** have three euros.*
Guy **ne** fait **que** m'ennuyer.	*Guy does **nothing but** bore me.*

⋅⋅⋅⁝ **Aucun(e)** is an adjective and must agree with the noun it modifies.

| Elle **n'**a **aucune** idée. | *She does **not** have **any** idea.* |
| On **ne** trouve **aucun** livre ici. | *We can't find **any** book here.* |

⋅⋅⋅⁝ Note that three negative words are required to express *neither . . . nor:* **ne… ni… ni.** Partitive and indefinite articles are not used.

| Je **n'**ai **ni** le temps **ni** la patience. | *I have neither the time nor the patience.* |
| Elle **n'**a **ni** stylo **ni** papier. | *She has neither pen nor paper.* |

⋅⋅⋅⁝ The placement of these negative expressions in the **passé composé** is similar to **ne… pas** with the exceptions of **ne… personne** and **ne… aucun(e),** which surround the entire verb.

—Vous avez **déjà** vu le spectacle?	*—You've **already** seen the show?*
—Non, nous **ne** l'avons **pas encore** vu.	*—No, we have **not** seen it **yet.***
Je **n'**ai **rien** trouvé aujourd'hui.	*I didn't find **anything** today.*
Elle **n'**a **plus** parlé de Jean.	*She didn't speak about Jean **anymore.***
Tu **n'**as écouté **personne.**	*You did not listen to **anyone.***
Il **n'**a eu **aucune** réponse.	*He didn't get a **single** response.*

⋅⋅⋅⁝ **Rien** and **personne** can also be the subject of a sentence.

—Que se passe-t-il ici?	*—What's going on here?*
—**Rien ne** se passe ici.	*—Nothing's going on here.*
—**Rien.**	*—Nothing.*
—Qui est là?	*—Who's there?*
—**Personne n'**est là.	*—Nobody / No one is here.*
—**Personne.**	*—Nobody / No one.*

⋅⋅⋅⁝ You can double up **jamais, personne, plus, aucun(e),** and **rien** with **ne.**

Vous **ne** travaillez **jamais** avec **personne.**	*You never work with anyone.*
Il **n'**y a **plus rien** à dire.	*There's nothing more to say.*
Elles **ne** font **jamais rien.**	*They never do anything.*
Aucun blog **ne** m'intéresse **jamais.**	*No blog ever interests me.*

⋅⋅⋅⁝ Like **quelque chose** and **quelqu'un, personne,** and **rien** can be modified with a masculine adjective after **de.**

| Il n'y avait **personne d'intéressant** à la fête. | *There was **no one interesting** at the party.* |
| Je ne trouve **rien de nouveau** ici. | *I am not finding **anything new** here.* |

⋅⋅⋅⁝ **Moi non plus** *(Me neither)* is the negative form of the common expression **moi aussi** *(me too).*

| —**Moi aussi.** | —**Moi non plus.** |

ACTIVITÉ J Qui le dirait? À votre avis, qui dirait chaque phrase suivante: **(a) un adolescent de 15 ans, (b) un adulte de 75 ans** ou **(c) tous les deux**?

1. Je **n'**aime **pas du tout** le microblogging.

2. Je **n'**ai **rien** lu **d'intéressant** sur mon réseau social aujourd'hui.

3. Je **n'**ai **pas encore** de Smartphone.

4. Je **ne** vois **plus** mes amis.

5. Je **ne** lis **jamais** le magazine *Reader's Digest*.

6. Je **n'**ai **ni** enfant **ni** petit-enfant.

7. Je **n'**ai reçu **aucun** texto aujourd'hui.

ACTIVITÉ K Comment était votre week-end?

Étape 1. Complétez chaque phrase avec **(a) Quelqu'un** ou **(b) Personne**. Puis, indiquez si la phrase est vraie ou fausse pour vous.

1. _____ m'a rendu visite.

2. _____ **ne** m'a téléphoné.

3. _____ **ne** m'a envoyé de courriel.

4. _____ **ne** m'a invité(e) à dîner.

5. _____ m'a invité(e) à aller au cinéma.

6. _____ **n'**a étudié avec moi.

 **Étape 2.** Demandez à un(e) partenaire si quelqu'un a fait ces activités avec ou pour lui/elle. Est-ce que votre partenaire était sociable ou solitaire le week-end dernier?

Modèle: É1: **Est-ce que quelqu'un t'a rendu visite le week-end dernier?**
É2: **Non, personne ne m'a rendu visite.**

ACTIVITÉ L Moi aussi! Moi non plus! Avec un(e) partenaire, indiquez si vous aimez ou si vous n'aimez pas ces choses.

Modèle: les revues
É1: **Moi, j'aime les revues. / Moi, je n'aime pas les revues.**
É2: **Moi aussi! / Moi non plus!**

1. les magazines de mode
2. le microblogging
3. les textos
4. le magazine *Sports Illustrated*
5. les réseaux sociaux
6. les potins

ACTIVITÉ M Les célébrités et vous Comparez votre vie avec celle des célébrités.

Modèle: Bill Gates a plus de dix maisons.   **Moi, je n'ai qu'une maison.**

1. Martha Stewart a plus de cinq frigos.

2. Katy Perry a plus de trois iPods.

3. Anderson Cooper a plus de huit Smartphones.

4. Donald Trump a plus de six voitures (*cars*).

Liaisons musicales

© Abdelhak Senna/AFP/Getty Images

Chanteur de raï et de pop et acteur français d'origine algérienne, Faudel chante en arabe et en français. Cherchez les paroles de sa chanson *Je n'ai que mon cœur* (2003) et trouvez une raison pour laquelle il n'a que son cœur à offrir à son amour.

ACTIVITÉ **N** **Kofi et Marie-Claire**

Étape 1. Kofi (l'oncle d'Abia du film *Liaisons*) et sa conjointe Marie-Claire se sont quittés parce qu'ils sont trop différents. Kofi est une personne positive et sociable mais Marie-Claire est très négative. Décrivez Marie-Claire.

Modèle: Kofi s'amuse souvent avec ses amis.
     Marie-Claire ne s'amuse jamais avec ses amis.

1. Kofi va souvent au cinéma.

2. Kofi voit encore ses amis de lycée.

3. Kofi aime danser et chanter.

4. Kofi a beaucoup d'amis.

5. Kofi adore faire la fête.

6. Kofi a toujours quelque chose de positif à dire.

Étape 2. Posez les questions à un(e) partenaire. Est-ce qu'il/elle est comme Kofi ou comme Marie-Claire?

Modèle: É1: **Est-ce que tu vas souvent au cinéma?**
     É2: **Oui, je vais souvent au cinéma. / Non, je ne vais jamais au cinéma.**

ACTIVITÉ **O** **La vie d'étudiant**

Étape 1. Écrivez quatre à cinq raisons de se plaindre de *(complain about)* sa vie d'étudiant en utilisant des expressions négatives.

Modèle: **Je n'ai jamais le temps de sortir avec mes amis.**

Étape 2. Montrez votre liste à un(e) partenaire. Êtes-vous d'accord avec les raisons de votre partenaire?

OUI, JE PEUX!   Here are two "can do statements" for you to check your progress so far. Look at each statement and rate yourself on how well you think you can perform the task. Then verify your ability with a partner. How did you do?

iLrn™

Are you looking for more practice? You can find it in **iLrn**.

1. **"I can say two things that I still or always do and two things that I no longer do or have not done yet."**

   I can perform this function
   ☐ with ease
   ☐ with some difficulty
   ☐ not at all

2. **"I can ask someone else about his/her activities and find out what that person does and no longer does."**

   I can perform this function
   ☐ with ease
   ☐ with some difficulty
   ☐ not at all

Avant de visionner

ACTIVITÉ **A** **Vous rappelez-vous?** Vous rappelez-vous ce qui s'est passé dans la Séquence 5 du film *Liaisons*? Pour chaque phrase, indiquez si c'est vrai ou faux.

	Vrai	Faux
1. Claire et Alexis se sont embrassés après leur rendez-vous.	☐	☐
2. Claire a vu un petit garçon qui pleurait dans une église.	☐	☐
3. Claire a appris que son oncle est mort.	☐	☐
4. Claire doit aller en France pour un enterrement.	☐	☐

ACTIVITÉ **B** **Une scène du film** Vous rappelez-vous cette scène? Claire et Alexis sont devant le Château Frontenac après leur rendez-vous. Écrivez les mots qui manquent *(are missing)*.

ALEXIS Il y a des choses que (1) _____ vous dire... mais...

CLAIRE (2) _____?

ALEXIS C'est que... (3) _____ que vous pourrez nous pardonner.

CLAIRE Pardonner? Pardonner à (4) _____? Alexis, que voulez-vous (5) _____?

ALEXIS (6) _____ moi. Ce n'est (7) _____. Je... La fatigue. Je divague *(am rambling)*. Bon. Je dois (8) _____. J'ai beaucoup de choses à faire très tôt demain.

▶ **Regarder la séquence**

Vous allez regarder la Séquence 5 du film *Liaisons*. Vérifiez vos réponses à l'Activité A et à l'Activité B.

Après le visionnage

ACTIVITÉ C Avez-vous une bonne mémoire?

Étape 1. Répondez aux questions pour voir si vous avez une bonne mémoire. Après, montrez vos réponses à un(e) partenaire. Avez-vous les mêmes réponses?

1. Est-ce que vous vous rappelez l'adresse de l'église où Claire a vu la petite fille?
2. La petite fille dans le rêve de Claire, elle avait environ (*approximately*) quel âge?
3. Comment s'appelle la femme qui a trouvé le corps (*body*) de l'oncle Michel?
4. Vers quelle heure l'oncle Michel est-il mort?

Étape 2. Avec votre partenaire, répondez à la question suivante: À votre avis, qu'est-ce qu'Alexis voulait dire à Claire devant le Château Frontenac après leur rendez-vous?

ACTIVITÉ D Résumé de la Séquence 5 Voici un résumé de la Séquence 5 du film. Choisissez les mots qui manquent.

Alexis   allé   Claire   devant   l'enveloppe   l'homme   rien   voulait

Après leur rendez-vous, Alexis (1) _____ dire quelque chose à (2) _____ mais il n'a (3) _____ dit. Quand Alexis s'en est (4) _____, Claire a vu l'homme qui lui a donné (5) _____. Claire a couru après (6) _____ et elle s'est retrouvée (7) _____ une église.

chambre   l'enterrement   Française   mort   petite   plus   rendu   rêve

Dans l'église, Claire a vu une (8) _____ fille qui pleurait. Claire s'est (9) _____ compte plus tard que ce n'était qu'un (10) _____. Plus tard dans sa (11) _____ d'hôtel, Claire a appris d'une (12) _____ que son oncle était (13) _____ à Paris. Claire doit aller à Paris pour (14) _____. Mais d'abord, elle doit aller à la Banque Nationale lundi.

Dans les coulisses

Directors use dream sequences to create a brief interlude from the main story. Dreams may be used to reveal information to viewers or to shed light on a character's psyche or thought processes. Can you think of films you've seen that included dream sequences? What was the purpose of those sequences? What do you think is the significance of the dream sequence in **Séquence 5** of the film *Liaisons*?

À DÉCOUVRIR: Le Togo et ses structures familiales

À DÉCOUVRIR: Le Togo

Pays: Le Togo
Géographie: L'Afrique occidentale; entre le Bénin et le Ghana
Climat: Tropical; chaud et humide dans le sud; semi-aride dans le nord
Population: Environ 7 millions
Capitale: Lomé

À DÉCOUVRIR: La ville de Lomé

Structure: Une grande ville moderne
Région: Région maritime
Population: Plus de 800 000
Réputation: La capitale économique, administrative et industrielle du Togo

Avant de lire

You will discover in this reading the issues of urbanization and family structures in Togo.

Que savez-vous déjà?

1. Que veut dire le terme «l'urbanisation»?
2. Quels sont quelques avantages ou désavantages de l'urbanisation pour un pays?
3. Quels effets l'urbanisation a-t-elle souvent sur la culture ou la société d'un pays?

OUTILS DE LECTURE
Using titles to predict content
You will increase your reading comprehension when you use a text's title as a clue to predicting its content. For example, try to predict some of the content of this reading based on its title: **Les structures et relations familiales changeantes.**

Les structures et relations familiales changeantes

© Robert Harding Picture Library Ltd/Alamy

Le Togo est l'un des plus petits pays de l'Afrique (environ la superficie° de la Virginie-Occidentale) et il a une population de sept millions d'habitants. C'est aussi un pays où on constate° une évolution des structures et relations familiales comme à travers° une grande partie du continent africain. Le processus d'urbanisation croissante° est en train de modifier les structures et parfois les relations familiales traditionnelles. Beaucoup de Togolais ont quitté leurs villages pour aller vivre dans les grandes villes, en particulier dans la capitale Lomé. Lors de° l'indépendance du pays en 1960, Lomé ne comptait qu'environ 100 000 habitants. Depuis, la population de la capitale a été multipliée par huit.

Ayant° quitté un mode de vie rural pour aller chercher du travail dans un milieu urbain, les nouveaux citadins° trouvent des conditions de logement très différentes. La famille élargie des sociétés traditionnelles de l'Afrique sub-saharienne, qui faisait cohabiter trois ou même quatre générations, a été progressivement transformée par les nouvelles réalités économiques et sociales des grandes villes. Au lieu de° vivre tous ensemble dans une concession°, aujourd'hui on trouve de plus en plus de familles nucléaires vivant séparément.

Au niveau des relations familiales, le respect pour les aînés° reste primordial, même dans les familles divisées entre la ville et la campagne. Ce respect représente toujours le facteur déterminant pour les liens° entre les générations. Donc, au lieu d'une transformation totale, il y a eu une diversification des modèles familiaux, et en particulier une augmentation° du nombre de familles monoparentales, dans lesquelles la mère est le chef de famille. Mais le contact quotidien avec la famille élargie a diminué°.

Adapted from: http://demoscope.ru/weekly/knigi/tours_2005/papers/iussp2005s51850.pdf – Communication présentée au XXVème congrès international de la famille (Tours 2005)

superficie *surface area* **constate** *observes* **à travers** *throughout* **croissante** *increasing* **Lors de** *At the time of* **Ayant** *Having* **citadins** *city-dwellers* **Au lieu de** *Instead of* **concession** *compound* **aînés** *elders* **liens** *relationships* **augmentation** *increase* **a diminué** *has decreased*

Après avoir lu

Compréhension

	Vrai	Faux
1. L'urbanisation est limitée au Togo.	☐	☐
2. La population de Lomé a triplé depuis 1960.	☐	☐
3. De plus en plus de familles nucléaires vivent séparément.	☐	☐
4. Le respect pour les aînés est toujours très important.	☐	☐

Share It!

Use **Share It!** in **iLrn** to express your reactions to the reading and to find out what your classmates think.

Et vous?

1. Est-ce que vous venez d'une région touchée par l'urbanisation?
2. Est-ce que vous avez grandi dans une maison multi-générationnelle?
3. Est-ce que le respect pour les aînés est important dans votre famille?
4. Est-ce que vous avez beaucoup de contacts avec votre famille élargie?

LA LECTURE ET L'ÉCRITURE
Une description des relations interpersonnelles

Descriptions of human relationships appear often in journalism, especially in human-interest stories. Here is a description of interpersonal relations in Togo from the perspective of Mawuli, a college student.

© Phil Borges/Danita Delimont/Alamy

Dans la culture togolaise et surtout dans ma famille, les relations interpersonnelles sont toujours très importantes et parfois compliquées. Nous avons des règles à respecter. Respecter les aînés (surtout les grands-parents), c'est important dans toute la société. Quand on reçoit des invités à la maison, ma mère leur offre toujours de l'eau et mon père leur pose des questions sur leur famille et leur santé. Mes parents s'entendent bien avec le copain de ma sœur aînée. Mon père organise ses visites à la maison mais mes parents ne croient plus au mariage arrangé. En général, aucune démonstration publique d'affection n'est pratiquée. Par exemple, ma sœur et son copain ne s'embrassent pas en public.

Avant d'écrire

1. What kinds of details appear in the description of Togolese interpersonal relations?

2. Answer the following questions to help you write your own description **des relations interpersonnelles.**

   a. Les rapports entre quelles deux (ou plus de deux) personnes voulez-vous décrire?

   b. Quels exemples de leur comportement *(behavior)* ensemble voulez-vous citer?

   c. Voulez-vous tirer *(draw)* une conclusion ou porter un jugement sur leurs relations interpersonnelles?

Écrire

Using information from **Avant d'écrire,** write your own description of a personal relationship you have with someone in 6–8 French sentences.

Après avoir écrit

Exchange your description with a partner. (1) Circle all the reflexive verbs and verify that your partner correctly conjugated them. (2) Underline all negative expressions and verify that they are all correct. (3) Double-check that your partner made all of the adjectives agree in number and gender. (4) Put a * next to the key phrase or key idea that best communicates your partner's description. (5) How would you characterize your partner's description: **perspicace** *(insightful)*, **objective, ennuyeuse, touchante, dérangeante, imaginative, drôle**? Discuss your reactions together and then write a second version of your description taking into account your partner's comments and corrections.

PARTIE 1 10–8

LES MODES DE VIE

les accros du shopping	shopaholics
les babas cool / les hippies	hippies
les bourreaux de travail	workaholics
les célibataires	single people
les écologistes / les écolos	ecologists, environmentalists
les fanas de la santé	health nuts
les femmes / les hommes au foyer	housewives, househusbands
les membres de la jet-set	jet setters
une mère active / un père actif	working mom / working dad
une mère célibataire / un père célibataire	single mother / single father
les retraités	retired people, retirees

NOMS

l'amitié (f.)	friendship
l'amour (m.)	love
le bonheur	happiness
l'environnement (m.)	environment
la fidélité / l'infidélité (f.)	loyalty / disloyalty
la moralité	morality
le prestige	prestige
la spiritualité	spirituality
le succès	success

ADJECTIFS

avare	stingy, miserly
bavard(e)	talkative, gossipy
bête	stupid, idiotic
bien habillé(e) / mal habillé(e)	well-dressed / poorly-dressed
égoïste	selfish
fidèle / infidèle	loyal / disloyal
gracieux / gracieuse	graceful, gracious
jaloux / jalouse	jealous
maladroit(e)	clumsy
prétentieux / prétentieuse	pretentious
simple	simple

VERBES

s'aimer	to like / love oneself / each other
se connaître	to know oneself / each other
se détester	to hate oneself / each other
se disputer	to argue with (each other)
s'embrasser	to kiss each other
s'énerver	to get upset
se fiancer	to get engaged to (each other)
se marier	to marry (each other)
se parler	to talk to oneself / each other
se quitter	to leave each other
se réconcilier	to make up with each other
se regarder	to look at oneself / each other
se rencontrer	to meet each other
se téléphoner	to telephone each other
se voir	to see oneself / each other

EXPRESSION

être bien dans sa peau	to have confidence in / to feel good about oneself

PARTIE 2 10–9

VERBES

s'appeler	to be named / called
appeler	to call
s'en aller	to go away
s'amuser	to have a good time
se demander	to wonder
se dépêcher	to hurry
se détendre	to relax, to take it easy
s'ennuyer	to be bored
s'entendre (bien / mal avec quelqu'un)	to get along (well / badly with someone)
s'excuser	to be sorry, to apologize
se fâcher	to get angry
s'inquiéter (de)	to worry (about)
s'installer (dans / à)	to move into, to settle into
s'intéresser (à)	to be interested (in)
se méfier (de)	to be suspicious (of)
se mettre (à)	to begin (to)
s'occuper (de)	to take care of
se passer	to happen
se perdre	to get lost
se promener	to take a walk, to stroll
se rappeler	to remember
rappeler	to call back
se rendre compte (de / que)	to realize
se reposer	to rest
se sentir	to feel
se souvenir (de)	to remember
se trouver	to be located
se tromper (de)	to be mistaken (about)
tromper	to cheat on (someone)

DIVERS

À mon (votre) avis	In my (your) opinion

RÉSUMÉ DE VOCABULAIRE

LA COMMUNICATION

un article	article
un blog	blog
un hebdomadaire	weekly (magazine, newspaper) publication
un journal intime	diary
un magazine (de mode)	magazine (fashion magazine)
un (magazine) mensuel	monthly (magazine) publication
le microblogging	Twitter-like messages
un (journal) quotidien	daily (newspaper) publication
un réseau social	social network
une revue	magazine
un site Web	website
un Smartphone	Smartphone

NOMS

une pensée	thought
les potins / un potin	gossip / piece of gossip
un sentiment	feeling

VERBES

déranger	to bother, to upset
exprimer	to express
pleurer	to cry
raconter	to tell (about), to narrate
regretter	to regret, to be sorry about
rendre quelqu'un (heureux)	to make someone (happy)
ressentir	to feel (emotion—sadness)
toucher	to touch, to deeply move

EXPRESSIONS

C'est dommage!	That's too bad!
Enfin!	Finally!
faire plaisir à quelqu'un	to please someone
Formidable! / Génial!	Great! / Awesome!
Je regrette. / Je suis désolé(e).	I'm sorry.
Merveilleux! / Super!	Marvelous! Wonderful! / Super!

ADVERBES

de temps en temps	from time to time
parfois / quelquefois	sometimes, at times
la plupart du temps	most of the time

LES EXPRESSIONS AFFIRMATIVES

déjà	already
encore	still
toujours	always

LES EXPRESSIONS NÉGATIVES

ne… aucun(e)	none, not any
ne… jamais	never
ne… ni… ni	neither . . . nor
ne… pas du tout	not at all
ne… pas encore	not yet
ne… personne	nobody, no one
ne… plus	no longer, no more
ne… que	only
ne… rien	nothing, not anything

La **vie** en **action**

En bref   In this chapter, you will:

- talk about transportation, the post office, traveling, clothing, and lifestyles

- learn the **futur simple** forms

- learn the relative pronouns **qui, que, dont,** and **où**

- learn some indefinite adjectives and pronouns

- learn about the sounds /z/ and /s/

- read about transportation, the post office, and travel in France and the Francophone world

 You will also watch **SÉQUENCE 6**: Une découverte of the film *Liaisons*.

Ressources

 audio   video   Share It!   iLrn⁻   🌐 http://www.cengagebrain.com

Les **modes de vie** et les **transports**

Lifestyles and transportation

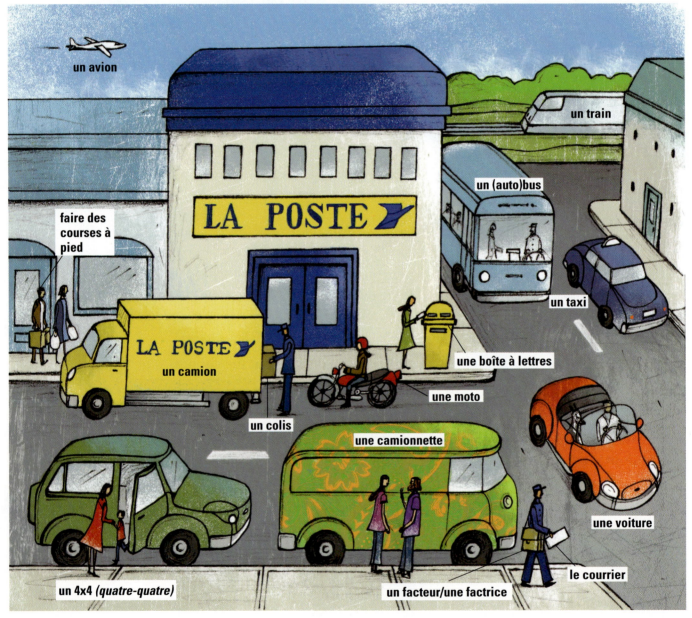

un avion

un train

un (auto)bus

faire des courses à pied

LA POSTE

un taxi

LA POSTE
un camion

une boîte à lettres

une moto

un colis

une camionnette

une voiture

un 4x4 *(quatre-quatre)*

un facteur/une factrice

le courrier

Ça bouge!

Vocabulaire complémentaire

une carte postale *postcard*	**bouger** *to move*
une enveloppe *envelope*	**conduire** *to drive*
un timbre *stamp*	**envoyer quelque chose en express** *to send something express*
le covoiturage *carpooling*	**faire le trajet (entre)** *to travel, to commute (between)*
le métro *subway*	**livrer** *to deliver goods / groceries*
les moyens (m.) **de transport** *means of transportation*	**transporter** *to transport*
un scooter *moped*	

- The prepositions **en** and **à** are used to express that you travel by a specific means of transportation. If you travel *in* this means of transportation, use **en.** If it's a means of transportation that you cannot be inside of, use **à.**

Ils voyagent souvent **en avion.**	*They often travel **by plane.***
Elle va à l'université **à pied.**	*She goes to the university **by foot.***
Il va au marché **à moto.**	*He goes to the market **by motorcycle.***

- Note that to express that you are sending something by a specific means of transportation, you use the preposition **par.**

Je veux envoyer cette lettre **par avion.**	*I want to send this letter **by air.***

Pour aller plus loin
Le verbe *conduire*

conduire *(to drive)*	
je **conduis**	nous **conduisons**
tu **conduis**	vous **conduisez**
il/elle/on **conduit**	ils/elles **conduisent**
PAST PARTICIPLE: **conduit**	

Other verbs conjugated like **conduire** are **construire** *(to construct)*, **détruire** *(to destroy)*, and **traduire** *(to translate)*.

Essayez! Complétez chaque phrase avec les formes appropriées des verbes **conduire, construire, détruire** ou **traduire** au présent.

1. L'orage _____ notre jardin.

2. Mon professeur _____ trop vite sa voiture.

3. Nous _____ ces phrases en anglais.

4. Mes frères _____ une nouvelle maison.

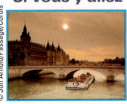

Si vous y allez

© Jon Arnold/Passage/Corbis

Si vous allez à Paris, découvrez la ville à bord d'un bateau-mouche. Vous pourrez découvrir les plus beaux monuments de Paris dans l'un des plus célèbres bateaux au monde. Le bateau-mouche vous offre aussi la possibilité d'un déjeuner ou d'un dîner élégant.

ACTIVITÉ A Marques et noms propres Quelle marque *(brand name)* ou quel nom propre *(proper name)* associez-vous à chaque moyen de transport mentionné?

11-1

Modèle: un bateau **Sea Ray**

1. **2.** **3.** **4.** **5.** **6.** **7.** **8.**

ACTIVITÉ B Les moyens de transport

11-2

Étape 1. Comment les personnes mentionnées font-elles leurs trajets quotidiens *(daily)*?

1. a. à scooter	b. en camionnette	**6.** a. à moto	b. en autobus
2. a. en camionnette	b. en avion	**7.** a. en 4X4	b. en métro
3. a. à moto	b. en taxi	**8.** a. en taxi	b. en covoiturage
4. a. à pied	b. en voiture	**9.** a. en camionnette	b. en autobus
5. a. en camionnette	b. en avion	**10.** a. en taxi	b. à moto

Étape 2. Complétez la phrase à propos de Claire Gagner du film *Liaisons*.

Claire a fait le trajet entre Montréal et Québec _____.

ACTIVITÉ C Les services de la poste Connaissez-vous bien les services de la poste? Essayez de répondre aux questions. Cherchez l'information sur Internet si nécessaire.

1. Combien coûte un timbre pour envoyer une carte postale du Texas en Floride?

2. Combien coûte un timbre pour envoyer une lettre des États-Unis en France?

3. Ça coûte combien pour envoyer une grande enveloppe en express aux États-Unis?

4. Combien coûte la location *(rental)* d'une boîte à lettres à la poste?

ACTIVITÉ D Comment les transporter?

Étape 1. Comment transporteriez-vous les objets ou animaux suivants?

Modèle: une commode de Paris à Québec **Je la transporterais par bateau.**

1. un divan de Detroit à New York	**5.** une guitare de Toronto à Montréal
2. un petit chien de Chicago à Paris	**6.** cinq chats de Boston à New York
3. cinq colis de Miami à Rome	**7.** dix tableaux d'art de Québec à Nice
4. un piano de New York à Paris	**8.** un téléviseur de Dallas à Austin

Étape 2. À tour de rôle, posez des questions basées sur l'Étape 1 à un(e) partenaire. Après, décidez qui serait un(e) bon(ne) expéditionnaire *(shipping clerk)*. Qui a répondu chaque fois avec un moyen de transport plus efficace?

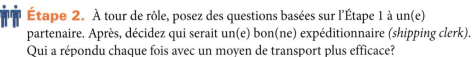

ACTIVITÉ **E** **Quel moyen de transport?**

Étape 1. Quel moyen de transport choisiriez-vous dans chaque situation?

Modèle: pour faire le trajet entre votre maison et le café   **Je prendrais l'autobus.**

1. votre maison et l'université
2. votre maison et le supermarché
3. votre maison et le cinéma
4. votre maison et la salle de sports
5. le cours de français et la bibliothèque
6. votre maison et une fête au centre-ville

Étape 2. Posez les questions à deux camarades de classe. Qui est le/la plus écologique? Qui est le plus paresseux / la plus paresseuse?

ACTIVITÉ **F** **Les habitudes de conduite**

Étape 1. Comment classifieriez-vous chaque situation? **(a) Pas de problème,** **(b) Ce n'est pas une bonne idée mais parfois c'est nécessaire** ou **(c) C'est dangereux et stupide.**

1. On conduit et on mange.
2. On conduit et on boit du café.
3. On conduit et on parle au téléphone.
4. On conduit et on écrit des textos.
5. On conduit quand on a sommeil.
6. On boit de l'alcool et on conduit.
7. On conduit quand il fait mauvais.
8. On conduit et on écoute de la musique.

Étape 2. Montrez vos réponses à un(e) partenaire pour voir si vous êtes d'accord. Puis, demandez à votre partenaire s'il/si elle fait ces activités pour déterminer s'il/si elle est un conducteur/une conductrice *(driver)* prudent(e) ou dangereux/dangereuse.

Modèle: **Est-ce que tu conduis et tu manges en même temps** *(at the same time)?*

Un mot sur la culture

Le TGV en France

Le train est un moyen de transport beaucoup plus utilisé en France qu'aux États-Unis. En effet, pour les Français, c'est un moyen de voyager qui est pratique et économique. En 1981, la SNCF (Société nationale des chemins de fer° français) a inauguré son premier train à grande vitesse°, le TGV. Grâce au° TGV, on peut faire le trajet entre Paris et Lyon en deux heures et entre Paris et Londres en moins de trois heures. Le TGV dessert le Royaume-Uni sous le nom Eurostar.

chemins de fer *railroad* **vitesse** *speed* **Grâce au** *Thanks to*

- Aimez-vous voyager en train? Quels avantages associez-vous à un voyage en train?

Pour parler de l'avenir

Le futur

DU FILM *LIAISONS*
....

Un coup d'œil sur la grammaire

Look at these photos from the film *Liaisons* and their captions.

CLAIRE Je t'appeller**ai** demain, d'accord?

ABIA Bon voyage. [...] Je m'occuper**ai** de Monsieur Émile.

1. What does **Je t'appellerai demain** mean?

2. What is the tense of the verb **appellerai** in the left caption?

3. What does **Je m'occuperai de Monsieur Émile** mean in the right caption?

❖ You learned how to express future events that *are going to happen* with the **futur proche** (the verb **aller** plus the infinitive form of a verb). To express future events that *will happen*, use the **futur simple**.

Marie **prendra** l'avion pour aller en Espagne.

*Marie **will take** the plane to Spain.*

❖ To form the **futur simple,** add the future endings to the future stem. The future verb stems are identical to the conditional verb stems.

<table>
<tr><th>s'amuser</th><th>sortir</th><th>prendre</th></tr>
<tr><td>je m'amuserai</td><td>je sortirai</td><td>je prendrai</td></tr>
<tr><td>tu t'amuseras</td><td>tu sortiras</td><td>tu prendras</td></tr>
<tr><td>il/elle/on s'amusera</td><td>il/elle/on sortira</td><td>il/elle/on prendra</td></tr>
<tr><td>nous nous amuserons</td><td>nous sortirons</td><td>nous prendrons</td></tr>
<tr><td>vous vous amuserez</td><td>vous sortirez</td><td>vous prendrez</td></tr>
<tr><td>ils/elles s'amuseront</td><td>ils/elles sortiront</td><td>ils/elles prendront</td></tr>
</table>

Note de **grammaire**
Note that, with the exception of the **nous** and **vous** forms, the future endings are identical to the present tense forms of the verb **avoir**.

❖ The irregular future stem forms are identical to the irregular conditional stem forms.

Luc **fera** le trajet en train.

*Luc **will make** the trip/**commute** by train.*

Elles n'**iront** pas en France l'été prochain.

*They **will** not **go** to France next summer.*

⸭ -**Er** verbs with spelling changes in the conditional form have the same spelling changes in the **futur simple.**

Nous **achèterons** une maison l'année prochaine.	We **will buy** a house next year.

⸭ The choice between the **futur proche** and the **futur simple** depends on how certain you are that the event will occur. If you think that the event will definitely occur, use the **futur proche.** If there is less certainty about the event occurring, use the **futur simple.** Compare the following sentences:

Je **ferai** mes devoirs ce soir.	I **will do** my homework tonight (maybe).
Je **vais faire** mes devoirs ce soir.	I **am going to do** my homework tonight (you're sure).
Il **étudiera** le chinois un jour.	He **will study** Chinese one day (thinks he will).
Il **va étudier** le chinois en mai.	He **is going to study** Chinese in May (definitely).

⸭ You learned in **Chapitre 9** that **si** clauses using the imperfect and conditional forms can be used to express hypothetical situations. You can also use **si** clauses to express events and conditions that are possible or likely to happen. In these cases, the **si** clause that expresses the condition is in the present tense and the main clause that expresses the possible outcome is in the **futur proche** or the **futur simple.**

Si tu ne **conduis** pas, je **prendrai** un taxi.	If you're not **driving**, I'**ll take** a taxi.
Si je **vais** à Paris, j'**irai** au Louvre.	If I **go** to Paris, I **will go** to the Louvre.

⸭ In French, if a clause begins with **quand, lorsque** (when), **dès que** (as soon as) or **aussitôt que** (as soon as), and a future event is implied, use the future tense. In English, the present tense is used.

Quand il **quittera** Paris, il **sera** triste.	**When** he **leaves** Paris, he'**ll be** sad.
Dès que j'**aurai** un chien, je l'**appellerai** Fido.	**As soon as** I **get** a dog, I'**ll call** it Fido.

⸭ If future time is not implied in clauses with **quand** or **dès que,** the verb may be in another tense.

Quand avez-vous étudié l'anglais?	**When did you study** English?
Dès qu'il est arrivé, on s'est mis à manger.	**As soon as he arrived,** we began to eat.

⸭ Note that **le futur** refers to the grammatical future only. If you are referring to future events that have not occured, you must use **l'avenir** (m.).

Claude s'inquiète de son **avenir.**	Claude is worried about his **future.**
On a étudié le **futur** en classe aujourd'hui.	We studied the **future tense** in class today.

ACTIVITÉ G **Les prédictions pour les modes de vie** À votre avis, est-ce que chaque prédiction sera vraie ou fausse?

Dans vingt ans…	Vrai	Faux
1. les mères célibataires **pourront** avoir une carrière plus facilement.	☐	☐
2. les bourreaux de travail **voudront** avoir plus d'enfants.	☐	☐
3. les fanas de la santé **vivront** moins longtemps.	☐	☐
4. les retraités **seront** plus pauvres.	☐	☐
5. il y **aura** moins de femmes au foyer.	☐	☐
6. les babas cool **n'existeront** plus.	☐	☐
7. il y **aura** plus de pères célibataires.	☐	☐
8. tout le monde **deviendra** plus écologiste.	☐	☐

ACTIVITÉ H **Dans dix ans** Un étudiant parle avec ses deux colocataires de ses prédictions pour l'avenir (dans dix ans). Choisissez le sujet de chaque phrase. Puis, indiquez si vous êtes d'accord avec les prédictions de cet étudiant.

1. _____ se**ra** uniquement électronique.   a. Le courrier   b. Les cartes postales

2. _____ n'ir**ons** plus à la poste.   a. Vous   b. Nous

3. _____ coûte**ra** plus cher.   a. Un timbre   b. Les enveloppes

4. _____ coûter**ont** moins cher.   a. L'autobus   b. Les taxis

5. _____ pourr**ons** conduire plus vite.   a. On   b. Nous

6. _____ devr**ai** payer plus pour l'essence *(gas)*.   a. Je   b. Tu

7. _____ attend**rez** le bus moins longtemps.   a. Les étudiants   b. Vous

8. _____ ne voudr**as** plus voyager en avion.   a. On   b. Tu

ACTIVITÉ I **Les prédictions pour les célébrités d'Hollywood**

Étape 1. Est-ce que chaque prédiction est probable ou pas probable? Si la prédiction n'est pas probable, faites une prédiction que vous pensez probable pour la célébrité.

1. Jeremy Lin **achètera** un stade de baseball.

2. Miley Cyrus **gagnera** un Grammy.

3. Lady Gaga **tombera** enceinte *(pregnant)*.

4. Martha Stewart **ira** en prison encore une fois.

5. Justin Bieber **aura** une nouvelle copine.

6. Daniel Radcliffe et Emma Watson **se marieront.**

7. Will Smith et Jada Pinkett Smith **se quitteront.**

8. Brad Pitt et Angelina Jolie **auront** un autre enfant.

Étape 2. Demandez à un(e) partenaire ce qu'il/elle pense de ces prédictions.

Modèle: É1: **Jeremy Lin achètera un stade. C'est probable ou pas probable?**
É2: **Ce n'est pas probable. Je pense qu'il achètera un restaurant.**

Étape 1. Avec un(e) partenaire, devinez *(guess)* si votre professeur fera les activités suivantes ce week-end.

Notre professeur…

1. **ira** au cinéma.
2. **fera** du shopping.
3. **conduira** à la campagne.
4. **s'amusera** avec des amis.

5. **verra** un spectacle.
6. **louera** un film français.
7. **prendra** un repas gastronomique.
8. **sortira** avec sa famille.

Étape 2. Votre professeur va vous donner ses réponses. Avez-vous bien deviné?

Étape 3. Demandez à votre partenaire s'il/si elle fera ces activités.

Modèle: **Est-ce que tu iras au cinéma ce week-end?**

Conclusion Qui passera un week-end plus intéressant? Votre professeur ou votre partenaire?

ACTIVITÉ **K** **Les événements possibles pour notre classe de français** Complétez chaque phrase avec un verbe au futur.

1. Si je ne peux pas conduire demain, je…
2. Si notre classe de français fait une excursion, nous…
3. Si mes camarades de classe veulent étudier ensemble, ils…
4. Si je veux apprendre une autre langue étrangère, je…
5. Si les cours sont annulés *(cancelled),* mon professeur…
6. Si notre professeur nous demande si nous voulons voir un film en classe, nous…
7. Si nous devons écouter de la musique française en classe, nous…
8. Si on invite quelqu'un de célèbre en cours de français, on…

ACTIVITÉ **L** **Les événements personnels possibles**

Étape 1. Complétez les phrases avec un verbe au présent ou au futur selon le cas pour décrire votre avenir.

1. Dès que je terminerai mes études,…
2. Je ferai un master si…
3. Je voyagerai en France si…
4. J'achèterai une maison quand…
5. Aussitôt que j'aurai un bon emploi…
6. J'achèterai une nouvelle voiture dès que…
7. Je me marierai si…
8. J'aurai des enfants si…

Étape 2. Montrez vos réponses à un(e) partenaire. Vos avenirs seront-ils similaires ou différents?

ACTIVITÉ **M** **L'avenir des modes de vie** Décrivez l'avenir de ces modes de vie dans dix ans en utilisant les expressions suivantes.

Possibilités

s'amuser plus/moins

avoir des enfants plus tôt/tard

avoir plus/moins d'enfants

avoir plus/moins de temps libre

dépenser plus/moins d'argent

devoir retourner au travail

s'ennuyer plus/moins

être plus/moins heureux/heureuse

être plus/moins riche

faire plus/moins de lessive

gagner plus/moins d'argent

manger plus/moins de produits bio

se marier plus tôt/tard

s'occuper plus/moins facilement de ses enfants

prendre plus/moins de jours de vacances

retourner à l'université

travailler plus/moins

voyager plus/moins facilement en avion

????

Modèle: **Les fanas de la santé seront moins heureux.**

1. Les mères actives _____
2. Les pères célibataires _____
3. Les mères célibataires _____
4. Les membres de la jet-set _____
5. Les accros du shopping _____

6. Les babas cool _____
7. Les bourreaux de travail _____
8. Les écologistes _____
9. Les femmes au foyer _____
10. Les retraités _____

ACTIVITÉ **N** **L'histoire de Roland**

Étape 1. Roland consulte une voyante *(fortune teller)* à propos de son avenir. Avec deux camarades de classe, écrivez une histoire *(story)* de cinq à six phrases sur l'avenir de Roland à l'aide de la photo suivante.

Étape 2. Lisez votre histoire à un autre groupe. Qui a une meilleure histoire?

© Pierre Roussel/Agence Quebec Presse/Newscom

ACTIVITÉ O Les péchés mignons

Étape 1. Décrivez trois péchés mignons *(guilty pleasures)* ou trois mauvaises habitudes *(habits)* que vous avez.

Modèle: J'achète beaucoup de chaussures *(shoes).* Je mange beaucoup de chips. Je fais la grasse matinée le samedi.

Étape 2. Lisez vos péchés mignons ou vos mauvaises habitudes à un(e) partenaire. Écoutez ceux/celles de votre partenaire. Dites à votre partenaire ce qui pourra se passer s'il/si elle n'a plus ces péchés mignons ou ces mauvaises habitudes.

Modèle: Si tu n'achètes plus de chaussures, tu auras plus d'argent pour acheter des choses plus importantes comme la nourriture. Si tu ne manges plus de chips, tu maigriras et tu seras en bonne santé. Si tu ne fais plus la grasse matinée, tu pourras finir tes devoirs plus tôt.

ACTIVITÉ P Quand les hommes vivront d'amour

Quand les hommes vivront d'amour est une chanson québécoise composée par Raymond Lévesque en 1956. Le refrain, *Quand les hommes vivront d'amour // il n'y aura plus de misère*, appelle à la paix et est resté populaire jusqu'à aujourd'hui. Décrivez comment notre monde pourra être quand les hommes vivront d'amour. Écrivez au moins *(at least)* quatre phrases.

Modèle: Quand les hommes vivront d'amour, **il n'y aura plus de violence.** Les enfants ne s'inquiéteront plus. Le monde sera plus beau.

Liaisons musicales

La chanson *Quand les hommes vivront d'amour* de Raymond Lévesque a été votée la chanson la plus chantée au Québec. Cette chanson a été traduite dans de nombreuses langues et de nombreux pays, et elle a été enregistrée *(recorded)* par beaucoup de chanteurs et chanteuses. Cherchez les paroles de cette chanson sur Internet.

OUI, JE PEUX!

Here are two "can do statements" for you to check your progress so far. Look at each statement and rate yourself on how well you think you can perform the task. Then verify your ability with a partner. How did you do?

1. **"I can tell someone three activities I will do in the next two weeks and what mode of transportation I will use to do these activities."**

   I can perform this function
   ☐ with ease
   ☐ with some difficulty
   ☐ not at all

2. **"I can ask someone else what activities he/she will do in the next two weeks and what mode of transportation he/she will use to do these activities."**

   I can perform this function
   ☐ with ease
   ☐ with some difficulty
   ☐ not at all

iLrn™

Are you looking for more practice? You can find it in **iLrn**.

VOCABULAIRE 2

🔊 Partons en vacances!

Let's go on vacation!

débarquer de l'avion

une porte d'embarquement

PORTE 23

un(e) agent(e) de la sécurité

un(e) agent(e) de bord

embarquer dans l'avion

la carte d'embarquement

un billet d'avion

une valise

une voyageuse (un voyageur)

un passeport

enregistrer les bagages

BA

À l'aéroport

> **Note de vocabulaire**
> **Un scanner corporel** is a body scanner, **un appareil de radiographie** is an x-ray machine; and **un détecteur de métaux** is a metal detector.

Vocabulaire complémentaire

à l'étranger *abroad/overseas*

un billet aller-retour *round-trip ticket*

un billet aller simple *one-way ticket*

un permis de conduire *driver's license*

une pièce d'identité *a form of identification*

un siège *seat*

un vol direct/une correspondance *direct/connecting flight*

---

la première classe *first-class*

la classe affaires *business class*

la classe économique *economy class*

---

un(e) agent(e) de voyages *travel agent*

un arrêt d'autobus *bus stop*

une auberge de jeunesse *youth hostel*

une chambre fumeurs/non-fumeurs *smoking/nonsmoking rom*

une chambre individuelle/double *single/double room*

une clé *key*

un(e) client(e) *client, guest*

une croisière *cruise*

une gare *(bus/train) station*

un gîte du passant *bed and breakfast*

un hôtel (trois/quatre/cinq étoiles) *(three/four/five star) hotel*

un hôtel de luxe *luxury hotel*

un lit simple/double *single/double bed*

le logement *lodging*

un motel *motel*

le service de chambre *room service*

une tente *tent*

aller en vacances (f.) *to go on vacation*

attacher la ceinture de sécurité *to fasten the seatbelt*

déclarer (vos achats) *to declare (your purchases)*

faire les valises *to pack*

passer à la douane *to go through customs*

passer au contrôle de sécurité *to go through security*

payer des frais (m.) supplémentaires *to pay extra fees*

© Courtesy of Wynne Wong

Si vous y allez

Si vous allez à Québec, visitez la Gare du Palais, une gare construite dans le même style que le Château Frontenac qui est desservie par *Via Rail Canada* et les autobus *Orléans Express*.

© Jeff Schultes / Shutterstock.com

Pour aller plus loin
Dans l'avion ou sur l'avion?

In French, to say that you are *on the plane, on the train,* or *on the bus,* you must use the preposition **dans**. **Sur l'avion** means there is something *on top of* the plane.

Je lis **dans** l'avion.	*I'm reading **on** the plane.*
Il y a un oiseau **sur** l'avion.	*There is a bird **on (top of)** the plane.*

Essayez! Répondez aux questions.

1. Qu'aimez-vous faire dans l'avion?

2. Qu'aimez-vous faire dans l'autobus?

ACTIVITÉ A **C'est où?** Complétez chaque phrase que vous entendez avec

11-3 **(a) l'aéroport, (b) l'arrêt d'autobus** ou **(c) la gare.**

1.　　　2.　　　3.　　　4.　　　5.　　　6.

ACTIVITÉ B **Les modes de vie et les voyages**

Étape 1. Qu'est-ce que vous associez à chaque mode de vie?

1. une retraitée	a. une auberge de jeunesse	b. un gîte du passant
2. un fana de la santé	a. une chambre fumeurs	b. une chambre non-fumeurs
3. une femme de la jet-set	a. un hôtel cinq étoiles	b. une tente
4. un homme d'affaires	a. la classe économique	b. la classe affaires
5. un baba cool	a. une tente	b. un hôtel de luxe
6. une mère et un père actifs	a. un lit simple	b. un lit double
7. une femme célibataire	a. une chambre double	b. une chambre individuelle
8. un étudiant	a. un motel	b. un hôtel cinq étoiles

Étape 2. Le Château Frontenac, c'est quel genre de logement *(accommodation)*?

© Maridav/Shutterstock.com

ACTIVITÉ C **Partir en vacances** La sœur d'Abia, Nadia, et leur cousin,

11-4 Jerome, veulent partir en vacances. Écoutez ce qu'ils disent à l'agent de voyages pour déterminer le meilleur vol et hébergement pour eux.

Voyage 1: Nadia

1. a. billet aller simple　　　　　b. billet aller-retour
2. a. vol national　　　　　　　　b. vol international
3. a. première classe　　　　　　b. classe économique
4. a. besoin d'enregistrer des valises　　b. pas besoin d'enregistrer de bagages
5. a. motel　　　　　　　　　　　b. hôtel 4 ou 5 étoiles
6. a. chambre fumeurs　　　　　b. chambre non-fumeurs
7. a. lit simple　　　　　　　　　b. lit double

Voyage 2: Jerome

1. a. billet aller-simple　　　　　b. billet aller-retour
2. a. vol national　　　　　　　　b. vol international
3. a. première classe　　　　　　b. classe économique
4. a. besoin d'enregistrer des valises　　b. pas besoin d'enregistrer de bagages
5. a. motel　　　　　　　　　　　b. hôtel 4 ou 5 étoiles
6. a. chambre fumeurs　　　　　b. chambre non-fumeurs
7. a. lit simple　　　　　　　　　b. lit double

ACTIVITÉ **D** **Savez-vous quoi faire à l'aéroport?**

Étape 1. Que devez-vous faire pour voyager en avion? Mettez les actions dans l'ordre.

a. _____ Vous donnez la carte d'embarquement à l'agent de bord.

b. _____ Vous attendez le vol à la porte d'embarquement.

c. _____ Vous débarquez de l'avion.

d. _____ Vous passez au contrôle de sécurité.

e. _____ Vous présentez une pièce d'identité et la carte d'embarquement à l'agent de sécurité.

f. _____ Vous embarquez dans l'avion.

g. _____ Vous mettez votre sac sous le siège devant vous et vous attachez votre ceinture de sécurité pour le décollage.

h. _____ Vous arrivez à l'aéroport et vous enregistrez vos valises.

Étape 2. Complétez les phrases.

1. S'il n'y a pas de vol direct,…   **3.** Si vous avez trois valises,…

2. Si vous voyagez à l'étranger,…   **4.** Si vous voulez transporter un couteau,…

 **Étape 3.** Montrez vos réponses à un(e) partenaire pour voir si vous êtes d'accord.

ACTIVITÉ **E** **Voyager à l'étranger**

Étape 1. Savez-vous quoi faire quand vous voyagez à l'étranger? Avec un(e) partenaire, décidez si chaque phrase est vraie ou fausse. Corrigez *(Correct)* les phrases qui sont fausses.

1. Il faut arriver à l'aéroport 30 minutes en avance.

2. On peut utiliser un permis de conduire comme pièce d'identité.

3. On peut fumer dans la section fumeurs de l'avion.

4. Il faut passer à la douane.

5. On peut rapporter *(bring back)* trois litres de vin ou de bière.

6. On peut rapporter du chocolat et des bonbons.

7. On peut rapporter du jambon et des steaks.

8. On ne déclare pas les produits qu'on achète au magasin hors taxe *(duty-free)*.

9. Il faut payer les frais de douane si on achète plus de 800 dollars U.S. de produits.

10. On peut aller en prison si on ment *(lie)* à l'agent de douane.

Étape 2. Discutez de ces questions avec votre partenaire.

1. Avez-vous voyagé à l'étranger? Où?

2. Avez-vous jamais menti à l'agent de douane?

ACTIVITÉ F Comment voyagez-vous?

Étape 1. Comment voyagez-vous typiquement? Notez vos réponses.

	Moi	Mon partenaire
1. Vous voyagez en première classe ou en classe économique?	_____	_____
2. Vous utilisez un(e) agent(e) de voyages ou Internet?	_____	_____
3. Vous préférez un siège près du hublot *(window)* ou un siège côté couloir *(aisle)*?	_____	_____
4. Quel type de logement choisissez-vous?	_____	_____
5. Vous préférez une chambre fumeurs ou non-fumeurs?	_____	_____
6. Vous perdez souvent votre clé d'hôtel?	_____	_____
7. Vous utilisez souvent le service de chambre?	_____	_____

Étape 2. Posez les questions à un(e) partenaire et notez ses réponses dans la deuxième colonne. Êtes-vous similaires ou différent(e)s? Pouvez-vous voyager ensemble?

Étape 3. Avec votre partenaire, devinez *(guess)* ce que *(what)* dirait votre professeur.

 ACTIVITÉ G Êtes-vous un(e) bon(ne) agent(e) de voyages?

Étape 1. Avec un(e) partenaire, discutez quel type de voyage serait idéal pour les personnes suivantes.

Nom: Mimi
Occupation: mère célibataire et secrétaire
Domicile: Tampa, FL.
Nombre de voyageurs: cinq (moi, mes trois enfants et ma sœur)
Durée du voyage: trois à cinq jours pour nous amuser
Argent à dépenser: 1000 dollars

Nom: Claude
Occupation: homme d'affaires célibataire et stressé
Domicile: Montréal, Québec
Nombre de voyageurs: un
Durée du voyage: une semaine pour me détendre et rencontrer une femme
Argent à dépenser: sans limite

Suggestions

aller à Disney	faire du camping	louer une voiture
descendre dans un hôtel de luxe	faire une croisière	louer un châlet

Questions à considérer
- Quel type de voyage proposez-vous? Où est-ce que les voyageurs iront?
- S'ils prennent l'avion, quel type de billets proposez-vous?
- Quel type de logement proposez-vous? Quels types d'activités sont possibles?

Étape 2. Avec votre partenaire, préparez un itinéraire pour Mimi et pour Claude.

Modèle: **Mimi peut faire du camping avec sa sœur et ses enfants à Wisconsin Dells...**

Étape 1. Indiquez si chaque situation s'applique *(applies)* au passé avant le 11 septembre 2001, au présent ou à l'avenir. Vous pouvez cocher *(check)* plus d'une catégorie.

	Le passé	Le présent	L'avenir
1. On peut passer au contrôle de sécurité sans carte d'embarquement.	_____	_____	_____
2. On peut apporter du vin dans les vols nationaux.	_____	_____	_____
3. On peut passer au contrôle de sécurité avec une bouteille d'eau.	_____	_____	_____
4. Il faut enlever *(remove)* les chaussures *(shoes)* au contrôle de sécurité.	_____	_____	_____
5. Il faut passer au scanner corporel au contrôle de sécurité.	_____	_____	_____
6. On ne paie pas de frais supplémentaires pour enregistrer les valises.	_____	_____	_____
7. On peut utiliser des couteaux en plastique dans l'avion.	_____	_____	_____
8. Les vols ont souvent du retard.	_____	_____	_____

Étape 2. Montrez vos réponses à un(e) partenaire pour voir si vous avez mis les mêmes choses. À votre avis, comment est-ce que les voyages en avion seront à l'avenir? Discutez de cette question avec votre partenaire.

Étape 3. Parlez avec votre partenaire d'un mauvais voyage en avion que vous avez fait.

© Vivafilm/Everett Collection

Un mot sur la culture

Les snowbirds en Floride

En Floride, il existe des villages québécois. En effet, en hiver, plus de cinq cent mille Québécois s'installent en Floride. On appelle ces Floriquébécois, dont la plupart° sont des retraités, des *snowbirds*. En Floride, on peut trouver des publications en français et on parle français dans plusieurs restaurants, épiceries et hôtels. L'âge moyen° des snowbirds est de 70 ans. En 1993, le cinéaste québécois George Mihalka a tourné° un film comique, *La Florida*, sur les snowbirds québécois.

plupart *most part* **moyen** *average* **a tourné** *produced*

• Connaissez-vous des quartiers québécois ou français aux États-Unis?

Pour relier deux idées

Les pronoms relatifs **qui, que, dont** et **où**

DU FILM _LIAISONS_

Un coup d'œil sur la grammaire

Look at these photos from the film _Liaisons_ and their captions.

CLAIRE C'est l'homme **qui** m'a donné l'enveloppe avec la réservation au Frontenac.

CLAIRE Et ici... c'est l'homme **que** j'ai rencontré...

1. What follows the relative pronoun **qui**? A verb or a subject?
2. What follows the relative pronoun **que**? A verb or a subject?
3. What do you think the two captions mean?

❖ Relative pronouns allow you to combine two ideas together into one sentence. Relative pronouns may be omitted in English, but they cannot be omitted in French.

La femme **qui** parle est ma tante. _The woman **who** is speaking is my aunt._
Le livre **que** j'ai lu était drôle.   _The book **(that)** I read was funny._

Les pronoms relatifs	
qui _who, that, which_	**dont** _that, (of) which, (of) whom, whose_
que _that, which_	**où** _where, when_

Note de **grammaire**
Qui may also be followed by a conjugated verb that has an object pronoun in front of it: **C'est l'homme qui m'a donné l'enveloppe.**

❖ **Qui** may refer to people or things and is used as the subject of a dependent clause. Because **qui** acts as the subject, it is always followed by a conjugated verb.

Tu vois l'homme **qui voyage** avec son chien?
Do you see the man **who is traveling** with his dog?

L'agente **qui a enregistré** mes valises est belle.
The agent **who checked** (in) my bags is beautiful.

❖ **Que** also refers to people or things and is used as the direct object of a dependent clause so **que** is always followed by a subject (not a verb). Note that **que** becomes **qu'** if the subject begins with a vowel sound.

C'est l'homme **qu'elle** a vu à l'hôtel! _That's the man **(that) she** saw at the hotel!_
J'ai lu le livre **que Luc** m'a donné. _I read the book **(that) Luc** gave me._

- Note that in the **passé composé**, the past participle after **que** agrees in number and gender with the direct object.

    La clé que Claire a trouvé**e** est pour un coffre-fort.

    The key that Claire found is for a safety deposit box.

- **Dont** replaces **de** plus a noun and can refer to people or things. Some expressions that contain **de** include **parler de, avoir besoin de, avoir peur de,** and **se souvenir de.**

    Voici la femme **dont** tu parlais.   *Here is the woman **whom** you were talking about.*

    Voici les livres **dont** j'ai besoin.   *Here are the books **(that)** I need.*

- **Dont** can also be used to refer to possessions. In this case, **dont** is followed by a definite article.

    Voici les gens **dont la** maison est grande.
    *Here are the people **whose** house is big.*

    J'ai rencontré une femme **dont le** mari est agent de bord.
    *I met a woman **whose** husband is a flight attendant.*

- Use **où** to refer to a place or a time.

    Je me rappelle le moment **où** il m'a dit qu'il m'aimait.
    *I remember the moment **when** he told me he loved me.*

    C'est une ville **où** il y a beaucoup de Français.
    *It's a city **where** there are lots of French people.*

ACTIVITÉ I Les films, les émissions et les personnes

Étape 1. Quel film ou quelle personne associez-vous à chaque description?

C'est un film…

1. **qui** est très drôle.
2. **qui** a gagné un Oscar.
3. **qui** est très mauvais.
4. **qui** vient de sortir.

C'est une personne…

5. **qui** voyage en première classe.
6. **qui** boit beaucoup d'alcool.
7. **qui** est très intelligente.
8. **qui** parle bien français.

Étape 2. Quelle émission ou quelle personne associez-vous à chaque description?

C'est une émission de télévision…

1. **que** les enfants aiment beaucoup.
2. **que** les gens aimaient dans les années 80.
3. **que** je regarderai cette semaine.
4. **que** je déteste.

C'est une personne…

5. **que** j'admire beaucoup.
6. **que** les adolescents aiment.
7. **que** j'aimerais rencontrer.
8. **que** tout le monde connaît.

Liaisons musicales

YP BO/Agence Quebec Presse/Newscom

Éric Lapointe (1969–) est un rockeur québécois dont les chansons se trouvent dans beaucoup de bandes sonores *(soundtracks)* de films populaires québécois comme *Les Boys* et *Bon cop, bad cop.* Cherchez une chanson d'Éric Lapointe sur Internet et décrivez son style.

ACTIVITÉ J **Les livres, les personnes et les villes** Quel livre ou quelle personne associez-vous à chaque description?

C'est un livre…

1. **dont** tout le monde **parle.**
2. **dont** les étudiants **ont besoin.**
3. **dont** les enfants **ont peur.**

C'est une personne…

4. **dont** les journaux **parlent.**
5. **dont** je **me souviens** bien.
6. **dont** j'**ai peur.**

C'est quelqu'un…

1. **dont** la maison est à Beverly Hills.
2. **dont** les cheveux sont blonds.
3. **dont** le mari est beau.

C'est une ville…

5. **où** on trouve les meilleurs restaurants.
6. **où** on peut parler français.
7. **où** il y a un aéroport international.

ACTIVITÉ K **Aimez-vous lire?**

Étape 1. Complétez les phrases avec **qui** ou **que** et indiquez si vous êtes d'accord avec chaque phrase.

J'aime les livres…

1. _____ J.K. Rowling écrit.
2. _____ parlent des extra-terrestres.
3. _____ le *New York Times* recommande.
4. _____ sont en français.
5. _____ ont beaucoup de dessins.
6. _____ mes amis aiment.
7. _____ je dois lire pour mes cours.
8. _____ ne coûtent pas cher.

Étape 2. Demandez à un(e) partenaire s'il/si elle aime ces livres.

Modèle: Est-ce que tu aimes les livres que J.K. Rowling écrit?

ACTIVITÉ L **Les femmes**

Étape 1. Complétez chaque phrase avec **que** ou **dont.** Ensuite, donnez le nom d'une femme qui correspond à chaque description.

Voici la femme…

1. _____ la mère est célèbre. _____
2. _____ le monde entier *(entire)* admire. _____
3. _____ les hommes adorent. _____
4. _____ les journaux parlent. _____
5. _____ la voix est très belle. _____
6. _____ les hommes ont peur. _____
7. _____ les parents détestent. _____
8. _____ on se souviendra toujours. _____

Étape 2. Posez les questions suivantes à un(e) partenaire.

1. Est-ce que tu connais quelqu'un que tous les parents adorent?
2. Est-ce que tu connais quelqu'un dont les enfants ont peur?
3. Est-ce que tu connais quelqu'un dont la voiture coûte très cher?

ACTIVITÉ **M** **Quel objet?** Utilisez les participes passés pour déterminer l'objet de chaque phrase. Puis, demandez à un(e) partenaire de vous donner un exemple de chaque chose qu'il/elle a lue, qu'il/elle a vue et qu'il/elle a essayée.

1. Nomme _____ que tu as lu**e**.   a. une revue   b. un journal   c. des livres
2. Nomme _____ que tu as vu**s**.   a. une émission   b. un spectacle   c. des films
3. Nomme _____ que tu as essayé.   a. une boisson   b. un dessert   c. des fruits

ACTIVITÉ **N** **L'agent de voyages** Nommez trois villes que vous trouvez intéressantes. Si vous étiez l'agent(e) de voyages, comment décririez-vous ces villes à votre partenaire? Utilisez le pronom relatif **où**. Décidez si vous voulez visiter les villes que votre partenaire a décrites.

Modèle: **Québec est une ville où on peut manger de la poutine. C'est aussi l'endroit où se trouve le Château Frontenac.**

ACTIVITÉ **O** **Les potins et les opinions** Créez des potins ou exprimez votre opinion sur ces sujets en utilisant les pronoms relatifs **qui, que, dont** et **où**. Dites vos potins/opinions à un(e) partenaire.

Modèle: **Ashton Kutcher est un acteur que ma sœur trouve stupide.** *Man of Steel* **est le plus mauvais film qui est sorti au cinéma. Boston est la ville où je suis né(e).**

1. Lupita Nyong'o / actrice
2. Mon/Ma voisin(e) / personne
3. Mon ex / personne
4. Las Vegas / ville
5. Le français / cours
6. Central Park / parc
7. Paul McCartney / chanteur
8. ??? / film
9. ???

OUI, JE PEUX!

Here are two "can do statements" for you to check your progress so far. Look at each statement and rate yourself on how well you think you can perform the task. Then verify your ability with a partner. How did you do?

1. **"I can say which place I would like to go to for vacation and what type of accommodations I would like and ask someone else what his/her preferences are."**

   I can perform this function
   ☐ with ease
   ☐ with some difficulty
   ☐ not at all

2. **"I can tell someone about a person that I admire and explain why, and ask someone else if there is a person that he/she admires."**

   I can perform this function
   ☐ with ease
   ☐ with some difficulty
   ☐ not at all

iLrn™

Are you looking for more practice? You can find it in **iLrn**.

🔊 Que **porter?**

What to wear?

une écharpe

un smoking

un bracelet

une robe du soir

un tee-shirt

un sweat (à capuche)

un chapeau

un manteau

des gants

un jean

un jogging

une casquette

un chemisier

un pull à col roulé

un costume

une chemise

un foulard

un tailleur

une robe

une (mini) jupe

une mallette

un pantalon

un short

des sandales (f.)

des chaussettes (f.)

des bottes (f.)

La réunion des anciens du lycée Gatineau

Note de **grammaire**
The plural forms of **chapeau** and **manteau** are **chapeaux** and **manteaux**.

442 *quatre cent quarante-deux* **CHAPITRE 11 La vie en action**

Vocabulaire complémentaire

un anorak *anorak*

des baskets *(f.) tennis shoes*

un blouson *windbreaker*

des chaussures *(f.)* à talon *high heel shoes*

un collier *necklace*

une cravate *tie*

un gilet *cardigan*

un imperméable *raincoat*

des lunettes *(f.)* (de soleil) *glasses (sunglasses)*

un maillot (de bain) *swimsuit*

une montre *watch*

un pantalon à pattes d'éléphant *bell bottom pants*

un pull-over *sweater*

un pyjama *pyjama*

un sous-vêtement *underwear*

une tenue *outfit*

un vêtement / les vêtements *an article of clothing / clothing*

une veste = jacket

des claquettes/ des tongs = flip flop

à la mode *stylish, fashionable*

ancien / ancienne *former*

bon marché *inexpensive*

cher / chère *expensive*

confortable *comfortable*

démodé(e) *old fashioned, out-of-date*

en solde *on sale*

porter *to wear*

Quelle est votre taille *(f.)*? *What size do you wear?*

Je fais du 32. *I'm a size 32.*

Quelle est votre pointure *(f.)*? *What is your shoe size?*

Je chausse du 36. *I wear a size 36 shoe.*

Ça vous va très bien. *That looks good on you.*

ajusté = skinny
droit = straight
coupe = cut
en cuir = leather

un haut
sans manches
= sleeveless top

Clair = light
vif = vibrant
marine
= navy
fluo = neon
foncé = dark
argent = silver
or = gold

🔊 **ACTIVITÉ A** **Classifiez les vêtements**

11-5 **Étape 1.** Indiquez si chaque vêtement mentionné est normalement pour **(a) une femme, (b) un homme** ou **(c) une femme ou un homme.**

1.   2.   3.   4.   5.   6.   7.   8.   9.   10.   11.   12.

11-6 **Étape 2.** Indiquez si chaque vêtement mentionné est **(a) un haut** *(top)* ou **(b) un bas** *(bottom)*.

1.   2.   3.   4.   5.   6.   7.   8.   9.   10.   11.   12.

11-7 **Étape 3.** Indiquez si chaque vêtement mentionné est normalement pour **(a) l'hiver, (b) l'été** ou **(c) l'hiver et l'été.**

1.   2.   3.   4.   5.   6.   7.   8.   9.   10.   11.   12.

VOCABULAIRE 3 *quatre cent quarante-trois* **443**

🔊 **ACTIVITÉ B Quel magasin?** Quel est votre magasin préféré pour acheter les
11-8 choses mentionnées?

Modèle: des chaussettes   **Kmart**

1.   2.   3.   4.   5.   6.   7.   8.   9.   10.   11.   12.

ACTIVITÉ C Au magasin Associez les éléments de la première colonne aux éléments de la deuxième colonne.

1. _____ Ça vous va très bien.
2. _____ Je fais du 36.
3. _____ Je chausse du 34.
4. _____ Oui, j'aimerais l'essayer.

a. Quelle est votre pointure?
b. Que pensez-vous?
c. Je peux vous aider?
d. Quelle est votre taille?

ACTIVITÉ D Est-ce que l'habit fait le moine?

> **Note de vocabulaire**
> **Est-ce que l'habit fait le moine?** is an idiomatic expression that means *Do the clothes make the man?*

Étape 1. Est-ce que l'habit *(clothing)* fait le moine *(monk)*? Quels vêtements associez-vous aux personnes suivantes?

Modèle: un professeur   **une chemise, un gilet, un pantalon et une cravate**

1. un acteur/une actrice
2. un(e) artiste
3. un(e) baba cool
4. un bourreau de travail
5. un(e) écologiste
6. un(e) fana de la santé

7. une femme active
8. un homme d'affaires
9. une femme au foyer
10. un(e) retraité(e)
11. un sportif/une sportive
12. un homme au foyer

 Étape 2. Regardez le dessin de la réunion des anciens du lycée Gatineau au début du **Vocabulaire 3** et répondez aux questions avec votre partenaire. Justifiez votre réponse.

Modèle: Qui pourrait être un homme au foyer?
L'homme qui porte des chaussettes avec un short et un pull-over.

1. Qui pourrait être un(e) baba cool?
2. Qui pourrait être une femme au foyer?
3. Qui pourrait être un sportif/une sportive?
4. Qui pourrait être un bourreau de travail?
5. Qui pourrait être un(e) fana de la santé?
6. Qui pourrait être un(e) artiste?

✈ ·····
Si vous y allez

© Charles Platiau /Reuters/ Corbis

Si vous allez à Paris, allez au grand magasin *Galeries Lafayette*. Situé sur le boulevard Haussmann dans le neuvième arrondissement, ce grand magasin a une sélection de vêtements à la mode pour hommes et femmes.

Étape 3. Dans le film *Liaisons*, Claire attend Alexis pour un rendez-vous. Qu'est-ce qu'ils portent? Est-ce que leurs vêtements sont à la mode ou démodés?

Que mettriez-vous dans votre valise?

Étape 1. Que mettriez-vous dans votre valise pour les événements suivants? Vous ne pouvez mettre que dix choses dans votre valise.

1. faire une croisière à la Martinique
2. aller au carnaval de Québec en février
3. aller à un mariage à Paris en mars
4. faire du ski en Suisse
5. faire du camping au Canada
6. fêter le Mardi gras à La Nouvelle-Orléans

 Étape 2. Montrez vos réponses à un(e) partenaire. Qui fait mieux ses valises?

ACTIVITÉ **F** **Que porteriez-vous?**

Étape 1. Que porteriez-vous dans les situations suivantes?

1. pour faire de la gym
2. pour aller à un restaurant élégant
3. pour aller à un mariage
4. pour aller à un entretien *(interview)*
5. pour passer au contrôle de sécurité à l'aéroport
6. pour aller à la plage
7. pour aller à une réunion d'anciens élèves du lycée
8. pour dormir

 Étape 2. Dites à un(e) partenaire ce que vous porteriez pour les situations de l'Étape 1 mais ne lui dites pas la situation. Votre partenaire va deviner *(guess)* la situation.

Modèle: É1: **Je porterais un tee-shirt, un short et des baskets.**
É2: **Tu vas à la plage?**

ACTIVITÉ **G** **Qu'est-ce qu'on porte en classe aujourd'hui?**

Étape 1. Notez combien de femmes et combien d'hommes dans la classe portent les vêtements suivants aujourd'hui.

1. un jean	5. une jupe	9. des baskets	13. un gilet
2. un tee-shirt	6. un sweat	10. un pull-over	14. une chemise
3. une casquette	7. un jogging	11. un foulard	15. des sandales
4. une cravate	8. des bottes	12. un chemisier	16. ???

Étape 2. Pour chaque vêtement, notez environ *(approximately)* combien vous en avez chez vous.

 Étape 3. Avec un(e) partenaire, comparez vos chiffres et répondez aux questions.

1. Y a-t-il une tenue typique pour les étudiants de notre classe? Décrivez-la.
2. Y a-t-il une différence entre ce que *(what)* les femmes et les hommes portent? Quelle est la différence?
3. Y a-t-il une différence entre les vêtements que vous avez chez vous et les vêtements que votre partenaire a chez lui/elle? Quelle est la différence?

ACTIVITÉ H **Avez-vous bon goût?**

Étape 1. Que porteriez-vous avec ces vêtements pour compléter la tenue?

Modèle: une mini-jupe noire
**Je porterais une mini-jupe noire avec un tee-shirt blanc,
des chaussures à talon noires et une ceinture.**

1. un pull à col roulé rouge
2. des bottes noires
3. un pull-over orange Gap
4. un chemisier/une chemise jaune
5. un pantalon à pattes d'éléphant
6. un gilet vert
7. un blouson noir
8. des chaussettes blanches

© Ekaterina Pokrovsky/Shutterstock.com

Étape 2. Posez les questions à un(e) partenaire. À votre avis, est-ce que les vêtements de votre partenaire sont à la mode ou démodés? Il/Elle a bon ou mauvais goût?

Étape 3. Toujours avec votre partenaire, décrivez une jolie tenue et une tenue laide que vous avez vue. Qui portait ces tenues?

Modèle: **J'ai vu une très jolie tenue à la télévision aux Oscars. Marion Cotillard portait une robe du soir violette avec des talons hauts, un collier et un bracelet. Mon voisin portait une tenue très laide. Il portait un tee-shirt jaune, un gilet marron, un short rouge, des baskets, des chaussettes blanches et une casquette des Dallas Cowboys.**

Un mot sur la culture

Coco Chanel

Quand on parle de la mode française, on pense tout de suite à la marque Chanel. Née à Saumur (Maine-et-Loire), Gabrielle «Coco» Chanel (1883–1971) a commencé sa carrière dans la confection de chapeaux où elle a rapidement connu le succès avant de se lancer dans la couture. On doit à Coco Chanel le pantalon pour femmes et le tailleur qui porte son nom. Coco Chanel a contribué à l'émancipation des femmes en créant des vêtements féminins confortables et pratiques dans un style qui était traditionnellement réservé aux hommes. Son parfum, Chanel N° 5, est l'un des parfums les plus célèbres au monde. La maison de mode Chanel est le symbole du goût et de l'élégance.

© Sasha/Stringer/Hulton Archive/Getty Images

• Avez-vous des produits Chanel? Quels produits Chanel aimeriez-vous avoir?

• Est-ce que vous avez vu le film *Coco avant Chanel* avec Audrey Tautou?

Liaisons avec les mots et les sons

11-9

Les sons /z/ et /s/

You already learned that the **s** sound in a **liaison** is pronounced /**z**/.

très occupé	deux écharpes	trois imperméables	vous aidez

An **s** is also pronounced /**z**/ when it occurs between two vowels.

un blouson	une chemise	Isabelle	un magasin

An **s** is pronounced /**s**/ when it occurs at the beginning of a word.

un sac	des sandales	un smoking	un siège

An **s** is pronounced /**s**/ before or after a pronounced consonant.

une casquette	un costume	transporter	Mustapha

A double **ss** is pronounced /**s**/.

les chaussures	les chaussettes	un passeport	les tissus

The following spellings also have the sound /**s**/: **ç, c** followed by **i** or **e**, and **t** in -**tion**.

Ça va	un bracelet	une ceinture	la natation

Pratique A. Écoutez et répétez ces mots de vocabulaire.

Le son /z/

1. deux agents
2. trois étoiles
3. vos achats
4. un chemisier
5. une croisière
6. une valise

Le son /s/

7. en solde
8. un sweat
9. passer
10. je chausse
11. ancien
12. un centime

Pratique B. Écoutez et répétez ces répliques de la Séquence 5 du film *Liaisons*. Relisez les répliques. Encerclez *(Circle)* tous les sons /z/ et soulignez *(underline)* tous les sons /s/.

MME PAPILLON C'est si triste. Mourir comme ça, tout seul, sans personne. Le médecin a dit qu'il était mort vers neuf heures du matin.

CLAIRE Vous..., vous avez dit vers neuf heures? Ça fait trois heures du matin au Québec. Mais il m'a appelé à cette heure. C'est pas possible...

À vos stylos! C'est l'heure de la dictée!

11-10

Vous allez entendre six phrases deux fois. La première fois, écoutez bien. La deuxième fois, écrivez les phrases.

Sujet Claire et Mme Papillon parlent au téléphone.

Pour parler des personnes et des choses non-spécifiées

Les adjectifs et les pronoms indéfinis

DU FILM *LIAISONS*

Un coup d'œil sur la grammaire

Look at these photos from the film *Liaisons* and their captions.

MME LEGRAND Hier j'ai égaré *(misplaced)* **toutes** mes cartes de crédit et maintenant ma clé.

MME LEGRAND À bientôt, Marie. À bientôt... Bonne journée à **tous**!

1. In the left caption, what is **toutes** referring to? And **tous** in the right caption?

2. What do you think **toutes** and **tous** mean in the captions?

Liaisons musicales

Luce Dufault (1966–) est une chanteuse québécoise de R'n'B qui a joué aussi dans des comédies musicales. *Tous ces mots* (1998) est une belle chanson sur un chagrin d'amour *(break-up)*. Écoutez la chanson sur Internet.

❖ Indefinite adjectives and pronouns allow you to refer to people, things, or qualities that are not specified. They also allow you to express sameness.

❖ **Tout** *(all)* may be used as an adjective or a pronoun. As an adjective, it must agree in number and gender with the noun it modifies and it can be followed by an article, a possessive adjective (**mon, ses...**), or a demonstrative adjective (**ce, cette...**).

J'ai vu **tous** mes amis.	*I saw **all** my friends.*
J'ai mangé **toute** la tarte.	*I ate **all** of the pie.*
Nous avons bu **tout** le café.	*We drank **all** the coffee.*
Toutes ces jupes sont belles.	***All** these skirts are beautiful.*

❖ The masculine form **tout** may be used as a pronoun to mean *all* or *everything.*

Tout va bien.	***Everything** is going well.*
Tout ça me fait peur.	***All** this scares me.*
J'aime **tout**.	*I like **everything**.*

❖ The pronouns **tous** and **toutes** mean *everyone, every one (of them),* or *all (of them).*

Tu vois ces robes? **Toutes** sont jolies.	*Do you see these dresses? **All** of them are pretty.*
Ces enfants veulent **tous** aller au parc.	*These children **all** want to go to the park.*

- Use the pronoun **tous** to refer to a group that includes at least one male. Use **toutes** to refer to a group that consists only of females.

Merci à **tous**!

*Thank you **everyone** (men only or men and women)!*

Toutes veulent venir.

***All of them** (only women) want to come.*

> **Note** de grammaire
> You may also hear **Merci à tous et à toutes!** from those who wish to be more politically correct.

- To say *everyone*, use the expression **tout le monde**.

Tout le monde est arrivé.

***Everyone** has arrived.*

- Here are other common expressions that may be used as adjectives or pronouns:

d'autres *(some) other(s)*	**certain(e)s (de)** *certain (of)*
l'autre/les autres *the other(s)*	**le/la/les même(s)** *the same*
un(e) autre *another*	**plusieurs (de)** *several (of)*

Les questions? **D'autres** sont plus faciles.

*The questions? **Some others** are easier.*

Il préfère **l'autre** chapeau.

*He prefers **the other** hat.*

Certaines chemises sont confortables.

***Certain** shirts are comfortable.*

Ces tee-shirts? **Certains** sont chers.

*These t-shirts? **Certain (ones)** are expensive.*

Les mêmes viennent toujours.

***The same ones** always come.*

Elle a acheté **plusieurs** bracelets.

*She bought **several** bracelets.*

- Some indefinites have different forms when used as adjectives and pronouns.

Adjectives	Pronouns
chaque *(+ noun) each, every*	**chacun/chacune (de)** *each (one) (of)*
quelques *(+ noun) some*	**quelques-uns/quelques-unes (de)** *some, a few (of)*

Chaque femme ici est belle.

***Every** woman here is beautiful.*

Chacune de ces femmes est française.

***Each one** of these women is French.*

J'ai **quelques** chemisiers.

*I have **some** blouses.*

Les chemisiers? **Quelques-uns** sont verts.

*The blouses? **A few of them** are green.*

ACTIVITÉ ❶ À la réunion des anciens élèves du lycée Gatineau

Complétez les conversations des anciens élèves du lycée Gatineau avec un adjectif ou avec un pronom indéfini.

1. ____ de mes copains est ici.   a. Chaque   b. Chacun   c. Chacune
2. ____ cours était intéressant.   a. Chaque   b. Chacun   c. Chacune
3. ____ de mes amis sont mariés.   a. Quelques   b. Quelques-uns   c. Quelques-unes
4. ____ camarades sont en Europe.   a. Quelques   b. Quelques-uns   c. Quelques-unes
5. Les femmes? ____ ont un MBA.   a. Quelques   b. Quelques-uns   c. Quelques-unes
6. Bonjour Mireille! ____ va bien?   a. Tout   b. Toute   c. Tous
7. Éric a perdu ____ ses cheveux.   a. tout   b. toutes   c. tous
8. Je suis sorti avec ____ les filles.   a. tout   b. toutes   c. tous

ACTIVITÉ J **Un potin à la réunion du lycée Gatineau** Complétez l'histoire avec la forme appropriée des mots suivants.

d'autres **l'autre** **un(e) autre**

(1) _____ jour, je suis allée à la réunion des anciens élèves du lycée Gatineau. Je n'ai pas vu mon professeur préféré, Monsieur Painchaud, mais j'ai parlé avec (2) _____ anciens professeurs. (3) _____ élève, Sandrine, voulait le voir aussi mais il n'est jamais venu.

certain(e)s **le/la/les même(s)** **plusieurs** **tout/toutes/tous/toutes**

(4) _____ amis ont dit qu'ils ont entendu un potin de (5) _____ élèves: la femme de M. Painchaud vient de le quitter. Mon amie Anne a dit qu'elle a entendu (6) _____ chose. C'est dommage. (7) _____ mes anciens camarades de classe sont tristes pour lui.

ACTIVITÉ K **Les confessions d'un accro du shopping** Un accro du shopping achète tout. Et vous? Utilisez les adjectifs indéfinis.

Modèle: Je veux acheter toutes les montres de Macy's.
        Moi, j'achèterais toutes les montres à Macy's aussi. / J'achèterais certaines montres à Macy's. / Je n'achèterais aucune montre à Macy's.

Je veux acheter tous/toutes…

1. les livres à Barnes and Noble
2. les chocolats Godiva
3. les glaces Ben & Jerry's
4. les écharpes à Kmart
5. les montres à T.J. Maxx
6. les iPods d'Apple

ACTIVITÉ L **Votre opinion**

Étape 1. Quelle est votre opinion sur les vêtements de ces magasins? Utilisez des adjectifs et des pronoms indéfinis.

Modèle: les pantalons de Walmart
        Certains pantalons de Walmart sont à la mode mais d'autres sont démodés. Tous leurs pantalons sont bon marché.

1. les lunettes de soleil de Target
2. les manteaux de Macy's
3. les chaussettes de T.J. Maxx
4. les chaussures de Sears
5. les jeans de Gap
6. les tee-shirts d'Urban Outfitters

Étape 2. Montrez vos réponses à un(e) partenaire. Êtes-vous d'accord avec les descriptions de votre partenaire?

✈ ·····
Si vous y allez

Courtesy of Gaëtan Paquet

Si vous avez envie de porter de belles lunettes, allez à la Lunetterie du Faubourg à Québec dans le Quartier Saint-Jean-Baptiste. Vous y trouverez une grande sélection de montures *(frames)* et de lunettes de soleil provenant *(originating from)* d'Europe et d'Amérique du Nord telles que J.F. Rey, Jean LaFont, Ray-Ban et Oakley.

Pour aller plus loin
Le pronom *lequel*

Lequel (laquelle, lesquels, lesquelles) means *which*. The different forms of **lequel** may be used as interrogative pronouns and must agree with the nouns they modify. They may also be used with prepositions. Note that **à** and **de** contract with **lequel.**

Laquelle de ces robes préférez-vous? La robe Chanel ou la robe Dior?
Which of these dresses do you prefer? The dress by Chanel or the dress by Dior?

Lesquels de ces tee-shirts aimez-vous? Les tee-shirts bleus ou les tee-shirts noirs?
Which of these t-shirts to you like? The blue t-shirts or the black t-shirts?

À laquelle pensez-vous? À la cravate Burberry ou à la cravate Dior?
Which tie are you thinking of? The Burberry tie or the Dior tie?

Vous parlez **duquel**? Du jean Gap ou du jean Calvin Klein?
Which one are you talking about? The Gap jeans or the Calvin Klein jeans?

Essayez! Complétez les phrases avec une forme de **lequel.**

1. _____ de ces jupes aimez-vous? Les jupes courtes ou les jupes longues?
2. _____ de ces pyjamas aimez-vous? Les pyjamas roses ou les pyjamas blancs?
3. _____ de ces chapeaux aimez-vous? Le chapeau noir ou le chapeau orange?
4. _____ de ces montres aimez-vous? La montre Cartier ou la montre Swatch?
5. _____ parlez-vous? De la chemise courte ou de la chemise longue?

OUI, JE PEUX!

Here are two "can do statements" for you to check your progress so far. Look at each statement and rate yourself on how well you think you can perform the task. Then verify your ability with a partner. How did you do?

1. **"I can say what I like to wear for different occasions and ask someone else what he/she likes to wear."**

   I can perform this function
   ☐ with ease
   ☐ with some difficulty
   ☐ not at all

2. **"I can describe what interesting clothes everyone, some, or several people were wearing at the last party I went to and ask someone else to do the same."**

   I can perform this function
   ☐ with ease
   ☐ with some difficulty
   ☐ not at all

iLrn™
Are you looking for more practice? You can find it in **iLrn**.

Avant de visionner

ACTIVITÉ A **Vous rappelez-vous?** Vous rappelez-vous qui a dit ces phrases dans la Séquence 5 du film *Liaisons:* Claire, Alexis ou Mme Papillon?

1. _____ La prochaine fois que vous êtes de passage […] au Québec, vous me le direz?
2. _____ Il y a des choses que j'aimerais vous dire… mais…
3. _____ C'est que… J'espère que vous pourrez nous pardonner…
4. _____ Ah, ma pauvre petite. J'ai une mauvaise nouvelle… Votre oncle est mort.
5. _____ Vous…vous avez dit neuf heures? […] C'est pas possible…
6. _____ Ah, ma pauvre petite. On se parlera quand vous arriverez…

> **Note** de **vocabulaire**
> The expression **être de passage** means *to pass through.*

ACTIVITÉ B **Devinez** Dans la Séquence 6 du film *Liaisons,* Claire va à la Banque Nationale avec sa clé mystérieuse. Devinez ce qui se passera. Complétez les phrases au futur simple avec les verbes donnés.

1. (parler) Claire _____.
2. (voir) Claire _____.
3. (trouver) Claire _____.
4. (apprendre) Claire _____.
5. (retourner) Claire _____.
6. (s'en aller) Claire _____.

ACTIVITÉ C **Un coup d'œil sur une scène** Voici une scène de la Séquence 6 du film *Liaisons.* Claire parle avec un employé de banque à la Banque Nationale. Avec un(e) partenaire, devinez le mot qui correspond à chaque espace *(space)* dans le dialogue. Vous allez vérifier vos réponses plus tard.

CLAIRE (1) _____.

EMPLOYÉ Bonjour, madame.

CLAIRE J'ai reçu cette (2) _____ et je voulais savoir si elle ouvre (3) _____ ici.

EMPLOYÉ Avez-vous (4) _____ du coffre?

CLAIRE Non. J'ai pas (5) _____, j'ai reçu (6) _____ avant-hier.

1. a. Bonjour   b. Excusez-moi   4. a. la clé   b. le numéro
2. a. clé   b. enveloppe   5. a. le numéro   b. une pièce d'identité
3. a. un coffre-fort   b. une porte   6. a. la clé   b. l'enveloppe

▶ **Regarder la séquence**
Vous allez regarder la Séquence 6 du film *Liaisons.* Vérifiez vos réponses à l'Activité B et à l'Activité C.

Après le visionnage

ACTIVITÉ **D** **L'avez-vous compris?** Pour chaque phrase, indiquez si c'est vrai ou faux.

	Vrai	Faux
1. Claire trouve des photos dans le coffre-fort.	☐	☐
2. Les documents dans le coffre-fort datent des années 90.	☐	☐
3. Claire trouve une autre clé dans le coffre-fort.	☐	☐
4. Claire s'en va en France.	☐	☐

ACTIVITÉ **E** **Un chiffre important**

Étape 1. Faites une liste des choses du film *Liaisons* qui sont associées au chiffre 315.

Étape 2. Montrez votre liste à un(e) partenaire. Avez-vous écrit les mêmes choses? Aimeriez-vous ajouter d'autres détails à votre liste? À votre avis, quelle est la signification du chiffre 315 dans le film?

ACTIVITÉ **F** **Utilisez le contexte**
Regardez bien le mot en caractère gras *(boldface)* et répondez à la question.

CLIENTE Bruno, je ne trouve pas ma clé. Où est-ce que je l'ai mise? **Cibole**!

- On utilise l'expression «Cibole!» quand on est calme ou quand on est énervé?

© Bill Greenblatt/UPI /Landov

Ciboire et calice

Liaisons avec la culture

La langue et les objets religieux au Québec

L'Église catholique a eu une influence considérable dans la société québécoise avant la Révolution tranquille. Pour cette raison, les noms de certains objets utilisés lors de la messe catholique peuvent avoir un double sens. Par exemple, à l'église, un ciboire° est un vase° où on met les hosties° consacrées° pendant la communion et un calice° est le vase pour le vin consacré. Pourtant, quand on est énervé et que l'on dit ces mots avec un point d'exclamation, ils peuvent représenter des gros mots°! D'autres termes religieux qui peuvent être des gros mots sont **baptême**, **hostie** et **tabernacle**. Il est donc très important de faire attention au contexte quand on utilise ces mots au Québec. Le mot «cibole!», que Madame LeGrand a utilisé, est un euphémisme du mot **ciboire** qui veut dire «darn it!» en anglais.

ciboire *ciborium* **vase** *vessel* **hosties** *holy bread* **consacrées** *blessed* **calice** *chalice* **gros mots** *curse words*

La mode: du transport à la haute couture

OUTILS DE LECTURE
Identifying previously learned vocabulary

When you read, it can be helpful to identify vocabulary you have already learned. Identifying previously learned words and expressions helps you remember their meanings better. In turn, these words can help you to guess the meaning of new words in a text and to predict a text's content.

1. Skim the text **La Poste et les services bancaires** and jot down the vocabulary words you have learned in this and previous chapters.

2. Look at your list of words. What do you think this text is about?

La Poste et les services bancaires

La Poste n'est pas uniquement un lieu où on achète des timbres et d'où on envoie des lettres et des colis. En France et dans plusieurs pays francophones, La Poste fonctionne également° comme une banque. Ouvrir un compte-chèques, un compte d'épargne, un plan-épargne-logement°, obtenir une carte bleue (carte de crédit) ou un prêt immobilier°, tout cela est possible au bureau de poste, ce qui fait de La Poste une des plus grandes banques françaises. Dans plusieurs pays africains, comme au Bénin ou au Cameroun, La Poste joue un rôle crucial dans l'économie, par exemple, en facilitant les transferts de fonds à travers les mandats° postaux.

© Jerome Chatin/Expansion-Rea/Redux Pictures

également *also* **un plan-épargne-logement** *mortgage savings account* **un prêt immobilier** *mortgage* **un mandat** *money order*

Vrai ou faux?

1. La Poste ne joue aucun rôle dans l'économie.   V / F

2. On peut acheter des timbres dans une banque.   V / F

3. On peut transférer des fonds en envoyant un mandat postal.   V / F

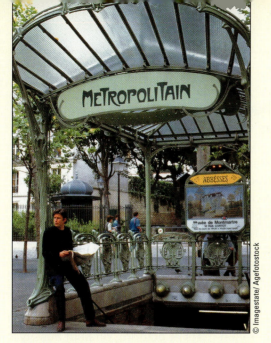

Le métro de Paris

Le métro (abréviation de «métropolitain») de Paris est un système populaire de transports desservant° la ville de Paris et son agglomération°. Le métro transporte plus de 4 millions de voyageurs par jour. Il dessert° 300 stations avec 384 points d'arrêt. Devenu un des symboles de Paris, il se caractérise par la densité de son réseau° au cœur de Paris et par son style architectural influencé par l'Art nouveau. La première ligne du métro de Paris a été inaugurée quelques mois après le début de l'Exposition universelle de 1900. Le métro parisien se classe, pour le nombre de voyageurs transportés, en quatrième position derrière Tokyo (3,2 milliards), Moscou (2,4 milliards) et Séoul (2 milliards).

Adapted from: France.fr

desservant *serving* **agglomération** *neighboring areas* **dessert** *serves* **réseau** *network*

Vrai ou faux?

1. Le métro de Paris a moins de 300 points d'arrêt.   V / F

2. Le métro parisien est un des symboles de Paris.   V / F

3. La première ligne du métro a été inaugurée en 1900.   V / F

La Belgique: destination populaire pour les vacances

La Belgique est une destination populaire pour les vacances, surtout chez les Européens parce que le pays est facile d'accès. Bruxelles, sa capitale, est une ville cosmopolite et l'un des sièges° de l'Union européenne. C'est également là que se trouve le siège de l'OTAN° (Organisation du traité de l'Atlantique Nord). Bruxelles accueille° beaucoup de manifestations culturelles. On y trouve aussi des lieux célèbres comme la Grand-Place, les Galeries royales Saint-Hubert, la fontaine Manneken-Pis et le Festival Couleur-Café. En gastronomie, la Belgique est connue pour son chocolat et ses gaufres°.

sièges *headquarters* **OTAN** *NATO* **accueille** *welcomes* **gaufres** *waffles*

Vrai ou faux?

1. Les Européens n'aiment pas voyager en Belgique.   V / F

2. Le siège de l'OTAN est à Bruxelles.   V / F

3. Bruxelles a beaucoup de manifestations culturelles.   V / F

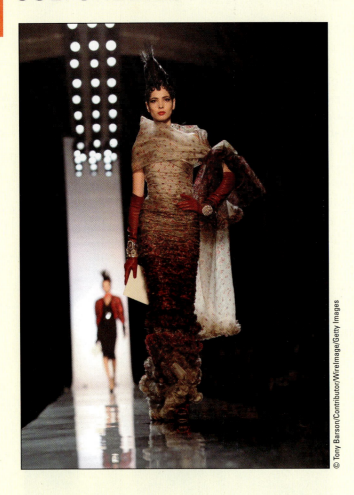

© Tony Barson/Contributor/WireImage/Getty Images

La Fédération Française de la Couture

La Fédération Française de la Couture, du Prêt-à-Porter des couturiers et des créateurs de Mode, a été fondée en 1973. Les missions principales de cette fédération sont d'établir les critères de la haute couture et de déterminer le calendrier des collections Printemps-Été et Automne-Hiver en ce qui concerne° la haute couture et le prêt-à-porter masculin et féminin. Paris accueille° chaque année, en janvier et en juillet, une trentaine de défilés° pendant la semaine de la Haute Couture. En mars et octobre, on peut aussi y voir plus d'une centaine de défilés de Prêt-à-Porter féminin. Les maisons les plus célèbres qui sont membres de cette fédération sont Chanel, Chloé, Christian Dior, Hermès, Jean-Paul Gaultier, Louis Vuitton et Yves Saint-Laurent, entre autres.

Adapted from: http://www.modeaparis.com/fr/la-federation/

en ce qui concerne *concerning* **accueille** *welcomes* **défilés** *fashion shows*

Vrai ou faux?

1. Chaque maison de mode décide de ses critères pour la haute couture.   V / F
2. La Fédération Française de la Couture établit le calendrier pour les collections.   V / F
3. La semaine de la Haute Couture est à Paris.   V / F

▶ LIAISONS CULTURELLES

Use **iLrn**™ to access the video **La mode** to learn more about French fashion. Be prepared to answer the question **Et vous? Quelles sont vos marques de vêtements préférées?** Share your responses with your classmates in **Share It!**

PARTIE 1 11–11

LES TRANSPORTS

un (auto)bus	bus
un avion	plane
un camion	truck
une camionnette	van, mini van
le covoiturage	carpooling
le métro	subway
une moto	motorcycle
les moyens (m.) de transport	means of transportation
à pied	on foot
un 4X4 (quatre-quatre)	SUV
un scooter	moped
un taxi	taxi
un train	train
une voiture	car

À LA POSTE

une boîte à lettres	mailbox
une carte postale	postcard
un colis	package
le courrier	mail
une enveloppe	envelope
un facteur/une factrice	mail carrier
la poste	post office
un timbre	stamp

VERBES

bouger	to move
conduire	to drive
construire	to construct
détruire	to destroy
envoyer quelque chose en express	to send something express
faire le trajet (entre)	to travel, to commute (between)
livrer	to deliver goods/groceries
traduire	to translate
transporter	to transport

PARTIE 2 11–12

À L'AÉROPORT

un aéroport	airport
un(e) agent(e) de bord	flight attendant
un(e) agent(e) de la sécurité	security agent
un billet d'avion	plane ticket
un billet aller-retour	round-trip ticket
un billet aller simple	one-way ticket
une carte d'embarquement	boarding pass
à l'étranger	abroad, overseas
un passeport	passport
un permis de conduire	driver's license

une pièce d'identité	a form of identification
une porte d'embarquement	departure gate
un siège	seat
une valise	suitcase
un vol direct/une correspondance	direct/connecting flight
un voyageur/une voyageuse	traveler
la première classe	first-class
la classe affaires	business class
la classe économique	economy class

LES VOYAGES

une auberge de jeunesse	youth hostel
une chambre fumeurs/non-fumeurs	smoking/nonsmoking rom
une chambre individuelle/double	single/double room
une clé	key
un(e) client(e)	client, guest
un gîte du passant	bed and breakfast
un hôtel (trois/quatre/cinq étoiles)	(three/four/five star) hotel
un hôtel de luxe	luxury hotel
un lit simple/double	single/double bed
un motel	motel
le logement	lodging
le service de chambre	room service
un(e) agent(e) de voyages	travel agent
un arrêt d'autobus	bus stop
une croisière	cruise
une gare	(bus/train) station
une tente	tent

VERBES

aller en vacances (f.)	to go on vacation
attacher la ceinture de sécurité	to fasten the seatbelt
débarquer de l'avion	to get off the plane
déclarer (vos achats)	to declare (your purchases)
embarquer dans l'avion	to board the plane
enregistrer (les valises)	to check in (luggage)
faire les valises	to pack
passer au contrôle de sécurité	to go through security
passer à la douane	to go through customs
payer des frais supplémentaires	to pay extra fees

LES PRONOMS RELATIFS

dont	that, (of) which, (of) whom
où	where, when
que	that, which
qui	who, that, which

PARTIE 3   11–13

LES VÊTEMENTS

un anorak	*parka*
des baskets *(f.)*	*sports shoes*
un blouson **(en cuir)**	*(leather) windbreaker*
des bottes *(f.)*	*boots*
un bracelet	*bracelet*
une casquette	*baseball cap*
un chapeau	*hat*
des chaussettes *(f.)*	*socks*
des chaussures *(f.)* **(à talon)**	*(high-heeled) shoes*
une chemise	*shirt*
un chemisier	*blouse*
un collier	*necklace*
un costume	*man's suit*
une cravate	*tie*
une écharpe	*scarf*
un foulard	*silk scarf*
des gants *(m.)*	*gloves*
un gilet	*cardigan sweater*
un imperméable	*raincoat*
un jean	*jeans*
un jogging	*sweatpants*
des lunettes *(f.)* **(de soleil)**	*(sun)glasses*
un maillot **(de bain)**	*swimsuit*
une mallette	*briefcase*
un manteau	*overcoat*
une (mini-)jupe	*(mini) skirt*
une montre	*watch*
un pantalon	*slacks*
un pantalon à pattes d'éléphant	*bell bottom pants*
un pull à col roulé	*turtle neck sweater*
un pull-over	*pullover sweater*
un pyjama	*pyjama*
une robe	*dress*
une robe du soir	*evening dress*
des sandales *(f.)*	*sandals*
un short	*shorts*
un smoking	*tuxedo*
un sous-vêtement	*underwear*
un sweat **(à capuche)**	*(hooded) sweatshirt*
un tailleur	*woman's suit*
un tee-shirt	*t-shirt*
une tenue	*outfit*
un vêtement / les vêtements	*an article of clothing / clothing*

ADJECTIFS

à la mode	*stylish, fashionable*
ancien/ancienne	*former*
bon marché	*inexpensive*
cher/chère	*expensive*
confortable	*comfortable*
démodé(e)	*old fashioned, out-of-date*

EXPRESSIONS

Quelle est votre taille *(f.)*?	*What size do you wear?*
Je fais du 32.	*I'm a size 32.*
Quelle est votre pointure *(f.)*?	*What is your shoe size?*
Je chausse du 36.	*I wear a size 36 shoe.*
Ça vous va très bien.	*That looks good on you.*

ADJECTIFS/PRONOMS INDÉFINIS

une autre/d'autres	*another/(some) other(s)*
l'autre/les autres	*the other(s)*
certain(e)s (de)	*certain (of)*
chacun/chacune (de)	*each (one) (of)*
chaque *(+ noun)*	*each, every*
le/la/les même(s)	*the same*
lequel/laquelle/ lesquels/lesquelles	*which*
plusieurs (de)	*several (of)*
quelques *(+ noun)*	*some*
quelques-uns/ quelques-unes (de)	*some, a few (of)*
tout/tous/toute/toutes	*all (of them)/everyone*
tout le monde	*everyone*

DIVERS

en solde	*on sale*
porter	*to wear*

La **santé**

En bref   In this chapter, you will:

- learn vocabulary to talk about health and hygiene

- learn parts of the body for humans and animals

- talk about similarities and differences between humans and animals

- learn reflexive verbs that pertain to hygiene and daily routines

- learn the present subjunctive

- learn expressions of volition, necessity, and emotions that take the subjunctive

- learn about the sounds **e caduc, e muet,** and **h**

- read about medical tourism in Tunisia

- write about your reaction to medical tourism

 You will also re-watch **SÉQUENCE 6: Une découverte** of the film *Liaisons*.

Ressources

 audio   video   Share It!   iLrn™   http://www.cengagebrain.com

© Stéphane Groleau / Alamy

VOCABULAIRE 1

L'hygiène **personnelle**

Personal hygiene

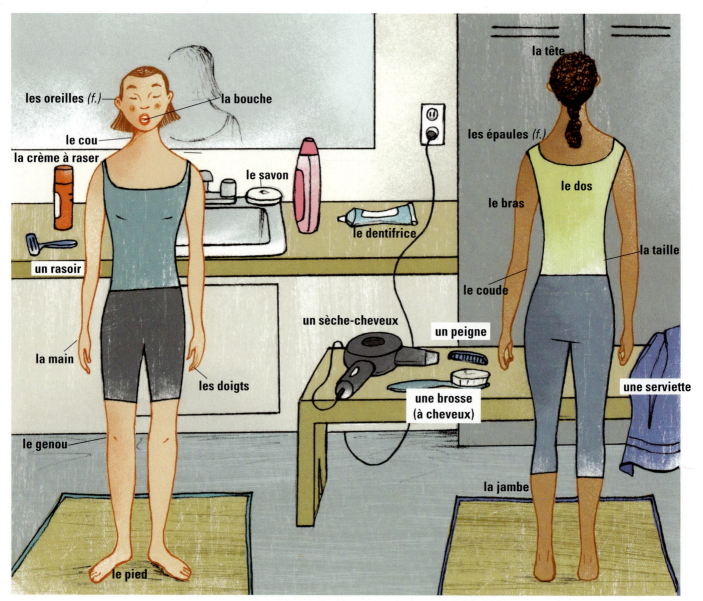

les oreilles *(f.)*

la bouche

le cou

la crème à raser

le savon

un rasoir

le dentifrice

la tête

les épaules *(f.)*

le dos

le bras

la taille

le coude

un sèche-cheveux

un peigne

la main

les doigts

une brosse
(à cheveux)

une serviette

le genou

la jambe

le pied

Dans le vestiaire *(locker room)* du centre sportif

Vocabulaire complémentaire

la cheville *ankle*
le corps *body*
les dents *(f.)* *teeth*
la gorge *throat*
la langue *tongue*
la poitrine *chest*
le ventre *abdomen, belly*

le visage / la figure *face*
_____
une brosse à dents *toothbrush*
l'hygiène *(f.)* *hygiene*
les produits *(m.)* de soin personnel
  personal care products
  la crème solaire *sunscreen*

la lotion *lotion*
le maquillage *makeup*
le shampooing *shampoo*
_____
utiliser *to use*

12-1

ACTIVITÉ **A** **Vêtements et accessoires** Quel vêtement ou accessoire associez-vous à la partie du corps mentionnée?

1.　　2.　　3.　　4.　　5.　　6.　　7.

ACTIVITÉ **B** **Les produits et les parties du corps**

Étape 1. Quelle partie du corps associez-vous aux produits suivants?

1. une brosse à dents　a. le dos　　　b. la cheville　c. la bouche

2. la crème à raser　　a. le visage　　b. la langue　　c. le ventre

3. le dentifrice　　　　a. le coude　　b. le genou　　c. les dents

4. le shampooing　　　a. la figure　　b. la tête　　　c. les mains

Étape 2. De quel produit de soin personnel est-ce qu'Alexis avait besoin à l'hôtel?

ACTIVITÉ **C** **Quelle partie du corps?**

Étape 1. Sur quelle partie du corps utilisez-vous ces produits ou appareils?

1. la lotion　　　　4. une serviette　　7. le shampooing

2. la crème solaire　5. le savon　　　　8. un peigne

3. un sèche-cheveux　6. le maquillage　　9. le déodorant

Étape 2. Posez les mêmes questions à deux camarades de classe, si possible un étudiant et une étudiante.

Étape 3. Est-ce que vos réponses et celles de vos camarades de classe sont semblables ou différentes? S'il y a des différences, décrivez-les.

Liaisons musicales

Images Distribution Canada/Agence Québec Presse Canada/Newscom

De la main gauche (1982) est une chanson de la chanteuse française Danielle Messia, décédée en 1985 d'une leucémie *(leukemia)*. La chanson parle de l'acceptation des différences et a été reprise en 1998 par la chanteuse québécoise Luce Dufault. Cherchez les paroles de cette chanson. Qu'est-ce que *la main gauche* symbolise dans la chanson?

ACTIVITÉ D **Les activités**

Étape 1. Quelles parties du corps est-ce qu'on utilise pour les activités suivantes?

Modèle: le bowling **On utilise les mains, les doigts, les bras et les jambes.**

1. écouter de la musique
2. regarder un film
3. manger un steak
4. faire de l'aérobic

5. jouer du violon
6. jouer au tennis
7. faire de la danse du ventre
8. faire du surf

Étape 2. Quelle est votre activité physique préférée? Quelles parties du corps utilisez-vous pour faire cette activité?

ACTIVITÉ E **Les produits de soin personnel**

© Cristi Matei/Shuttertock.com

Étape 1. Quels produits trouvez-vous…

1. chez un dentiste?
2. chez un coiffeur?
3. chez un coiffeur pour hommes?
4. chez le toiletteur *(dog groomer)*?
5. dans un institut de beauté?
6. dans une chambre d'hôtel?

Étape 2. Demandez à un(e) partenaire quels produits de soin personnel il/elle apporte au vestiaire *(locker room)* du centre sportif.

Conclusion Est-ce que votre partenaire est **propre, très propre** ou **obsessionnel(le)**?

ACTIVITÉ F **Vos marques préférées**

Étape 1. Quelle est votre marque *(brand)* préférée pour les produits suivants?

1. le dentifrice
2. le shampooing
3. le savon
4. le déodorant

5. le maquillage
6. les brosses à dents
7. la lotion
8. la crème solaire

Étape 2. Posez les questions à un(e) partenaire. Avez-vous choisi les mêmes marques? Quelles marques avez-vous en commun?

Étape 3. Avec votre partenaire, essayez de nommer une marque française pour chaque produit de l'Étape 1.

Étape 4. Si vous pouviez seulement emporter *(take)* trois produits de soin personnel pour faire du camping dans la forêt, lesquels emporteriez-vous?

Étape 1. Avec un(e) partenaire, indiquez si ces traits décrivent Lady Gaga, Adam Levine ou ni l'un ni l'autre *(neither)*.

	Lady Gaga	Adam Levine	Ni l'un ni l'autre
1. un gros ventre	_____	_____	_____
2. une taille fine *(slender)*	_____	_____	_____
3. les épaules larges *(broad)*	_____	_____	_____
4. les dents blanches	_____	_____	_____
5. un long cou	_____	_____	_____
6. de grands pieds	_____	_____	_____
7. une poitrine musclée	_____	_____	_____
8. un dos poilu *(hairy)*	_____	_____	_____
9. les oreilles percées *(pierced)*	_____	_____	_____
10. les jambes longues	_____	_____	_____
11. les cheveux parfois bleus	_____	_____	_____

Note de vocabulaire

Note that **cheveux** only refers to human hair on the head. To refer to human hair not on the head and animal hair or fur, use **les poils** *(hair)* or the adjective **poilu(e)(s)**.

Étape 2. Décrivez les traits physiques d'une autre personne célèbre.

Un mot sur la culture

Les critères de beauté

Dans les cultures occidentales°, être mince est à la mode. Pour être top-modèle, il faut avoir une taille fine et un ventre plat. Mais, dans certaines cultures africaines et asiatiques, on considère une femme charnue° belle parce que ce trait physique symbolise la fortune et la prospérité. Par exemple, en Mauritanie, un pays d'Afrique de l'Ouest, certaines femmes désirent grossir pour se préparer au mariage. Au Sénégal et en Côte d'Ivoire, il existe des concours de beauté° pour les femmes charnues. Cependant, en raison des influences internationales liées à la mode occidentale et à la télévision française, cette tradition devient moins populaire chez certaines jeunes filles.

occidentales *Western* **charnue** *plump* **concours de beauté** *beauty contests*

- Aimeriez-vous voir des concours de beauté pour les hommes?
- À votre avis, est-ce que les top-modèles des cultures occidentales sont trop minces?

Pour parler de l'hygiène personnelle et de la routine

Encore des verbes réfléchis

DU FILM *LIAISONS*
....

Un coup d'œil sur la grammaire

Look at these photos from the film *Liaisons* and their captions.

MME LEGRAND Je dois **m'habiller** [...] **me maquiller**...

MME LEGRAND Je dois rentrer chez moi pour **me préparer**.

1. What do the verbs **s'habiller** and **se maquiller** mean in the left caption?
2. What does the verb **se préparer** mean in the right caption?

:: In **Chapitre 10,** you learned about reflexive verbs. Many verbs used to express daily routines are also reflexive verbs since they convey what people do to or for themselves.

se brosser	*to brush*	**se laver**	*to wash (oneself)*
se coucher	*to go to bed*	**se lever**	*to get up*
se couper	*to cut (oneself)*	**se maquiller**	*to put on make-up*
se doucher	*to (take a) shower*	**se préparer**	*to get ready, to prepare*
s'endormir	*to go, fall asleep*	**se raser**	*to shave (oneself)*
s'habiller	*to get dressed*	**se réveiller**	*to wake up*
se déshabiller	*to (get) undress(ed)*	**se sécher**	*to dry (oneself)*

:: Many of these verbs can be used reflexively and non-reflexively. When the subject and object of the verb are the same, the verb is used reflexively. When the subject and the object of the verb are different, the verb is used non-reflexively.

Mme Laurent s'habille.	*Mme Laurent is getting dressed.*
Mme Laurent habille sa fille.	*Mme Laurent is dressing her daughter.*
Je me lave.	*I am washing up.*
Je lave mon chien.	*I am washing my dog.*

When a part of the body is used with a reflexive verb, it is usually preceded by the definite article, not the possessive adjective as in English.

Il se brosse les dents.	*He is brushing his teeth.*
Nous nous lavons les mains.	*We are washing our hands.*

As you learned in **Chapitre 10,** reflexive verbs always take **être** in the **passé composé,** and there is usually agreement between the past participle and the subject pronoun.

Nous nous sommes endormis.	*We fell asleep.*
Anne s'est habillée?	*Did Anne get dressed?*
Elles se sont réveillées à 8h30.	*They woke up at 8:30.*

If a reflexive verb in the **passé composé** is followed by a direct object, the past participle does not agree with the subject.

Elle s'est rasé les jambes.	*She shaved her legs.*
Ils se sont lavé les mains.	*They washed their hands.*
Nous nous sommes coupé les cheveux.	*We cut our hair.*

Remember that, if a verb is used non-reflexively instead of reflexively, it uses **avoir**—not **être**—as the auxiliary verb in the **passé composé.**

Marie s'est lavé les mains.	*but*	**Marie a lavé la vaisselle.**
Marie washed her hands.		*Marie washed the dishes.*

> **Note de grammaire**
> Remember that the past participle does not agree with verbs like **se parler** and **se téléphoner** that take indirect objects.

ACTIVITÉ H Votre routine

Étape 1. Dans quel ordre est-ce que vous faites ces activités le matin?

_____ Je me brosse les dents.   _____ Je me maquille.

_____ Je me douche.   _____ Je me rase.

_____ Je m'habille.   _____ Je me réveille.

_____ Je me lave le visage.   _____ Je me sèche les cheveux.

Étape 2. Est-ce qu'il y a des activités de l'Étape 1 que vous ne faites pas? Pourquoi pas?

ACTIVITÉ I Les parties du corps Complétez chaque phrase avec un verbe réfléchi au présent.

Modèle: les yeux   **Je me maquille les yeux.**

1. _____ les dents.   **4.** _____ les cheveux.

2. _____ les jambes.   **5.** _____ les pieds.

3. _____ le visage.   **6.** _____ les mains.

Si vous y allez

© Christophe Morin/Maxppp/Landov

Si vous allez en France, allez dans une boutique Yves Rocher pour les produits de beauté. L'entreprise française vous offre un vaste choix de produits pour le visage et le corps, des parfums et du maquillage.

ACTIVITÉ J Qu'est-ce qu'ils font? Décrivez les images suivantes avec une phrase complète au présent.

1. a.

b.

2. a.

b.

3. a.

b.

ACTIVITÉ K Les activités d'Abia et de Nadia Abia et sa sœur Nadia décrivent ce qu'elles ont fait hier. Complétez les phrases.

1. Nous nous sommes lavées _____.　　a. avant de partir　b. les mains

2. Nous nous sommes rasées _____.　　a. les jambes　　b. avec un nouveau rasoir

3. Nous nous sommes séché _____.　　a. les cheveux　　b. après la douche

4. Nous nous sommes brossé _____.　　a. les dents　　b. le chat de Patrick

5. Nous avons lavé _____.　　a. les cheveux　　b. la voiture de papa

Et vous? Quelles activités avez-vous faites hier?

ACTIVITÉ **L** **Qu'est-ce qu'ils ont fait?** Décrivez les images de l'Activité J au passé composé.

ACTIVITÉ **M** **Votre routine**

Étape 1. Répondez aux questions à propos de votre routine.

1. Est-ce que vous vous préparez rapidement ou lentement?
2. Est-ce que vous vous lavez les mains avant de manger?
3. Est-ce que vous vous brossez les dents tous les jours?
4. Est-ce que vous vous douchez tous les jours?
5. Est-ce que vous vous réveillez tôt ou tard?
6. Est-ce que vous vous endormez souvent devant la télé?
7. Est-ce que vous vous déshabillez avant de vous coucher?
8. Est-ce que vous vous couchez tôt ou tard?

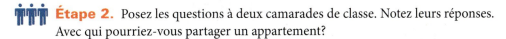

Étape 2. Posez les questions à deux camarades de classe. Notez leurs réponses. Avec qui pourriez-vous partager un appartement?

ACTIVITÉ **N** **Un jeu de charades** En groupes de trois à quatre personnes, vous allez jouer aux charades. Votre professeur va vous donner des expressions avec des verbes de cette leçon. Vous devez mimer vos expressions. Les autres personnes de votre groupe vont deviner votre expression. Qui sont les meilleurs acteurs de votre classe?

OUI, JE PEUX! Here are two "can do statements" for you to check your progress so far. Look at each statement and rate yourself on how well you think you can perform the task. Then verify your ability with a partner. How did you do?

iLrn™

Are you looking for more practice? You can find it in **iLrn**.

1. **"I can say two things that I do to get ready in the morning and I can ask others what they do to get ready."**

I can perform this function
☐ with ease
☐ with some difficulty
☐ not at all

2. **"I can say when I went to bed last night and when I got up this morning, and I can ask someone else when he/she did the same."**

I can perform this function
☐ with ease
☐ with some difficulty
☐ not at all

🔊 # Toutes les créatures

All creatures

L'homme et ses amis

Vocabulaire complémentaire

une animalerie *pet store*	**les poils** *(m.) animal hair, fur*
une créature *creature*	**un refuge** *(animal) shelter*
les moustaches *(f.) whiskers*	**un requin** *shark*
une patte *paw*	

ACTIVITÉ **A** Testez vos connaissances

Étape 1. Indiquez si chaque animal mentionné **(a) a une queue, (b) a des ailes** *(wings)* ou **(c) n'a ni l'un ni l'autre.**

1.   2.   3.   4.   5.   6.   7.   8.   9.   10.   11.   12.

Étape 2. Quel animal habite dans l'eau?

1. a. un hamster   b. un poisson
2. a. un lapin   b. un requin
3. a. un canard   b. une chèvre
4. a. une grenouille b. un ours

Étape 3. Quel animal a des pattes?

1. a. un lion   b. un poisson
2. a. une chèvre   b. un humain
3. a. un serpent   b. un lapin
4. a. un chien   b. un chat
5. a. un ours   b. un serpent
6. a. un requin   b. un tigre

Étape 4. Quel animal est plus féroce *(ferocious)*?

1. a. un oiseau   b. un serpent
2. a. une chèvre   b. un requin
3. a. un tigre   b. un chat
4. a. un rat   b. un hamster
5. a. un lapin   b. un ours
6. a. un humain   b. un lion

Étape 5. À quel pays associez-vous les animaux suivants?

1. le coq   2. le lion   3. l'aigle   4. le panda   5. la grenouille

ACTIVITÉ **B** Les animaux et les caractéristiques humaines

Étape 1. Dans les fables de l'écrivain français Jean de La Fontaine, les animaux ont des caractéristiques humaines. Quels traits et caractéristiques associez-vous aux animaux suivants?

Modèle: une chèvre   **Elle est têtue.**

1. un rat   3. un aigle   5. un cochon
2. un requin   4. un ours   6. un serpent

Étape 2. Montrez vos réponses à un(e) partenaire. Est-ce que vous êtes d'accord avec ses réponses?

Si vous y allez

Si vous allez à Anvers en Belgique, visitez le zoo d'Anvers. Créé *(Created)* au 19e siècle, le zoo d'Anvers est un des plus anciens et des plus célèbres en Europe. Plus de 5 000 animaux vous y attendent.

Le coq et le renard **de Jean de La Fontaine**

ACTIVITÉ C Le zodiaque chinois

Étape 1. Décrivez votre caractère avec cinq adjectifs.

Modèle: Je suis intelligent(e), patient(e), excentrique, optimiste et têtu(e).

Étape 2. Lisez les descriptions des animaux du zodiaque chinois. Quel animal est associé à votre année de naissance? Êtes-vous d'accord avec la description?

	Les rats (né[é] en 1936, 48, 60, 72, 84, 96) sont ambitieux et honnêtes. Ils aiment dépenser beaucoup d'argent. Rats célèbres: Shakespeare, Mozart.
	Les vaches *(cows)* (1937, 49, 61, 73, 85, 97) sont travailleuses, intelligentes, patientes et exigeantes. Vaches célèbres: Napoléon, Van Gogh.
	Les tigres (1938, 50, 62, 74, 86, 98) sont agressifs, courageux, passionnés et sensibles. Tigres célèbres: Marco Polo, Marilyn Monroe.
	Les lapins (1939, 51, 63, 75, 87, 99) sont talentueux, articulés et timides. Ils aiment faire la paix. Lapins célèbres: Confucius, Albert Einstein.
	Les dragons (1940, 52, 64, 76, 88, 2000) sont excentriques, extravertis, intelligents, indiscrets, exigeants et sains. Dragons célèbres: Jeanne d'Arc, Freud.
	Les serpents (1941, 53, 65, 77, 89, 2001) sont sages *(wise),* romantiques, beaux et ont le sens de l'humour. Ils sont aussi avares. Serpents célèbres: Darwin, A. Lincoln.
	Les chevaux (1942, 54, 66, 78, 90, 2002) sont populaires, beaux, intelligents et travailleurs mais aussi impatients et égoïstes. Chevaux célèbres: Rembrandt, Chopin.
	Les chèvres (1943, 55, 67, 79, 91, 2003) sont élégantes, créatives et timides. Parfois elles sont pessimistes. Chèvres célèbres: Michelangelo, Mark Twain.
	Les singes *(monkeys)* (1944, 56, 68, 80, 92, 2004) sont intelligents et ambitieux mais ils peuvent être facilement découragés *(discouraged).* Singe célèbre: Jules César.
	Les coqs (1945, 57, 69, 81, 93, 2005) sont créatifs, fiers, égoïstes et excentriques. Ils sont dévoués *(devoted)* à leur travail. Coq célèbre: Rudyard Kipling.
	Les chiens (1946, 58, 70, 82, 94, 2006) sont fidèles, honnêtes, têtus, idéalistes et parfois égoïstes. Ils s'inquiètent souvent. Chiens célèbres: Socrate, Benjamin Franklin.
	Les cochons (1947, 59, 71, 83, 95, 2007) sont intellectuels, sincères, optimistes et tolérants. Ils s'amusent et ils ont la joie de vivre. Cochon célèbre: Ernest Hemingway.

Étape 3. Décrivez votre caractère à deux camarades de classe et écoutez leurs descriptions. Devinez *(Guess)* quel animal est associé à leurs années de naissance. Avez-vous bien deviné?

Étape 4. Quel animal est associé aux enfants nés cette année? Quel animal sera associé aux enfants nés l'année prochaine? Utilisez Internet pour le découvrir.

vie et aux carrières suivants. Justifiez vos choix.

1. un gérant
2. un avocat
3. un écrivain
4. un homme politique
5. un baba cool

6. un bourreau de travail
7. un acteur
8. un accro du shopping
9. un professeur

 ACTIVITÉ D Les animaux et les humains Avec un(e) partenaire, dites en
quoi les animaux suivants sont similaires ou différents des humains.

Modèle: les chats **Les chats et les humains ont deux oreilles, deux yeux, un nez, une
bouche et une langue. Les chats sont différents des humains parce qu'ils ont
quatre pattes, des poils, des moustaches et une queue.**

1. les singes (*monkeys*)
2. les tigres

3. les chiens
4. les oiseaux

Conclusion À quel animal est-ce que les humains ressemblent (*resemble*) le plus?

ACTIVITÉ E Les animaux et vous Posez ces questions à un(e) partenaire.

1. Est-ce que tu as des animaux chez toi? Est-ce que tu as un(e) ami(e) qui a des
animaux chez lui/elle? Quel animal ou quels animaux?

2. Est-ce que tu (ou ton ami[e]) as (a) acheté l'animal dans une animalerie ou est-ce
que tu l'as (il/elle l'a) adopté dans un refuge pour animaux abandonnés?

3. À ton avis, quels animaux sont parfaits pour les étudiants?

LE LOUP ET L'AGNEAU

© The Art Archive/Private Collection/CCI/Picture Desk

Un mot sur la culture

Les animaux de Jean de La Fontaine

Jean de La Fontaine (1621–1695) est un écrivain français de la
période classique. Il est célèbre pour ses fables dans lesquelles
il personnifie les animaux pour donner des leçons de morale.
Quelques-unes de ses fables les plus connues sont: *La cigale*°
et la fourmi,° *Le corbeau*° *et le renard*, *La grenouille et le rat*, *Le
singe et le chat*, *Le cochon, la chèvre et le mouton* et *Le chat et
le vieux rat*.

cigale *grasshopper* **fourmi** *ant* **corbeau** *crow*

- Cherchez une fable de La Fontaine sur Internet. Quels
animaux sont dans cette fable? Quelle est la leçon de morale
de cette fable?

Pour exprimer les désirs et les obligations

Les verbes réguliers au subjonctif

DU FILM *LIAISONS*

Un coup d'œil sur la grammaire

Look at these photos from the film *Liaisons* and their captions.

CLIENTE [...] **il faut** donc **que** je **sorte** quelques bijoux *(jewels)* de mon coffre.

CLAIRE Quelqu'un **voulait que** je les **trouve.**

1. What verb follows **il faut que** in the left caption? What does the caption mean?
2. What verb follows **voulait que** in the right caption? What does the caption mean?

Note de grammaire
The subjunctive is not often used in English: *It's important that you not **be** sick. I wish that I **were** healthier.*

▸ You have used the indicative mood to state facts and ideas and to ask questions. You have used the imperative mood to express commands and the conditional mood to make suggestions and to express hypothetical situations. When you want to express will and influence (volition), desires, opinions, and obligations, you need to use the subjunctive mood, **le subjonctif.** The subjunctive is used quite frequently in French.

Il faut que je sorte avec Florian.   *It is necessary that I go out with Florian.*

Je veux que tu finisses tes devoirs.   *I want you to finish your homework.*

▸ The present subjunctive of most verbs is formed by dropping the **-ent** from the third person plural form **(ils/elles)** of the present indicative and adding the subjunctive endings **-e, -es, -e, -ions, -iez,** and **-ent.**

Note de grammaire
The **nous** and **vous** forms of the present subjunctive are identical to those of the imperfect.

Infinitive				
Stem	**regarder**	**vendre**	**choisir**	**connaître**
	(ils) **regard**ent	(ils) **vend**ent	(ils) **choisiss**ent	(ils) **connaiss**ent
... que je	regard**e**	vend**e**	choisiss**e**	connaiss**e**
... que tu	regard**es**	vend**es**	choisiss**es**	connaiss**es**
... qu'il/elle/on	regard**e**	vend**e**	choisiss**e**	connaiss**e**
... que nous	regard**ions**	vend**ions**	choisiss**ions**	connaiss**ions**
... que vous	regard**iez**	vend**iez**	choisiss**iez**	connaiss**iez**
... qu'ils/elles	regard**ent**	vend**ent**	choisiss**ent**	connaiss**ent**

Some verbs have two stems in the subjunctive: one stem for the **nous** and **vous** form and another stem for the **je, tu, il/elle/on,** and **ils/elles** forms.

	acheter	boire	prendre	venir
... que je/j'	achète	boive	prenne	vienne
... que tu	achètes	boives	prennes	viennes
... qu'il/elle/on	achète	boive	prenne	vienne
... que nous	achetions	buvions	prenions	venions
... que vous	achetiez	buviez	preniez	veniez
... qu'ils/elles	achètent	boivent	prennent	viennent

Other verbs that have two stems in the subjunctive include the following:

appeler: que j'appelle, que nous appelions

comprendre: que je comprenne, que nous comprenions

croire: que je croie, que nous croyions

devenir: que je devienne, que nous devenions

devoir: que je doive, que nous devions

essayer: que j'essaie, que nous essayions

payer: que je paie, que nous payions

préférer: que je préfère, que nous préférions

recevoir: que je reçoive, que nous recevions

voir: que je voie, que nous voyions

The subjunctive almost always occurs in sentences that contain a main clause and a dependent clause *and* in which the subject of the main clause is different from the subject of the dependent clause. The expression or verb in the main clause causes the subjunctive to be used in the dependent clause. The dependent clause begins with **que** *(that).*

Il faut **que vous lisiez** ce livre. — *It is necessary that you read this book.*

Il veut **que nous dormions** plus. — *He wants us to sleep more.*

The subjunctive commonly occurs after these verbs and expressions of volition, opinion, and obligation.

Il (ne) faut (pas) que	**aimer mieux que**
Il vaut mieux que	**désirer que**
Il (n') est (pas) nécessaire que	**préférer que**
Il (n') est (pas) important que	**vouloir que**

Il vaut mieux que vous payiez l'addition.
It's better that you pay the bill.

Je préfère que tu ne te lèves pas à midi.
I prefer that you don't get up at noon.

Il est important que tu te brosses les dents.
It's important for you to brush your teeth.

L'enfant veut que sa mère l'habille.
The child wants his mother to dress him.

ACTIVITÉ F Les désirs des activistes pour les droits des animaux

Indiquez si chaque phrase est vraie ou fausse.

Un activiste pour les droits des animaux…

	Vrai	Faux
1. **préfère que nous achetions** les chats dans une animalerie.	☐	☐
2. **désire que nous respections** les oiseaux.	☐	☐
3. **aime mieux que nous adoptions** les animaux d'un refuge.	☐	☐
4. **veut que vous apportiez** les chiens abandonnés à un refuge.	☐	☐
5. **désire que vous vendiez** des lapins pour la recherche (*research*).	☐	☐
6. **préfère que vous portiez** des manteaux de fourrure (*fur*).	☐	☐
7. **aime mieux qu'on abandonne** les vieux chevaux.	☐	☐
8. **veut qu'on vive** en paix avec les animaux.	☐	☐

Et vous? Êtes-vous un(e) activiste pour les droits des animaux?

ACTIVITÉ G Les animaux et les humains

Étape 1. Complétez les phrases avec le verbe approprié.

1. Il est important qu'un ours ____ beaucoup.   a. dorme   b. dort
2. Il ne faut pas qu'un chien ____ du chocolat.   a. prend   b. prenne
3. Il ne faut pas que nous ____ les animaux.   a. abandonnons   b. abandonnions
4. Il faut qu'on ____ les droits des animaux.   a. reconnaisse   b. reconnaît
5. Il ne faut pas que vous ____ du requin.   a. mangiez   b. mangez
6. Il vaut mieux que vous ne ____ pas avec les rats.   a. jouez   b. jouiez

Étape 2. Complétez les phrases avec **(a) Il faut, (b) Il ne faut pas, (c) Il vaut mieux, (d) Il n'est pas nécessaire** ou **(e) Il est important.**

1. _____ qu'un humain se brosse les dents.
2. _____ qu'on brosse les dents des chiens et des chats.
3. _____ qu'un humain prenne de la viande rouge.
4. _____ qu'une vache prenne de la viande rouge.
5. _____ qu'un humain boive de l'eau.
6. _____ qu'un canard boive de l'eau.
7. _____ qu'un humain se lave tous les jours.
8. _____ qu'un cochon se lave tous les jours.
9. _____ qu'un humain dorme le soir.
10. _____ qu'un rat dorme le soir.

Étape 3. Comparez vos réponses avec un(e) partenaire. Avez-vous les mêmes réponses? Avec votre partenaire, nommez deux similarités et deux différences entre un humain et un animal.

Liaisons musicales

© Jean Yves DesFoux/ Maxppp /Landov

Née Béatrice Martin (1989), Cœur de Pirate est une chanteuse et pianiste québécoise qui joue du piano depuis l'âge de trois ans. Elle a gagné le prix Félix de la Révélation de l'année avec son premier album *Cœur de pirate* (2008). *Corbeau*, une chanson de cet album, utilise la métaphore des oiseaux, (des corbeaux [*crows*]) pour décrire une rupture (*breakup*). Écoutez cette chanson sur Internet.

Étape 1. Le neveu et la nièce d'Abia du film *Liaisons,* Patrick et Aude, parlent de leurs désirs et de ceux des membres de leur famille. Complétez les phrases avec la forme appropriée du verbe qui convient.

1. Il vaut mieux que maman _____ un spectacle avec papa.
   a. chanter   b. danser   c. voir

2. Il faut que papa _____ «Je t'aime» à maman plus souvent.
   a. dire   b. écouter   c. parler

3. Patrick, il est important que tu _____ la lettre de l'oncle Jerome.
   a. entendre   b. lire   c. réussir

4. Aude, il ne faut pas que tu _____ les Coca de papa.
   a. boire   b. manger   c. mettre

5. Il faut que l'oncle Xavier _____ bientôt ses études.
   a. étudier   b. finir   c. sortir

6. Je désire que nous _____ plus souvent avec notre chat.
   a. s'amuser   b. se perdre   c. se demander

7. Je veux qu'on _____ bien avec l'ex-femme de l'oncle Kofi.
   a. s'entendre   b. se méfier   c. se mettre à

8. Nous préférons qu'Abia nous _____ des bonbons.
   a. acheter   b. manger   c. parler

9. Nous préférons que grand-mère nous _____ visite plus souvent.
   a. jouer   b. finir   c. rendre

10. J'aime mieux que l'oncle Xavier _____ nous voir ce soir.
    a. partir   b. prendre   c. venir

11. Papa ne veut pas que grand-maman _____ avec nous.
    a. connaître   b. essayer   c. vivre

12. Maman et papa veulent que nous _____ à nos examens.
    a. jouer   b. lire   c. réussir

Étape 2. Qu'est-ce que vous désirez de la part des personnes suivantes? Complétez les phrases avec les verbes donnés.

1. Je veux que mon/ma colocataire (écouter) _____.
2. J'aime mieux que mes voisins (s'entendre) _____.
3. Il vaut mieux que mon ami(e) (sortir) _____.
4. Je préfère que mon/ma colocataire (dormir) _____.
5. Je veux que ma famille (se sentir) _____.
6. Je désire que mon professeur (donner) _____.
7. Il vaut mieux que mes camarades de classe et moi, nous (regarder) _____.
8. Il est important que la classe et moi, nous (parler) _____.

Étape 3. Comparez vos réponses avec un(e) partenaire. Qui est plus exigeant(e) envers *(toward)* les autres? Vous ou votre partenaire?

ACTIVITÉ I Les personnages du film *Liaisons* Décrivez les photos avec les éléments donnés.

Modèle: Mme Gagner / Claire / rendre visite

Mme Gagner veut que Claire lui rende visite plus souvent.

1. Claire / la serveuse / servir

3. Claire / l'homme mystérieux / dire

2. la voisine de l'oncle Michel / Claire / venir

4. l'employé de la banque / Claire / donner

ACTIVITÉ J Les chefs

Étape 1. Que veulent les chefs? Choisissez un type de chef et complétez les phrases selon ses désirs. Utilisez le subjonctif.

Possibilités: le président de notre pays, un cadre d'entreprise, un président d'une chaîne de télé, un chef de cuisine, un professeur, le président de notre université, un membre du clergé, un parent,… veut…?

1. que nous (prendre) _____.

5. qu'on (apprendre) _____.

2. que nous (aider) _____.

6. qu'on (connaître) _____.

3. que les enfants (obéir) _____.

7. qu'on (essayer) _____.

4. que les jeunes (obtenir) _____.

8. qu'on (vivre) _____.

Conclusion Est-ce que vous voulez les mêmes choses que le type de chef que vous avez choisi?

Étape 2. Demandez à un(e) partenaire s'il/si elle veut les choses que vous avez écrites dans l'Étape 1.

Modèle: É1: **Est-ce que tu veux que nous prenions plus de vacances?**
É2: **Oui, je veux que nous prenions plus de vacances.**

Conclusion Est-ce que votre partenaire est comme le type de chef que vous avez choisi?

ACTIVITÉ K **Les demandes des étudiants** Avez-vous des demandes *(requests)* ou des suggestions pour votre professeur? Avec un(e) partenaire, écrivez une lettre de cinq à sept phrases à votre professeur avec les verbes donnés. Utilisez chaque verbe seulement *(only)* une fois.

Verbes possibles

acheter	écouter	lire	revenir
s'amuser	écrire	manger	sortir
apprendre	enseigner	prendre	travailler
boire	goûter	réfléchir	venir
commander	inviter	regarder	visiter
donner	jouer	répondre	voir

Modèle: Cher Monsieur/Chère Madame,
Il est nécessaire que vous nous écoutiez. Il faut que nous nous amusions plus en classe. Nous voulons que vous organisiez une fête pour la classe de français.

OUI, JE PEUX!

Here are two "can do statements" for you to check your progress so far. Look at each statement and rate yourself on how well you think you can perform the task. Then verify your ability with a partner. How did you do?

1. "I can name at least two favorite childhood pets or animals and ask others what animals they had or liked as children."

I can perform this function
☐ with ease
☐ with some difficulty
☐ not at all

2. "I can express at least one desire or obligation for this week (what it is necessary that I do or what I want to buy, watch, choose, take, drink, eat, try, see, etc.)."

I can perform this function
☐ with ease
☐ with some difficulty
☐ not at all

iLrn™

Are you looking for more practice? You can find it in **iLrn**.

Rester en forme

Staying healthy

un(e) patient(e)

le cœur

prendre la tension (artérielle)

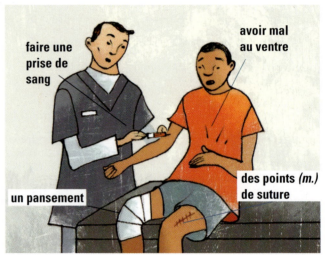

faire une prise de sang

avoir mal au ventre

des points *(m.)* de suture

un pansement

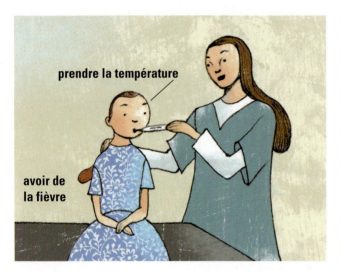

prendre la température

avoir de la fièvre

une allergie

un kleenex

être allergique à

Les maladies et les soins

Vocabulaire complémentaire

l'assurance-maladie *(f.)* health insurance

une blessure *wound*

la grippe *flu*

une intervention chirurgicale *surgery*

une maladie *illness*

un médicament *medication*

une radiographie *X-ray*

un rhume *cold*

le stress *stress*

un symptôme *symptom*

un traitement *treatment*

les urgences *(f.)* emergency room

tousser

le sirop contre la toux

une ordonnance

un(e) pharmacien(ne)

un cachet d'aspirine

ASPIRINE

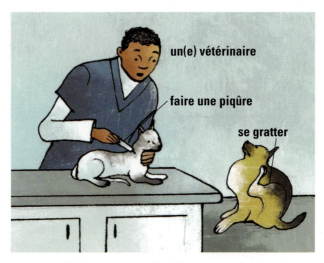

un(e) vétérinaire

faire une piqûre

se gratter

D'autres maladies et soins

Vocabulaire complémentaire	
aller aux urgences *to go to the emergency room*	**être en forme** *to be in good shape*
avoir mal à (la tête) *to hurt (to have a headache)*	**être / tomber malade** *to be / to get sick*
se casser (le bras) *to break one's (arm)*	**fatigué(e)** *tired*
conseiller *to advise*	**grave** *serious*
donner son sang *to give one's blood*	
être en bonne/mauvaise santé *to be in good/bad health*	**Qu'est-ce qui ne va pas?** *What's wrong?*

ACTIVITÉ A Qui le dit? Indiquez qui dit chaque phrase que vous entendez:
12-3 **(a) un médecin** ou **(b) un(e) patient(e).**

1.   2.   3.   4.   5.   6.   7.   8.   9.   10.   11.

ACTIVITÉ B C'est grave ou ce n'est pas grave? À votre avis, est-ce que chaque traitement suivant est pour une maladie qui **est très grave, peut-être un peu grave** ou **pas grave?**

Modèle: Prenez deux aspirines. **Ce n'est pas grave.**

1. Voici un pansement.
2. On va faire une radiographie.
3. Il faut faire une intervention chirurgicale.
4. Allez aux urgences!
5. Prenez du sirop pour votre toux.
6. Il faut faire dix points de suture.
7. Voici des médicaments pour vos allergies.

Et vous? Avez-vous jamais reçu ces soins?

ACTIVITÉ C Quelle activité?

Étape 1. Indiquez quelles activités ou situations vous associez aux symptômes de ces patients.

Modèle: Il est stressé.   **Il travaille trop.**

1. Il a un rhume.
2. Il a mal à la tête.
3. Il est toujours fatigué.

4. Il a une blessure au genou.
5. Il a la grippe.
6. Il s'est cassé le bras.

 Étape 2. Montrez vos réponses à un(e) partenaire. Avez-vous les mêmes réponses?

ACTIVITÉ D Les examens médicaux pour les animaux et pour nous

Étape 1. Indiquez qui dit chaque phrase: **(a) un médecin, (b) un vétérinaire** ou **(c) tous les deux.**

1. Est-ce qu'il a l'assurance-maladie?
2. Est-ce qu'il se gratte souvent?
3. Il faut lui donner du sirop contre la toux.
4. Il a des puces *(fleas).*
5. Je vais lui faire une piqûre.

6. Il a besoin d'un traitement.
7. Il a de la fièvre.
8. On va prendre sa tension.
9. Voudriez-vous donner votre sang?
10. Voici une ordonnance.

 Étape 2. Comparez vos réponses avec un(e) partenaire pour voir si vous êtes d'accord.

Étape 3. Avec votre partenaire, dites en quoi un examen médical est semblable et différent pour les humains et pour les animaux.

ACTIVITÉ E Les maladies

Étape 1. Quels problèmes pourraient avoir ces personnages du film *Liaisons* s'ils faisaient les activités suivantes?

Modèle: Robert a fait du vélo toute la journée. **Il va avoir mal aux jambes.**

1. Abia ne s'est pas séché les cheveux avant de sortir en hiver.
2. Robert est tombé du balcon de son appartement.
3. Claire a donné son sang à la Croix-Rouge *(Red Cross)*.
4. Claire a fait une nuit blanche *(all-nighter)* pour étudier pour ses examens.
5. Abia a bu du lait périmé *(expired)*.
6. Robert a mangé deux pizzas et a bu trois bouteilles de vin.

Étape 2. Quelle maladie associez-vous à ces symptômes?

1. Abia se gratte.
2. Claire a mal à la gorge et elle tousse.
3. Robert a mal à la tête, il a de la fièvre, il a froid et il a mal au ventre.

Étape 3. Montrez vos réponses à un(e) partenaire. Qui est le meilleur médecin? Avez-vous jamais eu ces symptômes?

ACTIVITÉ F Les remèdes de grand-mère

Étape 1. La grand-mère d'Abia connaît de bons remèdes *(remedies)*. Quelle maladie associez-vous à ces remèdes?

Il faut que tu…

1. boives du jus d'orange.
2. prennes de la soupe au poulet.
3. dormes beaucoup.
4. évites de t'énerver *(lose your temper)*.
5. boives de la tisane *(herbal tea)*.
6. te gargarises *(gargle)* avec de l'eau salée.

Étape 2. Montrez vos réponses à un(e) partenaire pour voir si vous êtes d'accord. Connaissez-vous de bons remèdes aussi?

ACTIVITÉ G Si vous étiez médecin Si vous étiez médecin, que suggéreriez-vous à ces patient(e)s?

1. J'ai de la fièvre.
2. J'ai mal à la gorge.
3. J'ai mal au ventre.
4. J'ai le nez bouché *(stuffy)*.
5. Je me suis coupé le doigt.
6. Je tousse beaucoup.

Si vous voyagez au Québec et si vous avez besoin d'aspirine ou de médicaments, allez à la pharmacie Brunet dont le slogan est: **En santé depuis 150 ans.**

ACTIVITÉ H **Le dossier médical**

Étape 1. Préparez le dossier médical *(medical history)* d'une personne célèbre. Répondez aux questions à sa place. **Suggestions:** Bart Simpson, Eric Cartman, Tom Cruise, Lindsay Lohan, Betty White, Robert Downey Jr., Oprah Winfrey, David Beckham

1. Est-ce que vous fumez? À quelle fréquence *(frequency)*? Avez-vous jamais fumé?

2. Est-ce que vous buvez de l'alcool? À quelle fréquence?

3. Mangez-vous très gras? À quelle fréquence?

4. Avez-vous jamais subi *(undergo)* une intervention chirurgicale? Pour quelle raison?

5. Avez-vous jamais eu une chirurgie esthétique *(plastic surgery)*? Pour quelle raison?

6. Prenez-vous des médicaments? Lesquels?

7. Avez-vous des allergies? Quelles allergies?

8. Êtes-vous jamais allé(e) aux urgences? Pour quelle raison?

 Étape 2. Comparez votre dossier médical avec ceux de deux camarades de classe.

ACTIVITÉ I **Êtes-vous en bonne santé cette année?**

Étape 1. Avez-vous eu ces problèmes de santé cette année? Répondez aux questions.

1. Vous avez eu mal à la tête?	4. Vous avez eu de la fièvre?
2. Vous avez eu mal à la gorge?	5. Vous avez eu des points de suture?
3. Vous avez eu un rhume?	6. Vous avez eu la grippe?

 Étape 2. Posez ces questions à un(e) partenaire. Qui est en meilleure forme cette année: vous ou votre partenaire?

Un mot sur la culture

L'assurance-maladie en France

En France, l'assurance-maladie fait partie de la Sécurité Sociale. Tous les salariés, français ou étrangers, peuvent bénéficier de la Sécurité Sociale pour la couverture des frais médicaux et dentaires (consultation de médecins généralistes et spécialistes, radiologie), des médicaments et des frais d'hospitalisation (chirurgie, maternité). Si vous êtes salarié(e), vous recevrez automatiquement votre carte d'assuré(e) social(e). La France a l'un des meilleurs systèmes d'assurance-maladie au monde.

© Carob Daily/Alamy

• Aimez-vous le système d'assurance-maladie de votre pays?

Liaisons avec les mots et les sons

La lettre *h,* le *e* caduc et le *e* muet

As you have seen, the **h** in French is usually silent and treated as a vowel.

l'homme	s'habiller	les humains	des heures

Some words have an *h* **aspiré.** This means the **h** is not treated as vowel, so it is not preceded by **l'** and there is no **liaison.**

le hockey	les haricots verts	le huit novembre	les héros

An unaccented **e** is usually pronounced like the **e** in the following words. This sound is called an *e* **caduc.**

ce	de	le	me	se regarder	cheveux

An *e* **caduc** is sometimes called *e* **muet** *(mute)* when it is silent. An *e* **muet** occurs at the end of words and when it is preceded by only one consonant.

coude	singe	tête	vache	logement	traitement

The *e* **caduc** sound is often dropped in spoken French.

Je ne sais pas.	Il ne se brosse pas les dents.	Je ne suis pas certain.

Pratique A. Écoutez et répétez ces mots de vocabulaire.

1. l'hygiène
2. s'habiller
3. le hamster
4. les hors-d'œuvre
5. se lever
6. le refuge
7. le requin
8. la brosse
9. un tigre

Pratique B. Écoutez ces répliques *(lines)* du film *Liaisons.* Ensuite, lisez-les et barrez *(cross out)* tous les *e* **muets.**

1. **EMPLOYÉ** Ça va bien, mon petit toutou *(doggy)*?
2. **MME LEGRAND** Je dois rentrer chez moi pour me préparer.
3. **CLAIRE** Je ne suis pas tombée sur ces documents par hasard.

🔊 12-5 **À vos stylos! C'est l'heure de la dictée!**

Vous allez entendre cinq phrases deux fois. La première fois, écoutez bien. La deuxième fois, écrivez les phrases.

Sujet Claire décrit à Abia les photos qu'elle a trouvées.

Pour exprimer la volonté et les émotions

Le subjonctif des verbes irréguliers

DU FILM *LIAISONS*

Un coup d'œil sur la grammaire

Look at these photos from the film *Liaisons* and their captions.

MICHEL (V.O.) Il faut que tu **ailles** à Québec.

CLAIRE Il faut que je **fasse** mes valises.

1. What is the infinitive form of **ailles** in the left caption? What does the caption mean?
2. What is the infinitive form of **fasse** in the right caption? What does the caption mean?

Some verbs have irregular subjunctive stems. With the exception of **avoir** and **être,** the endings themselves are regular.

	avoir	être	aller	faire
... que je/j'	aie	sois	aille	fasse
... que tu	aies	sois	ailles	fasses
... qu'il/elle/on	ait	soit	aille	fasse
... que nous	ayons	soyons	allions	fassions
... que vous	ayez	soyez	alliez	fassiez
... qu'ils/elles	aient	soient	aillent	fassent

	pouvoir	savoir	vouloir
... que je/j'	puisse	sache	veuille
... que tu	puisses	saches	veuilles
... qu'il/elle/on	puisse	sache	veuille
... que nous	puissions	sachions	voulions
... que vous	puissiez	sachiez	vouliez
... qu'ils/elles	puissent	sachent	veuillent

Il faut que j'**aille** aux urgences.   *I must go to the emergency room.*

Le médecin veut que je **fasse** de l'exercice.   *The doctor wants me to exercise.*

Here are some other verbs and expressions of volition, opinion, and obligation after which the subjunctive commonly occurs.

conseiller que *to advise that*	**souhaiter que** *to wish that*
demander que *to ask that*	**Il est essentiel que** *It is essential that*
exiger que *to demand that*	**Il est préférable que** *It is preferable that*

Mon mari **souhaite que je sois** plus heureuse.

My husband **wishes that I were** happier.

Je **demande que tu ailles** à l'hôpital.

*I **ask that you go** to the hospital.*

Il est préférable **qu'on ait** une voiture ici.

It is preferable that we have a car here.

Il est essentiel **que vous fassiez** attention!

It is essential that you pay attention!

The subjunctive is also used after verbs and expressions of emotion when there is a change in subject between the main clause and the dependent clause.

aimer que	**être heureux/heureuse que**
avoir peur que	**être surpris(e) que**
être content(e) que	**être triste que**
être désolé(e) que	**regretter que**
être furieux/furieuse que	

Je **regrette que tu sois** malade.
I'm sorry you are sick.

Anne **est surprise que nous ne sachions pas** parler anglais.
Anne is surprised that we don't know how to speak English.

Nous **sommes heureux que tu veuilles** donner ton sang.
We are happy that you want to give blood.

Liaisons musicales

© Bo-Yp/Agence Quebec Presse/Newscom

Kevin Parent est un chanteur québécois bilingue de la Gaspésie. Sa chanson *Seigneur (Lord)* lui a remporté le Félix de chanson de l'année en 1996: Seigneur, Seigneur// Qu'est-ce qu' tu veux que j' te dise? ...//Mon rôle dans la vie n'est pas encore défini//Pourtant je m'efforce pour qu'il soit accompli//Je le sais, faut tout que je recommence// Mais Seigneur j'ai pas envie… Cherchez un vidéoclip de cette chanson sur Internet.

ACTIVITÉ J **Un bon ou un mauvais médecin?** Indiquez qui dit chaque phrase: **(a) un bon médecin** ou **(b) un mauvais médecin**.

1. Je conseille que vous **alliez** manger à MacDo.
2. Il est préférable que vous **soyez** plus stressé(e).
3. Je recommande qu'on vous **fasse** une piqûre contre la grippe.
4. Je souhaite que vous **soyez** en bonne santé.
5. Je suis content que vous n'**ayez** pas d'assurance-maladie.
6. Il est préférable que vous **sachiez** prendre la tension.
7. Je suis heureux que vous **veuillez** fumer. Continuez.
8. Je suis content que vous **puissiez** donner votre sang. Merci.

Et vous? Vous avez un bon ou un mauvais médecin?

ACTIVITÉ **K** **Si vous étiez médecin ou parent...**

Étape 1. Que diriez-vous à vos patients si vous étiez médecin? Complétez les phrases suivantes.

Expressions utiles		
aimer que	être désolé(e) que	exiger que
avoir peur que	être furieux/furieuse que	souhaiter que
conseiller que	être heureux/heureuse que	regretter que
demander que	être surpris(e) que	Il est essentiel que
être content(e) que	être triste que	Il est préférable que

Modèle: (faire) de la gym   **Je conseille que vous fassiez de la gym.**

1. (être) allergique au chocolat
2. (faire) du yoga
3. (pouvoir) vous reposer plus
4. (savoir) bien manger
5. (vouloir) manger du poulet frit
6. (avoir) beaucoup de stress
7. (aller) souvent au centre sportif
8. (vouloir) éviter les matières grasses

Étape 2. Si vous étiez parent, que diriez-vous à votre enfant?

Modèle: (aller) à l'école   **J'exige que tu ailles à l'école.**

1. (pouvoir) réciter l'alphabet
2. (aller) dans ta chambre
3. (savoir) parler une langue étrangère
4. (vouloir) manger tes légumes
5. (avoir) beaucoup de bon(ne)s ami(e)s
6. (faire) la vaisselle
7. (être) impoli(e) avec tes ami(e)s
8. (avoir) une mauvaise note à l'examen

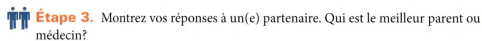 **Étape 3.** Montrez vos réponses à un(e) partenaire. Qui est le meilleur parent ou médecin?

 ACTIVITÉ **L** **Vous êtes en forme?** Posez ces questions à un(e) partenaire. Ensuite, réagissez *(react)* à sa réponse.

Modèle: É1: **Est-ce que tu es allergique aux chiens?**
 É2: **Non, je ne suis pas allergique aux chiens.**
 É1: **Je suis content(e) que tu ne sois pas allergique aux chiens.**

1. (être) allergique aux chats
2. (avoir) mal à la tête maintenant
3. (avoir) mal au ventre le matin ou le soir
4. (prendre) des vitamines
5. (aller) souvent aux urgences avec vos amis
6. (se brosser) les dents chaque jour
7. (boire) de l'alcool
8. (dormir) bien le soir
9. (se reposer) assez le week-end
10. (devoir) avoir une piqûre

Conclusion Qui est en meilleure forme? Vous ou votre partenaire?

ACTIVITÉ **M** **Les professeurs de français**

Étape 1. Quelles sont les pensées des professeurs de français? Complétez les phrases.

Modèle: Ils veulent que les étudiants **soient intelligents.**

1. Ils veulent que les étudiants…
2. Ils exigent que nous…
3. Ils ont peur que nous…
4. Ils sont parfois surpris que la classe…
5. Ils sont furieux que certains étudiants…
6. Ils sont contents que je…

Étape 2. Posez les questions à votre professeur.

Modèle: **Vous voulez que les étudiants soient intelligents?**

ACTIVITÉ **N** **Les personnages du film *Liaisons*** Complétez les phrases à propos des personnages du film *Liaisons*.

1. Claire regrette que sa mère…
2. Claire souhaite qu'Alexis…
3. Abia a peur que Claire…
4. Robert exige que Claire et Abia…
5. Robert est content que les clients…
6. Alexis est heureux que Claire…

ACTIVITÉ **O** **Un membre de ma famille** Faites une liste de cinq à six choses qu'un membre de votre famille fait que vous aimez ou que vous n'aimez pas.

Modèle: J'aime que ma sœur aille à l'église. Je regrette qu'elle soit paresseuse.

OUI, JE PEUX! Here are two "can do statements" for you to check your progress so far. Look at each statement and rate yourself on how well you think you can perform the task. Then verify your ability with a partner. How did you do?

1. **"I can say if I got sick this past year and what illness(es) I had or if I stayed healthy. I can find out if others also got sick or stayed healthy."**

   I can perform this function
   ☐ with ease
   ☐ with some difficulty
   ☐ not at all

2. **"I can advise new students with at least two suggestions (what they might have, be, do, be able to do, want, know, or where they might go)."**

   I can perform this function
   ☐ with ease
   ☐ with some difficulty
   ☐ not at all

iLrn™

Are you looking for more practice? You can find it in **iLrn**.

Avant de visionner

ACTIVITÉ A **Vous rappelez-vous?** Vous rappelez-vous ce qui s'est passé dans la Séquence 6 du film *Liaisons*? Choisissez la bonne réponse pour chaque phrase.

1. Le numéro du coffre-fort était _____.   a. 513   b. 315

2. Il y avait des photos et un _____ dans le coffre-fort.   a. testament   b. livre

3. L'une des personnes sur les photos ressemblait (*ressembled*) à _____.   a. Abia   b. Alexis

4. Claire devait aller à _____ de son oncle.   a. la fête   b. l'enterrement

ACTIVITÉ B **Une scène du film** Vous rappelez-vous cette scène? Claire et Abia se parlent à propos des photos que Claire a trouvées. Écrivez les mots qui manquent (*are missing*).

CLAIRE Et regarde cette (1) _____. C'est l'homme qui m'a donné (2) _____ avec la réservation au Frontenac. Il s'appelle Tremblay. Et ici... c'est (3) _____ que j'ai rencontré le soir où Tremblay m'a (4) _____ l'enveloppe, (5) _____.

ABIA Seigneur! Claire. C'est pas (6) _____. Cette photo date de (7) _____. Et tu m'avais dit qu'il était jeune et (8) _____.

CLAIRE Je (9) _____, je sais, Abia. Ça n'a aucun sens. C'est (10) _____ un mystère.

ABIA Mais si cette photo date de 1959, il devrait avoir 80 ans ou plus maintenant!

▶ **Regarder la séquence**

Vous allez regarder la Séquence 6 du film *Liaisons*. Vérifiez vos réponses à l'Activité A et à l'Activité B.

Après le visionnage

ACTIVITÉ C **Qu'est-ce qui n'a pas de sens?**

Étape 1. Dans la Séquence 6, Claire découvre des choses dans le coffre-fort qui sont encore plus mystérieuses et qui n'ont pas de sens. Avec un(e) partenaire, faites une liste des choses qui sont mystérieuses ou qui n'ont pas de sens.

Modèle: Claire a trouvé une photo de l'homme mystérieux qui lui a donné l'enveloppe à l'hôtel. La date sur la photo était 1959.

Étape 2. Montrez votre liste à une autre paire d'étudiant(e)s. Voulez-vous ajouter d'autres choses à votre liste?

Étape 1. Voici le testament que Claire a trouvé. Choisissez les mots qui manquent.

1930	15 mars	mort	dit	donné
fille	l'île d'Orléans	m'appelle	mariage	partager
pouvais	Québec	a épousé	six	sœurs

«Je (1) _____ Rémy Tremblay, frère et employé de Madeleine Tremblay, et je jure *(swear)* que ce testament repose sur la vérité...»

«Madeleine Tremblay a épousé Henri Prévost en (2) _____...»

«M. Prévost avait une (3) _____ adoptive d'un premier (4) _____. Elle s'appelait Claire-Angèle...»

«Née le (5) _____...»

«À la (6) _____ de M. Prévost, en 1933, Mme Prévost ne voulait pas (7) _____ ses biens *(assets)* avec Claire-Angèle et m'a (8) _____ l'ordre de la tuer *(kill)*...»

«... mais je ne (9) _____ pas le faire. La pauvre petite n'avait que (10) _____ ans...»

«Je suis venu à (11) _____ et j'ai amené la petite avec moi. Les bonnes (12) _____ de l'Église Notre-Dame-des-Victoires l'ont gardée...»

«Je ne lui ai rien (13) _____ sur son passé, pour la protéger...»

«Claire-Angèle (14) _____ un garçon de (15) _____ et ils ont eu un fils, Michel et une fille, Simone...»

Étape 2. Montrez vos réponses à un(e) partenaire et devinez les réponses aux questions suivantes.

1. Qui est Rémy Tremblay?
2. Qui est Madeleine Tremblay-Prévost?
3. Qui est Henri Prévost?
4. Qui est Claire-Angèle?

Dans les coulisses

In mystery genres, directors leave clues throughout a film to lead viewers to a discovery. The number 315 in the film is symbolic and is a clue that leads Claire to the testament and photos in the safety deposit box. Did you pick up on this clue in earlier segments of this film? What other films do you know that use numbers as clues?

À DÉCOUVRIR: La Tunisie et le tourisme médical

À DÉCOUVRIR: La Tunisie

Pays: La Tunisie
Géographie: L'Afrique du Nord (le Maghreb); entre l'Algérie et la Libye
Climat: Méditerranéen dans le nord; désertique dans le sud
Population: Plus de 10 millions
Capitale: Tunis

À DÉCOUVRIR: La ville de Tunis

Structure: Une grande ville moderne
Région: Bab el Bahr / Porte de France (dans le nord)
Population: Plus de 1 200 000 (en ville)
Réputation: La capitale administrative et politique de la Tunisie; le centre commercial et culturel

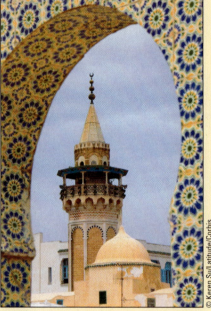

Avant de lire

You will discover in this reading the topic of medical tourism in Tunisia.

Que savez-vous déjà?

1. Qu'est-ce que le tourisme médical?

2. Quels sont quelques avantages ou désavantages du tourisme médical?

3. Pour quelles raisons est-ce qu'on s'intéresse au tourisme médical?

> **OUTILS DE LECTURE**
> **Preparing a summary of a text**
> You can have an easier time comprehending a text when you prepare a summary. To get started, skim the text **Le tourisme médical: la chirurgie esthétique** and jot down a few notes about its overall or general meaning.

Le tourisme médical: la chirurgie esthétique

© Sébastien Boisse/Photononstop/Glow Images

Le «tourisme médical» est un phénomène récent. La raison de son développement est simple: certains services médicaux—en particulier la chirurgie esthétique°—sont moins chers en dehors de l'Europe de l'Ouest. La Tunisie, pays ensoleillé et relativement proche de la France, est devenue une des premières destinations de ces touristes européens d'un nouveau genre.

De nombreux sites Web de cliniques tunisiennes proposent des formules «tous frais compris» (le voyage, l'hôtel, les repas et... l'intervention chirurgicale) qui, compte tenu du taux de change° de l'euro, sont (beaucoup) moins chères qu'une simple procédure médicale équivalente en France. Par exemple, une augmentation mammaire° et un *easy lift* coûteraient environ 9 000 euros en Tunisie tandis qu'°en Europe les deux mêmes opérations coûteraient approximativement 30 000 euros.

La majorité des médecins et chirurgiens tunisiens ont fait leurs études médicales en Europe ou aux États-Unis. Par conséquent, le niveau des soins médicaux dans certaines cliniques en Tunisie est à présent comparable à celui de la France, mais la période de récupération immédiate est bien différente. Les patients-touristes peuvent récupérer, après une liposuccion ou une rhinoplastie°, au bord de la piscine ou sur la plage de sable fin d'un hôtel quatre étoiles. Le phénomène du tourisme médical reste cependant minoritaire et concerne essentiellement les interventions chirurgicales à caractère purement esthétique (par opposition à la chirurgie réparatrice, par exemple après un accident), qui ne sont pas remboursées par la Sécurité Sociale en France.

Sources: http://www.cosmeticatravel.com/; http://www.estetikatour.com/

la chirurgie esthétique *cosmetic surgery* **le taux de change** *exchange rate*
une augmentation mammaire *breast augmentation* **tandis qu'** *whereas*
une rhinoplastie *"nose job"*

Après avoir lu

Compréhension

	Vrai	Faux
1. La Tunisie est déjà une destination touristique importante pour le tourisme médical.	☐	☐
2. Les procédures médicales sont moins chères en Tunisie.	☐	☐
3. Le tourisme médical concerne la chirurgie esthétique.	☐	☐

Et vous?

1. Est-ce que le tourisme médical est une bonne idée, à votre avis?

2. Est-ce que vous êtes pour ou contre la chirurgie esthétique?

3. Est-ce que vous auriez peur de recevoir des soins médicaux à l'étranger?

4. Est-ce que vous voudriez combiner des soins médicaux avec des vacances?

Share It!

Use **Share It!** in **iLrn™** to express your reactions to the reading and to find out what your classmates think.

The ability to express your personal reaction to a topic in an articulate manner is an important life skill. Here is a personal reaction to the topic of medical tourism.

À mon avis, la question du tourisme médical à caractère esthétique est très complexe. Premièrement, c'est une question personnelle. Si des gens veulent changer une partie de leur corps, c'est leur choix. Il est préférable qu'ils soient heureux. Mais deuxièmement, c'est aussi une question de santé. Il faut que les gens qui s'intéressent au tourisme médical réfléchissent beaucoup. Toutes les chirurgies, esthétiques ou réparatrices, sont dangereuses et une chirurgie à l'étranger pourrait avoir de plus grandes complications. Cette question du tourisme médical exige qu'un patient-touriste fasse attention.

Avant d'écrire

1. What kinds of statements appear in the personal reaction?
2. Answer the following questions to help you write your own **réaction personnelle.**

   a. Quelle est votre position au sujet du tourisme médical? Êtes-vous pour ou contre?

   b. Quelles sont deux ou trois raisons pour lesquelles vous avez cette position?

   c. Quel est votre «dernier mot»? Que voudriez-vous que les autres pensent du tourisme médical à la fin?

Écrire

Using information from **Avant d'écrire**, write you own personal reaction of 6–8 sentences in French.

Après avoir écrit

Exchange your **réaction personnelle** with a partner. (1) Underline any subjunctive expressions you see and verify that your partner correctly used them. (2) Circle all the subjunctive verbs and verify that they are all correctly conjugated. (3) Double-check that your partner correctly conjugated all other verbs and used infinitives when necessary. (4) Put a * next to the key phrase or key idea that best communicates your partner's personal reaction. (5) How would you characterize your partner's personal reaction: **neutre, forte, faible** (weak), **typique, unique,** etc.? Discuss your reactions together. Do you share the same personal reaction? Write a second version of your **réaction personnelle** taking into account your partner's comments and corrections.

RÉSUMÉ DE VOCABULAIRE

PARTIE 1 12–6

LES PARTIES DU CORPS

la bouche	mouth
le bras	arm
la cheville	ankle
le corps	body
le cou	neck
le coude	elbow
les dents (f.)	teeth
les doigts (m.)	fingers
le dos	back
les épaules (f.)	shoulders
le genou	knee
la gorge	throat
la jambe	leg
la langue	tongue
la main	hand
les oreilles (f.)	ears
le pied	foot
la poitrine	chest
la tête	head
le ventre	abdomen, belly
le visage / la figure	face

LES PRODUITS DE SOIN

une brosse (à cheveux)	hairbrush
une brosse à dents	toothbrush
la crème à raser	shaving cream
la crème solaire	sunscreen
le dentifrice	toothpaste
l'hygiène (f.)	hygiene
la lotion	lotion
le maquillage	makeup
un peigne	comb
les produits (m.) de soin personnel	personal care products
un rasoir	razor
le savon	soap
un sèche-cheveux	hairdryer
une serviette	towel
le shampooing	shampoo

VERBES

se brosser	to brush
se coucher	to go to bed
se couper	to cut (oneself)
(se) déshabiller	to (get) undress(ed)
se doucher	to shower
s'endormir	to fall asleep
(s')habiller	to (get) dress(ed)
se laver	to wash
se lever	to get up
se maquiller	to put on makeup
se préparer	to get ready, to prepare
se raser	to shave
se réveiller	to wake up
se sécher	to dry
utiliser	to use

PARTIE 2 12–7

LES ANIMAUX

un aigle	eagle
une chèvre	goat
un cochon	pig
un coq	rooster
une grenouille	frog
un hamster	hamster
un lapin	rabbit
un lion	lion
un oiseau	bird
un ours	bear
un rat	rat
un requin	shark
un serpent	snake
un tigre	tiger

DIVERS

une animalerie	pet store
une créature	creature
les humains (m.)	humans
les moustaches (f.)	whiskers
une patte	paw
les poils (m.)	animal hair, fur
la queue	tail
un refuge	(animal) shelter

LES EXPRESSIONS AVEC LE SUBJONCTIF

aimer mieux que	to like better that
désirer que	to desire that
préférer que	to prefer that
vouloir que	to want that
Il (ne) faut (pas) que	It is (not) necessary that
Il vaut mieux que	It is better that
Il (n')est (pas) nécessaire que	It is (not) necessary that
Il (n')est (pas) important que	It is (not) important that

PARTIE 3 12–8

LES SOINS MÉDICAUX

un cachet d'aspirine	aspirin
un examen médical	medical exam
une intervention chirurgicale	surgery

un médicament	*medication*
une ordonnance	*prescription*
un pansement	*bandage*
un point de suture	*stitch, suture*
une radiographie	*X-ray*
le sirop contre la toux	*cough syrup*
un traitement	*treatment*
les urgences (*f.*)	*emergency room*
aller aux urgences	*to go to the emergency room*
donner son sang	*to give one's blood*
faire une piqûre	*to give a shot*
faire une prise de sang	*to take one's blood*
prendre la température	*to take one's temperature*
prendre la tension (artérielle)	*to take one's blood pressure*

LES MALADIES

une allergie	*allergy*
une blessure	*wound*
la fièvre	*fever*
la grippe	*flu*
une maladie	*illness*
un rhume	*cold*
le stress	*stress*
un symptôme	*symptom*
avoir mal à (la tête)	*to hurt (to have a headache)*
avoir mal au ventre	*to have a stomach ache*
se casser (le bras)	*to break one's (arm)*
être allergique à	*to be allergic to*
être en bonne/mauvaise santé	*to be in good/bad health*

être en forme	*to be in shape*
être / tomber malade	*to be / to get sick*
se gratter	*to scratch*
tousser	*to cough*

DIVERS

l'assurance-maladie (*f.*)	*health insurance*
le cœur	*heart*
un kleenex	*tissue*
un(e) patient(e)	*patient*
un(e) vétérinaire	*vet*
fatigué(e)	*tired*
grave	*serious*
conseiller	*to advise*
Qu'est-ce qui ne va pas?	*What's wrong?*

LES EXPRESSIONS AVEC LE SUBJONCTIF

aimer que	*to love that*
avoir peur que	*to be afraid that*
conseiller que	*to advise that*
demander que	*to ask that*
être content(e) que	*to be happy that*
être désolé(e) que	*to be sorry that*
être furieux/furieuse que	*to be furious that*
être heureux/heureuse que	*to be happy that*
être surpris(e) que	*to be surprised that*
être triste que	*to be sad that*
exiger que	*to demand that*
regretter que	*to regret, to be sorry that*
souhaiter que	*to wish that*
Il est essentiel que	*It is essential that*
Il est préférable que	*It is preferable that*

Les sciences et la technologie dans la francophonie

Le tunnel sous la Manche

Un exemple d'une invention technologique importante en France est le tunnel sous la Manche, un tunnel ferroviaire° construit par la société franco-britannique Eurotunnel. Le tunnel sous la Manche relie le nord de la France et le sud-est de l'Angleterre. Il est long de 50,5 kilomètres. Les trains à grande vitesse qui utilisent le tunnel sous la Manche s'appellent Eurostar. Ils offrent 800 places pour les passagers et roulent à 160 km/h (99 m/h) à l'intérieur du tunnel et à 300 km/h (186 m/h) à l'extérieur du tunnel.

© PHILIPPE HUGUEN/Getty Images

ferroviaire *railway*

© Tischenko Irina/Shutterstock.com

Les cartes à puce

Contrairement aux cartes en plastique équipées d'une bande ou piste magnétique, les cartes à puce° contiennent au moins un circuit intégré (la «puce» électronique). Les premières versions de ces cartes ont été créées par l'inventeur français Roland Moreno en mars 1974. Depuis, les nouvelles versions des cartes à puce ont progressivement remplacé les cartes à piste magnétique, en particulier dans le domaine des cartes bancaires, qui nécessitent un niveau° de sécurité élevé. Selon la Banque de France, on compte 88,6 millions de cartes à puce à usage bancaire en France en 2010.

Adapted from: http://www.futura-sciences.com/magazines/maison/infos/dico/d/maison-carte-puce-11077/

une carte à puce *smart card* **un niveau** *level*

L'énergie solaire en Afrique

Le développement économique en Afrique repose sur l'accès à des sources d'énergie nouvelles, moins coûteuses° et moins polluantes. Grâce à son climat et à son niveau d'ensoleillement annuel, une grande partie du continent africain est particulièrement appropriée à l'exploitation de l'énergie solaire. En 2011, le Sénégal, avec l'aide d'une société° suisse et d'une société allemande, est devenu le premier pays sub-saharien à construire une usine de fabrication de panneaux solaires. En plus des panneaux solaires, d'autres produits adaptés aux réalités économiques africaines sont aujourd'hui développés, par exemple des lampes qui fonctionnent la nuit grâce à l'énergie solaire qu'elles ont captée° pendant la journée.

© Jenny Matthews/Alamy

coûteuses *costly* **une société** *a company* **captée** *captured*

Ariane

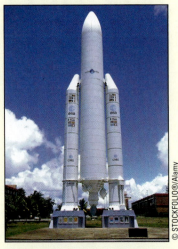

Le centre spatial en Guyane est situé près de la ville de Kourou. C'est de ce centre spatial que les fusées de l'Agence spatiale européenne sont lancées°, depuis une quarantaine° d'années. La Guyane, un département d'outre-mer français en Amérique du Sud, est proche de l'équateur, ce qui permet de lancer à plus bas prix des fusées transportant de gros satellites géostationnaires de télécommunications ou d'observation météorologique. Plusieurs centaines° de fusées Ariane ont été lancées du centre spatial guyanais.

lancées *launched* **quarantaine** *about 40* **centaines** *hundreds*

Le viaduc de Millau

Inauguré en 2004, le pont le plus haut du monde (343 mètres à son point culminant; donc un peu plus haut que la tour Eiffel) fait partie de l'autoroute A75, qui permet de relier° les villes de Clermont-Ferrand et de Béziers. Ce pont traverse° la vallée de la rivière Tarn et offre un panorama magnifique aux voyageurs. Il est aussi bien sûr tout près de Millau, Ville d'Art et d'Histoire. Comme le vent souffle° très fort à cette hauteur, le pont est équipé d'écrans brise-vent° spécifiquement conçus° pour protéger les véhicules et leurs passagers.

Source: http://www.tourisme-aveyron.com/fr/decouvrir/incontournables/viaduc-millau.php

relier *link* **traverse** *crosses* **souffle** *blows* **d'écrans brise-vent** *windscreens* **conçus** *designed*

Révision

1. Qu'est-ce que le tunnel sous la Manche?
2. Qui a inventé la carte à puce?
3. Pourquoi est-ce que l'énergie solaire est adaptée au continent africain?
4. Où se trouve la Guyane?
5. Pourquoi le viaduc de Millau est-il équipé d'écrans brise-vent?

▶ LIAISONS CULTURELLES

Vélib' - de vélo et liberté

Use **iLrn™** to access the video **Les moyens de transport** to learn more about transportation in France. Be prepared to answer the question **Alors, comment allez-vous vous déplacer la prochaine fois que vous êtes en France?** Share your responses with your classmates in **Share It!**

Les **innovations**

En bref   In this chapter, you will:

- learn about science, technology, and medical inventions

- learn expressions of opinion that take the subjunctive

- learn vocabulary for environmental and social concerns

- learn expressions of doubt that take the subjunctive

- distinguish between uses of the subjunctive and the indicative moods

- read about humanitarians in France and in the Francophone world

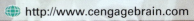
You will also watch **SÉQUENCE 7: Un nouveau chapitre** of the film *Liaisons.*

Ressources

 audio   video   Share It!   iLrn™   🌐 http://www.cengagebrain.com

VOCABULAIRE 1

La **technologie**

Technology

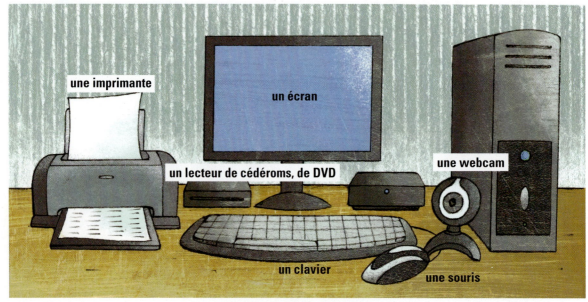

une imprimante

un écran

une webcam

un lecteur de cédéroms, de DVD

un clavier

une souris

Mon ordinateur

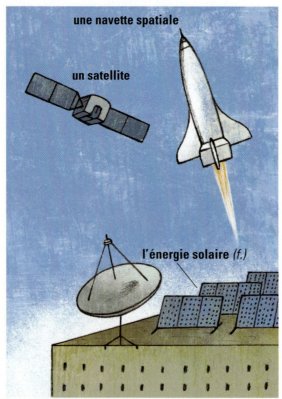

une navette spatiale

un satellite

l'énergie solaire *(f.)*

D'autres innovations technologiques

Vocabulaire complémentaire

le clonage *cloning*
un cœur artificiel *artificial heart*
une découverte *discovery*
un fichier *file*
un hybride *hybrid animal or plant*
une invention *invention*
un logiciel *software, program*
un mot de passe *password*
la réalité virtuelle *virtual reality*
un système GPS *GPS system*
le traitement de texte *word processing program*

le Wi-Fi *Wi-Fi*
_____

démarrer *to start up*
effacer *to delete, erase*
être en ligne (avec) *to be online (with)*
fermer / éteindre *to close / to shut off*
imprimer *to print*
sauvegarder *to save*
taper *to type*
télécharger *to download*

Note de grammaire
The present tense conjugation of **éteindre** is **j'éteins, tu éteins, il/elle/on éteint, nous éteignons, vous éteignez, ils/elles éteignent.** Its past participle is **éteint.**

ACTIVITÉ (A) Un ordinateur ou un iPhone? Décidez si on trouve chaque chose mentionnée sur **(a) un ordinateur, (b) un iPhone** ou **(c) les deux** *(both)*.

13-1

1.   2.   3.   4.   5.   6.   7.   8.   9.   10.   11.   12.

Conclusion Est-ce qu'un ordinateur est semblable à un iPhone ou est-ce que c'est très différent?

ACTIVITÉ (B) L'ordinateur

Étape 1. Est-ce que vous utilisez l'ordinateur pour faire vos devoirs? Mettez les étapes dans l'ordre.

a. _____ Choisissez un traitement de texte.

b. _____ Imprimez votre document.

c. _____ Éteignez l'ordinateur.

d. _____ Démarrez l'ordinateur.

e. _____ Tapez votre devoir sur le clavier.

f. _____ Sauvegardez votre document.

Étape 2. Répondez aux questions. Ensuite, posez les questions à un(e) partenaire.

1. Est-ce que vous avez une imprimante chez vous?
2. Quel logiciel utilisez-vous pour le traitement de texte?
3. Qu'est-ce que vous avez téléchargé récemment?
4. Est-ce que vous effacez les documents dont vous n'avez plus besoin?
5. Est-ce que vous avez le Wi-Fi chez vous?

Conclusion Vous servez-vous de *(Do you use)* l'ordinateur de la même manière que votre partenaire ou faites-vous des choses différemment?

ACTIVITÉ C Classez

Étape 1. Classez les découvertes et les inventions par ordre d'importance. Utilisez les chiffres 1–10.

_____ les animaux hybrides

_____ le système GPS

_____ le clonage

_____ le cœur artificiel

_____ l'énergie solaire

_____ le réseau Wi-Fi

_____ la navette spatiale

_____ la réalité virtuelle

_____ le satellite

_____ la voiture hybride

Étape 2. Comparez vos réponses avec un(e) partenaire.

Modèle: **J'ai mis le satellite en premier, le système GPS en deuxième, la voiture hybride en troisième…**

Étape 3. Posez les questions suivantes à deux camarades de classe. Ensuite, comparez les réponses de ces deux personnes.

1. Est-ce que tu as un système GPS?
2. Est-ce que tu as des gadgets qui utilisent l'énergie solaire? Lesquels?
3. Est-ce que tu as une voiture hybride? Est-ce que tu aimerais en avoir une?
4. Est-ce que tu aimerais avoir un chien hybride? Si oui, quel type de chien?
5. Est-ce que tu joues aux jeux de réalité virtuelle?

ACTIVITÉ D Une publicité pour un ordinateur

Étape 1. Décrivez quatre à cinq points forts de l'ordinateur que vous aimez.

- Intel Core i3 330M / 2.13 GHz
- Mémoire cache: 3 Mo - L3
- RAM: 4 Go (installé) / 8 Go (maximum)
- Lecteur de carte: Oui
- DVD±RW (±R DL) / DVD-RAM – integré
- Écran 15.5" TFT 1366 × 768 (WXGA)
- ATI Mobility Radeon HD 5650
- Mémoire vidéo: 1 Go
- Webcam: Intégrée - 0,3 Mégapixel
- Clavier, touchpad/ 4 ports USB
- Système d'exploitation: Microsoft Windows 8 Édition Familiale Premium 64 bits
- Microphone/Dolby Home Theater/ Carte son
- Carte Mémoire SD, Memory Stick, Memory Stick PRO-HG Duo

© Rick Wilking/Reuters/Landov

Sony - VAIO VPC-EB1M1E - Ordinateur Portable

Si vous y allez

© Christophe Lehenaff / Photononstop / Glow Images

Si vous allez à Paris, allez à la Cité des sciences et de l'industrie dans le XIXᵉ arrondissement. La Cité des sciences est un musée spécialisé dans la diffusion de la culture scientifique et technique. Les expositions permanentes sont organisées autour de thèmes: les mathématiques, l'océan, l'énergie, l'automobile, les étoiles et les galaxies.

Étape 2. Comparez votre ordinateur avec l'ordinateur Sony dans la publicité. (Écrivez deux à trois comparaisons.) Quel ordinateur préférez-vous?

 ACTIVITÉ **E** **Devant l'ordinateur**

Étape 1. Pendant combien de temps avez-vous fait ces activités hier devant l'ordinateur?

Modèle: lire des courriels   **Hier, j'ai lu mes courriels pendant quarante minutes.**

1. lire des courriels
2. être en ligne avec des amis
3. faire les devoirs
4. télécharger de la musique
5. imprimer des documents
6. naviguer sur Internet
7. jouer aux jeux vidéo
8. regarder un film

Étape 2. Posez les questions à deux camarades de classe.

Modèle: **Pendant combien de temps est-ce que tu as lu tes courriels hier?**

Conclusion Qui a passé le plus de temps devant l'ordinateur hier? Quelles activités étaient les plus populaires hier?

ACTIVITÉ **F** **Entretien: les innovations** Posez les questions à un(e) partenaire.

1. Quelles technologies ou quelles innovations pourraient sauver *(save)* des vies?
2. Quelles technologies ou quelles innovations sont controversées?
3. Quelle nouvelle découverte ou invention aimerais-tu voir dans l'avenir?

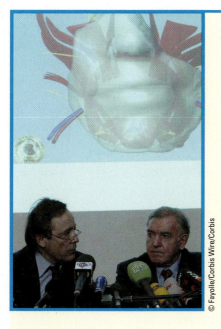

© Fayolle/Corbis Wire/Corbis

Un mot sur la culture

La greffe de visage: innovation médicale française

La France n'est pas seulement reconnue pour sa culture; on lui doit aussi beaucoup d'innovations médicales. Une innovation que les médias ont rendue célèbre est la greffe° de visage. En 2005, des chirurgiens français ont réalisé la première greffe partielle de visage au monde sur une femme de 38 ans, Isabelle Dinoire. Selon un communiqué de presse BBC, un an après l'opération, la patiente pouvait manger, parler, sourire° et sortir en public sans attirer l'attention. La greffe et ses suites° sont racontées dans un livre de Noëlle Châtelet, *Le Baiser d'Isabelle*.

Source: Noëlle Châtelet: *Le Baiser d'Isabelle—L'aventure de la première greffe du visage*
greffe *transplant* **sourire** *smile* **suites** *after-effects*

• Connaissez-vous d'autres innovations médicales françaises?

Pour exprimer les opinions

Le subjonctif et les opinions

DU FILM *LIAISONS*

Un coup d'œil sur la grammaire

Look at these photos from the film *Liaisons* and their captions.

MME PAPILLON C'est triste qu'il **soit** mort comme ça.

MME PAPILLON C'est dommage qu'on ne **puisse** pas parler plus longtemps.

1. Are the verbs **soit** and **puisse** in the subjunctive or the indicative?
2. Do the captions express opinions or facts?

In **Chapitre 12,** you learned that the subjunctive is used after verbs and expressions of volition, obligation, necessity, and emotion in a dependent clause that begins with **que.** The subjunctive is also similarly used after expressions of opinion.

<table>
<tr><td>Il est bizarre que</td><td>Il est merveilleux que</td></tr>
<tr><td>Il est bon que</td><td>Il est normal que</td></tr>
<tr><td>Il est dommage que</td><td>Il est possible que</td></tr>
<tr><td>Il est essentiel que</td><td>Il est stupide que</td></tr>
<tr><td>Il est juste (fair) / injuste (unfair) que</td><td>Il est triste que</td></tr>
<tr><td>Il est indispensable que</td><td>Il est utile / inutile que</td></tr>
</table>

Note de **grammaire**
These expressions are called *impersonal expressions* because they begin with **Il** *(It)*. Note that, in spoken French, **ce/c'** is often used instead of **il: c'est bizarre que, c'est dommage que, c'est triste que.**

Il est bizarre que tu ne **saches** pas utiliser un ordinateur.
*It's strange that you don't **know** how to use a computer.*

Il est bon qu'il **fasse** du soleil ce week-end.
It's good that it's sunny this weekend.

Il n'est pas bon que tu **sois** célibataire.
*It's not good that you **are** single.*

Il est injuste que nous ne **puissions** pas sortir ce soir.
*It's unfair that we **can't** go out tonight.*

© Graham Hughes/The
Canadian Press

ACTIVITÉ G **Qu'en pensez-vous?**

Étape 1. Indiquez si vous êtes d'accord ou pas d'accord avec les phrases suivantes.

1. Il est essentiel qu'on utilise l'énergie solaire.

2. Il est bon que les étudiants aient un système GPS.

3. Il est indispensable que le FBI nous surveille *(to keep watch on)* avec des satellites.

4. Il est inutile que les astronautes fassent des voyages en navette spatiale.

5. Il est stupide qu'on ait des voitures hybrides.

6. Il est injuste qu'on vende des chiens hybrides.

7. Il est dommage qu'on ait inventé la réalité virtuelle.

8. Il est utile que les scientifiques *(scientists)* fassent du clonage.

9. Il est bizarre que tout le monde n'ait pas de Wi-Fi.

10. Il est merveilleux qu'on puisse sauver des vies avec un cœur artificiel.

 Étape 2. Demandez à un(e) partenaire s'il/si elle est d'accord avec ces phrases.

Modèle: É1: **Est-ce qu'il est essentiel qu'on utilise l'énergie solaire?**

É2: **Non, à mon avis, il est utile mais pas essentiel qu'on utilise l'énergie solaire. Et toi?**

É1: **À mon avis, oui, il est essentiel qu'on utilise l'énergie solaire.**

> **Liaisons musicales**
>
> Luc De Larochellière (1966–) est un chanteur québécois. Plusieurs de ses chansons sont devenues des classiques québécois tels que *La machine est mon amie,* une chanson qui parle des effets de la technologie sur la société. Cherchez les paroles de cette chanson sur Internet. Quelles machines sont mentionnées dans la chanson?

ACTIVITÉ H **Deux colocataires et un ordinateur**

Étape 1. Deux colocataires vont partager un ordinateur. Complétez les phrases avec une expression de nécessité ou d'opinion.

Modèle: _____ que nous (ne pas être) _____ en ligne trop souvent.

Il est indispensable que nous ne soyons pas en ligne trop souvent.

1. _____ que nous (imprimer) _____ tous nos documents.

2. _____ que nous (acheter) _____ un bon traitement de texte.

3. _____ que nous (penser) _____ à un mot de passe qui soit facile à retenir *(retain).*

4. _____ que nous (avoir) _____ les meilleurs logiciels.

5. _____ que nous (installer) _____ le Wi-Fi.

6. _____ que nous (effacer) _____ les documents dont nous n'avons plus besoin.

7. _____ que nous (garder) *(keep)* _____ le clavier propre.

8. _____ que nous (sauvegarder) _____ les documents importants.

9. _____ que nous (ne pas télécharger) _____ trop de musique.

10. _____ que nous (éteindre) _____ l'ordinateur quand nous ne l'utilisons pas.

 Étape 2. Montrez vos réponses à un(e) partenaire. Aimeriez-vous partager un ordinateur avec cette personne?

ACTIVITÉ I La santé et vos opinions

Étape 1. Complétez les phrases suivantes.

Modèle: Cette patiente a mal à la tête. Il est indispensable qu'elle **se repose.**

1. Cette patiente a un rhume. Il est normal qu'elle _____.
2. Cette patiente a la grippe. Il est utile qu'elle _____.
3. Cette patiente a de la fièvre. Il est bon qu'elle _____
4. Cette patiente est allergique aux chats. Il est dommage qu'elle _____.
5. Cette patiente est allergique au chocolat. Il est stupide qu'elle _____.
6. Cette patiente a mal au ventre. Il n'est pas bon qu'elle _____.
7. Cette patiente est stressée. Il est indispensable qu'elle _____.
8. Cette patiente s'est cassé la jambe. Il est dommage qu'elle _____.
9. Cette patiente est en bonne santé. Il est merveilleux qu'elle _____.
10. Cette patiente est pauvre. Il est injuste qu'elle _____.

Étape 2. Complétez les phrases à propos des personnages du film *Liaisons*.

1. La mère de Claire souffre d'hallucinations. Il est normal qu'elle _____.
2. Robert, le patron de Claire et d'Abia, est allergique aux chiens. Il est bon qu'il _____.

ACTIVITÉ J Entretien

Étape 1. Répondez aux questions. Indiquez vos réponses dans la colonne **Moi.** Ensuite, posez les questions à deux camarades de classe. Notez leurs réponses.

	Moi	É1	É2
1. Est-ce que vous mangez trois repas par jour?	___	___	___
2. Est-ce que vous dormez huit heures par nuit?	___	___	___
3. Est-ce que vous mangez beaucoup de matières grasses?	___	___	___
4. Est-ce que vous buvez assez d'eau chaque jour?	___	___	___
5. Est-ce que vous mangez assez de fruits et de légumes?	___	___	___
6. Est-ce que vous achetez des plats préparés?	___	___	___
7. Est-ce que vous faites de la gym régulièrement?	___	___	___
8. Est-ce que vous consultez votre médecin régulièrement?	___	___	___

Étape 2. Écrivez un paragraphe de cinq à six phrases pour donner votre opinion à propos des réponses de vos deux camarades de classe.

Modèle: **Il est bon que Marc et André mangent trois repas par jour. Il est merveilleux que Marc dorme huit heures par jour. Il est dommage qu'André ne dorme pas assez. Il est indispensable qu'André dorme plus…**

Pour aller plus loin
L'infinitif ou le subjonctif?

When sentences with verbs of volition, emotion, or opinion have only one subject, the infinitive is used without **que**. With **avoir peur, regretter,** and expressions with **être,** use **de/d'** before the infinitive.

Je suis surpris que tu ne **viennes** pas.	***I'm surprised that you're** not **coming.***
Je suis surpris de voir Anne ce soir.	***I'm surprised to see** Anne tonight.*
Je regrette que tu sois malade.	***I'm sorry that you are** sick.*
Je regrette d'être en retard.	***I'm sorry to be** late.*

When impersonal expressions of emotion, opinion, or necessity do not specify a particular person or thing, they are followed by the infinitive without **que**. Add **de/d'** before the infinitive if the expression contains **être**.

Il est essentiel qu'il ait un ordinateur.	***It's essential that he has** a computer.*
Il est essentiel d'avoir un ordinateur.	***It's essential to have** a computer.*
Il faut qu'on lise les courriels.	***We must read** the e-mails.*
Il faut lire les courriels.	***We must read** the e-mails.*

Essayez! Complétez les phrases avec l'infinitif ou le subjonctif.

Modèle: Il est merveilleux d'**avoir** une voiture hybride.

1. Il est dommage **que les étudiants** _____.
2. Il est important **de/d'**_____.
3. Il est indispensable **que nous** _____.
4. Il faut _____.
5. Je suis content(e) **que mon professeur** _____.
6. J'ai peur **de/d'**_____.

OUI, JE PEUX!

Here are two "can do statements" for you to check your progress so far. Look at each statement and rate yourself on how well you think you can perform the task. Then verify your ability with a partner. How did you do?

1. **"I can describe and give my opinion about the computer that I currently have in my possession."**

   I can perform this function
   ☐ with ease
   ☐ with some difficulty
   ☐ not at all

2. **"I can ask others to describe their computer and have them offer their opinion about it so I can determine whose computer I prefer."**

   I can perform this function
   ☐ with ease
   ☐ with some difficulty
   ☐ not at all

iLrn™

Are you looking for more practice? You can find it in **iLrn**.

L'environnement et la **société**

The environment and society

les déchets domestiques *(m.)*

la déforestation

les déchets industriels *(m.)*

les espèces menacées *(f.)*

Quelques préoccupations écologiques et sociales

Note de **vocabulaire**
Use **être au chômage** to express *to be unemployed.* An unemployed person is **un chômeur / une chômeuse.**

Vocabulaire complémentaire

une ampoule basse consommation *energy saving lightbulb*
l'assistance sociale *(f.)* *social aid*
une association humanitaire *humanitarian association*
le chômage *unemployment*
l'effet de serre *(m.)* *greenhouse effect*
l'énergie renouvelable *(f.)* *renewable energy*

la faim *hunger*
la pauvreté *poverty*
une préoccupation (sociale) *(social) concern*
la préservation *preservation, protection*
un problème *problem*
une ressource naturelle *natural resource*
la société *society*
une solution *solution*

la pollution

un sans-abri / un SDF
(sans domicile fixe)

le réchauffement climatique

le recyclage

la surpopulation

les organismes *(m.)* génétiquement
modifiés (OGM)

D'autres préoccupations écologiques et sociales

Note de
grammaire
There is never an **s** at the
end of **OGM: les OGM.**

Vocabulaire complémentaire

écologique *ecological*	**jeter** *to throw (out)*
non biodégradable *nonbiodegradable*	**polluer** *to pollute*
	préserver *to preserve*
conserver *to conserve*	**protéger** *to protect*
faire du compost *to compost*	**protester** *to protest*
gaspiller *to waste*	**recycler** *to recycle*
interdire *to forbid*	**sauver** *to save, protect*

Note de
grammaire
The verb **interdire** is
conjugated like **dire:**
**j'interdis, tu interdis,
il/elle/on interdit,
nous interdisons, vous
interdisez, ils/elles
interdisent.** Its past
participle is **interdit.**

🔊 **ACTIVITÉ A Un problème ou une solution?** Indiquez si chaque mot ou
13-2 expression que vous entendez est **(a) un problème** ou **(b) une solution.**

    1.   **2.**   **3.**   **4.**   **5.**   **6.**   **7.**   **8.**   **9.**   **10.**   **11.**   **12.**   **13.**   **14.**

❖ **Et vous?** À votre avis, est-ce qu'il y a plus de problèmes ou plus de solutions dans
notre société?

🔊 **ACTIVITÉ B Une préoccupation écologique ou sociale?** Indiquez si
13-3 chaque préoccupation mentionnée est **(a) une préoccupation écologique, (b) une
préoccupation sociale** ou **(c) les deux.**

    1.   **2.**   **3.**   **4.**   **5.**   **6.**   **7.**   **8.**   **9.**   **10.**   **11.**   **12.**

❖ **Et vous?** À votre avis, quelles préoccupations sont plus importantes? Les
préoccupations écologiques ou les préoccupations sociales?

ACTIVITÉ C Classez!

Étape 1. Classez les préoccupations par ordre d'importance pour vous. Utilisez les
chiffres 1–10.

_____ le chômage	_____ la pauvreté
_____ la déforestation	_____ la pollution
_____ l'effet de serre	_____ le réchauffement climatique
_____ les espèces menacées	_____ les sans-abri / les SDF
_____ la faim	_____ la surpopulation

Étape 2. Comparez vos réponses avec un(e) partenaire. Avec lui/elle, décidez
quelles sont les trois préoccupations qui sont les plus importantes pour notre société
aujourd'hui.

ACTIVITÉ D Êtes-vous écologiste?

Étape 1. Indiquez si chaque phrase est vraie ou fausse pour vous.

1. J'éteins la lumière quand je quitte la pièce.

2. J'utilise des produits biodégradables.

3. J'éteins mon ordinateur quand je ne l'utilise pas.

4. Je ferme le robinet *(faucet)* quand je me brosse les dents.

5. Je recycle.

6. Je ne mange pas d'espèces menacées.

7. J'utilise des ampoules basse consommation.

8. Je fais du compost.

Conclusion Si vous avez dit **vrai** à plus de six phrases, vous êtes écologiste!

✈ ·····
Si vous y allez

Courtesy of Gaëtan Paquet

Si vous allez à Québec,
allez au restaurant Ô 6ième
sens. Les serveurs non-
voyants *(visually-impaired)*
vous serviront les plaisirs
de la table dans l'obscurité.
Cette expérience gourmande
activera votre sixième
sens et stimulera votre
imagination. Le restaurant
remet un pourcentage
de ses bénéfices *(profits)*
à des organisations qui
soutiennent les personnes
aveugles *(blind)*, une
préoccupation sociale
importante pour les
propriétaires du restaurant.

Étape 2. Demandez à un(e) partenaire s'il/si elle fait les choses de l'Étape 1.

Modèle: **Est-ce que tu éteins la lumière quand tu quittes la pièce?**

Conclusion Qui est le/la plus écologiste? Vous ou votre partenaire?

ACTIVITÉ **E** **Les meilleures solutions**

Étape 1. Décidez si chaque solution donnée est une bonne ou une mauvaise idée *(idea)* pour le problème indiqué.

	bonne idée	mauvaise idée
1. le chômage: On donne aux gens plus d'assistance sociale.	_____	_____
2. la surpopulation: On interdit aux gens d'avoir plus de deux enfants.	_____	_____
3. les espèces menacées: On interdit aux gens d'aller à la chasse.	_____	_____
4. le réchauffement climatique: On a besoin de ne rien faire.	_____	_____
5. les déchets domestiques: On jette les déchets dans la mer.	_____	_____
6. la faim: Les gens pauvres peuvent manger plus d'aliments OGM.	_____	_____
7. la pollution: On exige que les gens fassent du compost.	_____	_____
8. la pauvreté: On paie plus d'impôts *(taxes).*	_____	_____

 Étape 2. Montrez vos réponses à un(e) partenaire. Avez-vous les mêmes réponses? Pour chaque réponse où vous avez mis **mauvaise idée,** décidez quelle est la meilleure solution au problème avec votre partenaire.

Modèle: la pollution

On peut exiger que les gens recyclent. Nous pouvons faire du compost.

Un mot sur la culture

Greenpeace

Greenpeace, dont le siège est aujourd'hui basé à Amsterdam, est une organisation internationale présente sur tous les continents et sur tous les océans. Elle compte près de trois millions d'adhérents° à travers le monde. Selon son site Web officiel, Greenpeace est une organisation non-violente qui est indépendante des pouvoirs politiques et économiques. Sa mission est de dénoncer les atteintes° à l'environnement et d'apporter des solutions qui contribuent à la protection de l'environnement et à la promotion de la paix. Une préoccupation récente de Greenpeace France est la campagne° contre la dissémination des organismes génétiquement modifiés (OGM). Greenpeace France a réussi à obtenir plus de 100 000 signatures pour défendre l'interdiction du maïs OGM dans plusieurs pays européens.

Adapted from: http://2vancouver.com/fr/visiter/culture-locale/culture-verte/lemergence-du-mouvement-greenpeace-a-vancouver

adhérents *members* **atteintes** *attacks* **campagne** *campaign*

• Dans quels autres pays trouve-t-on l'organisation Greenpeace?

Pour exprimer le doute et la certitude
Le subjonctif et l'indicatif

DU FILM *LIAISONS*

Un coup d'œil sur la grammaire

Look at these photos from the film *Liaisons* and their captions.

ALEXIS Je **crois que** vous **comprenez**…

ABIA Hmm... je **ne suis pas certaine que** tu me **dises** la vérité…

1. Is the verb **comprenez** in the subjunctive or the indicative? Is Alexis expressing a belief or is he expressing a doubt?

2. Is the verb **dises** in the subjunctive or the indicative? Is Abia expressing certainty or doubt?

You learned that when you express desires, obligations, emotions, and opinions in a clause with **que,** you use the subjunctive. The subjunctive is also used to express doubt, uncertainty, and disbelief, and this is often conveyed by the following verbs and expressions.

douter que *to doubt that*	**ne pas être sûr(e) que** *not to be sure that*
ne pas croire que *not to believe that*	**Il est impossible que** *It is impossible that*
ne pas penser que *not to think that*	**Il n'est pas évident que** *It is not obvious that*
ne pas être certain(e) que *not to be certain that*	**Il n'est pas vrai que** *It is not true that*

On **ne pense pas** que Luc **fasse** du compost.

*We **don't think** Luc **composts**.*

Anne **n'est pas sûre** que Guy **comprenne.**

*Anne **is not sure** that Guy **understands**.*

Il **est impossible** qu'ils **aillent** à la chasse.

*It **is impossible** that they go **hunt**.*

The indicative is used after verbs and expressions that indicate certainty (**la certitude**) and beliefs such as the following.

Note de grammaire
Note that is it not possible to say **Il n'est pas clair que…**

croire que *to believe that*	**être sûr(e) que** *to be sure that*
penser que *to think that*	**Il est clair que** *It is clear that*
savoir que *to know that*	**Il est évident que** *It is obvious that*
être certain(e) que *to be certain that*	**Il est vrai que** *It is true that*

Je **crois** qu'il **a** faim.	*I **believe** he **is** hungry.*
Sara **sait** que tu **as** raison.	*Sara **knows** you **are** right.*
Il **est clair** que le chômage **est** un problème.	*It **is clear** that unemployment **is** a problem.*
Il **est vrai** qu'elle **fait** du compost.	*It **is true** that she **composts**.*

‣ A speaker may choose to use the subjunctive when asking a question with expressions of belief and certainty to indicate that he/she is unsure of the response.

Croyez-vous que le réchauffement climatique **soit** un gros problème?
Do you believe that global warming is a big problem?

Liaisons musicales

© Patrick Delecroix/Maxppp/Landov

La chanson *L'hymne à la beauté du monde* de Luc Plamondon nous demande d'être plus écologiques: *Ne tuons pas la beauté du monde // Faisons de la terre un grand jardin // pour ceux qui viendront après nous.* La chanson a été rendue célèbre par la chanteuse québécoise Isabelle Boulay. Écoutez la chanson sur Internet.

🔊 **ACTIVITÉ F** **Le doute ou la certitude?** Un écologiste parle à un groupe
13-4 d'étudiants. Vous allez entendre la première partie de chaque phrase. Choisissez la deuxième partie de chaque phrase.

1. a. … **recyclez** régulièrement.
   b. … **recycliez** régulièrement.
2. a. … **faites** du compost.
   b. … **fassiez** du compost.
3. a. … **achetez** des produits biodégradables.
   b. … **achetiez** des produits biodégradables.
4. a. … **éteignez** la lumière quand il faut.
   b. … **éteigniez** la lumière quand il faut.
5. a. … **conservez** l'eau.
   b. … **conserviez** l'eau.
6. a. … **protégez** les espèces menacées.
   b. … **protégiez** les espèces menacées.
7. a. … **prenez** des OGM.
   b. … **preniez** des OGM.
8. a. … **gaspillez** les ressources naturelles.
   b. … **gaspilliez** les ressources naturelles.

‣ **Et vous?** Quelles activités écologiques faites-vous?

🔊 **ACTIVITÉ G** **Le maire d'une ville** Un maire *(mayor)* parle aux habitants
13-5 de sa ville. Décidez s'il exprime le doute ou s'il exprime la certitude à propos des préoccupations de ses concitoyens *(fellow citizens)*.

1. a. Il est clair que…
   b. Il est impossible que…
2. a. Je crois que…
   b. Je ne crois pas que…
3. a. Il est certain que…
   b. Il n'est pas certain que…
4. a. Il est évident que…
   b. Il n'est pas évident que…
5. a. Je suis sûr que…
   b. Je ne suis pas sûr que…
6. a. Je sais que…
   b. Je doute que…
7. a. Je pense que…
   b. Je ne pense pas que…
8. a. Il est vrai que…
   b. Il n'est pas vrai que…

Conclusion Est-ce que ce maire est informé des préoccupations de ses concitoyens?

ACTIVITÉ **H** **Les personnages du film Liaisons**

Étape 1. Décidez si chaque phrase exprime une opinion, un doute ou une certitude à propos des personnages du film **Liaisons.**

1. … **aille** en France pour l'enterrement de son oncle.
   a. Il est évident que Claire   b. Il est bon que Claire

2. … **soit** une amie de Claire.
   a. Il est merveilleux qu'Abia   b. On sait qu'Abia

3. … **fait** ses devoirs avant de travailler à l'hôtel.
   a. Il est évident que Claire   b. Il n'est pas certain que Claire

4. … **doive** rester à l'hôpital.
   a. Il est dommage que Simone Gagner   b. Il est clair que Simone Gagner

5. … ne **prend** pas d'OGM.
   a. Il n'est pas vrai que Robert Levesque   b. On sait que Robert Levesque

6. … **est** français.
   a. Il n'est pas sûr qu'Alexis   b. Il est sûr qu'Alexis

7. … **ait** beaucoup d'amis à Montréal.
   a. Il est important qu'Abia   b. On pense qu'Abia

8. … **sache** faire la cuisine.
   a. Il est vrai que Claire   b. Il est utile que Claire

Étape 2. Complétez les phrases logiquement.

1. Je pense que Claire _____.   3. Il est bizarre qu'Alexis _____.
2. Je doute que Claire _____.   4. Il est évident qu'Abia _____.

Étape 3. Montrez vos réponses de l'Étape 2 à un(e) partenaire. Avez-vous écrit les mêmes choses?

ACTIVITÉ **I** **Le chat de Claire**

Étape 1. Monsieur Émile, le chat de Claire, est un chat spécial. Utilisez les verbes pour déterminer si chaque phrase exprime un fait *(fact)* (**Il est vrai que**) ou une opinion (**Il est bizarre que**) à propos de Monsieur Émile.

	Il est vrai que M. Émile…	Il est bizarre que M. Émile…
1. **sait** ouvrir la porte.	☐	☐
2. **fait** du jogging dans l'appartement.	☐	☐
3. **veuille** jouer avec les chiens.	☐	☐
4. **boive** du lait biologique.	☐	☐
5. **comprenne** le français.	☐	☐
6. **puisse** dormir sur la table de la cuisine.	☐	☐
7. **sache** danser.	☐	☐
8. **voit** parfois Mme Gagner avec Claire.	☐	☐

Étape 2. Complétez les phrases suivantes. Écrivez deux faits et deux opinions.

1. Il est vrai que je _____.

2. Il est vrai que mes amis et moi _____.

3. Il est bizarre que ma famille _____.

4. Il est bizarre que les étudiants _____.

ACTIVITÉ **J** **Votre camarade de classe** Dites à un(e) camarade de classe si vous croyez ou si vous ne croyez pas qu'il/elle fait (fasse) les activités suivantes. Votre camarade de classe va vous dire si vous avez raison ou si vous avez tort.

Modèle: (vouloir) recycler
   É1: **Je ne crois pas que tu veuilles recycler.**
   É2: **Tu as tort. Je veux recycler.**

1. (faire) du compost

2. (prendre) le temps de recycler

3. (avoir) des ampoules basse consommation

4. (savoir) conserver l'énergie

5. (donner) de l'argent aux associations humanitaires

6. (vouloir) manger des OGM

7. (avoir envie de) sauver les espèces menacées

8. (gaspiller) l'eau

© Lan O'Hanlon/Shutterstock.com

Conclusion Est-ce que votre camarade de classe est écologique?

ACTIVITÉ **K** **Je sais ou je doute?**

Étape 1. Connaissez-vous bien votre professeur? Complétez chaque phrase avec **Je sais que mon professeur** ou **Je doute que mon professeur.** Mettez les verbes à l'indicatif ou au subjonctif.

Modèle: (sortir) le lundi soir **Je doute que mon professeur sorte le lundi soir.**

1. (savoir) parler français

2. (prendre) du fromage français

3. (boire) du café italien

4. (faire) bien la cuisine

5. (comprendre) le chinois

6. (aller) en France chaque été

7. (devoir) travailler ce week-end

8. (avoir) un chat qui comprend le français

Étape 2. Montrez vos réponses à un(e) partenaire. Avez-vous écrit les mêmes choses?

Étape 3. Votre professeur va vous donner ses réponses. Écrivez quatre phrases pour donner votre opinion sur les activités de votre professeur.

Modèle: Il est dommage que mon professeur ne sorte pas le lundi soir.

ACTIVITÉ L Les potins

Étape 1. Vous êtes journaliste pour un magazine à potins. Écrivez huit phrases avec les éléments donnés à propos des vedettes d'Hollywood.

Il est bon que	avoir beaucoup de petit(e)s ami(e)s
Il n'est pas certain que	s'aimer beaucoup
Il est clair que	comprendre le français
Il est dommage que	connaître leurs fans
Il est évident que	écrire de belles chansons
Il est (im)possible que	être fidèle(s)/infidèle(s)
Il est nécessaire que	être heureux/heureuse
Il est stupide que	faire bien la cuisine
Il est sûr que	pouvoir chanter
Il est triste que	savoir danser
Je crois que	sortir avec quelqu'un de nouveau
Je doute que	vouloir avoir un chien hybride
Je sais que	???
Je veux que	???

Modèle: Emma Watson **Je veux qu'Emma Watson sorte avec Daniel Radcliffe.**

1. Miley Cyrus
2. Lady Gaga
3. Will Smith et Jada P. Smith
4. Brad Pitt et Angelina Jolie

5. Bruno Mars
6. LeBron James
7. ?
8. ?

 Étape 2. Montrez vos phrases à deux camarades de classe. Qui est le/la meilleur(e) journaliste?

ACTIVITÉ M Votre université

Étape 1. Qu'avez-vous à dire à propos de votre université? Complétez les phrases.

1. Il est évident que les cours…
2. Je veux que la nourriture…
3. Je doute que les étudiants…
4. Il est important que les professeurs…

5. Je pense que le campus…
6. Il faut que les frais de scolarité…
7. Je désire que le président…
8. Je crois que la bibliothèque…

Étape 2. Montrez vos réponses à un(e) partenaire. Êtes-vous d'accord avec les réponses de votre partenaire?

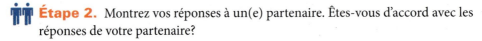

Pour aller plus loin

Espérer et souhaiter

The subjunctive is used after the verb **souhaiter** *(to wish)* in a clause with **que**.

Je **souhaite** que vous **puissiez** aller en France.
*I **wish** that you **could** go to France.*

Est-ce que tu **souhaites** que nous ne **gaspillions** pas nos ressources naturelles?
*Do you **wish** that we didn't **waste** our natural resources?*

The future indicative is used after the verb **espérer** in a clause with **que**.

J'**espère** que vous **pourrez** aller en France un jour.
*I **hope** you **will be able** to go to France one day.*

Nous **espérons** que tout le monde **recyclera** ses bouteilles.
*We **hope** that everyone **will recycle** their bottles.*

Essayez! Complétez les phrases avec le futur ou le subjonctif.

1. J'espère que mon professeur (faire) _____.

2. Mon professeur souhaite que nous (pouvoir) _____.

3. J'espère que mes amis _____.

4. Je souhaite que mon/ma colocataire _____.

OUI, JE PEUX!

Here are two "can do statements" for you to check your progress so far. Look at each statement and rate yourself on how well you think you can perform the task. Then verify your ability with a partner. How did you do?

1. **"I can say what I am certain will happen in our society and find out what someone else believes will happen."**

   I can perform this function
   ☐ with ease
   ☐ with some difficulty
   ☐ not at all

2. **"I can say what I doubt will happen in our society and find out what someone else doubts will happen."**

   I can perform this function
   ☐ with ease
   ☐ with some difficulty
   ☐ not at all

iLrn

Are you looking for more practice? You can find it in **iLrn**.

PROJECTION

Avant de visionner

ACTIVITÉ **A** **Devinez** Dans la Séquence 7 du film *Liaisons,* la dernière séquence, Claire va à Paris pour l'enterrement de son oncle. Devinez ce qui va se passer à Paris. Complétez les phrases.

1. Je pense que Claire _____.

3. Je ne pense pas que Claire _____.

2. Je crois que Claire _____.

4. Je ne crois pas que Claire _____.

ACTIVITÉ **B** **Un coup d'œil sur une scène** Voici une scène de la Séquence 7 du film *Liaisons.* Claire est à Paris chez Madame Papillon, la voisine de l'oncle Michel. Avec un(e) partenaire, devinez le mot qui correspond à chaque espace *(space)* dans le dialogue. Vous allez vérifier vos réponses plus tard.

CLAIRE Est-ce que (1) _____ vous parlait de la famille, de (2)_____, par exemple? Je (3) _____ que vous étiez son amie...

MME PAPILLON Je suis désolée, (4) _____. Michel était très (5) _____, vous savez. Il n'aimait pas parler (6) _____.

1. a. ma mère   b. mon oncle

2. a. ses amis   b. ses parents

3. a. doute   b. sais

4. a. Claire   b. mademoiselle

5. a. réservé   b. timide

6. a. avec moi   b. de sa vie privée

▶ **Regarder la séquence**

Vous allez regarder la Séquence 7 du film *Liaisons.* Vérifiez vos réponses à l'Activité A et à l'Activité B.

Après le visionnage

ACTIVITÉ **C** **Liaisons familiales** Dans la Séquence 7, Alexis parle de sa famille à Claire. Complétez les phrases.

1. Madeleine et Henri Prévost sont les parents _____.
   a. d'Alexis   b. de Tremblay

2. Claire-Angèle est la fille _____.
   a. biologique de Madeleine   b. adoptive d'Henri

3. Rémy Tremblay est _____.
   a. le frère d'Alexis   b. le frère et l'employé de Madeleine

4. Simone Gagner est la fille de _____.
   a. Claire-Angèle Prévost   b. Madeleine Prévost

5. Claire Gagner est la petite-fille de _____.
   a. Madeleine   b. Claire-Angèle

ACTIVITÉ **D** **L'avez-vous compris?** Avec un(e) partenaire, indiquez si chaque phrase est vraie ou fausse.

1. Madeleine Prévost voulait tuer *(kill)* Claire-Angèle pour garder la fortune familiale.

2. Claire-Angèle est la sœur adoptive d'Alexis Prévost.

3. Henri a emmené la petite Claire-Angèle à Québec pour lui sauver la vie.

4. Claire-Angèle est la sœur de Simone Gagner.

5. Madeleine a fait une confession à son fils Alexis avant sa mort.

6. Claire est l'héritière de la fortune familiale de la famille Prévost.

ACTIVITÉ **E** **Utilisez le contexte** Lisez bien ces répliques *(lines)* d'Alexis et de Claire. Que veulent dire les mots en caractères gras *(boldface)*?

ALEXIS Claire, vous êtes (1) **la petite-fille** de cette (2) **fillette** abandonnée, (3) **l'héritière** légitime de sa fortune. […]

ALEXIS Voilà, à présent (4) **vous êtes au courant** de tout. (5) **Quant à moi**, j'ai accompli ma mission.

CLAIRE Maman… ses hallucinations… Elle me parlait toujours des (6) **voix**, des visions… moi, je croyais que c'était à cause de sa (7) **folie**. De sa (8) **psychose**.

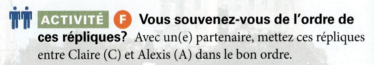

ACTIVITÉ **F** **Vous souvenez-vous de l'ordre de ces répliques?** Avec un(e) partenaire, mettez ces répliques entre Claire (C) et Alexis (A) dans le bon ordre.

a. **A** Qu'en pensez-vous? ____

b. **A** Ne soyez pas triste, Claire. On se reverra un jour. […] ____

c. **A** Non, ce n'est pas un rêve, Claire. […] ____

d. **A** Je sais que c'est difficile à comprendre. Je reviens du passé. ____

e. **C** Je ne sais pas… ____

f. **C** Vous allez me quitter maintenant? ____

g. **C** C'est pas possible. C'est un rêve. ____

h. **C** Alexis… et vous? Vous êtes un ange? Un esprit? ____

Et vous? Qu'en pensez-vous? Qui est Alexis? Un ange? Un esprit? Un rêve?

Dans les coulisses

In **Séquence 7**, when Claire discovers the tombstone, she is overcome by a startling revelation. Alexis tells her: "Je reviens du passé." What clues or hints surrounding the character of Alexis were provided throughout the movie to foreshadow this revelation?

LIAISONS
CULTURELLES

Ceux et celles qui travaillent pour l'humanité

OUTILS DE LECTURE
Recognizing related words

Recognizing words that are related to each other when you read can help you guess the meaning of words and improve reading comprehension. For example, a verb may have an adjective or a noun that is related. In the text *Une Française découvre le virus du sida,* the words **chercheuse** and **chercheur** appear. You have not learned these words but you do know the verb **chercher** which means *to look for.* Based on the meaning of the verb **chercher,** what do you think the nouns **chercheuse** and **chercheur** mean? Can you find other examples of related words in these texts?

Une Française découvre le virus du sida

Françoise Barré-Sinoussi, née en 1947 à Paris, est la troisième femme Nobel en France. Avec Luc Montaigner, elle a été récompensée par le prix Nobel de médecine pour l'identification du virus de l'immunodéficience humaine (VIH) en octobre 2008. Madame Barré-Sinoussi obtient son doctorat en 1974 à la Faculté des sciences de Paris. Chercheuse à l'Institut Pasteur à partir de 1975, elle mène° des travaux sur des thèmes liés au sida° (syndrome immunodéficitaire acquis). Depuis 2008, sa recherche se tourne vers les régulations congénitales des infections par le VIH. En 2012, elle est devenue présidente de l'International Aids Society, première société internationale indépendante de chercheurs et de médecins contre le VIH/sida.

Adapted from: http://www.aufeminin.com/portraits-de-femmes/francoise-barre-sinoussi-d48129.html

mène *leads, directs* **sida** *Aids*

© Pascal Le Segretain/Staff/Getty Images Entertainment/Getty Images

Vrai ou faux?

1. Françoise Barré-Sinoussi est la première Française à obtenir le prix Nobel.   V / F

2. Françoise Barré-Sinoussi a travaillé à l'Institut Pasteur.   V / F

3. Madame Barré-Sinoussi est devenue présidente de la première société internationale indépendante de médecins contre le sida en 2012.   V / F

© Sergio Gaudenti/Sygma/Kipa/Corbis

Aimé Césaire: fondateur de la négritude

Aimé Césaire (1913–2008) est un poète et homme politique français de Martinique. Il est, avec le Sénégalais Léopold Sédar Senghor, l'un des fondateurs du mouvement littéraire de la négritude et un anticolonialiste résolu. La négritude, un concept forgé par Aimé Césaire en réaction à l'oppression culturelle du système colonial français de l'époque, vise° à rejeter le projet français d'assimilation culturelle et à promouvoir° l'Afrique et sa culture. La pensée et la poésie de Césaire ont également marqué les intellectuels africains et les Noirs américains en lutte° contre la colonisation et l'acculturation.

Adapted from: http://www.rfi.fr/afrique/20130626-aime-cesaire-centenaire-mouvement-negritude/

vise *aims* **promouvoir** *promote* **en lutte** *struggling*

Vrai ou faux?

1. Aimé Césaire est de Paris.   V / F

2. La négritude rejette la colonisation française.   V / F

3. La poésie de Césaire influence aussi les Noirs américains.   V / F

La Fondation France Libertés

La Fondation France Libertés a été créée° en 1986 par Danielle Mitterrand, la veuve de l'ancien président de la République française, François Mitterrand. La fondation s'engage activement dans les grands combats, tels que le soutien° au peuple tibétain, et elle participe aux grands projets d'aide aux pays du Sud, comme la reconstruction du système éducatif au Cambodge ou la lutte° contre le sida en Afrique. Aujourd'hui, la défense des droits fondamentaux demeure° au cœur de l'action de la fondation. Le droit pour tous à disposer d'une eau potable°, libre et gratuite, est devenu un de leurs premiers combats.

© Lartige Christophe / SIPA / Newscom

Adapted from: www.france-libertes.org

créée *created* **soutien** *support* **lutte** *fight* **demeure** *remains* **potable** *drinkable*

Vrai ou faux?

1. Danielle Mitterrand est la fille de François Mitterrand.   V / F

2. La Fondation France Libertés a été créée par François Mitterrand.   V / F

3. Une préoccupation importante de la Fondation France Libertés est d'assurer l'accès à l'eau potable pour tout le monde.   V / F

UN DOCUMENTAIRE CHOC
de Richard Desjardins et Robert Monderie

L'Erreur boréale

« Un film de légitime défense. » — Richard Desjardins

© ACPAV Association coopérative de productions audiovisuelles

Richard Desjardins: chanteur et cinéaste pour l'environnement

Originaire de l'Abitibi-Témiscamingue (Québec), Richard Desjardins (1948–) est humaniste, chanteur et cinéaste. Il publie son premier recueil de poésie à l'âge de 23 ans. Son film (réalisé avec Robert Moderie), *L'Erreur boréale* (1999), expose le problème de la déforestation au Québec et lui a valu le prix Jutra du meilleur documentaire. Ce film a questionné la responsabilité citoyenne° face à la destruction de l'environnement. Aujourd'hui, le gouvernement reconnaît en partie le bien-fondé de ce documentaire et l'importance d'une gestion° plus responsable des forêts. En 2009, l'Université du Québec à Montréal lui décerne un doctorat honoris causa pour souligner son apport° exceptionnel en tant qu'artiste engagé dans la lutte pour la justice sociale et sa contribution essentielle à l'avènement° d'une éco-société.

Adapted from: http://www.uqam.ca/nouvelles/2009/09-152.htm

citoyenne *citizen* **gestion** *management* **apport** *contribution* **l'avènement** *arrival*

Vrai ou faux?

1. Richard Desjardins est un cinéaste québécois.   V / F
2. *L'Erreur boréale* est un film sur les sans-abri / les SDF au Québec.   V / F
3. Desjardins a reçu un doctorat honoris causa pour son travail pour l'environnement.   V / F

▶ LIAISONS CULTURELLES

l'énergie nucléaire

un satellite

Use **iLrn™** to access the video **La technologie** to learn more technology in the Francophone world. Be prepared to answer the question **Et vous? Comment est-ce que la technologie va changer votre vie dans l'avenir?** Share your responses with your classmates in **Share It!**

PARTIE 1　13–6

L'ORDINATEUR

un clavier	keyboard
un écran	computer screen
un fichier	file
une imprimante	printer
un lecteur de cédéroms	CD-ROM drive
un lecteur de DVD	DVD drive
un logiciel	software, program
un mot de passe	password
une souris	mouse
le traitement de texte	word processing program
une webcam	webcam
le Wi-Fi	Wi-Fi

LA TECHNOLOGIE ET LES INNOVATIONS

le clonage	cloning
un cœur artificiel	artificial heart
une découverte	discovery
l'énergie solaire (f.)	solar energy
un hybride	hybrid animal or plant
une invention	invention
une navette spatiale	space shuttle
la réalité virtuelle	virtual reality
un satellite	satellite
un système GPS	GPS system

VERBES

démarrer	to start up
effacer	to delete, erase
être en ligne (avec)	to be online (with)
fermer / éteindre	to close, to shut off
imprimer	to print
sauvegarder	to save
taper	to type
télécharger	to download

LES EXPRESSIONS D'OPINION

Il est bizarre que	It is bizarre that
Il est bon que	It is good that
Il est dommage que	It is too bad that
Il est essentiel que	It is essential that
Il est indispensable que	It is indispensable that
Il est juste / injuste que	It is fair / unfair that
Il est merveilleux que	It is wonderful that
Il est normal que	It is normal that
Il est possible que	It is possible that
Il est stupide que	It is stupid that
Il est triste que	It is sad that
Il est utile / inutile que	It is useful / not useful that

PARTIE 2　13–7

LES PRÉOCCUPATIONS ÉCOLOGIQUES

les déchets domestiques (m.)	domestic waste
les déchets industriels (m.)	industrial waste
la déforestation	deforestation
l'effet de serre (m.)	greenhouse effect
l'énergie renouvelable (f.)	renewable energy
les espèces menacées (f.)	endangered species
les organismes génétiquement modifiés (OGM) (m.)	genetically modified foods
la pollution	pollution
le réchauffement climatique	global warming

LES PRÉOCCUPATIONS SOCIALES

le chômage	unemployment
la faim	hunger
la pauvreté	poverty
une préoccupation (sociale)	(social) concern
un sans-abri / un SDF (sans domicile fixe)	homeless person
la surpopulation	overpopulation

NOMS

une ampoule basse consommation	energy saving lightbulb
l'assistance sociale (f.)	social aid
une association humanitaire	humanitarian association
la préservation	preservation, protection
un problème	problem
le recyclage	recycling
une ressource naturelle	natural resource
la société	society
une solution	solution

VERBES

conserver	to conserve
faire du compost	to compost
gaspiller	to waste
interdire	to forbid
jeter	to throw (out)
polluer	to pollute
préserver	to preserve
protéger	to protect
protester	to protest
recycler	to recycle
sauver	to save, protect

ADJECTIFS

écologique	*ecological*
non biodégradable	*nonbiodegradable*

LES EXPRESSIONS DE DOUTE

douter que	*to doubt that*
ne pas croire que	*not to believe that*
ne pas être certain(e) que	*not to be certain that*
ne pas être sûr(e) que	*not to be sure that*
ne pas penser que	*not to think that*
Il est impossible que	*It is impossible that*
Il n'est pas évident que	*It is not obvious that*
Il n'est pas vrai que	*It is not true that*

LES EXPRESSIONS DE CERTITUDE

croire que	*to believe that*
être certain(e) que	*to be certain that*
être sûr(e) que	*to be sure that*
penser que	*to think that*
savoir que	*to know that*
Il est clair que	*It is clear that*
Il est évident que	*It is obvious that*
Il est vrai que	*It is true that*

I. L'alphabet phonétique

Voyelles

[a] madame	[i] qui	[œ] sœur
[e] thé	[o] eau	[u] vous
[ɛ] être	[ɔ] porte	[y] sur
[ə] que	[ø] peu	

Semi-voyelles

[j] bien	[ɥ] puis	[w] oui

Voyelles nasales

[ɑ̃] quand	[ɛ̃] vin	[ɔ̃] non

Consonnes

[b] bleu	[l] lire	[s] sur
[d] dormir	[m] marron	[ʃ] chat
[f] faire	[n] nouveau	[t] triste
[ɥ] gris	[ɲ] enseigner	[v] vers
[ʒ] jaune	[p] parler	[z] rose
[k] quand	[ʀ] rester	

II. Les verbes réguliers

A. Conjugaison régulière

INFINITIF	PRÉSENT	INDICATIF		
		PASSÉ COMPOSÉ	IMPARFAIT	PLUS-QUE-PARFAIT
Verbes en -er **parler**	je parle	j' **ai** parl**é**	je parl**ais**	j' **avais** parlé
	tu parl**es**	tu **as** parl**é**	tu parl**ais**	tu **avais** parlé
	il/elle/on parle	il **a** parl**é**	il parl**ait**	il **avait** parlé
	nous parl**ons**	nous **avons** parl**é**	nous parl**ions**	nous **avions** parlé
	vous parl**ez**	vous **avez** parl**é**	vous parl**iez**	vous **aviez** parlé
	ils/elles parl**ent**	ils **ont** parl**é**	ils parl**aient**	ils **avaient** parlé
Verbes en -ir **finir**	je fin**is**	j' **ai** fini	je finiss**ais**	j' **avais** fini
	tu fin**is**	tu **as** fini	tu finiss**ais**	tu **avais** fini
	il/elle/on fin**it**	il **a** fini	il finiss**ait**	il **avait** fini
	nous fin**issons**	nous **avons** fini	nous finiss**ions**	nous **avions** fini
	vous fin**issez**	vous **avez** fini	vous finiss**iez**	vous **aviez** fini
	ils/elles fin**issent**	ils **ont** fini	ils finiss**aient**	ils **avaient** fini
Verbes en -re **répondre**	je répond**s**	j' **ai** répond**u**	je répond**ais**	j' **avais** répond**u**
	tu répond**s**	tu **as** répond**u**	tu répond**ais**	tu **avais** répond**u**
	il/elle/on répond	il **a** répond**u**	il répond**ait**	il **avait** répond**u**
	nous répond**ons**	nous **avons** répond**u**	nous répond**ions**	nous **avions** répond**u**
	vous répond**ez**	vous **avez** répond**u**	vous répond**iez**	vous **aviez** répond**u**
	ils/elles répond**ent**	ils **ont** répond**u**	ils répond**aient**	ils **avaient** répond**u**
Verbes pronominaux **se laver**	je me lave	je me **suis** lavé**(e)**	je me lavais	je m'**étais** lavé**(e)**
	tu te laves	tu t'**es** lavé**(e)**	tu te lavais	tu t'**étais** lavé**(e)**
	il/on se lave	il s'**est** lavé	il se lavait	il s'**était** lavé
	elle se lave	elle s'**est** lavée	elle se lavait	elle s'**était** lavée
	nous nous lavons	nous nous **sommes** lavé**(e)s**	nous nous lavions	nous nous **étions** lavé**(e)s**
	vous vous lavez	vous vous **êtes** lavé**(e)(s)**	vous vous laviez	vous vous **étiez** lavé**(e)(s)**
	ils se lavent	ils se **sont** lavés	ils se lavaient	ils s'**étaient** lavés
	elles se lavent	elles se **sont** lavées	elles se lavaient	elles s'**étaient** lavées

	LE SUBJONCTIF DES VERBES RÉGULIERS			
	REGARDER	VENDRE	CHOISIR	CONNAÎTRE
	(ils) **regardent**	(ils) **vendent**	(ils) **choisissent**	(ils) **connaissent**
... que je	regard**e**	vend**e**	choisiss**e**	connaiss**e**
... que tu	regard**es**	vend**es**	choisiss**es**	connaiss**es**
... qu'il/elle/on	regard**e**	vend**e**	choisiss**e**	connaiss**e**
... que nous	regard**ions**	vend**ions**	choisiss**ions**	connaiss**ions**
... que vous	regard**iez**	vend**iez**	choisiss**iez**	connaiss**iez**
... qu'ils/elles	regard**ent**	vend**ent**	choisiss**ent**	connaiss**ent**

B. Verbes à modification orthographique

INFINITIF	PRÉSENT	INDICATIF		
		PASSÉ COMPOSÉ	IMPARFAIT	PLUS-QUE-PARFAIT
acheter	j'achète	j'ai acheté	j'achetais	j'avais acheté
	tu achètes			
	il/elle/on achète			
	nous achetons			
	vous achetez			
	ils/elles achètent			
préférer	je préfère	j'ai préféré	je préférais	j'avais préféré
	tu préfères			
	il/elle/on préfère			
	nous préférons			
	vous préférez			
	ils/elles préfèrent			
payer	je paie	j'ai payé	je payais	j'avais payé
	tu paies			
	il/elle/on paie			
	nous payons			
	vous payez			
	ils/elles paient			
appeler	j'appelle	j'ai appelé	j'appelais	j'avais appelé
	tu appelles			
	il/elle/on appelle			
	nous appelons			
	vous appelez			
	ils/elles appellent			

INFINITIF		PRÉSENT	INDICATIF		
			PASSÉ COMPOSÉ	IMPARFAIT	PLUS-QUE-PARFAIT
amener	j'	**amène**	ai amené	amenais	avais amené
	tu	**amène**s	as amené	amenais	avais amené
	il/elle/on	**amène**	a amené	amenait	avait amené
	nous	amenons	avons amené	amenions	avions amené
	vous	amenez	avez amené	ameniez	aviez amené
	ils/elles	**amène**nt	ont amené	amenaient	avaient amené

		CONDITIONNEL			
		PRÉSENT	PASSÉ	FUTUR SIMPLE	IMPÉRATIF
	j'	**amène**rais	aurais amené	**amène**rai	
	tu	**amène**rais	aurais amené	**amène**ras	**amène**!
	il/elle/on	**amène**rait	aurait amené	**amène**ra	
	nous	**amène**rions	aurions amené	**amène**rons	amenons!
	vous	**amène**riez	auriez amené	**amène**rez	amenez!
	ils/elles	**amène**raient	auraient amené	**amène**ront	

		SUBJONCTIF	PARTICIPE PRÉSENT	PARTICIPE PASSÉ
	que j'	**amène**	amenant	amené
	que tu	**amène**s		
	qu'il/elle/on	**amène**		
	que nous	amenions		
	que vous	ameniez		
	qu'ils/elles	**amène**nt		

INFINITIF		PRÉSENT	INDICATIF	IMPARFAIT	PLUS-QUE-PARFAIT
			PASSÉ COMPOSÉ		
célébrer	je	**célèbr**e	ai célébré	célébrais	avais célébré
	tu	**célèbr**es	as célébré	célébrais	avais célébré
	il/elle/on	**célèbr**e	a célébré	célébrait	avait célébré
	nous	célébrons	avons célébré	célébrions	avions célébré
	vous	célébrez	avez célébré	célébriez	aviez célébré
	ils/elles	**célèbr**ent	ont célébré	célébraient	avaient célébré

		CONDITIONNEL		FUTUR SIMPLE	IMPÉRATIF
		PRÉSENT	PASSÉ		
	je	célébrerais	aurais célébré	célébrerai	
	tu	célébrerais	aurais célébré	célébreras	**célèbr**e!
	il/elle/on	célébrerait	aurait célébré	célébrera	
	nous	célébrerions	aurions célébré	célébrerons	célébrons!
	vous	célébreriez	auriez célébré	célébrerez	célébrez!
	ils/elles	célébreraient	auraient célébré	célébreront	

		SUBJONCTIF	PARTICIPE PRÉSENT	PARTICIPE PASSÉ
	que je	**célèbr**e	célébrant	célébré
	que tu	**célèbr**es		
	qu'il/elle/on	**célèbr**e		
	que nous	célébrions		
	que vous	célébriez		
	qu'ils/elles	**célèbr**ent		

INFINITIF		PRÉSENT	INDICATIF	IMPARFAIT	PLUS-QUE-PARFAIT
			PASSÉ COMPOSÉ		
espérer	j'	**espèr**e	ai espéré	espérais	avais espéré
	tu	**espèr**es	as espéré	espérais	avais espéré
	il/elle/on	**espèr**e	a espéré	espérait	avait espéré
	nous	espérons	avons espéré	espérions	avions espéré
	vous	espérez	avez espéré	espériez	aviez espéré
	ils/elles	**espèr**ent	ont espéré	espéraient	avaient espéré

		CONDITIONNEL		FUTUR SIMPLE	IMPÉRATIF
		PRÉSENT	PASSÉ		
	j'	espérerais	aurais espéré	espérerai	
	tu	espérerais	aurais espéré	espéreras	**espèr**e!
	il/elle/on	espérerait	aurait espéré	espérera	
	nous	espérerions	aurions espéré	espérerons	espérons!
	vous	espéreriez	auriez espéré	espérerez	espérez!
	ils/elles	espéreraient	auraient espéré	espéreront	

		SUBJONCTIF	PARTICIPE PRÉSENT	PARTICIPE PASSÉ
	que j'	**espèr**e	espérant	espéré
	que tu	**espèr**es		
	qu'il/elle/on	**espèr**e		
	que nous	espérions		
	que vous	espériez		
	qu'ils/elles	**espèr**ent		

INFINITIF		PRÉSENT	PASSÉ COMPOSÉ	IMPARFAIT	PLUS-QUE-PARFAIT
			INDICATIF		
répéter	je	**répèt**e	ai répété	répétais	avais répété
	tu	**répèt**es	as répété	répétais	avais répété
	il/elle/on	**répèt**e	a répété	répétait	avait répété
	nous	répétons	avons répété	répétions	avions répété
	vous	répétez	avez répété	répétiez	aviez répété
	ils/elles	**répèt**ent	ont répété	répétaient	avaient répété

		CONDITIONNEL			
		PRÉSENT	PASSÉ	FUTUR SIMPLE	IMPÉRATIF
	je	répéterais	aurais répété	répéterai	
	tu	répéterais	aurais répété	répéteras	**répèt**e!
	il/elle/on	répéterait	aurait répété	répétera	
	nous	répéterions	aurions répété	répéterons	répétons!
	vous	répéteriez	auriez répété	répéterez	répétez!
	ils/elles	répéteraient	auraient répété	répéteront	

		SUBJONCTIF	PARTICIPE PRÉSENT	PARTICIPE PASSÉ
	que je	**répèt**e	répétant	répété
	que tu	**répèt**es		
	qu'il/elle/on	**répèt**e		
	que nous	répétions		
	que vous	répétiez		
	qu'ils/elles	**répèt**ent		

INFINITIF		PRÉSENT	PASSÉ COMPOSÉ	IMPARFAIT	PLUS-QUE-PARFAIT
			INDICATIF		
ennuyer	j'	**ennui**e	ai ennuyé	ennuyais	avais ennuyé
	tu	**ennui**es	as ennuyé	ennuyais	avais ennuyé
	il/elle/on	**ennui**e	a ennuyé	ennuyait	avait ennuyé
	nous	ennuyons	avons ennuyé	ennuyions	avions ennuyé
	vous	ennuyez	avez ennuyé	ennuyiez	aviez ennuyé
	ils/elles	**ennui**ent	ont ennuyé	ennuyaient	avaient ennuyé

		CONDITIONNEL			
		PRÉSENT	PASSÉ	FUTUR SIMPLE	IMPÉRATIF
	j'	**ennui**erais	aurais ennuyé	**ennui**erai	
	tu	**ennui**erais	aurais ennuyé	**ennui**eras	**ennui**e!
	il/elle/on	**ennui**erait	aurait ennuyé	**ennui**era	
	nous	**ennui**erions	aurions ennuyé	**ennui**erons	ennuyons!
	vous	**ennui**eriez	auriez ennuyé	**ennui**erez	ennuyez!
	ils/elles	**ennui**eraient	auraient ennuyé	**ennui**eront	

		SUBJONCTIF	PARTICIPE PRÉSENT	PARTICIPE PASSÉ
	que j'	**ennui**e	ennuyant	ennuyé
	que tu	**ennui**es		
	qu'il/elle/on	**ennui**e		
	que nous	ennuyions		
	que vous	ennuyiez		
	qu'ils/elles	**ennui**ent		

essayer

INFINITIF		PRÉSENT	PASSÉ COMPOSÉ	IMPARFAIT	PLUS-QUE-PARFAIT
essayer	j'	essaie, essaye	ai essayé	essayais	avais essayé
	tu	essaies, essayes	as essayé	essayais	avais essayé
	il/elle/on	essaie, essaye	a essayé	essayait	avait essayé
	nous	essayons	avons essayé	essayions	avions essayé
	vous	essayez	avez essayé	essayiez	aviez essayé
	ils/elles	essaient, essayent	ont essayé	essayaient	avaient essayé

CONDITIONNEL

		PRÉSENT	PASSÉ	FUTUR SIMPLE	IMPÉRATIF
	j'	essaierais, essayerais	aurais essayé	essaierai, essayerai	
	tu	essaierais, essayerais	aurais essayé	essaieras, essayeras	essaie, essaye!
	il/elle/on	essaierait, essayerait	aurait essayé	essaiera, essayera	
	nous	essaierions, essayerions	aurions essayé	essaierons, essayerons	essayons!
	vous	essaieriez, essayeriez	auriez essayé	essaierez, essayerez	essayez!
	ils/elles	essaieraient, essayeraient	auraient essayé	essaieront, essayeront	

		SUBJONCTIF	PARTICIPE PRÉSENT	PARTICIPE PASSÉ
	que j'	essaie, essaye	essayant	essayé
	que tu	essaies, essayes		
	qu'il/elle/on	essaie, essaye		
	que nous	essayions		
	que vous	essayiez		
	qu'ils/elles	essaient, essayent		

envoyer

INFINITIF		PRÉSENT	PASSÉ COMPOSÉ	IMPARFAIT	PLUS-QUE-PARFAIT
envoyer	j'	envoie	ai envoyé	envoyais	avais envoyé
	tu	envoies	as envoyé	envoyais	avais envoyé
	il/elle/on	envoie	a envoyé	envoyait	avait envoyé
	nous	envoyons	avons envoyé	envoyions	avions envoyé
	vous	envoyez	avez envoyé	envoyiez	aviez envoyé
	ils/elles	envoient	ont envoyé	envoyaient	avaient envoyé

CONDITIONNEL

		PRÉSENT	PASSÉ	FUTUR SIMPLE	IMPÉRATIF
	j'	enverrais	aurais envoyé	enverrai	
	tu	enverrais	aurais envoyé	enverras	envoie!
	il/elle/on	enverrait	aurait envoyé	enverra	
	nous	enverrions	aurions envoyé	enverrons	envoyons!
	vous	enverriez	auriez envoyé	enverrez	envoyez!
	ils/elles	enverraient	auraient envoyé	enverront	

		SUBJONCTIF	PARTICIPE PRÉSENT	PARTICIPE PASSÉ
	que j'	envoie	envoyant	envoyé
	que tu	envoies		
	qu'il/elle/on	envoie		
	que nous	envoyions		
	que vous	envoyiez		
	qu'ils/elles	envoient		

INFINITIF		PRÉSENT	INDICATIF		
		PRÉSENT	PASSÉ COMPOSÉ	IMPARFAIT	PLUS-QUE-PARFAIT
jeter	je	**jett**e	ai jeté	jetais	avais jeté
	tu	**jett**es	as jeté	jetais	avais jeté
	il/elle/on	**jett**e	a jeté	jetait	avait jeté
	nous	jetons	avons jeté	jetions	avions jeté
	vous	jetez	avez jeté	jetiez	aviez jeté
	ils/elles	**jett**ent	ont jeté	jetaient	avaient jeté

		CONDITIONNEL			
		PRÉSENT	PASSÉ	FUTUR SIMPLE	IMPÉRATIF
	je	**jett**erais	aurais jeté	**jett**erai	
	tu	**jett**erais	aurais jeté	**jett**eras	**jett**e!
	il/elle/on	**jett**erait	aurait jeté	**jett**era	
	nous	**jett**erions	aurions jeté	**jett**erons	jetons!
	vous	**jett**eriez	auriez jeté	**jett**erez	jetez!
	ils/elles	**jett**eraient	auraient jeté	**jett**eront	

		SUBJONCTIF	PARTICIPE PRÉSENT	PARTICIPE PASSÉ
	que je	**jett**e	jetant	jeté
	que tu	**jett**es		
	qu'il/elle/on	**jett**e		
	que nous	jetions		
	que vous	jetiez		
	qu'ils/elles	**jett**ent		

INFINITIF		PRÉSENT	INDICATIF		
		PRÉSENT	PASSÉ COMPOSÉ	IMPARFAIT	PLUS-QUE-PARFAIT
se promener	je	me **promèn**e	me **suis** promené(e)	me promenais	m'**étais** promené(e)
	tu	te **promèn**es	t'**es** promené(e)	te promenais	t'**étais** promené(e)
	il/elle/on	se **promèn**e	s'**est** promené(e)	se promenait	s'**était** promené(e)
	nous	nous promenons	nous **sommes** promené(e)s	nous promenions	nous **étions** promené(e)s
	vous	vous promenez	vous **êtes** promené(e)(s)	vous promeniez	vous **étiez** promené(e)(s)
	ils/elles	se **promèn**ent	se **sont** promené(e)s	se promenaient	s'**étaient** promené(e)s

		CONDITIONNEL			
		PRÉSENT	PASSÉ	FUTUR SIMPLE	IMPÉRATIF
	je	me **promèn**erais	me **serais** promené(**e**)	me **promèn**erai	
	tu	te **promèn**erais	te **serais** promené(**e**)	te **promèn**eras	**promèn**e-toi!
	il/elle/on	se **promèn**erait	se **serait** promené(**e**)	se **promèn**era	
	nous	nous **promèn**erions	nous **serions** promené(**e**)s	nous **promèn**erons	promenons-nous!
	vous	vous **promèn**eriez	vous **seriez** promené(**e**)(s)	vous **promèn**erez	promenez-vous!
	ils/elles	se **promèn**eraient	se **seraient** promené(**e**)s	se **promèn**eront	

		SUBJONCTIF	PARTICIPE PRÉSENT	PARTICIPE PASSÉ
	que je	me **promèn**e	promenant	promené
	que tu	te **promèn**es		
	qu'il/elle/on	se **promèn**e		
	que nous	nous promenions		
	que vous	vous promeniez		
	qu'ils/elles	se **promèn**ent		

se rappeler

INFINITIF		PRÉSENT	PASSÉ COMPOSÉ	IMPARFAIT	PLUS-QUE-PARFAIT
			INDICATIF		
se rappeler	je	me **rappell**e	me **suis** rappelé(e)	me rappelais	m'**étais** rappelé(e)
	tu	te **rappell**es	t'**es** rappelé(e)	te rappelais	t'**étais** rappelé(e)
	il/elle/on	se **rappell**e	s'**est** rappelé(e)	se rappelait	s'**était** rappelé(e)
	nous	nous rappelons	nous **sommes** rappelé(e)s	nous rappelions	nous **étions** rappelé(e)s
	vous	vous rappelez	vous **êtes** rappelé(e)(s)	vous rappeliez	vous **étiez** rappelé(e)(s)
	ils/elles	se **rappell**ent	se **sont** rappelé(e)s	se rappelaient	s'**étaient** rappelé(e)s

		PRÉSENT	PASSÉ	FUTUR SIMPLE	IMPÉRATIF
			CONDITIONNEL		
	je	me **rappell**erais	me **serais** rappelé(e)	me **rappell**erai	
	tu	te **rappell**erais	te **serais** rappelé(e)	te **rappell**eras	**rappell**e-toi!
	il/elle/on	se **rappell**erait	se **serait** rappelé(e)	se **rappell**era	
	nous	nous **rappell**erions	nous **serions** rappelé(e)s	nous **rappell**erons	rappelons-nous!
	vous	vous **rappell**eriez	vous **seriez** rappelé(e)(s)	vous **rappell**erez	rappelez-vous!
	ils/elles	se **rappell**eraient	se **seraient** rappelé(e)s	se **rappell**eront	

	SUBJONCTIF	PARTICIPE PRÉSENT	PARTICIPE PASSÉ
que je	me **rappell**e	rappelant	rappelé
que tu	te **rappell**es		
qu'il/elle/on	se **rappell**e		
que nous	nous rappelions		
que vous	vous rappeliez		
qu'ils/elles	se **rappell**ent		

se lever

INFINITIF		PRÉSENT	PASSÉ COMPOSÉ	IMPARFAIT	PLUS-QUE-PARFAIT
			INDICATIF		
se lever	je	me **lèv**e	me **suis** levé(e)	me levais	m'**étais** levé(e)
	tu	te **lèv**es	t'**es** levé(e)	te levais	t'**étais** levé(e)
	il/elle/on	se **lèv**e	s'**est** levé(e)	se levait	s'**était** levé(e)
	nous	nous levons	nous **sommes** levé(e)s	nous levions	nous **étions** levé(e)s
	vous	vous levez	vous **êtes** levé(e)(s)	vous leviez	vous **étiez** levé(e)(s)
	ils/elles	se **lèv**ent	se **sont** levé(e)s	se levaient	s'**étaient** levé(e)s

		PRÉSENT	PASSÉ	FUTUR SIMPLE	IMPÉRATIF
			CONDITIONNEL		
	je	me **lèv**erais	me **serais** levé(e)	me **lèv**erai	
	tu	te **lèv**erais	te **serais** levé(e)	te **lèv**eras	**lèv**e-toi!
	il/elle/on	se **lèv**erait	se **serait** levé(e)	se **lèv**era	
	nous	nous **lèv**erions	nous **serions** levé(e)s	nous **lèv**erons	levons-nous!
	vous	vous **lèv**eriez	vous **seriez** levé(e)(s)	vous **lèv**erez	levez-vous!
	ils/elles	se **lèv**eraient	se **seraient** levé(e)s	se **lèv**eront	

	SUBJONCTIF	PARTICIPE PRÉSENT	PARTICIPE PASSÉ
que je	me **lèv**e	levant	levé
que tu	te **lèv**es		
qu'il/elle/on	se **lèv**e		
que nous	nous levions		
que vous	vous leviez		
qu'ils/elles	se **lèv**ent		

III. Les verbes auxiliaires

INFINITIF	PRÉSENT	INDICATIF		
		PASSÉ COMPOSÉ	IMPARFAIT	PLUS-QUE-PARFAIT
être	je suis tu es il/elle/on est nous sommes vous êtes ils/elles sont	j'ai été	j'étais	j'avais été
avoir	j'ai tu as il/elle/on a nous avons vous avez ils/elles ont	j'ai eu	j'avais	j'avais eu

IV. Les verbes irréguliers

INFINITIF	PRÉSENT		INDICATIF		
			PASSÉ COMPOSÉ	IMPARFAIT	PLUS-QUE-PARFAIT
aller	je vais tu vas il/elle/on va	nous allons vous allez ils/elles vont	je suis allé(e)	j'allais	j'étais allé(e)
s'asseoir	je m'assieds tu t'assieds il/elle/on s'assied	nous nous asseyons vous vous asseyez ils/elles s'asseyent	je me suis assis(e)	je m'asseyais	je m'étais assis(e)
boire	je bois tu bois il/elle/on boit	nous buvons vous buvez ils/elles boivent	j'ai bu	je buvais	j'avais bu
conduire	je conduis tu conduis il/elle/on conduit	nous conduisons vous conduisez ils/elles conduisent	j'ai conduit	je conduisais	j'avais conduit
connaître	je connais tu connais ill/elle/on connaît	nous connaissons vous connaissez ils/elles connaissent	j'ai connu	je connaissais	j'avais connu
courir	je cours tu cours il/elle/on court	nous courons vous courez ils/elles courent	j'ai couru	je courais	j'avais couru
croire	je crois tu crois il/elle/on croit	nous croyons vous croyez ils/elles croient	j'ai cru	je croyais	j'avais cru
devoir	je dois tu dois il/elle/on doit	nous devons vous devez ils/elles doivent	j'ai dû	je devais	j'avais dû
dire	je dis tu dis il/elle/on dit	nous disons vous dites ils/elles disent	j'ai dit	je disais	j'avais dit
écrire	j'écris tu écris il/elle/on écrit	nous écrivons vous écrivez ils/elles écrivent	j'ai écrit	j'écrivais	j'avais écrit

INFINITIF	PRÉSENT		PASSÉ COMPOSÉ	IMPARFAIT	PLUS-QUE-PARFAIT
envoyer	j'envoie tu envoies il/elle/on envoie	nous envoyons vous envoyez ils/elles envoient	j'ai envoyé	j'envoyais	j'avais envoyé
faire	je fais tu fais il/elle/on fait	nous faisons vous faites ils/elles font	j'ai fait	je faisais	j'avais fait
falloir	il faut		il a fallu	il fallait	il avait fallu
lire	je lis tu lis il/elle/on lit	nous lisons vous lisez ils/elles lisent	j'ai lu	je lisais	j'avais lu
mettre	je mets tu mets il/elle/on met	nous mettons vous mettez ils/elles mettent	j'ai mis	je mettais	j'avais mis
ouvrir	j'ouvre tu ouvres il/elle/on ouvre	nous ouvrons vous ouvrez ils/elles ouvrent	j'ai ouvert	j'ouvrais	j'avais ouvert
partir	je pars tu pars ill/elle/on part	nous partons vous partez ils/elles partent	je suis parti(e)	je partais	j'étais parti(e)
pleuvoir	il pleut		il a plu	il pleuvait	il avait plu
pouvoir	je peux tu peux il/elle/on peut	nous pouvons vous pouvez ils/elles peuvent	j'ai pu	je pouvais	j'avais pu
prendre	je prends tu prends il/elle/on prend	nous prenons vous prenez ils/elles prennent	j'ai pris	je prenais	j'avais pris
recevoir	je reçois tu reçois il/elle/on reçoit	nous recevons vous recevez ils/elles reçoivent	j'ai reçu	je recevais	j'avais reçu
savoir	je sais tu sais il/elle/on sait	nous savons vous savez ils/elles savent	j'ai su	je savais	j'avais su
suivre	je suis tu suis il/elle/on suit	nous suivons vous suivez ils/elles suivent	j'ai suivi	je suivais	j'avais suivi
venir	je viens tu viens il/elle/on vient	nous venons vous venez ils/elles viennent	je suis venu(e)	je venais	j'étais venu(e)
vivre	je vis tu vis il/elle/on vit	nous vivons vous vivez ils/elles vivent	j'ai vécu	je vivais	j'avais vécu
voir	je vois tu vois il/elle/on voit	nous voyons vous voyez ils/elles voient	j'ai vu	je voyais	j'avais vu
vouloir	je veux tu veux il/elle/on veut	nous voulons vous voulez ils/elles veulent	j'ai voulu	je voulais	j'avais voulu

INFINITIF		PRÉSENT	INDICATIF PASSÉ COMPOSÉ	IMPARFAIT	PLUS-QUE-PARFAIT
sortir	je	**sors**	**suis** sorti(e)	sortais	**étais** sorti(e)
	tu	**sors**	**es** sorti(e)	sortais	**étais** sorti(e)
	il/elle/on	**sort**	**est** sorti(e)	sortait	**était** sorti(e)
	nous	sortons	**sommes** sorti(e)s	sortions	**étions** sorti(e)s
	vous	sortez	**êtes** sorti(e)(s)	sortiez	**étiez** sorti(e)(s)
	ils/elles	sortent	**sont** sorti(e)s	sortaient	**étaient** sorti(e)s

		CONDITIONNEL PRÉSENT	PASSÉ	FUTUR SIMPLE	IMPÉRATIF
	je	sortirais	**serais** sorti(e)	sortirai	
	tu	sortirais	**serais** sorti(e)	sortiras	**sors**!
	il/elle/on	sortirait	**serait** sorti(e)	sortira	
	nous	sortirions	**serions** sorti(e)s	sortirons	sortons!
	vous	sortiriez	**seriez** sorti(e)(s)	sortirez	sortez!
	ils/elles	sortiraient	**seraient** sorti(e)s	sortiront	

		SUBJONCTIF	PARTICIPE PRÉSENT	PARTICIPE PASSÉ	
	que je	sorte	sortant	sorti	
	que tu	sortes			
	qu'il/elle/on	sorte			
	que nous	sortions			
	que vous	sortiez			
	qu'ils/elles	sortent			

INFINITIF		PRÉSENT	INDICATIF PASSÉ COMPOSÉ	IMPARFAIT	PLUS-QUE-PARFAIT
sentir	je	**sens**	ai senti	sentais	avais senti
	tu	**sens**	as senti	sentais	avais senti
	il/elle/on	**sent**	a senti	sentait	avait senti
	nous	sentons	avons senti	sentions	avions senti
	vous	sentez	avez senti	sentiez	aviez senti
	ils/elles	sentent	ont senti	sentaient	avaient senti

		CONDITIONNEL PRÉSENT	PASSÉ	FUTUR SIMPLE	IMPÉRATIF
	je	sentirais	aurais senti	sentirai	
	tu	sentirais	aurais senti	sentiras	**sens**!
	il/elle/on	sentirait	aurait senti	sentira	
	nous	sentirions	aurions senti	sentirons	sentons!
	vous	sentiriez	auriez senti	sentirez	sentez!
	ils/elles	sentiraient	auraient senti	sentiront	

		SUBJONCTIF	PARTICIPE PRÉSENT	PARTICIPE PASSÉ	
	que je	sente	sentant	senti	
	que tu	sentes			
	qu'il/elle/on	sente			
	que nous	sentions			
	que vous	sentiez			
	qu'ils/elles	sentent			

vendre

INFINITIF		INDICATIF			
		PRÉSENT	**PASSÉ COMPOSÉ**	**IMPARFAIT**	**PLUS-QUE-PARFAIT**
vendre	je	vends	ai vendu	vendais	avais vendu
	tu	vends	as vendu	vendais	avais vendu
	il/elle/on	vend	a vendu	vendait	avait vendu
	nous	vendons	avons vendu	vendions	avions vendu
	vous	vendez	avez vendu	vendiez	aviez vendu
	ils/elles	vendent	ont vendu	vendaient	avaient vendu

		CONDITIONNEL			
		PRÉSENT	**PASSÉ**	**FUTUR SIMPLE**	**IMPÉRATIF**
	je	vendrais	aurais vendu	vendrai	
	tu	vendrais	aurais vendu	vendras	vends!
	il/elle/on	vendrait	aurait vendu	vendra	
	nous	vendrions	aurions vendu	vendrons	vendons!
	vous	vendriez	auriez vendu	vendrez	vendez!
	ils/elles	vendraient	auraient vendu	vendront	

		SUBJONCTIF	**PARTICIPE PRÉSENT**	**PARTICIPE PASSÉ**
	que je	vende	vendant	vendu
	que tu	vendes		
	qu'il/elle/on	vende		
	que nous	vendions		
	que vous	vendiez		
	qu'ils/elles	vendent		

mourir

INFINITIF		INDICATIF			
		PRÉSENT	**PASSÉ COMPOSÉ**	**IMPARFAIT**	**PLUS-QUE-PARFAIT**
mourir	je	**meurs**	**suis mort(e)**	mourais	**étais mort(e)**
	tu	**meurs**	**es mort(e)**	mourais	**étais mort(e)**
	il/elle/on	**meurt**	**est mort(e)**	mourait	**était mort(e)**
	nous	mourons	**sommes mort(e)s**	mourions	**étions mort(e)s**
	vous	mourez	**êtes mort(e)(s)**	mouriez	**étiez mort(e)(s)**
	ils/elles	**meurent**	**sont mort(e)s**	mouraient	**étaient mort(e)s**

		CONDITIONNEL			
		PRÉSENT	**PASSÉ**	**FUTUR SIMPLE**	**IMPÉRATIF**
	je	mour**rais**	**serais mort(e)**	mour**rai**	
	tu	mour**rais**	**serais mort(e)**	mour**ras**	**meurs**!
	il/elle/on	mour**rait**	**serait mort(e)**	mour**ra**	
	nous	mour**rions**	**serions mort(e)s**	mour**rons**	mour**ons**!
	vous	mour**riez**	**seriez mort(e)(s)**	mour**rez**	mour**ez**!
	ils/elles	mour**raient**	**seraient mort(e)s**	mour**ront**	

		SUBJONCTIF	**PARTICIPE PRÉSENT**	**PARTICIPE PASSÉ**
	que je	**meure**	mourant	mort
	que tu	**meures**		
	qu'il/elle/on	**meure**		
	que nous	mour**ions**		
	que vous	mour**iez**		
	qu'ils/elles	**meurent**		

INFINITIF		PRÉSENT	PASSÉ COMPOSÉ	IMPARFAIT	PLUS-QUE-PARFAIT
			INDICATIF		
obtenir	j'	**obtiens**	ai obtenu	obtenais	avais obtenu
	tu	**obtiens**	as obtenu	obtenais	avais obtenu
	il/elle/on	**obtient**	a obtenu	obtenait	avait obtenu
	nous	obtenons	avons obtenu	obtenions	avions obtenu
	vous	obtenez	avez obtenu	obteniez	aviez obtenu
	ils/elles	**obtiennent**	ont obtenu	obtenaient	avaient obtenu

		CONDITIONNEL			
		PRÉSENT	PASSÉ	FUTUR SIMPLE	IMPÉRATIF
	j'	**obtiendrais**	aurais obtenu	**obtiendrai**	
	tu	**obtiendrais**	aurais obtenu	**obtiendras**	**obtiens!**
	il/elle/on	**obtiendrait**	aurait obtenu	**obtiendra**	
	nous	**obtiendrions**	aurions obtenu	**obtiendrons**	obtenons!
	vous	**obtiendriez**	auriez obtenu	**obtiendrez**	obtenez!
	ils/elles	**obtiendraient**	auraient obtenu	**obtiendront**	

		SUBJONCTIF	PARTICIPE PRÉSENT	PARTICIPE PASSÉ	
	que j'	**obtienne**	obtenant	obtenu	
	que tu	**obtiennes**			
	qu'il/elle/on	**obtienne**			
	que nous	obtenions			
	que vous	obteniez			
	qu'ils/elles	**obtiennent**			

INFINITIF		PRÉSENT	PASSÉ COMPOSÉ	IMPARFAIT	PLUS-QUE-PARFAIT
			INDICATIF		
devenir	je	**deviens**	**suis** devenu(e)	devenais	**étais** devenu(e)
	tu	**deviens**	**es** devenu(e)	devenais	**étais** devenu(e)
	il/elle/on	**devient**	**est** devenu(e)	devenait	**était** devenu(e)
	nous	devenons	**sommes** devenu(e)s	devenions	**étions** devenu(e)s
	vous	devenez	**êtes** devenu(e)(s)	deveniez	**étiez** devenu(e)(s)
	ils/elles	**deviennent**	**sont** devenu(e)s	devenaient	**étaient** devenu(e)s

		CONDITIONNEL			
		PRÉSENT	PASSÉ	FUTUR SIMPLE	IMPÉRATIF
	je	**deviendrais**	**serais** devenu(e)	**deviendrai**	
	tu	**deviendrais**	**serais** devenu(e)	**deviendras**	**deviens!**
	il/elle/on	**deviendrait**	**serait** devenu(e)	**deviendra**	
	nous	**deviendrions**	**serions** devenu(e)s	**deviendrons**	devenons!
	vous	**deviendriez**	**seriez** devenu(e)(s)	**deviendrez**	devenez!
	ils/elles	**deviendraient**	**seraient** devenu(e)s	**deviendront**	

		SUBJONCTIF	PARTICIPE PRÉSENT	PARTICIPE PASSÉ	
	que je	**devienne**	devenant	devenu	
	que tu	**deviennes**			
	qu'il/elle/on	**devienne**			
	que nous	devenions			
	que vous	deveniez			
	qu'ils/elles	**deviennent**			

LE SUBJONCTIF DES VERBES IRRÉGULIERS				
	AVOIR	**ÊTRE**	**ALLER**	**FAIRE**
... que je/j'	aie	sois	aille	fasse
... que tu	aies	sois	ailles	fasses
... qu'il/elle/on	ait	soit	aille	fasse
... que nous	ayons	soyons	allions	fassions
... que vous	ayez	soyez	alliez	fassiez
... qu'ils/elles	aient	soient	aillent	fassent
	POUVOIR	**SAVOIR**	**VOULOIR**	
... que je	puisse	sache	veuille	
... que tu	puisses	saches	veuilles	
... qu'il/elle/on	puisse	sache	veuille	
... que nous	puissions	sachions	voulions	
... que vous	puissiez	sachiez	vouliez	
... qu'ils/elles	puissent	sachent	veuillent	

VOCABULAIRE français-anglais

The French-English Vocabulary contains all the words and expressions included in the **Vocabulaire** sections at the end of each chapter. Entries are followed by the chapter number (**P** for **Chapitre préliminaire** and **F** for **Chapitre final**) where they appear. In addition, the French-English Vocabulary includes words and expressions used in the **Activités** sections.

Expressions are listed under their key word(s). In subentries, the symbol — indicates the repetition of the key word. Regular adjectives are given in the masculine form, with the feminine ending in parentheses. For irregular adjectives, the irregular ending of the feminine or the whole word is given. Irregular forms of the plural are also indicated. The gender of each noun is indicated after the noun. If the noun has both a masculine and a feminine form, both are listed. If the noun has an irregular form for the plural, this is also indicated in parentheses after the word.

The following abbreviations are used:

m.	masculine	*inv.*	invariable
f.	feminine	*n.*	noun
sing.	singular	*v.*	verb
pl.	plural	*adj.*	adjective
m. pl.	masculine plural	*adv.*	adverb
f. pl.	feminine plural		

A

à *to, in* 3
abord: d'— *first* 4
absolument *absolutely* 2
abstrait(e) *abstract* 9
accro du shopping *(m./f.) shopaholic* 10
acharné(e) *competitive, cutthroat* 7
acheter *to buy* 6
acteur *(m.) actor* 7
actif / active *active, working* 10; **mère** *(f.)* **active** *working mom* 10; **père** *(m.)* **actif** *working dad* 10
activement *actively* 2
actrice *(f.) actress* 7
actualité *(f.) current events*
addition *(f.) check* 6
adolescence *(f.) adolescence* 8
adolescent(e) *adolescent* 8
adorer *to adore* 1
adulte *(adj.) adult* 8; **âge** *(m.)* — *adulthood* 8
adulte *(m./f.) adult* 8
aérobic *(m.) aerobics* 2
aéroport *(m.) airport* 11
affaires *(f. pl.) things, stuff* 4, *business* 7; **homme** *(m.)* **d'**— *businessman* 7; **femme** *(f.)* **d'**— *businesswoman* 7
affiche *(f.) poster* P
Afrique *(f.) Africa* 3; — **du Nord** *North Africa* 3; — **de l'Ouest** *West Africa* 3
âge *(m.) age* 8; — **adulte** *adulthood* 8; **Moyen Âge** *Middle Ages*; **troisième** — *old age, the elderly* 8
agence *(f.) agency* 11
agent(e) *(m./f.) officer* 7, *agent* 11; — **de bord** *flight attendant* 11; — **de police** *police officer* 7; — **de la sécurité** *(m./f) security agent* 11; — **de voyages** *travel agent* 11
agneau *(m.) lamb* 5
agrafeuse *(f.) stapler* P

aider *to help* 8
aigle *(m.) eagle* 12
aigre *sour* 5
ail *(m.) garlic* 5
aimer *to like, to love* 1; — **bien** *to like* 1; — **mieux** *to prefer, to like better* 1; **s'**— *to like / love oneself / each other* 10
alcoolisé(e) *alcoholic* 5
aliment *(m.) particular food* 5; — **industriel** *processed food* 5
Allemagne *(f.) Germany* 3
allemand *(m.) German (language)* P
allemand(e) *German* 3
aller *to go* 2; — **bien** *to look good on someone* 11; — **à la chasse** *to go hunting, to hunt* 4; — **à la pêche** *to go fishing* 4; — **au spa** *to go to the spa* 2; — **en vacances** *to go on vacation* 11; **s'en** — *to go away* 10
allergie *(f.) allergy* 12
ambitieux / ambitieuse *ambitious* 1
amener *to bring someone* 6
amer / amère *bitter* 5
américain(e) *American* 3
Amérique *(f.) America* 3; — **du Nord** *North America* 3; — **du Sud** *South America* 3
ami(e) *friend* P; **petit(e)** — *boyfriend / girlfriend* P; **meilleur(e)** — *best friend* P
amitié *(f.) friendship* 10
amour *(m.) love* 10
amoureux / amoureuse (de) *in love (with)* 8; **tomber** — *to fall in love (with)* 8
amphithéâtre *(m.) lecture hall* 4
ampoule *(f.) lightbulb* F; — **basse consommation** *energy saving lightbulb* F
amusant(e) *funny* P
amuser *to amuse;* **s'**— *to have a good time* 10
an *(m.) year* 2

anchois *(m. pl.) anchovies*
ancien / ancienne *former* 11
anglais *(m.) English (language)* P
anglais(e) *British* 3
Angleterre *(f.) England* 3
animal domestique *(m.) pet* 3
animalerie *(f.) pet store* 12
animation *(f.) animation* 9; **film** *(m.)* **d'**— *(animated) cartoon / animated film* 9
année *(f.) year* 2; — **dernière / passée** *last year* 5; **Bonne** —! *Happy New Year!* 8
anniversaire *(m.) birthday* 2, *anniversary* 8; — **de mariage** *wedding anniversary* 8; **Bon / Joyeux** —! *Happy birthday!* 8; **C'est quand l'**— **de Samir?** *When is Samir's birthday?* 2; **C'est quand ton/ votre** —? *When is your birthday?* 2;
annoncer *to forecast* 2
annulé(e) *canceled*
anorak *(m.) parka* 11
antenne *(f.) antenna, dish* F
anthropologie *(f.) anthropology* P
août *August* 2
appareil *(m.) appliance, piece of equipment* 4; — **électroménager** *household appliance* 4
appartement *(m.) apartment* 4
appartenir (à) *to belong (to)*
appeler *to name, to call* 10; **s'**— *to be named / called* 10
appétit *(m.) appetite* 6; **Bon** —! *Enjoy (the meal)!* 6
applaudir *to applaud* 9
apporter *to bring something* 6
apprendre (à) *to learn (to)* 5
après *after* 1
après-midi *(m.) afternoon* 1; **de l'**— *in the afternoon* 1

VOCABULAIRE français-anglais

arbre (m.) tree 4
argent (m.) money 6
arrêt (m.) stop; — **d'autobus** bus stop 11
arriver to arrive 6
art (m.) art P; **galerie** (f.) **d'** — art gallery 9; **pop** — pop art 9
article (m.) article 10
artiste (m./f.) artist 9
Asie (f.) Asia 3
asperge (f.) asparagus 6
aspirateur (m.) vacuum 4; **passer l'** — to vacuum 4
assez enough 1
assiette (f.) plate 6
assistance sociale (f.) social aid F
assistant(e) social(e) social worker 7
assister (à) to attend
association (f.) association, organization F; — **humanitaire** humanitarian organization F
assurance-maladie (f.) health insurance 12
astronomie (f.) astronomy P
attacher to tie, to fasten 11; — **la ceinture de sécurité** to fasten the seatbelt 11
attendre to wait (for) 6
attentat terroriste (m.) terrorist attack
au revoir goodbye P
au(x) at 1; to, in 3
auberge (f.) hostel 11; — **de jeunesse** youth hostel 11
aubergine (f.) eggplant 6
audacieux / audacieuse daring
aujourd'hui today 1
aussi too, also P, as 7; —... **que** as ... as 7
autant as many, as much 7; — **de... que** as many, as much ... as 7
auteur (m.) author 9; **femme** (f.) — author (female) 9
autobus (m.) bus 11; **arrêt** (m.) **d'** — bus stop 11
automne (m.) fall 2
autre another, other 11
autrefois in the past, long ago 8
avancement (m.) promotion 8
avant before 1
avant-hier day before yesterday 5
avare stingy, miserly 10
avec with 1
avenir (m.) future
avion (m.) plane 11
avis (m.) opinion; **À mon (votre) avis...** In my (your) opinion . . . 10
avocat (m.) avocado 5
avocat(e) lawyer 7
avoir to have 1; —... **ans** to be ... years old 1; — **besoin de** to need 1; — **de la chance** to be lucky 1; — **chaud** to be hot 5; — **un cours de...** to have a . . . class 1; — **envie de** to feel like 1; — **faim** to be hungry 5; — **froid** to be cold 5; — **mal à la tête** to have a headache 12; — **mal au ventre** to have a stomach ache 12; — **peur de** to be afraid of 1; — **raison** to be right 1; — **soif** to be thirsty 5; — **sommeil** to be sleepy 1; — **tort** to be wrong 1
avril April 2

B

baba cool (m./f.) hippy 10
baccalauréat (m.) end-of-high-school exam 7
bague (f.) ring
baignoire (f.) bathtub 4
balcon (m.) balcony 4
ballet (m.) ballet 9
banane (f.) banana 5
banlieue (f.) suburbs 4
banque (f.) bank 4
banquet (m.) banquet 8
baptême (m.) baptism 8
barbe (f.) beard 3
barbecue (m.) BBQ 2; **faire un** — to have a BBQ 2
barrer to cross out
baseball (m.) baseball 2
basket-ball / basket (m.) basketball 2
baskets (f. pl.) sports shoes 11
bateau (m.) boat 4; — **à voile** sailboat 4; **faire du** — **(à voile) / faire du voilier** to go (sail)boating 4
bâtiment (m.) building 4
bavard(e) talkative, gossipy 10
beau / bel / belle handsome, beautiful, nice 2
beaucoup a lot 1
beau-fils (m.) stepson, son-in-law 3
beau-frère (m.) brother-in-law, stepbrother 3
beau-père (m.) father-in-law, stepfather 3
beaux-arts (m. pl.) fine arts 9
bel (m. before a vowel sound) handsome, beautiful, nice 2
belge Belgian 3
Belgique (f.) Belgium 3
belle (f.) beautiful, nice 2
belle-fille (f.) stepdaughter, daughter-in-law 3
belle-mère (f.) mother-in-law, stepmother 3
belle-sœur (f.) sister-in-law, stepsister 3
bête (adj.) stupid, idiotic 10
bête (f.) beast
beurre (m.) butter 5

bibliothèque (f.) library 1
bien fine P, good 1, well 2; — **sûr** of course 1
bientôt soon P; **À** —. See you soon. P
bière (f.) beer 5
billet (m.) bill, banknote 7, ticket 11; — **aller-retour** round-trip ticket 11; — **aller-simple** one-way ticket 11; — **d'avion** plane ticket 11
biodégradable biodegradable F; **non** — nonbiodegradable F
biologie (f.) biology P
biologique (bio) organic 6
biscuit (m.) cookie 5
bistro (m.) café-restaurant 4
bizarre bizarre F
blanc / blanche white 3
blessure (f.) wound 12
bleu(e) blue 3, rare (meat) 5
bleuet (m.) blueberry 5
blog (m.) blog 10
blond(e) (m./f.) blond person 3; (adj.) blond 3
blouson (m.) heavy jacket 11; — **en cuir** leather heavy jacket 11
blues (m.) blues, R&B 9
bœuf (m.) beef 6; — **haché** ground beef 6
boire to drink 5
bois (m. pl.) woods 4
boîte (de/d') (f.) box (of) 5; — **à lettres** mailbox 11; — **(de conserves)** can (canned goods) 6; — **de nuit** nightclub
bol (m.) bowl 6
bon / bonne good P, warm (weather) 2; **Bonne journée.** Good day. P; **Bonne nuit.** Good night. P
bonbon (m.) candy 5
bonheur (m.) happiness 8; **Au** — **de (qqn)!** To the happiness of (someone)! 8
bonjour hello P
bonsoir good evening P
bottes (f. pl.) boots 11
bouche (m.) mouth 12
boucherie (f.) butcher's shop 6
bouclé(e) curly 3
bouger to move 11
boulangerie (f.) bakery 6
boule (f.) ball; — **de cristal** crystal ball
bourreau de travail (m./f.) workaholic 10
bourse (f.) scholarship 7, stock market; — **(d'études)** scholarship 7
bout (m.) end 4
bouteille (de/d') (f.) bottle (of) 5
boutique (f.) store, boutique 4
bowling (m.) bowling 2
bracelet (m.) bracelet 11
bras (m.) arm 12

VOCABULAIRE français-anglais

Brésil *(m.)* *Brazil* 3
brésilien / brésilienne *Brazilian* 3
bricolage *(m.)* *tinkering, odd jobs* 2; **faire du —** *to tinker, to do odd jobs, to act the handyman/woman* 2
brillant(e) *brilliant* P
brioche *(f.)* *round egg bread* 6
brocoli *(m.)* *broccoli* 5
brosse *(f.)* *brush* 12; **— à cheveux** *hairbrush* 12; **— à dents** *toothbrush* 12
brosser *to brush* 12; **se — les cheveux / les dents** *to brush one's hair / teeth* 12
brun(e) *(adj.)* *brown* 3; *dark-haired person* 3
bureau *(m.)* *desk* P, *office* 1; **— de poste** *post office* 4
bus *(m.)* *bus* 11
but *(m.)* *goal*

C

cachet *(m.)* *pill, tablet* 12; **— d'aspirine** *aspirin* 12
cadeau *(m.)* *gift* 8
café *(m.)* *café* 1, *coffee* 5
cahier *(m.)* *notebook* P
calculatrice *(f.)* *calculator* P
camarade *(m./f.)* *mate, friend* P; **— de chambre** *roommate* P
camion *(m.)* *truck* 11
camionnette *(f.)* *van, mini van* 11
campagne *(f.)* *country(side)* 4
camping *(m.)* *camping* 2; **faire du —** *to go camping* 2
campus *(m.)* *campus* 4
Canada *(m.)* *Canada* 3
canadien / canadienne *Canadian* 3
canapé *(m.)* *couch* 4
canard *(m.)* *duck* 5
capacité *(f.)* *skill* 7; **—s de communication** *communication skills* 7
carotte *(f.)* *carrot* 5
carrière *(f.)* *career* 7
carte *(f.)* *card* 2; **— bancaire** *debit card* 7; **— de crédit** *credit card* 7; **— d'embarquement** *boarding pass* 11; **jouer aux —s** *to play cards* 2; **— postale** *(f.)* *postcard* 11; **— de vœux** *greeting card* 8
casquette *(f.)* *baseball cap* 11
casser *to break*; **se — (le bras)** *to break one's (arm)* 12
causerie *(f.)* *talk show* 9
ce *(m. sing.)* *this* 3
ceinture *(f.)* *belt*; **— de sécurité** *seatbelt*
célèbre *famous* P
célébrer *to celebrate* 6
célibataire *(adj.)* *single* 3; **mère** *(f.)* **—** *single mother* 10; **père** *(m.)* **—** *single father* 10

célibataire *(m./f.)* *single person* 10
celle *(f.)* *this one, that one* 9
celles *(f. pl.)* *these (ones), those (ones)* 9
celui *(m.)* *this one, that one* 9
cent *one hundred* 1; **— pour cent** *one hundred percent* 1
centième *hundredth* 8
centime *(m.)* *cent* 6
centre *(m.)* *center* 4; **— commercial** *shopping center / district* 4; **— sportif** *recreation center* 4; **—-ville** *downtown* 4
céréales *(f. pl.)* *cereal* 5
cérémonie *(f.)* *ceremony* 8; **— de remise des diplômes** *graduation ceremony* 8
cerise *(f.)* *cherry* 6
certain(e) *certain* F; **— (de)** *certain (of)* 11
cerveau *(m.)* *brain*
ces *these, those* 3
cet *(m. sing. before vowel)* *this* 3
cette *(f. sing.)* *this* 3
ceux *(m. pl.)* *these (ones), those (ones)* 9
chacun / chacune (de) *each (one) (of)* 11
chaise *(f.)* *chair* P
chambre *(f.)* *bedroom* 4, *room* 11; **— double** *double room* 11; **— fumeurs / non fumeurs** *smoking / nonsmoking room* 11; **— individuelle** *single room* 11
champignon *(m.)* *mushroom* 6
chance *(f.)* *luck* 8; **Bonne —!** *Good luck!* 8
chanceux / chanceuse *lucky*
chanson *(f.)* *song* 9
chanter *to sing* 1
chanteur *(m.)* *singer* 7
chanteuse *(f.)* *singer* 7
chapeau *(m.)* *hat* 11
chaque *(+ noun)* *each, every* 8
charcuterie *(f.)* *deli shop* 6
chariot *(m.)* *shopping cart* 6
charmant(e) *charming* P
chasse *(f.)* *hunt, hunting* 4; **aller à la —** *to go hunting, to hunt* 4
chat *(m.)* *cat* 3
chaud(e) *hot* 2
chausser *to wear shoe size . . .* 11; **Je chausse du 36.** *I wear a size 36 shoe.* 11
chaussures *(f. pl.)* *shoes* 11; **— à talons** *high-heeled shoes* 11
chauve *bald* 3
chef-d'œuvre *(m.)* *masterpiece* 9
chemise *(f.)* *shirt* 11
chemisier *(m.)* *blouse* 11
chèque *(m.)* *check* 7; **compte-—s** *(m.)* *checking account* 7; **payer par —** *to pay by check* 7

cher / chère *expensive* 11
chercher *to look for* 1
cheval *(m.)* *horse* 2; **faire du —** *to go horseback riding* 2
cheveux *(m. pl.)* *hair* 3; **— blonds** *blond hair* 3; **— bouclés / frisés** *curly hair* 3; **— bruns** *brown hair* 3; **— courts** *short hair* 3; **— longs et raides** *long straight hair* 3; **— noirs** *black hair* 3; **— ondulés** *wavy hair* 3; **— roux** *red hair* 3
cheville *(f.)* *ankle* 12
chèvre *(f.)* *goat* 12
chez *at the home / place of* 4
chien *(m.)* *dog* 3
chiffre *(m.)* *number* 7; **être bon / bonne avec les —s** *to be good with numbers* 7
chimie *(f.)* *chemistry* P
Chine *(f.)* *China* 3
chinois *(m.)* *Chinese (language)* P
chinois(e) *Chinese* 3
chips *(f. pl.)* *chips* 5
chœur *(m.)* *choir* 9
choisir *to choose* 4
chômage *(m.)* *unemployment* F
chorale *(f.)* *choir* 9
chose *(f.)* *thing* 4; **Autre —?** *Anything else?* 6
ciel *(m.)* *sky* 2; **Le — est couvert.** *It's cloudy / overcast.* 2
cinéma *(m.)* *movie theater* 4
cinéphile *(m./f.)* *film enthusiast*
cinq *five* P
cinquante *fifty* P
cinquième *fifth* 8
citron *(m.)* *lemon* 5; **— pressé** *lemonade* 5; **— vert** *lime* 5
clair(e) *clear* F
classe *(f.)* *class (of students)* P; **— affaires** *business class* 11; **— économique** *economy class* 11; **première — ** *first-class* 11
classer *to classify*
clavier *(m.)* *keyboard* F
clé *(f.)* *key* 11
client(e) *(m./f.)* *client, guest* 11
clonage *(m.)* *cloning* F
Coca *(m.)* *Coca-Cola* 5
cocher *to check*
cochon *(m.)* *pig* 12
cœur *(m.)* *heart* 12; **— artificiel** *artificial heart* F
coiffeur *(m.)* *hairdresser* 7
coiffeuse *(f.)* *hairdresser* 7
coin: au — (de) *on the corner (of)* 4
coincé(e) *uptight* 7
colis *(m.)* *package* 11
collège *(m.)* *junior high / middle school* 7
collier *(m.)* *necklace* 11
colocataire *(m./f.)* *roommate, housemate* P
colonie *(f.)* *colony* 8
colonisation *(f.)* *colonization* 8

VOCABULAIRE français-anglais

combien (de) *how much, how many*
4;**Ça fait —?** *How much is it?* 6; **C'est
—?** *How much is it?* 6; **— coûte(nt)... ?**
How much is/are . . . ? 6

comédie *(f.) comedy* 9; **— musicale**
musical (stage, film) 9

commander *to order* 2; **— une pizza** *to
order a pizza* 2

comme *like*

comment *how* P; **— allez-vous?** *(pl./sing.,
formal) How are you?* P; **— ça va?**
(sing., informal) How is it going? P; **—
s'appelle-t-elle?** *What is her name?* P;
— s'appelle-t-il? *What is his name?* P;
— t'appelles-tu? *What's your name?*
P; **— vas-tu?** *(sing., informal) How are
you?* P

commerce (international) *(m.)
business* P

commode *(f.) chest of drawers* 4

compléter *to fill in*

compositeur *(m.) composer* 9; **femme** *(f.)
— composer (female)* 9

compositrice *(f.) composer (female)* 9

compost: faire du — *to compost* F

comprendre *to understand* 5

compris(e) *included* 6; **Le service est
compris.** *The tip is included.* 6

comptabilité *(f.) accounting* P

comptable *(m./f.) accountant* 7

compte *(m.) account* 7; **—-chèques**
checking account 7; **— d'épargne**
savings account 7

concert *(m.) concert* 9

concombre *(m.) cucumber* 6

condoléances *(f. pl.) condolences* 8;
Mes —. *My condolences.* 8

conduire *to drive* 11

confiture *(f.) jam* 5

confortable *comfortable* 11

conjoint(e) *(m./f.) significant other,
(domestic) partner* 3

connaître *to know, to be familiar with* 8; **se
— to know oneself / each other** 10

connexion *(f.) connection* F

conseiller *to advise* 12

conserver *to conserve* F

console *(f.) console* 4; **— wii** *wii
game box* 6

constamment *constantly* 2

construire *to construct* 11

conte *(m.) tale* 9; **— de fées** *fairy tale* 9

content(e) *happy, content* P

continent *(m.) continent* 3

continuer *to go, to continue* 4

contre *against* 8

contrôle de sécurité *(m.) security check* 11;
passer au — *to go through security* 11

copain *(m.) friend* P

copine *(f.) friend* P

coq *(m.) rooster* 12

corps *(m.) body* 12

correspondance *(f.) connecting flight* 11

corriger *to correct*

costume *(m.) man's suit* 11

Côte d'Ivoire *(f.) Ivory Coast* 3

côté: à — (de) *next (to)* 4

côtelette *(f.) chop* 6; **— d'agneau / de porc**
(f.) lamb / pork chop 6

cou *(m.) neck* 12

coucher *to put to bed* 12; **se — to go to
bed** 12

coude *(m.) elbow* 12

couloir *(m.) hallway* 4

coup *(m.) blow, hit;* **— de foudre** *love
at first sight* 8; **tout d'un —** *all of a
sudden* 8

couper *to cut* 5; **se — to cut (oneself)** 12

couple *(m.) couple* 8

courageux / courageuse *courageous* 1

couramment *fluently* 2

courriel *(m.) email* 2

courrier *(m.) mail* 11

cours *(m.) class, course* P

course *(f.) errand* 2; **faire des —s** *to run
some errands* 2

court(e) *short (hair)* 3

cousin(e) *(m./f.) cousin* 3

couteau *(m.) knife* 6

coûter *to cost* 6

couvert(e) *cloudy, overcast* 2

couverts *(m. pl.) cutlery* 6

covoiturage *(m.) carpooling* 11

craie *(f.) chalk (piece of)* P

cravate *(f.) tie* 11

crayon *(m.) pencil* P

créatif / créative *creative* 7

créature *(f.) creature* 12

crème *(f.) cream* 5, *lotion* 12; **— à
raser** *shaving cream* 12; **— solaire**
sunscreen 12

crevette *(f.) shrimp* 6

critère *(m.) criteria*

critique *(f.) review, critique* 9

critique *(m./f.) reviewer, critic* 9

croire *to believe* F

croisière *(f.) cruise* 11

croissant *(m.) croissant* 5

cubiste *cubist* 9

cueillir *to pick*

cuillère *(f.) spoon* 5; **— (de/d')** *teaspoon (of)*
5; **— à soupe (de/d')** *table / soup spoon
(of)* 5

cuir *(m.) leather* 11

cuisine *(f.) cooking* 2, *kitchen* 4; **faire la —**
to cook 2

cuisiner *to cook* 1

cuisinier *(m.) cook* 7

cuisinière *(f.) stove* 4, *cook (female)* 7

cuisse *(f.) thigh, leg*

cuit(e) *cooked* 5; **bien-—** *well-done* 5

D

danse *(f.) dance, dancing* 2; **— classique**
classical dance 2; **— moderne** *modern
dance* 2

danser *to dance* 1

danseur *(m.) dancer (male)* 9

danseuse *(f.) dancer (female)* 9

date *(f.) date* 2; **Quelle est la —
(aujourd'hui)?** *What's the date (today)?* 2

davantage *more*

de *from* P; **—... à...** *from . . . until . . .* 1

débarquer *to get off* 11; **— de l'avion** *to
get off the plane* 11

débarrasser *to clear* 6

début *(m.) beginning* 9

décédé(e) *deceased* 3

décembre *December* 2

décès *(m.) death* 8

déchet *(m.) waste* F; **—s domestiques**
domestic waste F; **—s industriels**
industrial waste F

déclarer *to declare* 11; **— vos achats** *to
declare your purchases* 11

décolonisation *(f.) decolonization* 8

découverte *(f.) discovery* F

décrire *to describe*

déforestation *(f.) deforestation* F

déjà *already* 10

déjeuner *(m.) lunch* 5; **prendre le —** *to
have lunch* 5

déjeuner *(v.) to have lunch*

déloyal(e) *disloyal* 7

deltaplane *(m.) hang-gliding* 4; **faire du
—** *to go hang-gliding, to hang-glide* 4

demain *tomorrow* P; **À —.** *See you
tomorrow.* P

demande *(f.) request*

demander *to ask* 7; **se — to wonder** 10

démarrer *to start up* F

déménager *to move*

demi(e): et — half past 1

démodé(e) *old fashioned, out-of-date* 11

dent *(f.) tooth* 12

dentifrice *(m.) toothpaste* 12

dentiste *(m./f.) dentist* 7

dépêcher: se — to hurry 10

dépenser (de l'argent) *to spend (money)* 7

déposer (de l'argent) *to deposit (money)* 7

déprimé(e) *depressed*

depuis *for, since* 2; **— combien de temps**
for how long 2; **— quand** *how long,
since when* 6

déranger *to bother, to upset* 10

derrière *behind* 4

descendre *to go down (to), get off* 6

déshabiller *to undress* 12; **se — to get
undressed** 12

désirer *to desire* 6; **Vous désirez?** *What
would you like?* 6

désolé(e) *sorry* 12

dessert *(m.) dessert* 5

dessin *(m.) drawing;* **— animé** *(animated)
cartoon / animated film* 9

dessiner *to draw, to sketch* 2

dessous *underneath* 6; **au —— (de)** *below* 6

dessus *on top* 6; **au —** (**de**) *above* 6

destiné(e) *intended*

détendre: se — *to relax, to take it easy* 10

détester *to hate* 1; **se —** *to hate oneself / each other* 10

détruire *to destroy* 11

deux *two* P; **les —** *both*

devant *in front (of)* 4

devenir *to become* 3

deviner *to guess*

devoir *to have to, must, to owe* 7

devoirs (*m. pl.*) *homework* P

dieu (*m.*) *god*

difficile *difficult* P

dimanche *Sunday* 1

dinde (*f.*) *turkey* 5

dîner (*m.*) *dinner* 5; **prendre le —** *to have dinner* 5

dîner (*v.*) *to have dinner* 1

diplôme (*m.*) *diploma* 7; **cérémonie** (*f.*) **de remise des —s** *graduation ceremony* 8

dire *to say* 2

discours (*m.*) *speech*

disputer: se — *to argue with (each other)* 10

distrait(e) *absent-minded*

distributeur automatique (*m.*) *ATM* 7

divorce (*m.*) *divorce* 8

divorcé(e) *divorced* 3

dix *ten* P; **—-huit** *eighteen* P; **—-neuf** *nineteen* P; **—-sept** *seventeen* P

doctorat (*m.*) *doctorate, Ph.D.* 7

documentaire (*m.*) *documentary* 9

doigt (*m.*) *finger* 6

dommage *too bad;* **C'est —!** *That's too bad!* 10

donc *so, in that case, therefore* 1

donner *to give* 7

dont *that, (of) which, (of) whom* 11

dormir *to sleep* 3

dos (*m.*) *back* 12

douane (*f.*) *customs* 11; **passer à la —** *to go through customs* 11

douche (*f.*) *shower* 4

doucher *to shower* 12; **se —** *to shower* 12

doué(e) *gifted* P

douter *to doubt* F

douze *twelve* P

drame (*m.*) *drama* 9; **— psychologique** *psychological drama* 9

drapeau (*m.*) *flag*

droit (*m.*) *law* 7; **faculté** (*f.*) **de —** *law school* 7

droit *straight* 4; **tout —** *straight ahead* 4

droite (*f*) *right* 4; **à — (de)** *to/on the right (of)* 4

drôle *funny, odd* 7

du *from* 3

dynamique *dynamic* P

E

eau (*f.*) *water* 5; **— minérale** *mineral water* 5

écharpe (*f.*) *scarf* 11

échecs (*m. pl.*) *chess* 2; **jouer aux —** *to play chess* 2

éclair (*m.*) *eclair* 6

école (*f.*) *school* P; **— de commerce** *business school* 7; **— professionnelle** *professional / vocational school* 7

écolo(giste) (*m./f.*) *ecologist, environmentalist* 10

écologique *ecological* F

économie (*f.*) *economy* P

économies (*f. pl.*) *savings* 7; **faire des —** *to save money* 7

économiste (*m./f.*) *economist*

écouter (**de la musique**) *to listen (to music)* 1

écran (*m.*) *computer screen* P

écrire *to write* 2; **— des lettres** *to write letters* 2; **— des textos** *to write text messages* 2

écrivain / écrivaine *writer* 8

effacer *to delete, to erase* F

effet de serre (*m.*) *greenhouse effect* F

église (*f.*) *church* 4

égoïste *selfish* 10

embarquer *to board* 11; **— dans l'avion** *to board the plane* 11

embêtant(e) *annoying* P

embrasser *to kiss;* **s'—** *to kiss each other* 10

émission (*f.*) *broadcast, TV show* 9; **— de téléachat** *shopping network show* 9; **— de téléréalité** *reality TV show* 9; **— de variétés** *variety show* 9

empereur (*m.*) *emperor* 8

empire (*m.*) *empire* 8

emploi (*m.*) *job* 7

emploi du temps (*m.*) *schedule* 1

employé(e) *employee* 7

emprunter *to borrow* 7

en *to, in* 3; *of them/it, some* 7

enchanté(e) *pleased (to meet you)* P

encore *still* 10

endormir *to put to sleep* 12; **s'—** *to fall asleep* 12

endroit (*m.*) *location, place* 4

énergie (*f.*) *energy* F; **— renouvelable** *renewable energy* F; **— solaire** (*f.*) *solar energy* F

énergique *energetic* P

énerver *to upset;* **s'—** *to get upset* 10

enfance (*f.*) *childhood* 8

enfant (*m./f.*) *child* 3

enfin *finally* 4

ennuyer *to bore;* **s'—** *to be bored* 10

ennuyeux / ennuyeuse *boring* 1

enregistrer *to record, to check;* **— les valises** (*f. pl.*) *to check in luggage* 11

enseignant(e) *instructor, teacher* 7

ensuite *next, then* 4

entendre *to hear* 6; **s'— (bien / mal avec quelqu'un)** *to get along (well / badly with someone)* 10

enterrement (*m.*) *burial, funeral* 8

entre *between* 1

entrée (*f.*) *starter, appetizer* 5

entreprise (*f.*) *company* 7

entrer *to enter* 6

entretien (*m.*) *interview*

enveloppe (*f.*) *envelope* 11

environnement (*m.*) *environment* 10

envoyer *to send* 7

épargner *to save up (in a bank account)*

épaule (*f.*) *shoulder* 12

épicé(e) *spicy* 5

épicerie (*f.*) *small grocery store* 6

épinards (*m. pl.*) *spinach* 5

époque (*f.*) *time* 8; **à cette —-là** *at that time, in those days* 8; **— contemporaine** *contemporary time* 8

épouse (*f.*) *spouse (female)* 8

époux (*m.*) *spouse (male)* 8

équipe (*f.*) *team* 2

équipé(e) *equipped* 4; **bien —** *well equipped;* **mal —** *poorly equipped*

escalier (*m.*) *staircase* 4

espace (*m.*) *space*

Espagne (*f.*) *Spain* 3

espagnol (*m.*) *Spanish (language)* P

espagnol(e) *Spanish* 3

espèce (*f.*) *species* F; **—s menacées** *endangered species* F

espérer *to hope* 6

essayer (**de**) *to try (to)* 6

essentiel(le) *essential* 12

est (*m.*) *east* 4

et *and* P

étage (*m.*) *floor* 4; **premier —** *second floor (USA)* 4

étagère (*f.*) *bookshelf* 4

étape (*f.*) *stage* 8; **— de la vie** *stage of life* 8

États-Unis (*m. pl.*) *United States* 3

été (*m.*) *summer* 2

éteindre *to close, to shut off* F

étoile (*f.*) *star* 2

étranger: à l'— *abroad, overseas* 11

être *to be* P; **— allergique à** *to be allergic to* 12; **— en avance** *to be early* 1; **— bien dans sa peau** *to have confidence in / to feel good about oneself* 10; **— en forme** *to be in shape* 12; **— à l'heure** *to be on time* 1; **— en ligne (avec)** *to be online (with)* F; **— en retard** *to be late* 1

études (*f. pl.*) *studies* P; **— supérieures** *higher education* 7

étudiant(e) *student* P

étudier *to study* P

Europe (*f.*) *Europe* 3; **— de l'Est** *Eastern Europe* 3; **— de l'Ouest** *Western Europe* 3

évidemment *evidently* 2

évident(e) *obvious* F

éviter *to avoid* 5

examen (*m.*) *exam;* **— médical** *medical exam* 12

excentrique *eccentric* 7

excuser: s'— *to be sorry, to apologize* 10

exigeant(e) *demanding* 7

exiger *to demand* 12

explorateur (*m.*) *explorer (male)* 8

exploratrice (*f.*) *explorer (female)* 8

exposition (*f.*) *exhibition* 9

express: envoyer quelque chose en — *to send something express mail* 11
exprimer *to express* 10
extérieur (*m.*) *outside*
extraverti(e) (*adj.*) *extroverted* 7
extraverti(e) (*n.*) *extrovert* 7

F

face: en — (**de**) *across (from)* 4
fâcher: se — *to get angry* 10
facile *easy* P
facteur (*m.*) *mail carrier (male)* 11
factrice (*f.*) *mail carrier (female)* 11
faculté (*f.*) *school, college* 7; **— de droit** *law school* 7; **— de lettres et de sciences humaines** *liberal arts college* 7; **— de médecine** *medical school* 7; **— de sciences et de technologie** *science and technology college* 7
faim (*f.*) *hunger* F; **avoir —** *to be hungry* 5
faire *to do, to make* 2; **Ça fait … euros.** *That makes (It costs) . . . euros.* 6;**— du…** *to be a size . . .* 11; **— de l'aérobic** *to do aerobics* 2; **— attention (à)** *to pay attention (to)* 5; **— un barbecue** *to have a BBQ* 2; **— du bateau (à voile)** / **— du voilier** *to go (sail)boating* 4; **— du bowling** *to go bowling* 2; **— du bricolage** *to tinker, to do odd jobs, to act the handyman/woman* 6; **— du camping** *to go camping* 2; **— du cheval** *to go horseback riding* 2; **— du compost** *to compost* F; **— des courses** *to run some errands* 2; **— la cuisine** *to cook* 2; **— de la danse classique** *to do classical dance* 2; **— de la danse moderne** *to do modern dance* 2; **— … degrés** *to be . . . degrees* 2; **— la fête** *to party* 2; **— la grasse matinée** *to sleep in* 2; **— de la gym** *to work out, to exercise* 2; **— du jogging** *to go jogging* 2; **— du lèche-vitrine** *to window-shop* 2; **— la lessive** *to do the laundry* 4; **— de la marche** *to walk (for exercise)* 2; **— le ménage** *to do the housework* 4; **— de la natation** *to swim (for exercise)* 2; **— du patinage** *to ice skate, to go iceskating* 2; **— de la photo(graphie)** *to practice photography* 2; **— un pique-nique** *to (have / go on a) picnic* 2; **— plaisir à quelqu'un** *to please someone* 10; **— de la planche à voile** *to go wind-surfing* 2; **— la poussière** *to dust* 4; **— une promenade** *to take a walk (in town)* 2; **— de la randonnée** *to go hiking, to hike* 4; **— de la sculpture** *to sculpt* 9; **— du shopping** *to shop, to go shopping* 2; **— la sieste** *to take a nap* 2; **— du ski (alpin)** *to go*

(*downhill) skiing* 2; **— du ski de fond** *to go cross-country skiing* 2; **— du ski nautique** *to water-ski* 2; **— du sport** *to work out, to exercise* 2; **— du surf** *to surf* 2; **— la vaisselle** *to do the dishes* 4; **— les valises** *to pack* 11; **— du vélo** *to go bike riding* 2; **— un voyage** *to take a trip* 2; **— du yoga** *to do yoga* 2;
falloir *to be necessary* 12
famille (*f.*) *family* 3; **— élargie** *extended family* 3; **— proche** *immediate family* 3
fana (*m./f.*) *fan, nut* 10; **— de la santé** *health nut* 10
farce (*f.*) *prank*
farfelu(e) *scatter-brained* 7
farine (*f.*) *flour* 5
fascinant(e) *fascinating* P
fast-food (*m.*) *fast food* 5
fatigué(e) *tired* 12
fauteuil (*m.*) *armchair* 4
fée (*f.*) *fairy* 9; **conte** (*m.*) **de —s** *fairy tale* 9
félicitations (*f. pl.*) *congratulations* 8
femme (*f.*) *woman* P, *wife* 3; **— d'affaires** *businesswoman* 7; **— auteur** *author* 9; **— compositeur** *composer* 9; **— au foyer** *housewife* 10; **— ingénieur** *engineer* 7; **— médecin** *doctor* 7; **— plombier** *plumber* 7; **— poète** *poet* 8; **— politique** *politician* 8; **— pompier** *firefighter* 7; **— soldat** *soldier* 8
fenêtre (*f.*) *window* P
férié: jour (*m.*) **—** *holiday (legal)* 8
ferme (*f.*) *farm* 4
fermer *to close, to shut off* F
fête (*f.*) *party* 2, *holiday, celebration* 8; **faire la —** *to party* 2; **— des Mères** *Mother's Day* 8; **— nationale** *National Holiday* 8; **— des Pères** *Father's Day* 8; **— du Travail** *Labor Day* 8
fêter *to celebrate* 8
feu (*f.*) *fire;* **—x d'artifices** *fireworks*
feuille (*f.*) *sheet (paper)* P; **— de papier** *sheet of paper* P
feuilleton (*m.*) *soap opera* 9
février *February* 2
fiançailles (*f. pl.*) *engagement* 8
fiancer: se — *to get engaged to (each other)* 10
fibres (*f. pl.*) *fibers* 5
fichier (*m.*) *file* F
fidèle *loyal* 10
fidélité (*f.*) *loyalty* 10
fier / fière *proud* 1
fièvre (*f.*) *fever* 12

figure (*f.*) *face* 12
fille (*f.*) *girl* P, *daughter* 3
film (*m.*) *film, movie* 9; **— d'action** *action film* 9; **— d'animation** (*animated) cartoon / animated film* 9; **— d'horreur** *horror film* 9; **— romantique** *romance film* 9; **— de science-fiction** *sci-fi film* 9; **— à suspense** *suspense film* 9
fils (*m.*) *son* 3
fin (*f.*) *end, ending* 9
finir *to finish* 4
fleur (*f.*) *flower* 4
fleuve (*m.*) *river* 4
flexible *flexible* 7
fois (*f.*) *time;* **d'autres —** *other times* 10; **une —** *once* 8
fonder *to found* 8
football / foot (*m.*) *soccer* 2; **— américain** *football* 2
forêt (*f.*) *forest* 4
forme: être en — *to be in shape* 12
formidable *great, awesome* 10
foulard (*m.*) *silk scarf* 11
four (*m.*) *oven* 4; **au —** *baked* 5; **— (à) micro-ondes** *microwave* 4
fourchette (*f.*) *fork* 6
foyer (*m.*) *household;* **femme** (*f.*) **au —** *housewife* 10; **homme** (*m.*) **au —** *househusband* 10
frais (*m. pl.*) *fees* 11; **— de scolarité** *tuition* 7
frais / fraîche *cool (weather)* 2, *fresh, cool* 5
fraise (*f.*) *strawberry* 5
framboise (*f.*) *raspberry* 5
français (*m.*) *French (language)* P
français(e) *French* 3
France (*f.*) *France* 3
franquette: dîner (*m.*) **à la bonne —** *potluck*
fréquence (*f.*) *frequency*
frère (*m.*) *brother* 3
frigo (*m.*) *refrigerator / fridge* 4
frisé(e) *curly* 3
frit(e) *fried* 5
frites (*f. pl.*) *fries* 5
froid(e) *cold* 2; **avoir froid** *to be cold* 5
fromage (*m.*) *cheese* 5
fruit (*m.*) *fruit* 5; **—s de mer** *shellfish* 5
fumer *to smoke* 5
furieux / furieuse *furious* 12

G

gagner *to win, to earn* 7; **— de l'argent** *to earn money* 7; **— sa vie** *to earn a living* 7
galerie (*f.*) *gallery* 9; **— d'art** *art gallery* 9
gants (*m. pl.*) *gloves* 11
garage (*m.*) *garage* 4
garçon (*m.*) *boy* P
garderie (*f.*) *daycare center*
gare (*f.*) *(bus / train) station* 11
gaspiller *to waste* F

gâté(e) *spoiled*

gâteau *(m.) cake* 5

gauche *(f.) left* 4; **à — (de)** *to/on the left (of)* 4

général *(m.) general* 8

génial(e) *great / awesome* 10

génie *(m.) engineering* P; **— civil** *civil engineering* P; **— électrique** *electrical engineering* P; **— mécanique** *mechanical engineering* P

genou *(m.) knee* 12

genre *(m.) genre* 9

gens *(m. pl.) people* 1

gentil / gentille *nice* 1

gentiment *nicely* 2

gérant(e) *manager* 7

gérer *to manage*

gestion *(f.) business administration* P

gilet *(m.) cardigan sweater* 11

gîte du passant *(m.) bed and breakfast* 11

glace *(f.) ice cream* 5

glucides *(m. pl.) carbohydrates* 5

golf *(m.) golf* 2

gorge *(f.) throat* 12

goût *(m.) taste* 6; **avoir le — du travail** *to have good work ethic* 7; **C'est à votre —?** *Is it to your liking / taste?* 6

goûter *(m.) snack* 5

goûter *(v.) to snack, to taste* 6

gracieux / gracieuse *graceful, gracious* 10

grand(e) *big, tall* 3

grand-chose: Pas —. *Not much.* P

grandeur *(f.) greatness* 8

grandir *to grow up* 4

grand-mère *(f.) grandmother* 3

grand-père *(m.) grandfather* 3

grands-parents *(m. pl.) grandparents* 3

gras: en — *boldface*

gratter *to itch, to scratch* 12; **se — to scratch (oneself)** 12

grave *serious* 12

grenouille *(f.) frog* 12

grille *(f.) grid*

grillé(e) *grilled* 5

grippe *(f.) flu* 12

gris(e) *gray, dreary (weather)* 2

gros / grosse *fat* 3

grossir *to gain weight* 4

guerre *(f.) war* 8; **— mondiale** *world war*

H

habillé(e) *dressed* 10; **bien — well-dressed** 10; **mal — poorly-dressed** 10

habiller *to dress* 12; **s' — to get dressed** 12

habiter *to live (in a place), to reside* 1

habitude *(f.) habit;* **d' — usually** 8

hamburger *(m.) hamburger* 5

hamster *(m.) hamster* 12

Hanoukka *(f.) Hanukah* 8

haricot vert *(m.) green bean* 5

hebdomadaire *(m.) weekly (magazine, newspaper) publication* 10

héroïne *(f.) heroine* 8

héros *(m.) hero* 8

heure *(f.) hour, time* 1; **À quelle —... ?** *At what time . . . ?* 1; **Il est deux —s.** *It's two o'clock.* 1; **Il est une —.** *It's one o'clock.* 1

heureux / heureuse *happy* 1

hier *yesterday* 1; **— soir** *last night* 5

hip-hop *(m.) hip-hop* 9

hippy *(m./f.) (pl. hippies) hippy* 10

histoire *(f.) history, story* 9

hiver *(m.) winter* 2

hockey *(m.) hockey* 2

homard *(m.) lobster* 6

homme *(m.) man* P; **— d'affaires** *businessman* 7; **— au foyer** *househusband* 10; **— politique** *politician (male)* 8

hôpital *(m.) hospital* 4

horloge *(f.) clock* P

hors-d'œuvre *(m.) starter / appetizer* 5

hôte *(m.) host* 8

hôtel *(m.) hotel* 1; **— de luxe** *luxury hotel, resort* 11; **— trois / quatre / cinq étoiles** *three / four / five star hotel* 11

huile *(f.) oil* 5; **— d'olive** *olive oil* 5

huit *eight* P

humains *(m. pl.) humans* 12

humeur *(f.) mood* 7; **être de bonne — to be in a good mood** 7; **être de mauvaise — to be in a bad mood** 7

hybride *(m.) hybrid animal or plant* F

hygiène *(f.) hygiene* 12

hypermarché *(m.) hypermarket* 6

I

identité *(f.) identity* 11; **pièce** *(f.)* **d' — form of identification** 11

impatient(e) *impatient* P

impératrice *(f.) empress* 8

imperméable *(m.) raincoat* 11

important(e) *important* P

impressionniste *impressionist* 9

imprimante *(f.) printer* F

imprimer *to print* F

indépendance *(f.) independence* 8

indépendant(e) *independent* P

indiscret / indiscrète *indiscreet* 10

indispensable *indispensable* F

infidèle *disloyal* 10

infidélité *(f.) disloyalty* 10

infirmier *(m.) nurse (male)* 7

infirmière *(f.) nurse (female)* 7

inflexible *inflexible* 7

info(rmation)s *(f. pl.) news broadcast* 9

informaticien(ne) *computer specialist* 7

informatique *(f.) computer science* P

ingénieur *(m.) engineer* 7; **femme** *(f.)* **— engineer (female)** 7

ingrédient *(m.) ingredient* 5

inquiéter *to worry;* **s' — (de)** *to worry (about)* 10

installer: s' — dans / à *to move into, to settle into* 10

instant *(m.) instant;* **à l' — a few moments ago**

institut: — (m.) de beauté *spa, beauty parlor* 4

intellectuel / intellectuelle *intellectual* 1

intelligent(e) *intelligent* P

interdire *to forbid* F

intéressant(e) *interesting* P

intéresser: s' — (à) *to be interested (in)* 10

intervention chirurgicale *(f.) surgery* 12

introverti(e) *(adj.) introverted* 7

introverti(e) *(n.) introvert* 7

intrus(e) *one that does not belong*

inutile *not useful, useless* P

invention *(f.) invention* F

invité(e) *guest* 8

inviter *to invite* 1

iPod® *(m.) iPod®* P

irlandais(e) *Irish* 3

Irlande *(f.) Ireland* 3

Italie *(f.) Italy* 3

italien / italienne *Italian* 3

ivoirien / ivoirienne *of the Ivory Coast* 3

J

jaloux / jalouse *jealous* 7

jambe *(f.) leg* 12

jambon *(m.) ham* 5

janvier *January* 2

Japon *(m.) Japan* 3

japonais(e) *Japanese* 3

jardin *(m.) garden, lawn* 4

jardinage *(m.) gardening* 2; **faire du — to garden** 2

jaune *yellow* 3

jazz *(m.) jazz* 9

jean *(m.) jeans* 11

jeter *to throw (out)* F

jeu *(m.) game* 2; **—x de société** *board games* 2; **jouer aux —x de société** *to play board games* 2; **— télévisé** *game show* 9

jeudi *Thursday* 1

jeune *young* 3

jeunesse *(f.) youth* 8

jogging *(m.) jogging* 2, *sweatpants* 11

joli(e) *pretty* 3

jouer *to play* 1; **— de la batterie** *to play the drums* 2; **— aux cartes** *(f. pl.) to play cards* 2; **— de la guitare** *to play the guitar* 2; **— aux jeux de société** *(m. pl.) to play board games* 2; **— de la musique** *to play, to listen to music* 2; **— du piano** *to play the piano* 2; **— du violon** *to play violin* 2; **— du violoncelle** *to play cello* 2

joueur *(m.) player (male)* 2

joueuse *(f.) player (female)* 2

jour *(m.) day* 8; **— de l'Action de Grâce** *Thanksgiving* 8; **— de l'An** *New Year's Day* 8; **— férié** *legal holiday* 8

journal *(m.) newspaper* 2; **— intime** *diary* 10

journalisme *(m.) journalism* P

journaliste *(m./f.) journalist* 7

VOCABULAIRE français-anglais

journée (f.) day
juillet July 2
juin June 2
jupe (f.) skirt 11; **mini-—** (mini) skirt 11
jus (m.) juice 5; **— d'orange** orange juice 5
jusque until 4
juste / injuste fair / unfair F

K

karaoké (m.) karaoke 2; **faire du —** to do karaoke 2
kilo (de/d') (m.) kilogram (of) 5
kiosque: — (m.) **à journaux** newsstand 4
kleenex (m.) tissue 12

L

laboratoire (m.) laboratory 4
lac (m.) lake 4
laïc / laïque secular
laid(e) ugly 3
laisser to leave 6; **— un pourboire** to leave a tip 6
lait (m.) milk 5; **— de soja** soy milk 5
laitue (f.) lettuce 6
lampe (f.) lamp 4
langue (f.) language P, tongue 12
lapin (m.) rabbit 12
laquelle which (f. sing.) 11
lavabo (m.) bathroom sink 4
laver to wash 12; **se —** to wash (oneself) 12
laverie automatique (f.) laundromat 4
lèche-vitrine (m.) window-shopping 2; **faire du —** to window-shop 2
lecteur (m.) player (audiovisual equipment) 4; **— de cédéroms** CD-ROM drive F
légume (m.) vegetable 5
lentement slowly 2
lentilles (f. pl.) lentils 5
lequel which (m. sing.) 11
lesquelles which (f. pl.) 11
lesquels which (m. pl.) 11
lessive (f.) laundry 4; **faire la —** to do the laundry 4
lettres (f. pl.) liberal arts 7; **faculté** (f.) de **— et de sciences humaines** liberal arts college 7
leur their 3, them 7
lever to lift, to raise; **se —** to get up 12
liberté (f.) freedom 8
librairie (f.) bookstore 4
licence (f.) bachelor's degree (equivalent of) 7
lieu (m.) setting
lion (m.) lion 12
liquide (m.) cash 7; **payer en —** to pay cash 7
lire to read 2; **— les courriels** to read e-mail 2; **— le journal** to read the newspaper 2; **— un roman** to read a novel 2
lit (m.) bed 4; **— simple / double** single / double bed 11
littéraire literary 9

littérature (f.) literature P
livre (de/d') (f.) pound (of) 5
livre (m.) book P
livrer to deliver 11
location (f.) rental
logement (m.) lodging
logiciel (m.) software, program F
loi (f.) law 4
loin (de) far (from) 4
loisir (m.) leisure activity 2
long / longue long 3
lotion (f.) lotion 12
louer to rent 4
lourd(e) heavy, hot (weather), muggy (weather) 2
loyal(e) loyal, faithful 7
loyer (m.) rent 4
lui him, her 7
lundi Monday 1
lune (f.) moon 2
lunettes de soleil (f. pl.) sunglasses 11
lycée (m.) high school 4

M

ma my 3
madame (Mme) Ma'am, Mrs. P
madeleine (f.) madeleine cake 6
mademoiselle (Mlle) Miss P
magasin (m.) store 6; **— (de produits) bio** (m.) health / organic food store 6
magazine (m.): **— de mode** fashion magazine 10
mai May 2
maigrir to lose weight 4
maillot (de bain) (m.) swimsuit 11
main (f.) hand 12
maire (m.) mayor
maïs (m.) corn 6
mais but 1
maison (f.) house, home 4
mal badly 2, bad 7; **le plus —** the worst 7
malade sick 12; **tomber —** to get sick 12
maladie (f.) illness 12
maladroit(e) clumsy 10
malheureux / malheureuse unhappy 1
mallette (f.) briefcase 11
manger to eat 1
mangue (f.) mango 6
manteau (m.) overcoat 11
manuel (m.) textbook
maquillage (m.) makeup 12
maquiller to put on make-up (on someone) 12; **se —** to put on make-up 12
marché (en plein air) (m.) (open air) market 6
marche (f.) walking 2
marché: bon — inexpensive 11
marcher to walk 1
mardi Tuesday 1; **— gras** Mardi Gras 8
marelle (f.) hopscotch
mari (m.) husband 3
mariage (m.) marriage 8; **anniversaire** (m.) **de —** wedding anniversary 8
marié(e) married 3; **nouveaux mariés** (m. pl.) newly weds 8

marier: se — to marry (each other) 10
Maroc (m.) Morocco 3
marocain(e) Moroccan 3
marquant(e) memorable, important 8
marque (m.) brand
marron brown 3
mars March 2
master (m.) master's degree 7
match (m.) game, match 2; **— télévisé** televised game 9
mathématiques (f. pl.) mathematics P
matières grasses (f. pl.) fats 5
matin (m.) morning 1; **du —** in the morning 1; **être du —** to be a morning person 7
mauvais(e) bad 2; **le/la/les plus —(s)** the worst 7
mayonnaise (f.) mayonnaise 5
MBA (m.) MBA 7
me me 7
méchant(e) mean P
médecin (m.) doctor 7; **femme** (f.) **—** doctor (female) 7
médecine (f.) medicine; **faculté** (f.) **de —** medical school 7
médicament (m.) medication 12
méfier: se — (de) to be suspicious (of) 10
meilleur(e) best P, better 7
melon (m.) cantelope 6
membre (m./f.) member 10; **— de la jet-set** jet setter 10
même same 11; **le/la/les —s** the same 11
ménage (m.) housework 4; **faire le —** to do the housework 4
mensonge (m.) lie
mensuel (m.) monthly publication 10
menu (m.) menu 6
mer (f.) sea 4
merci thank you P
mercredi Wednesday 1
mère (f.) mother 3; **— active** working mom 10; **— célibataire** single mother 10
mériter to deserve
merveilleux / merveilleuse wonderful, marvelous, super F
mes my 3
message (m.) message 10
messagerie (m.) messaging 10
météo (f.) weather forecast 2
métro (m.) subway 11
mettre to place, to put, to set 6; **— la table** to set the table 6; **se — (à)** to begin (to) 10
meuble (m.) piece of furniture 4
mexicain(e) Mexican 3
Mexique (m.) Mexico 3
microblogging (m.) Twitter-like messages 10
micro-ondes (m.) microwave 4
midi (m.) noon 1
mieux better 7
milieu (m.) middle 6; **au — (de)** in the middle (of) 6
mille one thousand 4

milliard (m.) one billion 4
million (m.) one million 4
mince slim, lean, slender 3
ministre (m.) minister 8; **premier — ** prime minister 8
minuit (m.) midnight 1
miroir (m.) mirror 4
mode (f.) fashion; **à la —** stylish, fashionable 11
moderne modern P
modeste modest P
moi me P; **Pour —..., s'il vous plaît.** For me... please. 6
moins less, fewer 7; **— (de)... que** less, fewer... than 7; **le/la/les —** the least 7
mois (m.) month 2; **— dernier / passé** last month 5
mon my 3
monarchie (f.) monarchy 8
monsieur (M.) Sir, Mr. P.
montagne (f.) mountain 4
monter to go up, to climb, to get on 6
montre (f.) watch 11
montrer to show 7
moralité (f.) morality 10
mot (m.) word; **— de passe** password F
motel (m.) motel 11
moto (f.) motorcycle 11
moule (f.) mussel 6
mourir to die 6
moustaches (f. pl.) whiskers 12
moutarde (f.) mustard 5
mouvement (m.) movement 8
moyen de transport (m.) means of transportation 11
musclé(e) muscular 3
musée (m.) museum 4
musicien(ne) (n. & adj.) musician 7
musique (f.) music P; **— alternative** alternative 9; **— classique** classical 9; **— country** country 9; **— folk** folk 9; **—s du monde** world music 9; **— new age** new age music 9

N

naïf / naïve naive 1
nain(e) dwarf
naissance (f.) birth 8
naître to be born 6
natation (f.) swimming 2
nationalisme (m.) nationalism 8
nature (f.) nature; **— morte** still life 9
navette spatiale (f.) space shuttle F
naviguer: — sur Internet to surf the Internet 1
ne not P; **—... aucun(e)** none, not any 10; **—... jamais** never 1; **—... ni... ni** neither... nor 10; **—... pas du tout** not at all 10; **—... pas encore** not yet 10; **—... personne** nobody, no one 10; **—... plus** no longer, no more 10; **—... que** only 10; **—... rien** nothing, not anything 10
nécessaire necessary P

neige (f.) snow 2; **bonhomme** (m.) **de —** snowman
neiger to snow 2
neuf / neuve new P; **Quoi de neuf?** What's new? P
neuf nine P
neuvième ninth 8
neveu (m.) nephew 3
nez (m.) nose 3
nièce (f.) niece 3
noblesse (f.) nobility
Noël (m.) Christmas 8
noir(e) black 3
noix (f. pl.) walnuts 5
nom (m.) name P; **— de famille** last name P; **Mon — (de famille) est...** My (last) name is... P; **Quel est ton — (de famille)?** What is your (last) name? P
nord (m.) north 4
normal(e) normal F
nos our 3
notre our 3
nourriture (f.) food 5
nous us 7
nouveau / nouvel / nouvelle new 3
nouveaux mariés (m. pl.) newly weds 8
nouvel (m. before a vowel sound) new 3
nouvelle (f.) new 3
nouvelles (f. pl.) news, news items 9
novembre November 2
nuage (m.) cloud 2
nuit (f.) night 1

O

obéir (à) to obey 4
objet (m.) object 4
occuper: s'— (de) to take care of 10
octobre October 2
œuf (m.) egg 5
œil (m.) (pl. **yeux**) eye 3
œuvre (f.) work, masterpiece; **— d'art** work of art 9
oignon (m.) onion 5
oiseau (m.) bird 12
omelette (f.) omelet 5
oncle (m.) uncle 3
ondulé(e) wavy 3
onze eleven P
opéra (m.) opera 9
optimiste optimistic P
orage (m.) storm 2
orange (f.) orange 3; **jus d'— **(m.) orange juice 5
orchestre (m.) orchestra 9
ordinateur (m.) computer P; **— portable** laptop computer P;
ordonnance (f.) prescription 12
oreille (f.) ear 12
organisé(e) organized 7
organiser to organize, to throw (party) 8
organisme (m.) organism; **—s génétiquement modifiés (OGM)** genetically modified foods F
orgueilleux / orgueilleuse (very) proud 10

os (m.) bone
où where 4, when 11
ouest (m.) west 4
ouragan (m.) hurricane 2
ours (m.) bear 12
ouvrier (m.) worker (factory) (male) 7
ouvrière (f.) worker (factory) (female) 7

P

pacifique peaceful 8
pain (m.) bread 5; **— de campagne** country-style bread 6; **— au chocolat** croissant-type pastry filled with chocolate 6; **— complet** whole grain bread 5; **— de mie** loaf of sliced bread 6
paix (f.) peace 8
pamplemousse (m.) grapefruit 6
panier (m.) basket 6
pansement (m.) bandage 12
pantalon (m.) slacks 11; **— à pattes d'éléphant** bell bottom pants 11
papier (m.) paper P; **feuille** (f.) **de —** sheet of paper P
Pâques (m. pl.) Easter 8
parc (m.) park 1
parce que because 4
parents (m. pl.) parents, relatives 3
paresseux / paresseuse lazy 1
parfois sometimes, at times 1
parking (m.) parking lot 4
parler to speak, to talk 1; **se — ** to talk to oneself / each other 10
partager to share 4
partenaire (m./f.) significant other, (domestic) partner 3
partir to leave 3
pas not 1; **— du tout** not at all 1
passeport (m.) passport 11
passer to pass, to take 1; to spend; **— un examen** to take an exam 1; **— par** to pass by, to go by 6; **se —** to happen 10
passe-temps (m.) pastime, hobby 2
pastèque (f.) watermelon 6
pâtes (f. pl.) pasta 5
patiemment patiently 2
patient(e) (adj. & n.) patient P, 12
patinage (m.) iceskating 2
pâtisserie (f.) pastry shop, pastry 6
patron(ne) boss 7
patte (f.) paw 12
pauvreté (f.) poverty F
payer to pay 6; **— chacun sa part** to pay, to go Dutch 6; **— par carte de crédit** with a credit card 6; **— par chèque** to pay by check 7; **— en liquide** to pay cash 6
pays (m.) country 3
paysage (m.) landscape 9
peau (f.) skin; **être bien dans sa —** to have confidence in / to feel good about oneself 10
pêche (f.) fishing 4, peach 6; **aller à la —** to go fishing 4
peigne (m.) comb 12

peintre *(m./f.) painter* 9

peinture *(f.) paint* 2, *painting* 9; **faire de la —** *to paint* 2

peluche: animal *(m.)* **en —** *stuffed animal*

pendant *during, throughout* 1, *for* 6

pensée *(f.) thought* 10

penser *to think* 1

perdre *to lose* 6; **se —** *to get lost* 10

père *(m.) father* 3; **— actif** *working dad* 10; **— célibataire** *single father* 10

périmé(e) *spoiled*

permis *(m.) permit, license* 11; **— de conduire** *driver's license* 11

personnage *(m.) character* 9

personne *(f.) person* 1

pessimiste *pessimistic* P

petit déjeuner *(m.) breakfast* 5

petit(e) *small, short* 3

petite-fille *(f.) granddaughter* 3

petit-fils *(m.) grandson* 3

petits pois *(m. pl.) peas* 5

peu *little* 1; **un —** *a little* 1

peut-être *perhaps* 1

pharmacie *(f.) pharmacy* 4

philosophie *(f.) philosophy* P

photo(graphie) *(f.) photo(graph), photography* 2; **faire de la —** *to practice photography* 2

photographe *(m./f.) photographer* 9

photographier *to photograph* 9

physique *(f.) physics* P

pièce *(f.) room* 4, *piece, play* 9; **— de monnaie** *(f.) coin* 7; **— de théâtre** *play (theater)*

pied *(m.) foot* 12; **à —** *on foot* 11

pierre *(f.) stone*

piquant(e) *hot* 5

pique-nique *(m.) picnic* 2; **faire un —** *to (have/go on a) picnic* 2

piqûre *(f.) shot* 12; **faire une —** *to give a shot* 12

pire *worse* 7; **le/la/les —(s)** *the worst* 7

piscine (municipale) *(f.) (public) swimming pool* 4

pizza *(f.) pizza* 5

placard *(m.) closet* 4

plage *(f.) beach* 4

plaisir *(m.) pleasure* 2

plan *(m.) map (of a city)* 4

planche à voile *(f.) windsurfing board* 2

plante *(f.) plant* 4

plat *(m.) course (meals)* 5; **— principal** *main course, dish (kind of food)* 5

pleurer *to cry* 10

pleuvoir *to rain* 2

plombier *(m.) plumber* 7; **femme** *(f.)* **— plumber** *(female)* 7

plongée sous-marine *(f.) scuba diving* 2

pluie *(f.) rain* 2

plupart *(f.) most;* **la — du temps** *most of the time* 10

plus *plus, more* 7; **— (de)… que** *more . . . than* 7; **le/la/les —** *the most* 7

plusieurs *several* 11

poésie *(f.) poetry* 2

poète *(m.) poet (male)* 8; **femme** *(f.)* **— poet (female)** 8

poétique *poetic* 9

poids *(m.) weight*

poils *(m. pl.) animal hair, fur* 12

point *(m.) period, point* 4; **— de suture** *stitch, suture* 12; **à — medium (cooking)** 5

pointure *(f.) shoe size* 11; **Quelle est votre —?** *What is your shoe size?* 11

poire *(f.) pear* 6

poisson *(m.) fish* 5; **— d'avril** *April Fools' Day* 8

poissonnerie *(f.) fish and seafood shop* 6

poitrine *(f.) chest* 12

poivre *(m.) pepper* 5

poivron *(m.) pepper (bell)* 5; **— rouge / vert** *red / green pepper* 5

policier *(m.) crime / detective film* 9

poliment *politely* 2

politique *(f.) politics;* **homme** *(m.)* **— politician (male)** 8; **femme** *(f.)* **— politician (female)** 8

polluer *to pollute* F

pollution *(f.) pollution* F

pomme *(f.) apple* 5; **— de terre** *(f.) potato* 5

pompier *(m.) firefighter* 7; **femme** *(f.)* **— firefighter (female)** 7

pop *(f.) pop* 9

portable *(m.) cell phone, laptop computer* P; **ordinateur —** *(m.) laptop computer* P; **téléphone —** *(m.) cell phone* P

porte *(f.) door* P; **— d'embarquement** *departure gate* 11

porter *to wear* 11

portion *(f.) portion* 5

portrait *(m.) portrait* 9

poser: — des questions (à) *to ask questions* 4

poste *(f.) post office* 11

poste *(m.) position* 7

potin *(m.) piece of gossip* 10; **—s** *(m. pl.) gossip* 10

potiron *(m.) pumpkin* 6

poubelle *(f.) waste basket* P, *garbage, trash* 4; **sortir la —** *to take out the garbage, trash* 4

poulet *(m.) chicken* 5

pour *for* 2

pourboire *(m.) tip* 6; **laisser un —** *to leave a tip* 6

pourquoi *why* 4

poussière *(f.) dust* 4; **faire la —** *to dust* 4

pouvoir *to be able, can* 7

prairie *(f.) meadow, grassland, prairie* 4

pratique *practical* P

pratiquer *to practice, to do, to play (a sport)* 1; **— un sport** *to play sports* 1

précis(e) *precise, good with details* 7

préférable *preferable* 12

préférer *to prefer* 6

premier / première *first* 8

prendre *to take, to have* 5; **— le déjeuner / le dîner** *to have lunch / dinner* 5; **— son temps** *to take one's time* 5; **— un verre** *to have a drink* 5

prénom *(m.) first name* P

préoccupation *(f.) concern* F; **— sociale** *social concern* F

préparer *to prepare* 12; **se —** *to get ready* 12

près *near* 4

présenter *to introduce* P

préservation *(f.) preservation, protection* F

préserver *to preserve* F

président *(m.) president* 8

prestige *(m.) prestige* 10

prêt *(m.) loan* 7; **— étudiant** *student loan* 7

prêt(e) *ready*

prétentieux / prétentieuse *pretentious* 10

prêter (à) *to lend* 7

printemps *(m.) spring* 2

prise de sang *(f.) bloodwork* 12; **faire une —** *to take one's blood* 12

prix *(m.) price* 6

problème *(m.) problem* F

produit *(m.) product* 5; **— laitier** *dairy product* 5; **— de soin personnel** *personal care product* 12

professeur *(m.) professor, teacher* P

profession *(f.) profession* 7

professionnel(le) *professional* 7; **école** *(f.)* **professionnelle** *professional / vocational school* 7

promenade *(f.) walk* 2; **faire une — (en ville)** *to take a walk (in town)* 2

promener *to walk;* **se —** *to take a walk, to stroll* 10

propre *clean* 4

propreté *(f.) cleanliness*

protéger *to protect* F

protéines *(f. pl.) proteins* 5

protester *to protest* F

psychologie *(f.) psychology* P

psychologue *(m./f.) psychologist* 7

pub(licité) *(f.) commercial* 9

public / publique *public* 4

publier *to publish* 9

puis *next, then* 4

pull(-over) *(m.) (pullover) sweater* 11; **— à col roulé** *turtle neck sweater* 11

pyjama *(m.) pyjama* 11

Q

quand *when* 4

quarante *forty* P

quart: et — *a quarter past* 1; **moins le — a quarter to** 1

quartier *(m.) neighborhood* 4

quatorze *fourteen* P

quatre *four* P; **—-vingts** *eighty* 1; **—-vingt-dix** *ninety* 1

quatre-quatre (4 × 4) *(m.) SUV* 11

quatrième *fourth* 8

que *what* 1, *that, which* 11; **qu'est-ce — what** 1

Québec (m.) Quebec 3
québécois(e) from Quebec 3
quel(le) what, which 1; **Quelle heure est-il?** What time is it? 1; **Quel jour sommes-nous?** What day is it? 1
quelqu'un someone 7; — **de/d'** (+ adjective) someone (+ adjective) 7
quelque chose something; — **de/d'** (+ adjective) something (+ adjective) 5
quelquefois sometimes, at times 1
quelques some 11
quelques-uns / quelques-unes some, a few 11
queue (f.) tail 12
qui who(m) 4, that, which 11
quinze fifteen P
quitter to leave (a place / a person) 6; **se** — to leave each other 10
quoi (informal) what 4
quotidien (m.) daily publication 10

R

R'n'B (m.) blues, R&B 9
raconter to tell (about), to narrate 10
radiographie (f.) X-ray 12
radis (m.) radish 6
raide straight 3
raisin (m.) grapes 5
raisonnable sensible
randonnée (f.) hiking, hike 4; **faire de la** — to go hiking, to hike 4
ranger to pick up (the house), to put things away 4
rap (m.) rap 9
rapidement fast, quickly, hurry! 2
rappeler to call back 10; **se** — to remember 10
rarement rarely 1
raser to shave 12; **se** — to shave (one's face, legs, etc.) 12
rasoir (m.) razor 12
rat (m.) rat 12
rater to miss, to fail 1; — **un examen** to fail an exam 1
ravi(e) pleased P; — **de faire ta connaissance.** (sing., informal) Pleased to meet you. P; — **de faire votre connaissance.** (pl. / sing., formal) Pleased to meet you. P
rayon (m.) aisle, counter 6; — **audiovisuel** audio visual equipment aisle 6; — **boucherie** meat counter 6; — **boulangerie-pâtisserie** bakery-pastry aisle 6; — **charcuterie** deli aisle 6; — **poissons et fruits de mer** fish and seafood aisle 6; — **surgelés** frozen food aisle 6
réalisateur (m.) director (TV or movie) (male) 9
réalisatrice (f.) director (TV or movie) (female) 9
réalité (f.) reality; — **virtuelle** virtual reality F
récent(e) recent P
réception (f.) reception 8

recette (f.) recipe 5
recevoir to receive 9
réchauffement climatique (m.) global warming F
recherche (f.) research
réconcilier: se — to make up with each other 10
recruter to recruit
recyclage (m.) recycling F
recycler to recycle F
rédacteur (m.) writer (male)
rédactrice (f.) writer (female)
réfléchir (à) to reflect (upon), to consider 4
réforme (f.) reform 8
réfrigérateur (m.) refrigerator, fridge 4
refuge (m.) shelter (animal) 12
regarder to look; **se** — to look at oneself / each other 10
regarder to watch 1
régime (m.) diet 5; **être au** — to be on a diet 5
registre (m.) registry
règle (f.) rule 4
règlement (m.) agreements, rules 4
regretter to regret, to be sorry about 10
reine (f.) queen 8
rejoindre to join
relation (f.) relationship 8
rembourser to pay back 7
remède (m.) remedy
rencontrer to meet; **se** — to meet each other 10
rendez-vous (m.) date, appointment 8
rendre to give back, to return 6; — **quelqu'un (heureux)** to make someone (happy) 10; **se** — **compte (de / que)** to realize 10; — **visite à** to visit (someone) 6
rentrer to return, to go home 6
repas (m.) meal 5
répéter to repeat 6
répétition (f.) rehearsal; **salle** (f.) **de** — rehearsal room
réplique (f.) line (of a dialogue)
répondre (à) to answer 6
reposer: se — to rest 10
réputé(e) known
requin (m.) shark 12
réseau (m.) network F; — **social** social network 10
réservation (f.) reservation 6
réserver to reserve 6
résidence (f.) residence 4; — **universitaire** university / college residence hall 4
residentiel(le) residential 4
ressentir to feel (emotion—sadness) 10
ressource (f.) resource F; — **naturelle** natural resource F
restaurant (m.) restaurant 1; — **universitaire** (m.) campus cafeteria 4
rester to stay 6
retirer to withdraw 7; — **de l'argent** to withdraw money 7
retourner to return, to go back 6

retraite (f.) retirement 8; **Bonne —!** Happy retirement! 8; **prendre sa** — to retire (from a job) 8
retraité(e) (m./f.) retired person 10
réussir (à) to succeed (at, in) 4
réussite (f.) success 8; **À la** — **de (qqn, qqch)!** To the success of (someone, something)! 8
rêve (m.) dream
réveiller to wake up 12; **se** — to wake oneself up 12
revenir to come back 6
rêver (de) to dream (of, about) 8
revoir to see again 9
révolution (f.) revolution 8
revue (f.) magazine 10
rez-de-chaussée (m.) ground floor, first floor (USA) 4
rhume (m.) cold 12
rideau (m.) curtain 4
rien nothing; **De —.** You're welcome. P; — **de nouveau.** Nothing new. P
rivière (f.) river 4
riz (m.) rice 5
robe (f.) dress 11; — **du soir** evening dress 11
rock (m.) rock 9
roi (m.) king 8
rôle (m.) role 9
roman (m.) novel 2
rosbif (m.) roast beef 6
rose pink 3
rôti (m.) roast 5; — **de porc** pork roast 5
rouge red 3
roumain(e) Romanian 3
Roumanie (f.) Romania 3
rousse (f.) redhead (female) 3
roux (m.) redhead (male) 3
roux / rousse red (hair) 3
rue (f.) street 4
rugby (m.) rugby 2
russe (m.) Russian (language) P
russe Russian 3
Russie (f.) Russia 3

S

sa his/her/its 3
sac (m.) bag, purse P; — **de** bag (of) 5;
saignant(e) medium rare 5
sain(e) healthy 5
saint (m.) saint; **Saint-Sylvestre** (f.) New Year's Eve 8; **Saint-Valentin** (f.) St. Valentine's Day 8
saison (f.) season 2
salade (f.) salad 5
salaire (m.) salary, pay, wages 7
sale dirty 4
salé(e) salty 5
salir to dirty 4
salle (f.) room 4; — **à manger** (f.) dining room 4; — **de bains** bathroom 4; — **de répétition** rehearsal room; — **de séjour** (f.) living room, family room 4
salon (m.) salon, formal living room 4
salut hello, hi P

VOCABULAIRE français-anglais

samedi *Saturday* 1
sandales *(f. pl.) sandals* 11
sandwich *(m.) sandwich* 5; **— au fromage** *cheese sandwich* 5
sang *(m.) blood* 12; **donner son —** *to give one's blood* 12
sans *without*
sans-abri (sans domicile fixe) (SDF) *(m.) homeless person* F
santé *(f.) health* 5; **À votre —!** *To your health!* 6
satellite *(m.) satellite* F
saucisse *(f.) sausage* 5
saucisson *(m.) dry salami type sausage* 6
saumon *(m.) salmon* 6
sauvegarder *to save* F
sauver *to save, to protect* F
savoir *to know* F, *to know how to, to know by heart* 8
savon *(m.) soap* 12
science *(f.) science* P; **faculté** *(f.)* **de lettres et de —s humaines** *liberal arts college* 7; **faculté** *(f.)* **de —s et de technologie** *science and technology college* 7; **—s politiques** *political science* P
scientifique *(m./f.) scientist*
scooter *(m.) moped* 11
sculpteur *(m.) sculptor (male)* 9
sculptrice *(f.) sculptor (female)* 9
sculpture *(f.) sculpture* 9; **faire de la —** *to sculpt* 9
sèche-cheveux *(m.) hairdryer* 12
sécher *to dry* 12; **se —** *to dry oneself* 12
secrétaire *(m./f.) secretary* 7
sécurité *(f.) security* 11; **agent(e)** *(m./f.)* **de la —** *security agent* 11
seize *sixteen* P
sel *(m.) salt* 5
semaine *(f.) week* 1; **— dernière / passée** *(f.) last week* 5
semestre *(m.) semester, term* P
Sénégal *(m.) Senegal* 3
sénégalais(e) *Senegalese* 3
sens *(m.) sens;* **— de l'humour** *sense of humor* 7
sensible *sensitive* 7
sentiment *(m.) feeling* 10
sentir *to smell* 3; **se — to feel** 10
sept *sept* P
septembre *September* 2
série *(f.) serial sitcom or TV drama* 9
sérieusement *seriously* 2
sérieux / sérieuse *serious* 1
serpent *(m.) snake* 12
serveur *(m.) waiter* 6
serveuse *(f.) waitress* 6
servi(e) *served* 6; **C'est servi avec quoi?** *What does this come with?* 6
service *(m.) service* 6; **Le — est compris.** *The tip is included.* 6; **— de chambre** *room service* 11
serviette *(f.) napkin* 6, *towel* 12
ses *his/her/its* 3
seul(e) *alone*
shampooing *(m.) shampoo* 12

shopping *(m.) shopping* 2; **faire du —** *to shop, to go shopping* 2
short *(m.) shorts* 11
siège *(m.) seat* 11
sieste *(f.) nap* 2; **faire la —** *to take a nap* 2
simple *simple* 10
sirop *(m.) syrup* 12; **— contre la toux** *cough syrup* 12
site *(m.) site;* **— Web** *website* 10
six *six* P
ski *(m.) skiing* 2; **— alpin** *downhill skiing* 2; **— de fond** *cross-country skiing* 2; **— nautique** *water-ski* 2
Smartphone *(m.) Smartphone* 10
smoking *(m.) tuxedo* 11
sociable *sociable* P
société *(f.) society* F
sociologie *(f.) sociology* P
sœur *(f.) sister* 3
soins médicaux *(m. pl.) healthcare*
soir *(m.) evening* 1; **du —** *in the evening* 1; **être du —** *to be a night person* 7
soirée *(f.) party (evening)* 8
soixante *sixty* P; **—-dix** *seventy* 1; **—-quinzième** *seventy-fifth* 8
soldat *(m.) soldier* 8; **femme —** *(f.) soldier (female)* 8
solde: en — *on sale* 11
soleil *(m.) sun* 2; **Il fait (du) —.** *It's sunny.* 2
solution *(f.) solution* F
sombre *somber, dark* 9
son *his/her/its* 3
sondage *(m.) survey, poll*
sortir *to go out* 3, *to take out* 4; **— la poubelle** *to take out the garbage, trash* 4
soudain *suddenly* 8
souhaiter *to wish* 12
souligner *to underline*
soupe *(f.) soup* 5; **— à la tomate** *tomato soup* 5
souris *(f.) mouse* F
sous-sol *(m.) basement* 4
sous-vêtement *(m.) underwear* 11
souvenir: se — (de) *to remember* 10
souvent *often* 1
spécialisation *(f.) major* P; **Quelle est ta —?** *What's your major?* P
spectacle *(m.) show, performance* 9
spiritualité *(f.) spirituality* 10
sport *(m.) sport* 2; **faire du —** *to work out, to exercise* 2
sportif / sportive *athletic* 1
stade *(m.) stadium* 4
stage (de formation) *(m.) internship* 7
steak *(m.) steak* 5
stress *(m.) stress* 12
stressé(e) *stressed*
style *(m.) style* 9
stylo *(m.) pen* P
succès *(m.) success* 8; **Au — de (qqn, qqch)!** *To the success of (someone, something)!* 8
sucre *(m.) sugar* 5

sucré(e) *sweet* 5
sud *(m.) south* 4
suffisamment *sufficiently*
Suisse *(f.) Switzerland* 3
suisse *Swiss* 3
suivre *to follow*
sujet *(m.) subject* 9
super *marvelous, wonderful, super* 10
supermarché *(m.) supermarket* 6
supplémentaire *extra, additional* 11
sûr(e) *sure* F
surf *(m.) surfing* 2
surgelés *(m. pl.) frozen foods* 6; **rayon** *(m.)* **— frozen food aisle** 6
surpopulation *(f.) overpopulation* F
surpris(e) *surprised* 12
surréaliste *surrealist* 9
surveiller *to keep watch on*
sweat *(m.) sweatshirt* 11; **— à capuche** *hooded sweatshirt* 11
symptôme *(m.) symptom* 12
système GPS *(m.) GPS system* F

T

ta *(fam. & sing.) your* 3
table *(f.) table* P; **À —!** *Let's eat! / The food is ready!* 6
tableau *(m.) chalkboard* P, *painting* 9
tâche *(f.) chore, task* 4; **—s ménagères** *household chores* 4
taille *(f.) size* 11; **Quelle est votre —?** *What size do you wear?* 11
tailleur *(m.) woman's suit* 11
talentueux / talentueuse *talented* 1
talons: à — high-heeled 11
tante *(f.) aunt* 3
taper *to type* F
tapis *(m.) rug* 4
tapisserie *(f.) tapestry* 9
tard *later* P, *late* 4; **À plus —!** *See you later.* P; **plus — later** 4
tarte *(f.) pie* 5
tasse (de/d') *(f.) cup (of)* 5; **demi-—** *(f.) half-cup* 5
taxi *(m.) taxi* 11
te *you* 7
technologie *(f.) technology* P
tee-shirt *(m.) t-shirt* 11
téléachat *(m.) TV shopping* 9; **émission** *(f.)* **de — shopping network show** 9
télécharger *to download* F
téléfilm *(m.) made-for-TV film* 9
téléphone *(m.) phone* P; **— portable** *cell phone* P
téléphoner *to telephone* 1; **se — to telephone each other** 10
télévisé(e) *televised* 9; **jeu** *(m.)* **télévisé** *game show* 9; **match** *(m.)* **télévisé** *televised game* 9
télévision / télé *(f.) television / TV* 4
température *(f.) temperature* 2; **prendre la — to take one's temperature** 12; **Quelle — fait-il?** *What's the temperature?* 2

temps (m.) weather 2, time; **de — en —** from time to time 10; **la plupart du — ** most of the time 10; **Quel — fait-il?** What's the weather like? 2

tennis (m.) tennis 2; **— de table** ping-pong, table tennis 2

tension (artérielle) (f.) blood pressure 12; **prendre la —** to take one's blood pressure 12

tente (f.) tent 11

tenue (f.) outfit 11

tes (fam. & sing.) your 3

tête (f.) head 12

têtu(e) stubborn 7

thé (m.) tea 5

théâtre (m.) theater 9; **pièce** (f.) **de —** play (theater) 9

tigre (m.) tiger 12

timbre (m.) stamp 11

timide shy P

tissu (m.) fabric

tofu (m.) tofu 5

toi you (sing., informal) P

toile (f.) canvas

toilettes (f. pl.) restrooms 4

tolérance (f.) tolerance 8

tomate (f.) tomato 5

tomber to fall 6; **— amoureux / amoureuse (de)** to fall in love (with) 8; **— malade** to get sick 12

ton (fam. & sing.) your 3

tornade (f.) tornado 2

toucher to touch, to deeply move 10

toujours always 1

tour (m.) turn

tourner to turn 4; **— à droite / à gauche** to turn right / left 4

tous every 1, all, everyone (m. pl.) 11; **— les jours** everyday 1; **— les soirs** every evening 1

tousser to cough 12

tout (m. sing.) all 6, everyone 11; **C'est —!** That's all. 6; **— le monde** everyone 11

toute (f. sing.) all, everyone 11

toutes (f. pl.) all, everyone 11

toux (f.) cough 12; **sirop** (m.) **contre la —** cough syrup 12

traduire to translate 11

train (m.) train 11

traitement (m.) treatment 12; **— de texte** word processing program F

traiter to treat

trajet (m.) trip, commute 11; **faire le — (entre)** to travel, to commute (between) 11

transporter to transport 11

travail (m.) work 7

travailler to work 1

travailleur / travailleuse hard-working 1

traverser to cross 4

treize thirteen P

tremblement de terre (m.) earthquake

trente thirty P; **— et un** thirty-one P; **—-et-unième** thirty-first 8

très very P

triste sad 12

trois three P

tromper to cheat on (someone) 10; **se — (de)** to be mistaken (about) 10

trop too, too much 1

trouver to find 1; **se —** to be located 10

tuer to kill

Tunisie (f.) Tunisia 3

tunisien / tunisienne Tunisian 3

U

un one P

universitaire (adj.) college, university 4; **résidence** (f.) **—** university / college residence hall 4; **restaurant** (m.) **—** campus cafeteria 4

université (f.) university P

urgences (f. pl.) emergency room 12; **aller aux —** to go to the emergency room 12

utile useful F

utiliser to use 12

V

vacances (f. pl.) vacation; **aller en —** to go on vacation 11

vaisselle (f.) dishes 4; **faire la —** to do the dishes 4

valise (f.) suitcase 11; **faire les —s** to pack 11; **—s** luggage 11

vallée (f.) valley 4

valloir mieux to be better 12

vapeur: à la — steamed 5

veau (m.) veal 5

végétalien(ne) vegan 5

végétarien(ne) vegetarian 5

veille (f.) day before; **— de Noël** Christmas Eve 8

vélo (m.) bike, bicycle 2

vendeur (m.) salesman 7

vendeuse (f.) saleswoman 7

vendre to sell 6

vendredi Friday 1

venir to come 3; **— à l'esprit** to come to mind; **— de** to have just done something 3

vent (m.) wind 2; **Il fait du —.** It's windy. 2

ventre (m.) abdomen, belly 12

verglas (m.) (black) ice 2

vérité (f.) truth

verre (de/d') (m.) glass (of) 5; **— à vin** wine glass 6

vers around 1, towards 4

vert(e) green 3

vêtement (m.) article of clothing; **—s** clothing 11

vétérinaire (m.) vet 12

veuf / veuve widower / widow 3

viande (f.) meat 5

vie (f.) life 2

vieil (m. before a vowel sound) old 3

vieille (f.) old 3

vieillesse (f.) old age, the elderly 8

Viêt-Nam (m.) Vietnam 3

vietnamien / vietnamienne Vietnamese 3

vieux / vieil / vieille old 3

vif / vive bright, lively, colorful 9

ville (f.) city, town 4

vin (m.) wine 5

vinaigre (m.) vinegar 5

vingt twenty P; **— et un** twenty-one P; **—-et-unième** twenty-first 8; **—-deux** twenty-two P

violet(te) violet, purple 3

virgule (f.) comma 4

visage (m.) face 12

visiter to visit (something) 6

vite fast, quickly, hurry! 2

vivre to live 9

voici here is P

voilà there is P

voir to see 9; **se —** to see oneself / each other 10

voisin(e) (m./f.) neighbor 4

voiture (f.) car 11

voix (f.) voice; **à haute —** aloud

vol (m.) flight 11; **— direct** direct flight 11

volaille (f.) poultry 5

volley-ball (m.) volleyball 2

vos (formal sing. or pl.) your 3

votre (formal sing. or pl.) your 3

vouloir to want 7

vous you (pl./sing., formal) P

voyage (m.) trip 2; **faire un —** to take a trip 2; **— de noces** honeymoon 8

voyager to travel 1

voyageur (m.) traveler 11

voyageuse (f.) traveler 11

voyant(e) fortune teller

vrai(e) true F

vraiment really, truly 2

W

W.-C. (m. pl.) toilet (room), restrooms, water closet 4

webcam (f.) webcam F

week-end (m.) weekend 1

western (m.) western 9

Wi-Fi (m.) Wi-Fi F

Y

y there, of / about it 7

yaourt (m.) yogurt 5

yeux (m. pl.) eyes 3; **— bleus** blue eyes 3; **— yeux marron** brown eyes 3; **— yeux verts** green eyes 3

yoga (m.) yoga 2

Z

zéro zero P

INDEX

INDEX

PARTIE 1

OUI, JE PEUX!

Look at each statement and rate yourself on how well you think you can perform the task. Then verify your ability with a partner. How did you do?

1. **"I can say three things that I typically do and three things that I typically don't do during the school week."**

   I can perform this function
   ☐ with ease
   ☐ with some difficulty
   ☐ not at all

2. **"I can ask someone else if that person does particular activities or not to see if our activities are similar."**

   I can perform this function
   ☐ with ease
   ☐ with some difficulty
   ☐ not at all

Vocabulaire utile

chanter *to sing*

danser *to dance*

déjeuner *to have lunch*

étudier (à la bibliothèque) *to study (at the library)*

inviter des amis *to have friends over*

manger (au restaurant) *to eat (at the restaurant)*

marcher au parc *to walk in the park*

naviguer sur Internet *to surf the Internet*

pratiquer un sport *to play a sport*

regarder la télé *to watch TV*

travailler (dans un café, au bureau) *to work (in a café, at the office)*

voyager *to travel*

pendant la semaine *during the week*

Grammaire utile

•••❖ Les verbes du premier groupe en **-er**

travailler	
je travaille	nous travaillons
tu travailles	vous travaillez
il/elle/on travaille	ils/elles travaillent

Modèles

Je ne voyage pas pendant la semaine.

Est-ce que tu chantes?

Tu travailles pendant la semaine?

Richard et moi travaillons pendant la semaine.

PARTIE 2

OUI, JE PEUX!

Look at each statement and rate yourself on how well you think you can perform the task. Then verify your ability with a partner. How did you do?

1. **"I can say say two things that I do often, two things I sometimes do, and two things I rarely or never do."**

   I can perform this function
   ☐ with ease
   ☐ with some difficulty
   ☐ not at all

2. **"I can ask someone else about activities that person performs frequently, sometimes, or rarely/never."**

   I can perform this function
   ☐ with ease
   ☐ with some difficulty
   ☐ not at all

Vocabulaire utile

chercher (des livres à la bibliothèque) *to look for (books at the library)*

dîner au restaurant *to have dinner at the restaurant*

écouter la radio *to listen to the radio*

être en retard/en avance *to be late/early*

parler avec ma famille *to talk with my family*

passer un examen *to take an exam*

rater un examen *to fail an exam*

Est-ce que tu…? *Do you…?*

Qu'est-ce que vous faites? *What do you do?*

Grammaire utile

•••❖ Les adverbes

ne…jamais *never*
parfois *sometimes*
quelquefois *sometimes*
rarement *rarely*
souvent *often*
toujours *always*
tous les soirs *every evening*

Modèles

Mes amis et moi, nous dînons souvent au restaurant le vendredi soir.

Est-ce que tu écoutes la radio parfois?

Je rate rarement un examen.

PARTIE 3

OUI, JE PEUX!

Look at each statement and rate yourself on how well you think you can perform the task. Then verify your ability with a partner. How did you do?

1. **"I can describe my weekly schedule including when I have class, when I study, and so on, and indicate on which days I do what activities."**

   I can perform this function
   ☐ with ease
   ☐ with some difficulty
   ☐ not at all

2. **"I can ask someone else about his/her weekly schedule (classes, studying, other activities) and also find out on what days that person does what activities."**

   I can perform this function
   ☐ with ease
   ☐ with some difficulty
   ☐ not at all

Vocabulaire utile

lundi *Monday*

mardi *Tuesday*

mercredi *Wednesday*

jeudi *Thursday*

vendredi *Friday*

samedi *Saturday*

dimanche *Sunday*

à une heure *at one o'clock*

à deux heures *at two o'clock*

à midi/minuit *at noon/midnight*

　et quart *a quarter past*

　et demi(e) *half past*

　moins le quart *a quarter to*

　du matin *in the morning*

　de l'après-midi *in the afternoon*

　du soir *in the evening*

vers (8h30) *around (8:30)*

Grammaire utile

••• Le verbe **avoir** *(to have)*

avoir	
j'**ai**	nous **avons**
tu **as**	vous **avez**
il/elle/on **a**	ils/elles **ont**

Modèles

J'ai un cours de biologie le mardi à trois heures de l'après-midi.

Sarah dîne avec ses amis vers sept heures du soir le jeudi.

Est-ce que tu étudies à la bibliothèque le week-end?

ACTIVITÉ

Claire and Abia are talking about their week, but their sentences are not in order. Reassemble them in an order (1-6) that reconstructs their original conversation.

a. _____ **CLAIRE:** Non. J'ai besoin d'étudier un peu pour un examen lundi prochain, mais je suis libre *(free)* après 16h.

b. _____ **ABIA:** Claire, qu'est-ce que tu fais cette semaine?

c. _____ **CLAIRE:** Ah oui! Excellente idée. Merci beaucoup. J'aime toujours dîner avec ta famille.

d. _____ **ABIA:** Tu as envie de dîner avec ma famille et moi? C'est pour 19h samedi soir.

e. _____ **CLAIRE:** Beaucoup d'activités. Aujourd'hui, j'ai un cours à 10h et après je travaille à l'hôtel. Demain soir, je dîne avec ma mère et le jour après j'ai besoin de parler avec mon prof de psychologie. Et toi?

f. _____ **ABIA:** Moi, je travaille aussi cet après-midi avec toi et aussi demain et le jour après. J'invite ma famille ce week-end. Est-ce que tu travailles samedi?

••• **C'est à votre tour.** *(It's your turn.)* Does your week resemble Claire's or Abia's? Respond with your plans for the week and weekend, making sure to include any of the same or similar activities.

PARTIE 1

OUI, JE PEUX!

Look at each statement and rate yourself on how well you think you can perform the task. Then verify your ability with a partner. How did you do?

1. **"I can say one place where I am or am not going today and ask someone else if he/she is going there, too."**

   I can perform this function
   ☐ with ease
   ☐ with some difficulty
   ☐ not at all

2. **"I can say two things that I am going to do tomorrow if the weather is nice, sunny, rainy, and so on and ask someone else if he/she is going to do the same or different things."**

   I can perform this function
   ☐ with ease
   ☐ with some difficulty
   ☐ not at all

Vocabulaire utile

à la bibliothèque *at/to the library*

au cinéma *at/to the movies*

au restaurant *at/to the restaurant*

à l'université *at/to the university*

Il fait beau. *The weather is nice.*

Il fait du soleil. *It's sunny.*

Il neige. *It's snowing.*

Il pleut. *It's raining.*

aller (au parc) *to go (to the park)*

déjeuner (au café) *to have lunch (at a café)*

écouter de la musique avec des ami(e)s *to listen to music with friends*

étudier *to study*

pratiquer un sport avec des ami(e)s *to play a sport with friends*

Grammaire utile

Le verbe **aller** *(to go)*

aller	
je **vais**	nous **allons**
tu **vas**	vous **allez**
il/elle/on **va**	ils/elles **vont**

Modèles

Je ne vais pas à l'université aujourd'hui.

Est-ce que tu vas à la bibliothèque cet après-midi?

Je vais manger au restaurant *The Melting Pot* s'il pleut demain.

Est-ce que tu vas aller au parc demain s'il fait beau?

PARTIE 2

OUI, JE PEUX!

Look at each statement and rate yourself on how well you think you can perform the task. Then verify your ability with a partner. How did you do?

1. **"I can say two sports that I do and ask others what sports they do."**

   I can perform this function
   ☐ with ease
   ☐ with some difficulty
   ☐ not at all

2. **"I can ask someone else what he or she is going to do today, tonight, tomorrow, this weekend, and so on."**

   I can perform this function
   ☐ with ease
   ☐ with some difficulty
   ☐ not at all

Vocabulaire utile

faire de la gym / du sport *to exercise*

faire de la natation *to swim (for exercise)*

faire du patinage *to iceskate*

faire du ski *to ski, to go skiing*

faire du vélo *to go bike riding*

faire du yoga *to do yoga*

manger avec des ami(e)s *to eat with friends*

regarder un film au cinéma *to watch a film at the cinema*

Grammaire utile

Le verbe **faire** *(to do, to make)*

faire	
je **fais**	nous **faisons**
tu **fais**	vous **faites**
il/elle/on **fait**	ils/elles **font**

Modèles

Je fais de la natation et du patinage.

Fais-tu du ski?

Qu'est-ce que tu vas faire demain soir?

Que vas-tu faire ce week-end?

PARTIE 3

Look at each statement and rate yourself on how well you think you can perform the task. Then verify your ability with a partner. How did you do?

1. "I can say two activities that I do during my leisure time and ask others if they like the same or different activities."

   I can perform this function
   ☐ with ease
   ☐ with some difficulty
   ☐ not at all

2. "I can describe how I do different activities (patiently, quickly, seriously, well, badly, and so on)."

   I can perform this function
   ☐ with ease
   ☐ with some difficulty
   ☐ not at all

Vocabulaire utile

commander une pizza *to order a pizza*

écrire des textos *to write text messages*

faire la fête *to party*

faire un pique-nique *to have a picnic*

faire la sieste *to take a nap*

faire du shopping *to shop, to go shopping*

jouer aux cartes *to play cards*

jouer de la guitare *to play the guitar*

lire le journal *to read the newspaper*

lire un roman *to read a novel*

un loisir *a leisure activity*

Grammaire utile

•••> Les adverbes

activement *actively*
bien *well*
constamment *constantly*
gentiment *nicely*
lentement *slowly*
mal *badly*
patiemment *patiently*
rapidement, vite *fast, quickly*
sérieusement *seriously*

Modèles

J'étudie sérieusement pour les examens.

Je joue mal de la guitare.

Est-ce que tu aimes bien jouer aux cartes?

As-tu des loisirs préférés?

ACTIVITÉ

The following sentences are about the prologue and **Séquence 1** of the film *Liaisons*, but they are not in order. Reassemble them in an order (1-6) that reconstructs the original paragraph. The paragraph is started for you.

D'abord, Claire va à son cours de psychologie à l'Université McGill.

a. _____ Après la visite à l'hôpital, Claire va à l'hôtel Delta pour travailler.

b. _____ Claire dit que la vie de Simone est triste parce qu'elle n'a pas beaucoup de loisirs: «Elle mange, elle joue aux cartes, elle lit et elle dort. Elle mange, elle joue aux cartes, elle lit et elle dort. Elle existe, c'est tout. C'est trop triste...»

c. _____ Dans la scène suivante *(following)*, elle va rencontrer deux hommes mystérieux.

d. _____ Elle parle avec son amie, Abia, dans le vestiaire de l'hôtel.

e. _____ À l'hôpital, Claire parle gentiment avec sa mère et elle joue aux cartes patiemment avec elle.

f. _____ Ensuite, elle va à l'hôpital pour voir *(see)* sa mère, Simone.

•••> **C'est à votre tour.** Write a scene in which you explain to a friend a family member's or a roommate's activities (like Claire and Abia above). Explain how this person does them (that is, well, badly, slowly, etc.). Tell your friend what you think of this person's life based on his/her activities. Be prepared to act out the scene.

PARTIE 1

OUI, JE PEUX!

Look at each statement and rate yourself on how well you think you can perform the task. Then verify your ability with a partner. How did you do?

1. "I can tell someone where I am from and find out where he/she is from."

   I can perform this function
   ☐ with ease
   ☐ with some difficulty
   ☐ not at all

2. "I can tell someone three countries I am going to go to one day and find out which countries he/she is going to go to."

   I can perform this function
   ☐ with ease
   ☐ with some difficulty
   ☐ not at all

Vocabulaire utile

en/d'Allemagne (f.) to/from Germany
au/du Brésil to/from Brazil
au/du Canada to/from Canada
aux/des États-Unis to/from the United States
en/de France to/from France
en/d'Italie (f.) to/from Italy
au/du Japon to/from Japan
au/du Sénégal to/from Senegal
en/de Suisse to/from Switzerland

à/de Boston to/from Boston
à/de Montréal to/from Montreal
à/de New York to/from New York City
à/d'Ottawa to/from Ottawa
à/de San Diego to/from San Diego

Grammaire utile

⁂ Le verbe **venir** (to come)

venir	
je **viens**	nous **venons**
tu **viens**	vous **venez**
il/elle/on **vient**	ils/elles **viennent**

Modèles

Je viens d'Orlando, mais mes amis viennent du Brésil.

D'où viens-tu?

Un jour, je vais aller en France, au Canada et en Italie.

Où est-ce que tu vas aller un jour?

PARTIE 2

OUI, JE PEUX!

Look at each statement and rate yourself on how well you think you can perform the task. Then verify your ability with a partner. How did you do?

1. "I can say who is in my family and where these family members live."

   I can perform this function
   ☐ with ease
   ☐ with some difficulty
   ☐ not at all

2. "I can ask someone else about his/her family and where these family members live."

   I can perform this function
   ☐ with ease
   ☐ with some difficulty
   ☐ not at all

Vocabulaire utile

le beau-frère brother-in-law, stepbrother
le beau-père father-in-law, stepfather
la belle-mère mother-in-law, stepmother
la belle-sœur sister-in-law, stepsister
le frère brother
la grand-mère grandmother
le grand-père grandfather
la mère mother
l'oncle (m.) uncle
les parents (m.) parents
la sœur sister
la tante aunt

Grammaire utile

⁂ Les adjectifs possessifs

masculine singular	feminine singular	plural	
mon	ma	mes	my
ton	ta	tes	your (fam. & sing.)
son	sa	ses	his/her/its
notre	notre	nos	our
votre	votre	vos	your (fam. & pl.)
leur	leur	leurs	their

Modèles

Dans ma famille, il y a mon frère et mes parents.

Mon frère habite à Chicago. Mes parents habitent en Chine.

Est-ce que tu as des frères et des sœurs?

Où habite ta famille?

PARTIE 3

Look at each statement and rate yourself on how well you think you can perform the task. Then verify your ability with a partner. How did you do?

1. "I can describe the physical traits of two of my family members, including their size, height, hair, and eye color."

   I can perform this function
   ☐ with ease
   ☐ with some difficulty
   ☐ not at all

2. "I can ask someone else about the physical appearance of his/her family members (size, height, hair, and eye color)."

   I can perform this function
   ☐ with ease
   ☐ with some difficulty
   ☐ not at all

Vocabulaire utile

bouclé(e) / frisé(e) *curly*

chauve *bald*

court(e) *short*

long / longue *long*

mince *slim, lean, slender*

bleu(e) *blue*

blond(e) *blond*

brun(e) / marron *brown*

noir(e) *black*

vert(e) *green*

les cheveux courts *(m.)* *short hair*

les yeux bleus *(m.)* *blue eyes*

Grammaire utile

•••❖ Les adjectifs prénominaux

beau / bel / belle *handsome, beautiful*

grand(e) *big, tall*

jeune *young*

joli(e) *pretty*

petit(e) *small, short*

vieux / vieil / vieille *old*

Modèles

Ma mère est une belle femme. Elle est mince et elle a les cheveux frisés.

Décris les traits physiques de ton grand-père.

Mon grand-père est chauve. Ses yeux sont verts.

De quelle couleur sont les yeux de ton oncle?

ACTIVITÉ

A guest at the Hotel Delta, Madame Hastings, has been robbed and a detective is questioning her, but their sentences are not in order. Reassemble them in an order (1-6) that reconstructs their original conversation. The conversation is started for you.

INSPECTEUR: D'abord, votre nom et prénom, s'il vous plaît.

a. _____ **MME HASTINGS:** Il est grand et gros avec de petits yeux noirs comme un rat. Ses cheveux sont noirs, courts et bouclés.

b. _____ **MME HASTINGS:** Ah oui! Il a aussi un grand nez. Un très grand nez, un peu comme Cyrano de Bergerac.

c. _____ **INSPECTEUR:** Décrivez le voleur, s'il vous plaît. Il est grand? Petit?

d. _____ **MME HASTINGS:** Hastings. Beatrice Hastings.

e. _____ **INSPECTEUR:** A-t-il d'autres *(other)* traits particuliers?

f. _____ **INSPECTEUR:** Avec un trait comme ça, on va certainement trouver ce voleur!

•••❖ **C'est à votre tour.** Are you good at describing people? Think of someone you recently met or encountered (that is, a server, a cashier, someone on the street, etc.). Where do you think this person is from? Describe this person including as many details as you can of his/her physical traits.

PARTIE 1

OUI, JE PEUX!

Look at each statement and rate yourself on how well you think you can perform the task. Then verify your ability with a partner. How did you do?

1. **"I can describe my house, apartment, or room and find out what someone else's living space is like."**

   I can perform this function
   ☐ with ease
   ☐ with some difficulty
   ☐ not at all

2. **"I can say what tasks and household chore(s) I do each week and ask someone else if he/she does these chores or tasks as well."**

   I can perform this function
   ☐ with ease
   ☐ with some difficulty
   ☐ not at all

Vocabulaire utile

la chambre *bedroom*

la cuisine *kitchen*

la salle de bains *bathroom*

la salle de séjour *living room, family room*

les W.-C. *toilet (room), water closet*

les tâches ménagères *chores, housekeeping tasks*

faire la lessive *to do the laundry*

faire le ménage *to do the housework*

faire la vaisselle *to do the dishes*

passer l'aspirateur *to vacuum*

ranger (la maison) *to pick up (the house), to put things away*

sortir la poubelle *to take out the garbage, trash*

chaque semaine *each week*

Combien de pièces… ? *How many rooms . . . ?*

propre *clean*

sale *dirty*

Grammaire utile

••• L'expression **il y a** *(there is, there are)*

••• La préposition **chez** *(at the home, place of someone)*

Modèles

Il y a trois chambres, une cuisine et une salle de séjour chez moi.

Notre chambre est toujours propre et bien rangée.

Je sors la poubelle chaque semaine. Est-ce que tu sors aussi la poubelle?

Je passe l'aspirateur le vendredi après-midi. Et toi? Qu'est-ce que tu fais?

PARTIE 2

OUI, JE PEUX!

Look at each statement and rate yourself on how well you think you can perform the task. Then verify your ability with a partner. How did you do?

1. **"I can say what buildings and facilities are in my neighborhood and I can give directions to one of them."**

   I can perform this function
   ☐ with ease
   ☐ with some difficulty
   ☐ not at all

2. **"I can ask someone else if he/she has certain facilities in his/her neighborhood to determine whose neighborhood has more resources."**

   I can perform this function
   ☐ with ease
   ☐ with some difficulty
   ☐ not at all

Vocabulaire utile

le bureau de poste *post office*

un centre commercial *shopping center/district*

un centre sportif *recreation center*

des magasins *(m.) stores*

un musée *museum*

une piscine municipale *public swimming pool*

un quartier *neighborhood*

à côté (de) *next (to)*

à droite (de) *to/on the right (of)*

à gauche (de) *to/on the left (of)*

derrière *behind*

devant *in front (of)*

en face (de) *across (from)*

Grammaire utile

••• L'impératif

tourner	aller
(tu) **tourne**	(tu) **va**
(nous) **tournons**	(nous) **allons**
(vous) **tournez**	(vous) **allez**

Modèles

Il y a un musée, un cinéma et des magasins dans mon quartier.

Dans mon quartier, le bureau de poste est entre deux églises.

Est-ce qu'il y a une librairie dans ton quartier?

Pour aller au centre commercial, va en direction du centre-ville et tourne à gauche.

PARTIE 3

Look at each statement and rate yourself on how well you think you can perform the task. Then verify your ability with a partner. How did you do?

1. **"I can describe my favorite green spaces and state the types of activities I like to do there."**

   I can perform this function
   ☐ with ease
   ☐ with some difficulty
   ☐ not at all

2. **"I can ask someone else three information questions (for example, where, what, how many, which) about the types of green spaces in his/her hometown."**

   I can perform this function
   ☐ with ease
   ☐ with some difficulty
   ☐ not at all

Vocabulaire utile

la campagne *the country(side)*
une forêt *forest*
un lac *lake*
la mer *the sea*
une montagne *mountain*
la plage *the beach*

aller à la chasse *to go hunting*
aller à la pêche *to go fishing*
faire du bateau (à voile) / faire du voilier *to go (sail)boating*
faire du jardinage *to garden*
faire un pique-nique *to go on a picnic*
faire de la randonnée *to go hiking*
faire du vélo *to go biking*

Grammaire utile

••• Les mots d'interrogation

combien de *how many*
comment *how*
où *where*
pourquoi *why*
quand *when*
que/qu' *what*
quel(le)(s) *which*
qui *who(m)*

Modèles

J'aime mieux la plage et la mer pour aller à la pêche et nager.

La campagne est mon espace vert préféré. J'aime aller à la chasse.

Combien de lacs est-ce qu'il y a dans ta ville d'origine?

Où trouves-tu des arbres dans ta ville?

ACTIVITÉ

The following sentences are about the city and personal spaces seen in **Séquences 1** and **2** of the film *Liaisons*, but they are not in order. Reassemble them in an order (1-5) that reconstructs the original paragraph.

a. _____ Dans la Séquence 2, nous voyons l'appartement de Claire au premier étage du 4869 rue Rivard.

b. _____ L'hôtel Delta se trouve dans le quartier des Spectacles qui est le centre de la vie culturelle de Montréal, avec des musées, la place des Festivals et beaucoup d'autres endroits culturels.

c. _____ Au début de la Séquence 1, Claire tourne à gauche, au coin de la rue Président-Kennedy et de la rue de la Concorde pour entrer dans l'hôtel Delta.

d. _____ Son appartement est assez petit, propre, et simplement meublé et décoré avec une chambre, une cuisine, une salle de bains et une salle de séjour.

e. _____ Elle aime beaucoup lire et étudier dans sa salle de séjour sur son canapé confortable!

••• **C'est à votre tour.** What would the settings of a film being made about your life look like? Write a description in which you explain the spaces where you live, work, and/or study. Include how they are situated in relation to one another and the reputations of these spaces. Use the description above as a model.

PARTIE 1

OUI, JE PEUX!

Look at each statement and rate yourself on how well you think you can perform the task. Then verify your ability with a partner. How did you do?

1. **"I can tell someone what I typically eat for each meal during the week."**

   I can perform this function
   ☐ with ease
   ☐ with some difficulty
   ☐ not at all

2. **"I can ask someone else what he/she typically eats at each meal during the week and determine if we have similar eating habits."**

   I can perform this function
   ☐ with ease
   ☐ with some difficulty
   ☐ not at all

Vocabulaire utile

le petit déjeuner *breakfast*
le déjeuner *lunch*
le dîner *dinner*
les céréales (f.) *cereal*
les œufs (m.) *eggs*
le pain *bread*
le poulet *chicken*
la salade *salad*
un sandwich (au fromage) *(cheese) sandwich*
un yaourt *yogurt*
le café *coffee*
l'eau (minérale) (f.) *(mineral) water*
le jus d'orange *orange juice*
le lait *milk*
les habitudes alimentaires (f.) *eating habits*

Grammaire utile

❖❖❖ Les articles partitifs

LES ARTICLES PARTITIFS		Négatif
du (m. sing.)	Vous prenez **du** café? *Are you having (some) coffee?*	Vous ne prenez pas **de** café? *You're not having (any) coffee?*
de la (f. sing.)	Tu prends **de la** pizza? *Are you having (some) pizza?*	Tu ne prends pas **de** pizza? *You're not having (any) pizza?*
de l' (m. / f. vowel sound)	Je prends **de l'**eau. *I'm having some water.*	Je ne prends pas **d'**eau. *I'm not having (any) water.*

Modèles

Au petit déjeuner, je prends des œufs.
Je ne prends pas de café le matin.
Qu'est-ce que tu prends au dîner?
Nous avons des habitudes alimentaires similaires.

PARTIE 2

OUI, JE PEUX!

Look at each statement and rate yourself on how well you think you can perform the task. Then verify your ability with a partner. How did you do?

1. **"I can say what I like and do not like to eat and drink."**

   I can perform this function
   ☐ with ease
   ☐ with some difficulty
   ☐ not at all

2. **"I can ask someone else what he/she likes to eat and drink and determine if he/she eats well overall."**

   I can perform this function
   ☐ with ease
   ☐ with some difficulty
   ☐ not at all

Vocabulaire utile

le fast-food *fastfood*
les frites (f.) *fries*
les fruits de mer (m.) *seafood*
la glace *ice cream*
un hamburger *hamburger*
les légumes (m.) *vegetables*
les pâtes (f.) *pasta*
une pomme de terre *potato*
le steak *steak*
la tarte *pie*

la bière *beer*
le Coca *Coca-Cola*
le vin *wine*

manger bien *to eat well*

Grammaire utile

❖❖❖ Les préférences et les articles définis (**le, la, l,' les**)

Affirmatif	Négatif
Aimez-vous **les** aliments industriels? *Do you like processed foods?*	Je n'aime pas **les** aliments industriels. *I don't like processed food.*
Nous adorons **la** pizza végétarienne. *We adore vegetarian pizza.*	Nous n'adorons pas **la** pizza végétarienne. *We don't adore vegetarian pizza.*
Est-ce que tu détestes **le** tofu? *Do you hate tofu?*	Non, je ne déteste pas **le** tofu. *No, I don't hate tofu.*
J'aime mieux **l'**agneau. *I prefer lamb.*	Mon frère n'aime pas **l'**agneau. *My brother does not like lamb.*

Modèles

Qu'est-ce que tu aimes mieux boire au dîner?
J'aime boire du vin rouge et de l'eau.
Je déteste les haricots verts.
Nous mangeons bien.

PARTIE 3

Look at each statement and rate yourself on how well you think you can perform the task. Then verify your ability with a partner. How did you do?

1. **"I can say what I ate and drank for dinner last night."**

   I can perform this function
   ☐ with ease
   ☐ with some difficulty
   ☐ not at all

2. **"I can ask someone else what he/she ate and drank for dinner last night and determine who had a better dinner."**

   I can perform this function
   ☐ with ease
   ☐ with some difficulty
   ☐ not at all

Vocabulaire utile

une banane *banana*
les carottes *(f.)* *carrots*
un gâteau *cake*
les légumes *(m.)* à la vapeur *steamed vegetables*
le poisson au four *baked fish*
une pomme *apple*
le poulet frit *fried chicken*
le riz *rice*
un rôti de porc *roast pork*
la soupe *soup*
les tomates *(f.)* *tomatoes*

hier *yesterday*
hier soir *last night*

Grammaire utile

···▸ Le passé composé

manger	prendre	boire
j'ai mangé	j'ai pris	j'ai bu
tu as mangé	tu as pris	tu as bu
il/elle/on a mangé	il/elle/on a pris	il/elle/on a bu
nous avons mangé	nous avons pris	nous avons bu
vous avez mangé	vous avez pris	vous avez bu
ils/elles ont mangé	ils/elles ont pris	ils/elles ont bu

Modèles

Qu'est-ce que tu as mangé au dîner hier soir?

J'ai pris un steak grillé avec du riz et des légumes à la vapeur.

Je n'ai pas pris de café. J'ai bu du thé avec le dessert.

J'aime mieux ton dîner.

ACTIVITÉ

A guest at the Hotel Delta is talking about a restaurant where he dined, but his sentences are not in order. Reassemble them in an order (1-6) that reconstructs the original paragraph. The paragraph is started for you.

Hier soir, j'ai dîné dans un très bon restaurant avec ma femme, Louise.

a. _____ Louise a bu du vin blanc et j'ai bu un Coca parce que je n'aime pas les boissons alcoolisées.

b. _____ À la fin du repas, le serveur a dit que beaucoup de plats polynésiens sont influencés par la cuisine chinoise.

c. _____ Louise adore la cuisine polynésienne, donc on a choisi un restaurant polynésien, *La Terrasse tiki*, près de l'hôtel.

d. _____ Comme plat principal, Louise a pris du poisson mariné avec du jus de citron.

e. _____ On a commencé par des apéritifs.

f. _____ Louise a adoré son poisson mais moi, je n'aime pas les fruits de mer, donc j'ai pris du bœuf au lait de coco *(coconut)* avec du riz.

···▸ **C'est à votre tour.** Tell a classmate about a restaurant where you recently ate. Discuss what you ordered and whether or not you liked the food and drinks.

PARTIE 1

OUI, JE PEUX!

Look at each statement and rate yourself on how well you think you can perform the task. Then verify your ability with a partner. How did you do?

1. "I can tell someone what my favorite grocery store is and some unique or great things the store sells."

   I can perform this function
   ☐ with ease
   ☐ with some difficulty
   ☐ not at all

2. "I can ask someone else what his/her favorite grocery store is and what that store sells."

   I can perform this function
   ☐ with ease
   ☐ with some difficulty
   ☐ not at all

Vocabulaire utile

un hypermarché *hypermarket*
un supermarché *supermarket*

une boîte de conserves *canned goods*
une brioche *round egg bread*
le homard *lobster*
les madeleines *(f.) madeleine cakes*
un pain de campagne *country-style bread*
les pâtisseries *(f.) pastries*
le rayon audiovisuel *audio visual equipment aisle*
le rosbif *roastbeef*
un saucisson *dry salami type sausage*
le saumon *salmon*
les surgelés *(m.) frozen foods*

préféré(e) *favorite*

Grammaire utile

Le verbe **vendre** *(to sell)*

vendre	
je **vends**	nous **vendons**
tu **vends**	vous **vendez**
il/elle/on **vend**	ils/elles **vendent**

Modèles

Mon supermarché préféré est *Giant Eagle*.

Ce supermarché vend beaucoup de bons surgelés et de la bonne bière belge.

Quel est ton hypermarché ou supermarché préféré?

Que vend cet hypermarché ou ce supermarché?

PARTIE 2

OUI, JE PEUX!

Look at each statement and rate yourself on how well you think you can perform the task. Then verify your ability with a partner. How did you do?

1. "I can say when I last went to an outdoor market and what I bought there."

   I can perform this function
   ☐ with ease
   ☐ with some difficulty
   ☐ not at all

2. "I can ask someone else when he/she last went to an outdoor market and what he/she bought there."

   I can perform this function
   ☐ with ease
   ☐ with some difficulty
   ☐ not at all

Vocabulaire utile

les aubergines *(f.) eggplants*
les cerises *(f.) cherries*
les champignons *(m.) mushrooms*
les concombres *(m.) cucumbers*
la laitue *lettuce*
le maïs *corn*
les mangues *(f.) mangos*
les melons *(m.) melons*
les pêches *(f.) peaches*
les poires *(f.) pears*

Grammaire utile

Le passé composé avec **être**

Passé composé of *aller*	
je **suis allé(e)**	nous **sommes allé(e)s**
tu **es allé(e)**	vous **êtes allé(e)(s)**
il/elle/on **est allé(e)**	ils/elles **sont allé(e)s**

Modèles

Je suis allé(e) au marché en plein air la semaine dernière.

J'ai acheté des cerises, du maïs et de la laitue.

Quand est-ce que tu es allé(e) au marché en plein air?

Je ne suis jamais allé(e) au marché en plein air.

PARTIE 3

OUI, JE PEUX!

Look at each statement and rate yourself on how well you think you can perform the task. Then verify your ability with a partner. How did you do?

1. **"I can say what my favorite restaurant is, what my favorite thing to order is, and when I last ordered this item."**

   I can perform this function
   ☐ with ease
   ☐ with some difficulty
   ☐ not at all

2. **"I can ask someone else what his/her favorite restaurant is, what his/her favorite thing is to order, and when the last time was that he/she ordered this item."**

   I can perform this function
   ☐ with ease
   ☐ with some difficulty
   ☐ not at all

Vocabulaire utile

commander *to order*

être servi(e) avec… *to be served with…*

le plat préféré *favorite dish*

une assiette de fromages *cheese plate*
le beurre *butter*
le brocoli *broccoli*
une côtelette d'agneau/de porc *lamb/pork chop*
les crevettes *(f.)* *shrimp*
un éclair *eclair*
les épinards *(m.)* *spinach*
les moules *(f.)* *mussels*

Grammaire utile

Les pronoms compléments d'objet direct

Direct object pronouns			
Singular		**Plural**	
me/m'	*me*	**nous**	*us*
te/t'	*you*	**vous**	*you*
le/la/l'	*him/her/it*	**les**	*them*

Modèles

Mon plat préféré est les crevettes. Je les prends avec du beurre.

Je les ai commandées la semaine dernière.

Quel est ton restaurant préféré?

Qu'est-ce que tu as commandé?

ACTIVITÉ

The following sentences are about Claire's trip to Quebec in **Séquence 3** of the film *Liaisons*, but they are not in order. Reassemble them in an order (1-6) to reconstruct the original paragraph. The paragraph is started for you.

Claire est partie pour Québec.

a. _____ Quand la serveuse les a apportés à sa table, Alexis Prévost est arrivé.

b. _____ Claire l'a vu passer devant la fenêtre du café.

c. _____ En route pour sa destination, Claire a pris quelque chose à manger dans un café à Trois-Rivières, le café préféré de beaucoup de touristes.

d. _____ Quand Alexis est parti, l'homme mystérieux est passé par le café.

e. _____ Alexis a expliqué qu'il est venu au Canada pour des affaires de famille.

f. _____ Elle a commandé une tarte au sucre et un verre d'eau.

C'est à votre tour. Write a short script for this scene and act it out for your classmates.

PARTIE 1

OUI, JE PEUX!

Look at each statement and rate yourself on how well you think you can perform the task. Then verify your ability with a partner. How did you do?

1. "I can state the profession I would like to have and explain why."

   I can perform this function
   ☐ with ease
   ☐ with some difficulty
   ☐ not at all

2. "I can say two things that I loan or give to people and to whom I loan or give these things."

   I can perform this function
   ☐ with ease
   ☐ with some difficulty
   ☐ not at all

Vocabulaire utile

un(e) assistant(e) social(e) *social worker*

un(e) avocat(e) *lawyer*

un(e) comptable *accountant*

un(e) enseignant(e) *instructor, teacher*

un homme/une femme d'affaires *businessman/businesswoman*

un ingénieur/une femme ingénieur *engineer*

un(e) journaliste *journalist*

un(e) psychologue *psychologist*

une profession *profession*

un salaire *salary, pay, wages*

le travail *work*

parce que/qu' *because*

donner (à) *to give*

prêter (à) *to lend*

Grammaire utile

⟶ Les pronoms compléments d'objet indirect

INDIRECT OBJECT PRONOUNS	
singular	**plural**
me/m' *(to/for) me*	**nous** *(to/for) us*
te/t' *(to/for) you*	**vous** *(to/for) you*
lui *(to/for) him/her*	**leur** *(to/for) them*

Modèles

Je voudrais être acteur parce que j'adore chanter et danser.

Je vais devenir journaliste parce que le travail est intéressant.

Je prête souvent mon ordinateur et mes livres à ma colocataire.

Je lui donne souvent des stylos.

PARTIE 2

OUI, JE PEUX!

Look at each statement and rate yourself on how well you think you can perform the task. Then verify your ability with a partner. How did you do?

1. "I can name three professional skills or personality traits I have and find out if others have the same or different ones."

   I can perform this function
   ☐ with ease
   ☐ with some difficulty
   ☐ not at all

2. "I can state one thing I want to do, one thing I can do, and one thing I must do this week."

   I can perform this function
   ☐ with ease
   ☐ with some difficulty
   ☐ not at all

Vocabulaire utile

acharné(e) *competitive, cutthroat*

créatif/créative *creative*

organisé(e) *organized*

avoir de bonnes capacités de communication *to have good communication skills*

avoir le goût du travail *to have a good work ethic*

être bon/bonne avec les chiffres *to be good with numbers*

être du matin *to be a morning person*

être précis(e) *to be good with details*

Grammaire utile

⟶ Le verbe **vouloir** *(to want)*
je **veux,** tu **veux,** il/elle/on **veut,** nous **voulons,** vous **voulez,** ils/elles **veulent**

⟶ Le verbe **pouvoir** *(to be able to)*
je **peux,** tu **peux,** il/elle/on **peut,** nous **pouvons,** vous **pouvez,** ils/elles **peuvent**

⟶ Le verbe **devoir** *(to have to, must)*
je **dois,** tu **dois,** il/elle/on **doit,** nous **devons,** vous **devez,** ils/elles **doivent**

Modèles

Je suis créatif, flexible, mais un peu farfelu. Et toi?

Est-ce que tu es bonne avec les chiffres aussi?

J'ai de bonnes capacités de communication. Je suis précise et organisée aussi.

Je veux aller au cinéma, mais je dois étudier. Alors, je peux regarder un peu la télé.

PARTIE 3

OUI, JE PEUX!

Look at each statement and rate yourself on how well you think you can perform the task. Then verify your ability with a partner. How did you do?

1. **"I can name the type of institution in which I am studying and explain how I pay for my tuition."**

   I can perform this function
   □ with ease
   □ with some difficulty
   □ not at all

2. **"I can say if I study more, less or as much as another classmate and I can say who studies the most in the class."**

   I can perform this function
   □ with ease
   □ with some difficulty
   □ not at all

Vocabulaire utile

une école de commerce *business school*

une faculté de lettres et de sciences humaines *liberal arts college*

une faculté de sciences et de technologie *science and technology college*

une université (publique / privée) *(public/private) university*

une bourse d'études *scholarship*

une carte de crédit *credit card*

un prêt étudiant *student loan*

les frais de scolarité *(m.)* *tuition*

payer *to pay*

Grammaire utile

⋅⋅⋅ Les comparatifs (adverbes)
   autant que *as much as*
   plus que *more than*
   moins que *less than*

⋅⋅⋅ Les superlatifs (adverbes)
   le plus *the most*

Modèles

J'étudie dans une faculté de lettres et de sciences humaines.

Je paie mes frais de scolarité avec un prêt étudiant.

J'étudie moins que James et Bethany.

Noah, Leona, Sophie et Sarah étudient le plus dans la classe.

ACTIVITÉ

Two McGill University students are talking while waiting for the bus, but their sentences are not in order. Reassemble them in an order (1-4) that reconstructs their original conversation. The conversation is started for you.

CLAUDE: Est-ce que tu as choisi ta spécialisation, Julie?

a. _____ **CLAUDE:** Tu ne peux pas étudier les deux, le droit et la musique? Tu as le goût du travail et tu es une étudiante sérieuse et organisée. J'étudie moins que toi.

b. _____ **JULIE:** Oui, c'est une idée. Mais mon père est très têtu. Alors, peut-être que je peux lui rembourser cet argent à l'avenir parce que je n'aime pas vraiment le droit.

c. _____ **JULIE:** Oui et non. En fait *(Actually)*, je veux étudier la musique et devenir musicienne, mais mon père me dit que je dois étudier le droit parce qu'il paie pour mes études.

d. _____ **CLAUDE:** Tu dois lui parler. Tu veux faire des études et avoir une profession qui te plaisent *(please)*.

⋅⋅⋅ **C'est à votre tour.** Tell a classmate if you have or have not yet chosen a major and explain your decision or why you have not yet chosen.

PARTIE 1

OUI, JE PEUX!

Look at each statement and rate yourself on how well you think you can perform the task. Then verify your ability with a partner. How did you do?

1. "I can say three things that I did regularly when I was a child."

   I can perform this function
   ☐ with ease
   ☐ with some difficulty
   ☐ not at all

2. "I can ask someone else what he/she did regularly when he/she was a child to find out if we did similar activities when we were children."

   I can perform this function
   ☐ with ease
   ☐ with some difficulty
   ☐ not at all

Vocabulaire utile

aller à l'école *to go to school*

être enfant *to be a child*

jouer avec mes ami(e)s *to play with my friends*

manger des bonbons *to eat candy*

regarder des dessins animés *to watch cartoons*

chaque année / mois *each year / month*

d'habitude *usually*

le lundi, le samedi… *every Monday, every Saturday . . .*

souvent *often*

tous les jours *everyday*

Grammaire utile

❖ L'imparfait

regarder (regardons → regard-)	
je **regardais**	nous **regardions**
tu **regardais**	vous **regardiez**
il/elle/on **regardait**	ils/elles **regardaient**

The verb **être** is irregular in the imperfect: **j'étais, tu étais, il/elle/on était, nous étions, vous étiez, ils/elles étaient.**

Modèles

Quand j'étais enfant, je chantais souvent à l'église le dimanche.

Est-ce que tu mangeais des bonbons tous les jours quand tu étais petit?

Qu'est-ce que tu faisais souvent quand tu étais enfant?

Nous ne regardions pas de dessins animés quand nous étions petits.

PARTIE 2

OUI, JE PEUX!

Look at each statement and rate yourself on how well you think you can perform the task. Then verify your ability with a partner. How did you do?

1. "I can describe a holiday from my past and say three things that happened on this day that made it memorable."

   I can perform this function
   ☐ with ease
   ☐ with some difficulty
   ☐ not at all

2. "I can ask someone else what holiday was memorable for him/her and why it was memorable."

   I can perform this function
   ☐ with ease
   ☐ with some difficulty
   ☐ not at all

Vocabulaire utile

l'anniversaire *(m.) birthday*

la fête des Mères *Mother's Day*

la fête des Pères *Father's Day*

la fête nationale *National Holiday*

le jour de l'Action de Grâce *Thanksgiving*

le jour de l'An *New Year's Day*

Noël *Christmas*

la Saint-Sylvestre *New Year's Eve*

la Saint-Valentin *St. Valentine's Day*

Grammaire utile

❖ L'imparfait et le passé composé

Uses of the *imparfait*	Uses of the *passé composé*
1. To communicate that an event occurred repeatedly in the past (how things used to be)	1. Events that happened at a particular point in time
2. To describe or provide background information in the past	2. Sequence of actions in the past
3. To communicate that an event was in progress	3. To communicate actions interrupting something in progress or changes in states

Modèles

C'était mon anniversaire. J'avais dix ans. Ma famille a organisé une fête. Ma mère a préparé un gâteau. Mon père m'a donné un vélo rouge.

Quelle fête était mémorable pour toi? Pourquoi?

Ma fête préférée était la fête nationale de 2014. Il faisait beau. Je suis allé(e) au parc avec mes amis et nous avons fait un pique-nique. Nous avons beaucoup mangé.

OUI, JE PEUX!

Look at each statement and rate yourself on how well you think you can perform the task. Then verify your ability with a partner. How did you do?

1. "I can say two things one knows how to do during adolescence and during adulthood, and ask someone if he/she knows how to do some of these things."

   I can perform this function
   ☐ with ease
   ☐ with some difficulty
   ☐ not at all

2. "I can say that I know or do not know brilliant people and ask someone else if he/she knows brilliant people."

   I can perform this function
   ☐ with ease
   ☐ with some difficulty
   ☐ not at all

Vocabulaire utile

un(e) adolescent(e) *adolescent*
un(e) adulte *adult*

chercher un emploi *to find a job*
conduire *to drive*
faire la cuisine *to cook*
faire la vaisselle *to do dishes*
jouer de la flûte *to play the flute*
nager *to swim*
parler une deuxième langue *to speak a second language*

des gens brillants *brilliant people*
quelqu'un de brillant *someone brilliant*

Grammaire utile

•••• Les verbes **connaître** et **savoir**

Connaître means *to know or to be familiar with people, places, or things* and is followed by a direct object. **Savoir** *means to know facts, information, or how to do something* and may be followed by an infinitive.

connaître		savoir	
je **connais**	nous **connaissons**	je **sais**	nous **savons**
tu **connais**	vous **connaissez**	tu **sais**	vous **savez**
il/elle/on **connaît**	ils/elles **connaissent**	il/elle/on **sait**	ils/elles **savent**
PAST PARTICIPLE: **connu**		PAST PARTICIPLE: **su**	

Modèles

Les adultes savent conduire et faire la fête. Est-ce que tu sais conduire?

Je ne sais pas jouer du piano.

Je connais des gens brillants, ma mère et mon professeur.

Connais-tu quelqu'un de brillant?

ACTIVITÉ

The following sentences are about Claire's arrival in Quebec City in **Séquence 3** of the film *Liaisons*, but they are not in order. Reassemble them in an order (1-6) to reconstruct the original paragraph. The paragraph is started for you.

Claire est finalement arrivée au Château Frontenac à Québec.

a. _____ Claire était dans la salle de bains quand quelqu'un a remis une enveloppe sous sa porte.

b. _____ La réceptionniste lui a donné la clé de sa chambre, la chambre 315.

c. _____ Claire ne savait pas qui lui avait donné l'enveloppe donc elle a demandé au concierge s'il savait à quoi servait la clé.

d. _____ Malheureusement, Claire ne pouvait pas aller à la banque parce que c'était samedi et la banque était fermée.

e. _____ Le concierge lui a dit que c'était une clé pour un coffre-fort *(safe deposit box)* dans une banque.

f. _____ Il y avait une clé mystérieuse dans l'enveloppe.

•••• **C'est à votre tour.** Invent a different scenario that might have occurred when Claire arrived at the Château Frontenac in Quebec City. Write a description of this new scene in 5-6 sentences using the **passé composé** and the **imparfait**.

PARTIE 1

OUI, JE PEUX!

Look at each statement and rate yourself on how well you think you can perform the task. Then verify your ability with a partner. How did you do?

1. **"I can say the type of artist I would like to be and explain why."**

   I can perform this function
   ☐ with ease
   ☐ with some difficulty
   ☐ not at all

2. **"I can say three things that I should do this week and find out if others should also do these things or not this week."**

   I can perform this function
   ☐ with ease
   ☐ with some difficulty
   ☐ not at all

Vocabulaire utile

un(e) artiste *artist*
un(e) peintre *painter*
un(e) photographe *photographer*
un sculpteur / une sculptrice *sculptor*

abstrait(e) *abstract*
impressionniste *impressionist*
moderne *modern*

la photographie *photography*
un tableau *painting*

faire de la peinture *to paint*
prendre des photos *to take pictures*

Grammaire utile

⋯▸ Le conditionnel

aimer: j'aimer**ais**, tu aimer**ais**, il/elle/on aimer**ait**, nous aimer**ions**, vous aimer**iez**, ils/elles aimer**aient**

devoir: je devr**ais**, tu devr**ais**, il/elle/on devr**ait**, nous devr**ions**, vous devr**iez**, ils/elles devr**aient**

aller: j'ir**ais**, tu ir**ais**, il/elle/on ir**ait**, nous ir**ions**, vous ir**iez**, ils/elles ir**aient**

Modèles

J'aimerais être un(e) artiste d'art moderne parce que j'adore les tableaux abstraits.

Je serais sculpteur parce que j'adore l'artiste Rodin.

Cette semaine, je devrais faire le ménage, faire la lessive et téléphoner à ma mère.

Est-ce que tu devrais faire le ménage aussi?

PARTIE 2

OUI, JE PEUX!

Look at each statement and rate yourself on how well you think you can perform the task. Then verify your ability with a partner. How did you do?

1. **"I can say the type of show or performance I would go to if I had the money and find out if others would do the same."**

   I can perform this function
   ☐ with ease
   ☐ with some difficulty
   ☐ not at all

2. **"I can say the type(s) of music I would listen to if I were happy and sad."**

   I can perform this function
   ☐ with ease
   ☐ with some difficulty
   ☐ not at all

Vocabulaire utile

un ballet *ballet*
un concert *concert*
une pièce de théâtre *play*

le blues *blues*
le jazz *jazz*
la musique alternative *alternative music*
la pop *pop music*
le rap *rap music*
le rock *rock music*

avoir de l'argent *to have money*

Grammaire utile

⋯▸ Le conditionnel dans les phrases avec **si**

The **conditionnel présent** may be used to express what would happen if a hypothetical situation in a **si** clause were to occur. The verb in the **si** clause is in the **imparfait**.

Si j'**avais** plus d'argent, j'**achèterais** une nouvelle voiture.

Nous **irions** au cinéma **si** nous **avions** plus de temps.

Modèles

Si j'avais de l'argent, j'irais au concert de Lady Gaga.

Aimerais-tu aller au concert de Lady Gaga aussi?

J'écouterais de la musique country si j'étais triste.

Qu'est-ce que tu écouterais si tu étais content(e)?

PARTIE 3

OUI, JE PEUX!

Look at each statement and rate yourself on how well you think you can perform the task. Then verify your ability with a partner. How did you do?

1. **"I can name my three favorite types of TV shows and explain why they are my favorites."**

   I can perform this function
   ☐ with ease
   ☐ with some difficulty
   ☐ not at all

2. **"I can list the film genre(s) that I typically see in movie theaters and find out if others typically see the same or different genres of film."**

   I can perform this function
   ☐ with ease
   ☐ with some difficulty
   ☐ not at all

Vocabulaire utile

une causerie *talk show*

une comédie *comedy*

un drame psychologique *psychological drama*

une émission *show, program*

un film d'action *action film*

un film d'horreur *horror film*

un film romantique *romance film*

un film de science-fiction *science fiction film*

un film à suspense *suspense film*

un match télévisé *televised game*

une série *serial sitcom*

un genre de film *film genre*

Grammaire utile

Le verbe voir

voir *(to see)*	
je **vois**	nous **voyons**
tu **vois**	vous **voyez**
il/elle/on **voit**	ils/elles **voient**

Modèles

Mes émissions préférées sont les informations et les documentaires. Je suis une personne sérieuse et je n'ai pas beaucoup de temps pour regarder la télé.

En général, j'aime regarder des films d'action et des films d'horreur. Est-ce que tu regardes ces genres de films aussi?

Quels genres de film regardes-tu?

ACTIVITÉ

Two guests at the Château Frontenac, Élise and David, are talking about activities they could do in Quebec City, but their sentences are not in order. Reassemble them in an order (1-6) that reconstructs their original conversation. The conversation is started for you.

DAVID: Selon le journal *Voir Québec*, il y a plusieurs concerts en ville cette semaine. Aimerais-tu découvrir un peu la musique québécoise?

a. _____ **ÉLISE:** Si nous avions plus de temps, je voudrais tout faire mais comme nous partons dans deux jours…

b. _____ **DAVID:** Excellent! Il y plusieurs possibilités. Il y a un concert de Daniel Bélanger samedi soir. Les Sœurs Boulay donnent un spectacle aussi dimanche.

c. _____ **ÉLISE:** Oui, pourquoi pas? J'aimerais mieux connaître la chanson québécoise. Quel artiste aimerais-tu voir en spectacle?

d. _____ **DAVID:** D'accord. Je vois ce que *(what)* tu veux dire. On peut aller au musée dimanche matin et puis, on peut voir le concert des Sœurs Boulay le soir.

e. _____ **ÉLISE:** Je connais un peu Bélanger, mais pas les Sœurs Boulay. Quel genre de musique jouent-elles?

f. _____ **DAVID:** De la musique folk contemporaine et un peu de country. Il y a aussi plusieurs expositions au musée des Beaux-arts, comme celle sur l'artiste Alfred Pellan. C'est un peintre et sculpteur québécois.

C'est à votre tour. Tell a classmate about a show or exhibit you recently saw and describe it using as many details as possible.

PARTIE 1

OUI, JE PEUX!

Look at each statement and rate yourself on how well you think you can perform the task. Then verify your ability with a partner. How did you do?

1. **"I can say what lifestyle best characterizes me and explain why, and I can ask someone else to explain what lifestyle best characterizes him/her."**

   I can perform this function
   ☐ with ease
   ☐ with some difficulty
   ☐ not at all

2. **"I can say in what situations I have a good time and when I get bored, and I can ask someone else when he/she has a good time and gets bored to find out if we are similar."**

   I can perform this function
   ☐ with ease
   ☐ with some difficulty
   ☐ not at all

Vocabulaire utile

les accros du shopping *shopaholics*

les bourreaux de travail *workaholics*

les écologistes / les écolos *egologists, environmentalists*

les fanas de la santé *health nuts*

un mode de vie (actif) *(active) lifestyle*

le style de vie étudiant *student lifestyle*

décrire (quelqu'un) *to describe (someone)*

être bien dans sa peau *to have confidence in / to feel good about oneself*

s'amuser *to have a good time*

s'ennuyer *to get bored*

Grammaire utile

•••➤ Les verbes réfléchis

s'ennuyer	
je m'ennuie	nous nous ennuyons
tu t'ennuies	vous vous ennuyez
il/elle/on s'ennuie	ils/elles s'ennuient

Modèles

Je suis un accro du shopping parce que je fais du shopping dans les magasins ou sur Internet tout le temps.

Quel mode de vie te décrit le mieux?

Je m'amuse toujours quand j'invite des amis. Toi aussi?

Quand est-ce que tu t'ennuies? Moi, c'est pendant le cours d'histoire.

PARTIE 2

OUI, JE PEUX!

Look at each statement and rate yourself on how well you think you can perform the task. Then verify your ability with a partner. How did you do?

1. **"I can say three things that I did and three things that I did not do last week using reflexive verbs."**

   I can perform this function
   ☐ with ease
   ☐ with some difficulty
   ☐ not at all

2. **"I can ask someone else if he/she also did these activities last week to see if we did similar things."**

   I can perform this function
   ☐ with ease
   ☐ with some difficulty
   ☐ not at all

Vocabulaire utile

s'en aller *to go away*

se demander *to wonder*

se détendre *to relax, to take it easy*

se disputer *to argue with (each other)*

s'énerver *to get upset*

se fâcher *to get angry*

se mettre (à) *to begin (to)*

s'occuper (de) *to take care of*

se promener *to take a walk, to stroll*

se rendre compte (de/que) *to realize*

se tromper (de) *to be mistaken (about)*

Grammaire utile

•••➤ Les verbes réfléchis au passé composé

s'excuser *(to excuse oneself, to apologize)*	
je me suis excusé(e)	nous nous sommes excusé(e)s
tu t'es excusé(e)	vous vous êtes excusé(e)(s)
il/on s'est excusé	ils se sont excusés
elle s'est excusée	elles se sont excusées

Modèles

Mon amie et moi, nous nous sommes promenées au parc le week-end passé et nous nous sommes perdues. Nous nous sommes trompées de plan. Et toi, tu t'es promené?

Je me suis détendu, mais je me suis énervé quand la copine de mon colocataire est venue. Ils se sont disputés et je voulais regarder la télé. Est-ce que tu t'es détendue la semaine passée?

PARTIE 3

Look at each statement and rate yourself on how well you think you can perform the task. Then verify your ability with a partner. How did you do?

1. **"I can say two things that I still or always do and two things that I no longer do or have not done yet."**

   I can perform this function
   ☐ with ease
   ☐ with some difficulty
   ☐ not at all

2. **"I can ask someone else about his/her activities and find out what that person does and no longer does."**

   I can perform this function
   ☐ with ease
   ☐ with some difficulty
   ☐ not at all

Vocabulaire utile

un blog *blog*

un (magazine) mensuel *monthly (magazine) publication*

un réseau social *social network*

un site Web *website*

exprimer *to express*

faire plaisir à quelqu'un *to please someone*

pleurer *to cry*

raconter des potins *to gossip about*

regretter *to regret, to be sorry about*

rendre quelqu'un (heureux) *to make someone (happy)*

de temps en temps *from time to time*

parfois / quelquefois *sometimes, at times*

la plupart du temps *most of the time*

Grammaire utile

⚬⚬⚬ Les expressions négatives

The placement of these negative expressions is the same as **ne… pas**.

AFFIRMATIVE	NEGATIVE
encore *still*	**ne… plus** *no longer, no more*
toujours *always*	**ne… pas encore** *not yet*

Modèles

Je joue toujours du piano et je chante toujours, mais je ne fais plus de danse classique.

Est-ce que tu lis toujours des magazines de mode?

Je n'ai pas encore goûté les escargots. Tu les as déjà goûtés?

Je ne raconte plus de potins. Tu t'es arrêté aussi?

ACTIVITÉ

The following sentences are about the church to which Claire follows **l'homme mystérieux** in **Séquence 5** of the film *Liaisons*, but they are not in order. Reassemble them in an order (1-4) to reconstruct the original paragraph. The paragraph is started for you.

La petite église Notre-Dame-des-Victoires se trouve sur la place Royale dans le quartier historique du Vieux-Québec.

a. _____ Le Brézé était le bateau du Marquis de Tracy, seigneur français et militaire qui est arrivé en 1664. En 1666, il a battu *(defeated)* les Iroquois et a établi la paix à Québec.

b. _____ La décoration de l'intérieur de l'église est un témoignage *(testimony)* de cette période historique et de la foi *(faith)* des premiers Québécois. Il y a même une maquette *(model)* du Brézé suspendue au plafond *(ceiling)*.

c. _____ La place Royale est considérée comme la plus ancienne place française en Amérique et sa petite église catholique est considérée comme la plus vieille église en pierre au nord du Mexique.

d. _____ On s'est mis à construire l'église en 1688 mais elle a été détruite pendant le siège de Québec en 1759 quand les Anglais ont attaqué les Français pendant la Guerre de la Conquête *(French and Indian War)*. On l'a reconstruite en 1759.

⚬⚬⚬ **C'est à votre tour.** What important historic or sentimental site exists in your area? What do visitors see and do there? Are there any special traditions? Write a description of 5-6 sentences using **verbes réfléchis** if relevant.

PARTIE 1

OUI, JE PEUX!

Look at each statement and rate yourself on how well you think you can perform the task. Then verify your ability with a partner. How did you do?

1. **"I can tell someone three activities I will do in the next two weeks and what mode of transportation I will take to do these activities."**

   I can perform this function
   ☐ with ease
   ☐ with some difficulty
   ☐ not at all

2. **"I can ask someone else what activities he/she will do in the next two weeks and what mode of transportation he/she will take to do these activities."**

   I can perform this function
   ☐ with ease
   ☐ with some difficulty
   ☐ not at all

Vocabulaire utile

aller à la poste *to go to the post office*

faire des courses *to run errands*

faire du shopping en centre-ville *to do shopping downtown*

voyager à Paris *travel to Paris*

à pied *by foot*

à vélo *by bike*

en avion *by plane*

en bus *by bus*

en voiture *by car*

un moyen de transport *means of transportation*

dans deux semaines *in two weeks*

Grammaire utile

⋯⋙ Le futur

voyager: je voyager**ai**, tu voyager**as**, il/elle/on voyager**a**, nous voyager**ons**, vous voyager**ez**, ils/elles voyager**ont**

aller: j'ir**ai**, tu ir**as**, il/elle/on ir**a**, nous ir**ons**, vous ir**ez**, ils/elles ir**ont**

faire: je fer**ai**, tu fer**as**, il/elle/on fer**a**, nous fer**ons**, vous fer**ez**, ils/elles fer**ont**

Modèles

J'irai à l'université en bus.

Je ferai des courses à pied.

Je voyagerai à Boston en train pour voir mes parents.

Qu'est-ce que tu feras la semaine prochaine? Quel moyen de transport choisiras-tu?

PARTIE 2

OUI, JE PEUX!

Look at each statement and rate yourself on how well you think you can perform the task. Then verify your ability with a partner. How did you do?

1. **"I can say which place I would like to go to for vacation and the type of accommodations and ask someone else what his/her preferences are."**

   I can perform this function
   ☐ with ease
   ☐ with some difficulty
   ☐ not at all

2. **"I can tell someone about a person that I admire in my life and explain why, and ask someone else if there is a person that he/she admires."**

   I can perform this function
   ☐ with ease
   ☐ with some difficulty
   ☐ not at all

Vocabulaire utile

en classe économique

en première classe

une auberge de jeunesse *youth hostel*

un endroit *place*

un gîte du passant *bed and breakfast*

un hôtel (trois/quatre/cinq étoiles) *(three/four/five star) hotel*

un hôtel de luxe *luxury hotel*

un logement *lodging*

un motel *motel*

une tente *tent*

Grammaire utile

⋯⋙ Les pronoms relatifs

Les pronoms relatifs	
qui *who, that, which*	**dont** *that, (of) which, (of) whom, whose*
que *that, which*	**où** *where, when*

Modèles

J'aimerais aller dans un endroit où il fera beau tous les jours.

Quel type de logement choisirais-tu?

Je choisirais un logement qui ne coûte pas cher, un motel peut-être.

Une personne que j'admire beaucoup est ma sœur.

PARTIE 3

Look at each statement and rate yourself on how well you think you can perform the task. Then verify your ability with a partner. How did you do?

1. "I can say what I like to wear for different occasions and ask someone else what he/she likes to wear."

   I can perform this function
   ☐ with ease
   ☐ with some difficulty
   ☐ not at all

2. "I can describe what interesting clothes everyone, some, or several people were wearing at the last party I went to and ask someone else to do the same."

   I can perform this function
   ☐ with ease
   ☐ with some difficulty
   ☐ not at all

Vocabulaire utile

des bottes *(f.) boots*

un costume *man's suit*

une cravate *tie*

un jean *jeans*

une robe (du soir) *(evening) dress*

un tailleur *woman's suit*

un tee-shirt *t-shirt*

une tenue *outfit*

pour aller à l'université *to go to the university*

pour un dîner élégant *for an elegant dinner*

pour un entretien d'embauche *for a job interview*

pour une fête *for a party*

pour sortir avec des ami(e)s *to go out with friends*

Grammaire utile

❖ Les adjectifs et les pronoms indéfinis

d'autres *(some) other(s)*
l'autre/les autres *the other(s)*
certain(e)s (de) *certain (of)*
le/la/les même(s) *the same*
plusieurs (de) *several (of)*
tout le monde *everyone*

Modèles

Pour un dîner élégant avec mon petit ami, je porterais une belle robe et un collier.

Qu'est-ce que tu portes quand tu es en vacances?

À une fête la semaine dernière, j'ai vu plusieurs personnes avec de belles tenues. J'ai vu un homme qui portait un jean noir et une chemise chic. Il y avait une femme qui portait une mini-jupe noire et des bottes.

As-tu vu des tenues intéressantes récemment?

ACTIVITÉ

A hotel guest in New Orleans for a high school reunion is talking about her activities of the last two days, but her sentences are not in order. Reassemble them in an order (1-6) to reconstruct the original paragraph. The paragraph is started for you.

Je suis à La Nouvelle-Orléans pour une réunion des anciens élèves de mon lycée.

a. _____ J'ai vu plusieurs de mes anciens camarades de classe.

b. _____ Je lui écrirai un texto pour savoir s'il aimerait me revoir aussi.

c. _____ Je suis arrivée hier après-midi. J'ai pris le bus de Bâton Rouge à La Nouvelle-Orléans.

d. _____ Je me suis bien amusée avec André hier soir. J'aimerais le revoir.

e. _____ Certains ont beaucoup changé, mais d'autres n'ont pas changé du tout. Fred et Pierre portaient le même gilet rouge qu'ils portaient en cours de chimie.

f. _____ Après la soirée, j'ai pris un café avec André, un ami de mon cours de maths. Nous sommes allés au Vieux carré en taxi.

❖ **C'est à votre tour.** Tell a classmate about running into someone you had not seen in a while. Describe what happened. What was this person wearing? When will you see this person again? What will you do together?

PARTIE 1

OUI, JE PEUX!

Look at each statement and rate yourself on how well you think you can perform the task. Then verify your ability with a partner. How did you do?

1. **"I can say two things that I do to get ready in the morning and I can ask others what they do to get ready."**

   I can perform this function
   ☐ with ease
   ☐ with some difficulty
   ☐ not at all

2. **"I can say when I went to bed last night and when I got up this morning, and I can ask someone else when he/she did the same."**

   I can perform this function
   ☐ with ease
   ☐ with some difficulty
   ☐ not at all

Vocabulaire utile

se brosser (les dents) *to brush (one's teeth)*

se coucher *to go to bed*

se doucher *to (take a) shower*

s'habiller *to get dressed*

se laver *to wash (oneself)*

se maquiller *to put on make-up*

se raser *to shave (oneself)*

se réveiller *to wake up*

à quelle heure *at what time*

quand *when*

Grammaire utile

❖ Le verbe **se préparer** *(to get ready, to prepare)*

présent	passé composé
je me prépare	je me suis préparé(e)
tu te prépares	tu t'es préparé(e)
il/elle/on se prépare	il/elle/on s'est préparé(e)
nous nous préparons	nous nous sommes préparé(e)s
vous vous préparez	vous vous êtes préparé(e)(s)
ils/elles se préparent	ils/elles se sont préparé(e)s

Modèles

Tous les matins, je me brosse les dents et je m'habille.

Qu'est-ce que tu fais le matin pour te préparer?

Quand est-ce que tu t'es réveillé(e) ce matin?

Je me suis couché(e) à minuit hier.

PARTIE 2

OUI, JE PEUX!

Look at each statement and rate yourself on how well you think you can perform the task. Then verify your ability with a partner. How did you do?

1. **"I can name at least two favorite childhood pets or animals and ask others what animals they had or liked as children."**

   I can perform this function
   ☐ with ease
   ☐ with some difficulty
   ☐ not at all

2. **"I can express at least one desire or obligation for this week (what it is necessary that I do or what I want to buy, watch, choose, take, drink, eat, try, see, etc.)."**

   I can perform this function
   ☐ with ease
   ☐ with some difficulty
   ☐ not at all

Vocabulaire utile

un animal *animal*

un chat *cat*

un chien *dog*

une grenouille *frog*

un hamster *hamster*

un lapin *rabbit*

un oiseau *bird*

un serpent *snake*

Il est nécessaire que… *It is necessary that . . .*

désirer que *to desire that*

vouloir que *to want that*

Grammaire utile

❖ Les verbes réguliers au subjonctif

regarder: … que je regard**e**, … que tu regard**es**, … qu'il/elle/on regard**e**, … que nous regard**ions**, … que vous regard**iez**, … qu'ils/elles regard**ent**

acheter: … que j'ach**ète**, … que tu ach**ètes**, … qu'il/elle/on ach**ète**, … que nous achet**ions**, … que vous achet**iez**, … qu'ils/elles ach**ètent**

boire: … que je boi**ve**, … que tu boi**ves**, … qu'il/elle/on boi**ve**, … que nous buv**ions**, … que vous buv**iez**, … qu'ils/elles boi**vent**

Modèles

Quand j'étais petit(e), j'aimais les grenouilles et les hamsters.

Quels animaux est-ce que tu aimais quand tu étais enfant?

Cette semaine, il est nécessaire que j'achète un nouvel ordinateur.

Je ne veux pas que mon colocataire regarde le film *Frozen* chez nous cette semaine.

PARTIE 3

OUI, JE PEUX!

Look at each statement and rate yourself on how well you think you can perform the task. Then verify your ability with a partner. How did you do?

1. "I can say if I got sick this past year and what illness(es) I had or if I stayed healthy. I can find out if others also got sick or stayed healthy."

   I can perform this function
   ☐ with ease
   ☐ with some difficulty
   ☐ not at all

2. "I can advise new students with at least two suggestions (what they might have, be, do, be able to do, want, know, or where they might go)."

   I can perform this function
   ☐ with ease
   ☐ with some difficulty
   ☐ not at all

Vocabulaire utile

une allergie *allergy*

avoir de la fièvre *to have a fever*

avoir mal à (la tête) *to hurt, to have a (headache)*

avoir mal au ventre *to have a stomach ache*

être en bonne / mauvaise santé *to be in good / bad health*

être en forme *to be in shape*

être / tomber malade *to be / to get sick*

la grippe *flu*

un rhume *cold*

conseiller (de) *to advise (to)*

Grammaire utile

❖ Le subjonctif des verbes irréguliers

aller: … que j'**aille**, … que tu **ailles**, … qu'il/elle/on **aille**, … que nous **allions**, … que vous **alliez**, … qu'ils/elles **aillent**

avoir: … que j'**aie**, … que tu **aies**, … qu'il/elle/on **ait**, … que nous **ayons**, … que vous **ayez**, … qu'ils/elles **aient**

être: … que je **sois**, … que tu **sois**, … qu'il/elle/on **soit**, … que nous **soyons**, … que vous **soyez**, … qu'ils/elles **soient**

faire: … que je **fasse**, … que tu **fasses**, … qu'il/elle/on **fasse**, … que nous **fassions**, … que vous **fassiez**, … qu'ils/elles **fassent**

Modèles

Cette année, je suis souvent tombé malade. J'ai eu la grippe et j'ai souvent eu des allergies.

Et toi? Tu as été en bonne ou en mauvaise santé cette année?

Je conseille que vous ne mangiez pas au restaurant universitaire.

Je conseille que vous fassiez du yoga. C'est bon contre le stress.

ACTIVITÉ

The following sentences are about events that take place in **Séquence 6** of the film *Liaisons,* but they are not in order. Reassemble them in an order (1-6) to reconstruct the original paragraph. The paragraph is started for you.

Ce matin, Claire s'est réveillée tôt. Elle a une journée occupée.

a. _____ Claire retourne à Montréal et elle se prépare pour son voyage à Paris pour l'enterrement de son oncle.

b. _____ Ensuite, une femme entre dans la banque avec son chien.

c. _____ Quand Claire quitte la banque, elle se rend compte que le numéro 315 est important. L'employé lui donne le coffre et elle y trouve une photo d'Alexis Prévost.

d. _____ À la banque, l'employé dit qu'il est nécessaire qu'elle ait le numéro du coffre, mais Claire ne le connaît pas.

e. _____ Cette femme dit: «… Je dois aller à une autre soirée, un gala très important ce soir. Il faut donc que je sorte quelques bijoux de mon coffre.»

f. _____ Il faut qu'elle aille à la banque avec sa clé pour trouver le coffre-fort.

❖ **C'est à votre tour.** Write a short script for this scene (or part of the scene) and act it out for your classmates.

PARTIE 1

OUI, JE PEUX!

Look at each statement and rate yourself on how well you think you can perform the task. Then verify your ability with a partner. How did you do?

1. **"I can describe and give my opinion about the computer that I currently have in my possession."**

   I can perform this function
   ☐ with ease
   ☐ with some difficulty
   ☐ not at all

2. **"I can ask others to describe their computer and have them offer their opinion about it so I can determine whose computer I prefer."**

   I can perform this function
   ☐ with ease
   ☐ with some difficulty
   ☐ not at all

Vocabulaire utile

un clavier *keyboard*
un écran *monitor, screen*
une imprimante *printer*
un ordinateur *computer*
un ordinateur portable *laptop computer*
une souris *mouse*
une webcam *webcam*

Je trouve que... *I find/think that . . .*

aimer mieux *to like better*
penser de *to think about [to express an opinion]*
préférer *to prefer*

Grammaire utile

⋯▸ Le subjonctif et les opinions

Il est bizarre que...
Il est bon que...
Il est dommage que...
Il est essentiel que...
Il est inutile que...
Il est utile que...

Modèles

Je trouve que mon ordinateur est parfait pour moi. L'écran et le clavier sont de bonne qualité. Qu'est-ce que tu penses de ton ordinateur?

Il est bizarre que mon ordinateur n'ait pas de lecteur de cédéroms. Tu es d'accord?

Comment trouves-tu ton ordinateur? Comment est-il?

Il est essentiel que mon ordinateur soit nouveau. J'ai besoin de la webcam la plus récente.

PARTIE 2

OUI, JE PEUX!

Look at each statement and rate yourself on how well you think you can perform the task. Then verify your ability with a partner. How did you do?

1. **"I can say what I am certain will happen in our society and find out what someone else believes will happen."**

   I can perform this function
   ☐ with ease
   ☐ with some difficulty
   ☐ not at all

2. **"I can say what I doubt will happen in our society and find out what someone else doubts will happen."**

   I can perform this function
   ☐ with ease
   ☐ with some difficulty
   ☐ not at all

Vocabulaire utile

le chômage *unemployment*
l'énergie renouvelable (f.) *renewable energy*
une préoccupation (sociale) *(social) concern*
le réchauffement climatique *global warming*
le recyclage *recycling*

conserver *to conserve*
interdire *to forbid*
polluer *to pollute*
protéger *to protect*

Grammaire utile

⋯▸ Le subjonctif et l'indicatif

The subjunctive is used to express doubt, uncertainty, and disbelief.

douter que **ne pas être certain(e) que**
ne pas croire que **ne pas être sûr(e) que**

The indicative is used after verbs and expressions of certainty and belief.

croire que **être certain(e) que**
penser que **être sûr(e) que**

Modèles

Je suis certain que le réchauffement climatique va continuer à être une préoccupation importante. Toi aussi?

Je ne suis pas sûre que les gens trouvent une solution pour les déchets industriels. Qu'est-ce que tu crois?

Qu'est-ce que tu penses qu'il va se passer dans notre société à l'avenir?

Est-ce que tu crois que les gens vont moins polluer?

ACTIVITÉ

The following sentences come from a conversation between Claire and Alexis in **Séquence 7** of the film *Liaisons*, but they are not in order. Reassemble them in an order (1-6) that reconstructs their original conversation. The conversation is started for you.

ALEXIS: Claire, je sais que votre famille ne pourra jamais nous pardonner… mais je peux au moins essayer de vous remettre la fortune familiale à laquelle vous avez droit. […] Ce document devrait vous permettre de réclamer l'héritage auquel vous avez droit. […]

a. _____ **ALEXIS:** Je comprends. Parlez-en à votre mère. Elle comprendra.

b. _____ **CLAIRE:** Je ne sais pas quoi dire. C'est incroyable.

c. _____ **CLAIRE:** Maman… ses hallucinations… Elle me parlait toujours des voix, des visions… moi, je croyais que c'était à cause de sa folie. De sa psychose. Mais ce n'était pas la psychose… Alexis… et vous? Vous êtes un ange? Un esprit?

d. _____ **ALEXIS:** Je sais que c'est difficile à comprendre. Je reviens du passé. Mais, ce qui importe, c'est que maintenant je suis ici. Et ma tâche est terminée.

e. _____ **CLAIRE:** Je ne sais pas…

f. _____ **ALEXIS:** Qu'en pensez-vous?

C'est à votre tour. What are you certain about and what do you doubt regarding what Claire is going to do with the small fortune she has just inherited and must go claim? Write 5-6 predictions using expressions that indicate certainty or doubt.

NOTES

NOTES

NOTES

NOTES

NOTES

NOTES